PHILIP'S

STREET ATLAS
Cornwall
and Plymouth

www.philips-maps.co.uk
First published in 2003 by
Philip's, a division of
Octopus Publishing Group Ltd
www.octopusbooks.co.uk
Carmelite House
50 Victoria Embankment
London EC4Y 0DZ
An Hachette UK Company
www.hachette.co.uk

Fourth edition with interim revision 2015
First impression 2015
CORDA

978-1-84907-364-6 (spiral)

© Philip's 2015

Ordnance Survey®

This product includes mapping data licensed
from Ordnance Survey® with the permission
of the Controller of Her Majesty's Stationery
Office. © Crown copyright 2015. All rights
reserved. Licence number 100011710.

Contents

II	**Key to map pages**
IV	**Route planning**
VIII	Major administrative and Postcode boundaries
1	**Key to map symbols**
2	**Street maps** at 1¾ inches to 1 mile
104	**Street maps** at 3½ inches to 1 mile
148	**Street map of Plymouth city centre** at 7 inches to 1 mile
150	**Index** of towns, villages, streets, hospitals, industrial estates, railway stations, schools, shopping centres, universities and places of interest

D1326766

Key to map pages

80	Map pages at 1¾ inches to 1 mile
112	Map pages at 3½ inches to 1 mile
148	Map pages at 7 inches to 1 mile

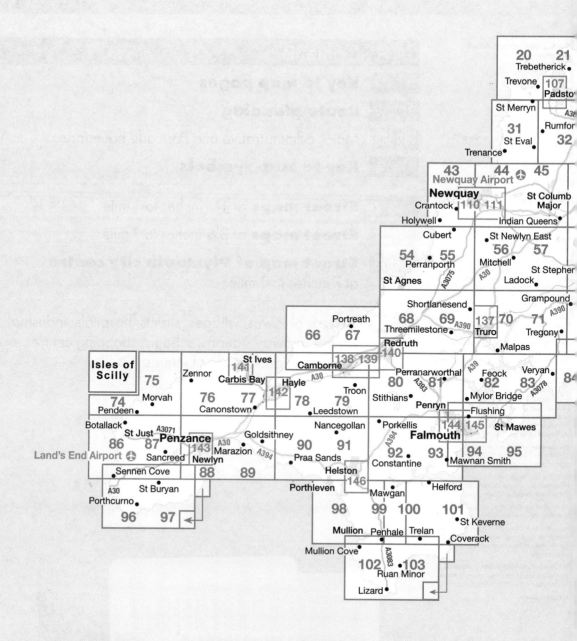

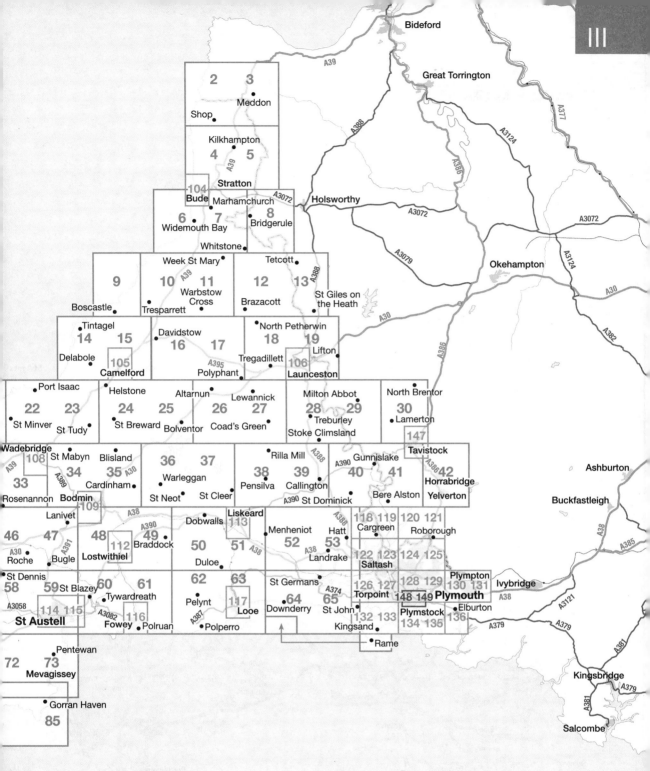

Bideford

Great Torrington

2 **3**
Meddon
Shop

Kilkhampton
4 **5**

104 Stratton
Bude Marhamchurch
6 **7** **8** Bridgerule
Widemouth Bay

Whitstone

Holsworthy

Week St Mary Tetcott
9 **10** **11** **12** **13**
Warbstow St Giles on
Boscastle Cross Brazacott the Heath
Tresparrett

Okehampton

Tintagel Davidstow North Petherwin
14 **15** **16** **17** **18** **19**
Lifton
Delabole Tregadillett
105 106
Camelford Polyphant Launceston

Port Isaac Helstone Altarnun Lewannick Milton Abbot North Brentor
22 **23** **24** **25** **26** **27** **28** **29** **30**
Treburley Lamerton
St Minver St Breward Bolventor Coad's Green Stoke Climsland
St Tudy

Wadebridge Rilla Mill Tavistock
108 St Mabyn Blisland **36** **37** 147
33 **34** **35** **38** **39** **40** **41** **42**
Warleggan Pensilva Callington Gunnislake Horrabridge
Rosenannon Cardinham Bere Alston Yelverton
Bodmin St Neot St Cleer St Dominick
109 Ashburton
Lanivet Liskeard 118 119 120 121
Dobwalls 113 Cargreen Roborough Buckfastleigh
46 **47** **48** **49** Menheniot **53** Hatt
112 Braddock **50** **51** **52** 122 123 124 125
Roche Bugle Lostwithiel Duloe Landrake Saltash
St Dennis 117 126 127 128 129 Plympton
58 **59** **60** **61** **62** **63** St Germans 130 131 Ivybridge
St Blazey Looe Torpoint 148 149 Plymouth
114 115 Pelynt 64 65 St John Plymstock Elburton
St Austell Fowey Polruan Downderry 132 133 134 135 136
116 Polperro Kingsand
Pentewan Rame
72 **73**
Mevagissey Kingsbridge

Gorran Haven
85

Salcombe

Scale

0   5   10   15   20   25 km

0   5   10   15 miles

Route planning

Scale

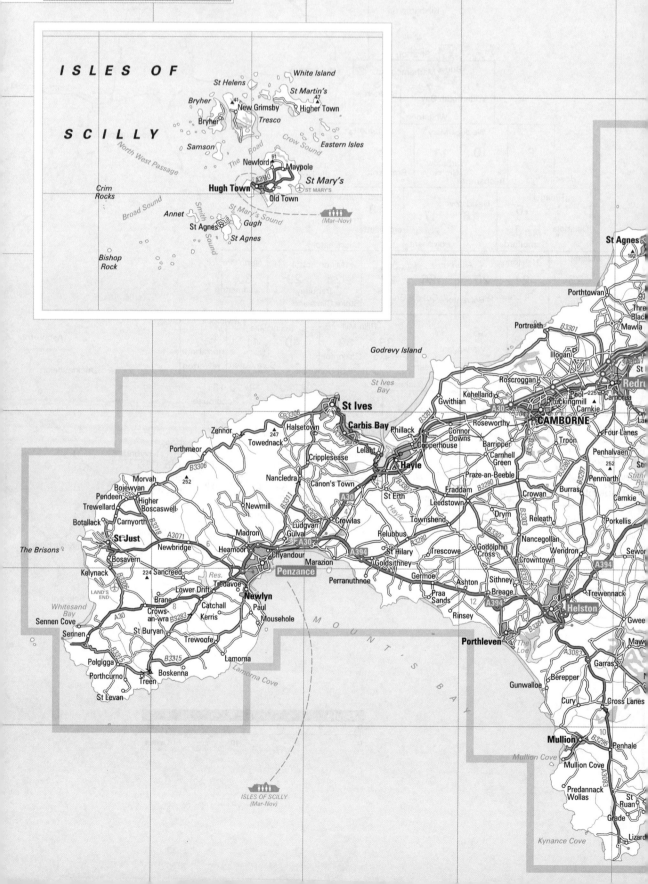

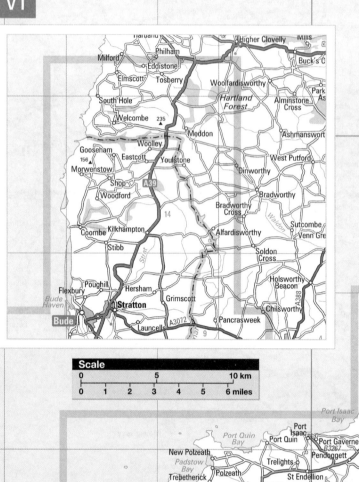

Scale
0   5   10 km
0   1   2   3   4   5   6 miles

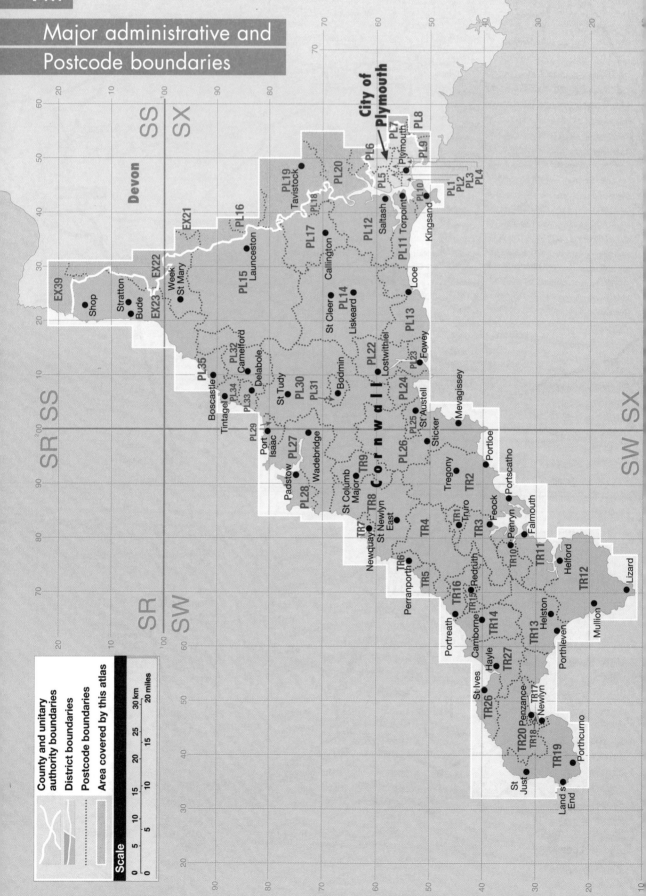

Key to map symbols

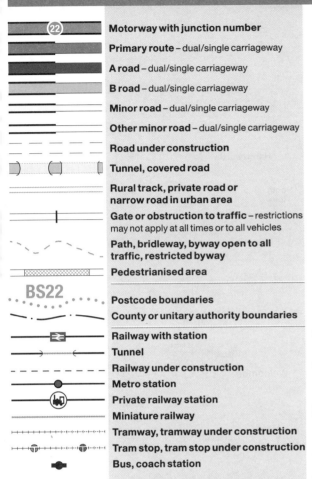

(22)	Motorway with junction number
	Primary route – dual/single carriageway
	A road – dual/single carriageway
	B road – dual/single carriageway
	Minor road – dual/single carriageway
	Other minor road – dual/single carriageway
	Road under construction
	Tunnel, covered road
	Rural track, private road or narrow road in urban area
	Gate or obstruction to traffic – restrictions may not apply at all times or to all vehicles
	Path, bridleway, byway open to all traffic, restricted byway
	Pedestrianised area
BS22	**Postcode boundaries**
	County or unitary authority boundaries
	Railway with station
	Tunnel
	Railway under construction
	Metro station
	Private railway station
	Miniature railway
	Tramway, tramway under construction
	Tram stop, tram stop under construction
	Bus, coach station

◆	**Ambulance station**
◆	**Coastguard station**
◆	**Fire station**
◆	**Police station**
✚	**Accident and Emergency entrance to hospital**
Ⓗ	**Hospital**
✛	**Place of worship**
𝒊	**Information centre** – open all year
🛒 Ⓟ	**Shopping centre, parking**
P&R PO	**Park and Ride, Post Office**
⚐ 🚐	**Camping site, caravan site**
► ✕	**Golf course, picnic site**
Church ROMAN FORT	**Non-Roman antiquity, Roman antiquity**
Univ	**Important buildings, schools, colleges, universities and hospitals**
	Woods, built-up area
River Medway	**Water name**
	River, weir
	Stream
	Canal, lock, tunnel
	Water
	Tidal water
58 ◄ **87** **246**	**Adjoining page indicators and overlap bands** – the colour of the arrow and band indicates the scale of the adjoining or overlapping page (see scales below)

The dark grey border on the inside edge of some pages indicates that the mapping does not continue onto the adjacent page

The small numbers around the edges of the maps identify the 1-kilometre National Grid lines

Abbreviations

Acad	**Academy**	Meml	**Memorial**
Allot Gdns	**Allotments**	Mon	**Monument**
Cemy	**Cemetery**	Mus	**Museum**
C Ctr	**Civic centre**	Obsy	**Observatory**
CH	**Club house**	Pal	**Royal palace**
Coll	**College**	PH	**Public house**
Crem	**Crematorium**	Recn Gd	**Recreation ground**
Ent	**Enterprise**	Resr	**Reservoir**
Ex H	**Exhibition hall**	Ret Pk	**Retail park**
Ind Est	**Industrial Estate**	Sch	**School**
IRB Sta	**Inshore rescue boat station**	Sh Ctr	**Shopping centre**
Inst	**Institute**	TH	**Town hall / house**
Ct	**Law court**	Trad Est	**Trading estate**
L Ctr	**Leisure centre**	Univ	**University**
LC	**Level crossing**	W Twr	**Water tower**
Liby	**Library**	Wks	**Works**
Mkt	**Market**	YH	**Youth hostel**

Enlarged maps only

	Railway or bus station building
	Place of interest
	Parkland

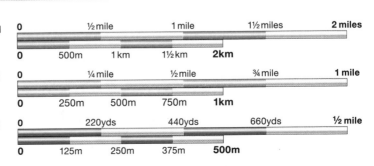

The map scale on the pages numbered in green is 1¾ inches to 1 mile
2.76 cm to 1 km • 1:36 206

0	½ mile	1 mile	1½ miles	**2 miles**
0	500m	1 km	1½ km	**2km**

The map scale on the pages numbered in blue is 3½ inches to 1 mile
5.52 cm to 1 km • 1:18 103

0	¼ mile	½ mile	¾ mile	**1 mile**
0	250m	500m	750m	**1km**

The map scale on the pages numbered in red is 7 inches to 1 mile
11.04 cm to 1 km • 1:9051

0	220yds	440yds	660yds	**½ mile**
0	125m	250m	375m	**500m**

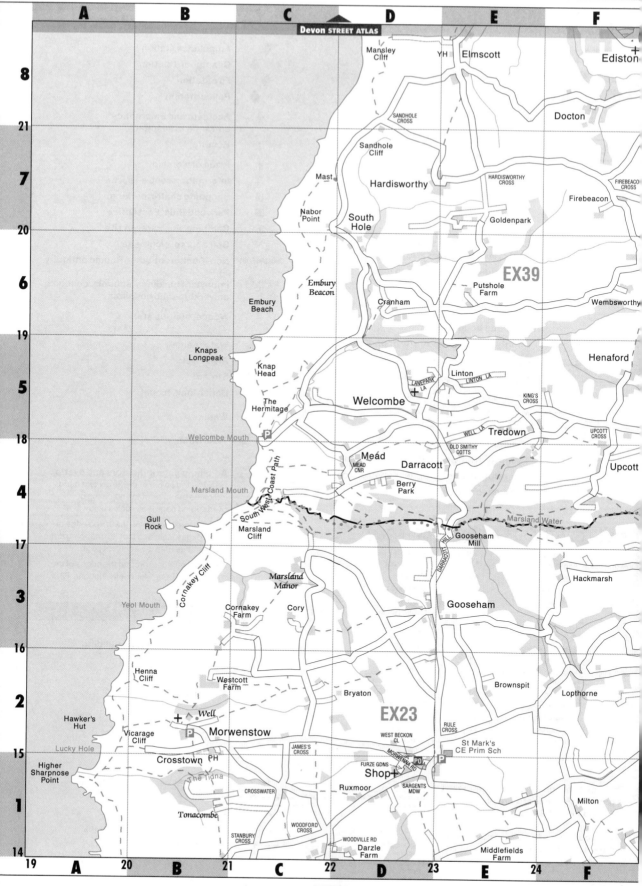

Devon STREET ATLAS

A   B   C   D   E   F

8

21

7

20

6

EX39

19

5

18

4

17

3

16

2

EX23

15

1

14

19   A   20   B   21   C   22   D   23   E   24   F

Mansley Cliff · YH · Elmscott · Ediston

Docton

SANDHOLE CROSS

Sandhole Cliff · Hardisworthy · HARDISWORTHY CROSS · FIREBEACO CROSS · Firebeacon

Mast · Nabor Point · South Hole · Goldenpark · Wembsworthy

Embury Beacon · Cranham · Putshole Farm

Embury Beach · Henaford

Knaps Longpeak · Knap Head · LANEPARK LA · Linton · LINTON LA · KING'S CROSS

The Hermitage · Welcombe · WELL LA · Tredown · UPCOTT CROSS

Welcombe Mouth · P · Meád · MEAD CNR · Darracott · OLD SMITHY COTTS · Upcott

Marsland Mouth · Berry Park · Marsland Water

South West Coast Path · Gooseham Mill · DARRACOTT HILL

Gull Rock · Marsland Cliff

Cornakey Cliff · Marsland Manor · Hackmarsh

Yeol Mouth · Cornakey Farm · Cory · Gooseham

Henna Cliff · Westcott Farm · Bryaton · Brownspit · Lopthorne

Hawker's Hut · Well · RULE CROSS · St Mark's CE Prim Sch

Vicarage Cliff · P · Morwenstow · WEST BECKON CL · P

Lucky Hole · Crosstown · PH · JAMES'S CROSS · MORWENNA RD · PO · Shop

Higher Sharpnose Point · The Tidna · FURZE GDNS · Ruxmoor · SARGENTS MDW · Milton

Crosswater · Middlefields Farm

Tonacombe · WOODFORD CROSS · WOODVILLE RD

STANBURY CROSS · Darzle Farm

4

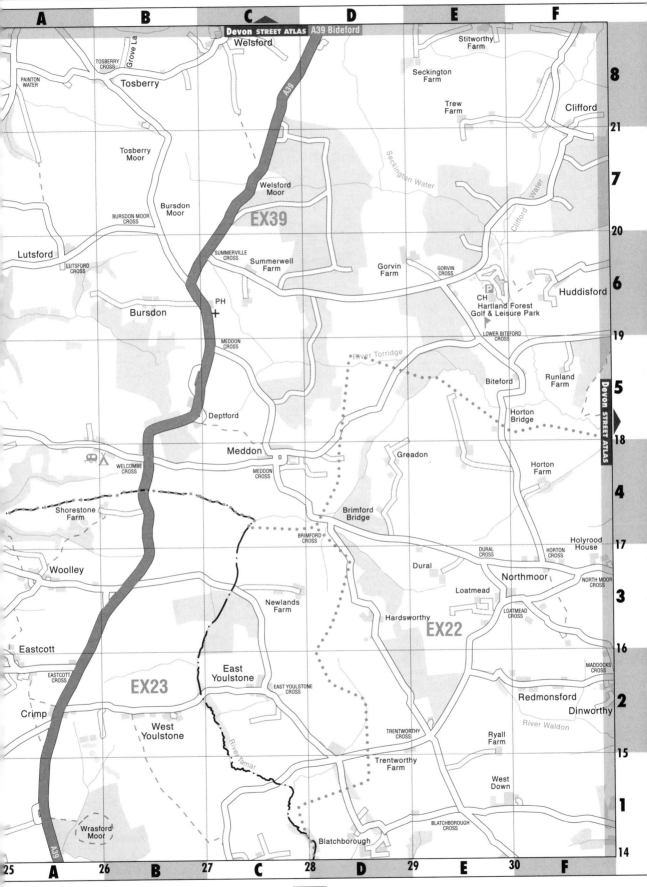

Devon STREET ATLAS A39 Bideford

Welsford

Stitworthy
Farm

Seckington
Farm

8

PAINTON
WATER

Tosberry

Trew
Farm

Clifford

21

Tosberry
Cross

Grove La

Tosberry
Moor

Welsford
Moor

7

Seckington Water

Clifford Water

Bursdon
Moor
Cross

Bursdon
Moor

EX39

20

Lutsford

Summerville
Cross

Summerwell
Farm

Gorvin
Farm

Gorvin
Cross

Huddisford

6

LUTSFORD
CROSS

CH
Hartland Forest
Golf & Leisure Park

Bursdon

PH

MEDDON
CROSS

LOWER BITEFORD
CROSS

19

River Torridge

Biteford

Runland
Farm

Devon STREET ATLAS

5

Deptford

Horton
Bridge

18

Meddon

Greadon

Horton
Farm

4

WELCOMBE
CROSS

MEDDON
CROSS

Shorestone
Farm

Brimford
Bridge

Holyrood
House

17

Woolley

BRIMFORD
CROSS

Dural
Cross

HORTON
CROSS

Newlands
Farm

Dural

Northmoor

NORTH MOOR
CROSS

3

Eastcott

Loatmead

LOATMEAD
CROSS

16

EX23

Hardsworthy

EX22

MADDOCKS
CROSS

EASTCOTT
CROSS

East
Youlstone

Redmonsford

2

Crimp

West
Youlstone

EAST YOULSTONE
CROSS

Dinworthy

River Waldon

TRENTWORTHY
CROSS

Ryall
Farm

15

River Tamar

Trentworthy
Farm

West
Down

1

Wrasford
Moor

BLATCHBOROUGH
CROSS

Blatchborough

14

A39

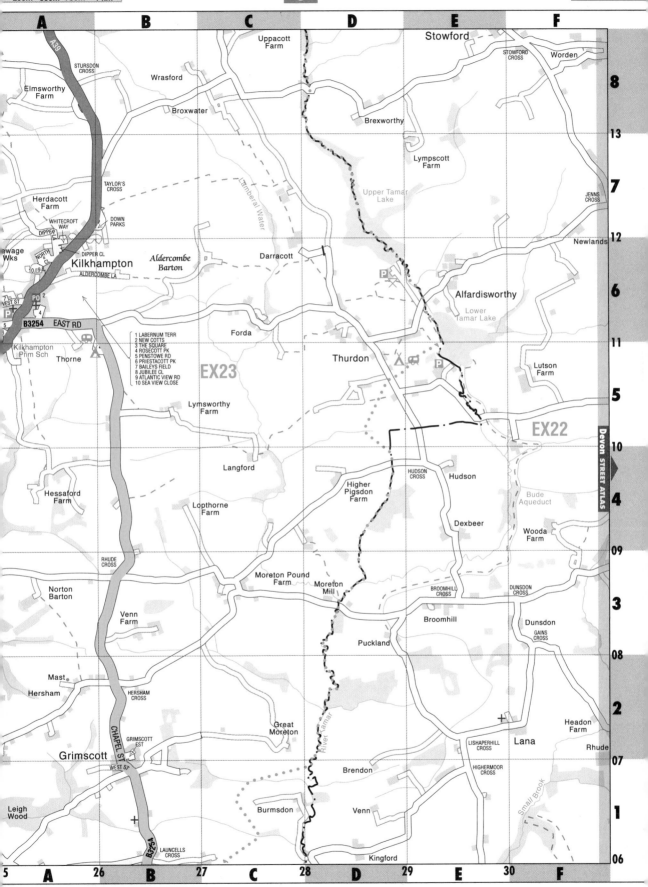

3

1 LABERNUM TERR
2 NEW COTTS
3 THE SQUARE
4 ROSECOTT PK
5 PENSTOWE RD
6 PRIESTACOTT PK
7 BAILEYS FIELD
8 JUBILEE CL
9 ATLANTIC VIEW RD
10 SEA VIEW CLOSE

Devon STREET ATLAS

Stowford
Stowford Cross
Worden
Uppacott Farm
Wrasford
Broxwater
Brexworthy
Lympscott Farm
Upper Tamar Lake
Jenns Cross
Elmsworthy Farm
Stursdon Cross
Herdacott Farm
Taylor's Cross
Down Parks
Whitecroft Way
Dipper Cl
Newlands
Darracott
Alfardisworthy
Kilkhampton
Aldercombe Barton
Aldercombe La
Lower Tamar Lake
West St
P
East Rd
B3254
Kilkhampton Prim Sch
Thorne
Forda
Thurdon
Lutson Farm
EX23
Lymsworthy Farm
EX22
Hessaford Farm
Langford
Higher Pigsdon Farm
Hudson Cross
Hudson
Bude Aqueduct
Lopthorne Farm
Dexbeer
Wooda Farm
Rhude Cross
Norton Barton
Moreton Pound Farm
Moreton Mill
Broomhill Cross
Dunsdon Cross
Venn Farm
Broomhill
Dunsdon
Gains Cross
Mast
Hersham
Hersham Cross
Puckland
Headon Farm
Great Moreton
Lishaperhill Cross
Lana
Rhude
Chapel St
Grimscott
Grimscott Est
West St
Brendon
Highermoor Cross
Small Brook
Leigh Wood
Burmsdon
Venn
B3254
Launcells Cross
River Tamar
Kingford

8

13

7

12

6

11

5

10

4

09

3

08

2

07

1

06

A   26   B   27   C   28   D   29   E   30   F

7   8

For full street detail of the highlighted area see page 104.

Scale: 1 inches to 1 mi

0 250m 500m 750m 1 km

Ebbingford Manor

Efford Beacon

Lynstone

Bude Canal (dis)

LYNSTONE RD

Upton

MARINE DR

COUNTY RD

Phillip's Point

Hotel

Phillips Farm

Higher Longbeak

Lower Longbeak

Salthouse Cottage

PH

BRAMBLE CL

1 ATLANTIC CL
2 CRESCENT CL

MADEIRA DR

ASHTON WLK
BRANDON WLK

Widemouth Sand

THE CRESCENT

LONGBEAK DR

Widemouth Bay

LEVERLAKE RD

Black Rock

Wanson Mouth

COMBE LA

Widemouth Farms

South West Coast Path

Foxhole Point

Penhalt Cliff

PH

Wanson

Millook Haven

EX23

Millook

Trevisick

BANGORS EST

Cancleave Strand

Bangors

Wanson Water

Dizzard Point

Millook Common

VICARAGE LA

Poundstock

Cemy Trekenard Farm

Trebarfoote

Chipman Strand

Long Cliff

Bynorth Cliff

Trevoulter Farm

Treskinnick Cross

Dizzard

The Den

Mas

Cleave Strand

Tregole

A39

A B C D E F
15 16 17 18 19 20

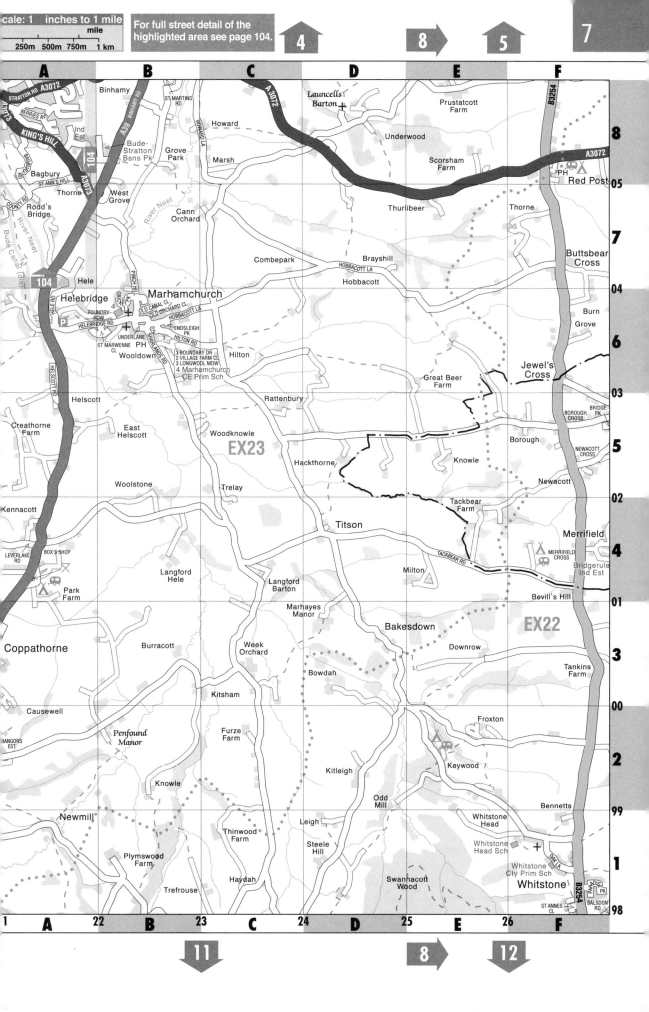

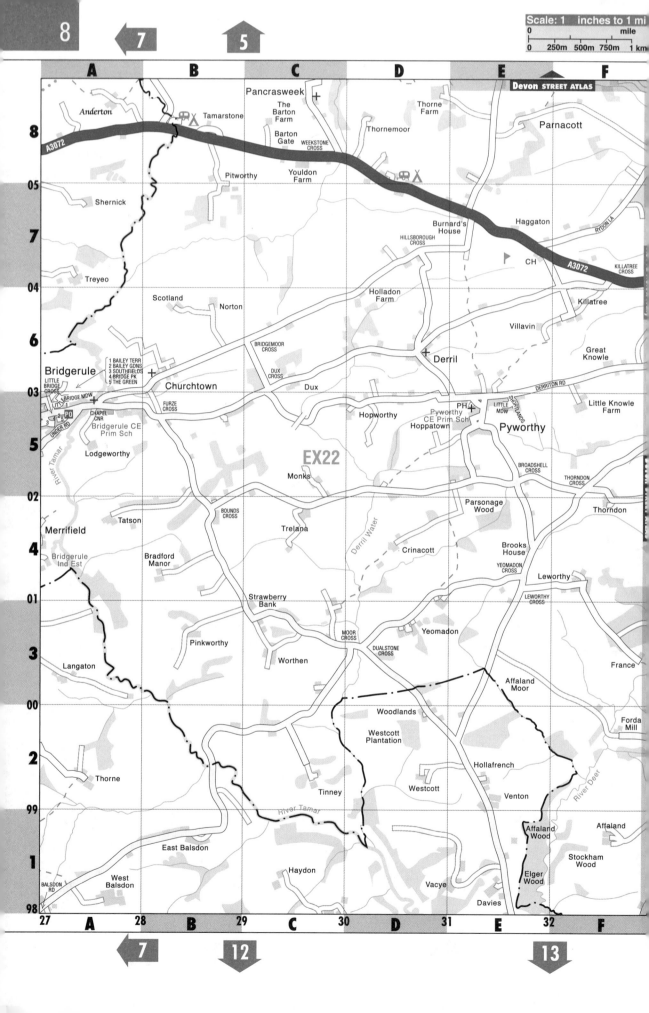

Scale: 1   inches to 1 mile
mile
250m 500m 750m 1 km

A B C D E F

8
97
7
96
6
95
5
94
4
93
3
92
2
91
90

Cambeak

Voter Run
EX23
High Cliff

Rusey Beach

Rusey Cliff

Buckator
Gull Rock

Beeny Sisters

Fire Beacon Point
Seals Hole

Beeny Cliff

Beeny

Trebyla Farm

B3263

Tremorle

Pentargon

Hillsborough

Trewannett

Mus of Witchcraft
VALENCY ROW

Penally Point

Penally Hill

PENALLY TERR

Penally House

PL35

Meachard

YH

Harbour

PENALLY CT

Tresuck

Newmills

River Valency

Trafalgar Farm

Willapark

Forrabury

Mast

Grower Rock

Boscastle

NEW RD

B3263

Visitor Ctr

MARINE TERR

Boscastle Com Prim Sch
FORE ST

Home Farm

Trebiffin

Short Island
Ladies Window

Firebeacon Hill
Long Island

Welltown Manor

TINTAGEL RD

UNDER RD

GREEN LA

CAMBER RD

BARN PARK RD

WILLAPARK VIEW

GIBBS

PARADISE RD

Paradise House

BUTT'S LA

HIGH ST

MOUNT PLEASANT

B3266

Trewold

Trevalga

B3263

14 15 10

C1
1 PENTARGON RD
2 EGLOS VIEW
3 TREFLEUR CL
4 LANGFORDS MDW
5 FORRABURY HILL
6 CLOVER LANE CL
7 WHITE SMOCK MDW
8 DOCTORS HILL
9 GUNPOOL LA

10 DUNN ST

C2
1 HOLLOWELL HO
2 BRIDGE WLK
3 THE OLD MILL

10

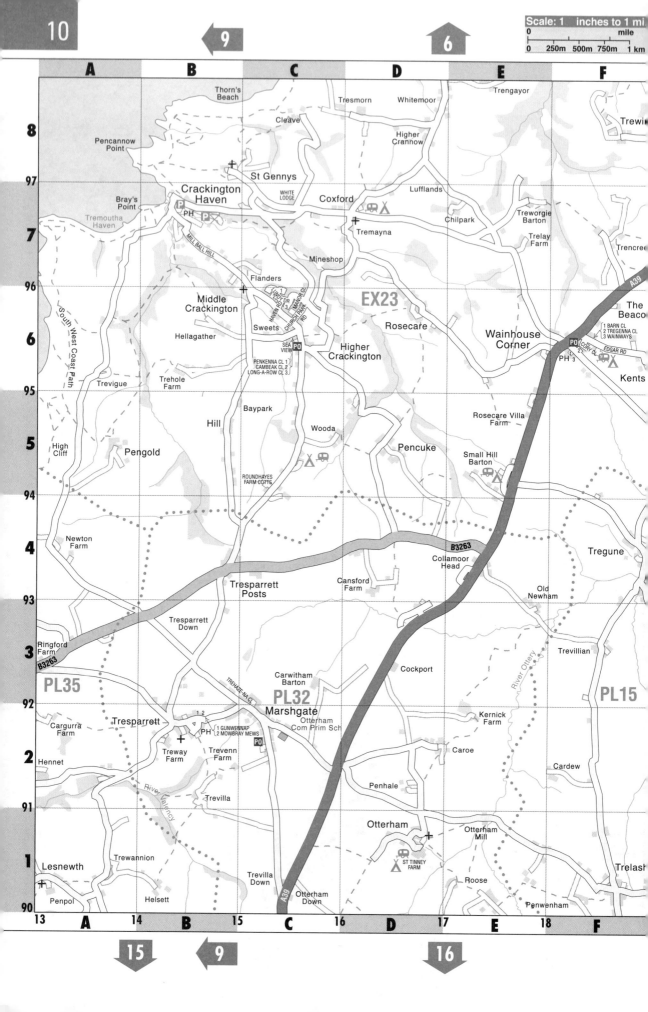

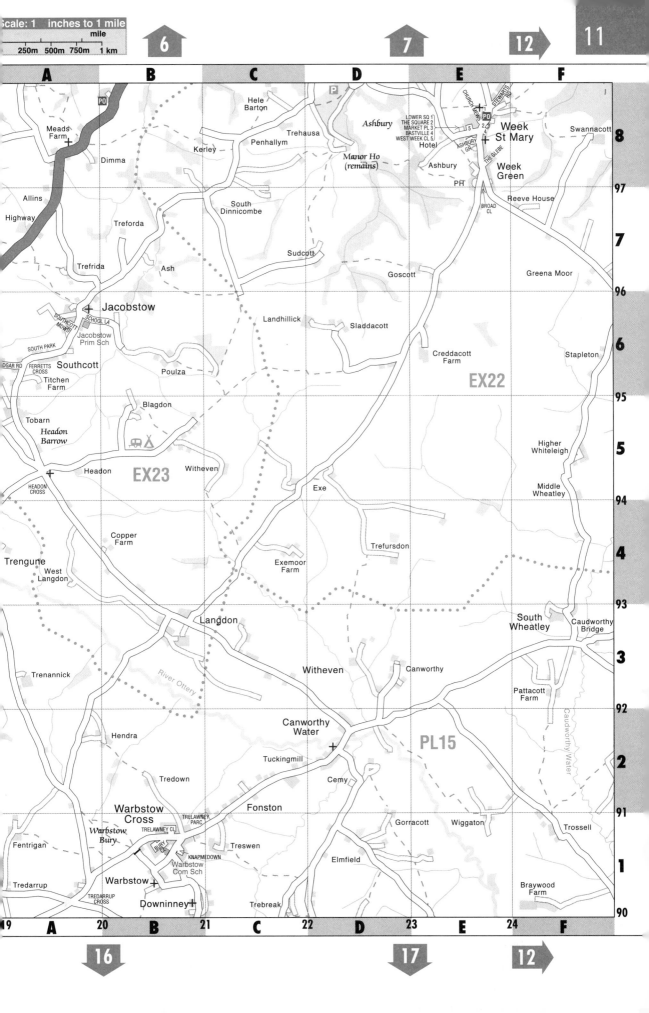

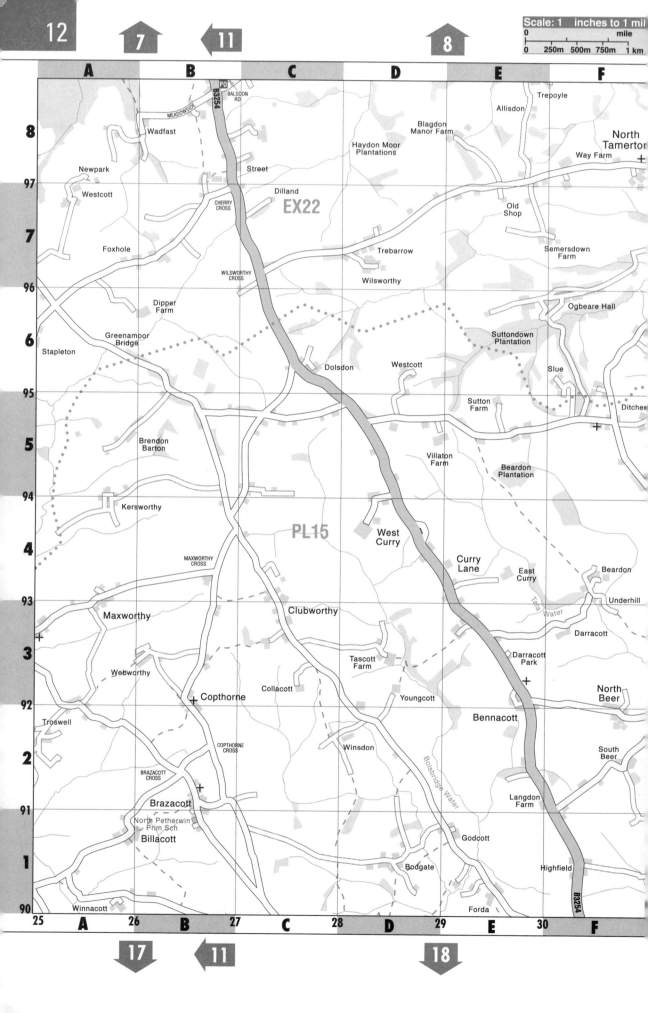

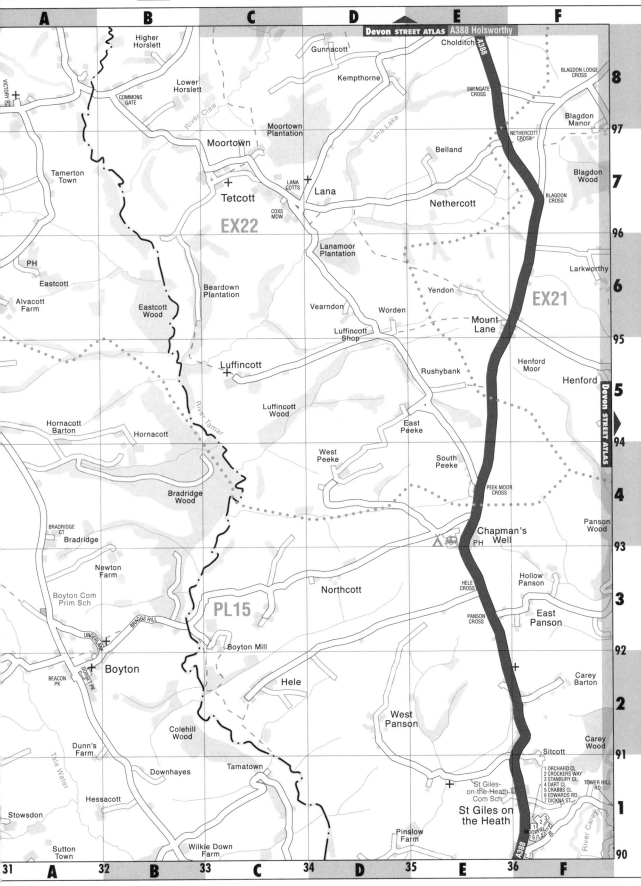

scale: 1   inches to 1 mile

mile

250m 500m 750m 1 km

8

A   B   C   D   E   F

Choldich

BLAGDON LODGE CROSS

Higher Horslett

Gunnacott

Kempthorne

SWINGATE CROSS

8

Blagdon Manor

97

Lower Horslett

VICTORY RD

COMMONS GATE

River Claw

Moortown Plantation

Lana Lake

NETHERCOTT CROSS

Belland

Blagdon Wood

7

Tamerton Town

Moortown

LANA COTTS

Lana

Nethercott

BLAGDON CROSS

EX22

Tetcott

COXS MDW

96

PH

Eastcott

Lanamoor Plantation

Larkworthy

6

Alvacott Farm

Beardown Plantation

Vearndon

Worden

Yendon

EX21

Eastcott Wood

Luffincott Shop

Mount Lane

95

Henford Moor

Luffincott

Rushybank

Henford

Devon STREET ATLAS

5

Hornacott Barton

Luffincott Wood

East Peeke

South Peeke

94

Hornacott

River Tamar

West Peeke

Panson Wood

Bradridge Wood

PEEK MOOR CROSS

4

BRADRIDGE CT

Bradridge

Newton Farm

Chapman's Well

PH

Hollow Panson

93

Boyton Com Prim Sch

BRAGGS HILL

Northcott

HELE CROSS

East Panson

PL15

UNDERLANE

Boyton Mill

PANSON CROSS

3

DORSET PK

Boyton

Hele

92

BEACON PK

Carey Barton

2

West Panson

Carey Wood

Colehill Wood

Sitcott

91

Dunn's Farm

Downhayes

Tamatown

1 ORCHARD CL
2 CROCKERS WAY
3 STANBURY CL
4 DART CL
5 CRABBS CL
6 EDWARDS RD
7 DICKNA ST

TOWER HILL RD

Tsla Water

Hessacott

St Giles-on-the-Heath Com Sch

1

Stowsdon

St Giles on the Heath

MOOR...

River Carey

Sutton Town

Wilkie Down Farm

Pinslow Farm

A388

90

31   A   32   B   33   C   34   D   35   E   36   F

Scale: 1 inches to 1 mil
0 mile
0 250m 500m 750m 1 km

A B C D E F

PL35

B3263

The Sisters
Lye Rock
Willapark
Gullastem
Bossiney Haven
Rocky Valley
ST PIRANS CT.
Trethevey
Bossiney
The Island
Castle
Monastery
Tintagel Head
Hotel
Mast
Hotel
St Nectan's Glen
Trewitten

C7
1 KNIGHTS CL
2 GAVERCOOMBE PK
3 CASTLE HTS
4 ATLANTIC WAY
5 KING ARTHURS TERR
6 TREVENA LODGE
7 KAYS MEWS
8 TREVENA DR
9 VICARAGE HILL

Barras Nose
THE BUNGALOWS
WESTGROUND WAY
LAURA CL
Castle
St Nectan's Kieve
Halgabron
Old Post Office
Toy Mus
Visitor Ctr
Fenterleigh
Glebe Cliff
Dovecote
PO
Tintagel
MERLINS WAY
TRENALE LA
Dunderhole Point
YH
DANMORE CL
TINTAGEL HTS
Tintagel Prim Sch
Trenale
Penhallic Point
Treven
PL34
Downrow
Tregatta
Truas
Hole Beach
South West Coast Path
PALMERS TERR
ATLANTIC
Treknow
TRELAKE LA
Trewarmett
PH
Trebarwith Strand
Gull Rock
Port William
ATLANTIC CL
PH
Prince of Wales Quarry Trail
Chy
P
Dennis Point
PH
PH
Penpethy
B3263
Backways Cove
Trebarwith
Start Point
Higher Trether Farm
Trecarne Farm
Trenouth Farm
B3314
Upton
TREBARWITH RD
Wind Farm
North Cornwall Short Stay School
Tregonnick Tail
TRECARNE GDNS
Rockhead
ROCKHEAD ST
HIGHER MEDROSE
Treligga
PL33
Delabole
Pengelly
Deli
The Mountain
PH
BELMONT CL
PH
HIGH ST
Tregardock Beach
ATLANTIC RD
TRELIGGA DOWNS RD
THE SIDINGS
Trerubies Cove
Tregardock Cliff
Tregardock
Delabole Prim Sch
ST JAMES CT
Cemy
BRIDGE HO
PL32
Trewen
Moonspark Farm
WESTDOWN RD
1 PLANET PK
2 ROUGHTOR VIEW
3 SLATE CL
4 MANDELEY CL
Wks
Jacket's Point
Tregragon
Delamere
Castle Goff
Westdowns
Helland Barton
Treveans
B3267
GYPSY LA
Newhall Manor
Dannonchapel
PL30
Higher Tynes
B3314
TREVILLEY LA
Trewalder
Lanteglos
BOWOOD PK

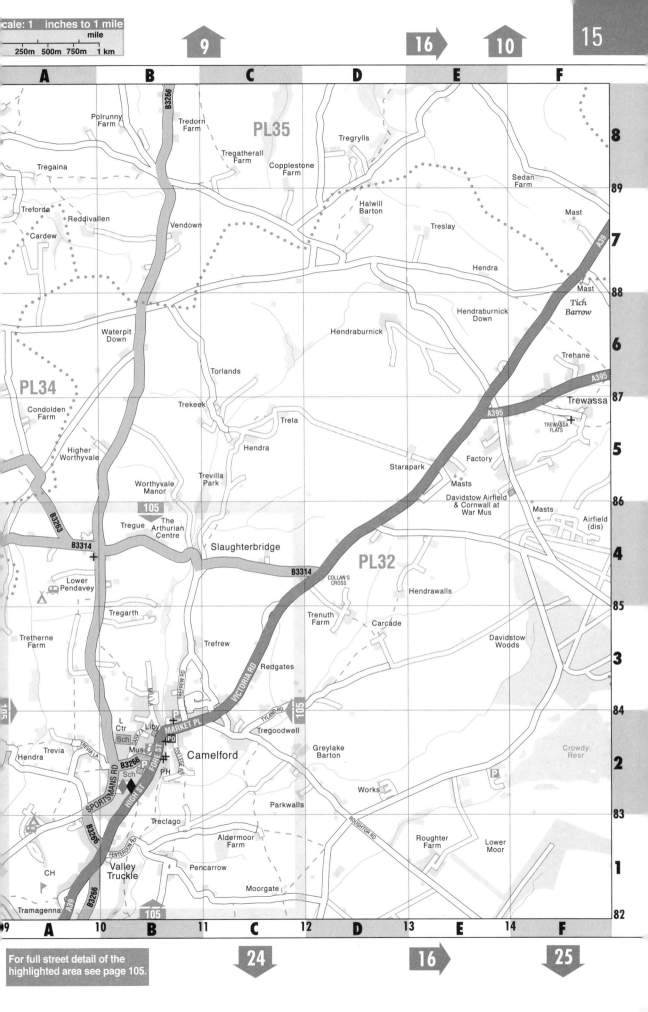

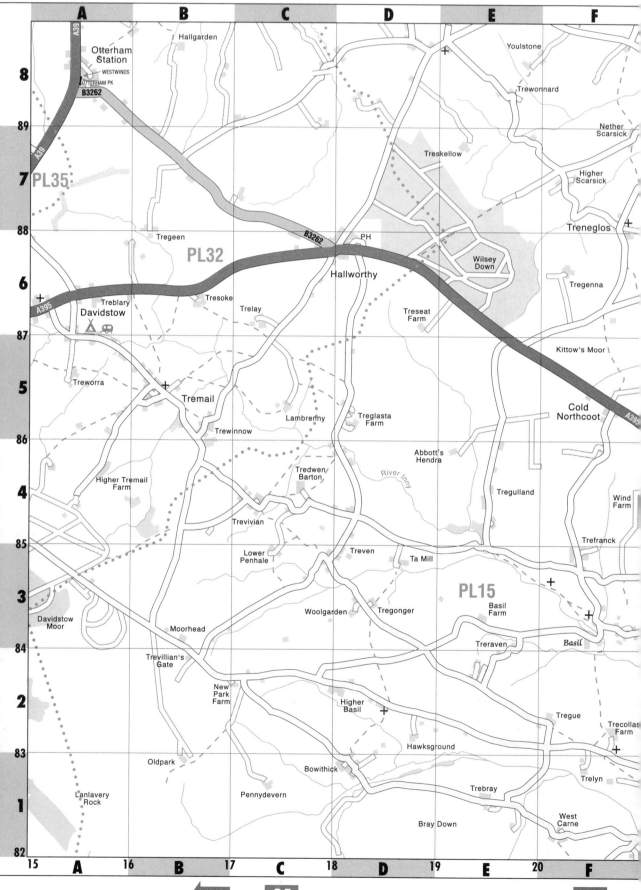

Scale: 1 inches to 1 mi
0   0   0   mile
0   250m 500m 750m   1 km

A   B   C   D   E   F

8
89
7 PL35
88
6
87
5
86
4
85
3
84
2
83
1
82

Hallgarden
Otterham Station
WESTWINDS
OTTERHAM PK
B3262
Tregeen
PL32
B3262
Treblary
Davidstow
Treworra
Tremail
Trewinnow
Higher Tremail Farm
Trevivian
Lower Penhale
Moorhead
Trevillian's Gate
New Park Farm
Oldpark
Lanlavery Rock
Davidstow Moor
Pennydevern
Bowithick
Tresoke
Trelay
Lambrenny
Tredwen Barton
Woolgarden
Treven
Treglasta Farm
Tregonger
Higher Basil
Hallworthy
PH
Youlstone
Trewonnard
Treskellow
Nether Scarsick
Higher Scarsick
Wilsey Down
Treneglos
Tregenna
Treseat Farm
Kittow's Moor
River Inny
Abbott's Hendra
Tregulland
Cold Northcoot
Ta Mill
PL15
Basil Farm
Wind Farm
Trefranck
Basil
Treraven
Hawksground
Tregue
Trecollas Farm
Trebray
Trelyn
Bray Down
West Carne
A39
B3262
A395
A395

15   A   16   B   17   C   18   D   19   E   20   F

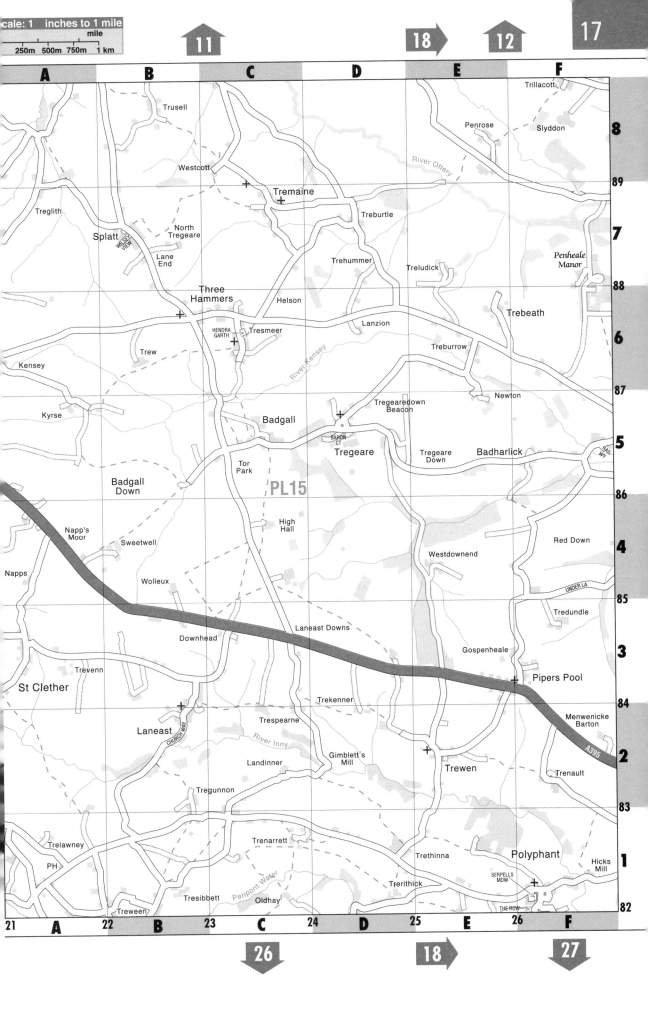

Scale: 1 inches to 1 mile

mile

250m   500m   750m   1 km

A   B   C   D   E   F

Trillacott

Trusell

Penrose

Slyddon

8

Westcott

River Ottery

Tremaine

89

Treglith

Treburtle

Splatt

North
Tregeare

WILSEY
VIEW

Penheale
Manor

7

Lane
End

Trehummer

Treludick

88

Three
Hammers

Helson

Trebeath

Lanzion

6

HENDRA
GARTH

Tresmeer

Treburrow

Trew

River Kensey

Kensey

Tregearedown
Beacon

Newton

87

Kyrse

Badgall

BARON
CT

Tregeare

Tregeare
Down

Badharlick

RAIL
WY

5

Tor
Park

PL15

Badgall
Down

86

Napp's
Moor

Sweetwell

High
Hall

Westdownend

Red Down

4

Napps

Wolleux

UNDER LA

85

Tredundle

Laneast Downs

Downhead

Gospenheale

3

St Clether

Trevenn

Trekenner

Pipers Pool

84

Laneast

CHURCH WAY

Trespearne

Menwenicke
Barton

A395

River Inny

Gimblett's
Mill

Trewen

2

Landinner

Trenault

Tregunnon

83

Trelawney

Trenarrett

Trethinna

Polyphant

Hicks
Mill

1

PH

SERPELLS
MDW

Trerithick

Tresibbett

Oldhay

THE ROW

82

Treween

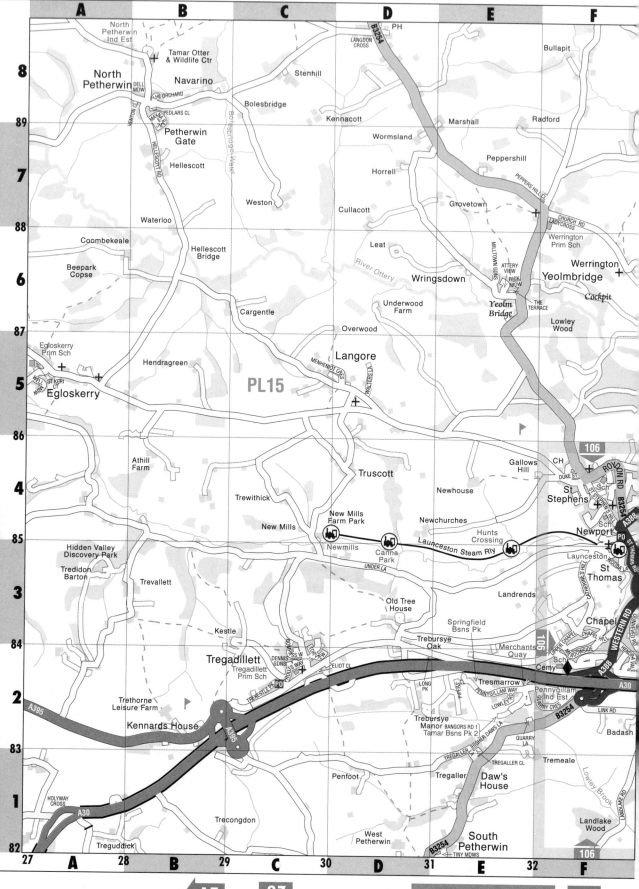

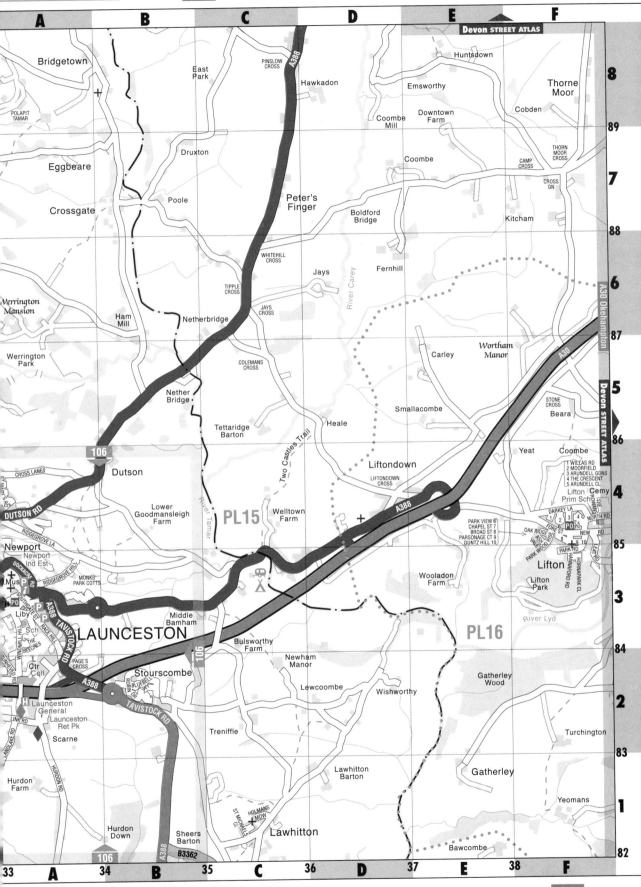

Scale: 1 inches to 1 mile

mile

250m 500m 750m 1 km

Devon STREET ATLAS

A **B** **C** **D** **E** **F**

Bridgetown

POLAPIT TAMAR

Eggbeare

Crossgate

Werrington Mansion

Werrington Park

East Park

PINSLOW CROSS

Druxton

Poole

WHITEHILL CROSS

TIPPLE CROSS

Ham Mill

Netherbridge

Nether Bridge

Hawkadon

Peter's Finger

JAYS CROSS

Jays

COLEMANS CROSS

Tettaridge Barton

Heale

Huntsdown

Emsworthy

Coombe Mill

Downtown Farm

Coombe

Boldford Bridge

River Carey

Fernhill

Liftondown

LIFTONDOWN CROSS

Thorne Moor

Cobden

THORN MOOR CROSS

CAMP CROSS

CROSS GN

Kitcham

Carley

Wortham Manor

Smallacombe

Beara

STONE CROSS

Yeat

Coombe

A30 Okehampton

Devon STREET ATLAS

Dutson

Lower Goodmansleigh Farm

PL15

Welltown Farm

Two Castles Trail

River Tamar

A388

1 WILLAS RD
2 MOORFIELD
3 ARUNDELL GDNS
4 THE CRESCENT
5 ARUNDELL CL

Lifton Prim Sch

Lifton Cemy

DARKEY LA

LITTLE RD NORTH RD THE ROWANS

FORE ST PO

Lifton

NEW

PARK VIEW 6
CHAPEL ST 7
BROAD ST 8
PARSONAGE CT 9
DUNTZ HILL 10

OAK RIDGE

NEW RD

HORNAPARK CL

HARNAFORD RD

LEAT RD

PARK RD

VALLEY

PARK WOOD

Lifton Park

CROSS LANES

DUTSON RD

RIDGEGROVE LA

Newport

Newport Ind Est

Mus

MONKS PARK COTTS

RIDGEGROVE HILL

Middle Bamham

LAUNCESTON

Liby

Sch

THE BEECHES

Ctr Call

PAGE'S CROSS

Stourscombe

TAVISTOCK RD

RACE HILL

A388

ROBIN DR

BLUEBELL

Launceston General

Launceston Ret Pk

LANDLAKE RD

LINK RD

HURDON RD

Scarne

Hurdon Farm

Hurdon Down

Sheers Barton

B3362

TAVISTOCK RD

Bulsworthy Farm

Newham Manor

Lewcoombe

Treniffle

ST MICHAELS CT

HOLMANS MDW

Lawhitton

Wishworthy

Wooladon Farm

Lawhitton Barton

River Lyd

PL16

Gatherley Wood

Gatherley

Bawcombe

Turchington

Yeomans

For full street detail of the highlighted area see page 106.

28

29

33 34 35 36 37 38

| | A | | B | | C | | D | | E | | F |

8

81

7

80

6

79   Gulland
                                                        Rock

5

78

4   Gunver
                                                                                     Head

77

Trevose   Cat's   Porthmissen
Head   Cove   Bridge

3   Stinking   Merope   Round
           Cove   Rocks   LB   Trevone   Hole   Porthmissen
                                       Sta   Bay
The Bull   Polventon or
Dinas Head   Round   Mother Ivey's Bay   Cataclews   ATLANTA 1
                      Hole   Point   ATLANTIC TERR 2   P
                                                                                    WEST VIEW 3
76
                                     Trevose   St Cadoc's   Newtrian
                                     Farm   Point   Bay

2   Booby's   Harlyn   South West Coast Path   Trevone
           Bay   Bay   IRB
                                                                    Sta   UPPER DOBBIN CL 1   THE CLOSE
                                                     SANDY LA   DOBBIN CL 2
                                                              PH   PARKENHEAD LA 3   SOUTHWAY
                                                     POLMARK HARLYN
                                                     DR   COTTS
75   St Constantine's   HARLYN   Harlyn   St Cadoc
                  Church   BARTON   Farm
           Constantine   Harlyn
           Bay   House   Polmark   Windmill
                                                                         Trenearne
1   TREVOSE   CH   Higher   PL28
                        CL   Harlyn   1 TRELANTIS
Treyarnon Point   Constantine   2 PEGUARRA CT   Trelowsa
                                   Bay   PH   Farm
74   Treyarnon Bay   YH   CRESCENT   Towan   HARLYN RD   B3276
84   A   85   B   86   RISE C   87   D   88   E   89   F

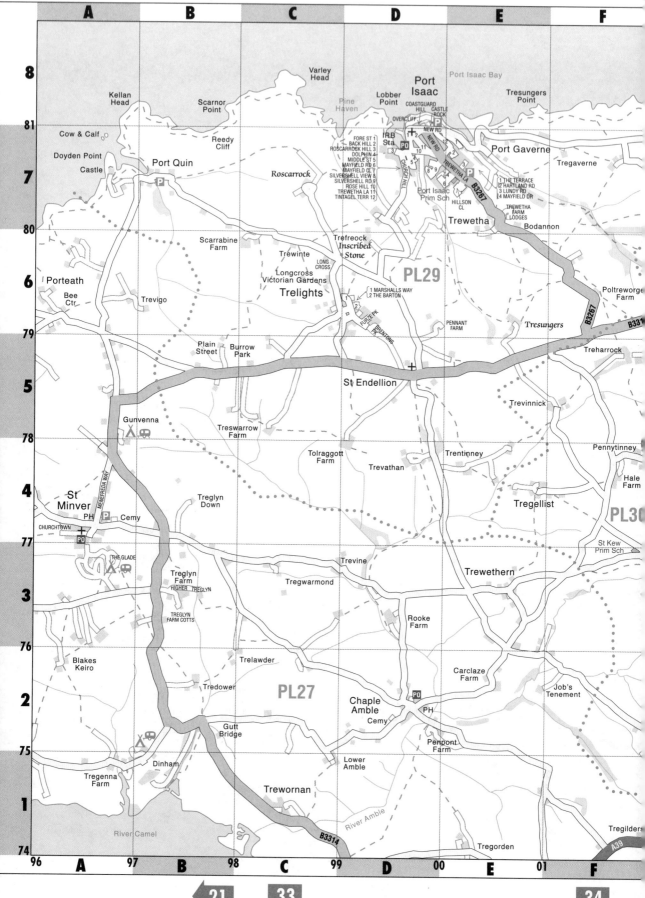

Scale: 1 inches to 1 mi

| | | A | | B | | C | | D | | E | | F |

8

81

7

80

6

79

5

78

4

77

3

76

2

75

1

74

Kellan Head

Cow & Calf

Doyden Point Castle

Port Quin

Porteath

Bee Ctr

Trevigo

St Minver

PH

CHURCHTOWN

PO

THE GLADE

Treglyn Farm

HIGHER TREGLYN

TREGLYN FARM COTTS

Blakes Keiro

Tredower

Gutt Bridge

Dinham

Tregenna Farm

Treworgan

River Camel

Scarnor Point

Reedy Cliff

Scarrabine Farm

Plain Street

Burrow Park

Gunvenna

Treswarrow Farm

Treglyn Down

Trelawder

Tregwarmond

Varley Head

Pine Haven

Roscarrock

Roscarrock

Trewinte

LONG CROSS

Longcross Victorian Gardens

Trelights

FURZE PK

BRENTONS PK

Trefreock Inscribed Stone

Trevine

Trelawder

Port Isaac Bay

Lobber Point

Port Isaac

COASTGUARD HILL

OVERCLIFF

CASTLE ROCK

NEW RD

IRB Sta

FORE ST 1
BACK HILL 2
ROSCARROCK HILL 3
DOLPHIN 4
MIDDLE ST 5
MAYFIELD RD 6
MAYFIELD CL 7
SILVERSHELL VIEW 8
SILVERSHELL RD 9
ROSE HILL 10
TREWETHA LA 11
TINTAGEL TERR 12

CHURCH HILL

Port Isaac Prim Sch

HILLSON CL

1 MARSHALLS WAY
2 THE BARTON

PENNANT FARM

St Endellion

Tolraggott Farm

Trevathan

Trevine

Rooke Farm

Chaple Amble

PO

PH

Cemy

Lower Amble

Penpont Farm

River Amble

Tresungers Point

Port Gaverne

Tregaverne

TREWETHA LA

B3267

1 THE TERRACE
2 HARTLAND RD
3 LUNDY RD
4 MAYFIELD DR

TREWETHA FARM LODGES

Trewetha

Bodannon

PL29

Tresungers

B3267

B33

Treharrock

Trevinnick

Trentinney

Tregellist

Poltreworge Farm

Pennytinney

Hale Farm

PL30

St Kew Prim Sch

Trewethern

Carclaze Farm

Job's Tenement

PL27

Tregorden

Tregilders

A39

B3314

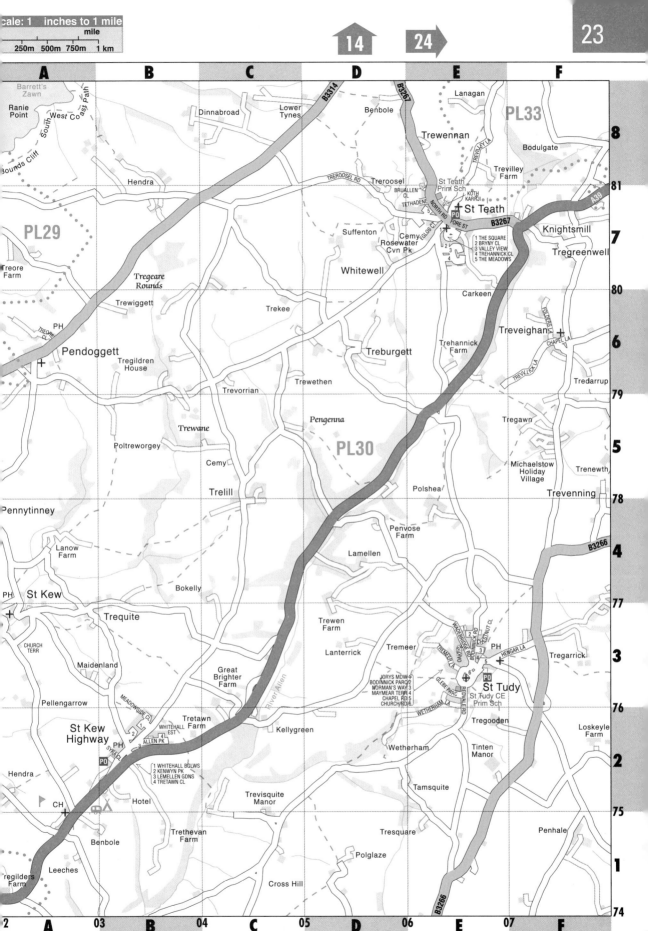

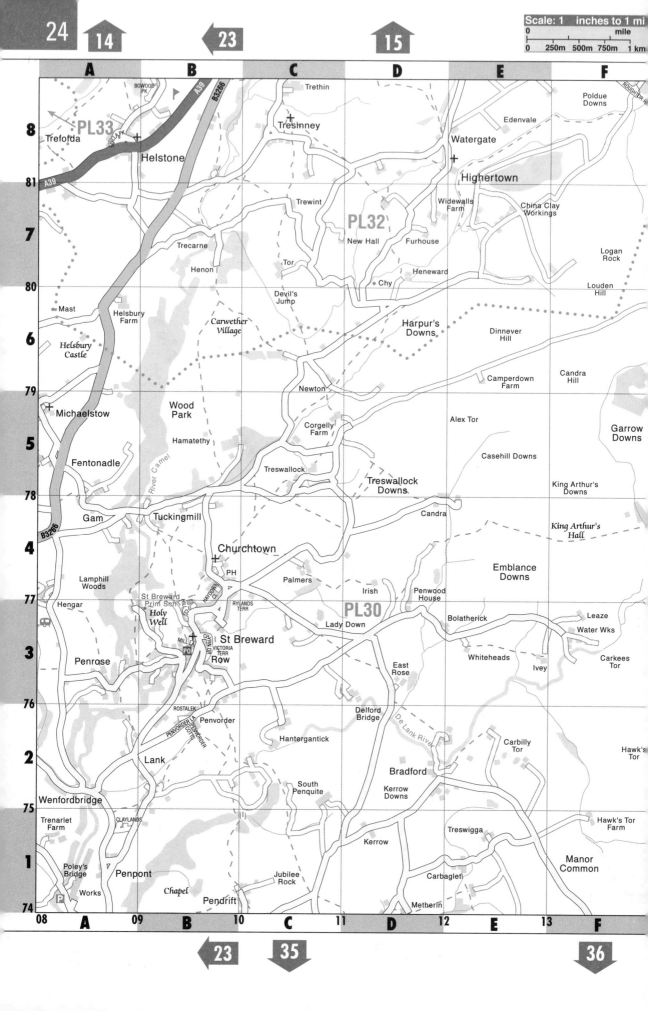

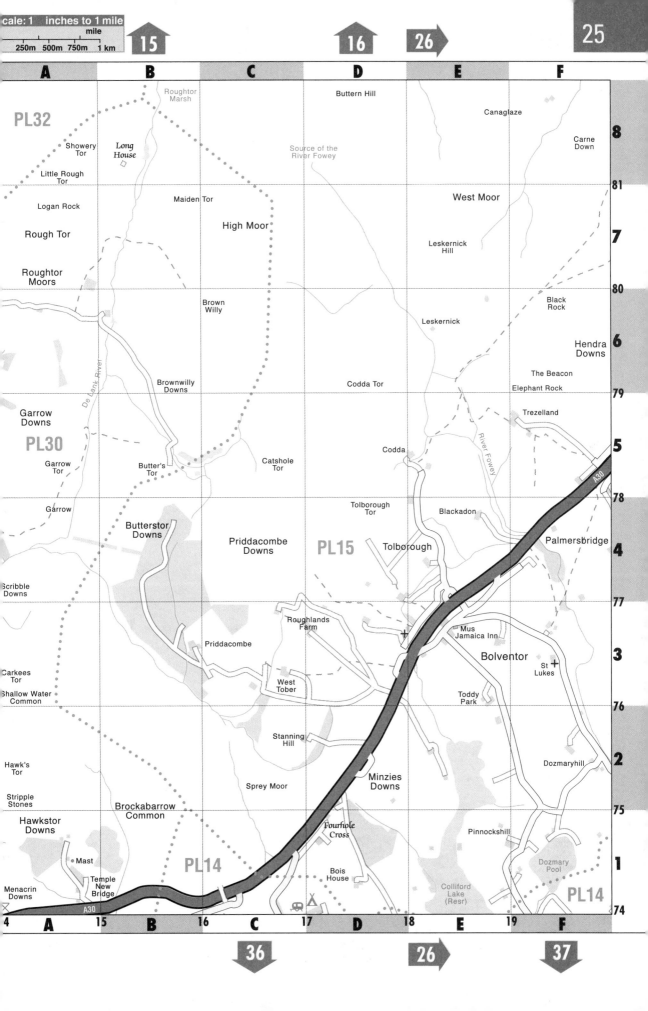

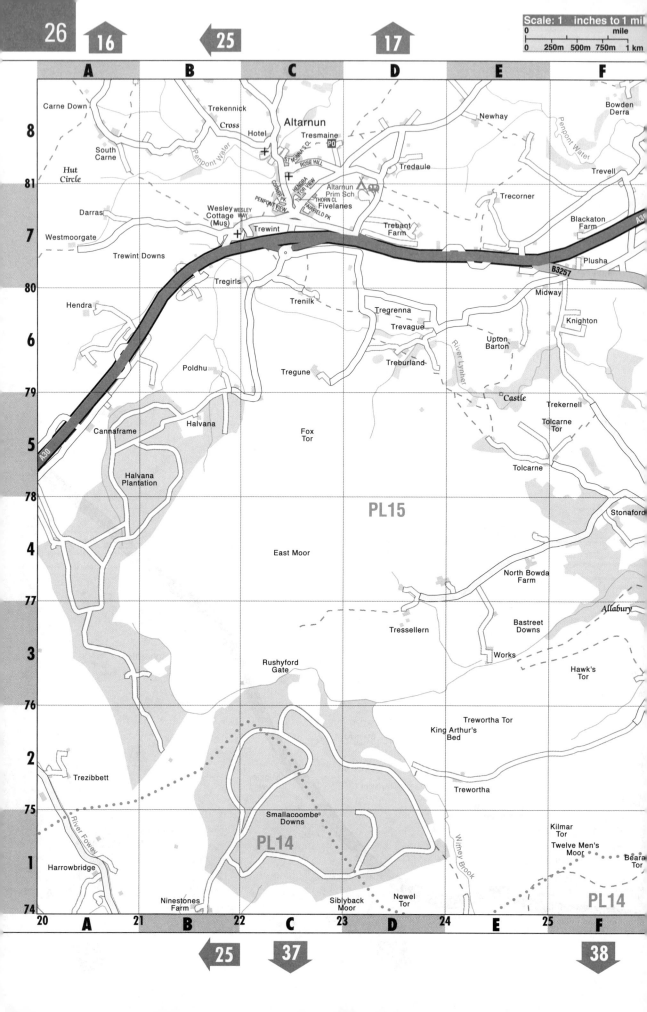

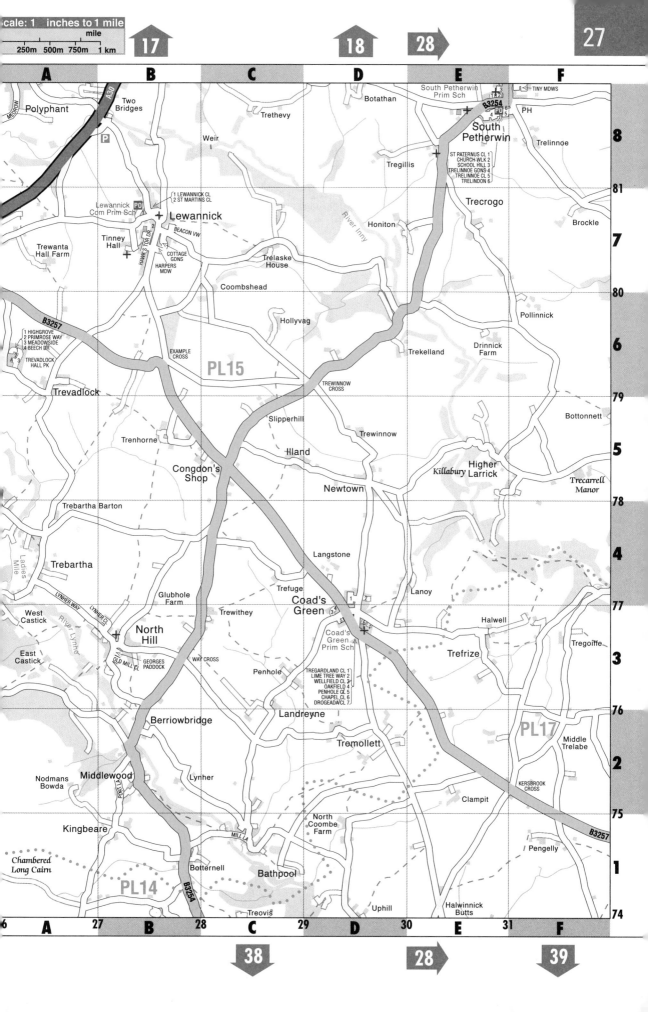

scale: 1 inches to 1 mile
mile
250m   500m   750m   1 km

A   B   C   D   E   F

17   18   28

Polyphant
Two Bridges
Weir
Trethevy
Botathan
South Petherwin Prim Sch
TINY MDWS
South Petherwin
PH
Trelinnoe

8

Tregillis
St PATERNUS CL 1
CHURCH WLK 2
SCHOOL HILL 3
TRELINNOE GDNS 4
TRELINNOE CL 5
TRELINDON 6
Brockle

81

1 LEWANNICK CL
2 ST MARTINS CL
Lewannick Com Prim Sch
Lewannick
River Inny
Honiton
Trecrogo

7

Trewanta Hall Farm
Tinney Hall
BEACON VW
COTTAGE GDNS
HARPERS MDW
Trelaske House
HAWK'S TOR DR

Coombshead
Pollinnick

80

B3257
1 HIGHGROVE
2 PRIMROSE WAY
3 MEADOWSIDE
4 BEECH DR
TREVADLOCK HALL PK
Hollyvag
Trekelland
Drinnick Farm

6

Trevadlock
EXAMPLE CROSS
PL15
TREWINNOW CROSS

79

Slipperhill
Trewinnow
Bottonnett

Trenhorne
Illand
Higher Larrick
Killabury
Trecarrell Manor

5

Congdon's Shop
Newtown

78

Trebartha Barton

Langstone

4

Ladies Mile
Trebartha
Lanoy

Glubhole Farm
Trefuge
77

LYNHER WAY
LYNHER CL
West Castick
Trewithey
Coad's Green
Trewinnow
Halwell
Tregoiffe

3

East Castick
OLD MILL PL
North Hill
GEORGES PADDOCK
WAY CROSS
Coad's Green Prim Sch
Trefrize

River Lynher
Penhole
TREGARDLAND CL 1
LIME TREE WAY 2
WELLFIELD CL 4
OAKFIELD 4
PENHOLE CL 5
CHAPEL CL 6
DROGEADA CL 7
76

Berriowbridge
Landreyne
PL17
Middle Trelabe

2

Nodmans Bowda
Middlewood
Lynher
Tremollett
KERSBROOK CROSS

PORT LA
75

Kingbeare
MILL LA
North Coombe Farm
Clampit
B3257

Chambered Long Cairn
Pengelly

1

PL14
B3254
Botternell
Bathpool
Uphill
Halwinnick Butts
74

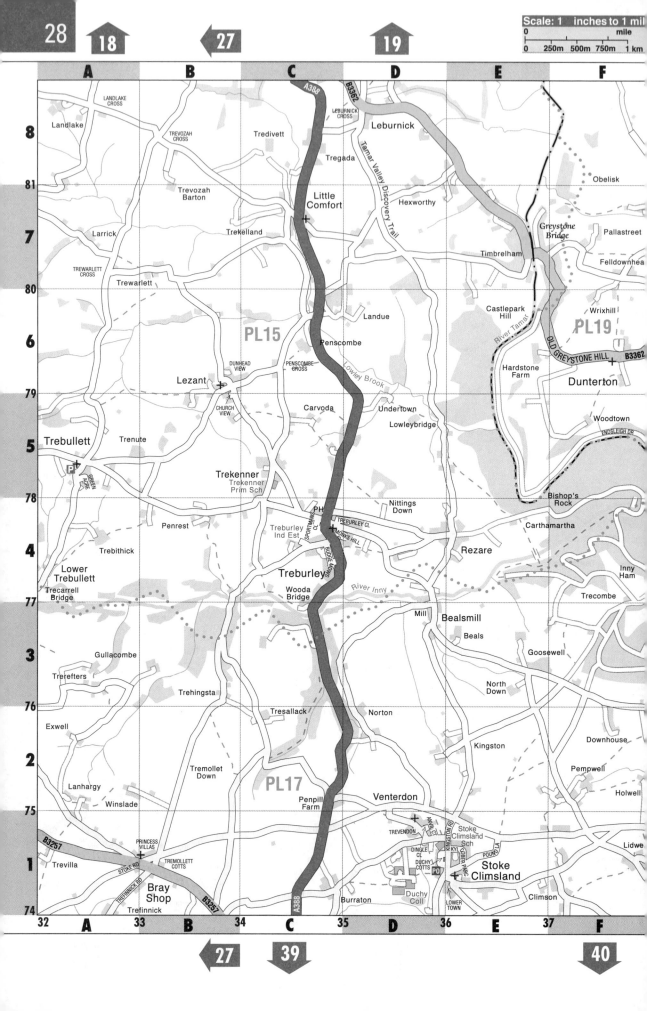

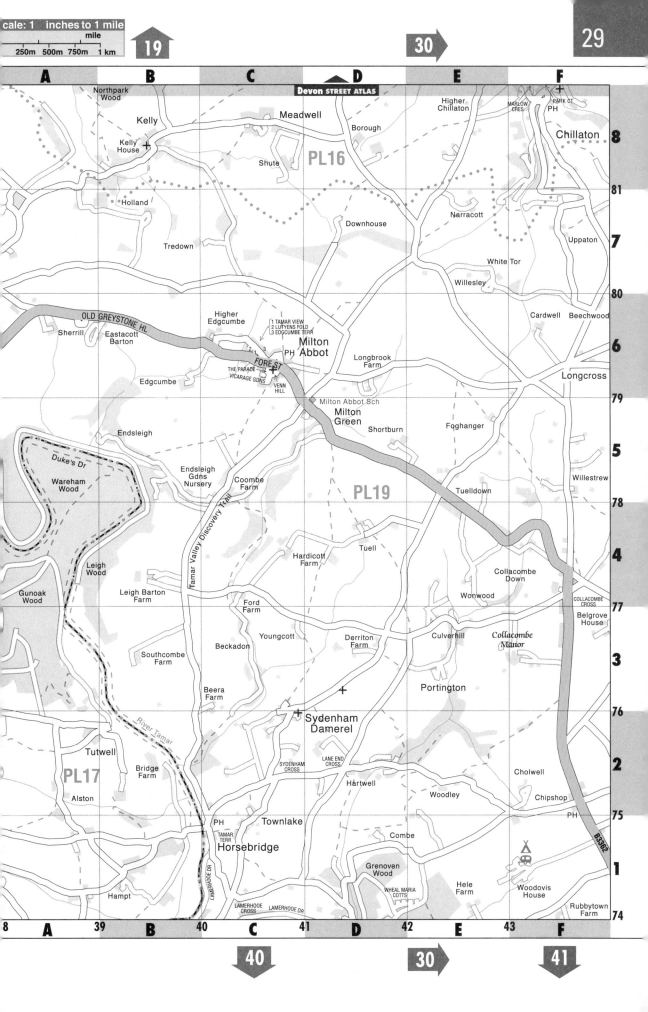

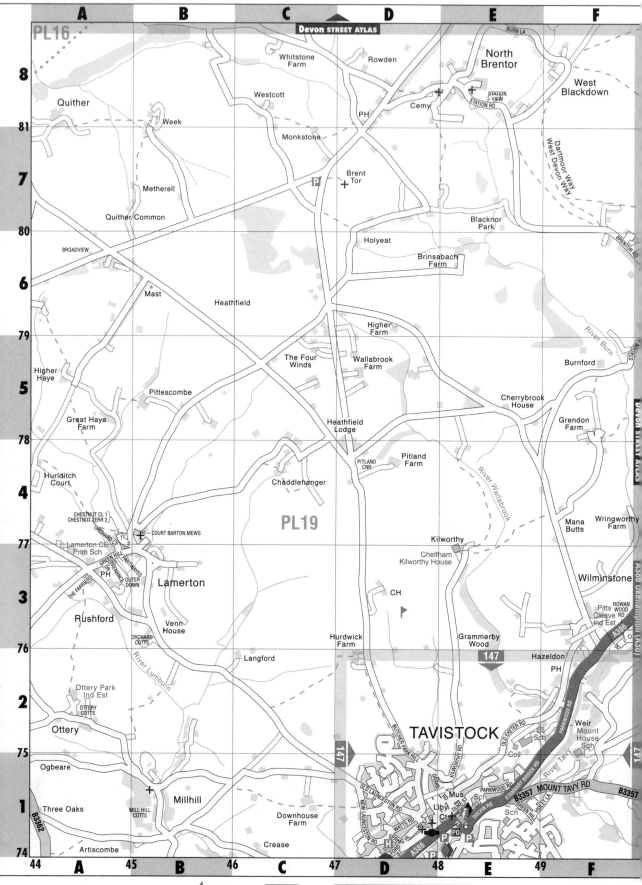

Scale: 1 inches to 1 mil

0   mile

0   250m   500m   750m   1 km

A   B   C   D   E   F

PL16

Devon STREET ATLAS

BURN LA

8

Quither

Whitstone Farm

Rowden

North Brentor

West Blackdown

Westcott

STATION VIEW

81

Week

Monkstone

PH

Cemy

STATION RD

Dartmoor Way
West Devon Way

7

Metherell

P

Brent Tor

Blacknor Park

BRENTOR RD

Quither Common

80

Holyeat

BROADVIEW

Brinsabach Farm

River Burn

6

Mast

Heathfield

Higher Farm

79

The Four Winds

Wallabrook Farm

Burnford

Higher Haye

Pittescombe

Cherrybrook House

Grendon Farm

5

Great Haye Farm

Heathfield Lodge

78

Hurlditch Court

Chaddlehanger

PITLAND CNR

Pitland Farm

River Wallabrook

Mana Butts

Wringworthy Farm

PL19

4

CHESTNUT CL 1
CHESTNUT TERR 2

ORCHARD CT

COURT BARTON MEWS

Kilworthy

Cheltham Kilworthy House

Wilminstone

77

Lamerton CE Prim Sch

GREEN HILL

EARTHWAYES

PH

OUTER DOWN

Lamerton

CH

Pitts Cleave Ind Est

ROWAN WOOD RD

A386 (Okehampton) (A30)

3

THE FARRIERS

Rushford

ORCHARD COTTS

Venn House

Hurdwick Farm

Grammerby Wood

A386

76

River Lumburn

Langford

147

Hazeldon

PH

2

Ottery Park Ind Est

OTTERY COTTS

Weir Mount House Sch

TAVISTOCK

Mount Tavy Rd

River Tavy

75

Ottery

BUTCHER PARK HILL

OLD EXETER RD

PARKWOOD RD

STANNARY BRIDGE RD

Coll

Sch

147

Ogbeare

OLD LAUNCESTON RD

DRAKE RD

KILWORTHY RD

PARKWOOD RD

GREEN HILL

B3357

MOUNT TAVY RD

B3357

1

Three Oaks

Millhill

MILL HILL COTTS

Downhouse Farm

NEW LAUNCESTON RD

WATTS RD

FORD ST

SPRING HILL

WEST ST

DOLVIN RD

DUKE ST

Mus

Liby

Ct

Sch

VIGO LA

Sch

B3362

Artiscombe

Crease

A386

PO

74

44   A   45   B   46   C   47   D   48   E   49   F

For full street detail of the highlighted area see page 147.

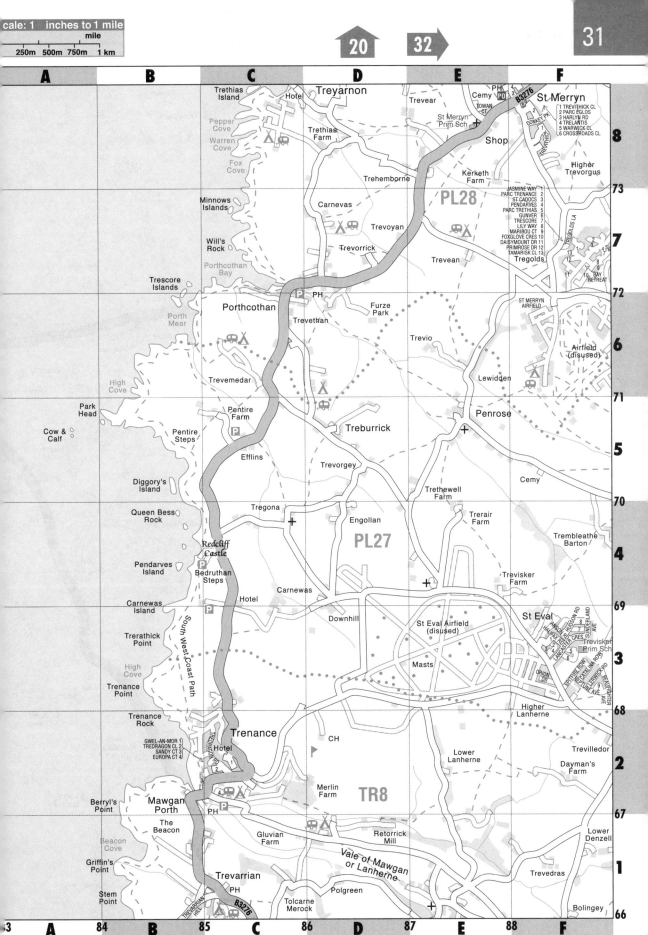

scale: 1   inches to 1 mile

mile

250m 500m 750m 1 km

A   B   C   D   E   F

Trethias
Island

Treyarnon

Trevear

Hotel

St Merryn

1 TREVITHICK CL
2 PARC EGLOS
3 HARLYN RD
4 TRELANTIS
5 WARWICK CL
6 CROSSROADS CL

Pepper
Cove

Trethias
Farm

St Merryn
Prim Sch

Cemy

PH
PO

B3276

TOWAN
CT

Warren
Cove

Shop

Higher
Trevorgus

8

Fox
Cove

Kerketh
Farm

JASMINE WAY   1
PARC TRENANCE 2
ST CADOCS   3
PENDARVES   4
PARC TRETHIAS 6
GUNVER   5
TRESCORE   7
LILY WAY   8
MARIBOU CT   9
FOXGLOVE CRES 10
DAISYMOUNT DR 11
PRIMROSE DR   12
TAMARISK CL   13

73

Minnows
Islands

Trehemborne

Carnevas

PL28

Trevoyan

Will's
Rock

Trevorrick

Trevean

TREGOLDS LA

Tregolds

13   12
11

9 8
10. BAY
    RETREAT

7

72

Trescore
Islands

Porthcothan
Bay

Porthcothan

Trevethan

Furze
Park

P   PH

ST MERRYN
AIRFIELD

Porth
Mear

Trevio

Airfield
(disused)

6

High
Cove

Trevemedar

Lewidden

71

Park
Head

Pentire
Farm

Treburrick

Penrose

5

Cow &
Calf

Pentire
Steps

P

Efflins

Trevorgey

Cemy

Diggory's
Island

Trethewell
Farm

70

Queen Bess
Rock

Tregona

Engollan

Trerair
Farm

Trembleathe
Barton

4

Pendarves
Island

Redcliff
Castle   P

PL27

Trevisker
Farm

Bedruthan
Steps   P

Carnewas

Carnewas
Island   P

Hotel

South West Coast Path

Downhill

St Eval Airfield
(disused)

St Eval

SUNDERLAND
AVE
RUDLOPH RD

HALIFAX RD
LANCASTER CRES
LENGTHER CRES

Trevisker
Prim Sch

69

Trerathick
Point

Masts

SPITFIRE ROW
CATALINA ROW

LERWICK RD
NEPTUNE AVE

BEAUFIGHTER
AVE

High
Cove

ORION
DR

3

Trenance
Point

Higher
Lanherne

68

Trenance
Rock

Trenance

CH

Trevilledor

2

GWEL-AN-MOR 1
TREDRAGON CL 2
SANDY CT 3
EUROPA CT 4

TREGRON RD

Hotel

Merlin
Farm

Lower
Lanherne

Dayman's
Farm

Berryl's
Point

Mawgan
Porth   P

TR8

67

Beacon
Cove

The
Beacon

PH

Gluvian
Farm

Retorrick
Mill

Lower
Denzell

Griffin's
Point

Vale of
Mawgan
or Lanherne

Trevedras

1

Stem
Point

Trevarrian

PH

Polgreen

Bolingey

66

TREVARRIAN HILL

B3276

Tolcarne
Merock

A   B   C   D   E   F

F3

1 BOTHA RD
2 WELLINGTON RD
3 MOSQUITO CRES
4 LIBERATOR ROW
5 WARWICK CRES
6 LINCOLN ROW
7 VILDEBEEST RD
8 BEAUFORT AVE
9 SHACKLETON CRES

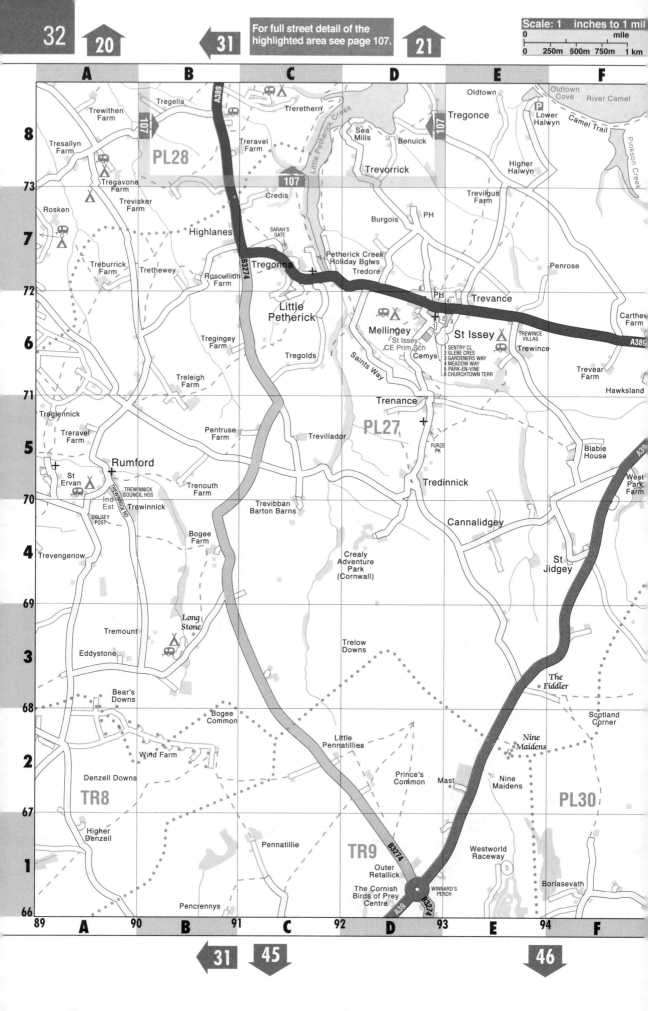

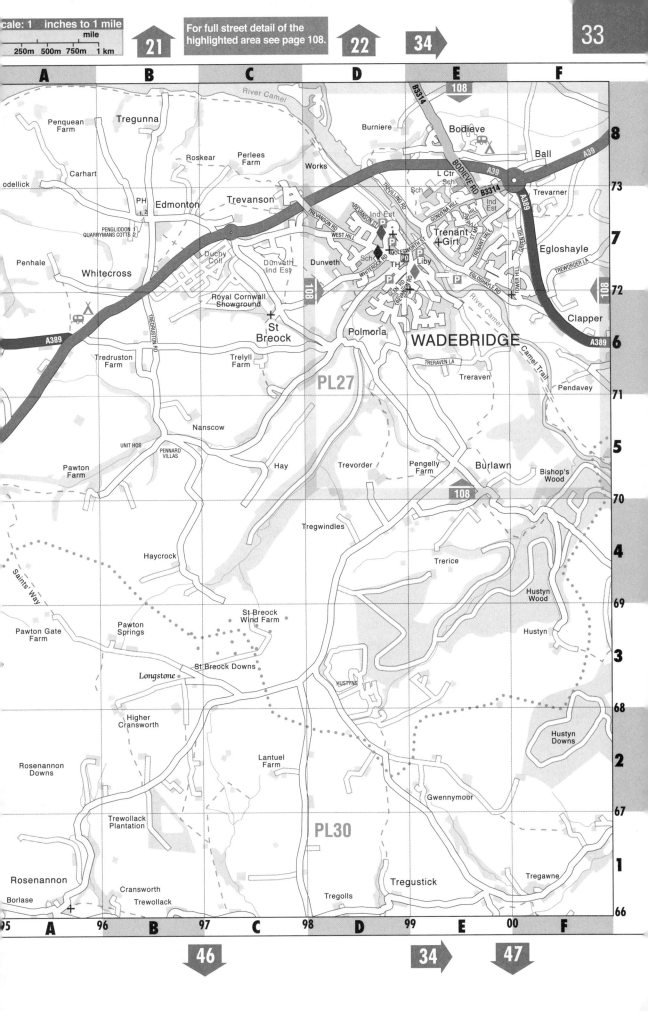

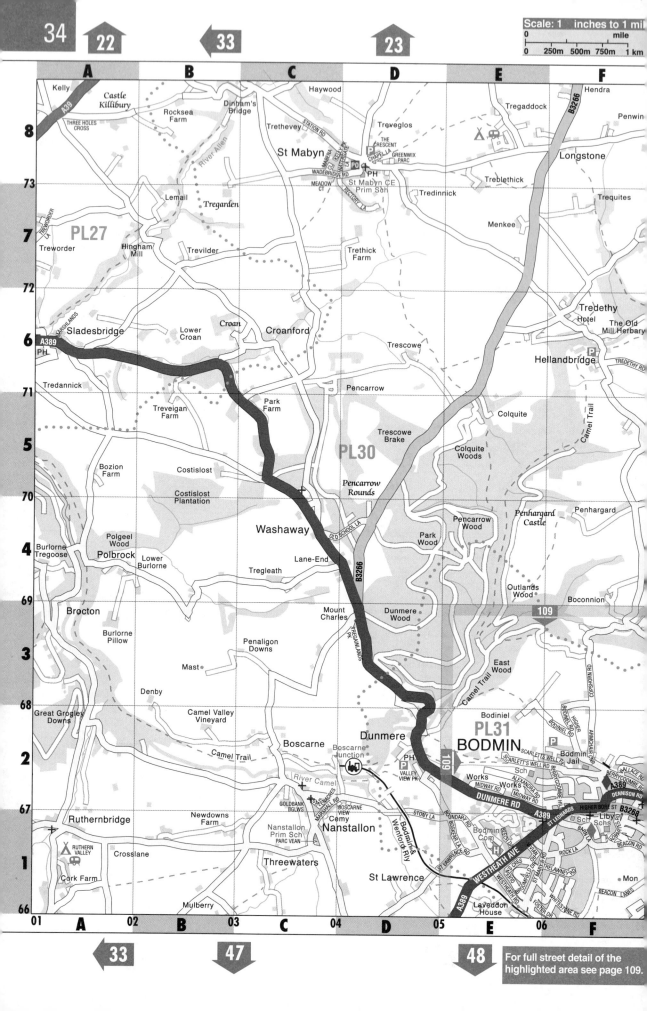

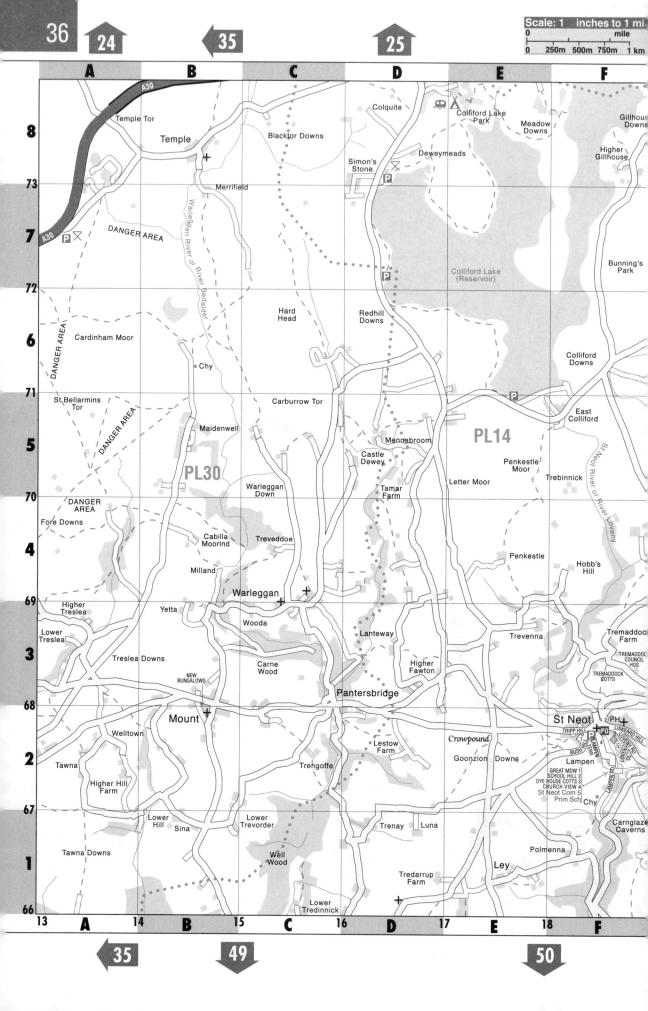

A   B   C   D   E   F

A30

Temple Tor

Temple

Colquite

Colliford Lake Park

Meadow Downs

Gillhous Downs

8

Blacktor Downs

Deweymeads

Higher Gillhouse

Merrifield

Simon's Stone

P

73

DANGER AREA

P

7

Colliford Lake (Reservoir)

Bunning's Park

72

Warleggan River or River Bedalder

Hard Head

Redhill Downs

P

6

DANGER AREA

Cardinham Moor

Colliford Downs

Chy

71

St Bellarmins Tor

Carburrow Tor

East Colliford

DANGER AREA

Maidenwell

Mennabroom

PL14

5

Penkestle Moor

Trebinnick

PL30

Castle Dewey

Warleggan Down

Tamar Farm

Letter Moor

70

DANGER AREA

Fore Downs

Cabilla Moorlnd

Treveddoe

Penkestle

Hobb's Hill

4

Milland

St Neot River or River Loveny

Warleggan

69

Higher Treslea

Yetta

Wooda

Lanteway

Trevenna

Tremaddoc Farm

Lower Treslea

Treslea Downs

Carne Wood

Higher Fawton

TREMADDOC COUNCIL HOS

3

NEW BUNGALOWS

Pantersbridge

TREMADDOCK COTTS

68

Mount

St Neot

PH

Welltown

Lestow Farm

Crowpound

TRIPP HILL

LISKEARD HILL

P PO

BUSH HILL

LAMPEN TERR

Tawna

Goonzion Downs

Lampen

LOVENY RD

2

Trengoffe

GREAT MDW 1
SCHOOL HILL 2
DYE HOUSE COTTS 3
CHURCH VIEW 4
St Neot Com 5
Prim Sch

LAMPEN RD

Chy

Higher Hill Farm

67

Lower Hill

Sina

Lower Trevorder

Trenay

Luna

Carnglaze Caverns

Polmenna

Tawna Downs

1

Well Wood

Ley

Tredarrup Farm

66

Lower Tredinnick

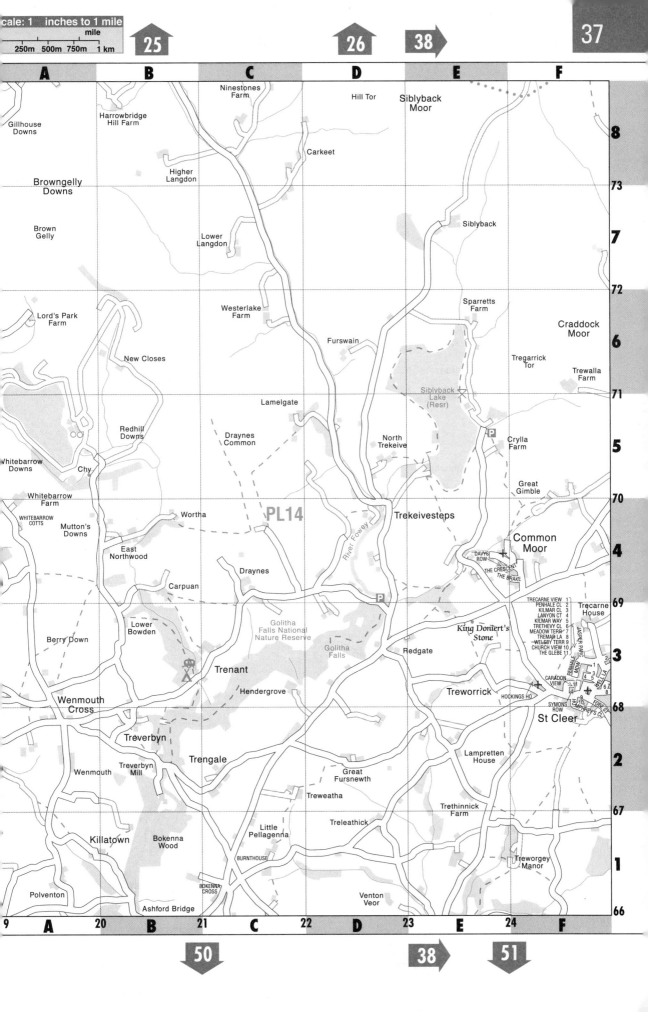

A   B   C   D   E   F

8
73
7
72
6
71
5
70
4
69
3
68
2
67
1
66

Gillhouse
Downs

Harrowbridge
Hill Farm

Ninestones
Farm

Hill Tor

Siblyback
Moor

Carkeet

Browngelly
Downs

Higher
Langdon

Siblyback

Brown
Gelly

Lower
Langdon

Lord's Park
Farm

Westerlake
Farm

Sparretts
Farm

Craddock
Moor

New Closes

Furswain

Tregarrick
Tor

Trewalla
Farm

Lamelgate

Siblyback
Lake
(Resr)

Redhill
Downs

Draynes
Common

North
Trekeive

Crylla
Farm

Whitebarrow
Downs

Chy

Great
Gimble

Whitebarrow
Farm

Wortha

PL14

Trekeivesteps

WHITEBARROW
COTTS

Mutton's
Downs

River Fowey

Common
Moor

East
Northwood

Draynes

DAVYS
ROW

THE CRESCENT
THE BRAKE

Berry Down

Lower
Bowden

Carpuan

Golitha
Falls National
Nature Reserve

Golitha
Falls

Redgate

King Doniert's
Stone

TRECARNE VIEW 1
PENHALE CL 2
KILMAR CT 3
LANYON CT 4
KILMAR WAY 5
TRETHEVY CL 6
MEADOW TERR 7
TREMAR LA 8
WELSBY TERR 9
CHURCH VIEW 10
THE GLEBE 11

Trecarne
House

Trenant

Hendergrove

Treworrick

HOCKINGS HO

CARADON
VIEW

SYMONS
ROW

HUMPHREY'S CL

St Cleer

Wenmouth
Cross

Treverbyn

Treverbyn
Mill

Trengale

Great
Fursnewth

Lampretten
House

Wenmouth

Treweatha

Trethinnick
Farm

Killatown

Bokenna
Wood

Little
Pellagenna

Treleathick

BURNTHOUSE

Polventon

BOKENNA
CROSS

Venton
Veor

Treworgey
Manor

Ashford Bridge

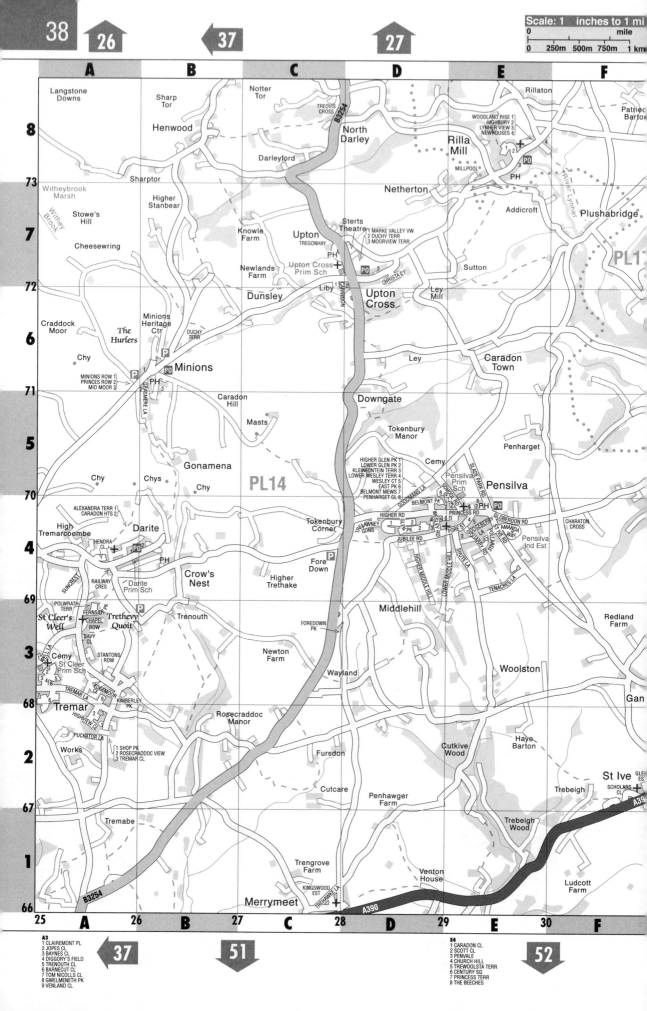

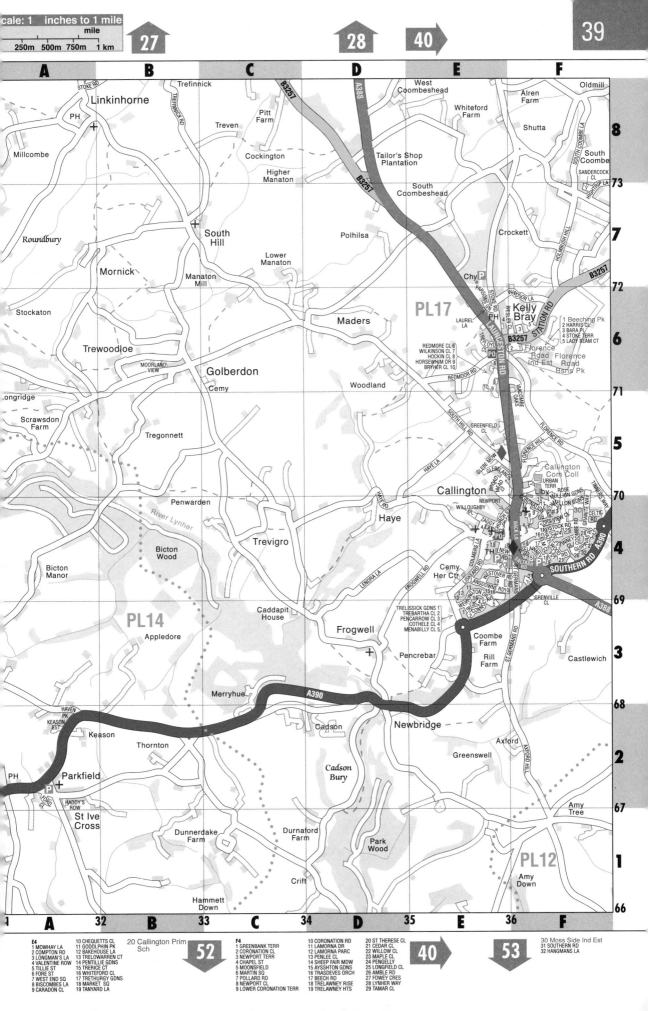

A B C D E F

8
73
7
72
6
71
5
70
4
69
68
3
2
67
1
66

Linkinhorne
PH
Millcombe
Stoke Rd
Trefinnick
Trennick Rd
Treven
Treven
B3257
A388
West Coombeshead
Whiteford Farm
Alren Farm
Oldmill
South Coombe
South Coombe La
Sandercock Cl
High Rip La
Shutta
Pitt Farm
Cockington
Higher Manaton
Tailor's Shop Plantation
South Coombeshead
Crockett
B3257
Roundbury
South Hill
Lower Manaton
Polhilsa
B3257
Kelly Bray
Windsor La
Wesley Rd
Stone Rd
Station Rd
Holmbush Hill
Mornick
Manaton Mill
PL17
Chy
Parsons Grn
Laurel La
PH
B3257
1 Beeching Pk
2 Harris Cl
3 Bara Pl
4 Stone Terr
5 Lady Beam Ct
Stockaton
Moorland View
Trewoodloe
Golberdon
Cemy
Maders
Woodland
Redmore Cl 6
Wilkinson Cl 7
Hockin Cl 8
Horsewhim Dr 9
Bryher Cl 10
Redmoor Rd
Florence Road
Florence Road
Florence Ind Est
Florence Bsns Pk
Laurel La
Treloyd
PO
ongridge
Scrawsdon Farm
Tregonnett
River Lynher
Penwarden
Haye Rd
Haye La
South Hill Rd
Greenfield Cl
Glebe Mdw
Glebelands
Broad Rd
Florence Hill
Florence Rd
Callington Com Coll
Liby
Urban Terr
Rose
Bullion Gdns
Mellon Gdns
Callington
Bicton Wood
Trevigro
Haye
Newport
Willoughby Pl
Zaggy Church Rd
New Rd
Back La
Coronation Rd
Tavistock Rd
Guys
Coombe Gdns
Granite Way
Celtic Rd
Tinney Way
A390
Bicton Manor
PL14
Appledore
Caddapit House
Frogwell
Cemy
Her Ctr
Colmers La
Iskard Rd
Lansdowne Rd
Westover Rd
Lendra La
Frogwell Rd
New
Trelissick Gdns 1
Trebartha Cl 2
Pencarrow Cl 3
Cothele Cl 4
Menabilly Cl 5
TH
P
Saltash Rd
Trelawny
St Germans Rd
Grenville Cl
A388
Coombe Farm
Rill Farm
Castlewich
Pencrebar
Newbridge
Axford
Greenswell
Axford Hill
Merryhue
A390
Cadson
Cadson Bury
Amy Tree
Haven Pk
Keason Est
Keason
Thornton
Ford Cl
Haddy's Row
PH
Parkfield
P
St Ive Cross
Dunnerdake Farm
Durnaford Farm
Park Wood
PL12
Amy Down
Hammett Down
Crift

A B C D E F

31 32 33 34 35 36

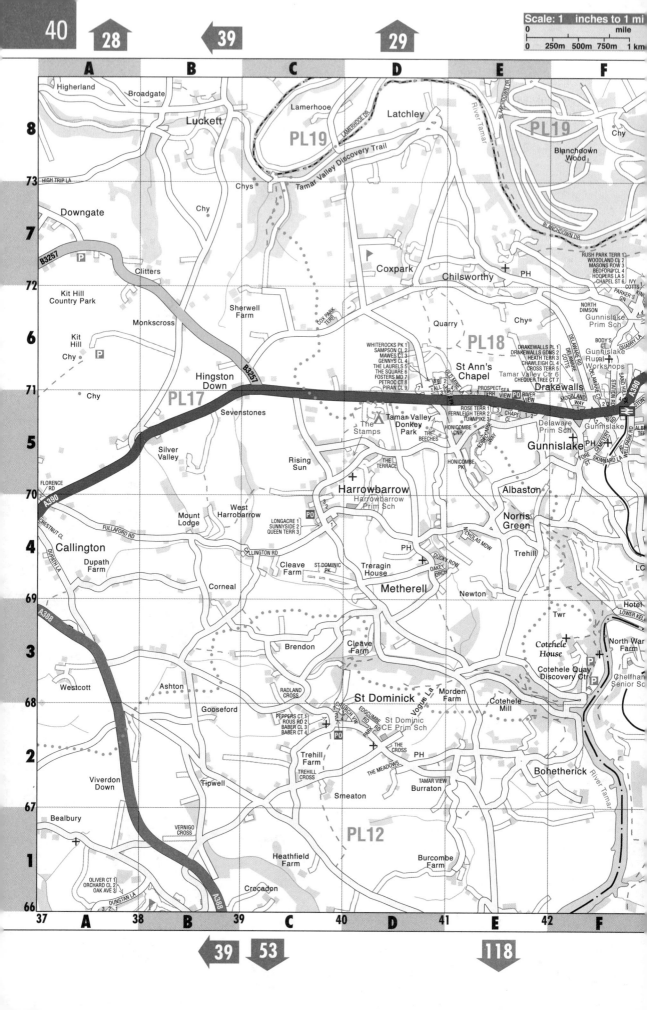

Scale: 1 inches to 1 mile

250m 500m 750m 1 km

For full street detail of the highlighted area see page 147.

29 30 42 41

A B C D E F

8
73
7
72
6
71
5
70
4
69
3
68
2
67
1
66

TAVISTOCK

B3362
B3257
Gulworthy
Gulworthy Cross
Gulworthy Prim Sch
Gulworthy Cotts
Saw Mill
New Bridge
Hatchwood House
Mast
Hatch Wood
Honeytor
Hawkmoor House Farm
NEWBRIDGE HILL
AND HILL FORE ST
PO

Newton Farm
Colcharton
River Lumburn
Hurlditch Horn
PH
The Rock
Morwelldown Plantation
Morwell Barton

BUCTOR PK 1
ABBOTSFIELD CL 2
ORCHARD CL
ABBOTSFIELD CRES
CREASE LA
URANDS
CALLINGTON RD
A390
A386
PIXON LA
Coll
Cemy
Brook
PLYMOUTH RD
BROOK LA
WHITCHURCH RD
A386

Parswell
Shillamill
Crowndale
147
Works
Rixhill
Anderton
Woodtown
West Devon Way
Birch Wood
Tor
Higher Walreddon
Mast
Walreddon
147

PL19

1 CLIFF VIEW TERR
2 CROCKER'S ROW
3 SIMMS TERR
4 EDGCUMBE CL
5 ALMA TERR
6 UNDER RD
7 PROSPECT TERR
8 THE ORCHARD
9 COMMERCIAL ST
10 THE CRESCENT
11 STAR PK
12 NEW COTTS
13 RODDA CL
14 MUDGES TERR
15 WOODLAND WAY
16 HIGHER TAMAR TERR
17 LOWER TAMAR TERR

Morwell Wood
Oakenhayes
Slimeford Farm
River Tamar
PL18

Morwell
Hartshole Farm
Broadwell
West Down
Double Waters
River Walkham

Power Sta
DUKES DR
Morwellham
Morwellham Quay
Harewood
Newquay
Maddacleave Wood
Hocklake Farm
Bucktor
River Tavy
Berra Tor
Alston
Coppicetown
St Andrew's CE Prim Sch

CHAPEL MDW 1
RICHMOND TERR 2
HILLSIDE CL 3
CUXTON MDWS 4
HILL VIEW 5
MODY
FORD WLK
THE VILLAGE

Chys
Gawton Farm
Rumleigh Farm
Balstone
Hatch Mill
Didham Farm
Denham Bridge

CHURCH HILL
ST ANDREW'S CL
ROWSE GDNS
HAREWOOD RD
ERIC RD
Calstock Prim Sch
LC
Calstock
CHURCH LA
STATION RD
MARSH LA
PO PH

1 ROSE HILL TERR
2 COTEHELE VIEW
3 TAMAR TERR
4 LANG GDNS
5 BAPTIST ST
6 PROVIDENCE PL
7 CHURCH ST
8 FORE ST
9 THE ADITS

Buttspill
Tuckermarsh
Helston Farm
Ashen
Braunder
Lockridge Farm
Whitsam
WHITSAM CROSS

Bere Alston
NEW RD
STATION RD
Chelfham
Bere Alston Prim Sch
Mount Tamar
PL20
Leigh
TAVISTOCK CROSS
QUARRY CNR
HUNTER'S OAK
Fishacre Wood
Milton Combe
CHURCH HILL
PH
ALLEY
Buckland Abbey

BROAD PARK RD
BEDFORD ST
PILGRIM
WOOLACOMBE RD
ALEXANDRA DR
B3257
THE DOWN
PENTILLIE RD
Woolacombe Farm
WOOLACOMBE CROSS
Tamar Valley Discovery Trail
Newhouse

20 TRINITY CL
21 HILLSIDE CT
22 PENTILLIE CT
23 PENTILLIE VW
24 CHESTNUT CL

B1
1 POUNDS PARK RD
2 JOHNSON CL
3 DRAKE'S PK
4 CHAPEL ST
5 WEST VIEW RD
6 BEDFORD PL
7 BEDFORD VILLAS
8 PARK LA
9 WHITEHALL DR
10 BEDFORD PK
11 PILGRIM CT
12 ST ANDREWS CL
13 LANGMAN CT
14 EDGCUMBE TERR
15 MARYTHORNE RD
16 THE SQUARE
17 THE CLOSE
18 TAMAR CL
19 MAYFLOWER CL

119 42 120

43 44 45 46 47 48

42

30

41

For full street detail of the highlighted area see page 147.

Scale: 1 inches to 1 mile
0 | mile
0 250m 500m 750m 1 km

C5
1 MADEIRA VILLAS
2 GREENWAY CL
3 KNIGHTON TERR
4 WALKHAM TERR
5 THE GREEN
6 SAMPFORD TERR

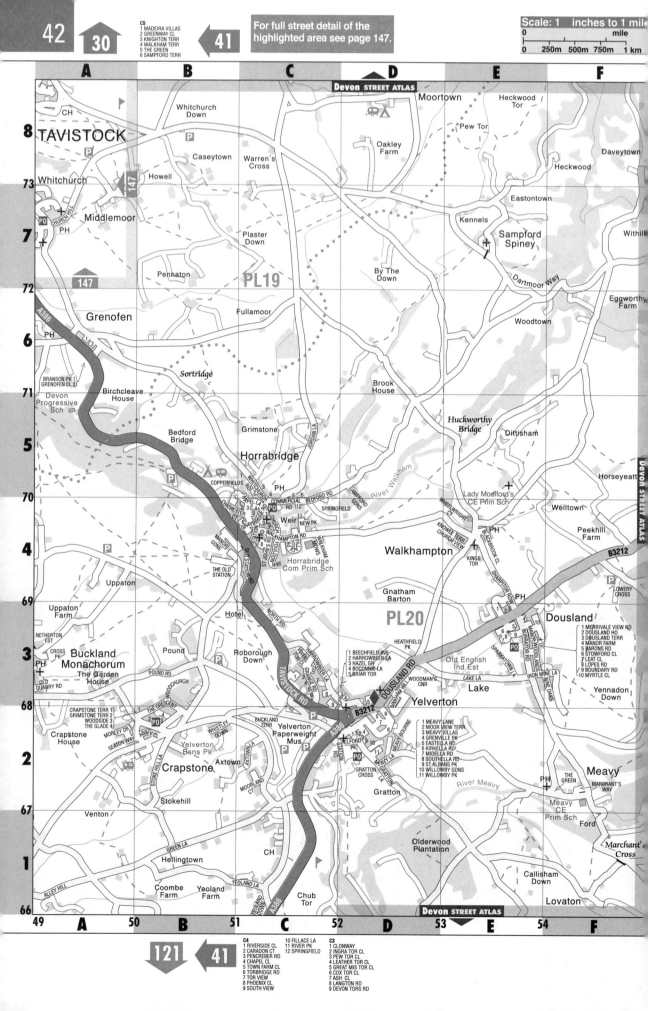

Devon STREET ATLAS

TAVISTOCK
Whitchurch
Middlemoor
Whitchurch Down
Caseytown
Warren's Cross
Howell
Pennaton
Plaster Down
PL19
Fullamoor
Grenofen
Sortridge
Birchcleave House
Devon Progressive Sch
Bedford Bridge
Grimstone
Horrabridge
Copperfields
Weir
Walkhampton
Horrabridge Com Prim Sch
Manor Gdns
Uppaton
Uppaton Farm
Netherton Est
Cross Pk
Buckland Monachorum
The Garden House
Old Quarry Rd
Crapstone Terr
Grimstone Terr
Woodside
The Glade
Crapstone House
Crapstone
Stoke Hill
Stokehill
Venton
Hotel
Roborough Down
Pound
Pound Rd
Woodchurch
The Crescent
Morley Dr
Abbey Cl
Seaton Way
Yelverton Bsns Pk
Whistley Down
Axtown
Moorland Ct
Hellingtown
Green La
Coombe Farm
Yeoland Farm
Yeoland La
Yeoland Down
CH
Chub Tor

Moortown
Heckwood Tor
Pew Tor
Oakley Farm
Daveytown
Heckwood
Eastontown
Kennels
Sampford Spiney
Withill
By The Down
Dartmoor Way
Eggworthy Farm
Woodtown
Brook House
Huckworthy Bridge
Dittisham
Horseyeatt
Lady Modiford's CE Prim Sch
Welltown
Wheelwright Ct
Knowle Terr Church View
Peekhill Farm
Kings Tor
Blackbrook Cl
PH
B3212
Sharpitor Rd
Lowery Cross
Dousland
Heathfield Pk
PL20
Old English Ind Est
Woodman's Cnr
Lake La
Lake
Iron Mine La
Yennadon Down
Yelverton
Meavy La
Elford
Gratton Cross
Gratton
Olderwood Plantation
River Meavy
Meavy
The Green
Marchant's Way
Meavy CE Prim Sch
Ford
Callisham Down
Lovaton
Marchant's Cross

Yelverton Paperweight Mus
Buckland Terr
Yelverton Terr
Axtown

Devon STREET ATLAS

121

41

C4
1 RIVERSIDE CL
2 CARADON CT
3 PENCREBER RD
4 CHAPEL CL
5 TOWN FARM CL
6 TORBRIDGE RD
7 TOR VIEW
8 PHOENIX CL
9 SOUTH VIEW
10 FILLACE LA
11 RIVER PK
12 SPRINGFIELD

C3
1 CLONWAY
2 INGRA TOR CL
3 PEW TOR CL
4 LEATHER TOR CL
5 GREAT MIS TOR CL
6 COX TOR CL
7 ASH CL
8 LANGTON RD
9 DEVON TORS RD

1 MEAVY LANE
2 MOOR VIEW TERR
3 MEAVY VILLAS
4 GRENVILLE PK
5 EASTELLA RD
6 KIRKELLA RD
7 MIDELLA RD
8 SOUTHELLA RD
9 ST ALBANS PK
10 WILLOWBY GDNS
11 WILLOWBY PK

1 MERRIVALE VIEW RD
2 DOUSLAND HO
3 DOUSLAND TERR
4 MANOR FARM
5 BARONS RD
6 STOWFORD CL
7 LEAT CL
8 LOPES RD
9 BOUNDARY RD
10 MYRTLE CL

1 BEECHFIELD AVE
2 HARROWBEER LA
3 HAZEL GR
4 BOCONNIC LA
5 BRIAR TOR

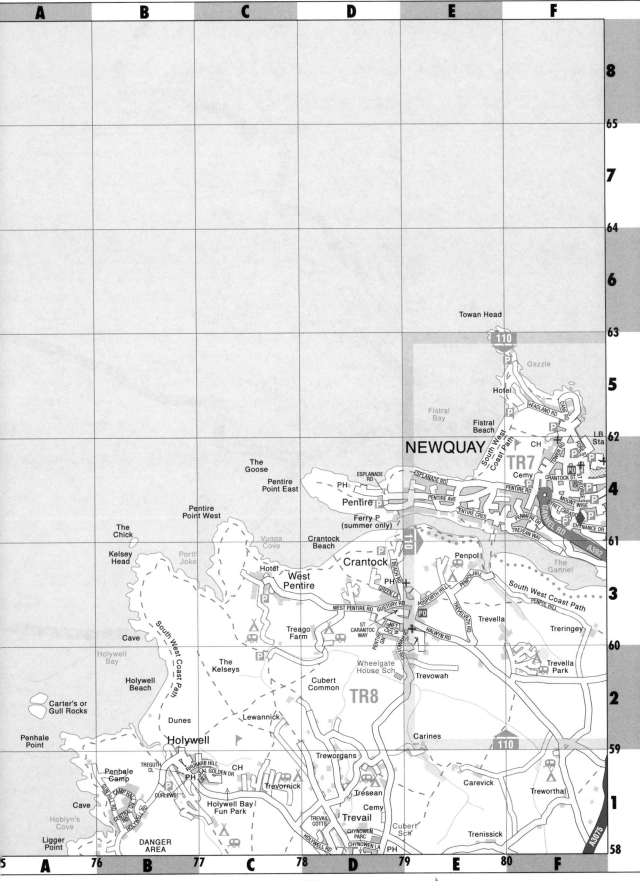

A B C D E F

8

65

7

64

6

Towan Head

63

110

Gazzle

5

Fistral
Bay

Hotel

Fistral
Beach

L.B.
Sta

62

NEWQUAY

South West Coast Path

TR7

CH

The
Goose

Pentire
Point East

PH

ESPLANADE
RD

ESPLANADE RD

Cemy

CRANTOCK ST

4

Pentire

Pentire Ave

Pentire RD

Mount
Wise

Ferry P
(summer only)

110

Pentire Cres

PENMERE DR

STRET CARADO

CHYNANCE DR

Pentire
Point West

The
Chick

Vugga
Cove

Crantock
Beach

TREVEAN WAY

CANNEL RD

A392

61

Kelsey
Head

Porth
Joke

Hotel

West
Pentire

Crantock

BEACH RD

PH

Penpol

GOSPORTH HILL

Trevella

PENPOL HILL

The
Gannel

South West Coast Path

3

GREEN LA

WEST PENTIRE RD

GUSTORY RD

PO

TREVELLICK RD

Cave

South West Coast Path

Treago
Farm

ST
CARANTOC
WAY

PENTIRE

HALWYN RD

Treringey

60

Holywell
Bay

The
Kelseys

Trevowah

Trevella
Park

Carter's or
Gull Rocks

Cubert
Common

Wheelgate
House Sch

TR8

2

Dunes

Lewannick

Carines

110

Penhale
Point

Holywell

59

Penhale
Camp

TREGUTH
CL

RHUBARB HILL

CH

Treworgans

Trevornick

Carevick

Treworthal

A3075

GOLDEN DR

PH

Cave

CURLEWS

Tresean

Trevail

1

Hoblyn's
Cove

Holywell Bay
Fun Park

TREVAIL
COTTS

Cemy

Cubert
Sch

Trenissick

Ligger
Point

DANGER
AREA

CHYNOWEN
PARC

HOLYWELL RD

CHYNOWEN LA

PH

58

A B C D E F

76 77 78 79 80

55 ↓

44 →

For full street detail of the
highlighted area see page
110.

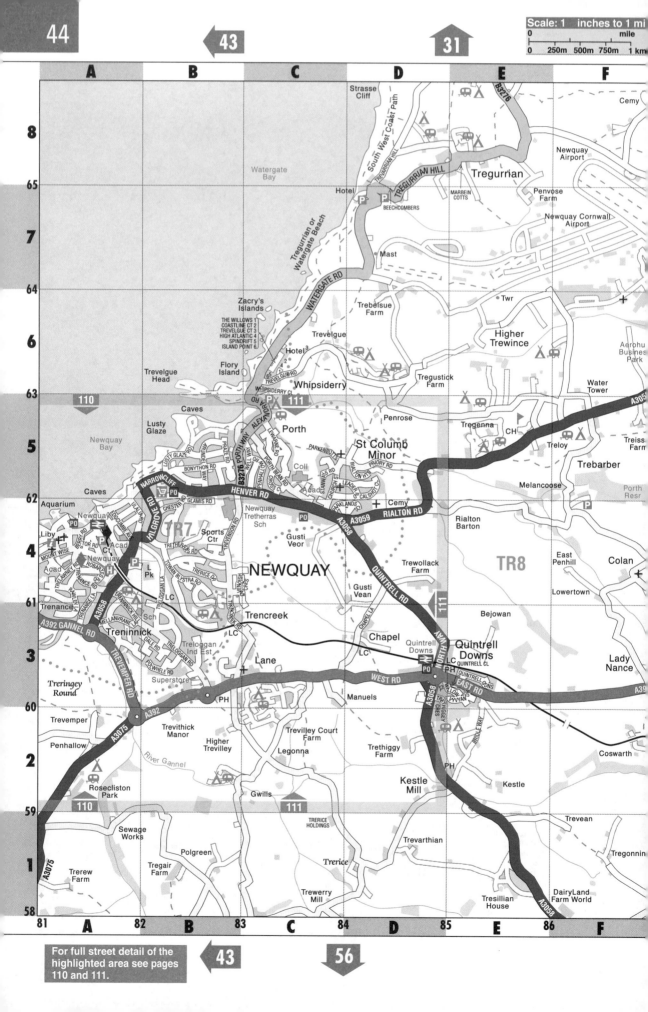

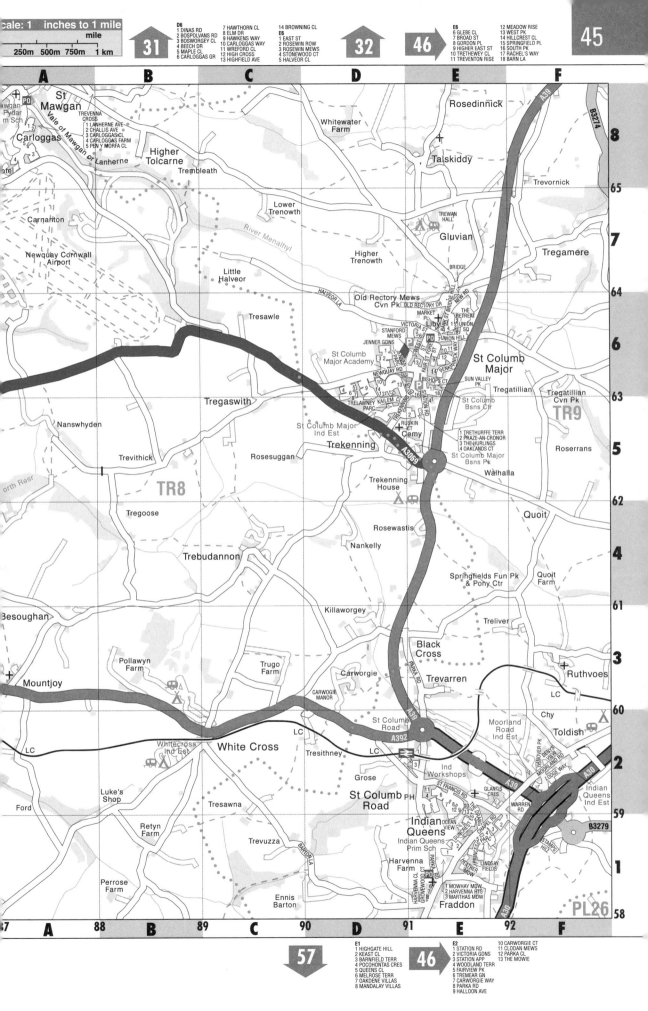

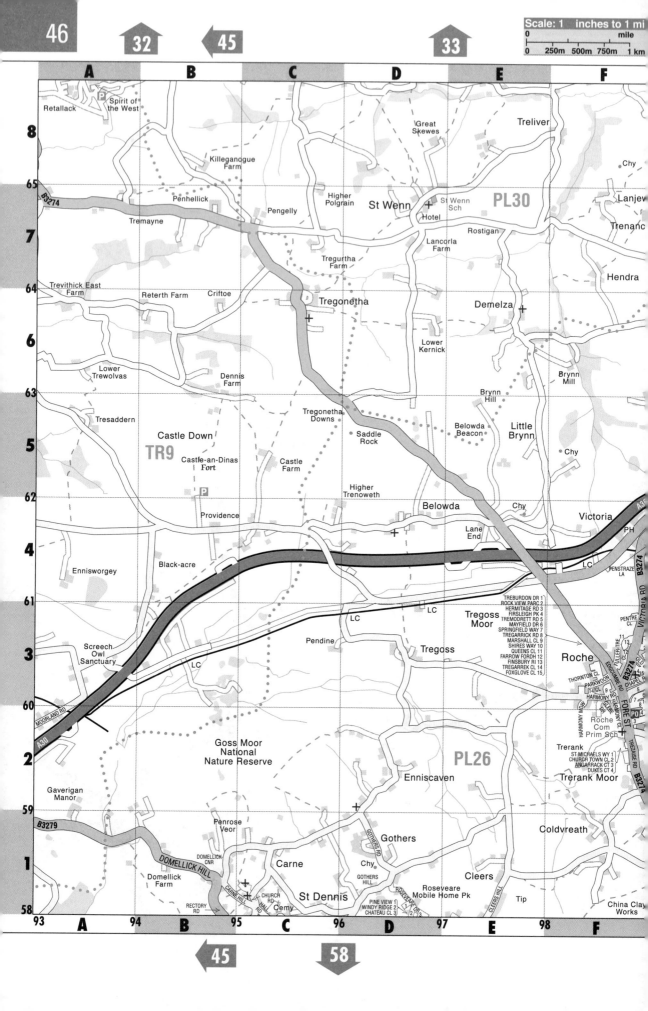

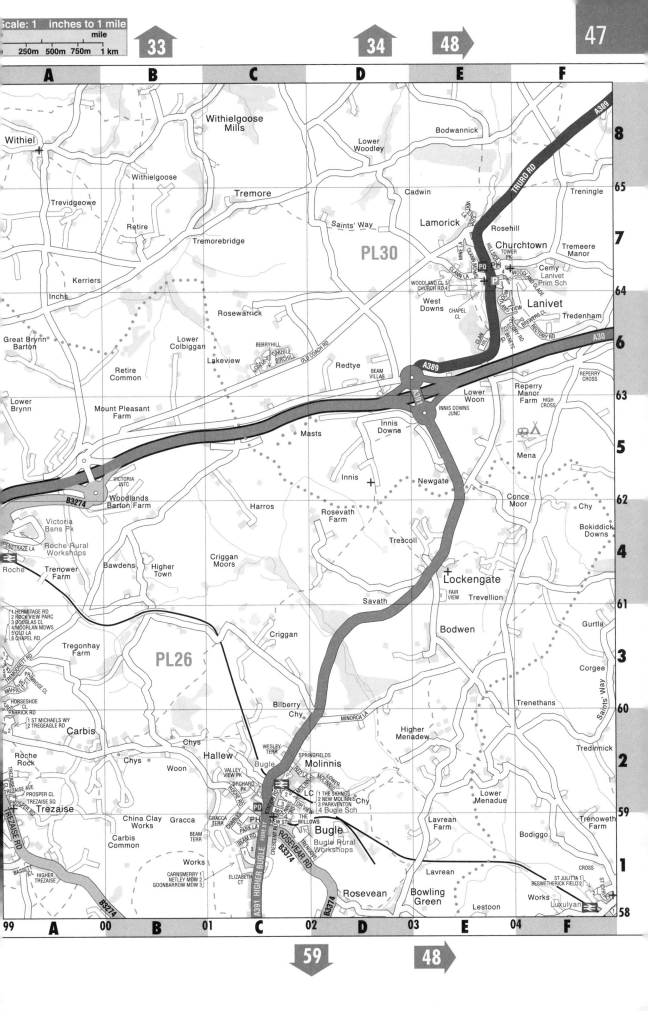

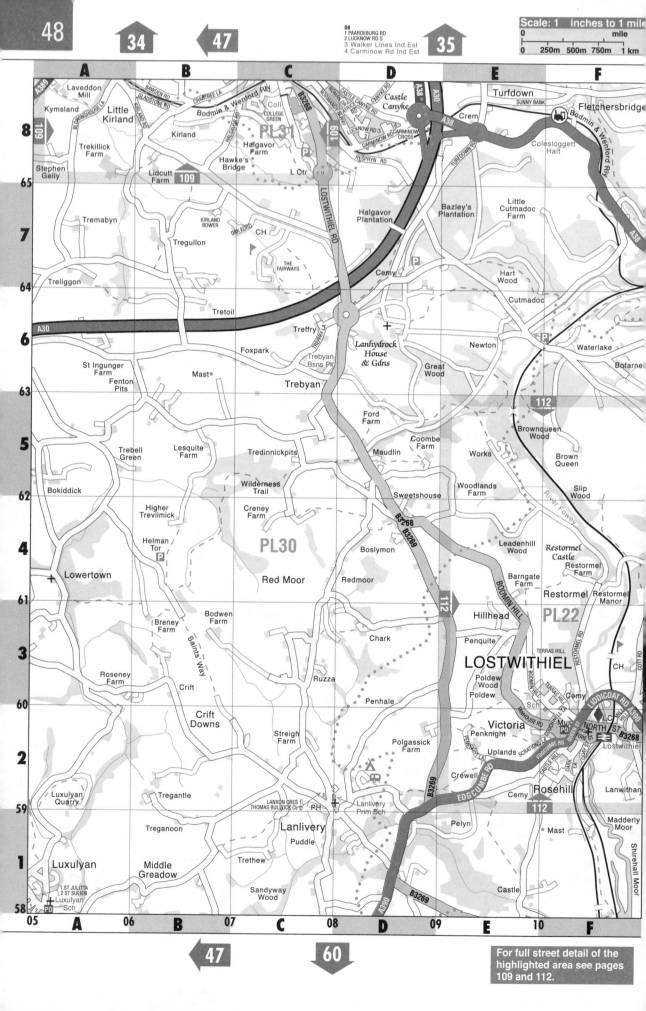

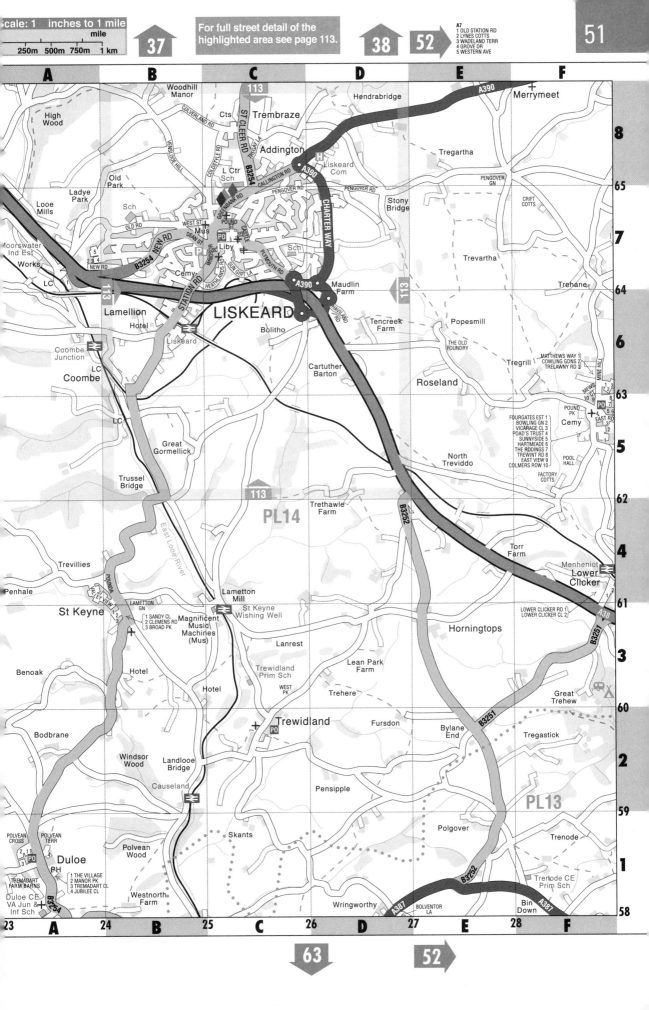

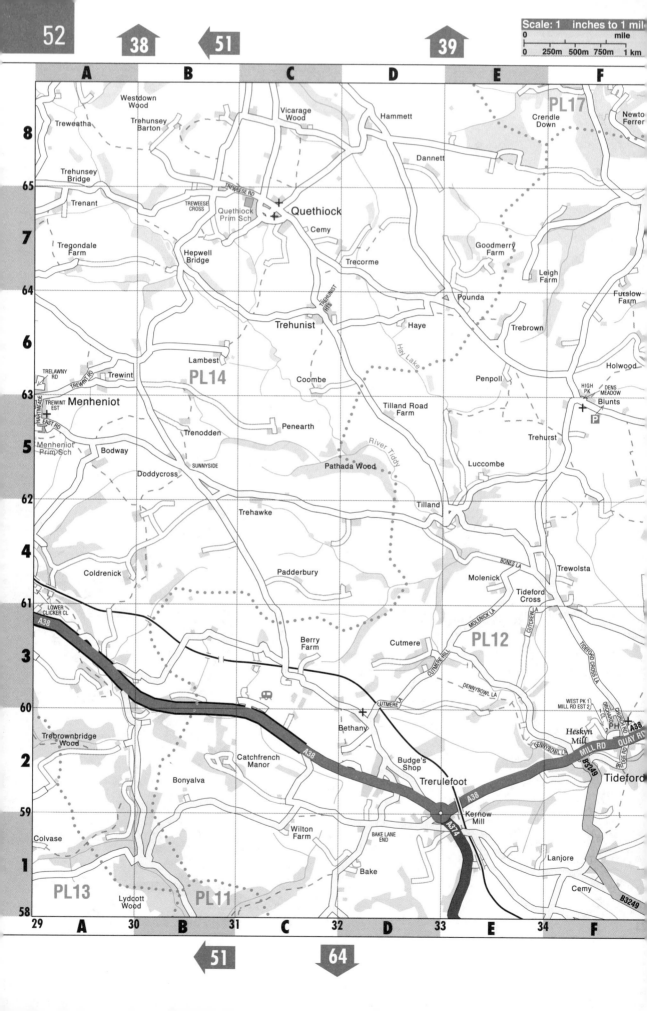

A B C D E F

PL17

Bramble Wood

New Down

Keason

St Mellion Park

KEASON HILL
LAKE VIEW
WOOD DR
1 THE ROWANS
2 ORCHARD CL
3 WOOD DR

Hotel

Woolaton

CHURCH PK

St Mellion CE Prim Sch

PH

St Mellion

Crocadon Wood

Halton Barton

8

Clapper Bridge

Herod Down

Tor

Trewashford

Mushton

THE GLEBE

Polborder

Tremoan

Mount Ararat

65

Herod Wood

MARY MOON CL
THE ROW
BRAMS PK
BARTON MDWS

Hotel

CHAPEL PL

Pillaton

Rowse

Trehill

BRISTON ORCH

PAYNTER'S CROSS

PAYNTER'S CROSS-COTTS

Pentillie Castle

7

64

Pillatonmill

Kernock

Sillaton

118

Stockadon Farm

6

Holwood

Coombe

Howton

Leigh Farm

LEIGH LA

Smeaton

Ellbridge

P

63

Cuttivett

River Lynher

Villaton

Hatt House

ANDREW PL

Bicton

PO

5

Trevashmond

PL12

Penquite

WOTTON CROSS

Wotton Farm

STUARTS WAY

VALLARD'S LA

BOADEN CL
FAIRMEAD CL 2
CARLTON VILLAS 3

MAYBANKS

Cross Farm

Rumbullion Farm

62

Trewandra Farm

TARTEN CROSS

DOLBEARE PK

COCA'S LA

NARROW LA

4

Brightor

Sir Robert Geffery's CE Prim Sch

FRENCHMAN'S LA

Notter Bridge

PH

Notter

Botusfleming

PH

61

Cutlinwith

LANTALLACK CROSS

POUND HILL
HOME PK

WEST LA

NEW ROAD TERR

Landrake

SCHOOL RD

PH

STONEY LANDS

QUARRY LA

PH

Broadmoor Farm

A388

3

QUAY RD

KILN LA

PENCAVO HILL

PO

ELFORD RD

BARTON RD

CHURCH ST

POSSESSION LA

LISKEARD RD

WHITY CROSS

60

THE CRESCENT 1
DUCKY LA 2
GEFFERY CL 3
BARTON MEWS 4
NORTH RD 5
THE SQUARE 6

7 JUBILEE COTTS
8 HOOPERS CL
9 MENHINICK CL
10 ADAMS BRCK
11 LITTLE ORCH
12 LOWERTOWN CL

POLDRISSICK LA

WOOD LA

DUCK LA

BROAD LA

TOWNSWELL LA

Trematon

122

B3271

Latchbrook

A38

2

Tredinnick

TREDINNICK LA

TREWINT LA

Trewint

POLDRISSICK HILL

POLDRISSICK LA

CUMBLE TOR LA

THORNWELL LA

Ind Ests

FELLDOWN RD

Penimble

River Tiddy

TIDEFORD DR

St Erney

Poldrissick

Treluggan Manor

VOSS RD

59

Lithiack

Berry Hill

Markwell

Trevollard

Burell House

Longlands

LONGLANDS LA

1

GALLERY LA

QUAY LA

TREVOLLARD LA

Trehan

58

A 36 B 37 C 38 D 39 E 40 F

For full street detail of the highlighted area see pages 118 and 122.

Scale: 1 inches to 1 mile

C1
1 BRECON CL
2 BEACONSFIELD PL
3 WHITE'S CL
4 ANGWIN AVE
5 CHURCHTOWN
6 CHEGWYN GDNS
7 KEMP'S CL
8 BOLSTER CL
9 PENWINNICK CL
10 TREGELLAS CL
11 POLBREEN LA
12 POLBREEN AVE

D1
1 PENGARTH
2 CASTLE MDWS
3 CASTLE MEADOWS CT
4 PENWINNICK PARC
5 MIDDLEGATES
6 GRENVILLE DR
7 LAMBOURNE AVE
8 ATLANTIC MEWS
9 HIGHFIELD CT
10 THE OLD SCHOOL
11 STIPPY STAPPY
12 MINERS WAY
13 KERENSA GDNS
14 PARKLANDS

Shag Rock
Shafts (dis)
Cligga Head
Cligga Workshops 1
ST GEORGE'S TERR 2
B3285
Shafts (dis)
Hotel
TR6
Hanover Cove
Anchor
South West Coast Path
Airfield
Green Island
Trevellas
Trevellas Porth
Cross Coombe
Chy
Blowinghouse
Newdowns Head
Trevaunance Cove
Heritage Trail
Blue Hills
Trevellas Coombe
Perran View Holiday Pk
TR5
Crams
New Downs
Chy
Shafts (dis)
PH
Wheal Kitty Workshops
Mithian Prim Sch
St Agnes Head
Wheal Kitty
Barkla Shop
Carn Gowla
Higher Bal
Chy
Peterville
Mithian
Tubby's Head
Chy
St Agnes Beacon
Liby
Mus
St Agnes Prim Sch
B3285
Town Hill
St Agnes
Goonown
Cemy
Bawden Rocks

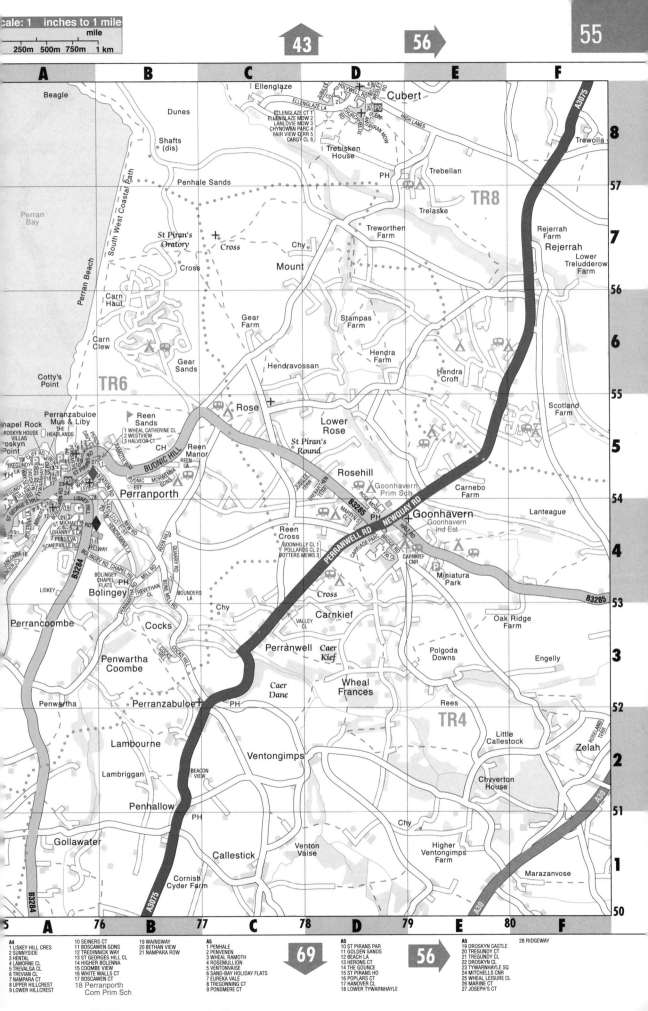

A4
1 LISKEY HILL CRES
2 SUNNYSIDE
3 HENTAL
4 LAMORNE CL
5 TREVALGA CL
6 TREVIAN CL
7 NAMPARA CT
8 UPPER HILLCREST
9 LOWER HILLCREST

10 SEINERS CT
11 BOSCAWEN GDNS
12 TREDINNICK WAY
13 ST GEORGES HILL CL
14 HIGHER BOLENNA
15 COOMBE VIEW
16 WHITE WALLS CT
17 BOSCAWEN CT
18 Perranporth
   Com Prim Sch

19 WAINSWAY
20 BETHAN VIEW
21 NAMPARA ROW

A5
1 PENHALE
2 PENVENEN
3 WHEAL RAMOTH
4 ROSEMULLION
5 VENTONVAISE
6 SAND-BAY HOLIDAY FLATS
7 EUREKA VALE
8 TREGONNING CT
9 PONSMERE CT

A5
10 ST PIRANS PAR
11 GOLDEN SANDS
12 BEACH LA
13 HERONS CT
14 THE GOUNCE
15 ST PIRANS HO
16 POPLARS CT
17 HANOVER CL
18 LOWER TYWARNHAYLE

A5
19 DROSKYN CASTLE
20 TREGUNDY CT
21 TREGUNDY CL
22 DROSKYN CL
23 TYWARNHAYLE SQ
24 MITCHELLS CNR
25 WHEAL LEISURE CL
26 MARINE CT
27 JOSEPH'S CT

28 RIDGEWAY

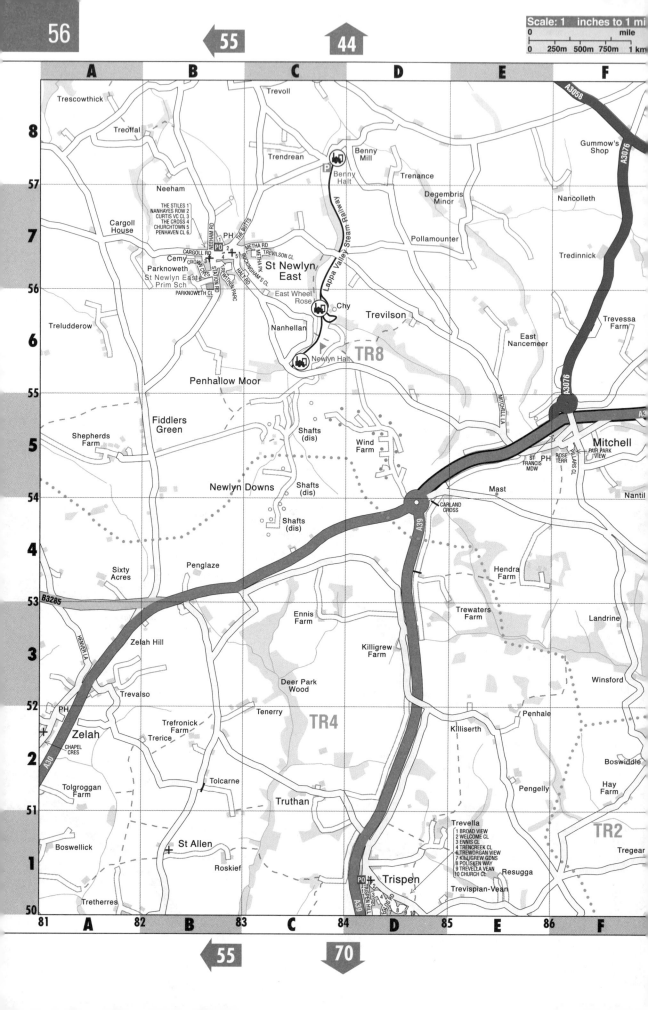

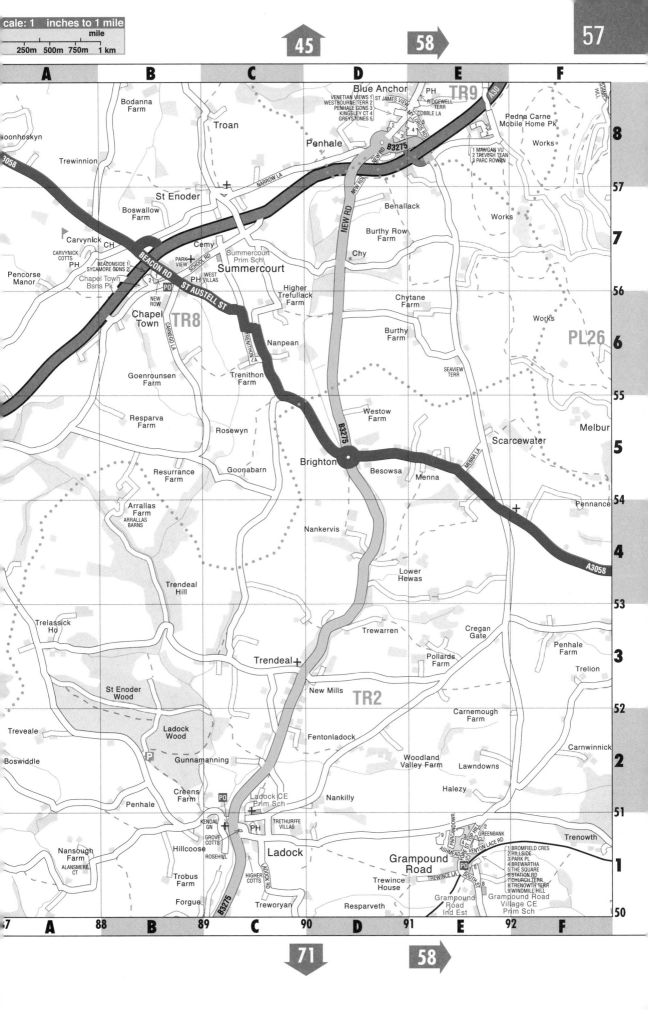

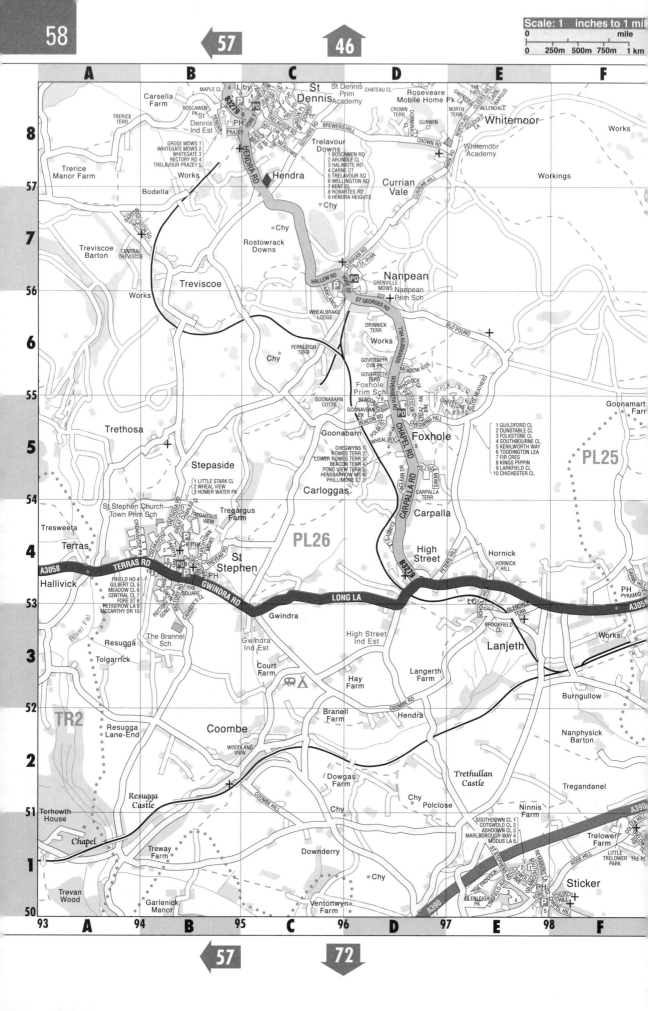

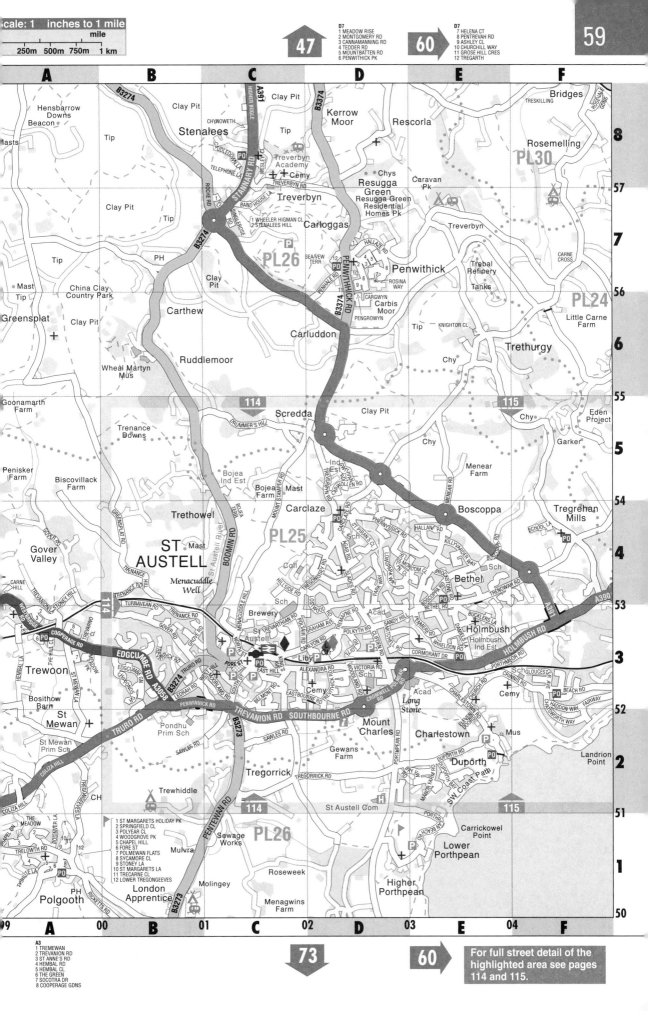

D7
1 MEADOW RISE
2 MONTGOMERY RD
3 CANNAMANNING RD
4 TEDDER RD
5 MOUNTBATTEN RD
6 PENWITHICK PK

D7
7 HELENA CT
8 PENTREVAH RD
9 ASHLEY CL
10 CHURCHILL WAY
11 GROSE HILL CRES
12 TREGARTH

60

A   B   C   D   E   F

Hensbarrow
Downs
Beacon

Bridges

Rosemelling

PL30

Masts

Stenalees

Clay Pit

Clay Pit

Kerrow
Moor

Rescorla

CHYNOWETH

HIGHER BUGLE

Treskilling

ROSEVALE GDNS

8

Tip

Tip

Treverbyn
Academy

Cemy

Resugga
Green
Resugga Green
Residential
Homes Pk

Chys

Caravan
Pk

Treverbyn

57

Clay Pit

Tip

Treverbyn

Carloggas

Carne
Cross

7

1 WHEELER HIGMAN CL
2 STENALEES HILL

SEA VIEW
TERR

Penwithick

Trebal
Refinery

Mast
Tip

China Clay
Country Park

Clay Pit

PL26

Clay Pit

Cargwyn
Carbis
Moor

Rosina
Way

Tanks

PL24

56

Greensplat

Carthew

Pengrowyn

Tip

Knightor Cl

Little Carne
Farm

Wheal Martyn
Mus

Ruddlemoor

Carluddon

Chy

Trethurgy

6

Goonamarth
Farm

114

Scredda

Clay Pit

115

Chy

Eden
Project

55

Trenance
Downs

DRUMMER'S HILL

Chy

Garker

Penisker
Farm

Biscovillack
Farm

Bojea
Ind Est

Bojea
Farm

Mast

Menear
Farm

Boscoppa

Tregrehan
Mills

5

Trethowel

Carclaze

PL25

SCHOOL LA

54

Gover
Valley

ST
AUSTELL

Mast

Bethel

Sch

4

Menacuddle
Well

Holmbush

A390

Holmbush
Ind Est

53

Trewoon

EDGCUMBE RD

A3058

Brewery

St
Austell

Liby

Acad

HOLMBUSH RD

Sch
GLOUCESTER
AVE

3

Bosithow
Barn

St
Mewan

TRURO RD

B3274

TREVANION RD SOUTHBOURNE RD

Long
Stone

Charlestown

Mus

52

St Mewan
Prim Sch

Pondhu
Prim Sch

Mount
Charles

Duporth

Landrion
Point

2

THE
MEADOW

Tregorrick

Gewans
Farm

SW Coast Path

Carrickowel
Point

Trelowth RD

Trewhiddle

114

St Austell Com

115

Lower
Porthpean

51

1 ST MARGARETS HOLIDAY PK
2 SPRINGHILL CL
3 POLYEAR CL
4 WOODGROVE PK
5 CHAPEL HILL
6 FORE ST
7 POLMEWAN FLATS
8 SYCAMORE CL
9 STONEY LA
10 ST MARGARETS LA
11 TRECARNE CL
12 LOWER TREGONGEEVES

PL26

Mulvra

Sewage
Works

Roseweek

Higher
Porthpean

1

PH

Polgooth

London
Apprentice

Molingey

Menagwins
Farm

50

09   A   00   B   01   C   02   D   03   E   04   F

A3
1 TREMEWAN
2 TREVANION RD
3 ST ANNE'S RD
4 HEMBAL RD
5 HEMBAL CL
6 THE GREEN
7 SOCOTRA DR
8 COOPERAGE GDNS

73

60

For full street detail of the
highlighted area see pages
114 and 115.

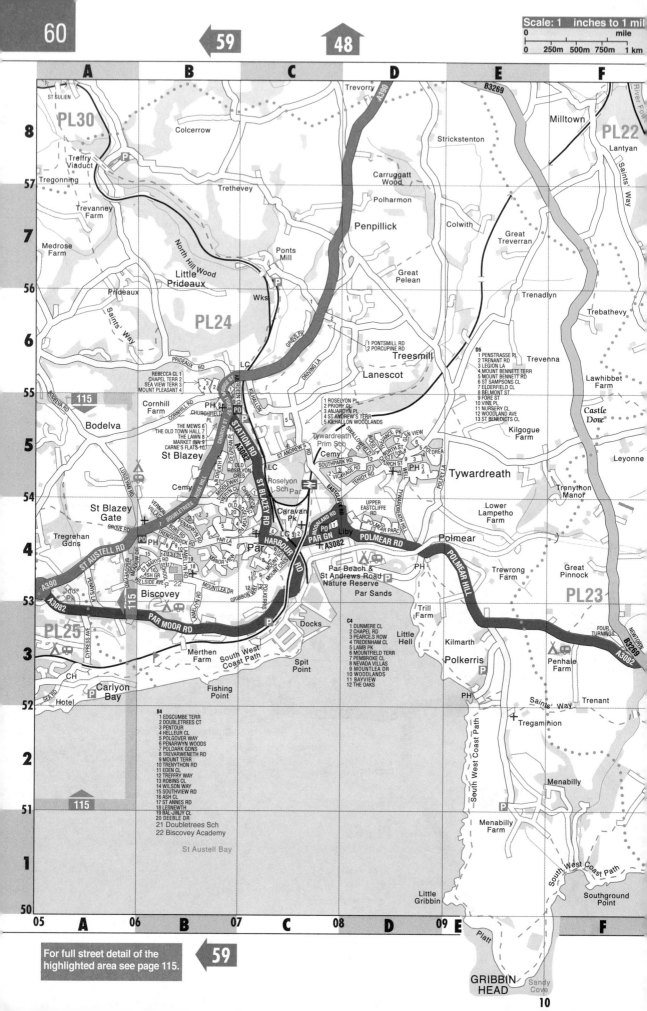

For full street detail of the
highlighted area see page 115.

← 59

PL30
St Sulien
Treffry Viaduct
Tregonning
Trevanney Farm
Medrose Farm
Colcerrow
Trethevey
North Hill Wood
Little Prideaux
Prideaux
Ponts Mill
Wks
PL24
Saints' Way
115
BODELVA RD
Bodelva
Cornhill Farm
PRIDEAUX RD
LC

REBECCA CL 1
CHAPEL TERR 2
SEA VIEW TERR 3
MOUNT PLEASANT 4

THE MEWS 6
THE OLD TOWN HALL 7
THE LAWN 8
MARKET INN 9
CARNE'S FLATS 10

St Blazey
Cemy
CHURCHFIELD RD
CORNHILL RD
OLD GREEN PL
PK
PO
STATION RD
A3082
ABBOTTS CL
BRIDGE ST
KILHALLON
LC

ST BLAZEY RD
OLD ROSELYON CRES
OLD ROSELYON RD
ROSE HILL
MIDDLEWAY
TREVITA CL
CHYVOGUE

St Blazey Gate
VERNON VILLAS
DOUBLETREES
PENARWIN RD
BORS RD
TRENOVISSICK RD
LAMELLYN RD
MANOR VIEW
ASH GR
ST MARYS RD
PAR LA
MOUNT CRES
HARBOUR RD
PAR
Caravan Pk
Roselyon L Sch
ST ANDREW'S RD
SWALLOWFIELD
Tywardreath Prim Sch
Cemy
SOUTHPARK RD
TEHIDY RD
VICARAGE RD

Treesmill
Lanescot
Penpillick
Polharmon
Carruggatt Wood
Great Pelean

1 PONTSMILL RD
2 PORCUPINE RD

1 ROSELYON PL
2 PRIORY CL
3 ANJARDYN PL
4 ST ANDREW'S TERR
5 KILHALLON WOODLANDS

D5
1 PENSTRASSE PL
2 TRENANT RD
3 LEGION LA
4 MOUNT BENNETT TERR
5 MOUNT BENNETT RD
6 ST SAMPSONS CL
7 ELDERFIELD CL
8 BELMONT ST
9 FORE ST
10 VINE PL
11 NURSERY CL
12 WOODLAND AVE
13 ST BENEDICTS CL

Strickstenton
Colwith
Great Treverran
Trenadlyn
Trebathevy

Milltown
PL22
Lantyan
Saints' Way

Castle Dore
Kilgogue Farm
Leyonne

Tywardreath
Lower Lampetho Farm
Trenython Manor

UPPER EASTCLIFFE RD
POLGAR PARC
EASTCLIFFE RD
TYWARDREATH HILL
POLMEAR RD
Polmear
PH
Trewrong Farm
Great Pinnock
PL23

Tregrehan Gdns
GROVE RD
ST AUSTELL RD
A390
A3082
Jdd Pk
PL25
CYPRESS AVE
CH
SEA RD
Carlyon Bay
Hotel

PENRWIN LA
BISCOVEY RD
115
HILLSIDE AVE
Biscovey
KILMARTH RD
MOUNTLEA DR
GRIBBIN RD
POLKERRIS
PAR MOOR RD

PO
PH
Par
MANOR VIEW
MOUNTLEA DR

Par Beach & St Andrews Road Nature Reserve
Par Sands
PH

Docks
Merthen Farm
South West Coast Path
Spit Point
Fishing Point

Trill Farm
Little Hell
Kilmarth
Polkerris
PH
PO

Four Turnings
NEWTOWN
B3269
A3082
Penhale Farm

B4
1 EDGCUMBE TERR
2 DOUBLETREES CT
3 PENTOUR
4 HELLEUR CL
5 POLGOVER WAY
6 PENARWYN WOODS
7 POLDARK GDNS
8 TREVARWENETH RD
9 MOUNT TERR
10 TRENYTHON RD
11 EDEN CL
12 TREFFRY WAY
13 ROBINS CL
14 WILSON WAY
15 SOUTHVIEW RD
16 ASH CL
17 ST ANNES RD
18 LESNEWTH
19 BAL-JINJY CL
20 DEEBLE DR
21 Doubletrees Sch
22 Biscovey Academy

C4
1 DUNMERE CL
2 CHAPEL RD
3 PEARCES ROW
4 TREDENHAM CL
5 LAMB PK
6 MOUNTFIELD TERR
7 PEMBROKE CL
8 NEVADA VILLAS
9 MOUNTLEA DR
10 WOODLANDS
11 BAYVIEW
12 THE OAKS

St Austell Bay

Saints' Way
Tregaminion
South West Coast Path
Menabilly
Menabilly Farm

Little Gribbin
South West Coast Path
Southground Point
Platt

GRIBBIN HEAD
Sandy Cove
Trenant

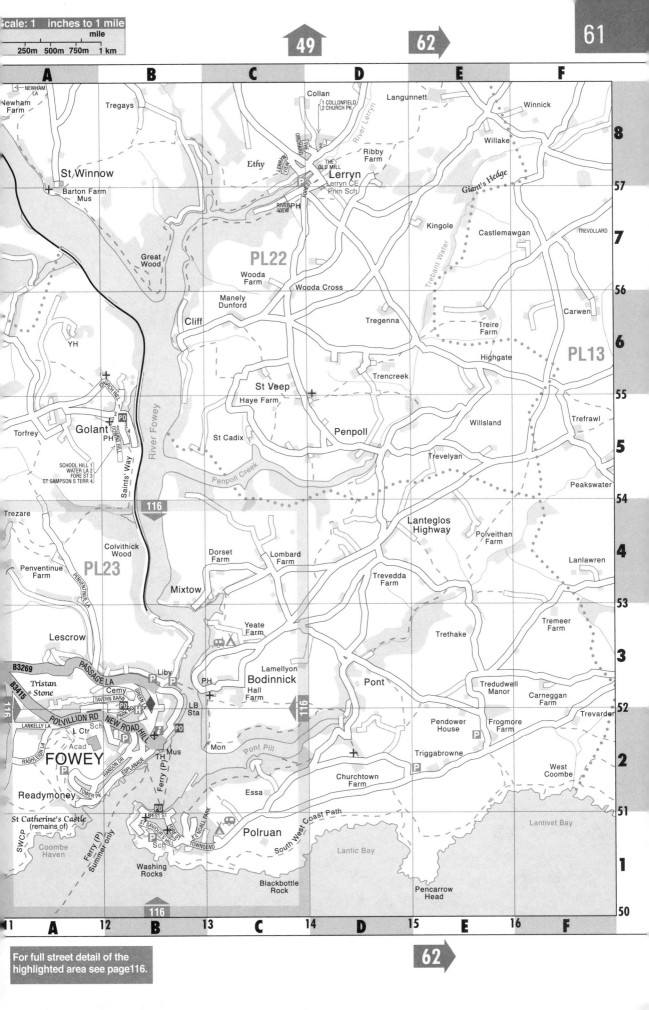

8

57

7

56

6

55

5

54

4

53

3

52

2

51

1

50

A B C D E F

Newham Farm
NEWHAM LA
St Winnow
Barton Farm Mus
Tregays
Collan
1 COLLONFIELD
2 CHURCH PK
Langunnett
Winnick
Willake
Ethy
River Lerryn
THE OLD MILL
Lerryn
Lerryn CE Prim Sch
RIVER VIEW PH
Ribby Farm
Kingole
Castlemawgan
TREVOLLARD
Giant's Hedge
PL22
Great Wood
Wooda Farm
Wooda Cross
Tregenna
Treire Farm
Carwen
Cliff
Manely Dunford
Trencreek
Highgate
PL13
YH
St Veep
Haye Farm
Willsland
Trefrawl
Torfrey
Golant
PH
St Cadix
Penpoll
Trevelyan
Trevarder
Peakswater
SCHOOL HILL 1
WATER LA 2
FORE ST 3
ST SAMPSON S TERR 4
River Fowey
Saints' Way
Penpoll Creek
Trezare
116
Lanteglos Highway
Polveithan Farm
Lanlawren
Penventinue Farm
PL23
Colvithick Wood
Dorset Farm
Lombard Farm
Trevedda Farm
Mixtow
Tremeer Farm
Lescrow
Yeate Farm
Trethake
Pont
Tredudwell Manor
Carneggan Farm
B3269
Tristan Stone
B3415
PASSAGE LA
Liby
Cemy
TAVERN BAR
PH
Bodinnick
Lamellyon Hall Farm
LB Sta
Pendower House
Frogmore Farm
Trevarder
POLVILLION RD
NEW ROAD HILL
Mon
Pont Pill
Triggabrowne
FOWEY
Acad
Mus
TH
ESPLANADE
Ferry (P)
Essa
Churchtown Farm
West Coombe
Readymoney
TOWER PK
St Catherine's Castle (remains of)
SWCP
Coombe Haven
Ferry (P) Summer only
WEST ST
ST SAVIOUR'S HILL
KENDALL PARK
TOWNSEND
Polruan
Sch
South West Coast Path
Lantivet Bay
Washing Rocks
Blackbottle Rock
Lantic Bay
Pencarrow Head

116

For full street detail of the highlighted area see page116.

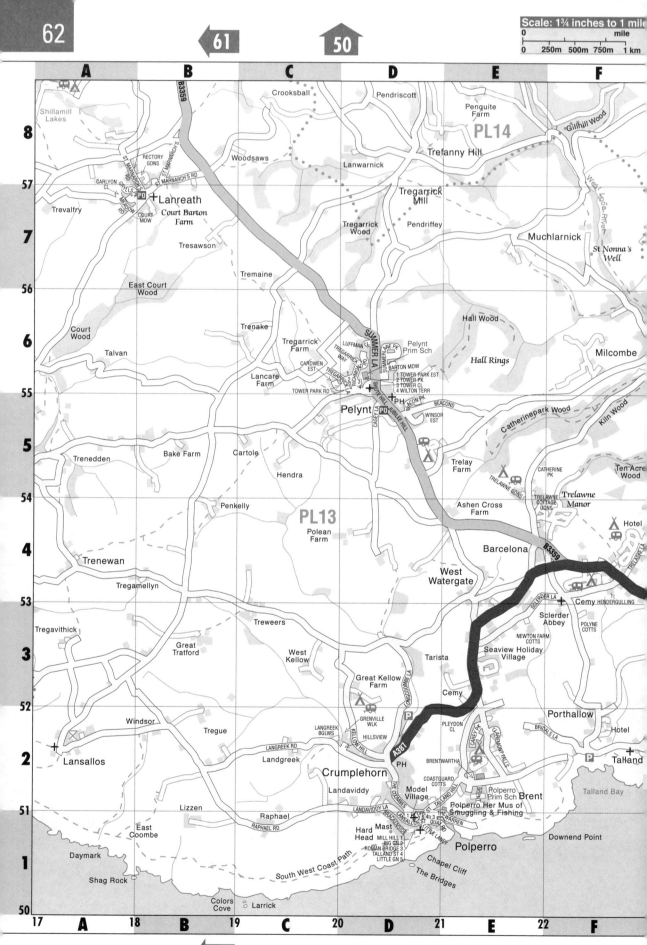

Scale: 1¾ inches to 1 mile

0   mile

0   250m   500m   750m   1 km

Shillamill
Lakes

ST MARNACH'S RD

GRIZLS CL
CARLYON CL

MEADOW RD

PO

RECTORY
GDNS

COURT
MDW

Lanreath

Court Barton
Farm

Trevalfry

Tresawson

B3359

Crooksball

Woodsaws

Pendriscott

Penquite
Farm

Gilhill Wood

PL14

Trefanny Hill

Lanwarnick

West Looe River

Tregarrick
Mill

Muchlarnick

St Nonna's
Well

Tregarrick
Wood

Pendriffey

East Court
Wood

Tremaine

Tregarrick
Farm

Trenake

Trenewan

LUFFMAN
CL

RICHMOND RD

TREGARRICK LA

SUMMER LA

ANE PK

TREWINTS

Pelynt
Prim Sch

Hall Wood

Milcombe

Court
Wood

Talvan

CARDWEN
EST

BARTON MDW

1 TOWER PARK EST
2 TOWER PK
3 TOWER CL
4 WILTON TERR

Hall Rings

Lancare
Farm

TOWER PARK RD

CASEY LA

SHUTE HILL

JUBILEE HILL

PH

PO

BEACON PK

BEACONS

WINSOR
EST

Catherinepark Wood

Kiln Wood

Trenedden

Bake Farm

Cartole

Pelynt

Trelay
Farm

CATHERINE
PK

Ten Acre
Wood

TRELAWNE GDNS

TRELAWNE
COTTAGE
GDNS

Trelawne
Manor

Hendra

PL13

Polean
Farm

Ashen Cross
Farm

Barcelona

B3359

Hotel

BELASKELA

Trenewan

Tregamellyn

West
Watergate

Penkelly

Tregavithick

Treweers

West
Kellow

Tarista

Cemy

HENDERGULLING

SCLERDER LA

Sclerder
Abbey

NEWTON FARM
COTTS

POLYNE
COTTS

Great
Tratford

Great Kellow
Farm

GRENVILLE
WLK

LONGCOOMBE LA

Seaview Holiday
Village

Lansallos

Windsor

Tregue

Landgreek

LANGREEK
BGLWS

HILLSVIEW

KELLOW HILL

Cemy

Porthallow

BRIDALS LA

Hotel

Talland

LANGREEK RD

Crumplehorn

Landaviddy

PLEYDON
CL

Brentwartha

CLAREMONT CLFFS

CAREY PK

BRENT

Polperro
Prim Sch

Brent

Talland Bay

P

A387

PH

THE COOMBES

Lizzen

Raphael

RAPHAEL RD

LANDAVIDDY LA

Model
Village

BRACKERSIDE

TALLAND HILL

FORE ST

4 3

QUAY RD

THE WARREN

Polperro Her Mus of
Smuggling & Fishing

Downend Point

East
Coombe

Hard
Head

Mast

MILL HILL 1
BIG GN 2
ROMAN BRIDGE 3
TALLAND ST 4
LITTLE GN 5

THE LANEY

COASTGUARD
COTTS

Polperro

Daymark

Shag Rock

South West Coast Path

Chapel Cliff

The Bridges

Colors
Cove

Larrick

Scale: 1 inches to 1 mile

250m 500m 750m 1 km

A B C D E F

ASTWOOD DEVELOPMENTS 1
CHAPEL ROW 2
TREMAYNE TERR 3
LYDCOTT CRES 4
MORVIEW RD 5
LYDCOTT CL 6
HARDING MD 7

B3254

Colhender Farm

Tredinnick

Tregarlandbridge

Plashford Farm

Tregarland

PH

Mast

CH

Widegates

Trenean Farms

8

PL14

Puffiland Farm

KIBBISDOME TERR

Highercliff
Sandplace

SHOEMAKERS ROW

Sandplace

Sandplace Hotel

Oaklands Bsns Pk

Morval

BINDOWN CT

PO

No Man's Land

57

Treworgey

Morval House

Cleese Farm

HOLLAND PK

P

SPRINGFIELD PK

BUCKLAWREN RD

PL13

7

Tredallett

Penarthtown

Tregoad

56

LC

SANDPLACE RD

117

Bucklawren

Penvith

6

Sowden's Bridge

TRENANT CROSS

East Looe River

St Martin

Great Tree

Windsworth

The Monkey Sanctuary

55

Ford

Polpever

Polpever

West Looe River

PL13

ST MARTIN'S RD

Acad

B3253

Millendreath

MAY LA

117

5

Kilminorth

Looe

SUNRISING EST

BARBICAN RD

Ind Est

Plaidy

Sch

P

54

117

PL13

Looe

STATION RD

Polean Trad Est

BODRIGAN RD

PO

HAY LA

BAY VIEW RD

East Looe

Millendreath Beach

4

POLPERRO RD

THE DOWNS

QUAY RD

PO
P

Mus

Limmicks Rd

West Looe

WEST LODGE HILL

HANNAFORE RD

LOOE

Looe Bay

53

A387

Tencreek

Portlooe

Hannafore

PORTVAN RD

MARINE DR

Hannafore Point

52

117

2

Portnadler Bay

St George's or Looe Island

PL13

51

Hore Stone

1

50

23 24 25 26 27 28

A B C D E F

For full street detail of the highlighted area see page 117.

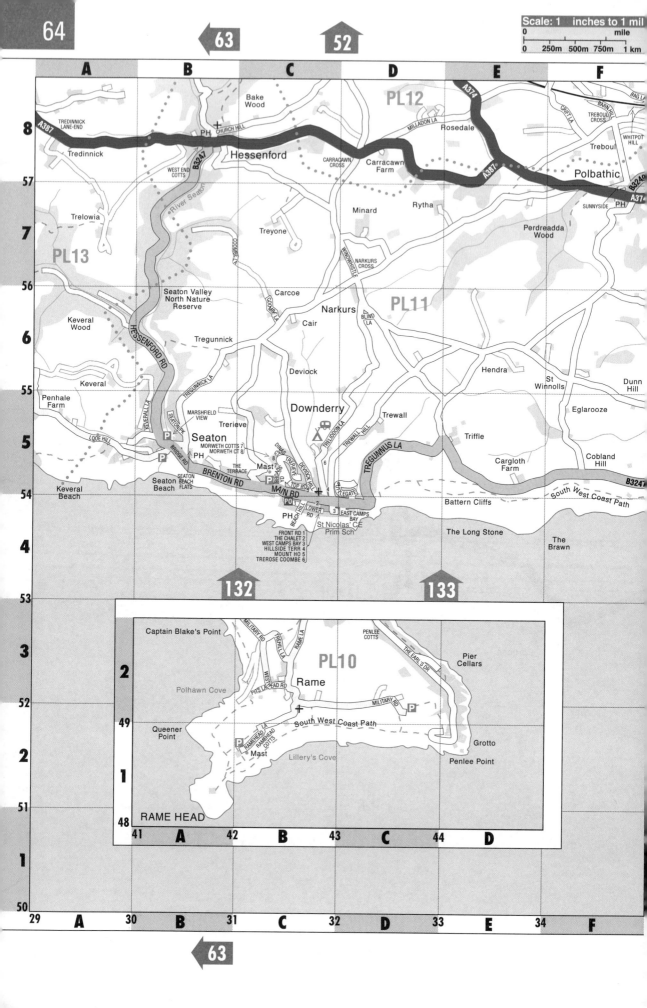

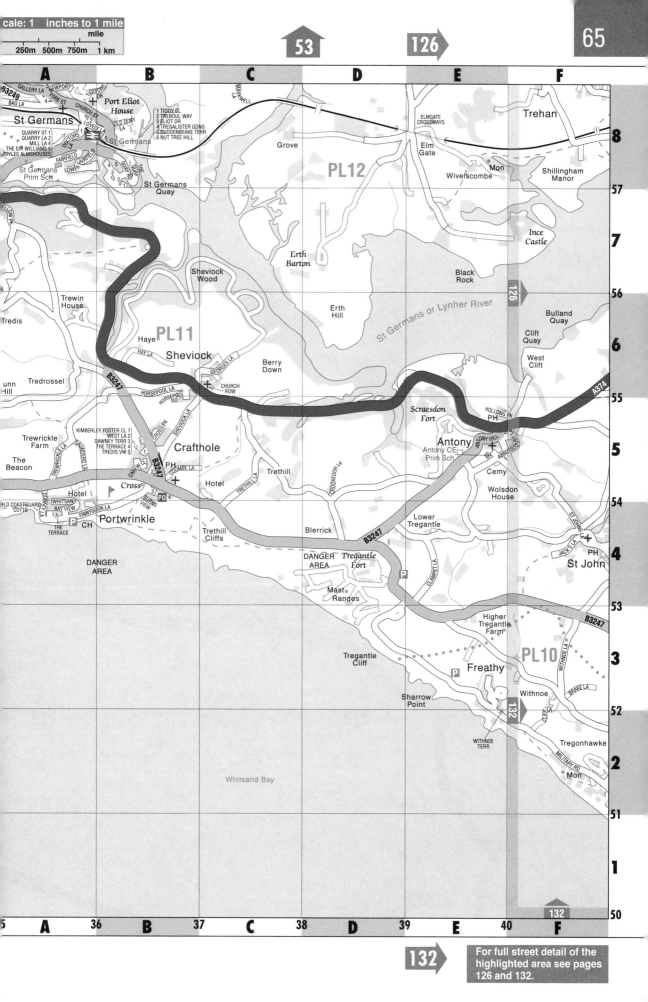

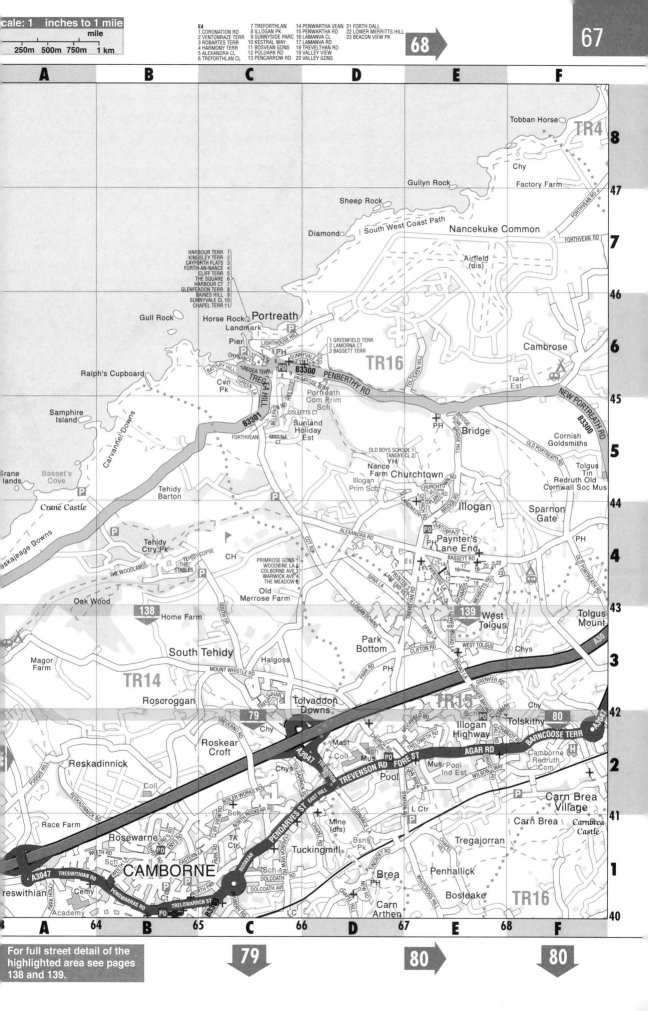

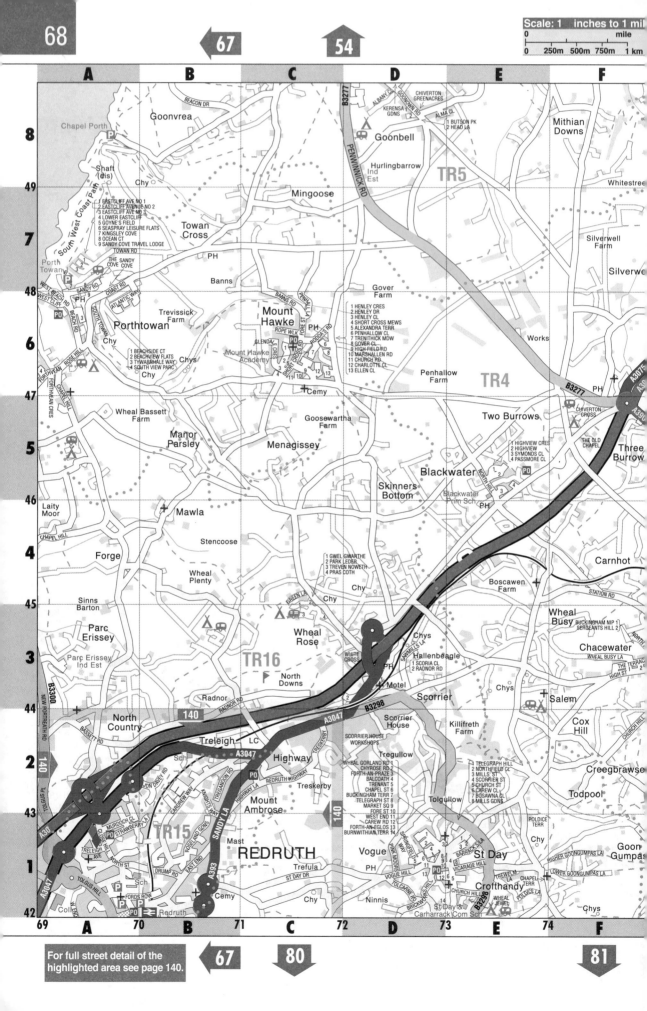

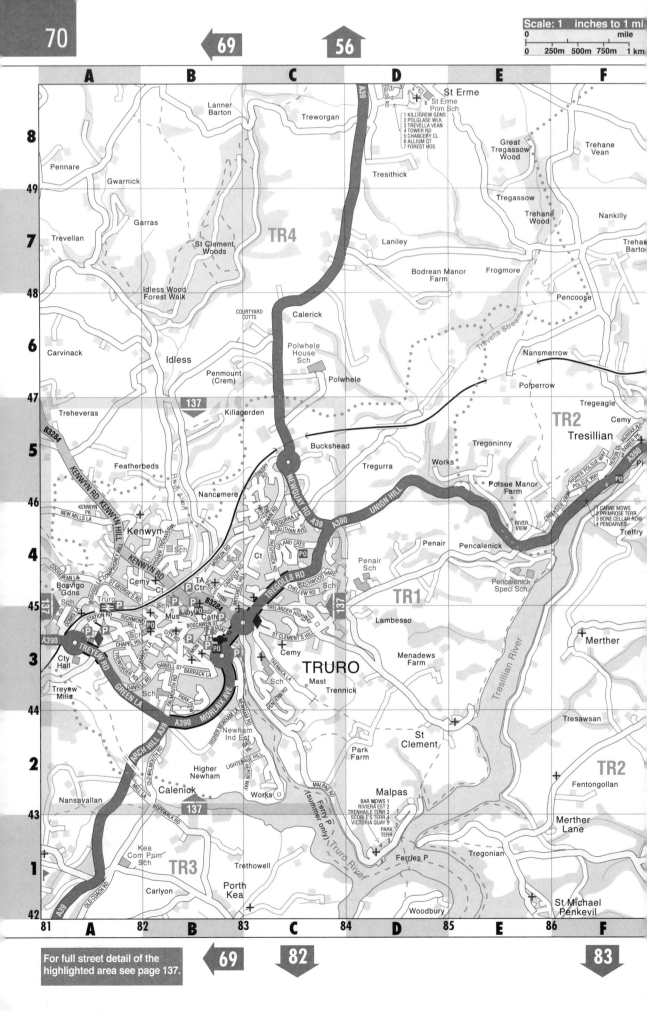

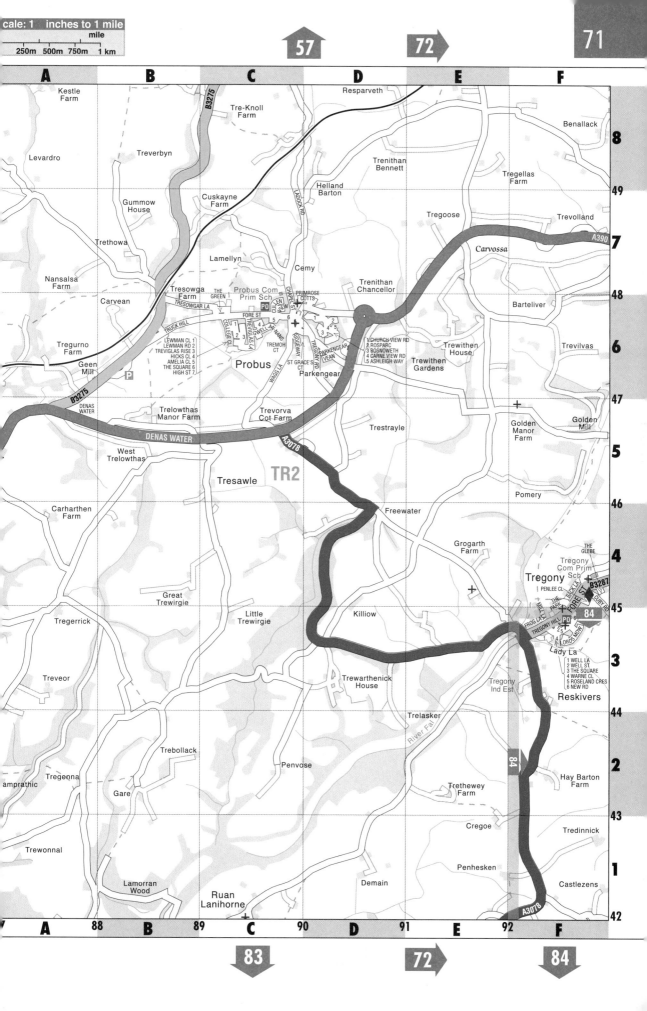

cale: 1   inches to 1 mile

mile

250m 500m 750m 1 km

A   B   C   D   E   F

Kestle Farm

Resparveth

Benallack

8

Levardro

Treverbyn

B3275

Tre-Knoll Farm

Helland Barton

Trenithan Bennett

Tregellas Farm

49

Gummow House

Cuskayne Farm

Cemy

Tregoose

Trevolland

7

A390

Lamellyn

LADOCK RD

Carvossa

Nansalsa Farm

Tresowga Farm

THE GREEN

Probus Com Prim Sch

PO

Primrose Cotts

Trenithan Chancellor

Barteliver

48

Carvean

TRESOWGAR LA

FORE ST

CHAPEL ST

RIDGEWAY

1 CHURCH VIEW RD
2 ROSPARC
3 BOSNOWETH
4 CARNE VIEW RD
5 ASHLEIGH WAY

Trewithen House

Trevilvas

6

Tregurno Farm

TRUCK HILL

COLLEGE CL

GWELL AF NANS

LEWMAN CL 1
LEWMAN RD 2
TREVIGLAS RISE 3
HICKS CL 4
AMELIA CL 5
THE SQUARE 6
HIGH ST 7

TREMOH CT

ST GRACE'S CT

PARKENGEAR VEAN

Trewithen Gardens

Geen Mill

B3275

DENAS WATER

P

Probus

WAGG LA

TREGONY RD

Parkengear

47

Trelowthas Manor Farm

Trevorva Cot Farm

Trestrayle

Golden Manor Farm

Golden Mill

DENAS WATER

A3078

West Trelowthas

TR2

Tresawle

Pomery

46

Carharthen Farm

Freewater

4

THE GLEBE

Tregony Com Prim Sch

Tregony

PENLEE CL

B3287

Great Trewirgie

Grogarth Farm

BRICKLA

FORE ST

QUAY RD

45

Little Trewirgie

Killiow

THE PARK

84

Tregerrick

MILL LA

TREGONY HILL

PO

LORD'S

1 WELL LA
2 WELL ST
3 THE SQUARE
4 WARNE CL
5 ROSELAND CRES
6 NEW RD

Lady La

3

Treveor

Trewarthenick House

Tregony Ind Est

Reskivers

Trebollack

Trelasker

River Fal

44

amprathic

Tregenna

Penvose

84

Trethewey Farm

Hay Barton Farm

2

Gare

Cregoe

Tredinnick

43

Trewonnal

Penhesken

1

Lamorran Wood

Ruan Lanihorne

Demain

A3078

Castlezens

42

A   88   B   89   C   90   D   91   E   92   F

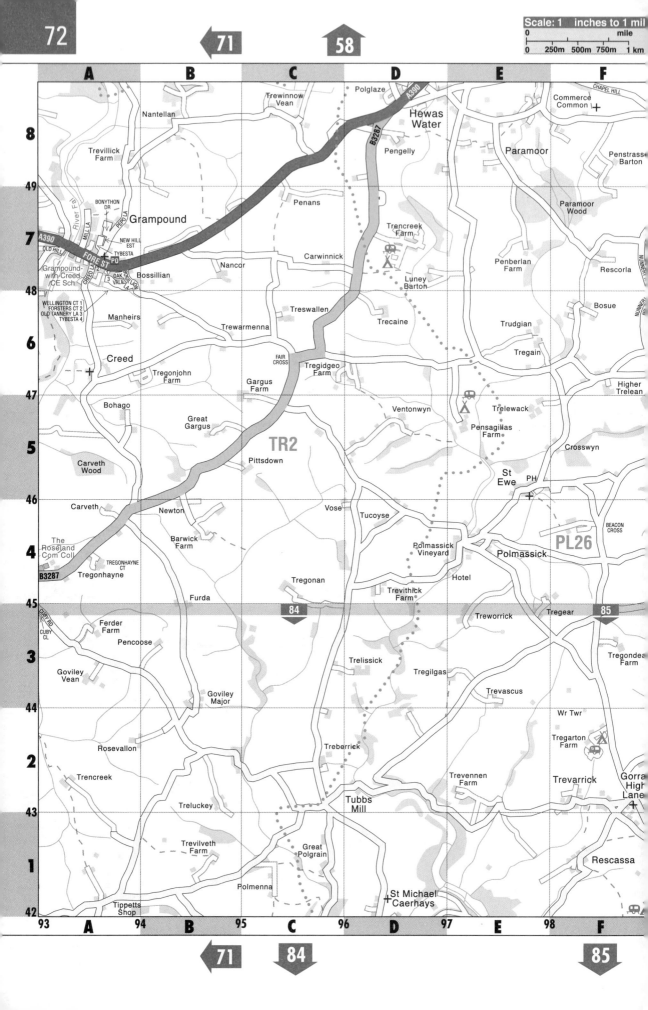

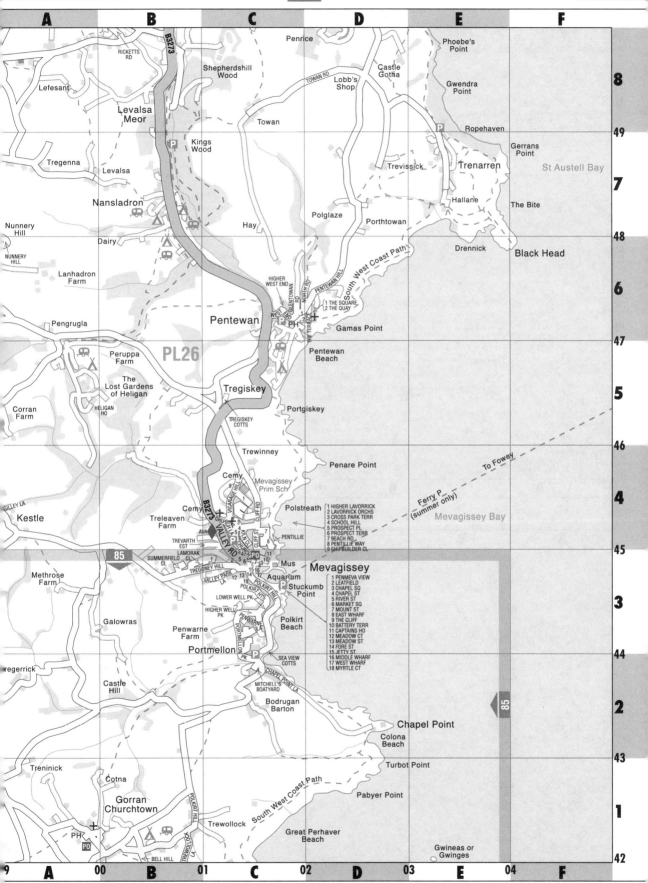

scale: 1 inches to 1 mile

mile

250m 500m 750m 1 km

A B C D E F

8

Phoebe's Point

Lefesant

RICKETTS RD

B3273

Shepherdshill Wood

Penrice

TOWAN RD

Lobb's Shop

Castle Gotha

Gwendra Point

49

Levalsa Meor

Kings Wood

P

Towan

Trevissick

Trenarren

Ropehaven

P

Gerrans Point

St Austell Bay

Tregenna

Levalsa

7

Nansladron

Hay

Polglaze

Porthtowan

Hallane

The Bite

Nunnery Hill

Dairy

Drennick

Black Head

48

NUNNERY HILL

Lanhadron Farm

HIGHER WEST END

GLENTOWAN RD

NORTH RD

PENTEWAN HILL

South West Coast Path

6

Pengrugla

WEST END

Pentewan

PH

THE TERRACE

1 THE SQUARE
2 THE QUAY

Gamas Point

Peruppa Farm

PL26

Pentewan Beach

47

The Lost Gardens of Heligan

HELIGAN HO

Tregiskey

Portgiskey

Corran Farm

TREGISKEY COTTS

5

To Fowey

46

Trewinney

Penare Point

GILLEY LA

Cemy

Mevagissey Prim Sch

Ferry P
(summer only)

Mevagissey Bay

4

Kestle

B3273

VICARAGE HILL

CLIFF RD

Cemy

Polstreath

1 HIGHER LAVORRICK
2 LAVORRICK ORCHS
3 CROSS PARK TERR
4 SCHOOL HILL
5 PROSPECT PL
6 PROSPECT TERR
7 BEACH RD
8 PENTILLIE WAY
9 SHIPBUILDER CL

Treleaven Farm

VALLEY RD

CHURCH ST

CLIFF ST

PENTILLIE

TREVARTH EST

AVA

CHURCH LA

11

45

LAMORAK CL

SUMMERFIELD CL

TREGONEY HILL

VALLEY PARK LA

POLKIRT HILL

P

Mus

Aquarium

Stuckumb Point

Mevagissey

1 PENMEVA VIEW
2 LEATFIELD
3 CHAPEL SQ
4 CHAPEL ST
5 RIVER ST
6 MARKET SQ
7 MOUNT ST
8 EAST WHARF
9 THE CLIFF
10 BATTERY TERR
11 CAPTAINS HO
12 MEADOW CT
13 MEADOW ST
14 FORE ST
15 JETTY ST
16 MIDDLE WHARF
17 WEST WHARF
18 MYRTLE CT

Methrose Farm

LOWER WELL PK

HIGHER WELL PK

PENWARNE LA

Polkirt Beach

3

Galowras

Penwarne Farm

PORTMELLON PK

Portmellon

P

SEA VIEW COTTS

Tregerrick

CHAPEL POINT LA

MITCHELL'S BOATYARD

Castle Hill

Bodrugan Barton

85

2

Chapel Point

Colona Beach

43

Treninick

Cotna

Turbot Point

POLKIRT HILL

TREWI... LA

South West Coast Path

Pabyer Point

1

Gorran Churchtown

PH

PO

BELL HILL

Trewollock

Great Perhaver Beach

Gwineas or Gwinges

42

9 A 00 B 01 C 02 D 03 E 04 F

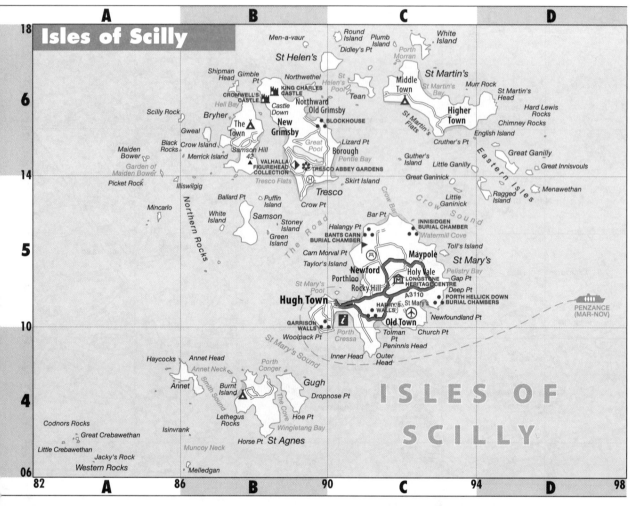

Isles of Scilly

A   B   C   D

18

Men-a-vaur
Round Island
White Island
Plumb Island
Porth Morran

St Helen's
Didley's Pt

Shipman Head
Gimble Pt
Northwethel
St Helen's Pool
Middle Town
St Martin's
Murr Rock
St Martin's Head

6
CROMWELL'S CASTLE
KING CHARLES CASTLE
Castle Down
Tean
St Martin's Bay
Higher Town
Hard Lewis Rocks

Hell Bay
Northward
Old Grimsby
Chimney Rocks

Scilly Rock
Bryher
New Grimsby
BLOCKHOUSE
St Martin's Flats
English Island

Gweal
The Town
Lizard Pt
Cruther's Pt
Great Ganilly

Black Rocks
Crow Island
Great Pool
Borough
Guther's Island
Great Innisvouls

Maiden Bower
Merrick Island
Samson Hill 42
VALHALLA FIGUREHEAD COLLECTION
TRESCO ABBEY GARDENS
Pentle Bay
Little Ganilly
Great Ganinick
Eastern Isles
Menawethan

14
Garden of Maiden Bower
Skirt Island
Great Ganinick
Ragged Island

Picket Rock
Illiswilgig
Ballard Pt
Puffin Island
Crow Pt
Tresco
Little Ganinick

Mincarlo
White Island
Samson
Stoney Island
Bar Pt
Crow Bay
Crow Sound

The Road
Green Island
Halangy Pt
INNISIDGEN BURIAL CHAMBER
Watermill Cove

5
BANTS CARN BURIAL CHAMBER
Maypole
Toll's Island

Carn Morval Pt
St Mary's

Taylor's Island
Newford
Holy Vale
Pelistry Bay

St Mary's Pool
Porthloo
Rocky Hill
LONGSTONE HERITAGE CENTRE
Gap Pt
Deep Pt

Hugh Town
A3110
PORTH HELLICK DOWN BURIAL CHAMBERS

HARRY'S WALLS
St Mary's
PENZANCE (MAR-NOV)

Newfoundland Pt

10
GARRISON WALLS
Old Town

Woolpack Pt
Porth Cressa
Tolman Pt
Church Pt

St Mary's Sound
Peninnis Head

Inner Head
Outer Head

Haycocks
Annet Head
Porth Conger

Annet Neck
Gugh

Annet
Smith Sound
Burnt Island
Dropnose Pt

4
Lethegus Rocks
The Cove
Hoe Pt

Codnors Rocks
Isinvrank
Horse Pt
St Agnes
Wingletang Bay

Great Crebawethan
Muncoy Neck

Little Crebawethan
Melledgan

Jacky's Rock
Western Rocks

06
82   A   86   B   90   C   94   D   98

ISLES OF SCILLY

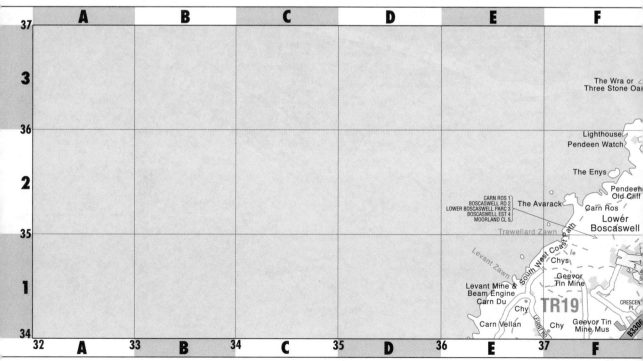

A   B   C   D   E   F

37

3
The Wra or Three Stone Oar

36
Lighthouse
Pendeen Watch

2
The Enys

Pendeen Old Cliff

CARN ROS 1
BOSCASWELL RD 2
LOWER BOSCASWELL PARC 3
BOSCASWELL EST 4
MOORLAND CL 5
The Avarack
Carn Ros
Lower Boscaswell

35
Trewellard Zawn

Levant Zawn
Chys

1
Levant Mine & Beam Engine
Carn Du
Geevor Tin Mine

TR19
CRESCENT PL

Carn Vellan
Chy
Chy
Geevor Tin Mine Mus

34
32   A   33   B   34   C   35   D   36   E   37   F

mile
250m 500m 750m 1 km

| A | B | C | D | E | F |

8
41
7
40
6
39

Porthglaze
Cove

Gurnard's
Head

5

38

Porthmeor
Point

TR26

TREEN
COTTS

Treen

Porthmeor
Cove

Great
Zawn

PH

B3306

4

Halldrine
Cove

Bosigran
Farm

Porthmeor

37

Porthmoina
Cove

Bosigran
Castle

Bosporthennis

Greeb
Point

Whirl
Pool

Rosemergy

P

Carn
Galver

Hannibal's
Carn

3

Long
Carn

South West Coast Path

Chair
Carn

Little
Galver

36

Portheras
Cove

Carn
Clough

Lower
Chypraze

Trevean

Watch
Croft

White
Downs

TR20

2

ENYS
COTTS

Pendeen
House

Morvah

Nine
Maidens

Portheras
Farm

TR19

ROSE
VALLEY

Trevowhan

35

St IVES RD

Keigwin

The
Carn

Bosullow
Common

Bosiliack

1

PONDS HILL

Pendeen

HIGHER
BOJEWYAN

Tor
Noon

Chun

Carn
Downs

Bosullow
Vean

Lanyon
Farm

B3318

Higher
Boscaswell

BOJEWYAN
STENNACK

Little
Bosullow

34

| A | 39 | B | 40 | C | 41 | D | 42 | E | 43 | F |

A1
1 PETERS ROW
2 PARK-AN-PYTH
3 TREASE
4 BOSCASWELL TERR
5 CALARTHA TERR
6 CRESCENT PL
7 THE SQUARE
8 ST JOHN'S TERR
9 GWEL-MOR
10 PORTHERRAS VILLAS
11 PORTHERRAS TERR

75

Scale: 1 inches to 1 mile
0 mile
0 250m 500m 750m 1 km

| A | B | C | D | E | F |

8

41

The Carracks

Carn Naun Point

Pen Enys Point

Hor Point

7

Mussel Point

South West Coast Path

Treveal

Trowan

Trevalgan

Wicca Pool

40

Trevessa Farm

Chy

B3306

6

TR26

Wicca

Trendrine Farm

Zennor Head

Porthzennor Cove

Chys

P

Tremedda Farm

Lower Tregerthen

Rosewall Hill

39

Pendour Cove

Carn Cobba

Culver House

Portglaze Cove

Giant's Rock

Zennor

Trendrine Hill

TOWEDNACK RD

5

Carnelloe Farm

Wayside Folk Mus

PH
P

Logan Stone

Sperris Quoit

Beagletodn Downs

Towednack
THE OLD VICARAGE

Breja Farm

High Bussow Farm

Trewey

38

Poniou

Zennor Quoit

Amalveor Downs

Amalveor

Chy

B3306

Kerrowe Farm

Foage Farm

Penderleath

4

Boswednack

Pennance

TREWEY HILL

Amalwhidden Farm

Chy

Embla

37

Trewey Common

Mill Downs

Nancledra Prim Sch

3

Higher Kerrowe

Lady Downs

Amalebra

B3311

Conquer Downs

Georgia

CHYPONS EST

36

Try Valley

Chy

Nancledra

BALDHU ROW

THE FIELD

Borea

NEW ROW

2

Mulfra Hill

Bodriffy

Mulfra Quoit

Carnaquidden Downs

TR20

Trenowin Downs

Castle-an-Dinas

Trye Farm

35

Tredinnick

Mulfra

Carnaquidden Farm

Chysauster Ancient Village

Settlement

Roger's Tower

TREDINNICK COTTS

Bosulval

Chysauster

Gulval Downs

1

Boskednan

Lower Ninnes

Trenowin Farm

34

Carfury

Trythall Prim Sch

Newmill

Boscreege Farm

Hellangove Farm

Castle Gate

B3311

| A | B | C | D | E | F |
44 45 46 47 48 49

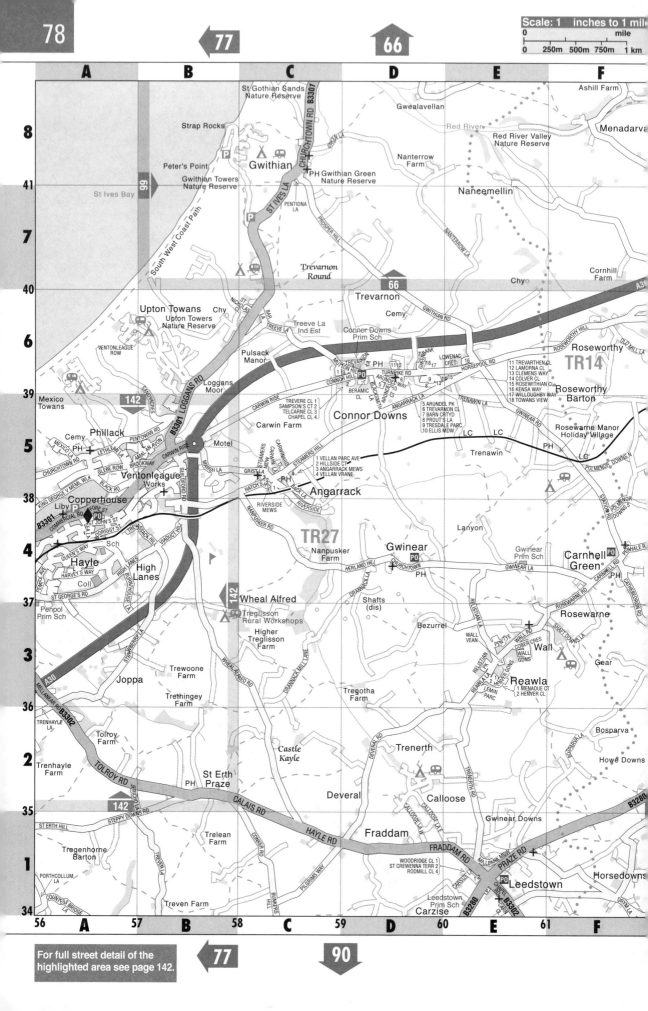

Scale: 1 inches to 1 mile
0   mile
0   250m   500m   750m   1 km

A   B   C   D   E   F

8

St Gothian Sands
Nature Reserve
Strap Rocks
Gwealavellan
Red River   Menadarva
Red River Valley
Nature Reserve
Peter's Point
Gwithian
41
St Ives Bay   Gwithian Towers   Nanterrow   Nancemellin
Nature Reserve   PH Gwithian Green   Farm
Nature Reserve
66
7
PENTIDNA   PROSPER HILL   NANTERROW LA   Cornhill
LA   Chyo   Farm
South West Coast Path   A30
Trevarnon
Round   66   Roseworthy
40   Trevarnon   TR14
Upton Towers   Chy   Treeve La   GWITHIAN RD   Roseworthy
Ind Est   Cemy   Barton
Upton Towers   Treeve La   Connor Downs   11 TREVARTHEN CL
6   Nature Reserve   Prim Sch   12 LAMORNA CL
VENTONLEAGUE   Pulsack Manor   ROSEWORTHY HILL   13 CLEMENS WAY
ROW   PH   11 12   14 COLVER CL
Mexico   Loggans   CARWIN RISE   LOWENAC   16   15 ROSEWITHIAN CL
39   Towans   142   Moor   CRES   16 KENSA WAY
Phillack   Cemy   TREVERE CL 1   17 WILLOUGHBY WAY
PH   Carwin Farm   SAMPSON'S CT 2   18 TOWANS VIEW
Mexico   Motel   TELCARNE CT 3   5 ARUNDEL PK
5   La   CHAPEL CL 4   Connor Downs   6 TREVARNON CL
Churchtown Rd   Rosewarne Manor   7 BARN CRTYD
LETHLEM   TRENAWIN LA   Holiday Village   8 PROUT'S LA
GLEBE ROW   MARSH LA   STEAMERS HILL   1 VELLAN PARC AVE   9 TRESDALE PARC
AMAL AN AVON   CARWIN RISE   GRIST LA   2 HILLSIDE CT   10 ELLIS MDW
Ventonleague   BROOKWAY   PH   3 ANGARRACK MEWS   Trenawin   LC   LC
BLACK RD   Works   HATCH LA   4 VELLAN VRANE   LC
38   King George V Meml Wlk   Angarrack   PH
Copperhouse   VIADUCT HILL   RIVERSIDE   Lanyon
P   SHORE ST   MEWS   RIVERSIDE
B3301   COMMERCIAL RD   ST JOHN'S ST   NANPUSKER RD
SORIGGY ST   TR27   Gwinear   Carnhell
4   QUEEN'S WAY   Nanpusker   PO   Green
Hayle   HIGH LANES   Farm   Churchtown   GWINEAR LA   CARNHELL RD   POWHALE RD
HARVEY'S WAY   High   HERLAND HILL   PH   Gwinear   PH
PERCIV AVE   Coll   Lanes   DRANNACK LA   Prim Sch   Rosewarne Rd
37   ST GEORGE'S RD   142   Wheal Alfred   Shafts   WALL   Rosewarne
Penpol   Treglisson   (dis)   RELISTIAN LA   VEAN   COBER CRES
Prim Sch   Rural Workshops   WALL   Wall
3   A30   STRAWBERRY LA   Higher   Bezurrel   GDNS   Gear
Treglisson   PEN TYE   WALL
Farm   RELISTIAN   Reawla   1 MENADUE CT
MELLANEAR RD B3302   WHEALACRED RD   Trewoone   PL   REWLA LA   2 HENVER CL
Joppa   Farm   LEMIN
2   Trethingey   PARC   Bosparva
Trenhayle   Farm   Trenerth
Farm   TOLROY RD   Castle   Howe Downs
36   Trenhayle   Kayle   Deveral   CALLOOSE LK   Gwinear Downs   B3280
LA   Calloose   B3280
Tolroy   St Erth   DEVERAL RD   TRENERTH RD   PRAZE RD   Horsedowns
Farm   Praze   Fraddam   MILLBANK   Leedstown
1   Trelean   PH   HAYLE RD   FRADDAM RD
Tregenhorne   Farm   CALAIS RD   WOODRIDGE CL 1   PO
Barton   STEPPY DOWNS RD   ST CREWENNA TERR 2   CHAPEL RD
JERICHO LA   TREVEN LA   PILGRIMS WAY   RODMILL CL 4   Leedstown   B3302
PORTHCOLLUM   BUNKERS   Prim Sch   Carzise   DRYM LA
34   COURTESS BRIDGE LA   Treven Farm   Carzise   B3280
56   A   57   B   58   C   59   D   60   E   61   F

For full street detail of the
highlighted area see page 142.

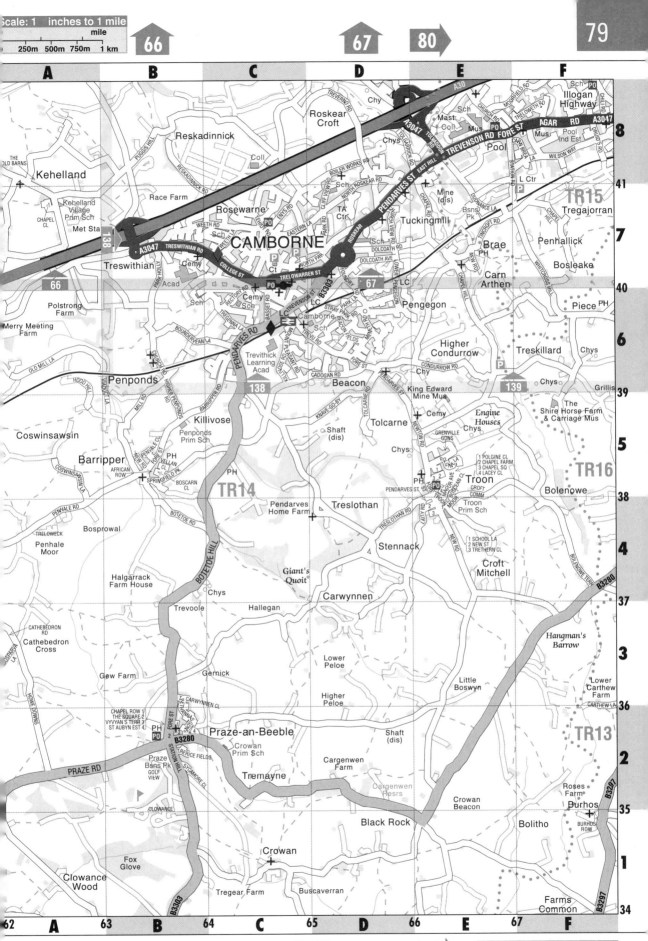

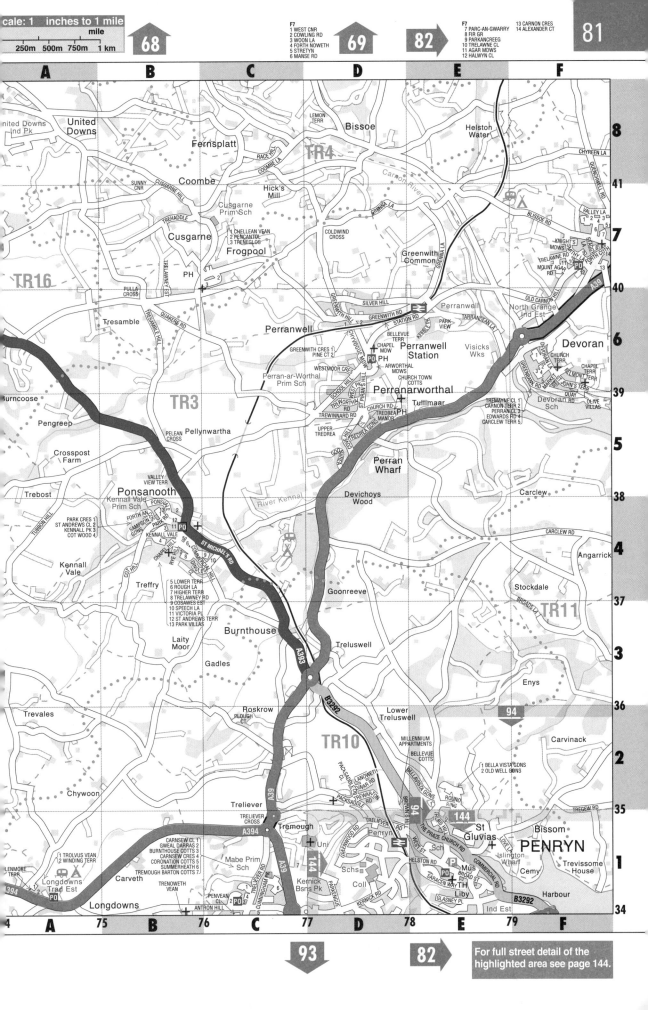

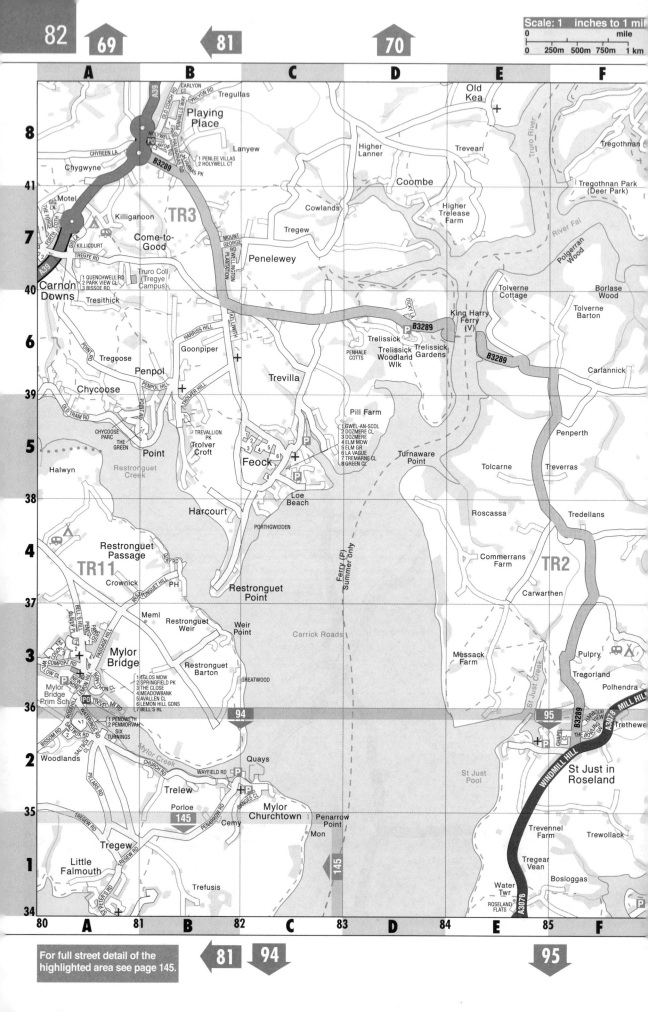

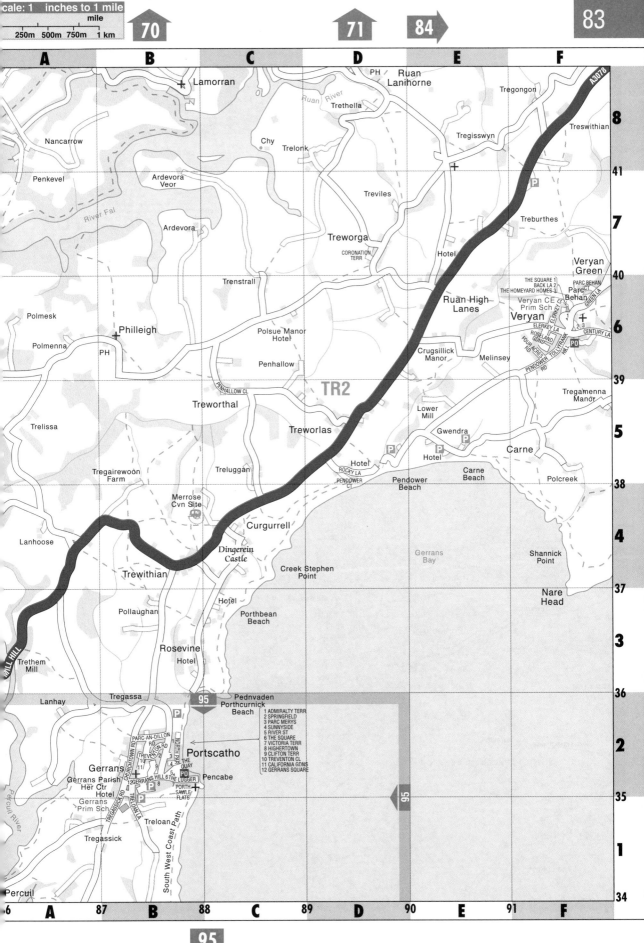

A B C D E F

Lamorran

Ruan
Lanihorne

8

Nancarrow
Trethella
Tregongon
Treswithian

Penkevel
Chy
Trelonk
Tregisswyn
41

Ardevora
Veor
Treviles
7

River Fal
Treworga
Hotel
Treburthes

Polmesk
Ardevora
CORONATION
TERR
Veryan
Green
40

Trenstrall
Ruan High
Lanes
THE SQUARE 1
BACK LA 2
THE HOMEYARD HOMES 3
PARC BEHAN
Parc
Behan

Philleigh
Polsue Manor
Hotel
Veryan CE
Prim Sch
6

Polmenna
PH
Penhallow
Crugsillick
Manor
Veryan
PO

Treworthal
PENHALLOW CL
Melinsey
39

TR2
Lower
Mill
Tregamenna
Manor

Trelissa
Treworlas
Gwendra
5

Tregairewoon
Farm
Treluggan
Hotel
ROCKY LA
PENDOWER
CT
Pendower
Beach
Carne
Carne
Beach
Polcreek

Merrose
Cvn Site
Hotel
Pendower
Beach
38

Lanhoose
Curgurrell
Shannick
Point
4

Trewithian
Dingerein
Castle
Creek Stephen
Point
Gerrans
Bay
Nare
Head
37

MILL HILL
Trethem
Mill
Hotel
3

Pollaughan
Rosevine
Hotel
Porthbean
Beach

Lanhay
Tregassa
95
Pednvaden
Porthcurnick
Beach
36

PARC-AN-DILLON
1 ADMIRALTY TERR
2 SPRINGFIELD
3 PARC MERYS
4 SUNNYSIDE
5 RIVER ST
6 THE SQUARE
7 VICTORIA TERR
8 HIGHERTOWN
9 CLIFTON TERR
10 TREVENTON CL
11 CALIFORNIA GDNS
12 GERRANS SQUARE
2

Gerrans
Portscatho
THE QUAY
THE LUGGER
Pencabe
95
Gerrans Parish
Her Ctr
Hotel
Gerrans
Prim Sch
PORTH
SAWLE
FLATS
35

Percuil River
Treloan
South West Coast Path

Tregassick
1

Percuil
34

6 A 87 B 88 C 89 D 90 E 91 F

95

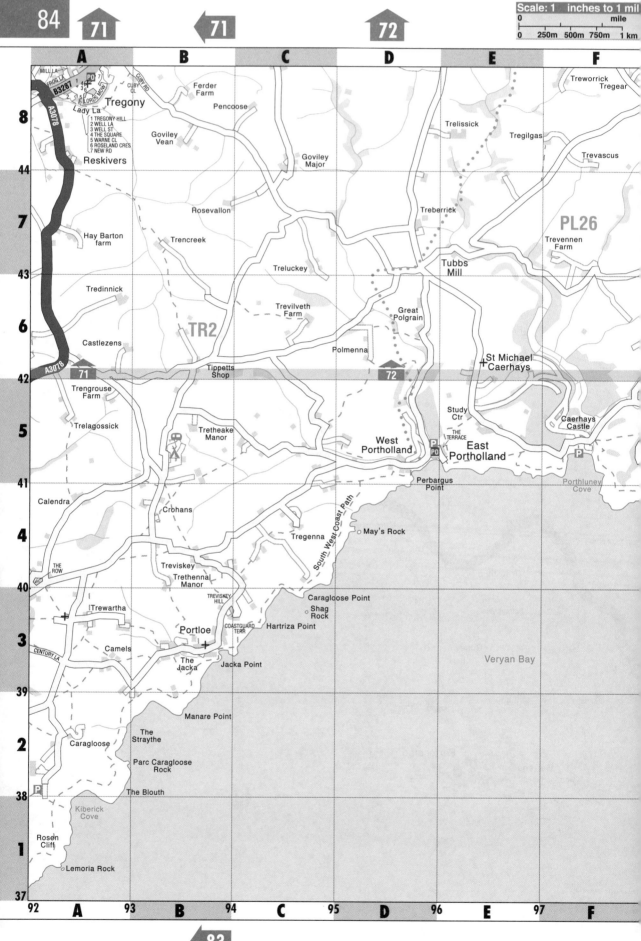

A **B** **C** **D** **E** **F**

MILL LA
FROG LA
B3287
A3078
Lady La
Tregony
1 TREGONY HILL
2 WELL LA
3 WELL ST
4 THE SQUARE
5 WARNE CL
6 ROSELAND CRES
7 NEW RD
Reskivers
CUBY CL
CUBY RD
Ferder Farm
Pencoose
Goviley Vean
Goviley Major
Treworrick Tregear
Trelissick
Tregilgas
Trevascus

8

44

Rosevallon
Treberrick
PL26
Trevennen Farm

7
Hay Barton farm
Trencreek
Treluckey

43
Tredinnick
Trevilveth Farm
Tubbs Mill

6
TR2
Great Polgrain

Castlezens
Polmenna
St Michael Caerhays

42
A3078
71
Tippetts Shop
72

Trengrouse Farm
Study Ctr
THE TERRACE
Caerhays Castle

5
Trelagossick
Tretheake Manor
West Portholland
East Portholland
PO
PO

41
Perbargus Point
Porthluney Cove

Calendra
Crohans
South West Coast Path
May's Rock

4
Tregenna

Treviskey
Trethennal Manor
TREVISKEY HILL
Caragloose Point

40
THE ROW
Trewartha
Shag Rock
Hartriza Point

3
CENTURY LA
Camels
Portloe
COASTGUARD TERR
Veryan Bay

The Jacka
Jacka Point

39
Manare Point

2
Caragloose
The Straythe
Parc Caragloose Rock

38
P
The Blouth
Kiberick Cove

1
Rosen Cliff
Lemoria Rock

37

A 92 **B** 93 **C** 94 **D** 95 **E** 96 **F** 97

A B C D E F

8

44

7

43

6

42

5

41

4

40

3

39

2

38

1

37

Mevagissey

Mevagissey Bay

1 PENMEVA VIEW
2 LEATFIELD
3 CHAPEL SQ
4 CHAPEL ST
5 RIVER ST
6 MARKET SQ
7 MOUNT ST
8 EAST WHARF
9 THE CLIFF
10 BATTERY TERR
11 CAPTAINS HO
12 MEADOW CT
13 MEADOW ST
14 FORE ST
15 JETTY ST
16 MIDDLE WHARF
17 WEST WHARF
18 MYRTLE CT

Mus
Aquarium
Stuckumb Point
Polkirt Beach

SUMMERFIELD CL
LAMORAK CL
TREGONEY HILL
VALLEY PARK LA
LOWER WELL PK
HIGHER WELL PK
POLKIRT HTS
POLKIRT HILL

PENWARNE LA
Penwarne Farm

Portmellon

SEA VIEW COTTS

CHAPEL POINT LA
MITCHELL'S BOATYARD
Bodrugan Barton

Chapel Point
Colona Beach

Methrose Farm
Galowras

Tregondean Farm

Wr Twr

Tregerrick
Castle Hill

egarton Farm

Trevarrick

Gorran High Lanes

Turbot Point

Pabyer Point

PL26

Treninick
Cotna

Rescassa

Gorran Churchtown

Trewollock

South West Coast Path

Great Perhaver Beach

Gwineas or Gwinges

PH
PO

72

73

Treveor

Trevesson Farm

Gorran Sch

TRELISPEN PARK DR
TRELISPEN PK
BELL HILL
PORTHEAST WAY
PORTHEAST WAY
WINDSOR
RICE LA

PERHAVER WAY
PERHAVER PK

CHUTE LA
CANTON
PO

CLIFF RD

Gorran Haven

1 QUILVER CL
2 RATTLE ST
3 CHURCH ST

Tregavarras
ROW
Tregavarras

Boswinger
YH

DERBY'S LA 1
WILLS MOOR 2
COOK'S LEVEL 3
TREWOLLOCK CL 4
PORTHEAST CL 5
LIGHTHOUSE LA 6

MOWHAY COTTS

Treveague Farm

FOXHOLE LA

Lamledra

Pen-a-maen or Maenease Point

Cadythew Rock

Hemmick Beach

Penare

Bow or Vault Beach

Penveor Point

Gell Point

High Point

Dodman Horse

Lizard Pool

Dodman Point

A 99 B 00 C 01 D 02 E 03 F

Scale: 1 inches to 1 mil
0 mile
0   250m   500m   750m   1 km

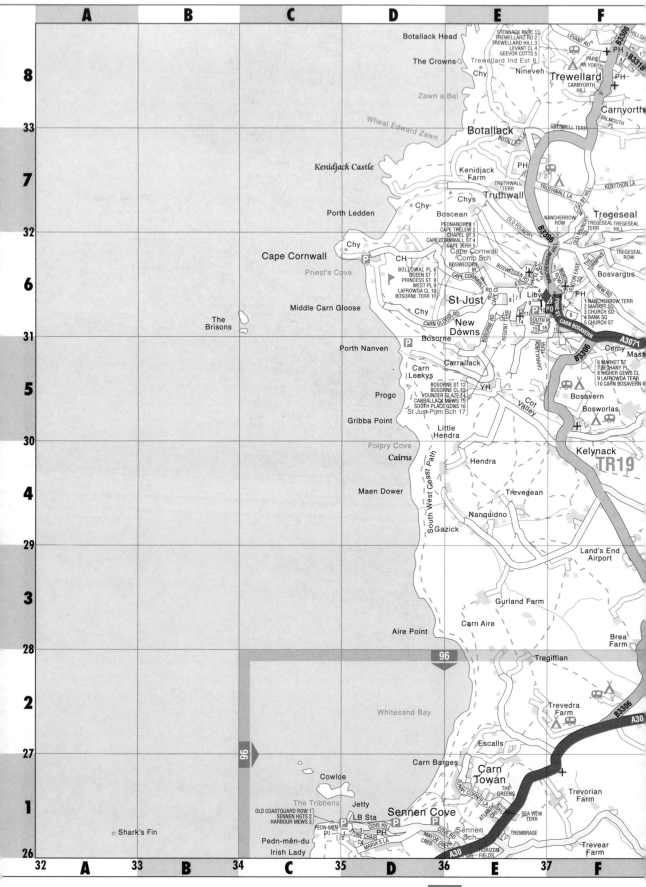

A **B** **C** **D** **E** **F**

8

33

7

32

6

31

5

30

4

29

3

28

2

27

1

26

32 **A** 33 **B** 34 **C** 35 **D** 36 **E** 37 **F**

Botallack Head
The Crowns
Zawn a Bal
Wheal Edward Zawn
Kenidjack Castle
Porth Ledden
Cape Cornwall
Priest's Cove
Middle Carn Gloose
The Brisons
Porth Nanven
Carn Leskys
Progo
Gribba Point
Polpry Cove
Cairns
Maen Dower
Gazick
Aire Point

STENNACK PARC 1
TREWELLARD RD 2
TREWELLARD HILL 3
LEVANT CL 4
GEEVOR COTTS 5
Trewellard Ind Est 6
Nineveh
Trewellard
Chy
CARNYORTH HILL
Carnyorth
FALMOUTH PL
Botallack
CRESWELL TERR
Kenidjack Farm
PH
TRUTHWALL TERR
Truthwall
TRUTHWALL LA
KENYTHON LA
Chys
Boscean
Chy
NANCHERROW ROW
Tregeseal
OLD FOUNDRY
TREGESEAL TREGESEAL TERR HILL
PEDNANDREA 1
CAPE TRELEW 2
CHAPEL ST 3
CAPE CORNWALL ST 4
CAPE TERR 5
Cape Cornwall Comp Sch
TREGESEAL ROW
Chy
CH
BOSWEDDEN PL
Bosvargus
BOLLOWAL PL 6
QUEEN ST 7
PRINCESS ST 8
WEST PL 9
LAFROWDA CL 10
BOSORNE TERR 11
CAPE CORNWALL RD
PH
St Just
Lib
1 NANCHERROW TERR
2 MARKET SQ
3 CHURCH SQ
4 BANK SQ
5 CHURCH ST
Chy
New Downs
Cemy
Mast
A3071
Bosorne
Carrallack
6 MARKET ST
7 BETHANY PL
8 HIGHER GEWS CL
9 LAFROWDA TERR
10 CARN BOSAVERN
BOSORNE ST 12
BOSORNE CL 13
VOUNDER GLAZE 14
CARRALLACK MEWS 15
SOUTH PLACE GDNS 16
St Just Prim Sch 17
YH
Bosavern
Cot Valley
Bosworlas
Little Hendra
Kelynack
TR19
Hendra
Trevegean
Nanquidno
Land's End Airport
Gurland Farm
Carn Aire
Brea Farm

96
Tregiffian
96
Whitesand Bay
Trevedra Farm
A30
B3306
Escalls
Carn Barges
Carn Towan
Trevorian Farm
THE GREENS
Cowloe
The Tribbens
Jetty
OLD COASTGUARD ROW 1
SENNEN HGTS 2
HARBOUR MEWS 3
LB Sta
Sennen Cove
Sennen Sch
SEA VIEW TERR
PEDN-MEN-DU
PH
COVE HILL
STONE CHAIR LA
MAYON GREEN
COVE RD
Trembrase
Shark's Fin
Pedn-mên-du
Irish Lady
MARIA'S LA
HORIZON FIELDS
A30
Trevear Farm

LEVANT RD
B3306
PH
HILLS
B3318
PH
PARC AN YORTH

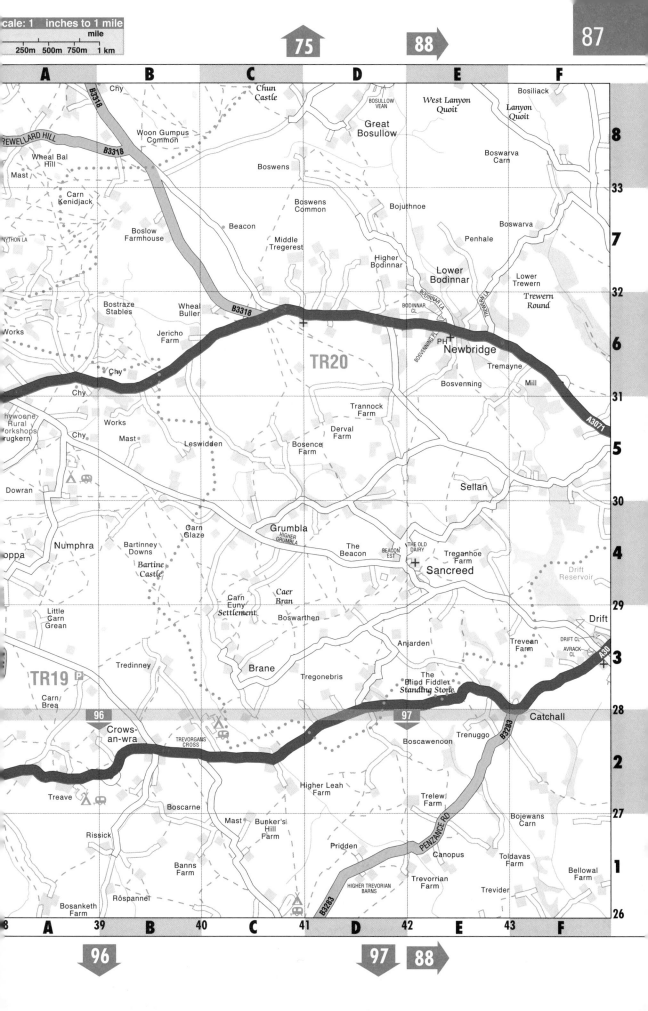

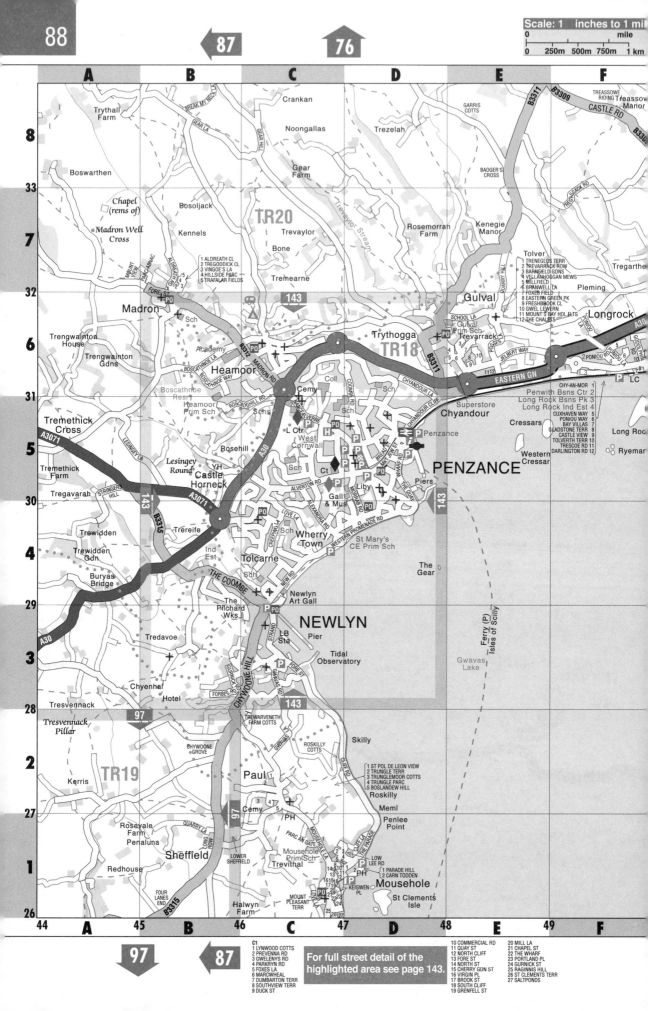

A   B   C   D   E   F

8

33

7

TR20

32

6

Madron

31

Tremethick
Cross

5

PENZANCE

30

4

NEWLYN

29

3

28

97

2

TR19

Paul

27

1

Sheffield

Mousehole

26

44   A   45   B   46   C   47   D   48   E   49   F

Area labels and selected place names:

Trythall Farm, Boswarthen, Chapel (rems of), Madron Well Cross, Crankan, Noongallas, Gear Farm, Trezelah, Bosoljack, Kennels, Trevaylor, Bone, Tremearne, Garris Cotts, Badger's Cross, Rosemorran Farm, Kenegie Manor, Treassowe Riding, Treassowe Manor, CASTLE RD, Tolver, Pleming, Gulval, Longrock, Trengwainton House, Trengwainton Gdns, Academy, Heamoor, Trythogga, TR18, Chyandour, Superstore, Chyandour, Cressars, Western Cressar, Long Roc, Ryemar, Heamoor Prim Sch, Boscathnoe Resr, Rosehill, Penzance, Tremethick Farm, Lesingey Round, Castle Horneck, West Cornwall, Liby, Gall & Mus, Piers, Tregavarah, Trewidden, Trereife, Wherry Town, St Mary's CE Prim Sch, The Gear, Trewidden Gdn, Buryas Bridge, Tolcarne, Newlyn Art Gall, The Pilchard Wks, The Coombe, Tredavoe, Chyenhal, Hotel, Pier, LB Sta, Tidal Observatory, Gwavas Lake, Ferry (P) Isles of Scilly, Tresvennack, Tresvennack Pillar, Trewarveneth Farm Cotts, Chywoone Grove, Skilly, Roskilly Cotts, Kerris, Paul, Roskilly, Meml, Penlee Point, Rosevale Farm Penaluna, Sheffield, Lower Sheffield, Trevithal, Mousehole Prim Sch, Mousehole, St Clements Isle, Redhouse, Four Lanes End, Halwyn Farm, Mount Pleasant Terr

Roads: A3071, A30, A3311, B3311, B3309, B3312, B3315, EASTERN GN

Boxed insets (numbered lists):

1 ALDREATH CL
2 TREGODDICK CL
3 VINGOE'S LA
4 HILLSIDE PARC
5 TRAFALAR FIELDS

CHY-AN-MOR 1
Penwith Bsns Ctr 2
Long Rock Bsns Pk 3
Long Rock Ind Est 4
CUXHAVEN WAY 5
PONIOU WAY 6
BAY VILLAS 7
GLADSTONE TERR 8
CASTLE VIEW 9
TOLVERTH TERR 10
TRESCOE RD 11
DARLINGTON RD 12

1 TRENEGLOS TERR
2 TREVARRACK ROW
3 BARNFIELD GDNS
4 VELLANHOGGAN MEWS
5 MILLFIELD
6 BRANWELL CL
7 FOXE'S FIELD
8 EASTERN GREEN PK
9 FRESHBROOK CL
10 GWEL LEWERN
11 MOUNT'S BAY HOL FLTS
12 THE CHALETS

1 ST POL DE LEON VIEW
2 TRUNGLE TERR
3 TRUNGLEMOOR COTTS
4 TRUNGLE PARC
5 BOSLANDEW HILL

1 PARADE HILL
2 CARN TODDEN

For full street detail of the highlighted area see page 143.

C1
1 LYNWOOD COTTS
2 PREVENNA RD
3 GWELENYS RD
4 PARKRYN RD
5 FOXES LA
6 MARCWHEAL
7 DUMBARTON TERR
8 SOUTHVIEW TERR
9 DUCK ST
10 COMMERCIAL RD
11 QUAY ST
12 NORTH CLIFF
13 FORE ST
14 NORTH ST
15 CHERRY GDN ST
16 VIRGIN PL
17 BROOK ST
18 SOUTH CLIFF
19 GRENFELL ST
20 MILL LA
21 CHAPEL ST
22 THE WHARF
23 PORTLAND PL
24 GURNICK ST
25 RAGINNIS HILL
26 ST CLEMENTS TERR
27 SALTPONDS

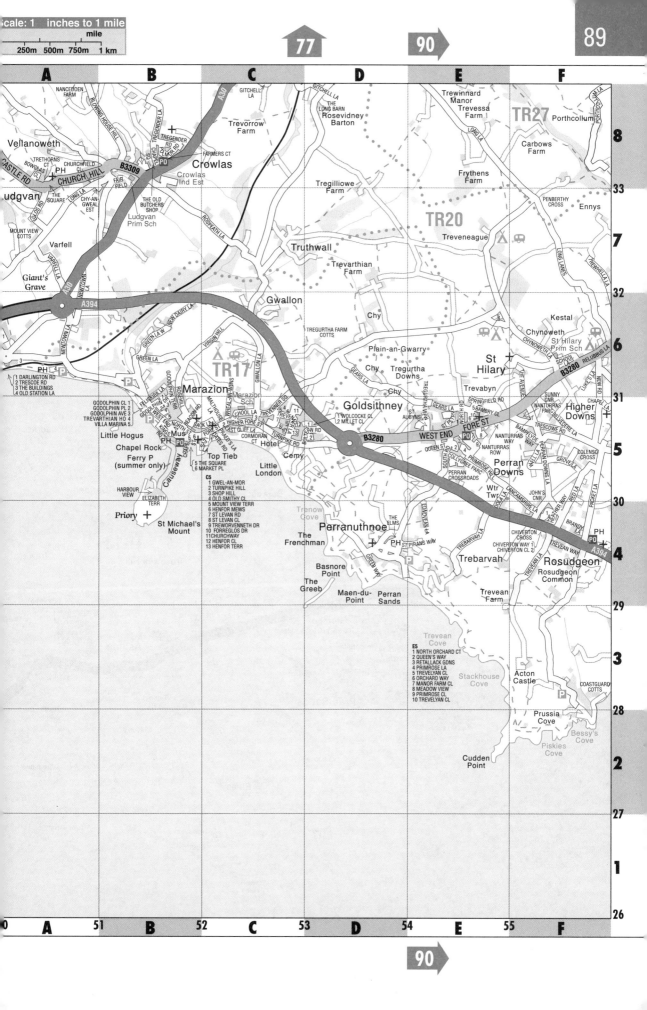

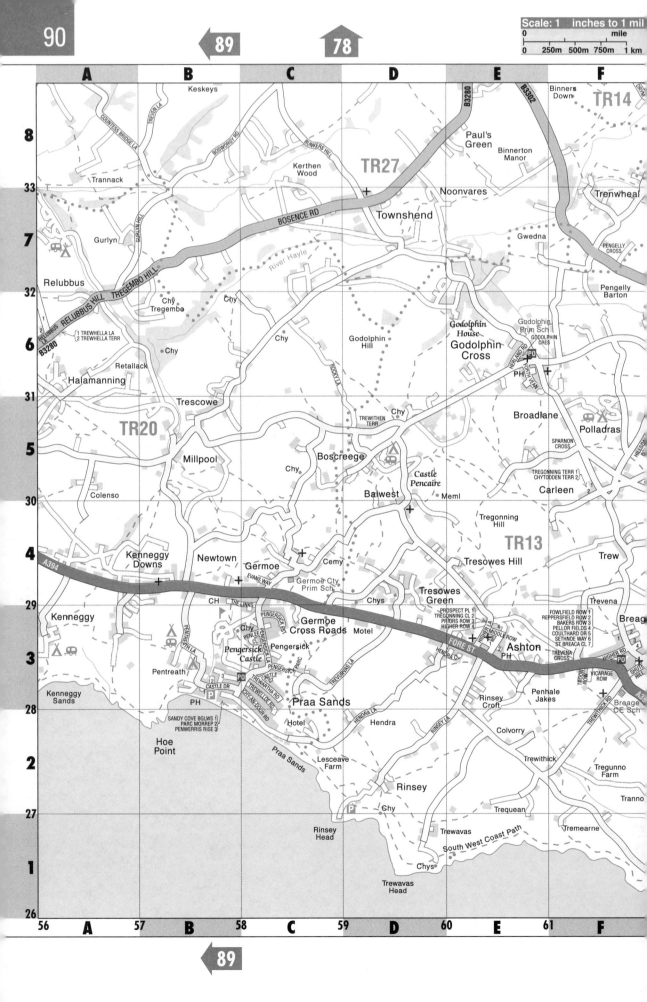

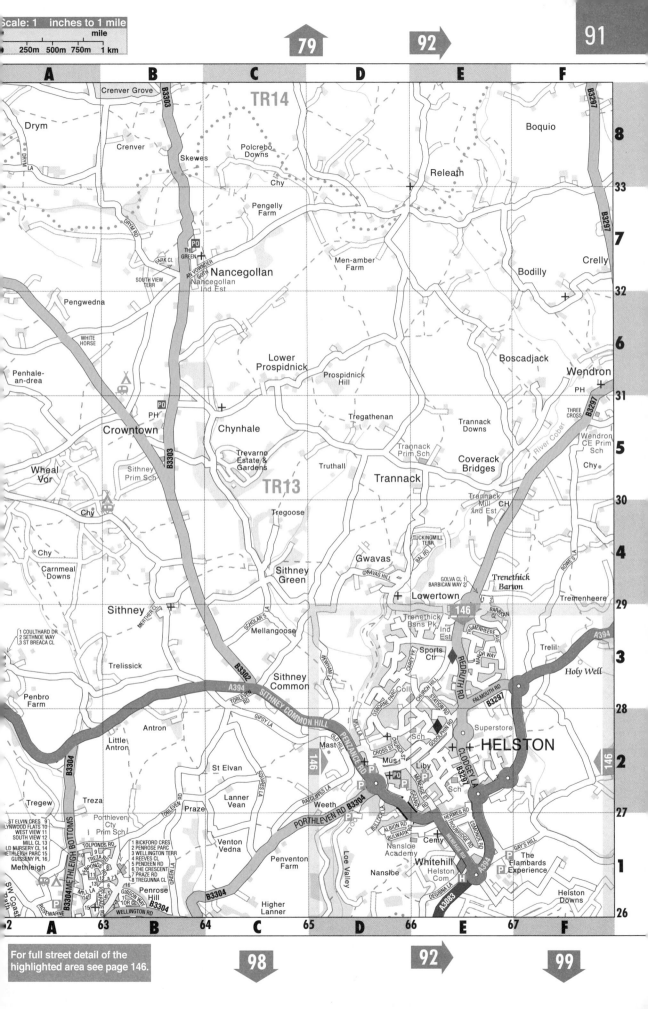

Scale: 1 inches to 1 mile
mile
250m 500m 750m 1 km

| A | B | C | D | E | F |

TR14

Drym

Crenver Grove

Boquio

8

Crenver

Skewes

Polcrebo
Downs

Releath

33

Chy

Pengelly
Farm

Men-amber
Farm

Crelly

7

PARK CL
THE
GREEN
PO
AN VOWNDER
GOTH
SOUTH VIEW
TERR

Nancegollan
Nancegollan
Ind Est

Bodilly

32

Pengwedna

Lower
Prospidnick

Boscadjack

Wendron

6

WHITE
HORSE

Prospidnick
Hill

PH

31

THREE
CROSS

Penhale-
an-drea

PO
PH

Crowntown

Chynhale

Tregathenan

Trannack
Downs

Wendron
CE Prim
Sch

River Cober

5

Wheal
Vor

Sithney
Prim Sch

Trevarno
Estate &
Gardens

Truthall

Trannack
Prim Sch

Coverack
Bridges

Chy

B3303

TR13

Trannack

30

Chy

Tregoose

Trannack
Mill
Ind Est

CH

TUCKINGMILL
TERR
BAL RD

4

Carnmeal
Downs

Sithney
Green

Gwavas

GWAVAS HILL

GOLVA CL 1
BARBICAN WAY 2

Trenethick
Barton

Tremenheere

1 COULTHARD DR
2 SETHNOE WAY
3 ST BREACA CL

Sithney

METHERS RD

Mellangoose

SCHOLAR'S LA

Lowertown

146

BARBICAN
CL
MENHEERE
AVE

Trelil

A394

3

Trelissick

B3302

Sithney
Common

KENWYN LA

Trenethick
Bsns Pk
Ind
Est

Sports
Ctr

CAREFY PK

MAJOR WAY

Holy
Well

A394

A394
SITHNEY COMMON HILL

TORLEVEN RD
GIPSY LA

Penbro
Farm

Antron

Little
Antron

St Elvan

SQUIRES LA

Mast

146

OLD PARK

PENZANCE RD

MILL LA

Osborne Parc Coll

CROSS ST

CHURCH ST

Sch

Mus

CHURCH HILL

STATION RD

GOODSHW RD

HELSTON

REDRUTH RD

FALMOUTH RD

Superstore

28

B3304

Tregew

Treza

TORLEVEN RD

Praze

Lanner
Vean

GREEN LA

Weeth

RATCLIFFES LA

PORTHLEVEN RD B3304

BULLOCK

Liby

MENAGE ST

COINAGEHALL ST

PO

Sch

CLODGEY LA

B3291

HERMES RD

2

ST ELVIN CRES 9
LYNWOOD FLATS 10
WEST VIEW 11
SOUTH VIEW 12
MILL CL 13
LD NURSERY CL 14
METHLEIGH PARC 15
GUISSENY PL 16
Methleigh

METHLEIGH BOTTOMS

B3304

Porthleven
Cty
Prim Sch

TOLPONDS RD
TREZA RD
RAPONDS RD

1 BICKFORD CRES
2 PENROSE PARC
3 WELLINGTON TERR
4 REEVES CL
5 PENDEEN RD
6 THE CRESCENT
7 PRAZE RD
8 TREGUNNA CL

Venton
Vedna

Loe Valley

Nansloe

ALBION RD

BULWARK

Cemy

FROUBRIDGE RD

ESMADE RD

Whitehill

Nansloe
Academy

Helston
Com

H

The
Flambards
Experience

GAY'S HILL
P

1

SW COAST PATH

ROSEWARNE

MILL LA

TOR CL

GIBSON WAY

WELLINGTON RD

GARAGE LA

Penrose
Hill

B3304
B3304

Higher
Lanner

Penventon
Farm

DEGIBNA LA

A3083

Helston
Downs

26

| A | 63 | B | 64 | C | 65 | D | 66 | E | 67 | F |

For full street detail of the
highlighted area see page 146.

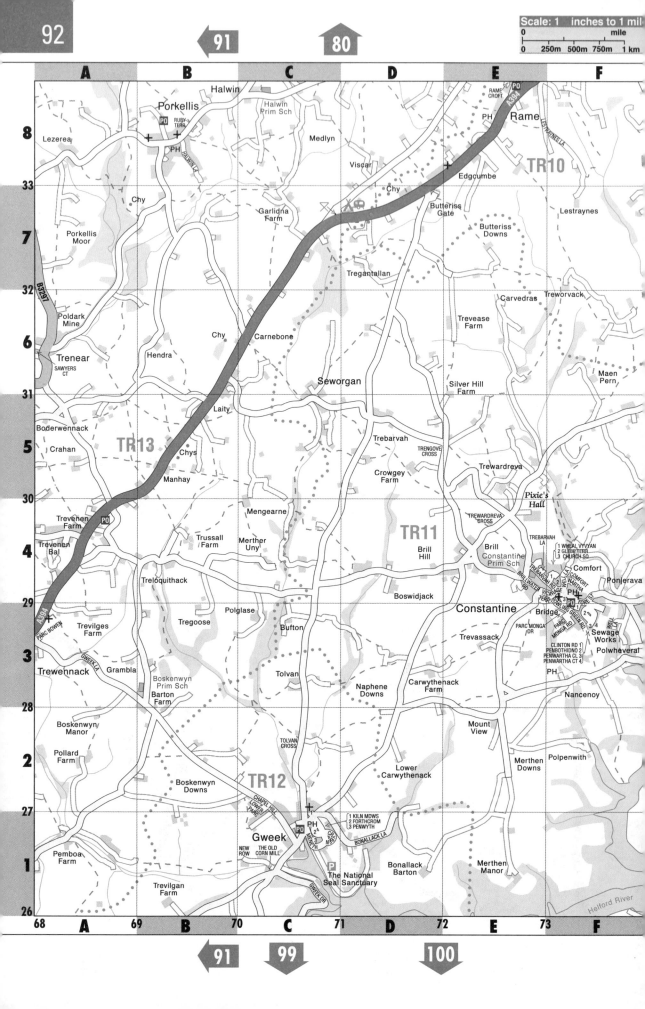

A B C D E F

Works

ANTRON HILL
Hantertavis

Trenoweth

TRENOWETH LA

Halvosso

TR10

Lower Spargo

Potter's

Trevone Farm

Higher Spargo

Job's Water

Helland Mill

Treverva

Helland House

Menallack Cheese Farm

Tresahor Vean

Bosvathick

Bosvarren House

Higher Treglidgwith Farm

Lower Treglidgwith

Treviades

HIGH CROSS

Drift Farm

Trenarth

TREWINCE LA
TREWINCE
INOW TERR

Porth Navas

Higher Calamansack

Lower Calamansack

Groyne Point

ORCHARD LA
Helford
PH

Treath

TR12

ANTRON WAY
ESTON CL 1
SPARGO CT 2
TRENOWETH RD
CHURCH RD
PENVEAN CL

Mabe Burnthouse

Antron Farm

College Resr

Argal Manor

Argal Resr

ARGAL VIEW
Lamanva
ELM GROVE COTTS

Higher Argal

Tresooth

Trewoon Farm

Bosawsack

Trecombe Farm

TR11

PENWARNE RD

Lower Tregarne

Treworval Farm

Bosanath Mill

Boskensoe Farm
GOLDMARTIN CL 1
CARLIDNACK CL 2
TREVENA GDNS 3
GOLDMARTIN SQ 4
GREENFIELDS CL 5
FIELD PL 6
ST MICHAELS CT 7
ROSEANNON 8
ROSCARRICK VILLAS 9
TREVANION CT 10

Lower Penpoll

DURGAN CROSSROADS

Glendurgan Garden

Durgan

Trebah Gardens

BAR RD
Hotel
CH
THE FAIRWAY
BUDOCK VEAN LA

Helford Passage
PH
COASTGUARD COTTS

Ferry (P)

Helford River

South West Coast Path

A B C D

Superstore

Resr

Tregonhaye

Higher Kergilliack

Sparnon

Trewen Farm

Tresooth Bungalow

Higher Crill Farm

Penwarne Manor

Penjerrick

Penjerrick Gdns

Penwarne Barton

Bareppa

CARLIDNACK RD

CHAPEL TOWN CLY

Carlidnack

CASTLE VIEW PK

SANDYS HILL
PARC AN MAINS
GROVE HILL
SHUTE HILL
ST ANNES

Mawnan Smith

Higher Penpoll

Mawnan Village CE Prim Sch

Bosveal

Bosveal

Polgwidden Cove

Porthallack

South West Coast Path

The Gew

77 78

Hillhead Farm

HILL HEAD RD
HILL RD
UNION RD
Mast
UNION CNR

Lower Kergilliack

SCHOOL LA

VICARAGE HILL

PO
PH

Budock Water

Menehay

TREWEN RD

Hotel

NO MANS LAND RD
PENJERRICK RD

Hotel

Tregedna

Rosemerryn Farm

MAENPORTH EST
P
Maenporth

High Cliff

Hotel

MAENPORTH RD
TRELISS CL

The Hutches

Bream Cove

Rosemullion

Trerose

OLD CHURCH RD
TREVANNEY CL
Carwinion Bamboo Gdn

Mawnan

P

Toll Point

Mawnan Shear

Parson's Beach

South West Coast Path

Rosemullion Head

94

P&R
Falmouth Wharves
FALMOUTH RD
Ponsharden Ind Est
DRACAENA AVE
OLD HILL
NORTH PAR

LARKS LA
TRESCOBEAS RD
Falmouth
H

CONWAY RD
Tregoniggie Ind Est
Bickland Ind est
BICKLAND HILL
Mongleath
LONGFIELD
Schs
MO NGL
KING LEITH
MONGLEATH RD
BOSLOWICK RD
SWINGATE HILL
MELVILL RD
Penmere

Swanvale
PO

BICKLAND WATER RD

FALMOUTH
Boslowick

SWANPOOL RD

ROSCARRACK RD

MAEN VALLEY PK
PENNANCE HILL
Trelevra Farm
TWINBROOK PK

Pennance Farm

Penrose

South West Coast Path

144

94

8

33

7

32

6

31

5

30

4

29

3

28

2

27

1

26

4 A 75 B 76 C 77 D 78 E 79 F

100

101

For full street detail of the highlighted area see page 144.

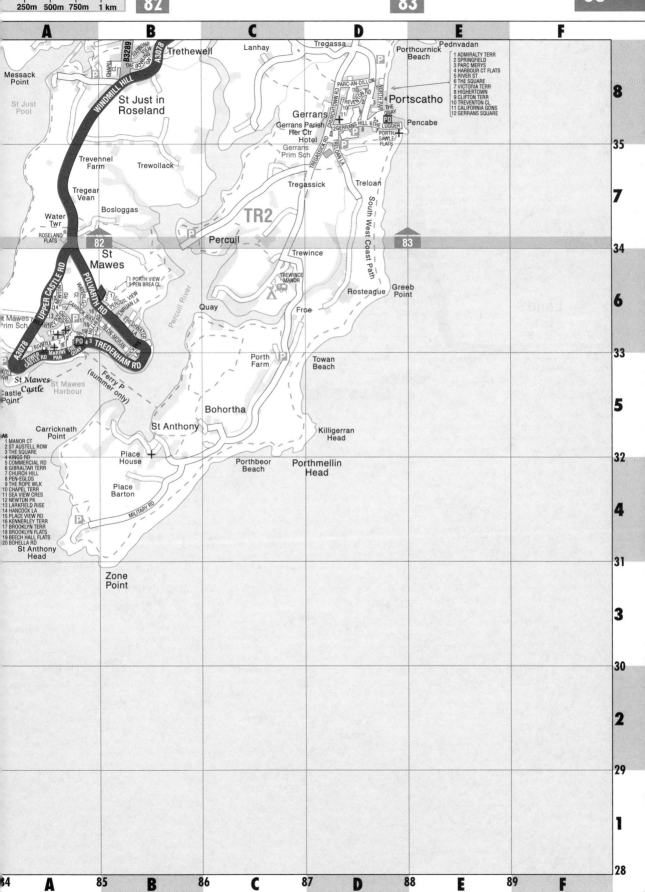

Messack Point

St Just Pool

Trethewell

St Just in Roseland

Trevennel Farm

Trewollack

Tregear Vean

Bosloggas

Water Twr

ROSELAND FLATS

St Mawes

Lanhay

Tregassa

Porthcurnick Beach

Pednvadan

Gerrans

Gerrans Parish Her Ctr Hotel

Gerrans Prim Sch

PARC-AN-DILLON

Portscatho

Pencabe

Pencable

1 ADMIRALTY TERR
2 SPRINGFIELD
3 PARC MERYS
4 HARBOUR CT FLATS
5 RIVER ST
6 THE SQUARE
7 VICTORIA TERR
8 HIGHERTOWN
9 CLIFTON TERR
10 TREVENTON CL
11 CALIFORNIA GDNS
12 GERRANS SQUARE

Tregassick

Treloan

TR2

Percuil

Trewince

TREWINCE MANOR

Rosteague

Greeb Point

St Mawes Prim Sch

Quay

Froe

Percuil River

South West Coast Path

Ferry P (summer only)

St Mawes Castle

St Mawes Harbour

Castle Point

Carricknath Point

Porth Farm

Towan Beach

Bohortha

St Anthony

Killigerran Head

A6
1 MANOR CT
2 ST AUSTELL ROW
3 THE SQUARE
4 KINGS RD
5 COMMERCIAL RD
6 GIBRALTAR TERR
7 CHURCH HILL
8 PEN-EGLOS
9 THE ROPE WLK
10 CHAPEL TERR
11 SEA VIEW CRES
12 NEWTON PK
13 LARKFIELD RISE
14 HANCOCK LA
15 PLACE VIEW RD
16 KENNERLEY TERR
17 BROOKLYN TERR
18 BROOKLYN FLATS
19 BEECH HALL FLATS
20 BOHELLA RD

Place House

Place Barton

Porthbeor Beach

Porthmellin Head

MILITARY RD

St Anthony Head

Zone Point

Scale: 1 inches to 1 mile
0 — mile
0 250m 500m 750m 1 km

A B C D E F

Tregiffian

Crows-an-wra

TREVORGAN CROSS

A30

Trevedra Farm

B3306

Treave

Boscarn

Escalls

Carn Barges

Carn Towan

THE GREENS

Rissick

Banns Farm

Cowloe

ST JUST CORNER LA

Trevorian Farm

The Tribbens

Jetty

Sennen Cove

SEA VIEW TERR

Róspannet

OLD COASTGUARD ROW 1
SENNEN HTS 2
HARBOUR MEWS 3

LB Sta

PH

COVE HILL

Trevear Farm

Bosanketh Farm

PEDN-MEN-DU

STONE CHAIR

COVE RD

MARIA'S LA

MAYON GREEN

86

PO

Pedn-mên-du

Irish Lady

Gamper

Mayon Cliff

Maen Castle

Mayon

CRES

MAYON FARM

Sennen Sch

HORIZON FIELDS

87

Dr Syntax's Head

Cemy

TOWER CL

Sennen

Mast

Penrose

TR19

Bosfranken Farm

Alsia Farm

The Peal

Dr Johnson's Head

ROSSITER HO

Brew

Hotel

HALLAN VEAN

PH

Carn Kez

Legendry Land's End

A30

B3315

Land's End

Trevescan

Skewjack Farm

Trengothal Farm

Crean

Carn Greeb

Trevilley

Trebehor

Bottoms

St Levan Prim Sch

Tresidder

B3283

Armed Knight

Enys Dodnan

SOUTH WEST COAST PATH

SCHOOL HILL

Sparnon

B3315

Pordenack Point

Zawn Reeth

Bosistow Farm

Polgigga

Trethewey

LITTLE TRETHEWEY EST

ST BURYAN HILL

Carn Boel

Mill Bay or Nanjizal

Raftra

Trendrennen Farm

TREEN HILL

PH

Carn Lês Boel

Arden-Sawah

OLD CABLE LA

Mast

Treen

Treryn Dinas

Inner Pendower Cove

Porthcurno Telegraph Mus

Zawn Kellys

Carn Barra

Róskestal

ZODIAC HO

THE VALLEY

Róspletha

Porthcurno

Mon

Folly Cove

Black Carn

St Levan

Minack Open Air Theatre

Logan Rock

Porth Curno

Horrace

Porth Loe

Porthgwarra

Vessacks

Pedn-mên-an-mere

Carn Scathe

Gwennap Head

Polostoc Zawn

Hella Point

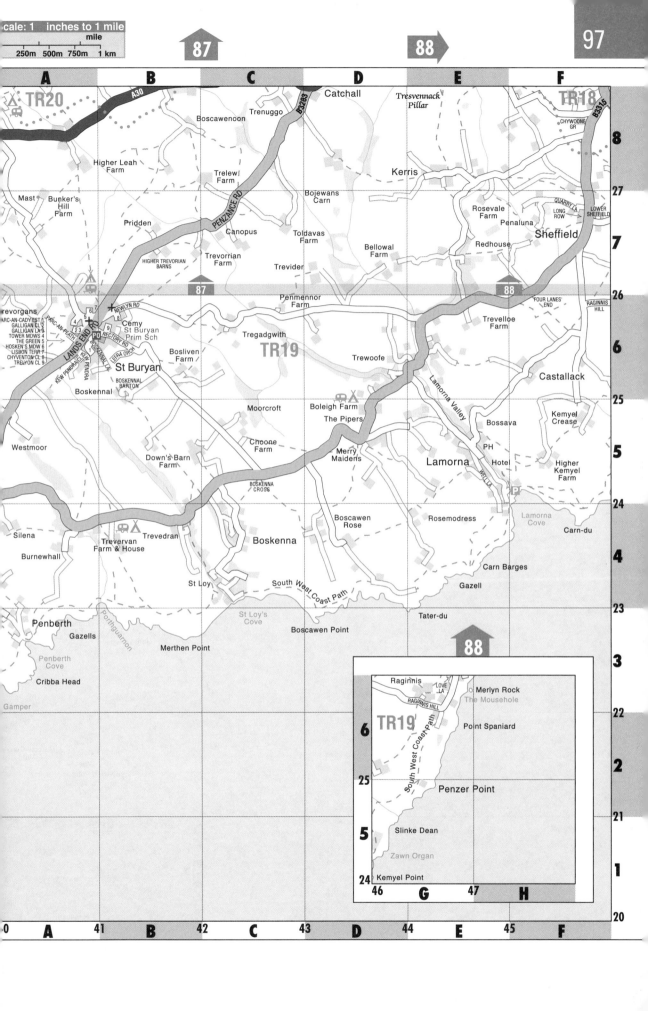

scale: 1 inches to 1 mile

mile

250m 500m 750m 1 km

87

88

A | B | C | D | E | F

TR20

A30

Catchall

Tresvennack Pillar

TR18

CHYWOONE GR

8

Boscawenoon

Trenuggo

B3283

Higher Leah Farm

Trelew Farm

Kerris

Rosevale Farm

Penaluna

QUARRY LA

LONG ROW

LOWER SHEFFIELD

27

Mast

Bunker's Hill Farm

Pridden

PENZANCE RD

Canopus

Bojewans Carn

Toldavas Farm

Bellowal Farm

Redhouse

Sheffield

B3315

7

Higher Trevorian Barns

Trevorrian Farm

Trevider

26

87

Penmennor Farm

88

FOUR LANES' END

RAGINNIS HILL

revorgans

PARC-AN-CADY EST

GALLIGAN CL 2

GALLIGAN LA 3

TOWER MDWS 4

THE GREEN 5

HOSKEN'S MDW 6

LISBON TERR 7

CHYVENTON CL 8

TRELYON CL 9

LANDS END RD

PARC-AN-PEATH

NEWLYN RD

Cemy

St Buryan Prim Sch

RECTORY RD

LETRA ORCH

PO

KEW PENGRACE

KEW PENDRA

BOSKENNAL LA

Tregadgwith

TR19

Trewoofe

Trevelloe Farm

6

Bosliven Farm

St Buryan

Boskennal

BOSKENNAL BARTON

Castallack

25

Moorcroft

Boleigh Farm

The Pipers

Lamorna Valley

Bossava

Kemyel Crease

Westmoor

Choone Farm

Merry Maiders

PH

Lamorna

Hotel

Higher Kemyel Farm

5

Down's Barn Farm

BOSKENNA CROSS

WELLA

P

24

Silena

Burnewhall

Trevervan Farm & House

Trevedran

Boskenna

Boscawen Rose

Rosemodress

Lamorna Cove

Carn-du

4

St Loy

South West Coast Path

Carn Barges

Gazell

23

Penberth

Gazells

St Loy's Cove

Boscawen Point

Tater-du

88

Porthguarnon

Merthen Point

Penberth Cove

Cribba Head

Gamper

22

Raginnis

LOVE LA

Merlyn Rock

The Mousehole

RAGINNIS HILL

South West Coast Path

Point Spaniard

2

TR19

6

25

Penzer Point

21

5

Slinke Dean

Zawn Organ

1

24

Kemyel Point

46

G

47

H

20

For full street detail of the highlighted area see page 146.

Scale: 1 inches to 1 mile

0 ___ mile

0   250m   500m   750m   1 km

A   **B**   **C**   **D**   **E**   **F**

B8
1 METHLEIGH BOTTOMS
2 METHLEIGH PARC
3 CHURCH ROW
4 FORE ST
5 HARBOUR VIEW
6 SHUTE LA
7 KESTREL CL
8 PROSPECT PL
9 CHAPEL TERR
10 SALT CELLAR HILL
11 MOUNT PLEASANT RD
12 HARBOURSIDE
13 BAY VIEW TERR
14 INSTITUTE HILL
15 WEST END
16 CLAREMONT TERR

C8
1 HOLMAN'S PL
2 THE GUE
3 ELLISTON GDNS
4 THOMAS ST
5 THOMAS TERR
6 FORTH SCOL
7 PEVERELL RD
8 SUNSET DR
9 SUNSET GDNS
10 MATELA CL
11 PARC-AN-MAEN
12 HAMMILLS DR
13 HAMMILL'S CL
14 ST PIRANS PARC
15 BALFIELD RD
16 TREMEARNE RD
17 TREGONNING VIEW
18 WARREN CL
19 WHEAL ROSE
20 MOUNT'S RD
21 MOUNT'S BAY TERR
22 OCEAN CRES
23 SUNNYBANK
24 HIGHBURROW
25 WESLEY CT

Mon   Mast   B3304   PO   B3304
Pier   Porthleven   UNITY ST
Tye Rocks

TR13   Penrose   Nancewidden
Degibna   Goonhusband
Penrose Walks   146
Higher Pentice
Tangies   Burnwic Farm
Carminowe Creek   Carminowe
Low Bar   South West Coast Path
Mon   Clies Farm
Chyvarloe   Burnow
Berepper Cross   Berepper   **TR12**
Gunwalloe   PARC-ASKELL CL
PH   Chyanvounder
Gunwalloe Fishing Cove
Trenoweth Farm
Baulk Head
Halzephron Cove   Hingey Farm
Green Rock
Halzephron Cliff
Pedngwinian
Winnianton Farm
Jangye-ryn   CH   The Towans
Church Cove
Poldhu Cove   POLDHU RD
Poldhu Point   Marconi Centre (Mus)
Masts
Mên-y-grib Point   Mon
102   LAELOUDER LA
Polurrian Cove
102
COASTGUARD COTTS 1
MULLION COVE BGLWS 2
Henscath   Hotel

Porthleven Sands
The Loe   146
A3083

8   25   7   24   6   23   5   22   4   21   3   20   2   19   1   18

61   **A**   62   **B**   63   **C**   64   **D**   65   **E**   66   **F**

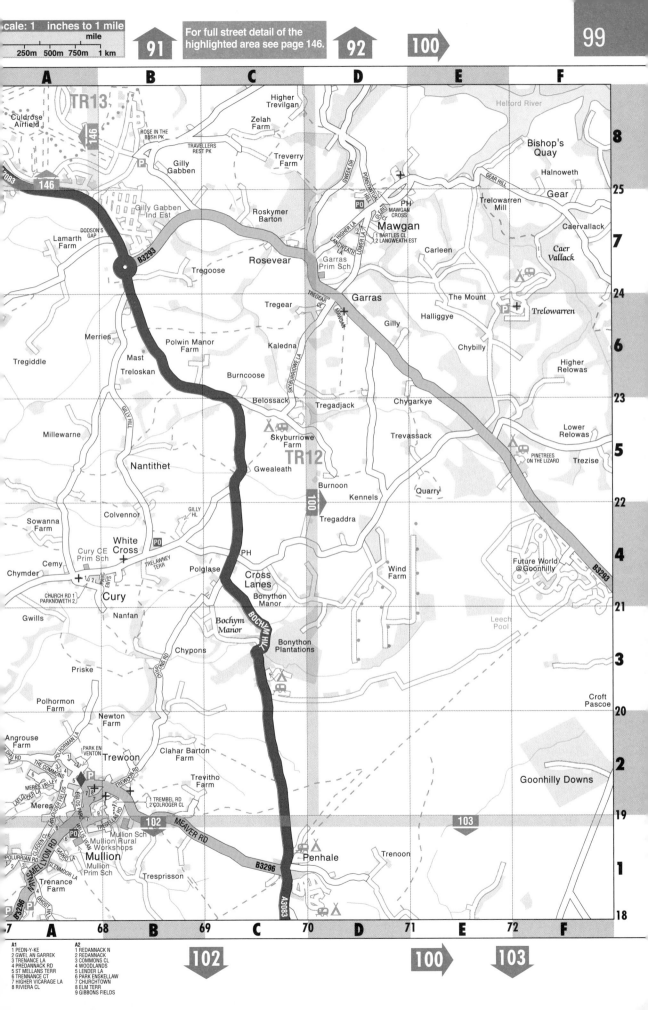

Scale: 1 inches to 1 mil
mile
0 250m 500m 750m 1 km

A B C D E F

8

Heltord River

Bishop's Quay

Tremayne
Trevedor
Kestle
Frenchman's Pill

25

Gear Hill
Halnoweth
Mudgeon Farm
Gear
Withan
Tregithew

PH
MAWGAN CROSS
Trelowarren Mill
PO

7

Mawgan
1 BARTLES CL
2 LANGWEATH EST
Carleen
Caer Vallack
Caervallack
Landrivick
Choon
Tregonwe

Garras Prim Sch

24

Garras
The Mount
Trelowarren
St Martin-in-Meneage Prim Sch
1 PORK ST
2 THE GREEN
3 BOSKERNOW
Tregevis Farm
Trevaddr

P

6

Gilly
Halliggye
Chybilly
St Martin
Higher Trenower

Higher Relowas
Trethewey
PH
Newtown-in-St Martin

23

Tregadjack
Chygarkye
Lower Relowas
Tregidder
Tregidden Hill

Trevassack
TR12
Tretharrup
Trewoon

5

PINETREES ON THE LIZARD
Trezise
Trewince
Trelaminney

Burnoon
Kennels
Quarry
Polkerth
Tregeague
Trelease Mill

22

Tregaddra
Wind Farm
Traboe
Trenithon

4

Future World @Goonhilly
Rosuick

21

Leech Pool
B3293
Grugwith

3

Traboe Cross
Roscrowgey
Roskilly
P
Kernewas

Croft Pascoe

20

Croft Pascoe Pool
Trelanvean

2

Goonhilly Downs
The Lizard Nature Reserve

19

102
103

Trelan

Trenoon

1

The Lizard Nature Reserve

18

70 A 71 B 72 C 73 D 74 E 75 F

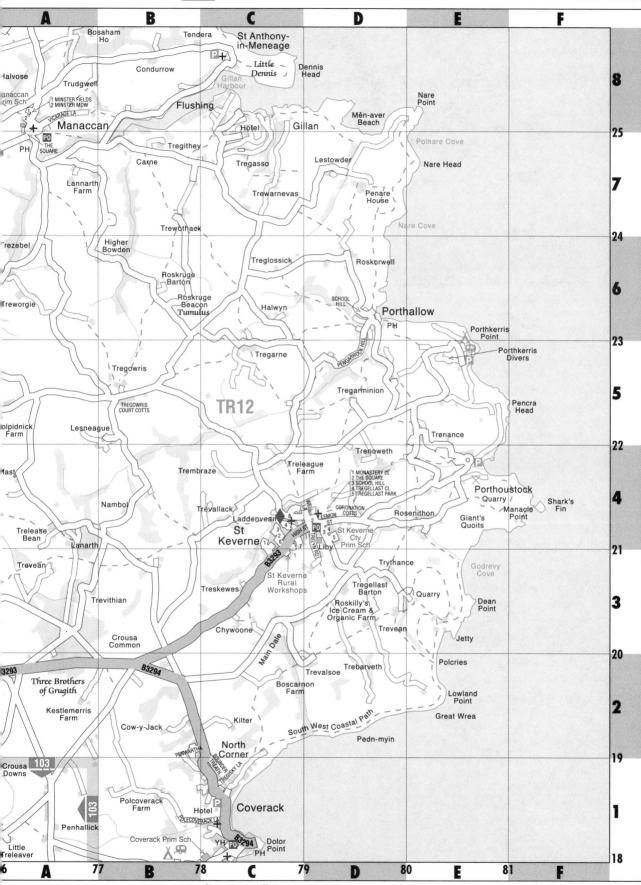

A B C D E F

8
25
7
24
6
23
5
22
4
21
3
20
2
19
1
18

C4
1 TRESKEWES EST
2 TREVALLACK VIEW
3 TREVALLACK PARC
4 LANHEVERNE PARC
5 DOCTORS HILL
6 POLVENTON PARC
7 PENMENNER EST
8 COMMERCIAL RD

C3
1 Treskewes Ind Est

Scale: 1 inches to 1 mile

mile

250m 500m 750m 1 km

100

101

101

103

A B C D E F

Crousa
Downs

Trelan

The Lizard
Nature Reserve

8

Penhallick

99

100

Little
Treleaver

18

Erisey
Barton

Gwente

Ponsongath

7

TR12

Arrowan
Common

Carnpessack

Trerise

17

Tresaddern
Farm

Trevenwith

Arrowan

Downas
Valley

Eastern Cliff

Poldowrian

The
Gaider

Poltesco Valley

PH

Gwendreath
Farm

P

Green
Saddle

fort

Beagles
Point

6

Crowgey
Farm

Spernic Cove

Carrick
Lûz

Pedn
Boar

Treal

Kuggar

Kennack Sands

Thorny
Cliff

16

Treveddon

Poltesco

Polbream Point

Carleon Cove

101

5

Treleague

Ruan
Minor

Perprean
Cove

7

Pednavounder

The Oxen

fort

15

LONG MOOR 1
MUNDYS FIELD 2
CHAPEL TERR 3
GLEBE TERR 4
HIGHER MOOR 5

Grade-Ruan
CE Prim Sch

South West Coast Path

Enys Head

HEADLAND
COTTS

Trewillis

Chynhalls
Point

St Ruah

TR12

4

St Ruan's
Well

LEDRA CL 1
RUMINELLA VIEW 2

PH

Kildown Point

17

Treleaver

South West Coast Path

Cadgwith

6

Ebber Rocks

14

Grade

Devil's Frying Pan

16

Treleaver
Cliff

Black Head

Gwavas

Carn
Barrow

77

G

78

H

3

Polbarrow

13

The
Chair

Whale
Rock

The
Balk

LB Sta

13

2

Church
Cove

Hot
Point

12

GREEN LA

Bass
Point

1

Pen Olver

11

1 A 72 B 73 C 74 D 75 E 76 F

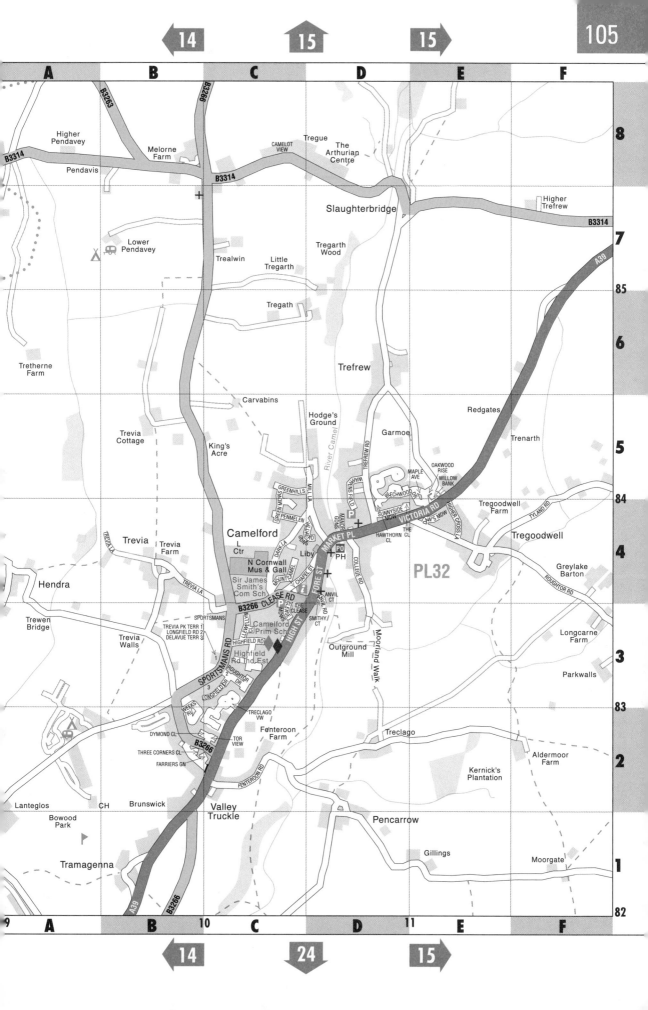

8

Higher
Pendavey

Melorne
Farm

Tregue

The
Arthurian
Centre

CAMELOT
VIEW

Pendavis

B3263

B3266

B3314

B3314

B3314

Slaughterbridge

Higher
Trefrew

B3314

7

Lower
Pendavey

Trealwin

Little
Tregarth

Tregarth
Wood

A39

85

Tregath

6

Tretherne
Farm

Trefrew

Carvabins

Hodge's
Ground

Redgates

Trevia
Cottage

King's
Acre

River Camel

Garmoe

Trenarth

5

Trevia
Farm

GREENHILLS

MILLIA

PENMELEN

MANOR
GDNS

OAKWOOD
RISE

WILLOW
BANK

MAPLE
AVE

BEECHWOOD

SUNNYSIDE
MDW

VICTORIA RD

Tregoodwell
Farm

TYLAND RD

84

Trevia

Camelford

L
Ctr

GREEN MDWS

DAIRY LA

MOUNT
CAMEL

Liby

N Cornwall
Mus & Gall

Sir James
Smith's
Com Sch

CHAPEL ST

FORE ST

MARKET PL

PO
PH

HAWTHORN
CL

THE
CL

COLLEGE RD

HIGHER CROSS LA

PL32

Tregoodwell

Greylake
Barton

ROUGHTOR RD

4

Hendra

TREVIA LA

TREVIA LA

B3266 CLEASE RD

ANVIL
CT

SMITHY
CT

ANVIL RD

Moorland Walk

Longcarne
Farm

Trewen
Bridge

Trevia
Walls

SPORTSMANS

TREVIA PK TERR 1
LONGFIELD RD 2
DELAVUE TERR 3

SPORTSMANS RD

Highfield
Rd Ind Est

HIGHFIELD RD

LLEWELLYN

HIGH ST

THE
CLEASE

Camelford
Prim Sch

Outground
Mill

Parkwalls

3

ROUGHTOR
DR

LONGFIELDER

WEEKS
RV

TRECLAGO
VW

Fenteroon
Farm

Treclago

83

DYMOND CL

TOR
VIEW

B3266

Kernick's
Plantation

Aldermoor
Farm

2

THREE CORNERS CL

FARRIERS GN

FENTEROON RD

Lanteglos

CH

Brunswick

Valley
Truckle

Pencarrow

Bowood
Park

Gillings

Moorgate

1

Tramagenna

A39

B3266

82

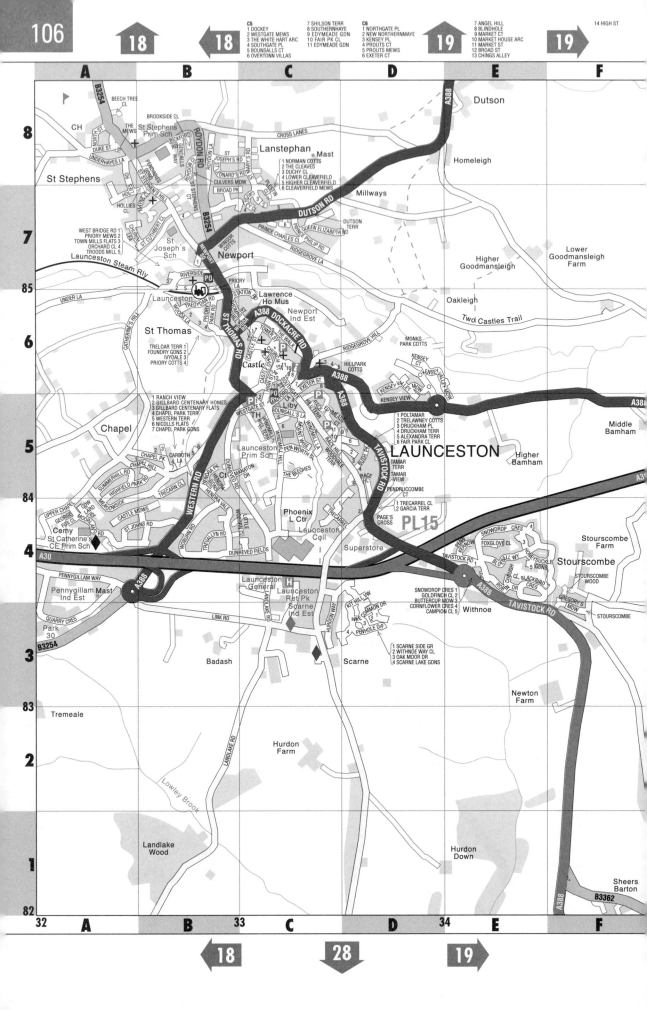

20 21 21

A B C D E F

8

Crugmeer

7

PL27

Tregirls
Farm

South West Coast Path

Gun
Point

St George's
Well

76

South West Coast Path

Meml

Ferry P
(Low Water)

6

P

ROCK RD

IRB Sta

Trethillick

Prideaux
Place

1 WATERS EDGE
2 THE OLD BOAT YARD

Ferry P
(High Water)

PL28

Cemy

B3276 A389

FENTONLUNA LA
ST SAVIOUR S LA

HIGH ST

CHURCH ST DUKE ST

CHURCH LA

Mus
Liby

LADYWELL

NORTH
QUAY

SOUTH
QUAY

STRAND

National
Lobster
Hatchery

RIVERSIDE

River Camel

1 OLD SCHOOL CT
2 ST EDMUNDS LA
3 COACHYARD MEWS
4 COMMERCIAL TERR
5 AVERY S ROW
6 STRAND ST
7 BROAD ST
8 CHAPEL CT
9 LANADWELL ST
10 MARKET PL
11 MARKET STRAND
12 MILL SQ
13 MIDDLE ST
14 ALMA PL
15 BARRY S LA
16 RUTHY S LA
17 CROSS ST

5

Treator

Treator
Cotts

B3276

P

St Petrocs
Mdw

DOWNSTREAM

GREWVILLE RD

HAWKINS RD

RALEIGH RD

BOYD AVE

RAN FIELDS

DRAKE RD

SCHOOL HILL

NEW ST

STATION RD

TREVERBYN RD

Padstow Harbour
Ind Est

75

B3276 A389

Trecerus
Ind Est

PERCY
MEWS

Padstow
Sch

PELLEW CL

POLPENNIC DR

SARAH'S CT

CODENEK AVE

SARAH'S LA

FREI/ANLEY RD

NETHER

GLYNN RD

DENNIS RD

ALAN RD

CAMEL CL

ANNETHY
LOWEN

MOYLE RD

EGERTON RD

PORTHILLY VIEW

Padstow
Workshop Units

B3276

MEADOW CT

PADSTOW

Dinas

SARAH'S
VIEW

SARAH'S
MDW

DINAS

LITT
DINAS

Town
Bar

4

Camel Trail

3

Dennis
Hill

Obelisk

74

Tregella

Little Petherick Creek

2

Trerethern

Saints Way

Sea
Mills

Benuick

Tregonce

Treravel
Farm

Trevorrick

PL27

1

73

0 A B 91 C D 92 E F

32 32 32

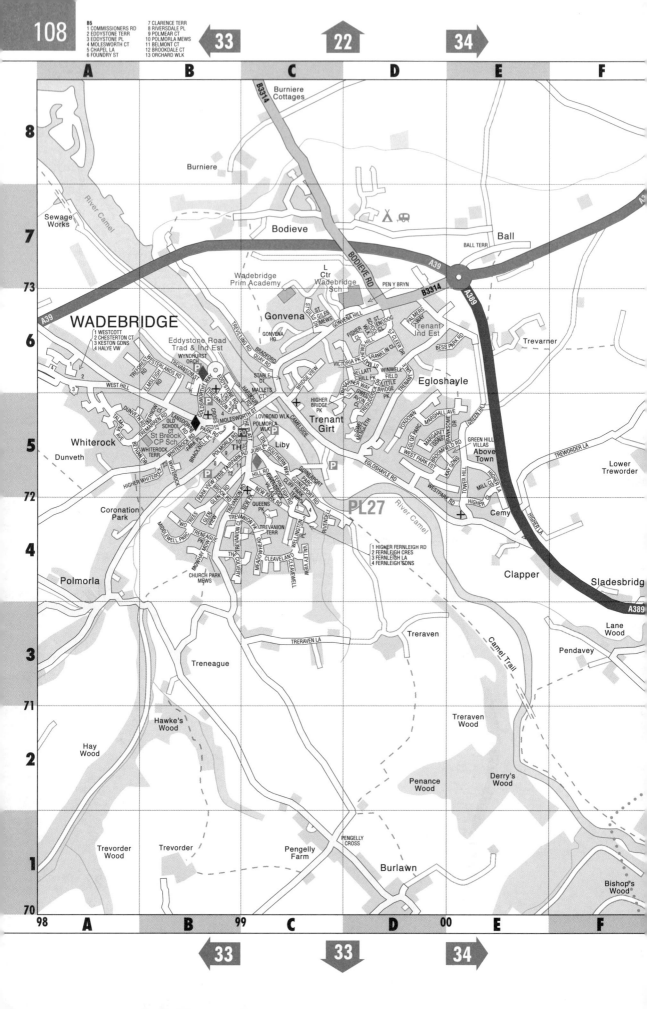

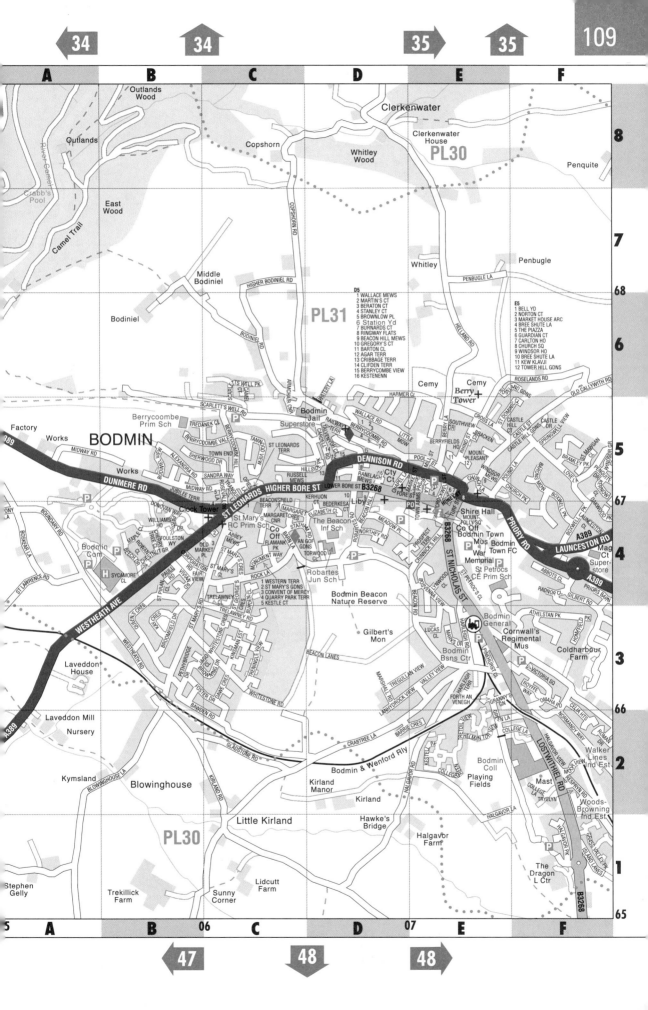

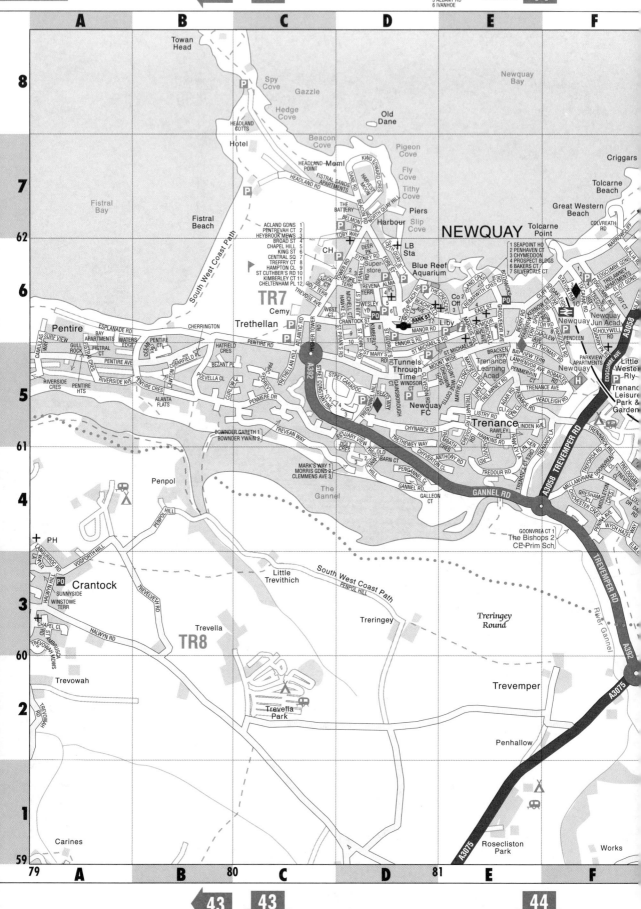

D5
1 CAERNARVON LODGE
2 ST MARY'S CT
3 BOWNDER SARRAS
4 BOWNDER MARHAUS

F6
1 TREVANION CT
2 WESTCOVE HO
3 STATION APP
4 ALBANY CT
5 ALBANY RD
6 IVANHOE

7 TOLCARNE MEWS
8 MORRAB CT
9 PERGOLLA CT
10 Newquay
   Adult Ed Ctr

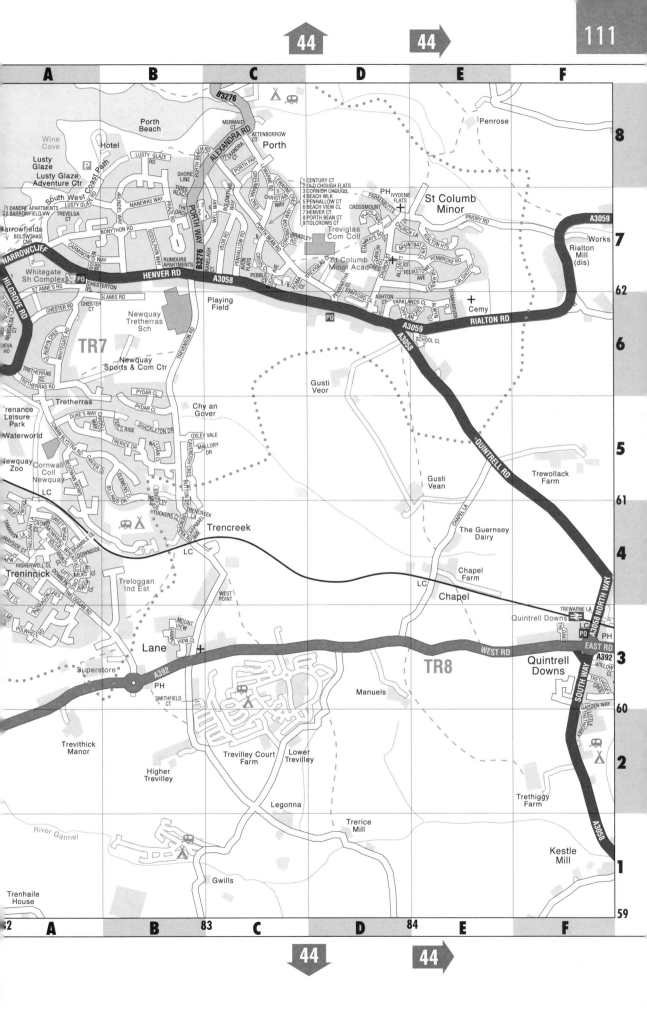

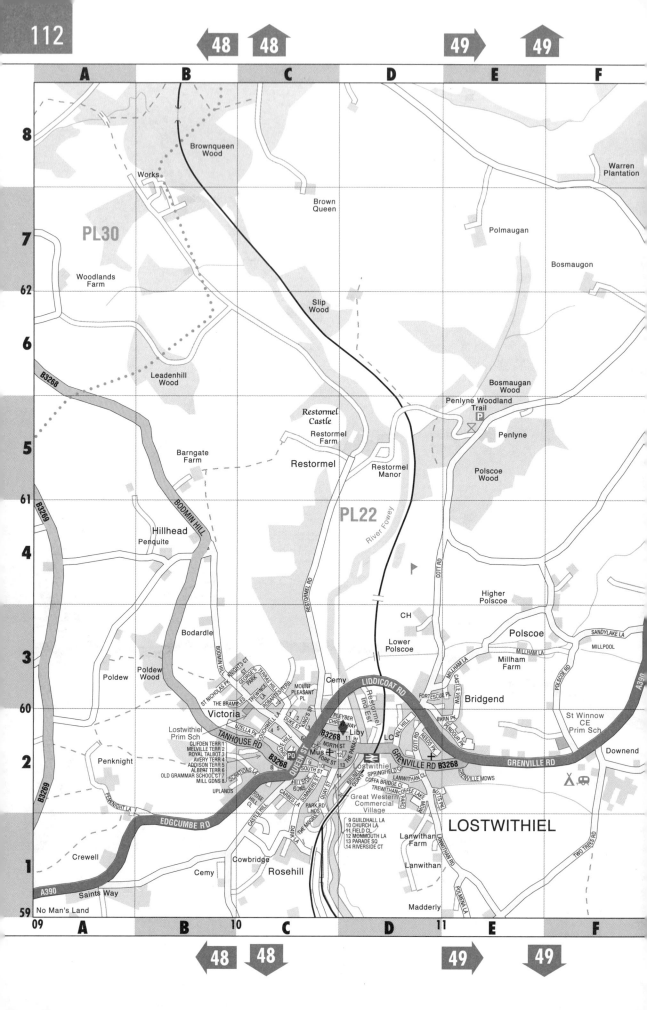

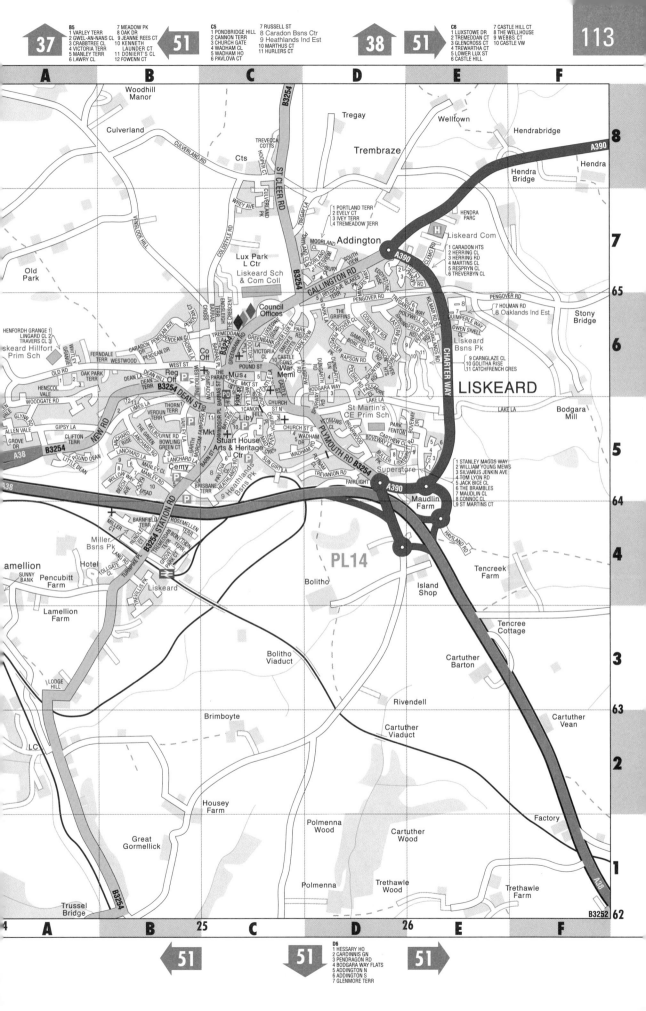

B5
1 VARLEY TERR
2 GWEL-AN-NANS CL
3 CRABBTREE CL
4 VICTORIA TERR
5 MANLEY TERR
6 LAWRY CL

7 MEADOW PK
8 OAK DR
9 JEANNE REES CT
10 KENNETH LAUNDER CT
11 DONIERT'S CL
12 FOWENN CT

C5
1 PONDBRIDGE HILL
2 CANNON TERR
3 CHURCH GATE
4 WADHAM CL
5 WADHAM HO
6 PAVLOVA CT

7 RUSSELL ST
8 CARADON BSNS CTR
9 HEATHLANDS IND EST
10 MARTHUS CT
11 HURLERS CT

C6
1 LUXSTOWE DR
2 TREMEDDAN CT
3 GLENCROSS CT
4 TOM LYON CT
5 LOWER LUX ST
6 CASTLE HILL

7 CASTLE HILL CT
8 THE WELLHOUSE
9 WEBBS CT
10 CASTLE VW

37 51 38 51

113

51 51 51

D6
1 HESSARY HO
2 CARDINNIS GN
3 PENDRAGON RD
4 BODGARA WAY FLATS
5 ADDINGTON N
6 ADDINGTON S
7 GLENMORE TERR

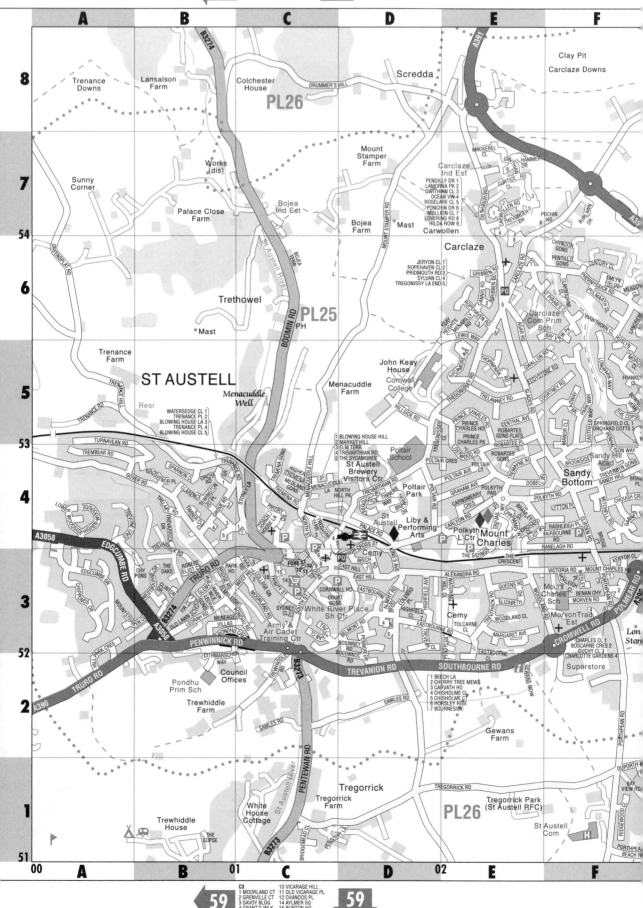

A B C D E F

8 Trenance Downs
Lansalson Farm
Colchester House
Scredda
Clay Pit
Carclaze Downs
PL26
DRUMMER'S HILL

B3274
A391

7 Sunny Corner
Works (dis)
Mount Stamper Farm
Carclaze Ind Est
PENDILLY DR 1
LAMORNA PK 2
GWITHIAN CL 3
OCEAN VW 4
ROSELARE CL 5
PONCHIN DR 6
MULLION CL 7
LOVERING RD 8
HILDA ROW 9
MACKEREL CL
GW
HAMMER DR
CURTICE RD
TREVORDER DR
POCHIN HO
BURLAWN DR
A3

Palace Close Farm
Bojea Ind Est

54 Bojea Farm
Mast
Carwollen
Carclaze
JERYON CL 1
ROPEHAVEN CL 2
PRIDMOUTH RD 3
SYLVAN CL 4
TREGONISSY LA END 5
CHYNOON GDNS
PENTILLIE GDNS
CENTURY CL
EMLYN FIELDS
MEADO

6 Trethowel
PL25
PH
BODMIN RD
ST AUSTELL RIVER
BOJEA TERR
Menacuddle Farm
GRIBBEN
PO
GRIBBEN RD
Carclaze Com Prim Sch
HAWTHORN CL
ROSLYN
LANDER

Mast

5 Trenance Farm
ST AUSTELL
Menacuddle Well
Resr
TRENANCE HILL
TRENANCE RD
John Keay House
Cornwall College
HILLSIDE RD
SYCAMORE AVE
PRINCE CHARLES RD
PRINCE CHARLES HO
PRINCE CHARLES PK
CENTRAL AVE
ROBARTES FLATS
ROBARTES PL
MANOR CL
THE COPSE
SPRINGFIELD CL 1
ORCHARD COTTS 3

WATERSEDGE CL 1
TRENANCE PL 2
BLOWING HOUSE LA 3
TRENANCE PL 4
BLOWING HOUSE CL 5

53 TURNAVEAN RD
TREMBEAR RD
1 BLOWING HOUSE HILL
2 MARKET HILL
3 ELM TERR
4 TREVARTHIAN RD
5 THE SYCAMORES
Poltair School
ROBARTES GDNS
Sandy Hill Acad
BROOKSIDE
TREVERBYN GDNS
Sandy Bottom
Sandy Hill

4 A3058
EDGCUMBE RD
GROSVENOR PL
CLARENCE PL
St Austell Brewery Visitors Ctr
Poltair Park
POLTAIR AVE
POLTAIR CRES
GRAHAM AVE
POLKYTH
CARNSMERRY CRES
Mount Charles
Polkyth L Ctr
Liby & Performing Arts
CLIFDEN RD
FAIRBOURNE RD
RANELAGH RD
CHOUGH CR
GANNET
St Austell

TRURO RD
B3274
A3058
THE OAKS
CHY PONS
CLINTON
PO
HIGH CROSS ST
BEECH
EAST HILL
Cemy
KING'S AVE
THE SIDINGS
THE CRESCENT
VICTORIA RD
MOUNT CHARLES RD
MORVEN RD
KEYROR CL
POLMEAR RD

3 EDGCUMBE GN
EDGCUMBE GN
CHIPPINS DR
B3274
A3058
OLD LAWN
MENEAGE VILLAS
TRURO RD
PENWINNICK RD
WEST HILL
MOORLAND RD
TRINITY ST
SOUTH ST
White River Place Sh Ctr
Cornwall Ho
Court GDNS
EASTBOURNE RD
HIGHFIELD AVE
HIGHFIELD CL
Cemy
TOLCARNE RD
WOODLAND CL
Mount Charles Sch
Morvon Trad Est
CROMWELL RD
Lon Star

Army & Air Cadet Training Ctr
SYDNEY ST
BELMONT RD
BOSINNEY RD
BOGANNOC RD
ALEXANDRA RD
QUEENS RD
ELIZABETH
MARGARET AVE
EASTBOURNE CL
CHARLES CL 1
BOSCARNE CRES 2
DUCHY CL 3
CHARLOTTE GARDENS 4
Superstore

52 TRURO RD
A390
PARK CRES
HILL PARK CRES
DITHMARSCHEN WAY
PONDHU CRES
B3273
TREVANION RD
SOUTHBOURNE RD
GEVANS MDW
i

Council Offices
Pondhu Prim Sch
Trewhiddle Farm
TREWIDDLE
B3273
SAWLES RD
1 BEECH LA
2 CHERRY TREE MEWS
3 CARVATH RD
4 CHISHOLME CL
5 CHISHOLME CT
6 HORSLEY RISE
7 BOURNESIDE
Gewans Farm

2 A390
SAWLES RD
PENTEWAN RD
ST AUSTELL RIVER

1 Trewhiddle House
White House Cottage
THE COPSE
Tregorrick
Tregorrick Farm
TREGORRICK RD
PL26
Tregorrick Park (St Austell RFC)
St Austell Com
H
DUPORTH
BAY VIEW RD
PORTHPEA BEACH RD

B3273
BRIDGEMEAD CL
PENSCULLA
RIDGEWOOD CL
PORTHPEA

51 A B 00 C 01 D 02 E F

C3
1 MOORLAND CT
2 GRENVILLE CT
3 SAVOY BLDG
4 GRANT'S WLK
5 BIDDICK'S CT
6 MARKET ST
7 CROSS LA
8 CHURCH ST
9 VICTORIA PL
10 VICARAGE HILL
11 OLD VICARAGE PL
12 CHANDOS PL
14 AYLMER SQ
15 BURTON HO
16 WEST HILL CT

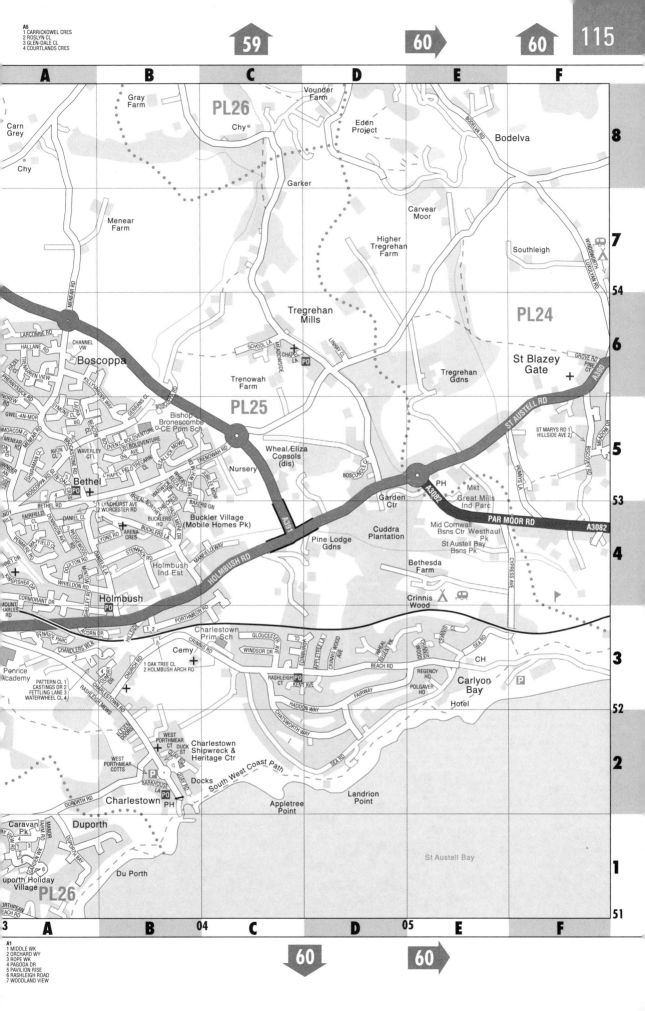

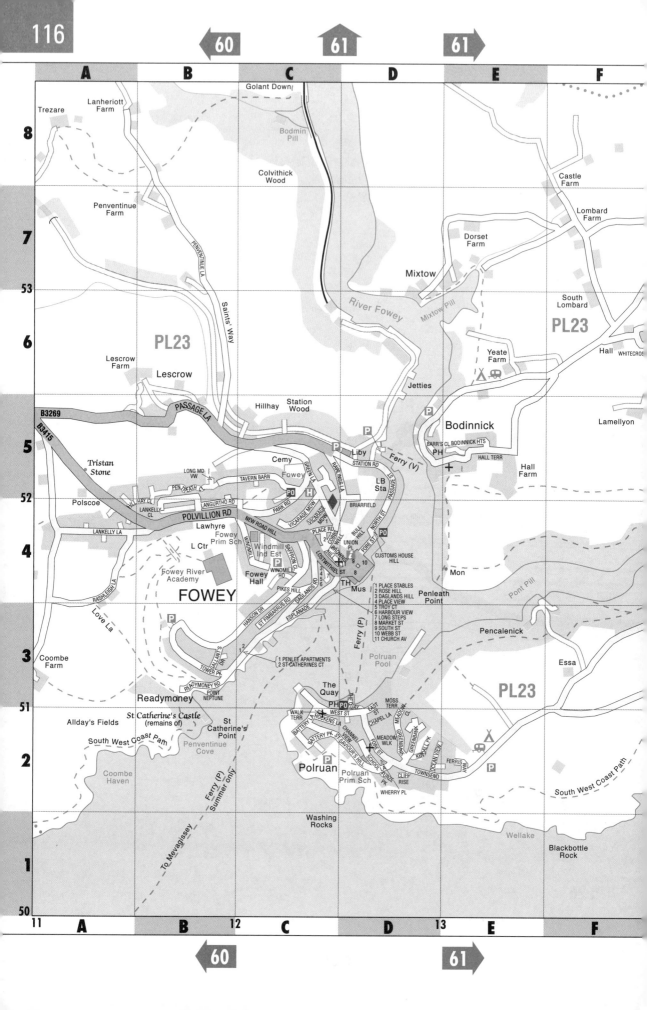

8

7

55

6

5

54

4

3

53

2

1

52

A B C D E F

PL14
Trenant Park

Hole
Trewith

Trenant
Barton

Prince's Briars
Wood

The Caers

Millhill
Wood

Longcoe
Wood

Longcoe
Farm

Great
Tree

Pendrym

LC
Terras
Bridge

Hall's
Wood

St Martin's
Wood

St Martin

PL13

East Looe River

ST MARTIN'S RD

SANDPLACE RD

Deerpark
Wood

RANNEYS
CL

KIMLERS WY

COLMER CL

LIMMOCKS RD

Looe
Com Acad

THE
BUNGALOWS

Barbican Rise
Ind Est

BARBICAN RD

FRANCISCAN C'
RAME VIEW

Millendreath

MAY LA

Quayfield
Wood

Kilminorth
Wood

Trenant
Wood

West Looe River

B3253

Hotel

RICHLANDS

SUNRISING EST

GLEBELANDS
FAIRFIELD

SPRINGFIELD RD

ST MARTIN'S RD
PLAIDY LA

MEADOW DR
BAY DOWN

1 HILLSIDE TERR
2 THE HILLOCKS
3 WESLEY TERR
4 LOWENNA GDNS
5 THE ORCHARD

HILLSIDE VILLAS 1
VALLEY BGLWS 2

Plaidy

Millendreath
Beach

PLAIDY PARK RD

Kilminorth Woods
Nature Reserve

Forest
Walks

Sewage
Works

Polean
Trad Est

BEECH TERR 1
TRELAWNEY TERR 2
POLVELLAN TERR 3
WEST DOWN CT 4
HIGHER BEECH TERR 5
FURZEDOWN TERR 6
BONSON CL 7
BELMONT 8

POLVELLAN
MANOR

POLEAN LA

WOODLANDS VIEW

Looe

STATION RD

Liby

SPRINGFIELD
GATE

BERKELEY
CT

CRAIGSIDE

NORTH VIEW

SHUTTA RD

SHUTTA RD

ELM TREE RD

CORMEL RD

ST GEORGE'S RD

Shutta

DAVES LA

SPRINGFIELD RD

BODRIGAN RD

PENDENNIS RD
BARBICAN CRESC

PH

PO

Looe
Prim Sch

CHANTRY LA

PLAIDY LA

Lower
Goonrea

POLPERRO RD

DOWNS RD

GOONRE

GOONWARTHA
CL Cemy

GOONWARTHA RD

PENARTH

PORTBYHAN

West
Looe

Mast

THE DOWNS

NORTH RD

QUAY RD

FORE ST

Hotel

P

ELM MEADOW
HILL

TH

i

Hotel

East
Looe

South West Coast Path

HAY LA

CUSTOM
HO DR

MEADOWAY

BAY VIEW DR

BAYVIEW DE PENDOVER
PENDOVER RD

CLEVELAND RD
COURTNEY
AVE

1 LOWER ST
2 CHURCH ST
3 BAY ST
4 THE BAY
5 LOWER CHAPEL ST
6 ST MARY'S
7 HIGHER CHAPEL ST
8 LOWER MARKET ST
9 MIDDLE MARKET ST
10 TOWER HILL
11 ADMIRALTY CT

TREETOPS
HILL

TREGARRICK

TREGARRICK
CT

A387

DOWNS LANE
PK

WEST LOOE HILL

DOWNS LA

TREMAINE

BARN MEADOW PK

WEST LOOE
CL

FORE ST

PO

DOWNS
VIEW

CASTLE ST

HIGHER MARKET ST

CHURCH END

PH

Mus

LOOE

IRB
Sta

Looe Bay

12 EAST QUAY HO
13 BULLER HO
14 SEA FRONT CT
15 QUAY ST
16 LOWER CHAPEL ST

HANNAFORE RD

HANNAFORE LA

DAWN RD

ROCK
TWRS

PL13

COASTGUARD STA FLATS 1
SUNNYCROFT 2
CHAPEL GROUND 3
PRINCES ST 4
PRINCES SQ 5
WEST LOOE SQ 6
CHURCH ST 7
HARBOUR SIDE 8
PORTBIGHAM 9
DINGLE'S FOLLY 10
WHITLIEBURN TERR 11

EDDYSTONE
CT

1 NAILZEE HO
2 ISLAND CT
3 NAILZEE POINT
4 ST GEORGES CT

Portlooe

Hannafore

STONEROCK
FLATS

THE CRESCENT

PORTUAN RD

Hannafore
Point

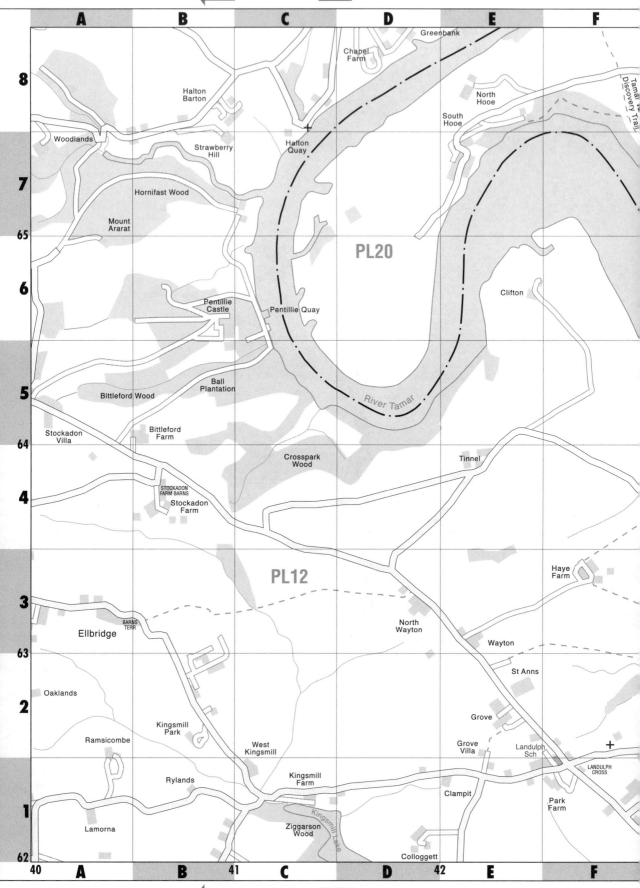

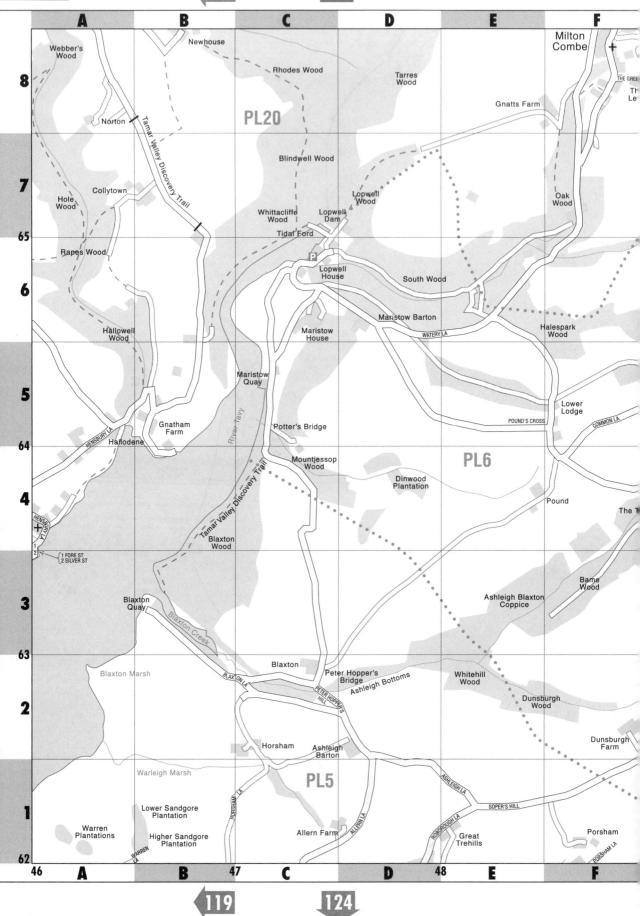

Milton Combe

THE GRE...
Th...
Le...

Webber's Wood

Rhodes Wood

Tarres Wood

PL20

Gnatts Farm

Norton

Blindwell Wood

Tamar Valley Discovery Trail

Oak Wood

Collytown

Hole Wood

Whittacliffe Wood

Lopwell Wood

Lopwell Dam

Rapes Wood

Tidal Ford

P

Lopwell House

South Wood

Hallowell Wood

Maristow Barton

Halespark Wood

Maristow House

WATERY LA

Maristow Quay

River Tavy

Lower Lodge

Gnatham Farm

Potter's Bridge

POUND'S CROSS

COMMON LA

HENSBURY LA

Hallodene

PL6

Mountjessop Wood

Dinwood Plantation

Tamar Valley Discovery Trail

Pound

HENSBURY LA

The T...

1 FORE ST
2 SILVER ST

Blaxton Wood

Bame Wood

Ashleigh Blaxton Coppice

Blaxton Quay

Blaxton Creek

Blaxton

Peter Hopper's Bridge

Whitehill Wood

Blaxton Marsh

BLAXTON LA

Ashleigh Bottoms

Dunsburgh Wood

PETER HOPPER'S HILL

Horsham

Ashleigh Barton

Dunsburgh Farm

Warleigh Marsh

HORSHAM LA

PL5

ASHLEIGH LA

Lower Sandgore Plantation

SOPER'S HILL

Warren Plantations

Higher Sandgore Plantation

Allern Farm

ALLERN LA

ROBOROUGH LA

Great Trehills

Porsham

WARREN...

BORSHAM LA

Uphill

Morey House

Hotel

PL20

Dashel

Bickham

Upper Road Plantation

Bickham

Bickham

Charity Bickham

Bulteel Bickham

Webbers

COMMON LA

Commonlane Plantation

Middlelodge Plantation

The Wilderness

Higher Park

Middle Lodge

DEVONPORT LEAT

Higher Lodge

Henshears

Combe Park Farm

Lower Upperton

Little Down

Welltown Bridge

PL6

Marrowpark Plantation

ROBOROUGH DOWN LA

UPPERTON LA

North Broadley

Coppers

Haxter Lodge

Roborough Plantation

Leigh

LITTLE DOWN LA

Broadley

Broadley Ind Pk

BROADLEY CT

Roborough Farm

Roborough House

HELE LA

Ten Acre Brake

PARKWOOD CL

BROADLEY PARK RD

TAMERTON RD

LEIGH LA

Vicarage

Porsham Plantation

Haxter Wood

PORSHAM CL

HAXTER CL

BELLIVER WAY

Belliver Ind Est

LADYWELL

OLD BELLIVER

LOPES DR 1
VILLAGE DR 2
CRAMBER CL 3
STAPLE CL 4

HESSARY DR

INSRA WLK

TAVISTOCK RD

STAPLE CL

PH

LEATSIDE

LEAF WLK

CARLTON LA

NEW RD

Roborough

BLACKEVEN HILL

JUMP CL

BICKLEIGH DOWN RD

BLACKEVEN CL

Coombe Barton

Hursley Bsns Pk

Coombe Wood

A386

53
118

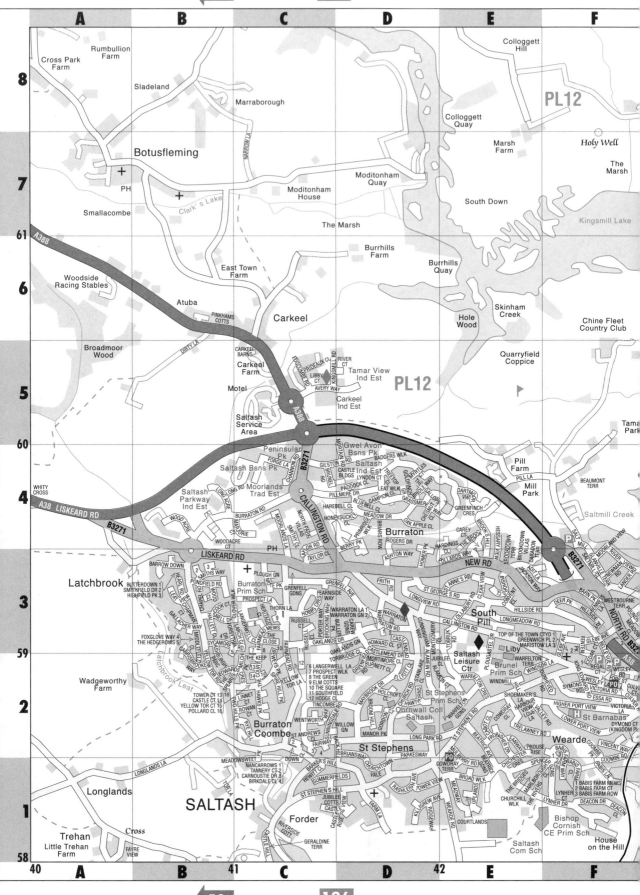

53
126

D1
1 Victoria Road
Prim Sch

A B C D E F

8

WARREN LA
OLD WARLEIGH LA
Warleigh Lodge
West Trehills
North Coombe Farm
Porsham Wood
LIZARD CL

7

Tamar Valley Discovery Trail
FRASER SQ
LINTON SQ
LINTON ON
Yappers Wood
WHITSON CROSS
Coombe Farm
Clittaford Cottage
Langley Plantation
KINNARD CRES
STROMA

Tamerton Foliot
Frenoes Farm
Mary Dean's CE Prim Sch
Hayesend Farm
WARING RD
Southway La
Beechwood Prim Sch
LUNDY CL
PENTLAND CL
ALDERNEY RD
INCHKEITH RD

61

Tor Plantation
OLD WARLEIGH LA
NURSERY LA
PO
SEVEN STARS LA
PH LA
LAMBERT RD
RIVERSIDE WLK
Cann House
PILLAR WLK 1
MOSES CT 2
ALGER WLK
BAMPFYLDE WAY
ROCKFIELD AVE

Tor Rock

6

STATION RD
TAMERTON FOLIOT RD
B3373
Cann Woods Nature Reserve
Southway
Southway Dr
PL6

Budshead Creek
LAKE VIEW
MILFORD CL
AYLESBURY CRES
Playing Fields
St Peter's RC Prim Sch
Whitleigh
Woodfield Prim Sch
Whitleigh Wood
TAMERTON FOLIOT RD
FRONTFIELD CRES
The Arbour
RAVEN DR
UPLAND DR

5

TAUNTON PL
HEREFORD RD
NEWCASTLE GDNS
Woodland Wood
St HELENS WLK
SHREWSBURY RD
Sir John Hunt Com Sports Coll
Woodlands Sch
Whitleigh Wood
Plymouth Whitleigh Prim Sch
Notre Dame RC Sch
NOTRE DAME CL

60

Budshead Wood
PL5
CANTERBURY DR
BUDSHEAD RD
WHITLEIGH GN
PO
TROWBRIDGE
READING WLK
HUNTINGDON GDNS
WHITLEIGH GDNS
WINDERMERE CRES
Water Works

4

1 BRANSCOMBE GDNS
2 QUEENS RD
3 KINGS RD
4 HIRMANDALE RD
5 HALDON PL
6 WOODLANDS CT
Brook Green Ctr for Learning
1 FOXTOR CL
2 MODBURY CL
3 MARLDON CL
4 BLACKTHORN CL
5 GUY MILES WAY
6 BOXHILL CL
LEWES GDNS
CHELMSFORD
IPSWICH CL
DERBY RD
APPLEBY WLK
DORCHESTER AVE
LANCASTER GDNS
KENDAL PL
Christian Mill Bsns Pk
BROOKLANDS CT

Plymouth Knowle Prim Sch
INSTOW WLK
Woodland Fort
Liby
1 BLAKE GDNS
2 CHESTERTON CL
3 CRASHAM CL
4 HOUSMAN CL
5 CONSTABLE CL
6 GOLDSMITH GDNS
7 WILMOT GDNS
8 SEDLEY WAY
BETJEMAN WLK
CARLISLE RD
BODMIN RD
WARWICK AVE
GUILDFORD
Crownhill Fort
SMALLACK CL 1
CHARLTON RD 2
LANSDOWNE RD 3

3

B3413
PO
Liby
ASHBURNHAM RD
OLD WOODLANDS RD
CROWNHILL RD
DUMFRIES RD
BUDSHEAD RD
B3373
OAK DR

West Park
COOMBE PARK LA
St FRANCIS CT
CAREW GDNS
WAVENEY GDNS
TRANSIT WAY
RUSKIN CRES
WHITLEIGH VILLAS
HAVISTOCK RD
SMALLACK DR
HUNTER CL

59

WANSTEAD GR
Shakespeare Prim Sch
BICKLEIGH
CARROLL
COWLEY RD
Crownhill

2

A38
DUNCOMBE AVE
EASTBURY AVE
Honicknowle
MOUNT PLEASANT
Hypermarket
PO
SHAKESPEARE RD
BYRON CL
Manadon Football Ctr
FROBISHER APP
WHITLEIGH AVE
WHITLEIGH COTTS
HEAVY WAY
PO
Alexandra Rd
CROWNHILL RD
FORT AUSTIN AVE
B341

QUARRY COTTS
BOSWELL CL 1
DEFOE CL 2
TENNYSON CL
BURNS AVE
SWIFT GDNS
St PETERS RD
CAXTON GDNS
RAMSEY GDNS
St Boniface RC Coll
CROSS PARK RD
Liby
TREWITH CT
WIDEY CROSS

1

A3064
WESTON MILL LA
Drake's Hill
Burrington Ind Est
Walkham Bsns Pk
THE PARKWAY
THACKERAY GDNS
BEDE GDNS
CHAUCER WAY
DRAYTON RD
CONGREVE GDNS
HILTON AVE
MACAULAY CRES
CONRAD RD
PL2
Manadon
St Boniface
GREAT BERRY
MORETON CL
Widey Court Prim Sch
Courtlands Specl Sch

PL2
BURRINGTON RD
Kestral Units
The All Saints CE Academy
BURRINGTON WAY
THE PARKWAY
SHIRLEY GDNS
SHERIDAN RD
COVERDALE PL
SWINBURNE GDNS
A38

58

A B C D E F

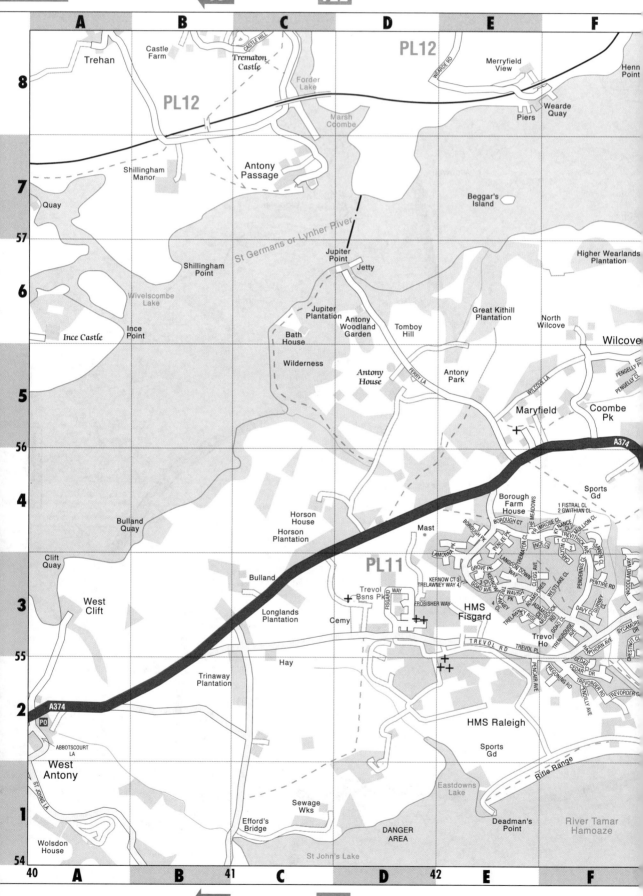

A   B   C   D   E   F

8   Trehan   Castle Farm   CASTLE HILL   Trematon Castle   PL12   Merryfield View   Henn Point

PL12   Forder Lake   Wearde Rd   Wearde Quay   Piers

Marsh Coombe

7   Shillingham Manor   Antony Passage   Beggar's Island   Higher Wearlands Plantation

Quay

57

6   Shillingham Point   St Germans or Lynher River   Jupiter Point   Jetty   North Wilcove   Wilcove

Wivelscombe Lake   Jupiter Plantation   Great Kithill Plantation

Ince Castle   Ince Point   Bath House   Antony Woodland Garden   Tomboy Hill   Antony Park   Maryfield   Coombe Pk

5   Wilderness   Antony House   Ferry La   Wilcove La

56

4   Bulland Quay   Horson House   Mast   Borough Farm House   Sports Gd   1 FISTRAL CL   2 GWITHIAN CL

Horson Plantation   BOROUGH CT   BOROUGH PK   PENLEE PK   PK IMROSE CL   TREMATON CL   K NANCE CL   MULLION CL   SENNEN CL   TREVITHICK AVE

Clift Quay   PL11   LAMORN PK   LANGDON DOWN WAY   INCE CL   PENDENNIS CL   PENTIRE RD   WOODLAND WAY

3   West Clift   Bulland   Trevol Bsns PK   FISGARD WAY   KERNOW CT 3   KENNARD   ADAMS CRES   WESTLAKE CL   DAVY CL   GURNEY   SYCAMORE DR

Longlands Plantation   Cemy   Frobisher Way   TRELAWNEY WAY 4   TRELAWNEY RISE   HMS Fisgard   Trevol Ho   CEDAR   CHESTNUT CT CL

55   Hay   Trinaway Plantation   TREVOL RD   TREVOL PL   TREGONING RD   TREVORDER G   TREVORDER G

2   A374   Abbotscourt La   PO   PENCAIR AVE   PENDILLY AVE   CEDAR DR

West Antony   St Johns La   HMS Raleigh   Sports Gd

Rifle Range

1   Efford's Bridge   Sewage Wks   DANGER AREA   Eastdowns Lake   Deadman's Point   River Tamar Hamoaze

Wolsdon House   St John's Lake

54

40   A   B   41   C   D   42   E   F

◆ 123
128 ▶

127

F5
1 NEPEAN ST
2 ADELAIDE ST
3 BRUNEL TERR
4 EPWORTH TERR
5 SUSSEX TERR
6 RAILWAY COTTS

7 YORK TERR
8 ST MAWES TERR

F3
1 CLARENDON HO
2 GARFIELD TERR
3 TRAFALGAR PL
4 THE MEWS
5 NELSON GDNS

6 BEYROUT PL
7 ST MICHAEL'S PL
8 ST MICHAEL'S TERR
9 PORTLAND CT
10 MOLYNEAUX PL
11 CLARENDON LA

F4
1 ST GEORGES CT
2 HORNBY ST
3 PHILLIMORE ST
4 FREMANTLE GDNS
5 FAIRFAX TERR

6 HARGOOD TERR
7 HARRISON ST
8 KEPPEL TERR
9 HEALY CT
10 BRUNSWICK PL

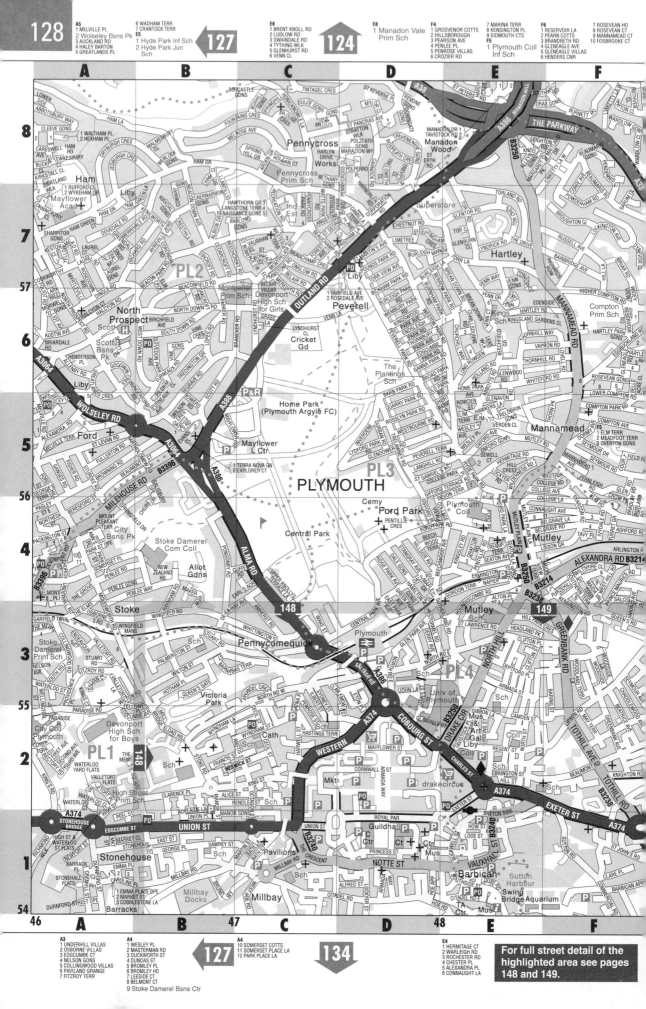

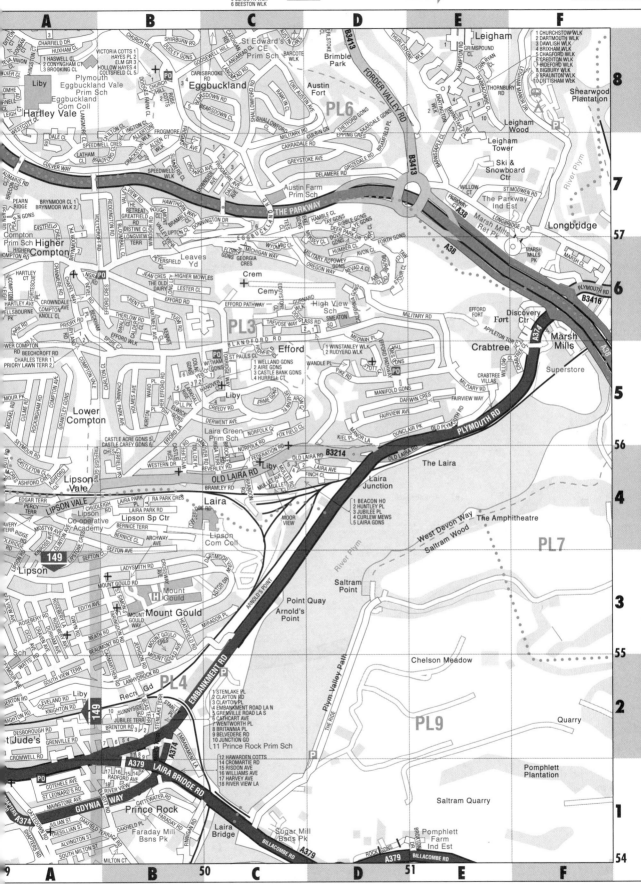

129

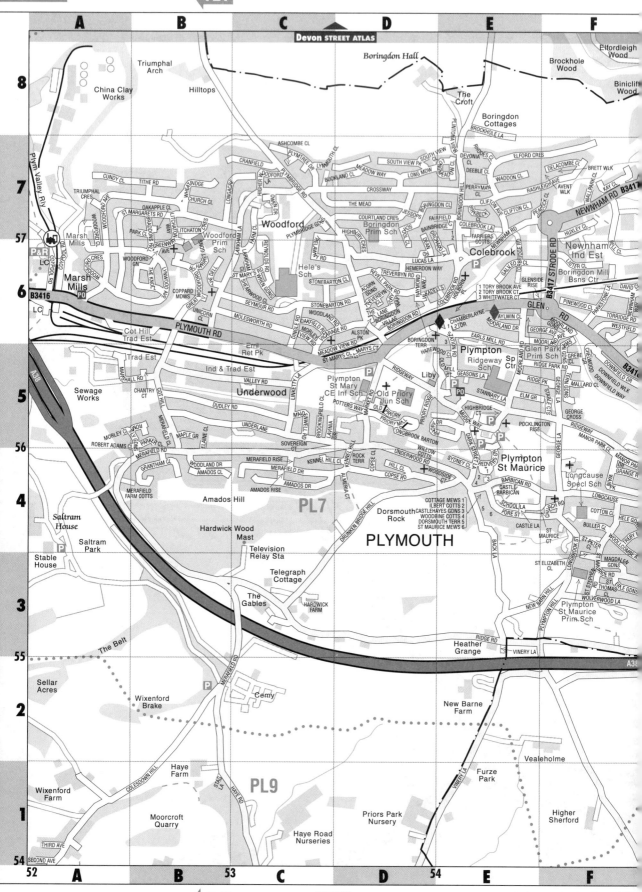

129

136

A B C D E F

8

Sparkwell
Farm

Newnham
Park

Furzeacre
Wood

Sparkwell

Windwhistle

B3417

Furzeacre
Bridge

Holly
Wood

Lowdamoor

HEMERDON LA

Hemerdon

Beechwood
Cross

Hemerdon
House

Beechwood

Old Newnham
Farm

Hemerdon
Farm

PH

Lodge

GALVA RD

LEDGATE LA

Old Newnham

Lodge

Sherwell

7

NEWNHAM RD

WEST PARK HILL

Sparkwell
Bridge

57

BIRCHWOOD GDNS

CORNFIELD
GDNS

Moor
Bridge

COMPASS DR

UPPER
RIDINGS

LOWER
RIDINGS

FURZEACRE CL

PRIDLE CL

LANGAGE
CROSS

6

Newnham
Ind Est

STOGGY LA

GREENWOOD PARK CL

WESTMOOR CL

HEMERDON HTS

LIDDLE WY

WALDON CL

GREENWOOD PARK RD

GLENHAVEN CL

MINERVA

KERSHAM

ALMOND DR

OAKFIELD CL

Langage
Science Pk

Higher
Langage

Combe
Farm

5

WESTFIELD

RALEIGH CL

GILBERT RD

ASHWOOD PARK RD

Chaddlewood

ROSECLAVE

WESTERN WOOD WAY

BEECHWOOD WAY

56

Chaddlewood
Prim Sch

WESTHOE

KINGSTON CL

ASPEN GDNS

FERN CL

POPLAR CL

WALNUT

Lower
Langage

HOLLAND RD

DEVERON CL

DENGIE

ROWAN

HICKORY DR

JASMINE CL

CLEMATIS WY

SUMMERLANDS GDNS

EASTERN WOOD RD

GARDEN CL

Applethorn
Slade

4

GLEN RD

HORSWELL
CHADDLEWOOD
HO

LARMER

PERIWINKLE CL

CELANDINE GDNS

Langage
Ind Est

MEADOW CL

PL7

Langage
Pk

Ley Farm

Voss

SANDY RD

EAGLE RD

BARN CL

PH

A38

3

DEEP LA

WOLVERWOOD CL

A38 Exeter, M5

B3416

Wiverton
House

Battisford
Pk

55

RIDGE RD

DEEP LA

Wiverton
Acre

Tuxton
Farm

Tuxton
Wood

Battisford

2

Butlas
Farm

Blackpool

1

East
Sherford

PL8

54

A 56 C D 57 E F

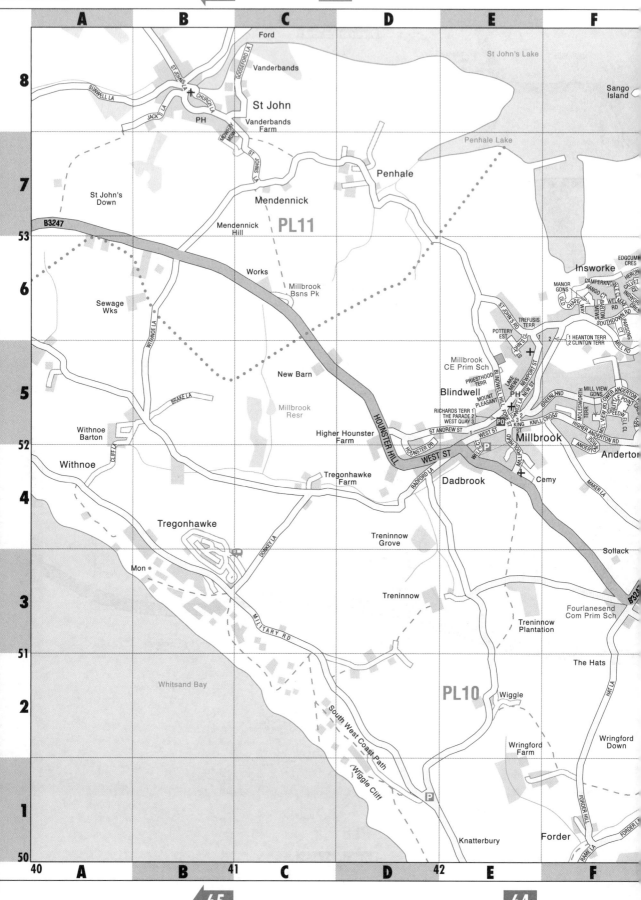

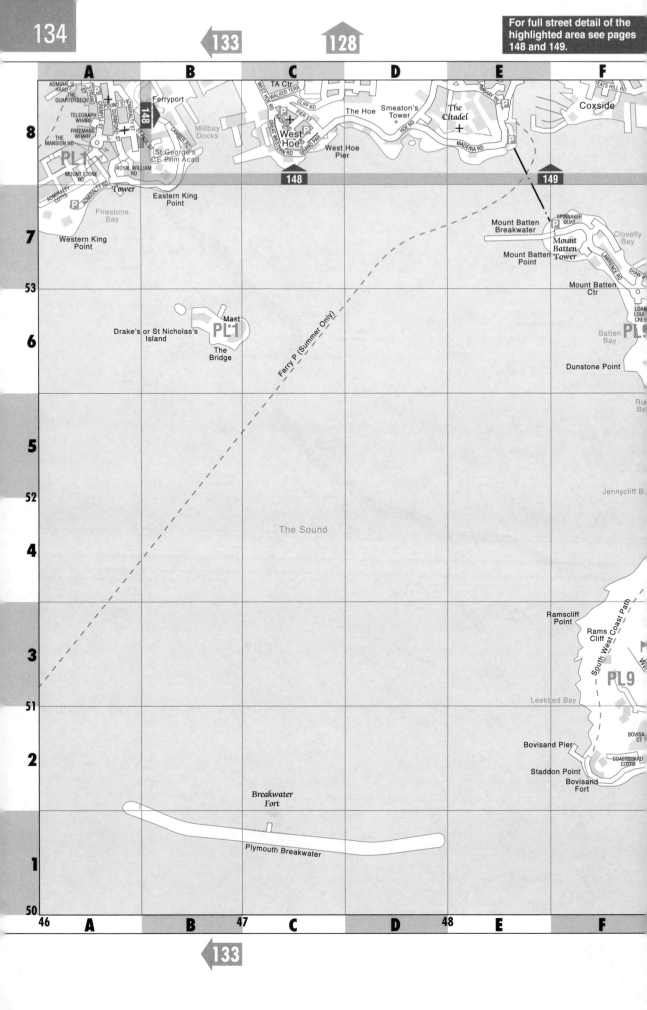

133

128

For full street detail of the highlighted area see pages 148 and 149.

A B C D E F

ADMIRAL'S HARD
THE QUARTERDECK
TELEGRAPH WHARF
FREEMANS WHARF
THE MANSION HO

TA Ctr
WEST HOE RD
WALKER TERR
CLIFF RD
PIER ST
The Hoe
Smeaton's Tower
The Citadel
Coxside
TEATS HILL RD
LABHAY RD
MADEIRA RD

Ferryport
148
CAMBER RD
Millbay Docks
West Hoe
St George's CE Prim Acad
GREAT WESTERN RD
RADFORD RD
GRAND PAR
West Hoe Pier
HOE RD

PL1
MOUNT STONE RD
ROYAL WILLIAM RD

148

149

Tower
ADMIRALTY COTTS
Eastern King Point
Firestone Bay

Mount Batten Breakwater
SPINNAKER QUAY
Clovelly Bay

8

Western King Point

7

Mount Batten Point
Mount Batten Tower
LAWRENCE RD
SHAW

Mount Batten Ctr
LORI LOUI CRES

53

Drake's or St Nicholas's Island
Mast
PL1
The Bridge

Batten Bay
PL9

6

Dunstone Point

Ferry P (Summer Only)

Ru Ba

5

52

Jennycliff B

The Sound

4

Ramscliff Point
Rams Cliff

South West Coast Path

3

PL9

51

Leekbed Bay

Bovisand Pier
BOVISA CT

2

Staddon Point
COASTGUARD COTTS
Bovisand Fort

Breakwater Fort

Plymouth Breakwater

1

50

46 A B 47 C D 48 E F

133

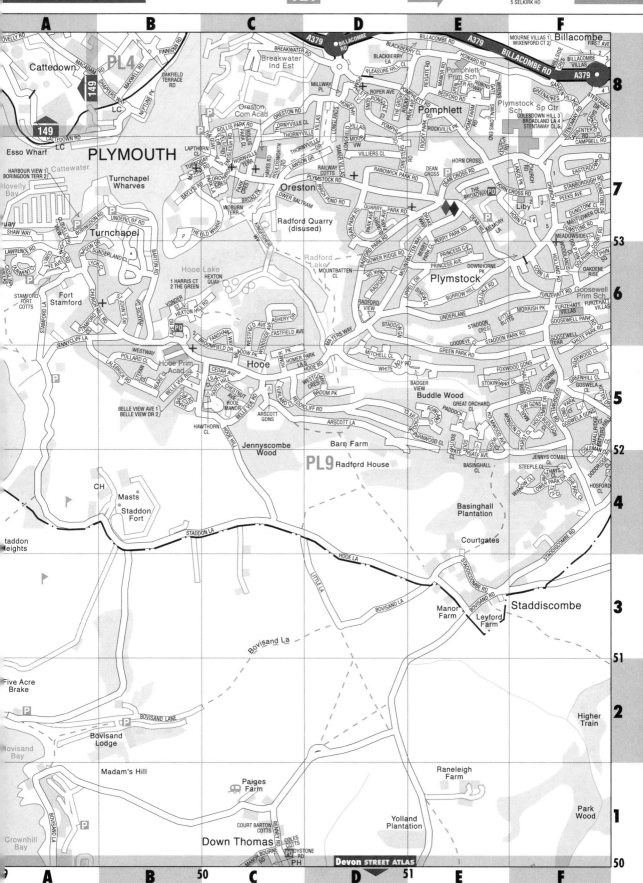

For full street detail of the highlighted area see page 149.

129

136

135

F5
1 CHALLGOOD CL
2 ORCHARDTON TERR

F7
1 THE DUKES RYDE
2 MAPLE CT
3 MAGNOLIA CT
4 HORN LANE FLATS
5 SELKIRK HO

A B C D E F

8
7
53
6
5
52
4
3
51
2
1
50

PL4

Cattedown

PLYMOUTH

Esso Wharf

Lovelly Bay

Quay

Shaw Way

Turnchapel Wharves

Turnchapel

Fort Stamford

Hooe Lake

Hooe

Hooe Prim Acad

Jennyscombe Wood

Staddon Heights

Masts

Staddon Fort

CH

Five Acre Brake

Bovisand Bay

Crownhill Bay

Bovisand Lodge

Madam's Hill

Paiges Farm

Down Thomas

Breakwater Ind Est

Oreston, Com Acad

Oreston

Lower Saltram

Radford Quarry (disused)

Billacombe

Billacombe Villas

Pomphlett

Pomphlett Prim Sch

Plymstock Sch

Liby

Plymstock

Goosewell Prim Sch

Buddle Wood

Barn Farm

PL9
Radford House

Courtgates

Manor Farm

Leyford Farm

Staddiscombe

Higher Train

Raneleigh Farm

Yolland Plantation

Park Wood

Basinghall Plantation

Bovisand La

Hooe La

Staddon La

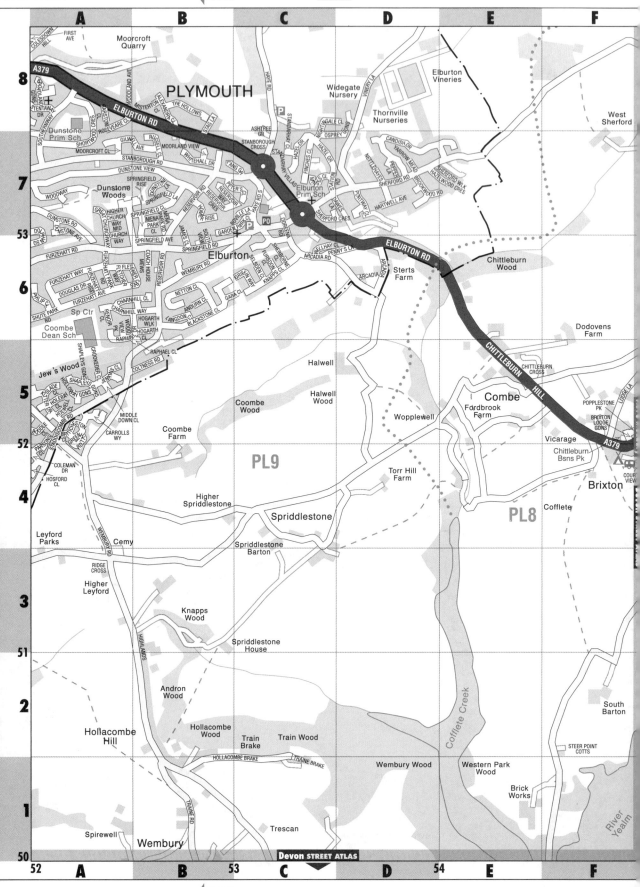

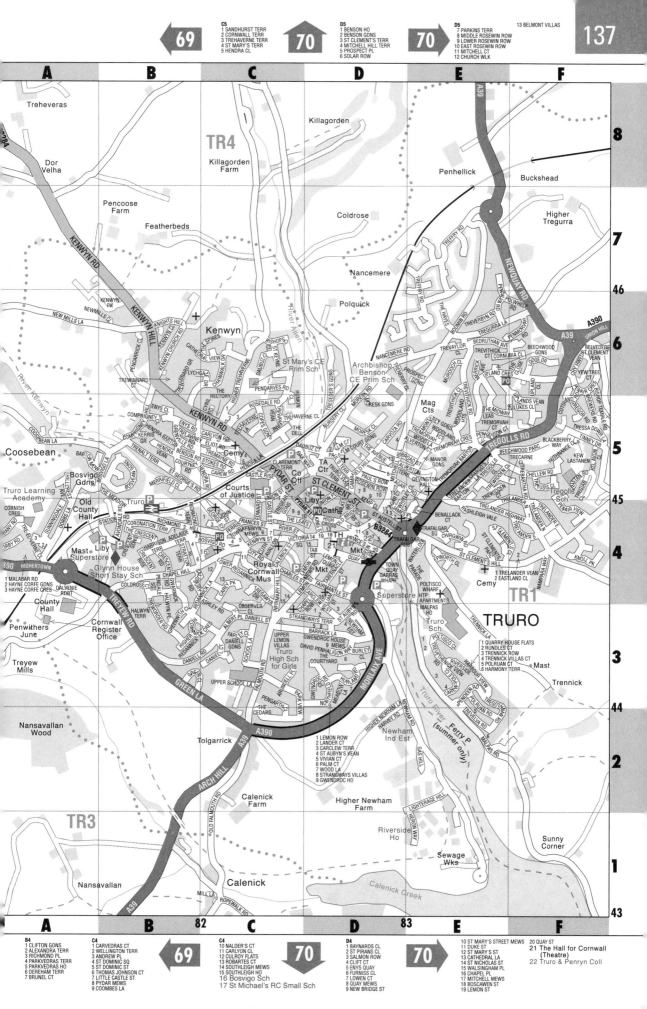

Oak Wood

Home Farm

Magor Plantation

Halgoss

Mount Whistle Farm

South Tehidy

Magor Farm

Roscroggan

Kieve Mill Cottage

Magor Downs

Rosewarne Farm

Depot

Tolvaddon

Roskear Croft

Roskear Croft

Kieve Hill Farm

Reskadinnick

North Rosewarne Farm

Rosewarne Terr

Duchy Coll Rosewarne

Forge Ind Pk

TR14

Higher Rosewarne

Race Farm

Rosemellin Prim Sch

New Downs Farm

Lower Rosewarne

Weeth Prim Sch

The Camborne Ctr

Treswithian Farm

A3047

TRESWITHIAN RD

Treswithian

Cemy

COLLEGE ST

TRELOWARREN ST

WESLEY ST

Superstore

Roskear Prim Sch

Treswithian

Treswithian Barns

Camborne Science & International Academy

The Corn Exchange

Crane

St Meriadoc CE VA Jun Sch

St Meriadocs CE Inf Sch

Cemy

Liby

TREVENSON ST

Camborne

Pengegon

CAMBORNE

Cogegoes Ind Pk

Cogegoes Farm

PENDARVES RD

SOUTH TERR

Trevithick Learning Academy

St Michael's Catholic Sec Sch

Penponds

Pendarves View

Mount Pleasant Farm

Beacon

Whe Harri

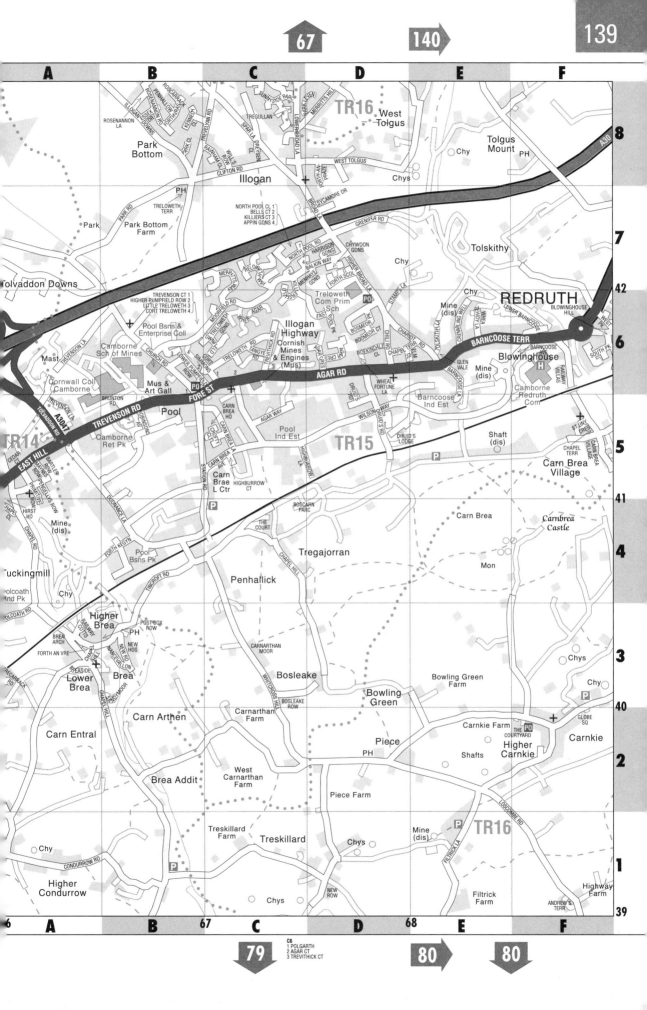

A	B	C	D	E	F

8

ROSENANNON LA

TR16 West Tolgus

Tolgus Mount Chy PH

Park Bottom

ROSCARROCK PENHALLOW ROSEMANOR
ILLOGAN DOWNS KENNETH PORTHTOWAN
ESSEX PORTHTOWAN

SUNNYSIDE PARC TREGULLAN

PARK CL PARK RD TREVELYAN RD WILL'S CL SPAR LA DREYSEN

CLIFTON RD RAILWAY CL RAW'S ROW

PH TRELOWETH TERR

WEST TOLGUS

Illogan

PORTH-AN-PRAZE Chys

7

Park Park Bottom Farm

PARK RD

NORTH POOL CL 1 BELLS CT 2 KILLIERS CT 3 APPIN GDNS 4

BROAD LA

GRENIFER RD

CHYWOON GDNS Chy Tolskithy

Tolvaddon Downs

Mast

TREVENSON LA

TREVENSON CT 1 HIGHER TRELOWETH 2 LITTLE TRELOWETH 3 CORT TRELOWETH 4

NORTH POOL RD TRELOWETH

HARRISON GDNS BALKIN WAY MENMATE GDNS FORTH SCOL HIGHER BROAD LA

Treloweth Com Prim Sch

PO

Chy

Mine (dis) CREMBLING WELL

Chy **REDRUTH**

42

Cornwall Coll Camborne

BRUNTON RD

Camborne Sch of Mines

Pool Bsns & Enterprise Coll

MERRITTS APP TRELOWETH GDNS MOORFIELD RD AGAR

CHURCH RD LOWER PUMPFIELD ROW SMITHING TRELOWETH TRELOWETH TANGYE TREVITHICK DR

Illogan Highway Cornish Mines & Engines (Mus)

BOSMEOR RD BOSMEOR CL ROCKINDALE CL CHAPEL

CHARIOT RD STAMPS LA TOLSKITHY RD

BARNCOOSE TERR

LOWER BARNCOOSE

Mine (dis) GLEN VALE

Blowinghouse H RAILWAY VILLAS

BLOWINGHOUSE HILL SOUTH PK WEST PK

Camborne Redruth Com

6

Mast Mus & Art Gall Pool

BARTLES ROW

Camborne Ret Pk

ROBINSONS RD

FORE ST TREVENSON RD A3047

AGAR RD

CARN BREA HO CARN BREA LA CROFT Pool Ind Est HIGHBURROW LA

DRUID'S RD WHEAL FORTUNE LA WILSON'S WAY BARNCOOSE LA

Barncoose Ind Est

DRUID'S LODGE

Shaft (dis)

ST JINY CRES CHAPEL TERR CARN BREA VILLAGE

5

TR14 EAST HILL

TOLVADDON RD

CEDAR CL

PRIMITIVE

HIRST HO

DUCHANGE LA

CARN BREA AVE SALTHOR RD CARN BREA L Ctr HIGHBURROW CT

THE COURT

BOSCARN PARC

Carn Brea

Carnbrea Castle

41

Mine (dis)

CHAPEL RD

uckingmill FORTH KEGYN Pool Bsns Pk

TINCROFT RD

CHAPEL HILL

Tregajorran

Mon

4

olcoath Ind Pk Chy

OLCOATH RD

Higher Brea RAILWAY COTTS POST BOX ROW NEW HOS

Penhallick

3

BREA ARCH FORTH AN VRE

SEASIDE Brea NANCEVALLON WHITCROSS HILL

Bosleake

Bowling Green Farm Chys

ARRECARRACK RD

Lower Brea CHAPEL HILL MOYMOOR

Bowling Green Chy P

40

Carn Entral

Carn Arthen

Carnarthan Farm

BOSLEAKE ROW

Carnkie Farm THE COURTYARD PO GLOBE SQ

Piece PH Shafts Higher Carnkie Carnkie

2

Brea Addit West Carnarthan Farm

Piece Farm

LOSCOMBE RD

1

Chy

CONDURROW RD

Treskillard Farm Treskillard Chys Mine (dis) TR16 P FILTRICK LA

Higher Condurrow Chys NEW ROW Filtrick Farm ANDREW'S TERR Highway Farm

39

A	B	C	D	E	F

C6
1 POLGARTH
2 AGAR CT
3 TREVITHICK CT

A B C D E F

B6
1 ST NICHOLAS CT
2 SAIL LOFT FLATS
3 THE ROPE WLK
4 ISLAND RD
5 PENAMEYNE CT
6 PORTHMEOR RD
7 BACK RD E
8 THE WHARF
9 FISH ST
10 BETHESDA PL
11 VICTORIA RD
12 VICTORIA PL
13 BARNALOFT
14 PIAZZA
15 NORTH PL
16 ST PETERS ST
17 BACK LA
18 CHURCH PL
19 CHY-AN-CHY
20 BAILEYS LA
21 PORTHMEOR SQ
22 BUNKERS HILL
23 ROSE LA
24 LOVE LA
25 THE DIGEY
26 VIRGIN ST
27 MEADOW FLATS
28 GODREVY TERR
29 BARNOON TERR
30 ACADEMY TERR
31 MARKET STRAND
32 LIFEBOAT HILL
33 MARKET SQ
34 BOWLING GN
35 BOWLING GN TERR
36 CARRACK DHU EST
37 CARRACK DHU
38 BELLAIR TERR
39 MOUNT PLEASANT
40 RICHMOND PL
41 TREWYN FLATS
42 BACK ST
43 ATLANTIC TERR
44 CLODGY VIEW
45 WEST PL
46 THE GALLERIES
47 THE MEADOW
48 CRUSOE FLATS
49 DIGEY FLATS
50 PORTHMEOR STUDIOS
51 PORTHMEOR CT
52 MOUNT ZION
53 WILLS LA

CARTHEW CT 1
CARTHEW TERR 2
AYR TERR 3
WHEAL AYR TERR 4
OCEAN VIEW TERR 5
PARC BEAN TERR 6
BELMONT TERR 7
CHANNEL VIEW 8
VENTNOR TERR 9
BELMONT PL 10
ALEXANDRA ROW 11

1 BEACH CT
2 PORTHGWIDDEN STUDIOS
3 CARNCROWS RD
4 CARNCROWS ST
5 TEETOTAL ST
6 ST EIA ST
7 BACK RD EAST
8 SEA VIEW PL

1 PENBEAGLE WAY
2 GWEL AN WHEAL
3 GWEL AN WHEAL CRES
4 PENWITH CL
5 PORTHIA CRES

1 MOONRAKERS
2 GODREVY CT
3 CARBIS BEACH APARTMENTS
4 RIVIERA APARTMENTS
5 GWELANMOR CL

1 HENDRAS CT
2 HEADLAND CT
3 KARENZA CT
4 TOLPEDN FLATS
5 NAMPARA CL
6 PORDENACK CL

HIGHER BOSKERRIS 1
BOSKERRIS MEWS 2
TREWARTHA FLATS 3
TREWARTHA EST 4
SHEILA'S CT 5
LOMOND HALL 6

Map labels: Mean Derrens · The Island or St Ives Head · Crowner Rocks · Carrick Du · Lookout Sta · Bamalûz Point · Mus · Porthmeor Beach · Tate St Ives (Gallery) · South West Coast Path · Cemy · Harbour · Pier · Smeaton's Pier · Pier LB Sta · **ST IVES** · Pedn Olva · St Ives · Porthminster Beach · Gwel-An-Mor Apartments · Porthminster Point · Edward Hain Com · Penbeagle · Bahavella Farm · St Ives Jun & Inf Schs · L Ctr · The Burrows · Corva Farm · St Ives Sch · Hotel · CH · **TR26** · Trelyon · Steeple Woodland Nature Reserve · Hendra · Carbis Bay · Barrepta Cove or Carbis Bay · Chy-an-Gweal · Knill's Mon · Superstore · Carbis Bay · Carrack Gladden · South West Coast Path · Vorvas Vean · Lower Vorvas · Carbis Water · Withen · Trewartha · Higher Vorvas · St Uny CE Prim Sch · Gonwin Farm · Longstone · Longstone Motel · Cemy

A
10 BOSTENNACK PL
11 BOSTENNACK TERR
12 PEARCE'S LA
13 MIDDLE STENNACK COTTS
14 STENNACK GDNS
15 SANDOWS LA
16 ROSEWALL COTTS
17 ROSEWALL TERR
18 FERN GLEN
19 LITTLE-IN-SIGHT

B5
1 ST ANDREW'S ST
2 REDFERN CT
3 STREET-AN-POL
4 TREGENNA PL
5 GABRIEL ST
6 BEDFORD PL
7 WESLEY PL
8 WINDSOR HILL
9 DRIFFIELD LA

B5
10 ALMA TERR
11 TRENWITH TERR
12 NORTH TERR
13 UMFULLA PL
14 TRENWITH PL
15 DOVE ST
16 TREGENNA HILL
17 STREET-AN-GARROW
18 SKIDDEN HILL

B5
19 FERN LEE TERR
20 SEA VIEW TERR
21 ALBERT PL
22 PADNOVER TERR
23 PORTHMINSTER TERR
24 PETES PL
25 CARRACK WIDDEN
26 ALBERT TERR
27 HARLEQUINS

B5
28 ROSEMORRAN
29 TALLAND CT
30 STONES CT

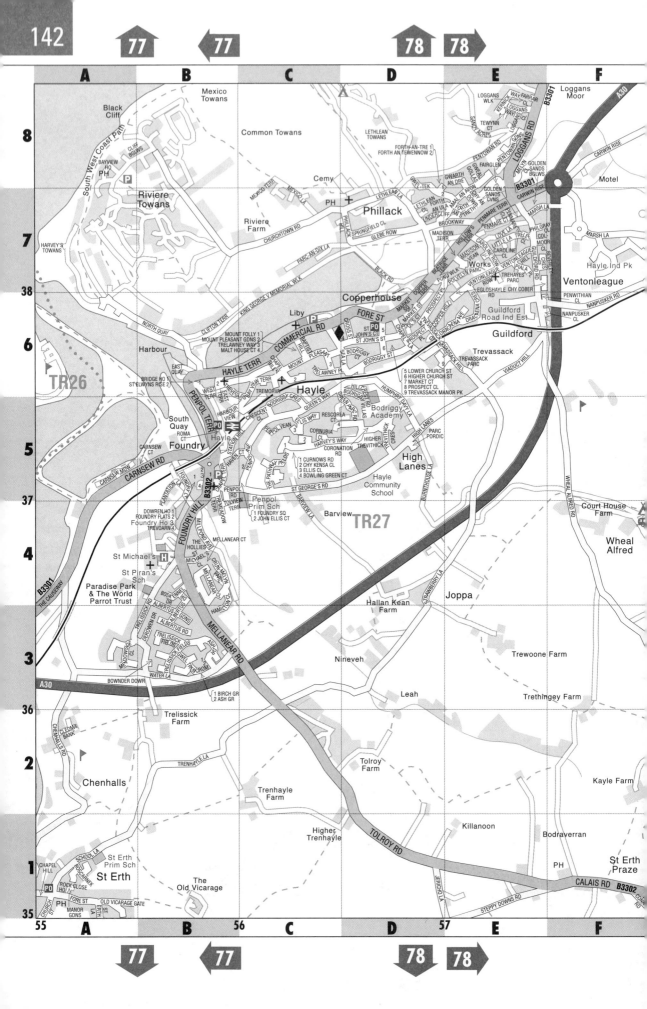

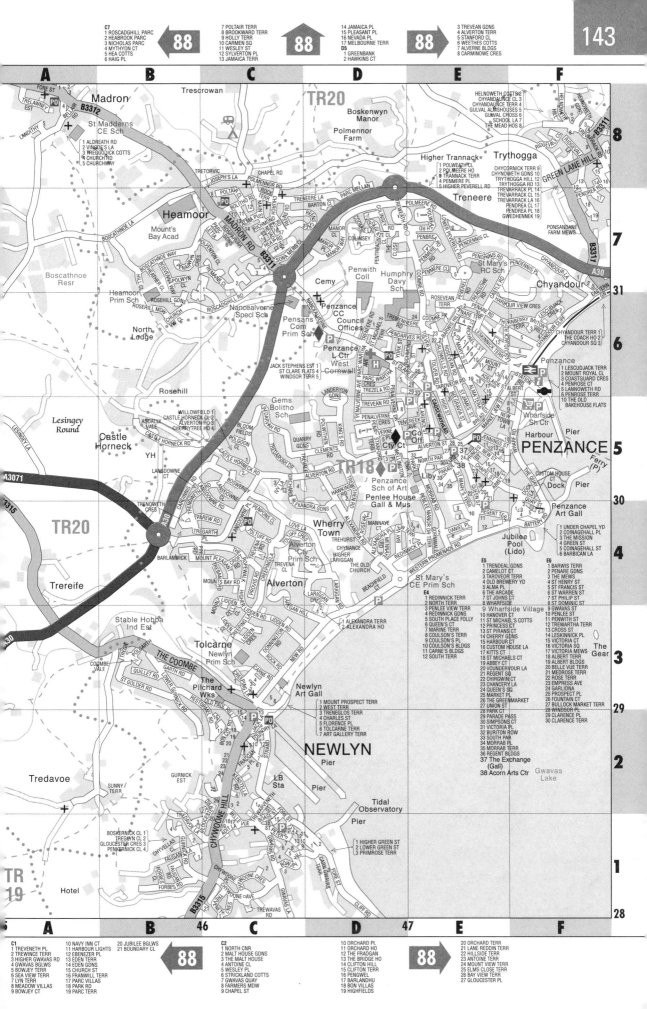

C7
1 ROSCADGHILL PARC
2 HEABROOK PARC
3 NICHOLAS PARC
4 MYTHYON CT
5 HEA COTTS
6 HAIG PL

7 POLTAIR TERR
8 BROOKWARD TERR
9 HOLLY TERR
10 CARMEN SQ
11 WESLEY ST
12 SYLVERTON PL
13 JAMAICA TERR

14 JAMAICA PL
15 PLEASANT PL
16 NEVADA PL
17 MELBOURNE TERR

D5
1 GREENBANK
2 HAWKINS CT

3 TREVEAN GDNS
4 ALVERTON TERR
5 STANFORD CL
6 WEETHES COTTS
7 ALVERNE BLDGS
8 CARMINOWE CRES

88 88 88

Madron
Trescrowan
TR20
Boskenwyn Manor
Polmennor Farm
Higher Trannack
Trythogga

St Madderns CE Sch
1 ALDREATH RD
2 VINGOE'S LA
3 TREGGODICK COTTS
4 CHURCH RD
5 CHURCHWAY

Heamoor
Mount's Bay Acad
Heamoor Prim Sch
North Lodge
Nancealverne Specl Sch

Penwith Coll
Humphry Davy Sch
St Mary's RC Sch

Boscathnoe Resr

Penzance CC Council Offices
Pensans Com Prim Sch
Penzance L Ctr West Cornwall
Cemy

JACK STEPHENS EST
ST CLARE FLATS 4
WINDSOR TERR 5

Lesingey Round
Castle Horneck
Rosehill
YH

Gems Bolitho Sch
WILLOWFIELD 1
CASTLE HORNECK CL 2
CHERRYTREE HO 3
CHERRYTREE 4

TR20
Trereife
Barlanwick

TR18

Penzance Sch of Art
Penlee House Gall & Mus

Wherry Town

Alverton Prim Sch
Alverton
The Old Church

St Mary's CE Prim Sch

Penzance Art Gall
Jubilee Pool (Lido)

1 UNDER CHAPEL YD
2 COINAGEHALL PL
3 THE MISSION
4 GREEN ST
5 COINAGEHALL ST
6 BARBICAN LA

E5
1 TRENDEAL GDNS
2 CAMELOT CT
3 TAROVEOR TERR
4 OLD BREWERY YD
5 ALMA PL
6 THE ARCADE
7 ST JOHNS CT
8 WHARFSIDE
9 WHARFSIDE VILLAGE
10 HANOVER CT
11 ST MICHAEL'S COTTS
12 PRINCESS CT
13 ST PIRANS CT
14 CHERRY GDNS
15 HARBOUR CT
16 CUSTOM HOUSE LA
17 KITTS CT
18 ST MICHAELS CT
19 ABBEY CT
20 VOUNDERVOUR LA
21 REGENT SQ
22 CHIRGWIN CT
23 CHANCERY LA
24 QUEEN'S SQ
25 MARKET PL
26 THE GREENMARKET
27 UNION ST
28 PARK CT
29 PARADE PASS
30 SIMPSONS CT
31 VICTORIA PL
32 BURITON ROW
33 SOUTH PAR
34 MORRAB PL
35 MORRAB TERR
36 REGENT BLDGS
37 THE EXCHANGE (Gall)
38 ACORN ARTS CTR

E6
1 BARWIS TERR
2 PENARE GDNS
3 THE MEWS
4 ST HENRY ST
5 ST FRANCIS ST
6 ST WARREN ST
7 ST PHILIP ST
8 ST DOMINIC ST
9 GWAVAS ST
10 PENLEE ST
11 PENWITH CT
12 TREWARTHA TERR
13 CROSS ST
14 LESKINNICK PL
15 VICTORIA CT
16 VICTORIA SQ
17 ALBERT TERR
18 ALBERT BLDGS
19 BELLE VUE TERR
20 MEDROSE TERR
21 ROSE TERR
22 EMPRESS AVE
23 GARLIDNA
24 PROSPECT PL
25 FOUNTAIN CT
26 BULLOCK MARKET TERR
27 WINDSOR PL
28 CLARENCE SQ
29 CLARENCE TERR

E4
1 REDINNICK TERR
2 NORTH TERR
3 PENLEE VIEW TERR
4 REDINNICK GDNS
5 SOUTH PLACE FOLLY
6 QUEEN'S CT
7 MARINE TERR
8 COULSON'S BANK
9 COULSON'S PL
10 COULSON'S BLDGS
11 CARNE'S BLDGS
12 SOUTH TERR

1 ALEXANDRA TERR
2 ALEXANDRA HO

1 MOUNT PROSPECT TERR
2 WEST TERR
3 TRENEGLOS TERR
4 CHARLES ST
5 FLORENCE PL
6 TOLCARNE TERR
7 ART GALLERY TERR

Stable Hobba Ind Est
Tolcarne
Newlyn Prim Sch
The Pilchard Wks
Newlyn Art Gall

NEWLYN
Pier

Tredavoe
Tidal Observatory
Pier

Gurnick Est

1 BOSKERNICK CL
2 TREGURN CL
3 GLOUCESTER CRES
4 PENKERNICK CL

1 HIGHER GREEN ST
2 LOWER GREEN ST
3 PRIMROSE TERR

TR19
Hotel
Gwavas Lake

PENZANCE
Chyandour
Penzance
Wharfside Sh Ctr
Harbour
Pier
Dock
Pier
Ferry (P)
Custom House
Dock
Pier
The Gear

Treneere
Ponsandane Farm Mews

Green Lane Hill

C1
1 TREVENETH PL
2 TREWINCE TERR
3 HIGHER GWAVAS RD
4 GWAVAS BGLWS
5 BOWJEY TERR
6 SEA VIEW TERR
7 LYN TERR
8 MEADOW VILLAS
9 BOWJEY CT

10 NAVY INN CT
11 HARBOUR LIGHTS
12 EBENEZER PL
13 EDEN TERR
14 EDEN GDNS
15 CHURCH ST
16 FRANWILL TERR
17 PARC VILLAS
18 PARK RD
19 PARC TERR

20 JUBILEE BGLWS
21 BOUNDARY CL

C2
1 NORTH CNR
2 MALT HOUSE GDNS
3 THE MALL
4 ANTOINE CL
5 WESLEY PL
6 STRICKLAND COTTS
7 GWAVAS QUAY
8 FARMERS MDW
9 CHAPEL ST

10 ORCHARD PL
11 ORCHARD HO
12 ORCHARD TERR
13 THE BRIDGE HO
14 CLIFTON HILL
15 CLIFTON TERR
16 PENGWEL
17 BARLANDHU
18 BON VILLAS
19 HIGHFIELDS

20 ORCHARD TERR
21 LANE REDDIN TERR
22 HILLSIDE TERR
23 ANTOINE TERR
24 MOUNT VIEW TERR
25 ELMS CLOSE TERR
26 BAY VIEW TERR
27 GLOUCESTER PL

88 88

◀ 81

81 ▲

C7
1 HARRIS CT
2 SLADES LA
3 BENNETTS COTTS
4 RUSSELL WAY
5 SARACEN HO
6 BANK COTTS

C8
1 Three Bridges
Specl Sch

A B C D E F

8

Falmouth University (Tremough Campus)

TREMOUGHDALE
THE PRAZE
West End
CHURCH RD
COMMERCIAL RD
Penryn
Penryn Jun Sch
Penryn Com Inf Sch

1 ST GLUVIAS PARC
2 BOHELLAND RISE

Round Ring
Bohelland Way

Bissom Farm
Bissom

St Gluvias
Islington Wharf

Gorran Gorras

TR11

Trevissome Farm

Trevissome House

7

Beehive Workshops
Kernick Bsns Pk
Kernick Ind Est

PENRYN
Penryn Coll

TR10

Cemy

1 CHARTER CT
2 BOHILL CT
3 SUMMERCOURT
4 SOUTH HARBOUR
5 DANIELS SAIL LOFT
6 FOXS YD
7 FOXSTANTON DR
8 CARN ROCK
9 TRESOOTH TERR
10 TRESOOTH CT
11 THE BAKEHOUSE

Lib
Quay Hill

FALMOUTH RD
B3292

Quay Harbour

Penryn River

Ponsharden

34

Superstore
Kernick GDNS
Kernick House

A39

Resr
College Resr

Hillhead Farm

P&R
Ponsharden Cotts
Homestead
Trevissome CT
NORTH PAR

Falmouth Wharves

Ponsharden Ind Est

6

Tregonhaye

Higher Kergilliack

Lower Kergilliack

Hillhead Farm

UNION RD
Mast

KERGILLIACK RD
OAKLAND PK
UNION CNR

Falmouth Com Sch

Pengelly
Lowenek
DRACAENA AVE

Penwerris Farm
Dracaena View

5

33

BICKLAND WATER
Bickland Water

THE NURSERIES
MANOR WAY
MANOR CRES

Trescobeas Rd

Falmouth

4

TR11

Nangitha Farm

Sparnon

Tregoniggie Ind Est

Bickland Ind Est

Empire Way
MOUNT STEPHENS LA 1
MEARWOOD LA 2
TRESIDDER
CHOUGH CL
LONGFIELD

Mongleath

Falmouth Bsns Pk

Penmere

Swanvale

3

Coronation Cotts
Nangitha Terr
Nangitha Cl
SCHOOL LA
Victoria Cotts
MERRY MIT MDW

VICARAGE HILL
CHURCH TOWN

Eglos Farm

St Francis CE Sch
CHURCH WAY
PITT MDW
GARDEN
St Mary's RC Prim Sch

Menehay

MONGLEATH RD
MONGLEATH AVE

QUEEN ANNE RD

MARGARET PL

32

MENHAY VIEW
PO
PH
ROSE EGLOS
WATERSHEAD PARC
TREVONEY
TREWEN TERR
STEPHNEY CL

Budock Water

Rose Eglos

Roscarrack House

BOSMEOR RD
BOSMEOR RD

Boslowick

2

Trewen House

TRELIL LA
CONDOR COTTS
PARC SIGHNEY
TREVERN PARC
TREWEN RD

Higher Roscarrack Farm

MESSACK CL
CARRICK CL
SPEAR'S TERR

TREMORVAH CT

1

Tresooth Bungalow

PENWARNE RD

Trewen Farm

Higher Crill Farm

CRILL CNR
PENBRICK HILL
CRILL RD

BAY VIEW TERR

Hotel

MAEN VALLEY PK

Trelevra Farm

GOLDEN BANK PK
SWANPOOL RD
CH

TREMORVAH PK

31

77 A 78 B C 78 D 79 E F

◀ 93

93 ▲

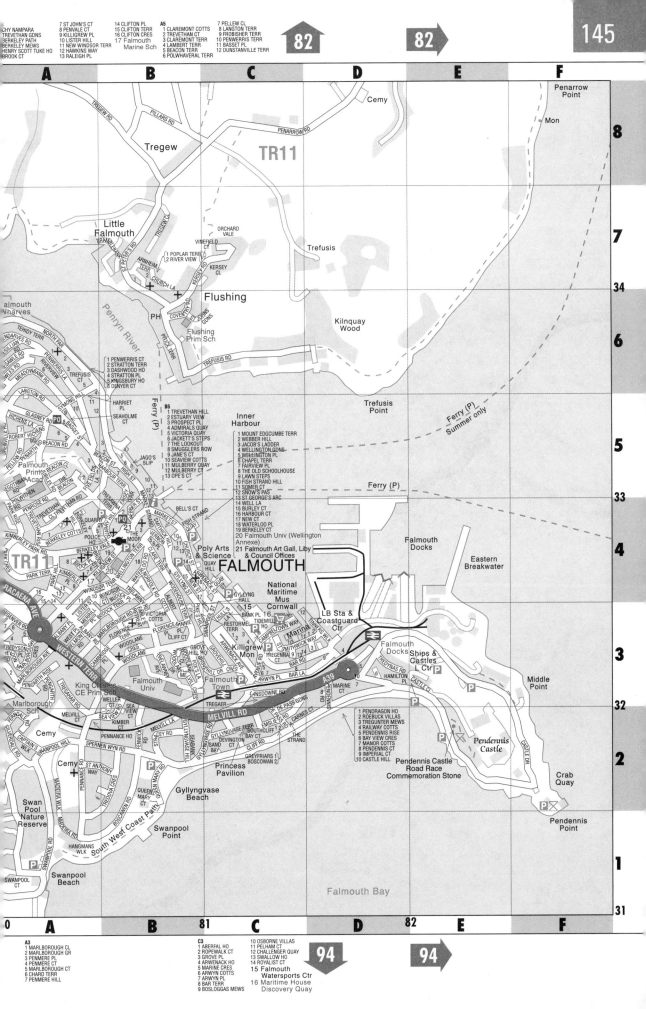

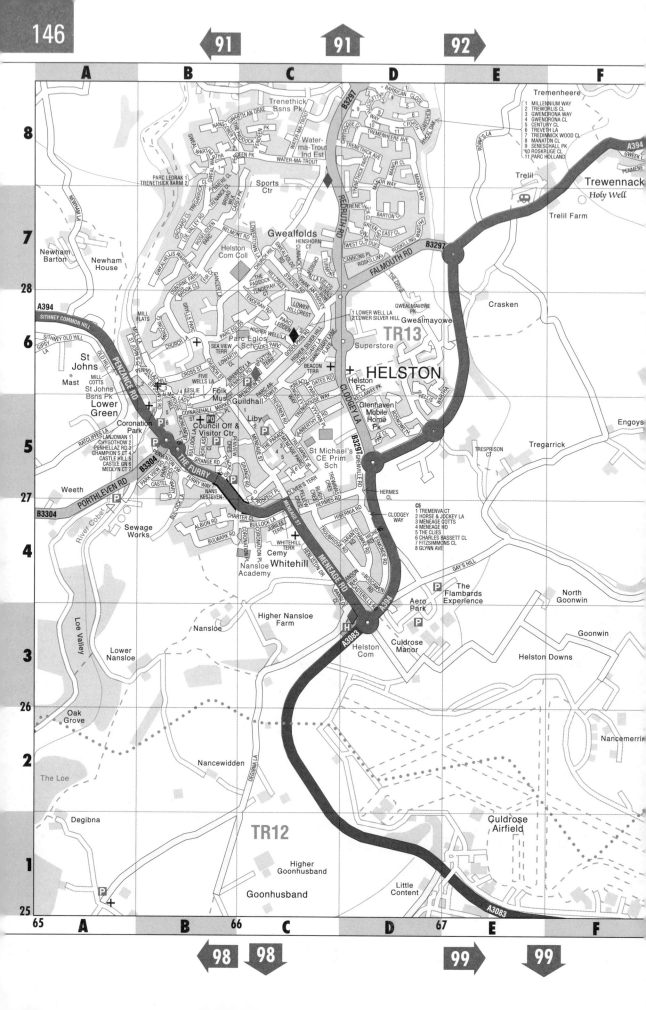

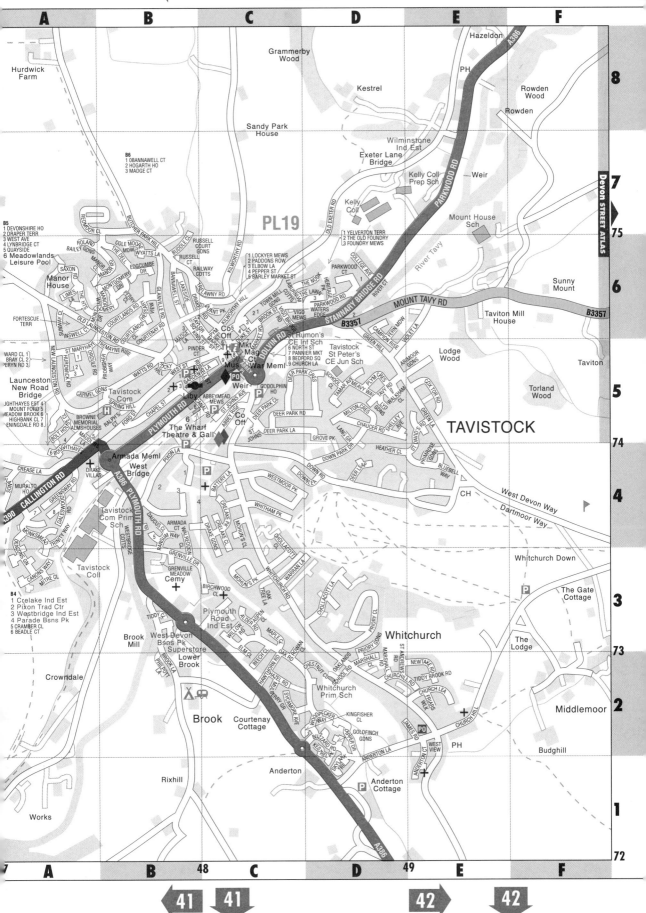

Devon STREET ATLAS

A B C D E F

8
7
75
6
5
74
4
3
73
2
1
72

Hurdwick
Farm

Grammerby
Wood

Hazeldon

A396

Kestrel

Rowden
Wood

Rowden

Sandy Park
House

PH

Wilminstone
Ind Est

PARKWOOD RD

Weir

Kelly Coll
Prep Sch

B6
1 OBANNAWELL CT
2 HOGARTH HO
3 MADGE CT

Exeter Lane
Bridge

Mount House
Sch

Kelly
Coll

PL19

Sunny
Mount

River Tavy

B5
1 DEVONSHIRE HO
2 DRAPER TERR
3 WEST AVE
4 LYNBRIDGE CT
5 QUAYSIDE
6 Meadowlands
Leisure Pool

1 LOCKYER MEWS
2 PADDONS ROW
3 ELBOW LA
4 PEPPER ST
5 BARLEY MARKET ST

Parkwood
CT

College Ave

STANNARY BRIDGE RD

MOUNT TAVY RD

B3357

Taviton Mill
House

B3357

Manor
House

1 YELVERTON TERR
2 THE OLD FOUNDRY
3 FOUNDRY MEWS

The Nook

Lodge
Wood

Taviton

FORTESCUE
TERR

St Rumon's
CE Inf Sch

Tavistock
St Peter's
CE Jun Sch

Torland
Wood

WARD CL 1
BRAY CL 2
PERYN RD 3

Tavistock Com

Launceston
New Road
Bridge

Co
Off

Mkt
Mag
Ct
War Meml

5 DEER PARK CL
6 NORTH ST
7 PANNIER MKT
8 BEDFORD SQ
9 CHURCH LA

Godolphin
Ho

TAVISTOCK

JGHTHAYES EST 4
MOUNT FORD 5
MEADOW BROOK 6
HIGHBANK CL 7
ENINGDALE RD 8

PLYMOUTH RD

H

Liby

Mus

Weir

Abbeymead
Mews

Co
Off

Deer Park Rd

Deer Park La

CH

West Devon Way

Dartmoor Way

CALLINGTON RD

A390

A396

PLYMOUTH RD

The Wharf
Theatre & Gall

Armada Meml
West
Bridge

Drake
Villas

Pixon La

Battery La

WHITHAM PK

Westmoor Pk

DEER LEAP

Down Rd

Whitchurch Down

The Gate
Cottage

CREASE LA

MURALTO
HO

Tavistock
Com Prim
Sch

Crelake La

Crelake Av

Mohun's Ct

DRAKE GDNS

WARREN PK

P

The Lodge

MONKSMEAD
TRINITY WAY

B4
1 Crelake Ind Est
2 Pixon Trad Ctr
3 Westbridge Ind Est
4 Parade Bsns Pk
5 CRAMBER CL
6 BEADLE CT

Tavistock
Coll

Armada
CT

Grenville Dr

Birchwood
CL

OAK TREE LA

Whitchurch

St Andrew's Rd

Churchill Rd

NEWTAKE
Tiddy Brook Rd

Middlemoor

Crowndale

Grenville
Meadow
Cemy

TIDDY CL

Brook
Mill

West Devon
Bsns Pk
Superstore

Lower
Brook

Plymouth
Road
Ind Est

ALDER
ASPEN

WILLOW

ELM CL

BEECH CL

OAK RD

PRIORY CL

Priory Gdns

Marshall La

MARSHALL CL

Friars
Wlk

Church Lea

Church Hill

PH

West
View

The
Lodge

Brook

Rixhill

Courtenay
Cottage

Whitchurch
Prim Sch

KINGFISHER
CL

Goldfinch
Gdns

Anderton

Anderton
Cottage

Budghill

Works

A386

A B C D E F

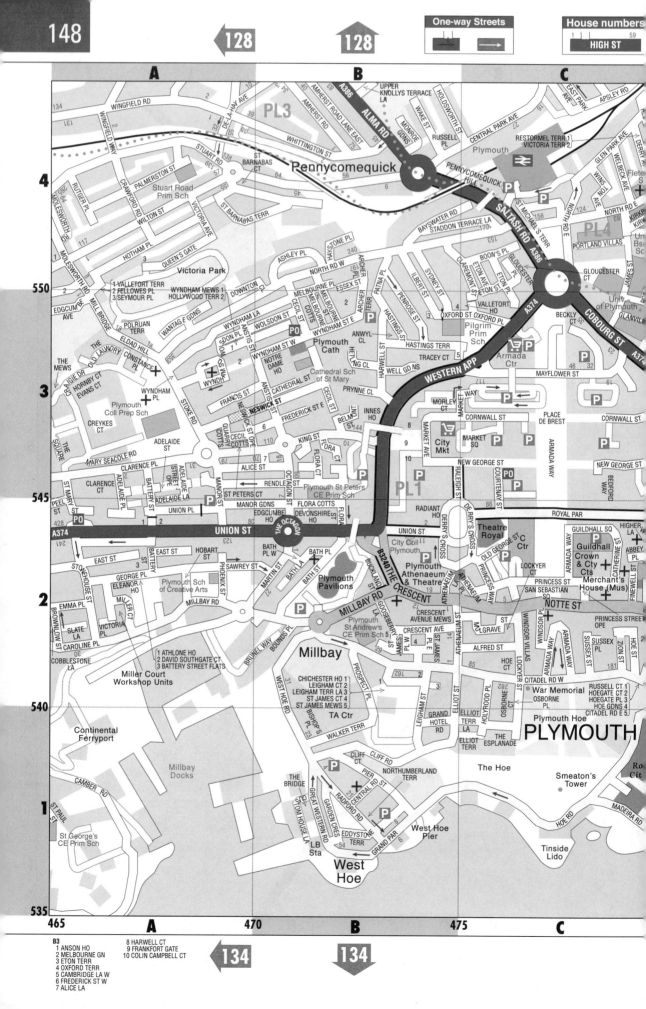

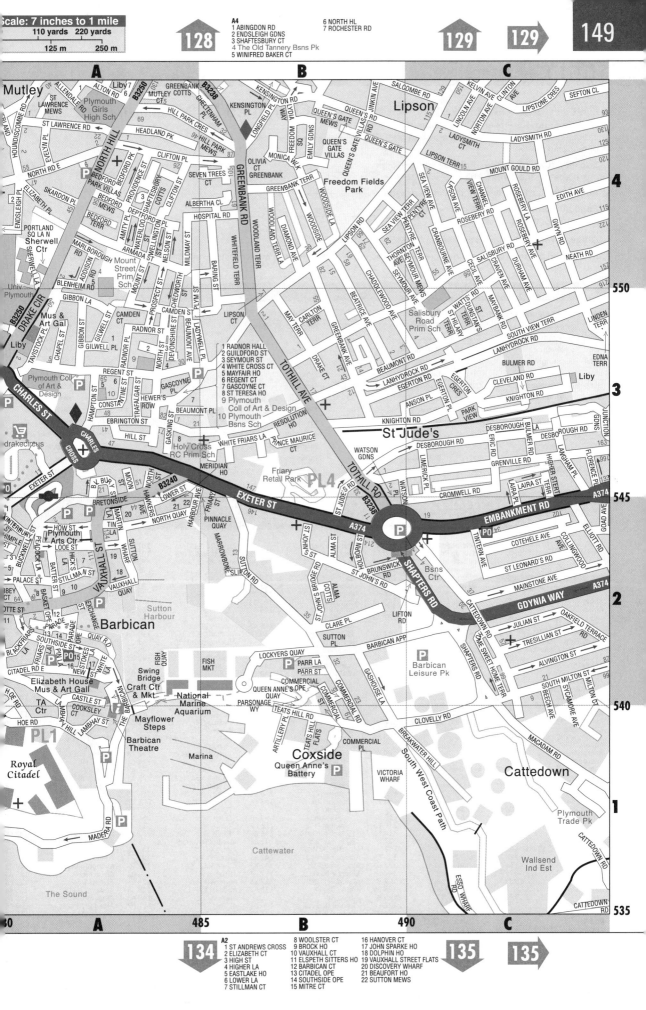

Index

Place name May be abbreviated on the map → **Church Rd** **6** Beckenham BR2.........**53** C6

Location number Present when a number indicates the place's position in a crowded area of mapping

Locality, town or village Shown when more than one place has the same name

Postcode district District for the indexed place

Page and grid square Page number and grid reference for the standard mapping

Cities, towns and villages are listed in CAPITAL LETTERS

Public and commercial buildings are highlighted in **magenta**   **Places of interest** are highlighted in blue with a star★

Abbreviations used in the index

Acad	**Academy**	Comm	**Common**	Gd	**Ground**	L	**Leisure**	Prom	**Promenade**
App	**Approach**	Cott	**Cottage**	Gdn	**Garden**	La	**Lane**	Rd	**Road**
Arc	**Arcade**	Cres	**Crescent**	Gn	**Green**	Liby	**Library**	Recn	**Recreation**
Ave	**Avenue**	Cswy	**Causeway**	Gr	**Grove**	Mdw	**Meadow**	Ret	**Retail**
Bglw	**Bungalow**	Ct	**Court**	H	**Hall**	Meml	**Memorial**	Sh	**Shopping**
Bldg	**Building**	Ctr	**Centre**	Ho	**House**	Mkt	**Market**	Sq	**Square**
Bsns, Bus	**Business**	Ctry	**Country**	Hospl	**Hospital**	Mus	**Museum**	St	**Street**
Bvd	**Boulevard**	Cty	**County**	HQ	**Headquarters**	Orch	**Orchard**	Sta	**Station**
Cath	**Cathedral**	Dr	**Drive**	Hts	**Heights**	Pal	**Palace**	Terr	**Terrace**
Cir	**Circus**	Dro	**Drove**	Ind	**Industrial**	Par	**Parade**	TH	**Town Hall**
Cl	**Close**	Ed	**Education**	Inst	**Institute**	Pas	**Passage**	Univ	**University**
Cnr	**Corner**	Emb	**Embankment**	Int	**International**	Pk	**Park**	Wk, Wlk	**Walk**
Coll	**College**	Est	**Estate**	Intc	**Interchange**	Pl	**Place**	Wr	**Water**
Com	**Community**	Ex	**Exhibition**	Junc	**Junction**	Prec	**Precinct**	Yd	**Yard**

Index of towns, villages, streets, hospitals, industrial estates, railway stations, schools, shopping centres, universities and places of interest

Abb–Amb

A

Abbey Cl PL20 .... 42 B2
Abbey Ct
  19 Penzance TR18...... 143 E5
  Plymouth PL1........... 149 A2
Abbey Hill TR26....... 77 E3
Abbey Mdw TR26...... 77 E4
Abbeymead Mews PL19 . 147 C5
Abbey Mews PL31...... 109 C4
Abbey Pl
  Plymouth PL1........... 148 C2
  Tavistock PL19.......... 147 C5
Abbey Rise PL19 .... 147 C5
Abbey St TR18 .... 143 E5
Abbotsbury Way PL2 ... 127 F8
Abbots Cl PL31 .... 109 F4
Abbotsfield Cl PL19 .... 41 D8
Abbotsfield Cres PL19... 41 D8
Abbotts Rd PL3 .... 128 E6
Aberdeen Ave PL5 ..... 124 D1
Aberdeen Cl PL24...... 60 B6
Aberfal Ho **1** TR11..... 145 C4
Abingdon Rd **1** PL4.... 149 A4
Abney Cres PL6........ 125 B6
Above Town Cl PL27 ... 21 F3
Abscott La PL9......... 135 C5
Acacia Rd TR11 .... 144 F5
Academy Terr **30** TR26 .. 141 B6
Acklington Pl PL5...... 123 E4
Acland Cl EX23 .... 104 E7
Acland Gdns TR7 ★...... 110 D6
Acorn Arts Ctr ★ **38** TR18 143 E5
Acorn Dr PL25......... 115 A3
Acorn Gdns PL7........ 130 D6
Acre Cotts PL1......... 127 F3
Acre Pl PL1............ 127 F3
Adams Cl
  Plymouth PL5......... 123 F1
  Torpoint PL11 .... 126 F3
Adams Cres PL11 ...... 126 E3
ADDINGTON 113 D7
Addington N **5** PL14 .... 113 D6
Addington S **6** PL14 .... 113 D6
Addison Rd PL4........ 149 A4
Addison Terr PL22...... 112 C2
Adelaide La PL1........ 148 A2

Adelaide Pl PL1....... 148 A3
Adelaide Rd TR15....... 140 C4
Adelaide St
  Camborne TR14........ 138 E3
  Penzance TR18......... 143 E6
  2 Plymouth, Ford PL2 ... 127 F5
  Plymouth PL1.......... 148 A3
Adelaide Street Ope PL1 148 A3
Adelaide Terr TR1 ..... 137 B4
Adela Rd PL11......... 127 A3
Adit La
  Newlyn TR18.......... 143 C1
  Saltash PL12.......... 122 E3
Adits The PL18.......... 41 A3
Admiral's Hard PL1..... 134 A8
Admirals Quay **4** TR11.. 145 B5
Admiralty Cotts PL1..... 134 A7
Admiralty Ct PL13...... 117 D3
Admiralty Rd
  Plymouth, Millbay PL1... 134 A8
  Plymouth, St Budeaux PL5 123 C2
Admiralty St
  Plymouth, Keyham PL2 ... 127 E6
  Plymouth, Millbay PL1... 134 A8
Admiralty Terr TR2..... 83 B2
Aerohub Business Park
  TR8.................. 44 F6
African Row TR14...... 79 B5
Agar Cres TR15........ 139 D6
Agar Ct
  2 Camborne TR15...... 139 C6
  Truro TR1............. 137 D5
Agar Mdws **11** TR3 .... 81 F7
Agar Rd
  Camborne TR15........ 139 D6
  Newquay TR7.......... 110 E5
  St Austell PL25 .... 114 E6
  Truro TR1............. 137 C5
Agar Terr **12** PL31...... 109 D5
Agar Way TR15......... 139 C5
Agaton Rd PL5......... 123 E3
Agnes Cl EX23 .... 104 F4
Ainslie Terr PL2........ 127 E7
Airborne Dr PL6........ 125 B4
Aire Gdns PL3......... 129 B5
Alamein Ct PL12....... 122 E2
Alamein Rd PL12....... 122 D2
Alan Harvey Cl **14** TR26.. 77 A6
Alan Rd PL28 .... 107 D4
Alansmere Ct TR2...... 57 A1
Alanta Flats TR7....... 110 B5
Albany Cl
  Redruth TR15.......... 140 C3

Albany Cl continued
  Redruth TR15.......... 140 C3
  St Agnes TR5.......... 68 D8
Albany Ct
  4 Newquay TR7...... 110 F6
  Redruth TR15.......... 140 D3
Albany Gdns TR15...... 140 C3
Albany La TR15........ 140 C4
Albany Pl TR11........ 145 A3
Albany Rd
  Falmouth TR11......... 145 A3
  5 Newquay TR7...... 110 F6
  Redruth TR15.......... 140 C4
  Truro TR1............. 137 A4
Albany St PL1.......... 127 E2
Albany Terr TR26 ..... 141 B4
ALBASTON 40 E5
Albemarle Villas PL1... 127 F3
Albert Bldgs **19** TR18 ... 143 E6
Albert Cotts TR11 ..... 145 B4
Albertha Cl PL4........ 149 B4
Albert Pl
  Camborne TR14........ 138 E3
  21 St Ives TR26...... 141 B6
  Truro TR1............. 137 C3
Albert Rd
  Plymouth PL2......... 127 F3
  Saltash PL12.......... 123 A2
  St Austell PL25 .... 114 D3
  St Ives TR26.......... 141 B5
Albert St
  Camborne TR14........ 138 E3
  Penzance TR18......... 143 F6
Albert Terr
  Gunnislake PL18 ...... 40 F5
  Lostwithiel PL22 ...... 112 C2
  18 Penzance TR18 .... 143 E6
  26 St Ives TR26..... 141 B5
Albertus Dr TR27...... 142 B3
Albertus Gdns TR27.... 142 B3
Albertus Rd TR27...... 142 B3
Albert Villas PL2....... 127 E4
Albion Ct PL11......... 127 B3
Albion Dr PL2.......... 128 B7
Albion Rd
  Helston TR13.......... 146 B4
  Torpoint PL11 .... 127 B3
Albion Row TR16....... 80 F8
Alcester Cl PL2........ 127 E4
Alcester St PL2........ 127 F4
Alden Wlk PL6......... 129 B7
Aldercombe La EX23 ... 5 A6
Alderney Rd PL6 ...... 124 F7

Alder Rd PL19 .... 147 C3
Aldersley Wlk PL6 ..... 125 A1
Aldreath Cl TR20....... 88 B7
Aldreath Rd TR20 ...... 88 B7
Alexander Ct
  14 Carnon Downs TR3... 81 F7
  Gorran Haven PL26..... 85 D5
Alexandra Cl
  5 Illogan TR16....... 67 E4
  Plymouth PL9.......... 136 B8
  St Ives TR26.......... 77 A7
Alexandra Ct TR7...... 111 C8
Alexandra Dr PL20..... 41 C1
Alexandra Gdns TR18 ... 143 D4
Alexandra Ho TR18..... 143 D3
Alexandra Pl
  Penzance TR18......... 143 D4
  5 Plymouth PL4..... 128 C4
  St Ives TR26.......... 77 A7
Alexandra Rd
  Bodmin PL31.......... 109 B5
  Illogan TR16.......... 67 D4
  Newquay TR7.......... 111 C8
  Penzance TR18......... 143 D4
  Plymouth, Crownhill PL6 .. 124 F2
  Plymouth, Ford PL2 .... 127 F5
  Plymouth, Mutley PL4 ... 128 F4
  St Austell PL25 .... 114 E3
  St Ives TR26.......... 77 A7
Alexandra Sq PL12..... 123 A2
Alexandra Terr
  Mount Hawke TR4 ...... 68 C6
  Penzance TR18......... 143 D3
  Plymouth PL2.......... 127 F5
  St Ives TR26.......... 141 A5
  Tremar PL14 .... 38 A4
  2 Truro TR1........ 137 B4
ALFARDISWORTHY 5 E6
Alford Cl EX23 .... 104 F5
Alfred Pl PL2.......... 127 F5
Alfred Rd PL2.......... 127 F5
Alfred St PL1.......... 148 C2
Alger Wlk PL6......... 124 E6
Alice La **7** PL1....... 148 B3
Alice St PL1........... 148 A3
Alldritt Cl TR7........ 111 D7
Allenby Rd PL2........ 128 A6
Allendale PL26......... 58 E8
Allendale Rd PL4...... 149 A4
Allen Pk PL30.......... 23 B2
Allen Vale PL14 .... 113 A5
Allern La PL5.......... 120 D1
Allerton Wlk PL6....... 129 B7

Alley Hill PL20 .... 42 A1
Alleyn Gdns PL3 .... 128 E8
Allium Ct TR4.......... 70 D8
All Saints Pk PL18...... 40 E5
Alma Cl TR5........... 68 D8
Alma Cotts PL4 .... 149 B2
Alma Pl
  Heamoor TR18......... 143 C7
  Newquay TR7.......... 110 D6
  Padstow PL28 .... 107 D5
  5 Penzance TR18 .... 143 E5
  Redruth TR15.......... 140 B5
Alma Rd
  Plymouth PL3.......... 128 C4
  Truro TR1............. 69 F3
Alma St PL4 .... 149 B2
Alma Terr
  Carharrack TR16....... 80 F8
  Gunnislake PL18 ...... 41 A6
  Penzance TR18......... 143 E5
  10 St Ives TR26 .... 141 B5
Almeria Ct PL7........ 130 C4
Almond Dr PL7......... 131 B6
Almshouse Hill TR13 ... 146 B5
Alston Pk PL7.......... 130 D6
ALTARNUN 26 C8
Altarnun Prim Sch PL15.. 26 C7
Alton Pl PL4........... 128 E4
Alton Rd PL4.......... 149 A4
Alverne Bldgs **7** TR18.. 143 D5
ALVERTON 143 C4
Alverton Ct TR1........ 137 E5
Alverton Cty Prim Sch
  TR18................. 143 C4
Alverton Ho TR18...... 143 C5
Alverton Rd TR18...... 143 D5
Alverton St TR18....... 143 E5
Alverton Terr
  4 Penzance TR18..... 143 D5
  Truro TR1............. 137 D5
Alvington St PL4....... 149 C2
Alwin Pk PL6.......... 125 A5
Alwyn Cl TR7.......... 111 E6
Amacre Dr PL9......... 135 B6
Amados Cl PL7......... 130 B4
Amados Dr PL7........ 130 C4
Amados Rise PL7 ...... 130 C4
Amal An Avon TR27.... 142 E7
ALVERTON 76 F3
AMALEBRA 76 E4
Amanda Way PL14 .... 38 E4
Amble Rd **26** PL17..... 39 F4
Ambrose Ct TR15 ...... 140 C4

Amelia Cl TR2 71 C6
Amherst Rd PL3 148 B4
Amherst Road Lane East
PL3 148 B4
Amity Pl PL4 149 A4
ANDERTON 132 F4
Anderton Ct PL19 147 E2
Anderton La PL19 147 D2
Anderton Rise PL10 132 F4
Andrewartha Rd TR10 144 B8
Andrew Pl 3 TR1 137 C4
Andrew's Terr TR16 139 F1
Andrews Way PL12 53 E5
Andurn Cl PL9 136 B6
Aneray Rd TR14 138 D4
ANGARRACK 78 C5
Angarrack Ct PL26 46 F2
Angarrack La TR27 78 D5
Angarrack Mews TR27 78 C5
Angavran Mdw TR8 55 D8
Angel Hill 7 PL15 106 C6
An Gof Gdns PL31 109 C4
Angwin Ave 4 TR5 54 C1
Anjardyn Pl PL24 60 C5
Ankervis La TR16 140 F1
Annear Rd TR10 144 A6
Ann's Pl PL3 128 A4
Anson Ho 1 PL1 148 B3
Anson Pl
Plymouth, Devonport
PL2 127 F4
Plymouth, St Jude's PL4 149 C3
Anson Rd PL27 31 F3
Anson Way TR13 146 D4
Anstis St PL1 148 A3
Anthony Cl EX23 4 C3
Anthony Lowen PL28 107 D4
Anthony Rd TR7 110 E4
Antoine Cl 4 TR18 143 C2
Antoine Terr 23 TR18 143 C2
ANTONY 65 E5
Antony CE Prim Sch PL11 65 E5
Antony Gdns PL2 128 C8
Antony Hill PL11 65 E5
Antony House* PL11 126 D5
Antony Rd PL11 127 B3
Antony Woodland Gdn*
PL11 126 D6
Antron Hill TR10 81 B1
Antron La TR10 93 C8
Antron Way TR10 93 C8
Anvil Ct
Camelford PL32 105 D3
Venterdon PL17 28 D1
Anvil Rd PL32 105 D4
An Vownder Goth TR13 91 B7
Anwyl Cl PL1 148 B3
Anzac Ave PL5 124 A4
Appin Gdns TR15 139 C7
Appleby Wlk PL5 124 D4
Appleton Tor Cl PL3 129 F5
Appletree La PL25 115 D3
Apsley Rd PL4 128 D4
Arbour The PL6 124 E5
Arcade The 6 TR18 143 E5
Arcadia PL9 136 D6
Arcadia Rd PL9 136 C6
Archbishop Benson CE Prim
Sch TR1 137 D6
Archer Pl PL1 148 B4
Archer Terr PL1 148 B3
Arch Hill TR1 137 C2
Architects Way PL5 127 B8
Arch La TR27 77 D1
Archway Ave PL4 129 B3
Arden Gr PL2 128 C8
Arena Cres PL25 115 B4
Argal View TR10 93 B6
Arimoor Gdns PL19 147 E5
Ark Royal Cl PL5 127 D8
Arkwright Gdns PL5 123 F2
Arley Cl PL6 125 B6
Arlington Rd PL4 128 F4
Armada Ct PL19 147 B4
Armada Ctr PL1 148 C3
Armada Rd PL10 133 A1
Armada St PL4 149 A4
Armada Way PL1 148 C2
Armchair Cnr PL31 109 C5
Arnheim Terr TR11 145 B7
Arnison Cl PL9 135 F5
Arnold's Point PL4 129 C3
Arnside Cl PL6 125 D3
Arrallas Barns TR2 57 B4
Arscott Gdns PL9 135 C5
Arscott La PL9 135 D5
Art Gallery Terr TR18 143 C3
Arthurian Ctr The*
PL32 105 D8
Arthur Terr PL11 127 B2
Artillery Pl PL4 149 B1
Arun Cl PL3 129 C5
Arundel Ct TR27 78 D6
Arundell Cl PL16 19 F4
Arundell Gdns
Falmouth TR11 144 E6
Lifton PL16 19 F4
Arundell Pl TR1 137 C3
Arundel Pk TR27 78 D6
Arundel Terr
Bude EX23 104 D4
Plymouth PL2 127 F4
Arundel Way
Connor Downs TR27 78 D6
Newquay TR7 111 B7
Arundle Cl PL26 58 C8
Arwenack Ave TR11 145 C3
Arwenack Ho 4 TR11 145 C3
Arwenack St TR11 145 C4
Arworthal Mdws TR3 81 D6
Arwyn Cotts 6 TR11 145 C3
Arwyn Pl 7 TR11 145 C3
Asdally Vale TR18 143 B5
Ashburgh Parc PL12 122 B3
Ashburnham Rd PL5 124 A3
Ashbury Cl PL14 113 D7
Ashbury Gr EX22 11 E8
Ash Cl
16 Par PL24 60 B4
7 Yelverton PL20 42 C3
Ashcombe Cl PL7 130 C7
Ashdown Cl
Plymouth PL6 125 E3
Sticker PL26 58 E1
Ashdown Wlk PL6 125 E3
Ash Dr TR27 142 B3
Ashery Dr PL9 135 C6
Ashfield Gdns TR11 144 E6
Ashfield Rd TR11 144 F6
Ashfield Villas TR11 144 F6
Ashford Cl PL3 129 A4
Ashford Cres PL3 129 A4
Ashford Hill PL4 129 A4
Ashford Rd PL4 128 F4
Ash Gr
Hayle TR27 142 B3
Par PL24 60 B4
Plymouth PL2 127 F7
Ashleigh Cl PL5 124 C7
Ashleigh La PL5 120 D1
Ashleigh Way
Plymouth PL7 131 C4
Probus TR2 71 D6
Ashley Cl 9 PL26 59 D7
Ashley Pl PL1 148 B4
Ashley Rd
Shortlanesend TR4 69 F6
Truro TR1 137 C4
Ashmead TR2 57 E1
Ashridge Gdns PL5 124 B2
ASHTON 90 E3
Ashton Cl PL6 125 C6
Ashton Ct TR7 111 D6
Ashton Way PL12 122 D3
Ashton Wlk EX23 6 F5
Ashtree Cl PL6 125 D7
Ashtree Gr PL9 136 C8
Ash Vale PL16 19 F4
Ashwood Cl PL7 131 B5
Ashwood Park Rd PL7 131 C6
Aspen Cl PL19 147 C3
Aspen Gdns PL7 131 B5
Astor Dr PL4 129 C3
Astwood Developments
PL13 63 F8
Athelstan Pk PL31 109 F3
Athenaeum La PL1 148 B2
Athenaeum Pl PL1 148 C2
Athenaeum St PL1 148 B2
Atherton Pl PL2 127 E4
Athlone Ho PL1 148 A2
Atlanta PL28 20 E2
Atlantic Cl
Camborne TR14 138 E2
Treknow PL34 14 C5
Widemouth Bay EX23 6 F5
Atlantic Cres TR19 96 C7
Atlantic Mews
New Polzeath PL27 21 D6
8 St Agnes TR5 54 D1
Atlantic Rd
Delabole PL33 14 D2
Newquay TR7 110 C6
Tintagel PL34 14 C7
Atlantic Terr
Camborne TR14 138 E2
New Polzeath PL27 21 D6
43 St Ives TR26 141 B6
Trevone PL28 20 E2
Atlantic View Rd EX23 5 A6
Atlantic Way
Porthtowan TR4 68 A6
4 Tintagel PL34 14 C7
Attenborrow Ct TR7 111 C8
Attery View PL15 18 E6
Auckland Rd 3 PL2 128 A5
Audierne TR10 144 C7
Austin Ave PL2 128 A6
Austin Cres PL6 125 C1
Austin Farm Prim Sch
PL6 129 C7
Ava PL26 73 C4
Avallen Cl TR11 82 A3
Avent Wlk PL7 130 F7
Avenue Rd TR11 145 C3
Avenue The
St Hilary TR20 89 F6
Truro TR1 137 D5
Avery's Row PL28 107 D5
Avery Terr PL22 112 C2
Avery Way PL12 122 C5
Avon Cl
Plymouth PL3 129 D6
St Austell PL25 115 A5
Avondale Rd TR1 137 B4
Avon Flats TR7 111 C7
Avrack Cl TR19 87 F3
Axe Cl PL3 129 D6
Axford Hill PL17 39 F2
Axtown La PL20 42 C2
Aycliffe Gdns PL7 131 A3
Aylesbury Cres PL5 124 B5
Aylmer Sq 14 PL25 114 C3
Aylwin Cl PL7 130 E6
Ayr Ct 1 TR26 141 A5
Ayreville Rd PL2 128 B7
Ayr La TR26 141 B6
Ayr Terr TR26 141 A6
Aysshton Gdns 15 PL17 39 F4

B

Babbacombe Cl PL6 129 E8
Baber Cl PL12 40 C2
Baber Ct PL12 40 D2
Babis Farm Cl PL12 122 F1
Babis Farm Ct PL12 122 F1
Babis Farm Mews PL12 122 F2
Babis Farm Row PL12 122 F1
Babis Farm Way PL12 122 F2
Babis La PL12 122 F1
Baby Beach La PL27 21 D6
Back Hill
Port Isaac PL29 22 D7
Saltash PL12 122 D2
Back La
Angarrack TR27 78 C5
Callington PL17 39 F4
Marazion TR17 89 B5
Plymouth PL7 130 E4
St Erth TR27 77 D2
17 St Ives TR26 141 B6
Tintagel PL34 14 D7
Tregony TR2 71 F4
Veryan TR2 83 F6
Back Lane W TR15 140 B4
Back Quay TR1 137 D4
Back Rd PL18 41 A3
Back Road E 7 TR26 141 B6
Back Road W TR26 141 B6
Back St 42 TR26 141 B6
BADGALL 17 C5
Badger's Cross TR20 88 E8
Badgers Wlk PL12 122 D4
Badger View PL9 135 E5
BADHARLICK 17 E5
Bagbury Rd EX23 104 E3
Bag La
Polbathic PL12 64 F8
St Germans PL12 65 A8
Bahavella Dr TR26 141 B4
Bailey Gdns EX22 8 A5
Baileys Field 7 EX23 5 A6
Baileys La 20 TR26 141 B6
Bailey Terr EX22 8 A5
Bainbridge Ave PL3 128 F7
Bainbridge Ct PL7 130 E7
Baines Hill TR16 67 C6
Bakehouse La 12 PL17 39 E4
Bakehouse The TR10 144 D7
Bake Lane End PL12 52 D1
Bakers Cl PL7 131 C5
Bakers Ct TR7 110 E6
Bakers Gn PL25 115 B4
Bakers Pl PL1 127 F1
Bakers Row TR13 90 F3
BAKESDOWN 7 D3
Balcoath TR16 68 D1
BALDHU 69 C1
Baldhu Row TR 20 76 F2
Balfield Rd 15 TR13 98 C8
Balfour Terr PL2 127 E4
Bal-Jinjy Cl 19 PL24 60 B4
Balkin Way TR15 139 D7
BALL 108 E7
Ballard Cl TR16 80 B5
Ballard Est TR16 80 B5
Ball Terr PL27 108 E7
Balmoral Ave PL2 127 F5
Balmoral Pl 3 TR15 140 B5
Balmoral Terr 4 TR15 140 B5
BALNOON 77 A5
Balnoon Flats TR26 77 A4
Bal Rd TR13 91 E4
BALWEST 90 D5
Bambry Cl TR20 89 E5
Bampflyde Way
Goldsithney TR20 89 F5
Plymouth PL6 124 D6
Bampton Rd PL6 125 E1
Band House La PL26 59 C7
BANGORS 6 F2
Bangors Est EX23 6 F2
Bangors Rd PL15 18 E2
Bank Cotts 6 TR10 144 C7
Bank Pl TR11 145 C3
Bank Sq TR19 86 F6
Bank St
Newquay TR7 110 D6
St Columb Major TR9 45 E6
Bannawell Ct 1 PL19 147 B6
Bannawell St PL19 147 B6
Banns Rd TR4 68 C6
Baptist Hill TR27 142 C6
Baptist St PL17 41 A3
Bara Pl PL17 39 F6
Barbara Hepworth Mus &
Sculpture Gdn* TR26 141 B6
BARBICAN 149 A2
Barbican App PL4 149 B2
Barbican Cl
Helston TR13 146 D8
Looe PL13 117 D4
Barbican Ct
Looe PL13 117 D5
12 Plymouth PL4 149 A2
Barbican Hill PL13 117 D4
Barbican La TR18 143 F4
Barbican Leisure Pk PL4 149 C2
Barbican Rd
Looe PL13 117 E6
Plymouth PL7 130 E4
Barbican Rise Ind Est
PL13 117 E5
Barbican The PL1 149 A2
Barbican Theatre PL1 149 A1
Barbican Way TR13 91 E4
Barbury Cres PL6 125 B8
BARCELONA 62 E4
Barcote Wlk PL6 129 C8
Bardsey Cl PL6 125 A7
BAREPPA 93 D4
Baring St PL4 149 B4
Barker's Hill PL12 122 C1
Barkhouse La PL25 115 B2
BARKLA SHOP 54 E1
Bar La
Connor Downs TR27 78 C6
Falmouth TR11 145 C3
Barlandhu 17 TR18 143 C2
Barlanwick TR18 143 B4
Barley Market St PL19 147 C6
Barlowena TR14 138 D1
Barlow Gdns PL2 128 B7
Bar Mdws TR1 70 D2
Barnaloft 13 TR26 141 B6
Barn Cl
Plymouth PL7 131 D4
Wainhouse Corner EX23 10 F6
Barncoose Ave TR15 139 F6
Barncoose Ind Est TR15 139 E5
Barncoose La TR15 139 E6
Barncoose Terr TR15 139 E6
Barn Courtyard TR27 78 D6
Barndale Cres PL6 125 B6
BARNE BARTON 127 C8
Barne Cl PL5 127 C8
Barnecut Cl 6 PL14 38 A3
Barne La PL5 123 D1
Barne Rd PL5 127 C8
Barnfield Dr PL7 131 C5
Barnfield Gdns TR18 88 E6
Barnfield Pk EX23 4 E1
Barnfield Terr
3 Indian Queens TR9 45 E1
Liskeard PL14 113 B4
Barn Hill
Cadgwith TR12 103 B4
Polbathic PL12 64 F8
Tideford PL12 52 F1
Barningham Gdns PL6 125 B6
Barn La
Bodmin PL31 109 C4
18 St Columb Major TR9 45 E6
Barn Meadow Pk PL13 117 B2
Barnoon Hill TR26 141 B6
Barnoon Terr 29 TR26 141 B6
Barn Park La PL31 35 B2
Barnpark Rd PL35 9 C1
Barn Park Rd PL3 128 D6
Barn Pk
Lostwithiel PL22 112 E2
Saltash PL12 122 F3
Barn St PL14 113 C5
Barnstaple Cl PL6 129 E7
Barns Terr PL12 118 A3
Barnwood Cl PL9 135 E5
Baron Ct PL15 17 D5
Barons Mdw PL31 109 F5
Barons Rd PL20 42 E3
Barossa Rd PL11 127 B3
Barrack La TR1 137 D3
Barrack Pl PL1 128 A1
Barrack's La TR16 68 E1
Barrack St PL1 127 E2
Barras Cross PL14 113 C6
Barras Pl PL14 113 C6
Barras St PL14 113 C6
Bar Rd
Falmouth TR11 145 C3
Mawnan Smith TR11 93 C2
Barrepta Cl TR26 141 D1
Barrie Cres PL31 109 E2
BARRIPPER 79 B5
Barripper Rd
Camborne TR14 138 C1
Penponds TR14 79 C5
Barrow Down PL12 122 B3
Barrowfield View TR7 111 A7
Barr's Cl PL23 116 D5
Barry's La PL28 107 D5
Bar Terr 8 TR11 145 C3
Bartholomew Rd PL2 128 B5
Bartles Cl TR12 99 D7
Bartles Ind Est TR15 140 B6
Bartles Row TR14 139 A5
Bartlett Ave EX23 104 F5
Barton Ave PL2 127 E5
Barton Cl
11 Bodmin PL31 109 D5
Heamoor TR18 143 D7
Helston TR13 146 D7
Landrake PL12 53 C3
Plymouth PL7 131 C5
Barton Ct PL26 58 A7
Barton La TR9 45 D1
Barton Mdw
Pelynt PL13 62 D6
Truro TR1 137 A5
Barton Mdws PL12 53 B7
Barton Mews
Landrake PL12 53 C3
Millbrook PL10 132 F6
Barton Rd
Plymouth PL9 135 B6
St Dennis PL26 58 A7
Barton The PL29 22 D6
Barview La TR27 142 C4
Barwis Hill TR18 143 E6
Barwis Terr 1 TR18 143 E6
Basinghall Cl PL9 135 E5
Basket Ope PL4 149 A2
Basset Rd TR14 138 D2
Basset St
Camborne TR14 138 D2
Falmouth TR11 145 A5
Redruth TR15 140 C4
Bassett Cl PL26 47 A1
Bassett Pl 11 TR11 145 A5
Bassett Rd
Illogan TR16 67 E4
Redruth TR15 140 B8
Bassett Terr TR16 67 D6
Bastville EX22 11 E8
Bath La PL1 148 B2
Bath Pl PL1 148 B2
Bath Place W PL1 148 B2
BATHPOOL 27 C1
Bath St PL1 148 B2
Battershall Cl PL9 135 F5
Batter St PL4 149 A2
Battery Hill TR16 67 C6
Battery La
Polruan PL23 116 C2
Tavistock PL19 147 C4
Battery Mill La TR27 77 E1
Battery Pk PL23 116 C2
Battery Rd TR18 143 F4
Battery St PL1 148 A2
Battery Street Flats PL1 148 A2
Battery Terr PL26 73 C3
Battery The TR7 110 D7
Battisford Pk PL7 131 E3
Bawden Rd PL31 109 B3
Bay Apartments TR7 110 A6
Bay Ct TR11 145 C2
Baydon Cl PL6 125 C1
Bay Down PL13 117 D5
Bayly's Rd PL9 135 B7
Baynards Cl 1 TR1 137 D4
Baynes Cl 3 PL14 38 A3
Bay Rd PL28 20 F2
Bay Retreat PL28 31 F7
Bay St PL13 117 D3
Bayswater Rd PL1 148 B4
Bay The PL13 117 D3
Baytree Cl PL6 125 D6
Bay Tree Cotts 3 EX23 4 D1
Baytree Gdns PL2 128 A7
Baytree Hill PL14 113 C5
Bayview 11 PL24 60 C4
Bay View Cres TR11 145 D3
Bayview Dr PL13 117 E4
Bayview Ho TR27 142 A8
Bay View Pk PL25 114 F6
Bay View Rd
Looe PL13 117 D4
St Austell PL26 115 A1
Bay View Terr
Budock Water TR11 144 C1
Hayle TR27 142 C6
26 Newlyn TR18 143 C2
Newquay TR7 110 E5
Penzance TR18 143 D4
13 Porthleven TR13 98 B8
Bay Villas TR20 88 F6
Beach Ct TR26 141 C6
Beachfield Ave TR7 110 D6
Beachfield Ct TR18 143 D4
Beach Hill PL11 64 C4
Beach La 12 TR6 55 A5
Beach Rd
Carbis Bay TR26 141 D2
Crantock TR8 43 D3
Mevagissey PL26 73 C4
Newquay TR7 110 D6
Perranporth TR6 55 A5
Porthtowan TR4 68 A6
St Austell PL25 115 D3
St Ives TR26 141 A6
Trevone PL28 20 F2
Beachside Ct TR4 68 A6
Beach View Cl TR7 111 C7
Beachview Flats TR4 68 A6
Beach Wlk TR7 111 C7
BEACON 138 F1
Beacon Cl
Falmouth TR11 145 A5
St Austell PL25 115 A5
Beacon Cross PL26 72 F4
Beacon Down Ave PL2 128 B7
Beacon Dr TR5 54 B1
Beacon Est TR20 87 D4
Beacon Farm TR5 54 C1
Beaconfield Rd PL2 128 B7
Beacon Fields TR14 138 E2
Beacon Hill PL31 109 D4
Beacon Hill Mews 9
PL31 109 D5
Beacon Ho PL3 129 D4
Beacon Inf Sch The
PL31 109 D4
Beacon Lanes PL31 109 D3
Beacon Parc TR13 146 C6
Beacon Park Rd PL2 128 B7
Beacon Pk
Boyton PL15 13 A2
Pelynt PL13 62 D5
Beacon Rd
Bodmin PL31 109 E3
Falmouth TR11 145 A5
Foxhole PL26 58 D5
Marazion TR17 89 B5
Newquay TR7 110 D7
Porthleven TR13 98 B8

Beacon Rd *continued*
St Agnes TR5 . . . . 54 C1
Summercourt TR8 . . . . 57 B7
Beacons PL13 . . . . 62 E5
Beaconsfield Pl **2** TR5 . . . 54 C1
Beaconsfield Terr PL31. . 109 C5
Beaconside
Foxhole PL26 . . . . 58 D5
Summercourt TR8 . . . . 57 B7
Beacon Sq TR14 . . . . 138 F1
Beacon St TR11 . . . . 145 B5
Beacon Terr
Camborne TR14 . . . . 138 E1
5 Falmouth TR11 . . . . 145 A4
Foxhole PL26 . . . . 58 D5
Helston TR13 . . . . 146 C6
Lizard TR12 . . . . 102 F2
Beacon The TR11 . . . . 145 A5
Beacon View TR4 . . . . 55 B2
Beacon View Pk **23** TR16 . 67 E4
Beacon Vw PL15 . . . . 27 B7
Beadle Ct **6** PL19 . . . . . . 147 B4
BEALSMILL 28 E3
Bealswood Cl PL18 . . . . . . 41 A6
Bealswood Rd PL18 . . . . . 41 A6
Beam Rd PL26 . . . . 47 C1
Beam Terr PL26 . . . . 47 B1
Beam Villas PL30 . . . . 47 D5
Beare Cl PL9 . . . . 135 D5
Bearsdown Cl PL6 . . . . . . 129 C8
Bearsdown Rd PL6 . . . . . 129 C8
Bears Terr TR16 . . . . 80 E7
Beatrice Ave
Plymouth, Keyham PL2 . . 127 C5
Plymouth, St Jude's PL4 . 149 B3
Saltash PL12 . . . . 122 E2
Beatrice Gdns PL12 . . . . 122 E1
Beatrice Rd PL31 . . . . 48 D8
Beatrice Terr TR27 . . . . . 142 D7
Beattie Rd PL5 . . . . 127 B8
Beatty Cl PL6 . . . . 125 A4
Beauchamp Cres PL2 . . . 128 C7
Beauchamp Rd PL2 . . . . . 128 C7
Beauchamps Mdw TR7 . . 140 D2
Beaudyn Wlk **5** PL6 . . . . 129 C7
Beaufighter Ave PL27 . . . 31 F3
Beaufort Ave **8** PL27. . . . 31 F3
Beaufort Ho **21** PL4 . . . . 149 A2
Beauly Cl PL7 . . . . 131 A5
Beaumaris Gdns PL3 . . . 128 F8
Beaumaris Rd PL3 . . . . . . 128 F8
Beaumont Ave PL4 . . . . . 149 A3
Beaumont Pl PL4 . . . . 149 A3
Beaumont Rd PL4 . . . . . . 149 B3
Beaumont St PL2 . . . . 128 A5
Beaumont Terr PL12 . . . . 122 F4
Beck Adams PL12 . . . . 53 C3
Beckett Cl TR15 . . . . 140 C4
Beckford Cl PL7 . . . . 131 A5
Beckham Pl PL3 . . . . 129 A6
Beckly Ct PL1 . . . . 148 C3
Bede Gdns PL5 . . . . 124 C1
Bede Haven Cl EX23 . . . . 104 E4
Bederkesa Ct PL31 . . . . . 109 D4
Bedford Cl PL18 . . . . 40 F6
Bedford Mews PL4 . . . . . 149 A4
Bedford Park Villas PL4 . 149 A4
Bedford Pk
10 Bere Alston PL20 . . . . 41 B1
Plymouth PL4 . . . . 149 A4
Bedford Pl
6 Bere Alston PL20 . . . . 41 B1
6 St Ives TR26 . . . . 141 B5
Bedford Rd
Horrabridge PL20 . . . . . . 42 C4
Plymouth PL9 . . . . 135 E8
St Ives TR26 . . . . 141 B5
Bedford Sq PL19 . . . . 147 C5
Bedford St
Bere Alston PL20 . . . . 41 B1
Plymouth PL2 . . . . 127 F5
Bedford Units PL18 . . . . . 40 F5
Bedford Villas **7** PL20 . . 41 B1
Bedford Way PL1 . . . . 148 C3
Bedowan Mdws TR7 . . . . 111 A4
Bedruthan Ave TR1 . . . . . 137 E6
Bedruthan Steps★ PL27 . 31 B4
Beech Ave
Liskeard PL14 . . . . 113 B5
Plymouth PL4 . . . . 149 C2
Beech Cl
Falmouth TR11 . . . . 144 F5
Tavistock PL19 . . . . 147 C2
Torpoint PL11 . . . . 127 A3
Beechcombers TR8 . . . . . 44 D7
Beechcroft Rd
Plymouth, Lower Compton
PL3 . . . . 129 A6
Plymouth, North Prospect
PL2 . . . . 128 B7
Beech Ct PL6 . . . . 125 D5
Beech Dr
Bodmin PL31 . . . . 109 B4
Lewannick PL15 . . . . 27 A6
4 St Columb Major TR9 . . 45 D6
Beeches The
Launceston PL15 . . . . . . 106 C5
8 Pensilva PL14 . . . . . . 38 E4
Beechfield Ave PL20 . . . . 42 D3
Beechfield Gr PL3 . . . . . . 128 E6
Beech Hall Flats **19** TR2 . 95 A6
Beeching Pk PL17. . . . . . . 39 F6
Beech La PL25 . . . . 114 D3

Beech Rd
17 Callington PL17 . . . . . . 39 F4
Falmouth TR11 . . . . 144 F5
St Austell PL25 . . . . 114 D3
Beech Terr PL13 . . . . 117 C4
Beech Tree Cl PL15 . . . . . 106 A8
Beechwood Ave PL4 . . . . 128 D4
Beechwood Cross PL7 . . 131 F7
Beechwood Dr PL32 . . . . 105 D5
Beechwood Gdns TR1 . . 137 E6
Beechwood Parc TR1 . . . 137 F5
Beechwood Prim Sch
PL6 . . . . 124 E6
Beechwood Rise PL6 . . . 125 E1
Beechwood Terr PL4 . . . . 128 D4
Beechwood Way PL7 . . . . 131 D5
Beehive Workshops
TR10 . . . . 144 A7
BEENY 9 E3
Beeston Wlk **6** PL6 . . . . 129 C7
Behenna Dr TR1 . . . . 69 F3
Bekelege Dr TR14 . . . . . . 138 F1
Belair Rd PL2 . . . . 128 C7
Belair Villas PL2 . . . . 128 C7
Belbay TR10 . . . . 144 C8
Belerion Rd TR16 . . . . 67 C5
Belgrave La PL4 . . . . 128 F4
Belgrave Rd PL4 . . . . 128 F4
Belgrave Terr PL14 . . . . . 113 D6
Belgravia St PL18 . . . . . . 143 E5
Belhay TR10 . . . . 144 C8
Bellair Rd TR20 . . . . 143 A8
Bellair Terr **38** TR26 . . . 141 B6
Bellamy Cl PL6 . . . . 125 A1
Bellatt PL27 . . . . 108 D6
Bella Vista Gdns TR10 . . . 81 E2
Bell Cl PL7 . . . . 130 F6
Belle Acre Cl PL3 . . . . 128 F6
Bellever Parc TR14 . . . . . 138 F4
Belle Vue
Bude EX23 . . . . 104 D6
Newlyn TR18 . . . . 143 C1
Belle Vue Ave
Bude EX23 . . . . 104 D6
Plymouth PL9 . . . . 135 B5
Bellevue Cotts TR10 . . . . 81 E2
Belle Vue Dr PL9 . . . . 135 B5
Belle Vue La EX23 . . . . . . 104 D6
Belle Vue Rd
Plymouth PL9 . . . . 135 C5
Saltash PL12 . . . . 122 F2
Belle Vue Rise PL9 . . . . . 135 B5
Bellevue Sq PL11 . . . . . . 127 B2
Bellevue Terr **20** TR18 . . 143 E6
Bellflower Cl PL6 . . . . 121 C1
Bell Hill PL26 . . . . 85 C5
Bellers La TR26 . . . . 141 B5
Bellingham Cres PL7 . . . 131 C4
Belliver Ind Est PL6 . . . . 121 B1
Belliver Way PL6 . . . . 121 B1
Bell La
Bodmin PL31 . . . . 109 E5
Lanner TR16 . . . . 80 D6
Bells Ct TR15 . . . . 139 C7
Bell's Ct TR11 . . . . 145 B4
Bell's Hill
Falmouth TR11 . . . . 82 A3
Mylor Bridge TR11 . . . . . . 82 A3
Bell Veor TR16 . . . . 80 E6
Bell Yd **1** PL31 . . . . 109 E5
Belmont PL13 . . . . 117 C4
Belmont Cl PL33 . . . . 14 D2
Belmont Ct
8 Plymouth PL3 . . . . . . 128 A4
11 Wadebridge PL27 . . . 108 B5
Belmont Mews PL14 . . . . 38 D4
Belmont Pk PL14 . . . . 38 D4
Belmont Pl
Newquay TR7 . . . . 110 D7
Plymouth PL3 . . . . 128 A4
St Ives TR26 . . . . 141 A6
Belmont Rd
Falmouth TR11 . . . . 145 A4
Helston TR13 . . . . 146 B7
St Austell PL25 . . . . 114 C3
Belmont St
Plymouth PL1 . . . . 148 B3
8 Tywardreath PL24 . . . 60 D5
Belmont Terr
Devoran TR3 . . . . 81 F6
St Ives TR26 . . . . 141 A6
Belmont Villas **13** TR1 . . 137 D5
BELOWDA 46 D4
Belstone Cl PL5 . . . . 124 A3
Belvedere TR1 . . . . 137 F6
Belvedere La TR20 . . . . . . 89 F5
Belvedere Rd PL4 . . . . . . 129 B2
Belyars Ct TR26 . . . . 141 B4
Belyars La TR26 . . . . 141 B4
Benallack Ct TR1 . . . . 137 E4
Benan Chy PL25 . . . . 114 F3
Benbow St PL2 . . . . 127 F4
Bencoolen Rd EX23 . . . . 104 D5
Beneathway PL14 . . . . . . 50 E7
BENNACOTT 12 E2
Bennets La PL13 . . . . 127 E1
Bennetts Cotts **3** TR10. . 144 C7
Bennett St PL1 . . . . 127 E1
Benny Halt Sta★ TR8. . . . 56 C8
Benson Gdns **2** TR1 . . . 137 D5
Benson Ho **1** TR1 . . . . . 137 D5
Benson Rd TR1 . . . . 137 B5
Bentley Dr **5** EX23 . . . . . 4 D1
Beramic Ct TR27 . . . . 78 D6
Beraton Ct **3** PL31 . . . . 109 D5
BERE ALSTON 41 B1
Bere Alston Sta PL20 . . . . 41 B2

BERE FERRERS 119 E3
Bere Ferrers Sta PL20 . . 119 E3
BEREPPER 98 F5
Berepper Cross TR12 . . . . 98 E5
Beresford St PL2 . . . . 128 A4
Berkeley Cl EX23 . . . . 4 D1
Berkeley Cotts TR11 . . . . 145 A4
Berkeley Ct
Falmouth TR11 . . . . 145 B4
Looe PL13 . . . . 117 C5
Berkeley Hill TR11 . . . . . . 145 A4
Berkeley Mews TR11 . . . 145 A4
Berkeley Path **3** TR11 . . 145 A4
Berkeley Vale TR11 . . . . . 145 A4
Berkshire Dr PL2 . . . . 127 F5
Bernice Cl PL4 . . . . 129 B4
Bernice Terr PL4 . . . . 129 B4
Berries Ave EX23 . . . . . . 104 E4
Berries Mount EX23 . . . . 104 F4
Berriowbridge 27 B2
Berrow Park Rd PL3 . . . . 128 E6
Berrycombe View **16**
PL31 . . . . 109 D5
Berrycoombe Hill PL31 . . 109 C5
Berrycoombe Prim Sch
PL31 . . . . 109 B5
Berrycoombe Rd PL31 . . 109 D5
Berrycoombe Vale PL31 . 109 C5
Berryfields Ho PL31 . . . . 109 E5
Berry Head Gdns PL6 . . . 124 E1
Berryhill PL30 . . . . 47 C6
Berry La PL31 . . . . 109 E5
Berryman Cres TR11 . . . 144 F3
Berry Park Cl PL9 . . . . . . 135 E6
Berry Park Rd PL9 . . . . . . 135 E7
Berry Pk PL12 . . . . 122 D4
Berry Rd TR7 . . . . 110 E6
Berthon Rd PL5 . . . . 127 C8
Berveth Cl TR3 . . . . 69 D3
Berwick Ave PL5 . . . . 124 E3
BESOUGHAN 45 A3
Bess Park Rd PL27 . . . . . 108 E6
Beswetherick Field PL30 . 47 F1
Bethan Dr PL27 . . . . 108 E5
Bethan View **20** TR6 . . . 55 A4
Bethany Homes **1** TR14. 138 C2
Bethany Pl TR19 . . . . 86 F6
BETHEL 115 A5
Bethel Rd PL25 . . . . 115 A4
Bethesda Pl **10** TR26 . . 141 B6
Betjeman Wlk PL5 . . . . . . 124 C3
Beverley Cres TR27 . . . . . 142 E7
Beverley Rd PL3 . . . . 129 C4
Beverston Way PL6 . . . . . 125 B8
Beweys Pk PL12 . . . . 122 C2
Beyrout Pl **6** PL1 . . . . . . 127 F3
Bezant Pl TR7 . . . . 110 B5
Bickern Rd PL11 . . . . 127 B3
Bickford Cres TR13 . . . . . . 91 B1
Bickford Rd PL15 . . . . . . 106 B8
BICKHAM 121 A7
Bickham Park Rd PL3 . . . 128 D7
Bickham Rd PL5 . . . . 123 D2
Bickland Hill TR11 . . . . . 144 D4
Bickland Ind Est TR11 . . 144 D4
Bickland Water Rd TR11 . 144 D2
Bickland Wlk TR11 . . . . . 144 D4
Bickleigh Cl PL6 . . . . 125 A1
Bickleigh Down Bsns Pk
PL6 . . . . 125 D8
Bickleigh Down CE Prim Sch
PL6 . . . . 125 D7
Bickleigh Down Rd PL6 . 121 D7
Bicton Cl PL6 . . . . 125 D1
Biddick Dr PL2 . . . . 127 F6
Biddick's Ct **5** PL25 . . . 114 C3
Bideford Mews **13** EX23 . . 4 E1
Bideford Wlk PL6 . . . . . . 129 E8
Bigbury Wlk PL6 . . . . 129 E8
Biggin Hill PL5 . . . . 123 F4
Big Gn PL13 . . . . 62 D1
Bilbury St PL4 . . . . 149 A3
BILLACOMBE 135 F8
Billacombe Rd PL9 . . . . . 129 E1
Billacombe Villas PL9 . . . 135 F8
BILLACOTT 12 B1
Billings Cl PL6 . . . . 124 D6
Billings Dr TR7 . . . . 111 B5
Billington Ct PL6 . . . . 129 B7
Bindown Ct PL13 . . . . 63 E8
Binhamy Cl EX23 . . . . . . 104 F4
Binhamy Rd EX23 . . . . 7 B8
Binkham Hill PL20 . . . . . . 42 D3
Bircham View PL6 . . . . . . 125 C1
Birch Cl PL6 . . . . 125 E7
Birches The PL6 . . . . 125 D6
Birchfield Ave PL2 . . . . . 128 B6
Birch Gr TR27 . . . . 142 B3
Birchill PL30 . . . . 47 C6
Birch Pond Rd PL9 . . . . . 135 D7
Birchwood Cl PL19 . . . . . 147 C3
Birchwood Gdns PL7 . . . 131 A7
Birkbeck Cl PL7 . . . . 130 E7
Birkdale Cl PL12 . . . . 122 C2
Biscombe Gdns PL26 . . . 123 A2
Biscombes La **8** PL17. . . 39 E4
BISCOVEY 60 B4
Biscovey Academy **22**
PL24 . . . . 60 B4
Biscovey Rd PL24 . . . . . . 115 F5
Bishop Bronescombe CE
Prim Sch PL25 . . . . 115 B5
Bishop Cornish CE Prim Sch
PL12 . . . . 122 F1
Bishops Cl
Saltash PL12 . . . . 122 E3
Truro TR1 . . . . 137 C6
Bishops Ct TR9 . . . . 45 E6

Bishop's Hill Rd PL27 . . . 21 D6
Bishop's Pl PL1 . . . . 148 B1
BISHOP'S QUAY 99 F8
Bishop's Rd TR26 . . . . . . 141 B5
Bishop Temple Rd TR1 . . 137 F6
BISSOE 81 D8
BISSOM 144 E8
Bissom Rd TR10 . . . . 81 F2
Blackberry Cl PL9 . . . . . . 135 E8
Blackberry La PL9 . . . . . . 135 E8
Blackberry Way TR1 . . . . 137 F5
Blackbird Cres PL15 . . . . 106 E4
Blackbrook Cl PL20 . . . . . 42 E4
BLACK CROSS 45 E3
Blackerry Cl TR16 . . . . . . 140 F1
Blackeven Cl PL6 . . . . . . 121 C1
Blackeven Hill PL6 . . . . . 121 C1
Blackfriars La PL1 . . . . . . 149 A2
Blackhall Gdns PL6 . . . . 124 D6
Blackmore Cres PL6 . . . . 124 D6
Black Rd TR27 . . . . 142 D7
BLACK ROCK 79 D1
Blacksmith La TR27 . . . . . 78 D6
Blackstone Cl PL9 . . . . . . 136 B6
Blackthorn Cl
Plymouth, Honicknowle
PL5 . . . . 124 B3
Plymouth, Woolwell PL6 . 125 D8
BLACKWATER 68 D5
Blackwater Prim Sch TR4 . 68 E5
Bladder La PL5 . . . . 124 E2
Blagdon Cross EX21 . . . . 13 F7
Blagdon Lodge Cross
EX21 . . . . 13 F8
Blairgowrie Rd PL5 . . . . . 123 C2
Blake Gdns PL5 . . . . 124 C3
Blakes Pk PL14 . . . . 113 D7
Blanchard Pl **2** PL7 . . . . 130 E7
Blanchdown Dr PL18 . . . . 40 F7
Blanchminster Rd EX23 . 104 E5
Blandford Rd PL3 . . . . . . 129 C6
Blatchborough Cross EX22 .3 E1
Blaxton La PL5 . . . . 120 C2
Blenheim Rd PL4 . . . . 149 A4
Bligh Cres TR13 . . . . 146 C5
Blight's Row TR15 . . . . . . 140 B5
Blindhole **8** PL15 . . . . . 106 C6
Blind La PL11 . . . . 64 D6
BLINDWELL 132 E5
Blindwell Hill PL10 . . . . . 132 E5
BLISLAND 35 D8
Blisland Prim Sch PL30 . . 35 D7
Blissoe Rd TR3 . . . . 81 F7
Bloomball Ct PL3 . . . . . . 129 B6
Bloom Fields TR18 . . . . . 143 C5
BLOWINGHOUSE
Bodmin. 109 B2
Redruth 139 F6
Blowing House Cl PL25 . . 114 B4
Blowinghouse Hill TR15 . 140 A4
Blowing House Hill
Crowlas TR20 . . . . 89 B8
Hayle TR20 . . . . 77 A1
St Austell PL25 . . . . 114 C4
Blowinghouse La PL30 . . 109 B2
Blowing House La PL25 . 114 B4
BLUE ANCHOR 57 D8
Bluebell Cl PL12 . . . . 122 D4
Bluebell Way
Launceston PL15 . . . . . . 106 E4
Tavistock PL19 . . . . 147 E4
Blue Haze Cl PL6 . . . . . . 125 D5
Blue Reef Aquarium★
TR7 . . . . 110 D6
Blunt's La PL6 . . . . 125 C3
Boaden Cl PL12 . . . . 53 E5
Boase St TR18 . . . . 143 C1
Bobs Rd PL24 . . . . 60 B4
Bochym Hill TR12 . . . . 99 C3
Boconnic La PL20 . . . . . . 42 D3
Boconnoc Ave PL17 . . . . . 39 F3
Boconnoc Rd PL25 . . . . . 114 D2
BODELVA 115 B8
Bodelva Rd PL24 . . . . 115 B8
Bodgara Way PL14 . . . . . 113 D6
Bodgara Way Flats **4**
PL14 . . . . 113 D6
BODIEVE 108 C7
Bodieve Rd PL27 . . . . 108 D7
BODILLY 91 F7
Bodinar Rd TR10 . . . . 81 D2
Bodiniel Rd PL31 . . . . . . 109 C6
Bodiniel View PL31 . . . . . 109 B5
Bodinnar Cl TR20 . . . . . . 87 E6
Bodinnar La TR20 . . . . . . 87 E6
BODINNICK 116 B5
Bodinnick Hts PL23 . . . . 116 B5
Bodinnick Parc PL30 . . . . 23 E3
Bodinnick Rd PL30 . . . . . 23 E3
BODMIN 109 B5
Bodmin Beacon Nature
Reserve★ PL31 . . . . . . 109 D4
Bodmin Bsns Ctr PL31. . 109 E3
Bodmin Bsns Pk PL31 . . 35 B2
Bodmin Coll PL31 . . . . . . 109 B4
Bodmin Community Hospital
PL31 . . . . 109 B4
Bodmin General Sta★
PL31 . . . . 109 E3
Bodmin Hill PL22 . . . . . . 112 B4
Bodmin Jail★ PL31 . . . . . 109 D5
Bodmin Parkway Sta
PL30 . . . . 49 A7
Bodmin Rd
Plymouth PL5 . . . . 124 D1
St Austell PL25 . . . . 114 C6
Truro TR1 . . . . 137 E6
Bodmin Ret Pk PL31 . . . . 35 B1

Bodmin Town Mus★
PL31 . . . . 109 E4
Bodmin & Wenford Rly★
PL30 . . . . 109 D2
Bodrigan Rd PL13 . . . . . . 117 C5
Bodriggy Academy PL27 . 145 D5
Bodriggy Cres TR27 . . . . 142 C5
Bodriggy Ct TR27 . . . . . . 142 D6
Bodriggy St TR27 . . . . . . 142 D6
Bodriggy Villas TR27 . . . 142 D6
BODWEN 47 E3
Body's Ct PL18 . . . . 40 F6
Bohella Rd TR10 . . . . 144 D8
Bohella Rise TR10 . . . . . 144 D8
Bohella Way TR10 . . . . . 144 D8
Bohella Rd **20** TR2 . . . . . 95 A6
BOHETHERICK 40 E7
Bohill TR10 . . . . 144 D7
Bohill Ct TR10 . . . . 144 D7
BOHORTHA 95 C5
Boiler Works Rd TR14 . . . 138 E5
Bojea Ind Est PL25 . . . . . 114 C7
Bojea Terr PL25 . . . . 114 C7
Bojewan Stennack TR19. . 75 B1
Bokenna Cross PL14 . . . . 37 C1
Boldventure Ave PL25 . . . 115 B5
Boldventure Cl PL25 . . . . 115 B5
Bolenna La TR6 . . . . 55 A4
BOLENOWE 79 F5
Bolenowe Terr TR14 . . . . 79 F4
BOLINGEY 55 B4
Bolingey Chapel Flats
TR6 . . . . 55 B4
Bolingey Rd TR6 . . . . 55 A4
BOLITHO 79 F1
Bolitho Rd PL18 . . . . 143 C7
Bollowal Pl TR19 . . . . 86 E6
Bolowthas Cnr TR7 . . . . 111 A7
Bolowthas Way TR7 . . . . 111 C7
Bolster Cl **8** TR5 . . . . . . 54 C1
Boltern Rd TR17 . . . . 89 C5
Bolt House Cl PL19 . . . . . 147 A5
BOLVENTOR 25 E3
Bolventor La PL13 . . . . . . 63 E8
Bonallack La TR12 . . . . . . 92 D1
Bon Cot Rd TR18 . . . . . . 143 C2
Bond St
Plymouth PL6 . . . . 124 E6
6 Redruth TR15 . . . . . . 140 B4
Bone Cellar Row TR2. . . . 70 F5
Bone Mill Rd TR6 . . . . 55 B4
Bones La PL12 . . . . 52 E4
Bonson Cl PL3 . . . . 117 C4
Bon Villas **18** TR18 . . . . 143 C4
Bonville Rd PL6 . . . . 124 E6
Bonython Cl TR11 . . . . . . 82 A3
Bonython Dr TR2 . . . . 72 A7
Bonython Rd TR7 . . . . . . 111 B7
Bonython Terr PL14 . . . . 113 B4
Boon's Pl PL1 . . . . 148 C4
BOQUIO 91 F8
BOREA 76 F2
Borgwitha TR16 . . . . 80 B5
Boringdon Ave PL5 . . . . . 127 D8
Boringdon Cl PL7 . . . . . . 130 D7
Boringdon Hill PL7 . . . . . 130 E7
Boringdon Mill Bsns Ctr
PL7 . . . . 130 F6
Boringdon Prim Sch
PL7 . . . . 130 D7
Boringdon Rd
Plymouth, Plympton PL7 . 130 D7
Plymouth, Turnchapel PL9 . 135 A7
Boringdon Terr
Plymouth, Plympton PL7 . 130 D7
Plymouth, Turnchapel PL9 . 135 A7
Boringdon Villas PL7 . . . . 130 D7
Borlase Cl TR13 . . . . 146 B5
Borough Cross EX22 . . . . . 7 F5
Borough Ct PL11 . . . . 126 E4
Borough Pk PL11 . . . . 126 E4
Borrowdale Cl PL6 . . . . . 124 D5
Bosawna Ct TR16 . . . . 68 E1
BOSCADJACK 91 F6
Boscarn Cl TR14 . . . . 79 B5
BOSCARNE 34 C2
Boscarne Cres PL25 . . . . 114 F3
Boscarne Junction Sta★
PL30 . . . . 34 D2
Boscarnek TR27 . . . . 142 A1
Boscarne View PL30 . . . . 34 D2
Boscarn Parc TR15 . . . . . 139 C4
Boscarn Rd TR15 . . . . . . 140 D6
BOSCASTLE 9 C1
Boscastle Com Prim Sch
PL35 . . . . 9 C1
Boscastle Gdns PL2 . . . . 128 C8
Boscastle Visitor Ctr★
PL35 . . . . 9 D2
Boscaswell Downs TR19 . 75 A1
Boscaswell Est TR19 . . . 74 F1
Boscaswell Rd TR19 . . . . 75 A1
Boscaswell Terr **4** TR19 . 75 A1
Boscathnoe La TR18 . . . 143 B7
Boscathnoe Way TR18 . . 143 B7
Boscawen Ct **17** TR6 . . . 55 A4
Boscawen Gdns **11** TR6 . 55 A4
Boscawen Pk PL26 . . . . . 58 B8
Boscawen Pl PL2 . . . . . . 127 C4
Boscawen Rd
7 Chacewater TR4 . . . . . 69 A3
Falmouth TR11 . . . . 145 A4
Helston TR13 . . . . 146 D4
Perranporth TR6 . . . . 55 A4
St Dennis PL26 . . . . 58 C8
Boscawen St **18** TR1 . . . 137 D4
Boscean Cl TR14 . . . . 79 E4

BOSCOPPA 115 A6
Boscoppa Cl TR15....... 140 D7
Boscoppa Rd
  St Austell, Bethel PL25...115 A5
  St Austell, Boscoppa PL25. 115 B5
Boscowan TR11........... 145 C2
BOSCREEGE 90 C5
Boscundle Ave TR11..... 144 F1
Boscundle Cl PL25...... 115 D5
Boscundle Row PL12..... 123 A2
Bosence Rd TR27........ 90 C7
Bosillion La TR2........ 72 A7
Bosinney Rd PL25....... 114 D3
Bosinver La PL26........ 59 A1
Boskear La PL31........ 109 A4
BOSKEDNAN............. 76 A1
Boskenna 97 C4
Boskenna Cross TR19.... 97 C5
Boskennal Barton TR19.. 97 B6
Boskennal La TR19...... 97 B6
Boskennal Rd TR16...... 80 A5
Boskennel Dr TR27...... 142 B4
Boskenwyn Prim Sch
  TR13.................. 92 B3
Boskenza Ct TR26....... 141 C2
Boskernick Cl TR18..... 143 B1
Boskernow TR12......... 100 D6
Boskerris Cres TR26.... 141 D2
Boskerris Mews TR26.... 141 D1
Boskerris Rd TR26...... 141 D2
Boslandew Hill TR19.... 88 C2
BOSLEAKE 139 C3
Bosleake Row TR15...... 139 C3
Bosloggas Mews 9
  TR11.................. 145 C3
BOSLOWICK 144 F2
Boslowick Cl TR11...... 144 F3
Boslowick Ct TR11...... 144 E2
Boslowick Rd TR11...... 144 E2
Bosmeor Cl TR11........ 144 E2
Bosmeor Ct TR15........ 139 D6
Bosmeor Pk TR15........ 139 D6
Bosmeor Rd TR11........ 144 E3
Bosoweth
  Helston TR13.......... 146 D5
  Probus TR2............ 71 D6
Bosorne Cl TR19........ 86 E6
Bosorne Rd TR19........ 86 E6
Bosorne St TR19........ 86 E6
Bosorne Terr TR19...... 86 E6
Bosparva La
  Leedstown TR27........ 78 F1
  Praze-an-Beeble TR14... 79 A3
Bospolvans Rd 2 TR9... 45 D6
Bospowis TR14.......... 138 C3
BOSSINEY 14 D8
Bossiney Rd PL34....... 14 D7
Bostennack Pl 10 TR26. 141 A5
Bostennack Terr 11
  TR26.................. 141 A5
Bosuen Rd TR7.......... 111 A7
Bosullow Vean TR20..... 87 D8
Bos Vean TR12.......... 102 F2
Bosvean Gdns
  11 Illogan TR16....... 67 E4
  Truro TR1............. 137 B5
Bosvean Rd TR4......... 69 F6
Bosvenna View PL31..... 109 E4
Bosvenna Way TR18..... 143 B7
Bosvenning Pl TR20..... 87 D6
Bosvigo Gdns* TR1..... 137 A5
Bosvigo La TR1......... 137 B5
Bosvigo Rd TR1......... 137 C4
Bosvigo Sch 16 TR1.... 137 C4
Boswedden Pl TR19..... 86 E6
Boswedden Rd TR19..... 86 E6
BOSWEDNACK........... 76 A4
Boswell Cl PL5......... 124 B2
Boswergy TR18.......... 143 C5
BOSWINGER 85 B5
Boswithian Rd TR14.... 138 F6
Boswargey Cl 3 TR9.... 45 D6
Boswargy Rd TR20, TR27.. 90 B8
BOTALLACK 86 E7
Botallack La TR19...... 86 E7
Botetoe Hill TR14...... 79 C4
Botetoe Rd TR14........ 79 B4
Botha Rd 1 PL27....... 31 F3
Bothwicks Rd TR7...... 110 E6
BOTTOMS 96 E5
BOTUSFLEMING 122 B7
Boughthayes Est PL19... 147 A5
Boulden Cl PL7......... 131 C5
Boulter Cl PL6......... 121 C1
Boundary Cl 21 PL18... 143 C1
Boundary Dr EX23....... 7 B6
Boundary Rd
  Bodmin PL31........... 109 A4
  Dousland PL20......... 42 E3
Bounders La TR6........ 55 B4
Bounder Treath TR12.... 101 C1
Boundervean La TR14.... 138 B2
Bounds Cross EX22....... 8 B4
Bounds Pl PL1.......... 148 B2
Bounsalls Ct 5 PL15... 106 C5
Bounsall's La PL15..... 106 C5
Bourne Cl PL3.......... 129 D6
Bourneside PL25........ 114 D3
Boveway Dr PL14........ 113 E5
Boveway La PL14........ 113 D5
Boville La PL9......... 136 C2
Bovey Cl PL9........... 134 F2
Bovisand La
  Down Thomas PL9....... 135 B2
  Staddiscombe PL9...... 135 D3
Bovisand Pk PL9........ 135 A1

Bovisand Rd PL9........ 135 E3
Bowden 10 EX23........ 4 D1
Bowden Park Rd PL6.... 125 A1
Bowdens Row TR15...... 140 A4
Bowers Rd PL2.......... 128 B5
Bowers Park Dr PL6.... 125 E7
Bowglas LE TR20....... 89 A8
Bowhays Wlk 2 PL6.... 129 C7
Bowjey Ct 9 TR18..... 143 C1
Bowjey Hill TR18...... 143 C1
Bowjey Terr 5 TR18... 143 C1
Bow La EX23............ 4 D2
Bowles Rd TR11........ 145 A6
Bowling Gn
  Menheniot PL14........ 51 F5
  34 St Ives TR26...... 141 B6
Bowling Gn The TR2.... 82 F2
BOWLING GREEN
  Bugle................. 47 E1
  Redruth............... 139 D3
Bowling Green Ct
  Hayle TR27............ 142 D5
  Liskeard PL14......... 113 B5
Bowling Green Rd TR11.. 92 F3
Bowling Green Terr 35
  TR26................. 141 B6
Bownder Dowr TR27..... 142 B3
Bownder Gareth TR7.... 110 C5
Bownder Marhaus 4
  TR7.................. 110 D5
Bownder Sarras 3 TR7. 110 D5
Bownder Vean PL25..... 115 A5
Bownder Ywain TR7..... 110 C5
Bowood Pk
  Delabole PL33......... 14 F1
  Helstone PL32......... 24 B8
Boxhill Cl PL5......... 124 B3
Boxhill Gdns PL2....... 128 C8
Box's Shop EX23........ 7 A4
Boxwell Pk PL31........ 109 F4
Boyd Ave PL28.......... 107 C5
BOYTON 13 B2
Boyton Com Prim Sch
  PL15................. 13 A3
Bracken Cl
  Bodmin PL31........... 109 E5
  Plymouth PL6.......... 125 D8
Brackenside PL13....... 62 D1
Bracken Terr TR7...... 110 E5
Brackwell Pl TR27..... 108 B5
BRADDOCK 49 F5
Braddock CE Prim Sch
  PL14................. 50 B6
Braddock Cl PL26...... 58 D6
Braddons Hill PL7..... 130 B7
Bradfield Cl PL6....... 125 E1
BRADFORD 24 D2
Bradford Cl PL6........ 129 B7
Bradford Quay Rd PL27.. 108 C6
Bradley Rd
  Newquay TR7........... 111 C7
  Plymouth PL4.......... 128 F4
Bradridge Ct PL15...... 13 A4
Braemar Cl PL7......... 131 C4
Braeside Pk PL14....... 50 E8
Braggs Hill PL15....... 13 B3
Brake La PL10.......... 132 B5
Brake The PL14......... 37 F4
Bramblebank TR11....... 145 B7
Bramble Hill EX23..... 104 E5
Brambles The
  Liskeard PL14......... 113 C5
  Lostwithiel PL22...... 112 C3
Bramble Wlk 1 PL6.... 129 C7
Bramfield Pl PL6....... 129 D7
Bramley Cl PL25........ 114 E4
Bramley Pk PL31........ 109 F5
Bramley Rd PL3......... 129 C5
Brancker Rd PL2........ 128 C6
Brandon Rd PL3......... 129 C4
Brandon Wlk PL3........ 6 F5
Brandreth Rd 3 PL3... 128 F6
Brandy La TR20......... 89 F4
BRANE 87 C3
Branksome Dr PL27..... 108 C5
Brannel Sch The PL26.. 58 B3
Branscombe Gdns PL5... 124 A3
Branson Ct 9 PL7..... 131 C5
Branson Pk PL19....... 42 A6
Branwell La TR18...... 88 E6
Braunton Wlk PL6...... 129 E8
Bray Cl PL19........... 147 A5
Brayford Cl PL5........ 124 C1
Bray Rise TR16......... 80 A5
BRAY SHOP 28 B1
Bray's Pl PL14......... 114 F4
Brays Terr 2 TR16.... 140 F1
Brazacott 12 B2
Brazacott Cross PL15... 12 B2
Bread St TR18.......... 143 E5
Brea Arch TR14......... 139 A3
Bread St TR18.......... 143 E5
BREAGE 90 F3
Breage CE Sch TR13.... 90 F3
Break My Neck La TR20. 88 B8
Breakwater Hill PL4... 149 C1
Breakwater Ind Est PL9. 135 C8
Breakwater Rd
  Bude EX23............. 104 D5
  Plymouth PL9.......... 135 C8
Brean Down Cl PL3..... 128 E6
Brean Down Rd PL3..... 128 E7

Brea Rd PL27........... 21 D2
Breaside TR14.......... 139 A3
Brecon Cl
  Plymouth PL3.......... 129 A7
  1 St Agnes TR5....... 54 C1
Bredon Ct TR7.......... 110 C6
Bree Shute La
  4 Bodmin PL31........ 109 E5
  10 PL31.............. 109 E5
BRENT 62 E2
Brentford Ave PL5..... 124 B5
Brent Knoll Rd 1 PL3. 128 E6
Brenton Rd PL11....... 64 B5
Brentons Pk PL29...... 22 D6
Brentor Rd
  Mary Tavy PL19....... 30 F6
  Plymouth PL4.......... 129 B2
Brent Tor* PL19....... 30 D7
Brentwartha PL13...... 62 E2
Brest Rd PL6........... 125 A3
Brest Way PL6.......... 125 A3
Bretonside PL4......... 149 A2
Brett Wlk PL7.......... 130 F7
Brewartha TR2.......... 57 E1
Brewers Cl PL30........ 47 F6
Brewers Hill PL26..... 58 C8
Brewers Rd TR1........ 137 F5
Brewery Hill TR26..... 77 E4
Brewery La TR13....... 146 B6
Briansway PL12......... 122 D2
Briardale Rd PL2...... 127 E6
Briarleigh Cl PL6..... 125 F2
Briar Rd
  Bude EX23............. 104 E4
  Plymouth PL3.......... 128 F7
Briars Row PL12....... 122 D4
Briars Ryn PL12....... 53 B7
Briar Tor PL20......... 42 D3
Briarwood PL14......... 113 D5
Brickfields Sp Ctr PL1. 127 F2
Brickworks Hill TR16.. 68 D1
Bridals La PL13........ 62 E2
BRIDGE 67 E5
Bridge TR9............. 45 E7
Bridge Cl TR7.......... 111 A4
Bridge Ct PL25........ 114 F4
Bridge Hill
  Illogan TR16.......... 67 E5
  St Columb Major TR9.. 45 E6
Bridge Ho
  Delabole PL33......... 14 E2
  Hayle TR27............ 142 B6
Bridge Ho The 13 TR18. 143 C2
Bridge La PL12......... 53 A3
Bridgemead Cl PL26.... 114 C1
Bridgemoor Cross EX22. 8 C6
Bridge Pk EX22........ 8 A5
Bridge Rd
  Goonhavern TR4........ 55 D4
  Illogan TR16.......... 67 E4
  Seaton PL11........... 64 B5
  St Austell PL25....... 114 B3
  Tideford PL12......... 52 F2
Bridge Row TR16....... 67 E5
BRIDGERULE 8 A6
Bridgerule CE Prim Sch
  EX22................. 8 A5
Bridgerule Ind Est EX22. 7 F4
BRIDGES 59 F8
Bridge St
  Par PL24.............. 60 B6
  7 Stratton EX23...... 4 D1
Bridges The PL12...... 122 E1
Bridge The PL1........ 148 B1
BRIDGETOWN 19 B8
Bridge View
  PL5.................. 127 D8
  Wadebridge PL27....... 108 C6
Bridge Wlk 2 PL35.... 9 C2
Bridgwater Cl PL6..... 125 B1
Bridle Cl PL7.......... 131 B7
Bridle Way
  Quintrell Downs TR8... 44 E3
  Saltash PL12.......... 122 D4
Bridwell Cl PL5........ 127 E8
Bridwell Lane N PL5... 127 E8
Bridwell Rd PL5....... 127 E8
BRIGHTON 57 D5
Brillwater Rd TR11.... 92 E4
Brimford Cross EX22... 3 D4
Brimhill Cl PL7....... 131 B3
Brisbane Terr PL14.... 113 C5
Brismar Wlk 3 PL6.... 129 C7
Briston Orch PL12..... 53 E7
Britannia Pl PL4...... 129 B2
Britcheston Cl PL9.... 136 A5
British Rd TR5......... 54 D1
Briton's Hill TR18.... 143 F6
Brixham Wlk PL6....... 129 E8
BRIXTON 136 F5
Brixton Lodge Gdns PL8. 136 F5
Brixton Terr TR13..... 146 C6
Broad Cl EX22.......... 11 E7
Broadclose Hill EX23.. 104 E6
Broad La
  Illogan TR15.......... 139 D7
  Trematon PL12......... 53 D3
Broadland Gdns PL9.... 136 A8
Broadland La PL9...... 135 F8
Broadlands Cl PL7..... 131 A3
BROADLANE 90 E5
Broadley Cl PL6....... 121 B2
Broadley Ind Pk PL6... 121 B2
Broadley Park Rd PL6.. 121 B2
Broad Mead PL17....... 39 E5

Broad Park Rd
  Bere Alston PL20...... 41 B2
  Plymouth PL3.......... 128 D6
Broad Pk
  Launceston PL15....... 106 B7
  Plymouth PL9.......... 135 C7
  St Keyne PL14......... 51 B3
Broadshell Cross EX22.. 8 E5
Broads La TR11......... 81 B7
Broad St
  12 Launceston PL15... 106 C6
  Lifton PL16........... 19 F4
  Newquay TR7........... 110 D6
  Padstow PL28.......... 107 D5
  Penryn TR10........... 144 D7
  7 St Columb Major TR9. 45 E6
  Truro TR1............. 137 C5
Broads Yd PL11........ 64 C5
Broadview PL19........ 30 A6
Broad View TR4........ 56 D1
Broadway The PL9...... 135 E7
Broad Wlk
  Helston TR13.......... 146 B7
  Saltash PL12.......... 122 E1
Brock Ho 9 PL4....... 149 A2
Brockhole La PL7...... 130 E8
Brockley Rd PL3....... 129 C4
Brocks La PL10........ 132 F5
Brockstone Rd PL25.... 115 A5
Brockton Gdns PL6..... 125 B6
BROCTON 34 A3
Bromfield Cres TR2.... 57 E1
Bromhead Cl TR6...... 129 A8
Bromley Ho 6 PL2..... 128 A4
Bromley Pl 5 PL2..... 128 A4
Bronescombe Cl TR10... 144 D7
Bronte Pl PL5......... 124 D1
BROOK 147 B2
Brook Cl
  Helston TR13.......... 146 B7
  Plymouth PL7.......... 131 A3
Brook Ct 6 TR11...... 145 A4
Brookdale Ct 12 PL27. 108 B5
Brookdown Terr PL12... 122 E3
Brookdown Villas PL12. 122 E3
Brook Dr EX23......... 104 E7
Brooke Cl PL12........ 123 A2
Brookfield Cl
  Lanjeth PL26.......... 58 E3
  Plymouth PL7.......... 131 B5
Brookfields PL11...... 127 F1
Brook Green Ctr for Learning
  PL5.................. 124 B4
Brooking Cl PL6....... 129 A8
Brookingfield Cl PL7.. 130 C5
Brooking Way PL12.... 122 C3
Brook La PL19......... 147 B2
Brooklands PL27....... 21 D6
Brooklands Ct PL6..... 124 C3
Brooklyn Flats 18 TR2. 95 A6
Brooklyn Terr 17 TR2. 95 A6
Brook Pl
  Falmouth TR11......... 145 A4
  Penryn TR10........... 144 C7
Brook Rd
  Falmouth TR11......... 144 F3
  Wadebridge PL27....... 108 B5
Brooks PL22............ 49 E3
Brookside PL25........ 114 F4
Brookside Cl PL15..... 106 B8
Brook St
  Falmouth TR11......... 145 A4
  17 Mousehole TR19.... 88 C1
  Tavistock PL19........ 147 C6
Brook The PL12........ 122 E4
Brookward Terr 8 TR18. 143 C7
Brookway TR7.......... 142 E7
Brookwood Rd PL9..... 136 D7
Broomfield Dr
  Bodmin PL31........... 109 B3
  Plymouth PL9.......... 135 C5
Broomfield Rd PL27.... 108 D5
Broom Hill PL12....... 122 D2
Broomhill Cross EX22.. 5 E3
Broomhill La EX23...... 4 D2
Broom Pk PL9.......... 135 D5
Broughton Cl PL3...... 128 F7
Browne Memorial
  Almshouses PL19...... 147 A5
Browning Cl 14 TR9... 45 D6
Browning Dr PL31...... 109 C3
Browning Rd PL2....... 128 A5
Brownlow Pl 5 PL31... 109 D5
Brownlow St PL1....... 148 A2
Browns Hill PL23...... 116 C4
Brown's Hill TR10..... 144 C8
Broxton Dr PL9........ 129 E1
Bruallen Cl PL30...... 23 E7
Brunel Ave PL2........ 127 F5
Brunel Ct 1 TR1...... 137 B4
Brunel Prim Sch PL12.. 122 E4
Brunel Quays PL12..... 112 D2
Brunel Rd PL12........ 122 C4
Brunel Terr 3 PL2.... 127 F5
Brunel Way PL1........ 148 A2
BRUNNION 77 A3
Brunswick Pl 10 PL2.. 127 F4
Brunswick Rd PL4..... 149 B2
Brunton Rd TR15....... 23 B5
Brush End TR26........ 77 E4
Bryher Cl PL17........ 39 E6
Brymon Way PL6....... 125 B4
Brynmoor Cl PL3....... 129 A6
Brynmoor Pl PL3....... 129 A6
Brynmoor Wlk PL3..... 129 A6
Bryny Cl PL30......... 23 E7
Buckett's Hill TR15... 140 C2
Buckeys La TR2........ 95 B6

Buckfast Cl PL2....... 128 A8
Buckingham Nip TR4.... 68 F3
Buckingham Pl PL5..... 123 E2
Buckingham's Cl TR8... 56 B7
Buckingham Terr TR16.. 68 D1
Buckland Abbey* PL20.. 41 F1
Buckland Cl PL7....... 130 D7
BUCKLAND
  MONACHORUM.......... 42 A3
Buckland St PL1....... 148 B2
Buckland Terr PL20.... 42 C2
Bucklawren Rd PL13.... 63 E7
Bucklers Ho PL25...... 115 B4
Bucklers La PL25...... 115 B4
Buckler Village (Mobile
  Homes Pk) PL25...... 115 B4
Buckwell St PL1, PL4.. 149 A2
Buctor Pk PL19........ 41 D8
Buddle Cl
  Plymouth PL9.......... 136 A5
  Tavistock PL19........ 147 B6
BUDE 104 E6
Budehaven Com Sch
  EX23................ 104 F5
Budehaven L Ctr EX23.. 104 F5
Bude Ind Est EX23..... 104 E5
Bude Inf Sch EX23..... 104 E5
Bude Jun Sch EX23..... 104 E5
BUDOCK WATER......... 144 B2
Budock Vean La TR11... 93 B2
Budge Mdws PL15...... 28 C4
Budleigh Cl PL9....... 135 F5
Budnic Est TR6........ 55 B5
Budnic Hill TR6....... 55 B5
Budock Pl TR11........ 145 B4
Budock Terr TR11...... 145 B4
BUDOCK WATER......... 144 B2
Buena Vista Cl PL6.... 125 D6
Buena Vista Dr PL6.... 125 C6
Buena Vista Gdns PL6.. 125 C6
Buena Vista Way PL6... 125 D6
BUGLE 47 D1
Bugle Rural Workshops
  PL26................ 47 C1
Bugle Sch PL26........ 47 C1
Bugle Sta PL26........ 47 C2
Buildings The TR20.... 89 A6
Bullan's La TR26...... 141 A5
Bullans Terr 5 TR26.. 141 A5
Bulleid Cl PL2........ 127 F7
Bulleid Way EX23...... 104 E4
Buller Cl
  Plymouth PL7.......... 130 F4
  Torpoint PL11......... 127 A3
Buller Hill TR16...... 80 B6
Buller Ho PL13........ 117 D3
Buller Pk
  Liskeard PL14......... 113 D5
  Saltash PL12.......... 122 D3
Buller Rd PL11........ 127 C3
Buller St PL13........ 117 C3
Bull Hill PL23........ 116 D4
Bullock La
  Helston, Lower Green
    TR13............... 146 B5
  Helston, Whitehill TR13. 146 C4
Bullock Market Terr 27
  TR18................ 143 E6
Bulmer Rd PL4......... 149 C3
Bulteel Gdns PL6...... 124 E7
Bulwark Rd TR13....... 146 B4
Bungalows The
  Looe PL13............. 117 D6
  Tintagel PL34......... 14 D7
Bunkers Hill
  22 St Ives TR26...... 141 B6
  Townshend TR27........ 90 C8
Bunyan Cl PL3......... 124 C2
Burden Cl PL31........ 109 C4
Burgess Cl EX23....... 4 D2
BURHOS 79 F2
Burhos Row TR15....... 79 F1
Buriton 32 TR18....... 143 E5
BURLAWN 108 D1
Burlawn Dr PL25....... 114 F7
Burleigh La PL3....... 128 C4
Burleigh Manor PL3.... 128 D7
Burleigh Park Rd PL3.. 128 D6
Burley Cl TR11........ 137 D3
Burley Ct TR11........ 145 B4
Burnard Cl PL6........ 124 E7
Burnards Ct 7 PL31... 109 D5
Burnett Cl PL12....... 122 D2
Burnett Rd PL6........ 128 F8
Burnham Park Rd PL3... 128 C4
Burniston Cl PL7...... 131 A3
Burnistone Cl PL7..... 131 A3
Burn La PL19.......... 30 E8
Burns Ave PL5......... 124 C2
Burns View PL11....... 65 B5
Burnthouse TR16....... 37 C1
Burnthouse Cotts TR10. 81 C1
Burnthouse Terr TR27.. 142 D5
Burn View EX23........ 104 D6
Burnwithian Terr TR16. 68 D1
BURRATON 122 D4
BURRATON COOMBE..... 122 C2

Burraton Prim Sch PL12 . 122 C3
Burraton Rd PL12 . . . . . 122 C4
Burrator Rd PL20 . . . . . . 42 E3
Burrington Ind Est PL5 . . 124 A1
Burrington Rd PL5 . . . . . 124 A1
Burrington Way PL5 . . . . 124 B1
Burrow Hill PL9 . . . . 135 E6
Burrows The TR26 . . . . 141 A5
BURSDON 3 B6
Bursdon Moor Cross EX39 . 3 B7
Burthallan La TR26 . . . . . 77 A7
Burton Cl PL6 . . . . 125 B6
Burton Ho **15** PL25 . . 114 C3
Burwell Cl PL15 . . . . . . 125 E4
Bury Cl PL15 . . . . 11 B1
Bush Hill PL14 . . . . 36 F2
Bush Pk
  Launceston PL15 . . . . . 106 C5
  Plymouth PL6 . . . . . . 125 F3
BUSVEAL 140 F4
Butcher Park Hill PL19 . 147 B7
Bute Rd PL4 . . . . 129 A4
Butler Cl PL6 . . . . 125 B6
Butney Cnr TR14 . . . . . . 66 E3
Butson Pk TR5 . . . . 68 D8
Buttercup Mdw PL15 . . . 106 E4
Butterdown PL12 . . . . . . 122 B3
Buttlegate PL11 . . . . 64 D5
Button Dr TR8 . . . . 111 B5
Butt Park Rd PL5 . . . . . 124 B3
BUTTSBEAR CROSS 7 F7
Butts La PL35 . . . . 9 D1
Butts Pk PL22 . . . . 112 D2
Butts The
  St Newlyn East TR8 . . . . 56 B7
  Tintagel PL34 . . . . 14 D7
Buzzard Rd PL19 . . . . . 147 D2
Byard Cl PL5 . . . . 123 E1
Byland Rd PL3 . . . . 129 A6
Byron Ave PL5 . . . . 124 C2

C

Cabot Cl PL12 . . . . 122 E2
Cades Parc TR13 . . . . . 146 C6
CADGWITH 103 B4
Cadoc Cl PL28 . . . . 20 E1
Cadogan Cl TR14 . . . . . 138 E1
Cadogan Dr TR14 . . . . . 138 E1
Cadogan Rd TR14 . . . . . 138 E1
Cadover Cl PL6 . . . . . . 125 A1
Caernarvon Gdns PL2 . . 128 B7
Caernarvon Lodge **1**
  TR7 . . . . 110 D5
Calais Rd TR27 . . . . 78 C2
Calartha Rd TR19 . . . . . 75 A1
Calartha Terr **5** TR19 . . 75 A1
Calder Cl PL3 . . . . 129 B6
Caldicot Gdns PL6 . . . . 125 C8
Caledonia Cl **1** PL7 . . 131 B5
CALENICK 137 C1
Calenick St TR1 . . . . . . 137 C4
Cal Hill TR16 . . . . 140 D3
California Gdns
  Plymouth PL3 . . . . . . 129 C6
  Portscatho TR2 . . . . . . 83 B2
CALLESTICK 55 C1
CALLINGTON 39 E5
Callington Com Coll PL17 39 F5
Callington Her Ctr★ PL17 39 E4
Callington Prim Sch **20**
  PL17 . . . . 39 E4
Callington Rd
  Harrowbarrow PL17 . . . 40 C4
  Liskeard PL14 . . . . . . 113 D7
  Saltash PL12 . . . . 122 E3
  Tavistock PL19 . . . . . 147 A4
CALLOOSE 78 D2
Calloose Lane E TR27 . . 78 D1
Calloose Lane W TR27 . . 78 D1
Callywith Gate Ind Est
  PL31 . . . . 35 B2
Calshot Cl TR7 . . . . 111 E7
CALSTOCK 41 A3
Calstock Prim Sch PL18 . 41 A3
Calstock Rd PL18 . . . . . . 41 A6
Calstock Sta PL17 . . . . . 41 A3
Calumet Rd TR14 . . . . . 138 E3
Calver Cl TR10 . . . . . . 144 C8
Calvez Cl PL10 . . . . . . 132 F6
Camaret Dr TR26 . . . . . 141 B4
Cambeak PL35 . . . . 9 C1
Cambeak Cl EX23 . . . . . 10 C6
Camber Rd PL1 . . . . . . 148 A1
CAMBORNE 138 B2
Camborne Cl PL5 . . . . . 124 A5
Camborne Ctr The★
  TR14 . . . . 138 E3
Camborne Geological Mus &
  Art Gal★ TR14 . . . . . 139 B6
Camborne Redruth Com
  Hospl TR15 . . . . 139 C6
Camborne Ret Pk TR15 . 139 B5
Camborne Sch of Mines
  TR15 . . . . 139 B6
Camborne Science &
  International Academy
  TR14 . . . . 138 B3
Camborne Sta TR14 . . . 138 E3
Cambridge La W **5** PL1 . 148 B3
Cambridge Pl TR11 . . . . 145 A3
Cambridge Rd PL2 . . . . 127 F5
CAMBROSE 67 F6

Camden Ct PL4 . . . . . . 149 A3
Camden St PL4 . . . . . . 149 A3
Camel Cl PL28 . . . . 107 D4
Camel Cl PL30 . . . . 109 C6
CAMELFORD 105 C4
Camelford L Ctr PL32 . . 105 C4
Camelford Prim Sch
  PL32 . . . . 105 C3
Camelot Ct **2** TR18 . . 143 E5
Camelot View PL32 . . . 105 C8
CAMELS HEAD 127 E7
Camelside PL27 . . . . . . 108 C5
Camel Valley Vineyard★
  PL30 . . . . 34 B2
Cameo Ct TR14 . . . . . . 138 F4
Cameron Cl EX23 . . . . . 104 D7
Cameron Way PL6 . . . . 125 B1
Camilla Terr PL2 . . . . . 128 D7
Campbell Rd PL9 . . . . . 135 F7
Campbeltown Way TR11 . 145 C3
Camp Cross PL15 . . . . . . 19 F7
Camperdown St PL2 . . . 127 F4
Camperknowle Cl PL10 . 132 F6
Campfield Hill TR1 . . . . 137 D5
Camp Hall Rd TR8 . . . . . 43 B1
Campion Cl
  PL15 . . . . 106 E4
  7 Plymouth PL7 . . . . 131 C5
  Saltash PL12 . . . . 122 D4
Campion Rise PL19 . . . 147 D6
Campion View PL6 . . . . 125 E8
Camullas Way TR7 . . . . 110 A5
Canal Rd PL19 . . . . 147 B5
Candish Dr PL9 . . . . . . 136 D7
Canefields Ave PL7 . . . 131 B3
Canhaye Cl PL7 . . . . . . 131 A3
CANNALIGGEY 32 E4
Cannamanning Rd **3**
  PL26 . . . . 59 D7
Canna Park Sta★ PL15 . . 18 D3
Cann Gdns PL6 . . . . . . 124 D6
Cannis Rd PL25 . . . . . . 114 E6
Cannon Hill PL14 . . . . . 113 C5
Cannons Pl TR13 . . . . . 146 D7
Cannon St PL1 . . . . 127 D2
Cannon Terr **2** PL14 . . 113 C5
Cann Woods Nature
  Reserve★ PL5 . . . . . . 124 C6
Cann Wood View PL6 . . 125 E7
CANONSTOWN 77 C2
Canons Way PL19 . . . . . 147 A3
Canterbury Dr PL5 . . . . 124 B4
Cantillion Cl PL27 . . . . . 21 E3
Canton PL26 . . . . 85 D5
Canyke Rd PL31 . . . . . . 48 D8
Cape Cl TR19 . . . . 86 E6
Cape Cornwall Comp Sch
  TR19 . . . . 86 E6
Cape Cornwall Rd TR19 . 86 E6
Cape Cornwall St TR19 . 86 E6
Cape Terr TR19 . . . . 86 E6
Cape Trelew TR19 . . . . . 86 E6
Captains Gdns PL5 . . . . 124 E1
Captains Ho PL26 . . . . . 73 C3
Captain's Wlk TR11 . . . 145 A2
Caradon Bsns Ctr **8**
  PL14 . . . . 113 C5
Caradon Cl
  9 Callington PL17 . . . 39 E4
  1 Pensilva PL14 . . . . 38 E4
  Plymouth PL6 . . . . . . 125 A5
Caradon Ct **2** PL20 . . . 42 C4
Caradon Dr PL14 . . . . . 113 B6
Caradon Hts
  Liskeard PL14 . . . . . . 113 D7
  Tremar PL14 . . . . 38 B4
Caradon Terr PL12 . . . . 122 E3
CARADON TOWN 38 E6
Caradon View PL14 . . . . 37 F3
Carbeile Rd PL11 . . . . . 127 A2
Carbes La PL22 . . . . . . 112 C2
CARBIS 47 A2
CARBIS BAY 141 D3
Carbis Bay Sta TR26 . . 141 D2
Carbis Ct TR15 . . . . . . 140 A5
Carboth La PL15 . . . . . 106 B5
CARCLAZE 114 E6
Carclaze Com Prim Sch
  PL25 . . . . 114 E6
Carclaze Ind Est PL25 . . 114 E7
Carclaze Rd PL25 . . . . . 114 E6
Carclew Ave TR7 . . . . . 110 C6
Carclew Rd TR11 . . . . . . 81 F4
Carclew St TR1 . . . . . . 137 D3
Carclew Terr
  Devoran TR3 . . . . 81 F6
  Truro TR1 . . . . 137 D3
Cardell Rd PL31 . . . . . . 109 D5
Cardell Way TR7 . . . . . 111 A5
Cardiff Cl PL7 . . . . 131 B4
Cardigan Rd PL6 . . . . . 125 C1
Cardinal Ave PL5 . . . . . 127 D8
CARDINHAM 35 E3
Cardinham Prim Sch
  PL30 . . . . 35 E3
Cardinham Woods Forest
  Walks★ PL30 . . . . 35 C1
Cardinnis Gn **2** PL14 . . 113 D6
Cardinnis Rd TR18 . . . . 143 B5
Cardrew Cl TR15 . . . . . 140 B6
Cardrew Dr TR15 . . . . . 140 D6
Cardrew Ind Est TR15 . . 140 C7
Cardrew La **1** TR15 . . . 140 D7
Cardrew Terr TR15 . . . . 140 D6
Cardrew Way TR15 . . . . 140 D7
Cardwen Est PL13 . . . . . 62 C6

Careswell Ave PL2 . . . . 127 F8
Carew Ave PL5 . . . . 124 B3
Carew Cl
  Crafthole PL11 . . . . 65 B5
  St Day TR16 . . . . 68 E1
Carew Gdns
  Plymouth PL5 . . . . . . 124 B3
  Saltash PL12 . . . . 122 D3
Carew Gr PL5 . . . . 124 B3
Carew-Pole Cl TR1 . . . . 137 E3
Carew Rd
  St Day TR16 . . . . 68 D1
  Truro TR1 . . . . 137 C5
Carew Terr PL11 . . . . . . 127 B2
Carew Wharf PL11 . . . . 127 C2
Carew Wharf Bsns Ctr
  PL11 . . . . 127 C2
Carey Ct PL12 . . . . 122 E3
Carey Pk
  Helston TR13 . . . . 146 B7
  Polperro PL13 . . . . 62 E2
  Truro TR1 . . . . 137 C4
CARFURY 76 A1
Cargoll Rd TR8 . . . . 56 B7
CARGREEN 119 A2
Cargwyn PL26 . . . . 59 D6
Cargy Cl TR8 . . . . 55 D8
CARHARRACK 80 F8
Carisbrooke Rd PL6 . . . 125 C1
Carkeek's Cl PL26 . . . . . 58 B3
CARKEEL 122 C5
Carkeel Barns PL12 . . . 122 C5
Carkeel Ind Est PL12 . . 122 D5
Carknown Gdns TR15 . . 140 D3
Carland Cross TR8 . . . . . 56 D4
CARLEEN 90 F5
CARLIDNACK 93 E4
Carlidnack Cl TR11 . . . . 93 D3
Carlidnack La TR11 . . . . 93 D4
Carlidnack Rd TR11 . . . . 93 E4
Carlisle Rd PL5 . . . . . . 124 D3
CARLOGGAS
  Foxhole 58 C5
  Penwithick 59 D7
  St Mawgan 45 A8
Carloggas Cl TR8 . . . . . . 45 A8
Carloggas Farm TR8 . . . 45 A8
Carloggas Gr **6** TR9 . . . 45 D6
Carloggas Way **10** TR9 . 45 D6
Carlton Cl PL3 . . . . 129 B5
Carlton Ho **7** PL31 . . . 109 E5
Carlton Terr
  Plymouth, Lipson PL4 . . 149 B3
  Plymouth, Weston Mill PL5 127 E8
Carlton Vills PL12 . . . . . 53 E4
CARLUDDON 59 D6
CARLYON BAY 115 E3
Carlyon Cl
  Looe PL13 . . . . 62 A7
  Threemilestone TR3 . . . 69 D3
  Torpoint PL11 . . . . . . 126 F4
  11 Truro TR1 . . . . . . 137 C4
Carlyon Ct TR3 . . . . 82 B8
Carlyon Ho TR1 . . . . 69 E4
Carlyon Rd
  Playing Place TR3 . . . . . 82 B8
  St Austell PL25 . . . . . . 114 E4
  Truro TR1 . . . . 137 C5
Carmarthen Rd PL4 . . . 129 B2
Carmel Gdns PL11 . . . . 147 A5
Carmen Sq **10** TR18 . . 143 C7
Carminow Cross PL30 . . 48 D8
Carminowe Cres **8**
  TR18 . . . . 143 D5
Carminow Rd PL31 . . . . 48 D8
Carminow Way TR7 . . . 111 A7
Carnanton Moor TR15 . . 139 C3
Carn ARTHEN 139 B2
Carnarthen Rd **1** TR14 . 138 E2
Carnarthen St TR14 . . . 138 E2
Carn Ave TR14 . . . . 138 F4
Carn Bargus PL26 . . . . . 58 E8
Carn Bosavern TR19 . . . 86 F6
Carn Bosavern Cl TR19 . 86 F6
Carn Brae L Ctr TR15 . . 139 C5
Carn Brea Ho TR15 . . . . 139 C5
Carn Brea La TR15 . . . . 139 C5
CARN BREA VILLAGE . . . 139 F5
Carn Brea Village TR15 . 139 F5
Carn Cl TR27 . . . . 78 E1
Carncrows Rd TR26 . . . 141 C6
Carncrows St TR26 . . . . 141 C6
CARNE
  St Dennis 46 C1
  Veryan 83 F5
Carne Cross PL24 . . . . . 59 F7
Carne Ct PL26 . . . . 58 C8
Carnedon PL14 . . . . 38 C7
Carnego La TR8 . . . . 57 B6
Carne Hill
  St Dennis PL26 . . . . . . 46 C1
  Trewoon PL25 . . . . 58 F4
Carnellis Rd **7** TR26 . . 141 A5
Carne Mdws TR2 . . . . . . 70 F5
CARN ENTRAL 139 A2
Carne Rd TR18 . . . . 143 C3
Carne's Bldgs **11** TR18 . 143 E4
Carnes Ct TR11 . . . . . . 145 C2
Carne's Flats TR24 . . . . 60 B5
Carneton Cl TR8 . . . . . . 43 D4
Carn Euny Settlement★
  TR20 . . . . 87 C3
Carne View Cl TR14 . . . 138 F5
Carne View Rd PL14 . . . 71 D6
Carnglaze Caverns★ PL14 36 F1

Carnglaze Cl PL14 . . . . 113 E6
Carn Gloose Rd TR19 . . . 86 D6
Carn Gwavas Terr TR18 . 143 D1
CARNHELL GREEN 78 F4
Carnhell Rd TR14, TR27 . 78 F4
CARNHOT 68 F4
Carninney La TR26 . . . . 141 C1
CARNKIE 139 F2
CARNKIEF 55 D3
Carn Marth La TR16 . . . 140 E2
Carnock Rd PL2 . . . . . . 128 D8
Carnon Cres **13** TR3 . . 81 F7
CARNON DOWNS 82 A7
Carnon Terr TR3 . . . . . . 81 F6
Carnoustie Dr PL12 . . . 122 C2
Carn Rock TR10 . . . . . . 144 D7
Carn Ros TR19 . . . . 74 F1
Carnsew Cl TR10 . . . . . . 81 C1
Carnsew Cres TR10 . . . . 81 C1
Carnsew Ct TR27 . . . . . 142 B5
Carnsew Mdw TR27 . . . 142 A5
Carnsew Rd TR27 . . . . . 142 A5
Carnsmerry PL26 . . . . . . 47 C1
Carnsmerry Cres PL25 . 114 E4
Carnstabba Rd **13** TR26 . 77 A6
Carntiscoe Workshops
  TR27 . . . . 77 C2
Carn Todden TR19 . . . . . 88 D1
CARN TOWAN 96 C7
Carn View TR16 . . . . 80 F6
Carn View Terr TR19 . . . 75 A1
CARNYORTH 86 F8
Carnyorth Hill TR19 . . . . 86 F8
Carnyorth Terr TR19 . . . 86 F8
Carolina Gdns PL2 . . . . 127 F7
Caroline Cl TR27 . . . . . 142 E7
Caroline Row TR27 . . . . 142 E7
CARPALLA 58 D4
Carpalla Rd PL26 . . . . . . 58 D5
Carpalla Terr PL26 . . . . . 58 D5
Carpenter Rd PL9 . . . . . 135 F8
Carpmael Ave TR8 . . . . 111 B4
Carracawn Cross PL12 . . 64 D8
Carrack Dhu **37** TR26 . . 141 B6
Carrack Dhu Est **36** TR26 141 B6
Carrack Gladden TR26 . . 141 D2
Carradale Rd PL6 . . . . . 129 C7
Carrack Widden **25** TR26 141 B5
Carrallack Mews TR19 . . 86 E6
Carrallack Terr TR19 . . . 86 E5
Carriage Ho The TR3 . . . 69 F1
Carriage Parc TR4 . . . . . 55 D4
Carrickowel Cres **1**
  PL25 . . . . 115 A5
Carrick Rd TR11 . . . . . . 144 E2
Carrick Way TR2 . . . . . . 95 A6
Carrine Rd TR1 . . . . 69 F3
Carrisbrooke Way PL12 . 122 B3
Carrnown Gdns TR15 . . 140 D3
Carroll Rd PL5 . . . . 124 C2
Carrolls Way PL9 . . . . . 136 A5
Carron La PL6 . . . . 121 D1
Carsize La TR27 . . . . 78 E1
Carter Cl TR7 . . . . 111 A5
Carteret Rd EX23 . . . . . 104 C3
CARTHEW 59 B6
Carthew Cl
  Liskeard PL14 . . . . . . 113 D5
  St Ives TR26 . . . . 141 A6
Carthew Ct TR26 . . . . . 141 A6
Carthew La
  Four Lanes TR13 . . . . . 80 A3
  Praze-an-Beeble TR13 . . 79 F2
Carthew Terr TR26 . . . . 141 A6
Carthew Way TR26 . . . . 141 A6
Carvath Ho PL25 . . . . . 114 D3
Carvedras Ct **1** TR1 . . 137 C4
Carvossa St TR20 . . . . . 89 B8
Carvoza Rd TR1 . . . . . . 137 D5
Carvynick Cotts TR8 . . . 57 A7
Carwinard Cl TR27 . . . . . 78 C5
Carwinion Bamboo Gdn★
  TR11 . . . . 93 E3
Carwinion Rd TR11 . . . . 93 E3
Carwin La TR27 . . . . 78 C5
Carwin Rise
  Angarrack TR27 . . . . . . 78 C5
  Hayle TR27 . . . . 142 E7
Carwollen Rd PL25 . . . . 114 E7
Carworgie Ct **10** TR9 . . 45 E2
Carworgie Manor TR8 . . 45 D3
Carworgie Way **7** TR9 . 45 E2
CARWYNNEN 79 B3
Carwynnen Cl TR14 . . . . 79 B3
CARZISE 78 C1
Casey La PL13 . . . . 62 D5
CASTALLACK 97 F6
Castel Wary Cl TR13 . . . 146 B5
Casterills Rd TR13 . . . . 146 D4
Castings Dr **2** PL25 . . . 115 A3
Castle Acre Gdns PL3 . . 129 B5
Castle Bank Gdns PL3 . . 129 B5
Castle Barbican PL7 . . . 130 E4
Castle Bldgs PL12 . . . . 122 D4
Castle Canyke Rd PL31 . 109 F3
Castle Carey Gdns PL3 . 129 B5
Castle Cl TR11 . . . . 145 E3
Castle Ct
  Praa Sands TR20 . . . . . 90 C3
  Saltash PL12 . . . . 122 C2
Castle Dr
  Bodmin PL31 . . . . 109 F5
  Falmouth TR11 . . . . . 145 F2
  Praa Sands TR20 . . . . . 90 B3
  St Mawes TR2 . . . . 94 F5
Castle Dyke PL15 . . . . . 106 C6
CASTLE GATE 76 F1

Castle Gdns PL14 . . . . . 113 C6
Castle Gn TR13 . . . . . . 146 B5
Castlehayes Gdns PL7 . . 130 E4
Castle Hill
  Falmouth TR11 . . . . . 145 D3
  Helston TR13 . . . . 146 B5
  6 Liskeard PL14 . . . . 113 C6
  Lostwithiel PL22 . . . . . 112 C2
  Truro TR1 . . . . 122 C1
Castle Hill Ct
  Bodmin PL31 . . . . 109 E5
  7 Liskeard PL14 . . . . 113 C6
Castle Hill Gdns PL31 . . 109 F5
CASTLE HORNECK 143 B5
Castle Horneck Cl TR18 . 143 C5
Castle Horneck Rd TR18 . 143 C5
Castle Hts **3** PL34 . . . . 14 C7
Castle La
  Liskeard PL14 . . . . . . 113 C6
  Plymouth PL7 . . . . . . 130 E4
Castle Mdws
  Launceston PL15 . . . . 106 A4
  2 St Agnes TR5 . . . . 54 D1
Castlemead Cl PL12 . . . 122 D3
Castlemead Dr PL12 . . . 122 D3
Castle Meadows Ct **3**
  TR5 . . . . 54 D1
Castle Rd
  Longrock TR20 . . . . . . 88 F8
  Ludgvan TR20 . . . . 89 A8
  Penzance TR18 . . . . . 143 E7
  Tintagel PL34 . . . . 14 C7
Castle Rise
  Plymouth PL3 . . . . . . 129 B4
  Saltash PL12 . . . . 122 D1
Castle Rock PL29 . . . . . . 22 D8
Castle St
  Bodmin PL31 . . . . 109 F5
  Launceston PL15 . . . . 106 C6
  Liskeard PL14 . . . . . . 113 C6
  Looe PL13 . . . . 117 D3
  Plymouth PL1 . . . . . . 149 A2
  Truro TR1 . . . . 137 C4
Castleton Cl PL3 . . . . . 129 A4
Castle View
  10 Liskeard PL14 . . . 113 C6
  Longrock TR20 . . . . . . 88 F6
  Lostwithiel PL22 . . . . . 112 E3
  Saltash PL12 . . . . 122 D1
  Tintagel PL34 . . . . 14 C7
Castle View Cl TR15 . . . 140 B6
Castle View Pk TR11 . . . 93 D3
Caswarth Terr PL28 . . . 107 D5
Catalina Row PL27 . . . . 31 F3
Catalina Vills PL9 . . . . . 135 A6
CATCHALL 97 D8
Catchfrench Cres PL14 . 113 E6
Cathcart Ave PL4 . . . . . 129 B2
Cathebedron Rd
  Carnhell Green TR14 . . . 78 F4
  Praze-an-Beeble TR14 . . 79 A3
Cathedral Church of the
  Blessed Virgin Mary★
  TR1 . . . . 137 D4
Cathedral La **13** TR1 . . 137 D4
Cathedral of St Mary &
  St Boniface PL1 . . . . 148 B3
Cathedral School of St Mary
  PL1 . . . . 148 B3
Cathedral St PL1 . . . . . 148 B3
Cathedral View TR1 . . . 137 C6
Catherine Cl EX23 . . . . 104 F4
Catherine Pk PL13 . . . . . 62 E5
Catherine's Hill PL15 . . 106 A6
Catherine St PL1 . . . . . 148 C2
CATTEDOWN 149 C1
Catterick Cl PL5 . . . . . 123 E5
Cattewater Rd PL4 . . . . 129 B1
Caudledown La PL26 . . . 59 C8
Caunter Rd PL14 . . . . . 113 D6
Causeland Sta PL14 . . . . 51 B2
Causeway Ho PL1 . . . . . 137 D4
Causewayhead TR18 . . . 143 E5
Causeway The
  Falmouth TR11 . . . . . 144 F4
  Hayle TR27 . . . . 142 A4
Causley Cl PL15 . . . . . . 106 C7
Cavendish Cres TR7 . . . 111 B5
CAWSAND 133 B2
Caxton Gdns PL5 . . . . . 124 C1
Cayforth Flats TR16 . . . . 67 C6
Cayley Way PL5 . . . . . . 123 F2
Cecil Ave PL4 . . . . 149 C4
Cecil Cotts PL1 . . . . . . 148 A3
Cecil St PL1 . . . . 148 B3
Cedar Ave PL9 . . . . 135 C5
Cedar Cl
  21 Callington PL17 . . 39 F4
  Torpoint PL11 . . . . . . 126 F2
Cedarcroft Rd PL2 . . . . 128 B7
Cedar Dr
  Camborne TR14 . . . . . 139 A5
  Saltash PL12 . . . . 122 F2
Cedar Dr PL11 . . . . 126 F2
Cedar Gr EX23 . . . . 104 F4
Cedar House Flats TR26 . 77 E4
Cedars The TR1 . . . . . . 137 C2
Celandine Gdns PL7 . . . 131 C5
Celia Hts PL31 . . . . 109 F2
Celtic Rd PL17 . . . . 39 F4
Cemetery Rd PL18 . . . . . 40 F5
Centenary Row Middle
  TR14 . . . . 138 E3
Centenary Row W **2**
  TR14 . . . . 138 E3
Centenary St TR14 . . . . 138 E3
Central Ave PL25 . . . . . 114 E5
Central Cl PL26 . . . . 58 B4

Cen–Chy 155

Central Park Ave PL4 .... 148 C4
Central Rd
Holywell TR8 .... 43 B1
Plymouth PL1 .... 148 B1
Central Sq TR7 .... 110 D6
Central Treviscoe PL26 ... 58 A7
Century Cl
Helston TR13 .... 146 D8
St Austell PL25 .... 114 F6
Century Ct TR7 .... 111 C7
Century La TR2 .... 83 F6
Century Sq 6 PL14 .... 38 E4
CHACEWATER 68 F3
Chacewater Hill TR4 .... 69 A3
Chacewater Prim Sch
TR4 .... 69 A3
CHADDLEWOOD 131 B6
Chaddlewood Ave PL4 .... 149 B3
Chaddlewood Cl PL7 .... 131 A4
Chaddlewood Ho PL7 ... 131 B5
Chaddlewood Prim Sch
PL7 .... 131 A5
Chadwick Parc TR15 .... 140 B6
Chagford Wlk PL6 .... 129 E8
Chainwalk Dr TR1 .... 137 C6
Chalets The TR18 .... 88 E6
Chalet The PL11 .... 64 C4
Challacombe Gdns TR10. 144 C8
Challenger Quay 12
TR11 .... 145 C3
Challgood Cl 1 PL9 .... 135 F5
Challgood Rise PL9 .... 135 F5
Challis Ave TR8 .... 45 A8
Challock Cl PL6 .... 125 D4
Chamberlayne Dr PL7 ... 130 E6
Champion's Ct TR13 .... 146 B6
Chancery Cl TR4 .... 70 D8
Chancery La 23 TR18 .... 143 E5
Chandlers Wlk PL25 .... 115 A3
Chandos Pl 12 PL25 .... 114 C3
Channel Park Ave PL3 ... 129 B5
Channel View
Polruan PL23 .... 116 D2
St Austell PL25 .... 115 A6
St Ives TR26 .... 141 A6
Channel View Terr
Plymouth PL4 .... 149 C4
4 Redruth TR15 .... 140 C4
Channon Rd PL12 .... 122 C4
Chantry Ct PL7 .... 130 B5
Chantry La PL13 .... 117 E4
CHAPEL
Launceston 106 A5
Quintrell Downs 111 E4
Chapel Cl
Camborne, Kehelland
TR14 .... 66 F1
Camborne, Tuckingmill
TR14 .... 139 A4
Coad's Green PL15 .... 27 D3
Connor Downs TR27 .... 78 D6
Crantock TR8 .... 110 A3
Gunnislake PL18 .... 40 E5
4 Horrabridge PL20 .... 42 C4
Lanivet PL30 .... 47 E6
St Just in Roseland TR2 .... 82 F2
Chapel Cnr EX22 .... 8 A5
Chapel Cotts EX23 .... 4 C8
Chapel Cres TR4 .... 56 A2
Chapel Ct
Camborne TR14 .... 138 F4
Padstow PL28 .... 107 D5
9 Redruth TR15 .... 140 B5
Chapeldown Rd PL11 .... 127 A2
Chapel Farm TR14 .... 79 E5
Chapel Field PL25 .... 115 B5
Chapel Gn PL26 .... 59 A1
Chapel Ground PL13 .... 117 C3
Chapel Hill
Camborne, Brea TR14 .... 139 A3
Camborne, Tregajorran
TR15 .... 139 C4
Gweek TR12 .... 92 C2
Hayle TR27 .... 142 C6
Lanner TR16 .... 80 D6
Launceston PL15 .... 106 B5
Newquay TR7 .... 110 D6
Perranporth TR6 .... 55 B4
Polgooth PL26 .... 59 A1
Ponsanooth TR3 .... 81 B4
Porthtowan TR4 .... 68 A5
Redruth TR16 .... 68 A4
St Erth TR27 .... 142 A1
Sticker PL26 .... 58 F1
Truro TR1 .... 137 B4
Chapel La
Bodmin PL31 .... 109 D5
Goldsithney TR20 .... 89 F5
Hayle TR27 .... 142 D6
Horrabridge PL20 .... 42 C4
Lizard TR12 .... 102 F2
Penryn TR10 .... 144 C7
Polruan PL23 .... 116 D2
St Austell PL25 .... 115 C6
St Mabyn PL30 .... 34 D8
St Teath PL30 .... 23 F6
5 Wadebridge PL27 .... 108 B5
Chapel Mdw
Buckland Monachorum
PL20 .... 41 F3
Perranarworthal TR3 .... 81 D6
Chapel Park Gdns PL15 .. 106 B5
Chapel Park Terr PL15 .. 106 B5
Chapel Pk PL15 .... 106 B5
Chapel Pl
Pillaton PL12 .... 53 B7
16 Truro TR1 .... 137 D4
Chapel Point La PL26 .... 73 C2
Chapel Rd
Camborne TR14 .... 139 A4
Foxhole PL26 .... 58 D5
Heamoor TR18 .... 143 C8
Indian Queens TR9 .... 45 E1
Leedstown TR27 .... 78 E1
2 Par PL24 .... 60 C4
Roche PL26 .... 46 F3
Saltash PL12 .... 122 B3
St Just TR19 .... 86 E6
St Tudy PL30 .... 23 E3
Chapel Row
Praze-an-Beeble TR14 .... 79 B2
2 Redruth TR15 .... 140 B5
Tremar PL14 .... 38 A3
Truro TR1 .... 137 D4
Widegates PL13 .... 63 F8
Chapel Sq
Crowlas TR20 .... 89 B8
Mevagissey PL26 .... 73 C3
Troon TR14 .... 79 E5
Chapel St
4 Bere Alston PL20 .... 41 B1
4 Callington PL17 .... 39 F4
Camborne TR14 .... 138 D2
Camelford PL32 .... 105 C4
Grimscott EX23 .... 5 B2
Gunnislake PL18 .... 40 F6
Lifton PL16 .... 19 F4
Marazion TR17 .... 89 B5
Mevagissey PL26 .... 73 C3
21 Mousehole TR19 .... 88 C1
9 Newlyn TR18 .... 143 C2
Penzance TR18 .... 143 E5
Plymouth, Mount Wise PL1 127 E2
Plymouth PL4 .... 149 A3
Probus TR2 .... 71 C6
Redruth TR15 .... 140 B5
St Day TR16 .... 68 D1
St Ives TR26 .... 141 B5
St Just TR19 .... 86 E6
Tavistock PL19 .... 147 B5
Chapel Terr
Camborne TR15 .... 139 D6
Devoran TR3 .... 81 F6
Falmouth TR11 .... 145 B4
Hayle TR27 .... 142 B5
Par PL24 .... 60 B6
9 Porthleven TR13 .... 98 B8
Portreath TR16 .... 67 C6
Redruth, Carn Brea Village
TR15 .... 139 F5
Redruth TR15 .... 140 D2
Ruan Minor TR12 .... 103 A5
St Day TR16 .... 68 E1
10 St Mawes TR2 .... 95 A6
Trewellard TR19 .... 86 F8
CHAPEL TOWN 57 B6
Chapel Town Bsns Pk
TR8 .... 57 B7
Chapel Town Cl TR11 .... 93 D4
Chapel Way PL3 .... 129 A6
CHAPLE AMBLE 22 D2
Chapman Ct PL12 .... 122 B3
Chapmans Ope PL1 .... 127 D2
CHAPMAN'S WELL 13 E4
Chapmans Wy PL25 .... 114 E4
Charaton Cross PL14 .... 38 F4
Chard Barton PL5 .... 124 B3
Chard Rd PL5 .... 123 D2
Chard Terr 6 TR11 .... 145 A3
Charfield Dr PL6 .... 129 A8
Chariot Rd TR15 .... 139 E6
Charles Ave TR11 .... 144 E2
Charles Bassett Cl 6
TR13 .... 146 C5
Charles Cl PL25 .... 114 F3
Charles Cross PL4 .... 149 A3
Charles St
Bugle PL26 .... 47 C1
Newlyn TR18 .... 143 C3
Plymouth PL4 .... 149 A3
Truro TR1 .... 137 C4
Charles Terr PL3 .... 129 A6
CHARLESTOWN 115 B2
Charlestown Prim Sch
PL25 .... 115 C3
Charlestown Rd PL25 ... 115 B3
Charlestown Shipwreck &
Heritage Ctr* PL25 .... 115 B2
Charlotte Cl TR4 .... 68 C6
Charlotte Gardens PL25 . 114 F3
Charlotte St PL2 .... 127 E4
Charlton Cres PL6 .... 125 A2
Charlton Rd PL6 .... 125 A3
Charnhill Cl PL9 .... 136 A6
Charnhill Way PL9 .... 136 A6
Charter Cl TR13 .... 146 C4
Charter Ct TR10 .... 144 D7
Charter Way PL14 .... 113 E6
Chateau Cl PL26 .... 46 D1
Chatsworth Gdns PL5 ... 123 F3
Chatsworth Way PL25 ... 115 C2
Chaucer Rd PL19 .... 147 D5
Chaucer Way PL5 .... 124 C1
Chawleigh Cl PL18 .... 40 F5
Chedworth St PL4 .... 149 A3
Chegwin Gdns TR7 .... 110 E5
Chegwins Hill PL26 .... 58 D5
Chegwyn Gdns 6 TR5 .... 54 C1
Chegwyns PL26 .... 58 D5
Chelfham Bere Alston Prim
Sch PL20 .... 41 B1
Chelfham Kilworthy House
PL19 .... 30 E3
Chelfham Senior Sch
PL20 .... 40 F3
Chellean Vean TR4 .... 81 C7
Chellew Rd TR1 .... 137 F5
Chelmer Cl PL7 .... 131 A5
Chelmsford Pl PL5 .... 124 C4
Chelson Gdns PL6 .... 125 E3
Cheltenham Pl
Newquay TR7 .... 110 D6
Plymouth PL4 .... 149 B4
Chelwood Gr PL7 .... 130 F5
CHENHALLS 142 A2
Chenhalls Cl TR27 .... 77 E2
Chenhalls Rd TR27 .... 142 A2
Chenoweth Cl TR14 .... 138 C4
Chepstow Ave PL6 .... 125 C8
Chequer Tree Ct PL18 .... 40 F5
Chequetts Cl 10 PL17 .... 39 E4
Cheriton Cl PL5 .... 124 A3
Cherrill Gdns EX23 .... 104 E7
Cherrington TR7 .... 110 B5
Cherry Cross EX22 .... 12 B7
Cherry Gdns 14 TR18 .... 143 E5
Cherry Gdn St 15 TR19 ... 88 C1
Cherry Pk PL7 .... 131 A3
Cherry Tree Cl PL31 .... 109 B4
Cherrytree Ho TR18 .... 143 C5
Cherry Tree La PL7 .... 131 A4
Cherry Tree Mews PL25 . 114 D3
Cheshire Dr PL6 .... 124 D6
Chesnut Cl PL12 .... 122 D4
Chester Ct TR7 .... 111 A6
Chesterfield Rd PL3 .... 129 B4
Chester Pl 4 PL4 .... 128 E4
Chester Rd TR7 .... 111 A6
Chesterton Cl PL5 .... 124 C3
Chesterton Ct PL27 .... 108 A6
Chesterton Pl TR7 .... 111 A7
Chestnut Ave PL9 .... 135 C5
Chestnut Cl
Callington PL17 .... 40 A4
Falmouth TR11 .... 144 F5
Lamerton PL19 .... 30 A4
St Tudy PL30 .... 23 E3
Tavistock PL19 .... 147 D2
Torpoint PL11 .... 126 F3
24 Yelverton PL20 .... 41 B1
Chestnut Gr PL31 .... 109 B4
Chestnut Rd PL3 .... 128 D7
Chestnut Terr PL19 .... 30 A4
Cheviot Rd TR7 .... 110 E4
Chichester Cl PL26 .... 58 E5
Chichester Cres
Newquay TR7 .... 110 F4
Saltash PL12 .... 122 E1
Chichester Ct PL20 .... 42 C4
Chichester Ho PL1 .... 148 B2
Childrey Gdns PL6 .... 125 C1
Childrey Wlk PL6 .... 125 C1
Chili Rd TR15 .... 139 D6
CHILLATON 29 F8
CHILSWORTHY 40 E7
Chilton Cl PL6 .... 129 B7
China Clay Ctry Pk* PL26 59 A7
Chings Alley 13 PL15 .... 106 C6
Chipponds Dr PL25 .... 114 A3
Chirgwin Ct 22 TR18 .... 143 E5
Chirgwin Rd TR1 .... 137 E4
Chisholme Cl PL25 .... 114 D3
Chisholme Ct PL25 .... 114 D3
Chittleburn Bsns Pk PL8 136 F6
Chittleburn Cross PL8 ... 136 E5
Chittleburn Hill PL8 .... 136 E5
Chivenor Ave PL5 .... 123 D4
Chiverton Cl TR20 .... 89 F4
Chiverton Cross
Blackwater TR4 .... 68 F5
Rosudgeon TR20 .... 89 F4
Chiverton Greenacres
TR5 .... 68 D8
Chiverton Way TR20 .... 89 F4
Chollacott Cl PL19 .... 147 C4
Chollacott La PL19 .... 147 D3
Chough Cl
Falmouth TR11 .... 144 E4
Launceston PL15 .... 106 E4
Chough Cres PL25 .... 114 F4
Choughs Cl TR14 .... 138 B3
Christa Ct PL14 .... 38 D7
Christian Mill Bsns Pk
PL6 .... 124 E4
Christian Way TR7 .... 111 C7
Chubb Dr PL3 .... 128 B4
Chudleigh Rd PL4 .... 129 A4
Chun Castle* TR20 .... 87 C8
Church Av PL23 .... 116 D4
CHURCHBRIDGE 50 F1
Church Cl
Blisland PL30 .... 35 D8
Lelant TR26 .... 77 E4
Plymouth PL7 .... 130 B7
Trispen TR4 .... 56 D1
CHURCH COMBE 140 A2
CHURCH COVE 103 A2
Church Cove Rd TR12 ... 103 A2
Church Ct PL6 .... 125 A7
Church End PL13 .... 117 D3
Churchfield Cl TR20 .... 89 A8
Churchfield Pl PL24 .... 60 B5
Churchfields Rd TR8 .... 55 D8
Church Gate 3 PL14 .... 113 C5
Church Hill
Calstock PL18 .... 41 A3
Chacewater TR4 .... 68 F2
Golant PL23 .... 61 B6
Helston TR13 .... 146 C7
Herodsfoot PL14 .... 50 E3
Hessenford PL11, PL12 .... 64 B8
Ludgvan TR20 .... 89 A8
Milton Combe PL20 .... 41 F1
Penryn TR10 .... 144 D8
Church Hill *continued*
4 Pensilva PL14 .... 38 E4
Plymouth PL6 .... 125 B1
Port Isaac PL29 .... 22 D7
St Day TR16 .... 68 E1
Sticker PL26 .... 58 F1
7 St Mawes TR2 .... 95 A6
Tavistock PL19 .... 147 E2
Tintagel PL34 .... 14 C7
Church Hill Rd PL9 .... 135 A6
Church Ho PL12 .... 123 A2
Churchill Rd PL19 .... 147 D2
Churchill Way
10 Penwithick PL26 .... 59 D7
Plymouth PL3 .... 128 E6
Churchill Wlk PL12 .... 122 E1
Church La
Bodmin PL31 .... 109 E5
Bude EX23 .... 104 D5
Calstock PL18 .... 41 A3
Camborne TR14 .... 138 D3
Cargreen PL12 .... 119 A1
Flushing TR11 .... 145 B7
Helston TR13 .... 146 B6
Lelant TR26 .... 77 E4
Lostwithiel PL22 .... 112 C2
Mevagissey PL26 .... 73 C4
Padstow PL28 .... 107 D5
St Columb Minor TR7 .... 111 E7
St John PL11 .... 132 B8
Tavistock PL19 .... 147 C5
Churchlands PL13 .... 117 D5
Churchlands Cl PL6 .... 125 E7
Churchlands Rd PL6 .... 125 E8
Church Lea
Launceston PL15 .... 106 A7
Tavistock PL19 .... 147 E2
Church Mews
Stithians TR3 .... 80 F3
Week St Mary EX22 .... 11 E8
Church Park Ct PL6 .... 125 E8
Church Park Mews PL27. 108 B4
Church Park Rd
Crackington Haven EX23 ... 10 C6
Plymouth PL6 .... 125 E8
Church Path EX23 .... 104 C5
Church Pk
Bodmin PL31 .... 109 F5
Horrabridge PL20 .... 42 C4
Lerryn PL22 .... 61 D8
St Mellion PL12 .... 53 D8
Church Pl
Liskeard PL14 .... 113 C5
18 St Ives TR26 .... 141 B6
Church Rd
Camborne TR15 .... 139 B6
Cury TR12 .... 99 A4
Four Lanes TR16 .... 80 A5
Heamoor TR18 .... 143 C7
Illogan TR16 .... 67 E4
Lanivet PL30 .... 47 E7
Launceston PL15 .... 18 F6
Lelant TR26 .... 77 E4
Mabe Burnthouse TR10 .... 93 C8
Madron TR20 .... 143 A8
Mount Hawke TR4 .... 68 C6
Mylor Bridge TR11 .... 82 B2
Pendeen TR19 .... 75 A1
Penponds TR14 .... 138 B1
Penryn TR10 .... 144 C8
Perranarworthal TR3 .... 81 D5
Plymouth, Plympton PL7 .. 130 F4
Plymouth, Plymstock PL9 . 135 F7
Saltash PL12 .... 122 D2
Shortlanesend TR4 .... 69 F6
St Austell PL25 .... 115 B3
St Dennis PL26 .... 46 C1
Stithians TR3 .... 80 F4
St Tudy PL30 .... 23 E3
Tideford PL12 .... 52 F2
Church Row
Carharrack TR16 .... 80 F8
Lanner TR16 .... 80 D6
3 Porthleven TR13 .... 98 B8
Sheviock PL11 .... 65 C6
Church Row La PL5 .... 124 C6
Church Sq
8 Bodmin PL31 .... 109 E5
Constantine TR11 .... 92 F4
St Just TR19 .... 86 F6
4 Stratton EX23 .... 4 E1
Church St
Callington PL17 .... 39 E4
Calstock PL18 .... 41 A3
Camborne TR14 .... 138 D3
Carharrack TR16 .... 80 F8
Falmouth TR11 .... 145 B4
Gorran Haven PL26 .... 85 D5
Helston TR13 .... 146 B6
Landrake PL12 .... 53 C3
Launceston PL15 .... 106 C6
Liskeard PL14 .... 113 C5
Looe, East Looe PL13 .... 117 D3
Looe, West Looe PL13 .... 117 C3
Mevagissey PL26 .... 73 C3
15 Newlyn TR18 .... 143 C1
Padstow PL28 .... 107 D5
Par PL24 .... 60 B5
Plymouth PL3 .... 128 A4
Poughill EX23 .... 4 D2
8 St Austell PL25 .... 114 C3
St Columb Minor TR7 .... 111 D7
St Day TR16 .... 68 E1
St Erth TR27 .... 142 A1
St Germans PL12 .... 65 A8
St Just TR19 .... 86 F6
5 Stratton EX23 .... 4 E1
Tywardreath PL24 .... 60 D5
Churchstow Wlk PL6 .... 129 E8
Church Street N PL14 ... 113 C5
Church Street S PL14 ... 113 C5
Church Terr
Devoran TR3 .... 81 F6
Grampound Road TR2 .... 57 E1
St Kew PL30 .... 23 A3
CHURCHTOWN
Bridgerule 8 B6
Camborne 67 E5
Lanivet 47 E7
St Breward 24 B4
CHURCH TOWN 140 A3
Churchtown
Cardinham PL30 .... 35 F3
Gwinear TR27 .... 78 D4
7 Mullion TR12 .... 99 A2
5 St Agnes TR5 .... 54 C1
St Minver PL27 .... 22 A4
St Newlyn East TR8 .... 56 B7
Church Town TR11 .... 144 D3
Church Town Cl PL26 .... 46 F2
Church Town Cotts TR3 .. 81 D5
Churchtown Mdws PL26 .. 58 B4
Churchtown Mews PL30 .. 35 C8
Churchtown Rd
Gwithian TR27 .... 66 B2
Illogan TR16 .... 67 E5
Phillack TR27 .... 142 C7
Portscatho TR2 .... 83 B2
St Stephen PL26 .... 58 B4
Churchtown Terr PL27 ... 32 D6
Churchtown Vale PL12 .. 122 D1
Church View
St Cleer PL14 .... 37 F3
St Dominick PL12 .... 40 D2
St Neot PL14 .... 36 F2
Treburley PL15 .... 28 B5
Walkhampton PL20 .... 42 E4
Church View Cl TR18 .... 143 B6
Church View Rd
Camborne TR14 .... 138 F4
Probus TR2 .... 71 D6
Churchway
Madron TR20 .... 143 A8
11 Marazion TR17 .... 89 C5
Church Way
Falmouth TR11 .... 144 E3
Plymouth PL5 .... 127 E8
St Clether PL15 .... 17 B2
Church Wlk
Redruth TR15 .... 140 A5
South Petherwin PL15 .... 27 E8
12 Truro TR1 .... 137 D5
Chute La PL26 .... 85 D5
Chy-an-Chy 19 TR26 .... 141 B6
Chyandaunce Cl TR18 .... 143 F8
Chyandaunce Terr TR18 . 143 F8
Chyandor Cl PL24 .... 60 C4
CHYANDOUR 143 F7
Chyandour TR15 .... 140 A4
Chyandour Cl 1 TR26 .... 77 A6
Chyandour Cliff TR18 ... 143 F6
Chyandour La TR18 .... 143 F7
Chy-an-Dour Rd TR20 .... 90 C3
Chyandour Sq TR18 .... 143 F7
Chyandour Terr TR18 .... 143 F7
Chy an Dowr TR27 .... 142 E7
CHY-AN-GWEAL 141 B2
Chy-an-Gweal Est TR20 .. 89 A7
Chy-an-Mor TR20 .... 88 F6
Chy Cober TR27 .... 142 E7
CHYCOOSE 82 A6
Chycoose Parc TR3 .... 82 A5
Chycornick Terr TR18 ... 143 F8
Chygothow TR13 .... 146 B6
Chy Hwel TR1 .... 137 F6
Chy Kensa Cl TR27 .... 142 C5
Chylan Cres TR7 .... 111 E6
Chymeddon TR7 .... 110 E6
Chy Nampara 1 TR11 ... 145 A4
Chynance
Penzance TR18 .... 143 D4
Portreath TR16 .... 67 C6
Chynance Dr
Newquay TR7 .... 110 D5
TR7 .... 43 F4
CHYNHALE 91 C5
Chynoon Gdns PL25 .... 114 F6
Chynowen La TR8 .... 43 D1
Chynowen Parc TR8 .... 43 D1
Chynoweth PL26 .... 59 C8
Chynoweth Gdns TR18 .. 143 F8
Chynoweth La TR20 .... 89 F6
Chy Pons PL25 .... 114 A4
Chypons Est TR 20 .... 76 F3
Chypons Rd TR12 .... 99 B3
Chypraze Ct TR14 .... 138 B3
Chyreen La
Carnon Downs TR3 .... 81 F8
Playing Place TR3 .... 82 A8
Chyrn Dr PL30 .... 24 B3
Chyrose Rd TR16 .... 68 D1
Chysauster Ancient Village*
TR 20 .... 76 D2
Chytodden Terr TR13 .... 90 F5
Chytroose Cl TR13 .... 146 D8
Chyvelah Ope TR1 .... 69 E3
Chyvelah Rd TR3 .... 69 D4
Chyvelah Vale TR1 .... 69 E3
Chyvellas Cl TR18 .... 143 B1
Chyventon Cl TR19 .... 97 B6
Chyventon Ho TR15 .... 140 B5
Chyverton Cl TR7 .... 110 D4
Chyvogue Mdw TR3 .... 81 D6

Chywoone Ave TR18 . . . . . **143** C1
Chywoone Cres TR18 . . . **143** C1
Chywoone Gr TR19 . . . . **97** F8
Chywoone Hill TR18 . . . . **143** C1
Chywoone Pl TR18 . . . . . . **143** C1
Chywoon Gdns TR15 . . . **139** D7
Chywoon Rural Workshops
  TR19 . . . . **87** A5
Citadel Ope 13 PL1 . . . . . **149** A2
Citadel Road E PL1 . . . . . **149** A2
Citadel Road W PL1 . . . . **148** C2
Citadel The★ PL1 . . . . **149** A1
City Bsns Pk PL3 . . . . **128** A4
City Coll Plymouth (Kings
  Road Ctr) PL1 . . . . **128** A2
City Coll Plymouth (Learning
  Warehouse) PL1 . . . . . . **148** B2
City Rd TR1 . . . . **137** C4
Clairemont Pl 1 PL14 . . . **38** A3
Clampet La PL11 . . . . **65** E4
Clann Hl PL30 . . . . **47** E7
Clann La PL30 . . . . **47** E7
Clann Mdws PL30 . . . . . . **47** E7
CLAPPER **108** E4
Claremont Cotts 1
  TR11 . . . . **145** A5
Claremont Falls PL13 . . **62** E2
Claremont Mews TR15 . **140** B5
Claremont Rd TR15 . . . . **140** B5
Claremont St PL1 . . . . . . **148** C4
Claremont Terr
  3 Falmouth TR11 . . . . . **145** A5
  16 Porthleven TR13 . . . . **98** B8
  Truro TR1 . . . . **137** C5
Clarence Ct PL1 . . . . **148** A3
Clarence Pl
  29 Penzance TR18 . . . . . **143** E6
  Plymouth, Morice Town
   PL2 . . . . **127** C4
  Plymouth, Stonehouse PL1 **148** A3
Clarence Rd
  St Austell PL25 . . . . **114** B4
  Torpoint PL11 . . . . **127** B3
Clarence St TR18 . . . . . . **143** E5
Clarence Terr
  30 Penzance TR18 . . . . . **143** E6
  7 Wadebridge PL27 . . **108** B5
Clarence Villas TR18 . . **143** E6
Clarendon Ho 1 PL1 . . . **127** F3
Clarendon La 11 PL3 . . . **127** F3
Clare Pl PL4 . . . . **149** B2
Clare Terr TR11 . . . . **145** B4
Claybourne Cl PL25 . . . **114** F6
Claylands PL30 . . . . **24** A1
Claytonia Cl PL6 . . . . . . **121** C1
Clayton Pl PL4 . . . . **129** B2
Clayton Rd PL4 . . . . **129** B2
Clearbrook Ave PL5 . . . **123** E1
Clear View PL12 . . . . **122** E3
Clease Mdws PL32 . . . . . **105** C3
Clease Rd PL32 . . . . **105** C4
Clease The PL32 . . . . **105** C3
Cleave Cres EX23 . . . .**4** B8
Cleaveland PL27 . . . . **108** C4
Cleaverfield Mews PL15 . **106** C7
Cleaves The PL15 . . . . . . **106** C7
Cleave The PL10 . . . . **133** B2
Cleavewell PL27 . . . . **108** C4
Cledma Bank TR27 . . . . . **142** A2
CLEERS **46** E1
Cleers Hill
  St Dennis PL26 . . . . **46** E1
  Whitemoor PL26 . . . . . . **58** E8
Cleeve Gdns PL2 . . . . . . **128** A8
Clegg Ave PL11 . . . . **126** E3
Clemens Cl TR7 . . . . **111** B5
Clemens Rd PL14 . . . . . . **51** B3
Clemens Way TR27 . . . . . **78** D6
Clement Rd PL7 . . . . **131** B5
Clements Rd TR18 . . . . . **143** D5
Clemmens Ave TR7 . . . . **110** D4
Clemo Rd PL14 . . . . **113** E7
CLERKENWATER **109** D8
Clevedon Park Ave PL2 . **128** B6
Clevedon Rd TR7 . . . . . . **110** D5
Cleveland Ave PL13 . . . **117** D4
Cleveland Rd PL4 . . . . . . **149** C3
Clies The 5 TR13 . . . . . **146** C5
Clifden Cl
  Mullion TR12 . . . . **99** A1
  Newquay TR7 . . . . **110** E5
Clifden Dr PL27 . . . . **21** D6
Clifden Rd PL25 . . . . **114** F4
Clifden Terr
  14 Bodmin PL31 . . . . . . **109** D5
  Lostwithiel PL22 . . . . . . **112** C2
CLIFF **61** B6
Cliff Bglws TR27 . . . . . . **142** A8
Cliff Ct
  Falmouth TR11 . . . . **145** B3
  Plymouth PL1 . . . . **148** B1
Cliff La
  Millbrook PL10 . . . . **132** A4
  Mousehole TR19 . . . . . . **88** D1
  New Polzeath PL27 . . . . **21** D6
CLIFFORD **3** F8
Clifford Cl PL5 . . . . **123** E2
Cliff Park Terr PL27 . . . **108** C5
Cliff Rd
  Falmouth TR11 . . . . **145** C2
  Gorran Haven PL26 . . . . **85** D5
  Mevagissey PL26 . . . . . **73** C4
  Mousehole TR19 . . . . . . **88** D2
  Newlyn TR18 . . . . **143** D1
  Newquay TR7 . . . . **110** F6

Cliff Rd *continued*
  Perranporth TR6 . . . . . . **55** A5
  Plymouth PL1 . . . . **148** B1
  Porthleven TR13 . . . . . . **98** B8
Cliff Rise PL23 . . . . **116** D2
Cliff St PL26 . . . . **73** C4
Cliff Terr TR16 . . . . **67** C6
Cliff The PL26 . . . . **73** C4
Cliff View Rd TR14 . . . . **138** E4
Cliff View Terr TR14 . . . **138** E4
Clift Ct 4 TR1 . . . . **137** D4
Clifton Ave PL7 . . . . **130** E7
Clifton Cl PL7 . . . . **130** E7
Clifton Cres 16 TR11 . . **145** A4
Clifton Gdns 1 TR1 . . . **137** B4
Clifton Hill 14 TR18 . . . **143** C2
Clifton Pl
  14 Falmouth TR11 . . . . **145** A4
  Plymouth PL4 . . . . **149** A4
Clifton Rd TR15 . . . . **139** C8
Clifton St PL4 . . . . **149** A4
Clifton Terr
  15 Falmouth TR11 . . . . **145** A4
  Hayle TR27 . . . . **142** B6
  Liskeard PL14 . . . . **113** A5
  16 Newlyn TR18 . . . . . **143** C2
  Portscatho TR2 . . . . **83** B2
Cligga Workshops TR6 . **54** F4
Clijah Cl TR18 . . . . **140** C2
Clijah La TR18 . . . . **140** D2
Clinton Ave PL4 . . . . **129** A4
Clinton Cl
  Bude EX23 . . . . **104** E4
  Redruth TR15 . . . . **140** C3
Clinton Dr PL25 . . . . **114** B3
Clinton Pas 4 TR15 . . . . **140** B4
Clinton Rd
  Constantine TR11 . . . . . **92** F3
  Redruth TR15 . . . . **140** C4
Clinton Terr PL10 . . . . . **132** F6
Clittaford Rd PL6 . . . . . . **124** F7
Clittaford View PL6 . . . . **124** E7
Cloake Pl PL12 . . . . **119** A2
Clodan Mews 11 TR9 . . . **45** E2
Clodgey La TR13 . . . . . . **146** D5
Clodgey Way TR13 . . . . **146** D4
Clodgy View 4 TR26 . . **141** B6
Clonway 1 PL20 . . . . **42** C3
Close Hill TR15 . . . . **140** B6
Close The
  17 Bere Alston PL20 . . . **41** B1
  Lanner TR16 . . . . **80** E6
  Mylor Bridge TR11 . . . . **82** A3
  Penzance TR18 . . . . . . **143** D7
  Saltash PL12 . . . . **122** C3
  Trevone PL28 . . . . **20** F2
  Truro TR1 . . . . **137** F6
Clos Trevithick 4 TR14 **138** F2
Clovelly Rd PL4 . . . . **149** C1
Clovelly View PL9 . . . . . **135** F4
Clover Lane Cl 6 PL35 . . **9** C1
Clover Rise PL6 . . . . **125** E8
Clover Wlk PL12 . . . . . . **122** C3
Clowance Ave TR14 . . . . **79** B2
Clowance Cl PL1 . . . . . . **127** F1
Clowance La PL1 . . . . . . **127** E1
Clowance St PL1 . . . . . . **127** F1
CLOWANCE WOOD **79** A1
CLUBWORTHY **12** C3
Clyde St PL2 . . . . **127** F5
Coach Ho The
  Penryn TR10 . . . . **144** D7
  Penzance TR18 . . . . . . **143** F7
Coach House La PL25 . . **114** C4
Coach House Mews PL9 . **136** B6
Coach La TR15 . . . . **140** A4
Coachyard Mews PL28 . **107** D5
COAD'S GREEN **27** D4
Coad's Green Prim Sch
  PL15 . . . . **27** D3
Coastguard Cotts
  Down Thomas PL9 . . . . **134** F2
  Mawnan Smith TR11 . . . **93** C1
  Mullion TR12 . . . . **98** F1
  Polperro PL13 . . . . **62** E2
  Rosudgeon TR20 . . . . . . **89** F3
Coastguard Cres TR18 . **143** F6
Coastguard Hill PL29 . . **22** D8
Coastguard Hos PL26 . . **21** B4
Coastguard Sta Flats
  PL13 . . . . **117** C3
Coastguard Terr TR2 . . . **84** B3
Coastline Ct TR8 . . . . . . **44** C6
Coast Rd TR4 . . . . **68** A7
Cobbett Rd PL5 . . . . **124** B2
Cobb La PL9 . . . . **135** F6
Cobble La TR9 . . . . **57** E8
Cobblestone La PL1 . . . **128** A1
Cobbs Well PL23 . . . . . . **116** C4
Cober Cres TR27 . . . . . . **78** E3
Cobourg St PL1 . . . . **148** C3
Cockington Cl PL6 . . . . . **125** E1
Cockington Wlk PL6 . . . **125** C1
Cocklawelva PL27 . . . . . . **21** D2
COCKS **55** B3
Cocks Hill TR6 . . . . **55** B3
Cock's Lake La PL12 . . . **53** D4
COCKWELLS **77** C1
Cockwells Cnr TR26 . . . . **77** C1
Codiford Cres TR14 . . . **138** E4
Coffa Bridge Cl PL22 . . **112** D2
Coffee Lake Mdw PL22 . **112** D2
Cogegos Ind Pk TR14 . . **138** A2
Cogos Pk TR11 . . . . **82** A3
Coinagehall Pl TR18 . . . **143** F4
Coinagehall St
  Helston TR13 . . . . **146** B5
  Penzance TR18 . . . . . . **143** F4

COLAN **44** F4
Colborne Ave TR16 . . . . . **67** D4
Colborne Rd PL6 . . . . . . **125** A2
COLD NORTHCOTT **16** F5
Coldrenick St PL5 . . . . . **123** D1
Coldrose Ct TR1 . . . . . . **137** B4
Coldstyle Rd PL14 . . . . . **113** C7
Coldwind Cross TR3 . . . **81** D7
COLEBROOK **130** E6
Colebrook Cl TR15 . . . . **140** A5
Colebrook La PL7 . . . . . **130** E7
Colebrook Rd
  Plymouth, Plympton PL7 . **130** E6
  Plymouth, St Budeaux PL5 **123** D1
Coleman Dr PL9 . . . . **135** F4
Colemans Cross PL15 . . . **19** C5
Cole Moore Mdw PL19 . . **147** B6
Colenso Cross TR20 . . . **89** F5
Colenso Pl PL25 . . . . **114** D3
Coleridge Ave PL6 . . . . **124** F2
Coleridge Rd PL4 . . . . . **129** A4
Coles Cotts PL9 . . . . **135** C1
Colesdown Hill PL9 . . . **130** A1
Colesloggett Halt Sta★
  PL30 . . . . **48** F8
Colin Campbell Ct 10
  PL1 . . . . **148** B3
Colinsey Pl TR18 . . . . . . **143** D7
Colinsey Rd TR18 . . . . . **143** D7
Coliza Hill PL26 . . . . **59** A2
Collacombe Cross PL19 . **29** F4
Collaford Cl PL7 . . . . **131** A4
Collan's Cross TR32 . . . **15** D4
College Ave
  Plymouth PL3 . . . . **128** E5
  Tavistock PL19 . . . . **147** D6
College Cl TR2 . . . . **71** C6
College Dean Cl PL6 . . . **125** C5
College Gn
  Bodmin PL31 . . . . **109** E2
  St Austell PL25 . . . . **114** C3
College Green PL31 . . . **109** E2
College Hill TR10 . . . . . **144** C7
College La
  Bodmin PL31 . . . . **109** F2
  Plymouth PL4 . . . . **128** F4
  Redruth TR15 . . . . **140** E7
College Ope TR10 . . . . . **144** D7
College Park Pl PL3 . . . **128** E5
College Rd
  Camelford PL32 . . . . . . **105** D4
  Plymouth PL2 . . . . **127** E5
College Road Prim Sch
  PL2 . . . . **127** E5
College St TR14 . . . . **138** C3
College View PL3 . . . . . **128** E4
College Way TR1 . . . . . . **69** E3
Colletts Ct TR16 . . . . . . **67** C5
Colliford Lake Pk★ PL14 . **36** E8
Collin Cl PL5 . . . . **123** D1
Collingwood Ave PL4 . . **149** C2
Collingwood Rd PL1 . . . **128** A3
Collingwood Villas 5
  PL1 . . . . **128** A3
Collins Parc TR3 . . . . . . **80** F3
Coll of St Mark & St John
  PL6 . . . . **125** C4
Collon Field PL22 . . . . . **61** D8
Collorian La TR26 . . . . . **77** C1
Collygree Parc TR20 . . . **89** E5
Colmer Cl PL13 . . . . **117** D6
Colmers La PL17 . . . . . . **39** E4
Colmers Row PL14 . . . . . **51** F5
Col-Moor Cl TR27 . . . . **142** E7
Colne Gdns PL3 . . . . **129** B5
Colroger Cl TR12 . . . . . . **99** B2
Colston Cl PL6 . . . . **125** B6
Coltishall Cl PL5 . . . . . . **123** F4
Coltness Rd PL9 . . . . . . **136** B5
Coltsfield Cl PL6 . . . . . . **129** B8
Columbus Cl PL5 . . . . . **123** C2
Colver Cl TR27 . . . . **78** D6
Colvreath Rd TR7 . . . . . **110** F6
Colwill Rd PL6 . . . . **125** E3
Colwill Wlk PL6 . . . . **125** F3
Colworth Ave TR11 . . . . **144** F3
Colwyn Rd PL11 . . . . . . **127** A3
COMBE **136** E5
Combe La EX23 . . . .**6** F4
Combley Dr PL6 . . . . **125** D4
COME-TO-GOOD **82** B7
COMFORD **80** F6
Comfort Rd TR11 . . . . . . **82** A3
Comfort Wartha TR11 . . **92** F4
Commercial Hill TR3 . . . **81** B4
Commercial Ope PL4 . . . **149** B2
Commercial Pl PL4 . . . . **149** B1
Commercial Rd
  Calstock PL18 . . . . **41** A3
  Hayle TR27 . . . . **142** C6
  Horrabridge PL20 . . . . . **42** C4
  10 Mousehole TR19 . . . . **88** C1
  Penryn TR10 . . . . **144** D7
  Plymouth PL4 . . . . **149** B2
  8 St Keverne TR12 . . . . **101** C4
  5 St Mawes TR2 . . . . . . **95** A6
Commercial Sq 3 TR14 . **138** D3
Commercial St
  Camborne TR14 . . . . . . **138** D3
  Gunnislake PL18 . . . . . . **41** A4
  Plymouth PL4 . . . . **149** B2
Commercial Terr PL28 . **107** D5
Commissioners Rd 1
  PL27 . . . . **108** B5
Common La PL6 . . . . **121** B5
COMMON MOOR **37** F4
Commons Cl 3 TR12 . . . **99** A2

Commons Gate EX22 . . . **13** B8
Commons The TR12 . . . . **99** A2
Compass Dr PL7 . . . . . . **131** A7
Compass Point TR26 . . . **141** D2
Compass W PL15 . . . . . . **18** C2
Comprigney Cl TR1 . . . . **137** B5
Comprigney Hill TR1 . . . **137** B5
Compton Ave PL3 . . . . . **129** A5
Compton Knoll Cl PL3 . . **129** A6
Compton Leigh PL3 . . . . **129** A6
Compton Park Rd PL3 . . **128** F5
Compton Prim Sch PL3 . **129** A6
Compton Rd 2 PL17 . . . . **39** E4
Compton Vale PL3 . . . . . **129** A5
CONDON'S SHOP **27** B5
Condor Cotts TR11 . . . . **144** C2
Condurrow Rd TR14 . . . **139** A1
Congreve Gdns PL5 . . . **124** C1
Coniston Gdns PL6 . . . . **124** F4
Conker Rd TR27 . . . . **78** C1
Connaught Ave PL4 . . . **128** F4
Connaught La 6 PL4 . . . **128** E4
Connoc Cl PL14 . . . . **113** D5
CONNOR DOWNS **78** D5
Connor Downs Prim Sch
  TR27 . . . . **78** D6
Connor Hill TR27 . . . . . . **78** D6
Conqueror Dr PL5 . . . . . **124** E1
Conrad Rd PL5 . . . . **124** D1
Consols Rd TR16 . . . . . . **80** F8
Consort Cl PL3 . . . . **128** E2
Consort Ho PL5 . . . . **123** B2
Constable Cl PL5 . . . . . . **124** D3
Constance Pl PL1 . . . . . . **148** A3
CONSTANTINE **92** E3
CONSTANTINE BAY **20** D1
Constantine Prim Sch
  TR11 . . . . **92** E3
Constantine St PL4 . . . . **149** A3
Convent Cl PL12 . . . . . . **122** E3
Convent of Mercy PL31 . **109** C4
Conway Cl TR11 . . . . **144** E4
Conway Gdns
  Falmouth TR11 . . . . **144** D4
  Plymouth PL2 . . . . **128** D4
Conway Rd TR11 . . . . . . **144** D4
Conyngham Ct PL6 . . . . **129** A8
Cooban Ct TR1 . . . . **137** F5
Cook Ct PL12 . . . . **122** B3
COOKSLAND **35** B2
Cooksland Ind Est PL31 . **35** B2
Cooksland La PL31 . . . . . **35** B2
Cooksland Rd PL31 . . . . . **35** B1
Cook's Level PL26 . . . . . **85** C5
Cooksley Cl TR1 . . . . . . **149** A1
Cookworthy Rd PL2 . . . **127** F6
COOMBE
  Camborne **66** F3
  Perranarworthal **81** B8
  Playing Place **82** D8
  St Stephen **58** D3
Coombe Dean Sch PL9 . **136** A6
Coombe Dean Sp Ctr
  PL9 . . . . **136** A6
Coombe Dr PL12 . . . . . . **119** A2
Coombe Hill PL26 . . . . . **58** C2
Coombe Junction Halt
  PL14 . . . . **51** A6
Coombe La
  Cargreen PL12 . . . . **119** A2
  Crafthole PL11 . . . . **65** B5
  Penzance TR18 . . . . . . **143** D7
  Plymouth PL5 . . . . **124** D7
  Seaton PL11 . . . . **64** B7
  Truro TR1 . . . . **81** C8
Coombe Park Cl PL10 . . **133** A2
Coombe Park La PL5 . . . **124** A3
Coombe Pk
  Camborne TR14 . . . . . . **66** F3
  Kingsand PL10 . . . . **133** A2
  Penzance TR18 . . . . . . **143** E6
  Saltash PL12 . . . . **122** F2
Coombe Rd
  Callington PL17 . . . . **39** E4
  Lanjeth PL26 . . . . **58** D3
  Penzance TR18 . . . . . . **143** E7
  Saltash PL12 . . . . **123** A2
Coombes La 9 TR1 . . . . **137** C4
Coombe The
  Crumplehorn PL13 . . . . . **62** D2
  Newlyn TR18 . . . . **143** B3
Coombe Vale TR18 . . . . **143** B3
Coombe View
  15 Perranporth TR6 . . . . **55** A4
  Plymouth PL2 . . . . **127** F7
Coombe Way PL5 . . . . . **123** F1
Cooperage Gdns 8 PL25 . **59** A3
Cooperage Rd PL25 . . . . **59** A3
Cooper's La TR13 . . . . . . **98** C8
COOSEBEAN **137** A5
Coosebean La TR4 . . . . **137** A5
Copes Gdns TR1 . . . . . . **137** C5
Copleston Rd PL6 . . . . . **124** E5
Coppard Mdws PL7 . . . . **130** B6
COPPATHORNE **7** A3
Copper Beech Way PL6 . **125** C7
Copperfields PL20 . . . . . **42** B5
Copper Hill TR27 . . . . . . **142** D6
COPPERHOUSE **142** D6
Copper Pk PL13 . . . . **148** A3
Copper Terr TR27 . . . . . **142** D7
Coppice Gdns PL5 . . . . . **124** E2
Coppice Wood Dr PL6 . . **125** C7
Copse Cl PL7 . . . . **130** D4
Copse Rd PL7 . . . . **130** D4

Copse The
  St Austell, Sandy Bottom
   PL25 . . . . **114** F5
  St Austell, Tregorrick PL26 **114** B1
Copshorn Rd PL31 . . . . . **109** C7
COPTHORNE **12** B3
Copthorne Cross PL15 . . **12** B2
Copthorne Gdns PL9 . . **135** F5
Corea Terr PL1 . . . . **128** A2
Corfe Ave PL3 . . . . **128** F8
Coringdean Cl PL6 . . . . **125** B6
Cormoran Ct TR17 . . . . . **89** C5
Cormorant Dr PL25 . . . . **115** A4
Corner Brake PL6 . . . . . . **125** D7
Corner Gdns EX23 . . . .**4** D1
Corner Pk PL15 . . . . **26** C7
Cornerstone Ct PL11 . . **127** B3
Cornfield Gdns PL7 . . . . **131** B7
Cornflower Cres PL15 . . **106** E4
Cornhill Rd PL24 . . . . . . **60** B5
Cornish Birds of Prey Ctr
  The★ TR9 . . . . **32** D1
Cornish Chough TR7 . . **110** E6
Cornish Cider Farm★ TR4 **55** B1
Cornish Cres TR1 . . . . . . **69** F4
Cornish Goldsmiths★
  TR16 . . . . **67** F5
Cornish Mines & Engines
  (Mus)★ TR15 . . . . **139** C6
Cornubia Cl
  Hayle TR27 . . . . **142** C5
  Truro TR1 . . . . **137** F6
Cornwall Beach PL1 . . . **127** D2
Cornwall Coll Camborne
  TR15 . . . . **139** B6
Cornwall Coll Newquay
  TR7 . . . . **111** A5
Cornwall Coll St Austell
  PL25 . . . . **114** D5
Cornwall Coll Saltash
  PL12 . . . . **122** D2
Cornwall Ctr★ TR15 . . . . **140** B4
Cornwall Ho PL25 . . . . . **114** C3
Cornwallis TR26 . . . . . . **141** E2
Cornwall's Regimental Mus
  (Duke of Cornwall's Light
  Infantry Mus)★ PL31 . . **109** F3
Cornwall St
  Bere Alston PL20 . . . . . **41** B1
  Plymouth, Morice Town
   PL1 . . . . **127** D2
  Plymouth PL1 . . . . **148** C3
Cornwall Terr
  Penzance TR18 . . . . . . **143** E4
  2 Truro TR1 . . . . **137** C5
Cornwood Rd PL7 . . . . . **131** B4
Cornworthy Cl PL2 . . . . **128** A7
Coronation Ave TR14 . . **138** A4
Coronation Cl 2 PL17 . . . **39** F4
Coronation Cotts
  Budock Water TR11 . . . . **144** C3
  Mabe Burnthouse TR10 . **81** C1
  St Keverne TR12 . . . . . **101** C4
Coronation Pl
  Helston TR13 . . . . **146** C4
  Plymouth PL5 . . . . **127** E8
Coronation Rd
  10 Callington PL17 . . . . **39** F4
  Hayle TR27 . . . . **142** D5
  1 Illogan TR16 . . . . . . **67** E4
  Redruth TR15 . . . . **140** D4
Coronation Terr
  Truro TR1 . . . . **137** B4
  Veryan TR2 . . . . **83** D7
Coronation Way TR7 . . . **111** C7
Corondale Rd PL2 . . . . . **128** B7
Corporation Rd
  Bodmin PL31 . . . . **109** B4
  Plymouth PL2 . . . . **128** D7
Corsham Cl PL6 . . . . **125** B6
Cort Simmons TR15 . . . **139** C6
Cort Treloweth TR15 . . **139** B6
Corva Cl 11 TR26 . . . . . . **77** A6
Corva Rd 9 TR26 . . . . . . **77** A6
Cory Cl EX23 . . . . **10** F6
Cosawes Est TR3 . . . . . . **81** B4
Cosdon Pl PL6 . . . . **124** F1
COSWINSAWSIN **79** A5
Coswinsawsin La TR14 . . **79** A5
Cotehele Ave
  Plymouth, Keyham PL2 . **127** F5
  Plymouth, Prince Rock PL4 **149** C2
Cotehele Ho★ PL12 . . . . . **40** F3
Cotehele Quay Discovery
  Ctr★ PL12 . . . . **40** F3
Cotehele View PL18 . . . . **41** A3
Cothele Cl PL17 . . . . **39** E3
Cot Hill
  Plymouth PL7 . . . . **130** B5
  Ponsanooth TR3 . . . . . . **81** B4
  2 Stratton EX23 . . . . **4** E1
Cot Hill Trad Est PL7 . . **130** B6
Cot Rd TR15, TR16 . . . . . **67** D4
Cotsland Rd TR1 . . . . . . **137** F5
Cotswold Ave PL26 . . . . **58** E1
Cotswold Cl PL26 . . . . . . **58** E1
Cottage Gdns PL15 . . . . **27** B7
Cottage Mews PL7 . . . . **130** E4
Cotton Cl PL7 . . . . **130** F4
Cott Rd
  Lostwithiel PL22 . . . . . . **112** D2
  Lostwithiel, Polscoe PL22 . **112** E2
Cotts PL20 . . . . **119** B7
Cot Wood PL3 . . . . **81** B4
Couchwell La PL22 . . . . **112** C2
Coulson's Bldgs 10 TR18 **143** E4
Coulson's Pl 9 TR18 . . . **143** E4
Coulson's Terr 8 TR18 . . **143** E4

Cou–Diz 157

Coulthard Dr TR13 91 A3
Countess Bridge La TR27 90 A8
Count House La TR26 141 C2
County Cl PL7 131 A5
County Rd EX23 104 E2
Court Barton Cotts PL9 135 C1
Court Barton Mews PL19 30 B4
Courtenay Rd PL19 147 B6
Courtenay St PL1 148 C3
Courtfield Rd PL3 128 F5
Court Gdns PL25 114 C3
Courtland Cres PL7 130 D7
Courtlands PL12 122 E1
Courtlands Cl PL19 147 B6
Courtlands Cres 4 PL25 115 A5
Courtlands Rd PL19 147 B6
Courtlands Specl Sch PL6 124 F1
Court Mdw PL13 62 B7
Courtnay Cl PL13 117 D4
Courtney Ho PL5 124 B2
Courtney Rd
  Liskeard PL14 113 D6
  St Austell PL25 114 F5
  Truro TR1 137 B5
Court The
  Camborne TR15 139 C4
  Plymouth PL6 125 C7
  Saltash PL12 122 C2
Court View PL8 136 F4
Courtyard Cotts TR4 70 C6
Courtyard The
  Redruth TR16 139 F2
  Truro TR1 137 D3
Cove Hill
  Perranarworthal TR3 81 D5
  Sennen Cove TR19 96 B7
Cove Mdw PL11 127 A6
Coventry Rd TR11 145 B6
COVERACK 101 C1
COVERACK BRIDGES 91 E5
Coverack Prim Sch TR12 101 C1
Cove Rd TR19 96 C7
Coverdale Pl PL5 124 C1
Cove The TR4 68 A7
Cowdray Cl PL12 122 E2
Cowdray Terr PL12 122 E1
Cow Lard Cl PL15 106 A4
Cowley Rd PL5 124 D3
Cowling Gdns PL14 51 F6
Cowling Rd 2 TR3 81 F7
COXFORD 10 D7
COX HILL 68 F2
COXPARK 40 D7
Cox Park Terr PL18 40 C6
Cox's Cl PL6 125 B1
COXSIDE 149 B1
Coxs Mdw EX22 13 C7
Cox Tor Cl 6 PL20 42 C3
Cox Tor Rd PL19 147 E5
Coypool Rd PL7 130 A6
Crabbs Cl PL15 13 F1
Crabbtree Cl 3 PL14 113 B5
CRABTREE 129 E5
Crabtree Cl PL3 129 F5
Crabtree La PL30, PL31 109 D2
Crabtree Villas PL3 129 E5
CRACKINGTON HAVEN 10 B7
Crackston Cl PL6 129 B7
CRAFTHOLE 65 B5
Craigie Dr PL1 148 A3
Craigmore Ave PL2 127 F5
Craigside PL13 117 D4
Cramber Cl
  Roborough PL6 125 C8
  5 Tavistock PL19 147 B4
Cranberry Rd TR14 138 B3
Cranbourne Ave PL4 149 C4
CRANE 138 C2
Crane Manor Ct TR14 138 C2
Crane Rd TR14 138 C2
Cranfield PL7 130 C7
Cranfield Rd TR14 138 B3
Cranmere Rd PL3 129 A6
CRANTOCK 43 D3
Crantock St TR7 110 D6
Crantock Terr 7 PL2 128 A5
CRAPSTONE 42 B2
Crapstone Terr PL20 42 B2
Crashaw Cl PL5 124 D3
Craven Ave PL4 149 C4
Crawford Rd PL1 148 A4
Creakavose PL26 58 B4
Creakavose Pk PL26 58 A4
Crealy Adventure Park (Cornwall)★ PL27 32 D4
CREAN 96 F5
Crease La PL19 147 A4
Creathorne Rd EX23 104 E7
Creative Unit (Krowji)★ TR15 140 A4
Creaz-an-Bre PL26 58 D5
Crediton Wlk PL6 129 E8
CREED 72 A6
Creed La TR2 72 A7
Creedy Rd PL3 129 C5
CREEGBRAWSE 68 F2
Creekside View TR2 70 F4
Creeping La
  Newlyn TR18 143 C3
  Penzance TR18 143 C4
Crelake Cl PL19 147 C4
Crelake Ind Est 1 PL19 147 B4
Crelake Pk PL19 147 C4
Crellow Fields TR3 80 F3
Crellow Hill TR3 80 F3
Crellow La TR3 80 F3
Crellow Terr TR3 80 F3
Crellow Vale TR3 80 F3
CRELLY 91 F7
Crembling Well TR15 139 E6
CREMYLL 133 E7
Cremyll Rd PL11 127 B2
Cremyll St PL1 134 A8
Crescent Ave PL1 148 B2
Crescent Avenue Mews PL1 148 B2
Crescent Cl
  Hayle TR27 142 C5
  Widemouth Bay EX23 6 F5
Crescent Gdns TR1 137 B4
Crescent Pl 6 TR19 74 F1
Crescent Rd
  Bugle PL26 47 C1
  Truro TR1 137 B4
Crescent Rise
  Constantine Bay PL28 20 C1
  Truro TR1 137 B4
Crescent The
  Bude EX23 104 D5
  Camborne TR14 138 D4
  Carbis Bay TR26 77 C4
  Common Moor PL14 37 F4
  Crapstone PL20 42 B3
  Gunnislake PL18 41 A6
  Landrake PL12 53 C3
  Lifton PL16 19 F4
  Liskeard PL14 113 C6
  Looe PL13 117 D1
  Newquay TR7 110 E6
  Plymouth PL1 148 B2
  Porthleven TR13 91 B1
  St Austell PL25 115 B5
  St Ives TR26 77 A7
  St Mabyn PL30 34 D8
  Truro TR1 137 B4
  Widemouth Bay EX23 6 F5
Cressbrook Cl PL6 125 F2
Cressbrook Dr PL6 125 F2
Cressbrook Wlk PL6 125 E2
Cresthill Rd PL2 128 B7
Creswell Terr TR19 86 F7
Creykes Ct PL1 148 A3
Cribbage Terr 13 PL31 109 D5
Cricketers Hollow PL27 21 E3
Cricket Pk EX23 7 B6
Crift Cotts PL14 51 F7
Crift La PL12 64 F8
Crill Cnr TR11 144 C1
CRIMP 3 A2
Crinnick's Hill PL31 109 E4
Crinnis Cl PL25 115 E3
Crinnis Rd PL25 115 B3
Crinnis Wood PL25 115 E3
Crinnis Wood Ave PL25 115 D3
CRIPPLESEASE 77 A3
CROANFORD 34 C6
Crocker's Row PL18 41 A6
Crockers Way PL15 13 F1
Crockwell St PL31 109 E5
Croft Comm TR14 79 E5
CROFTHANDY 68 E1
Croftlands PL27 21 E3
CROFT MITCHELL 79 E4
Croft Parc TR12 102 F2
Croft Pk PL6 125 C7
Croft Rd TR18 143 C4
Croft Row TR16 80 F8
Crofty Cl TR15 139 C5
Cromartie Rd PL4 129 B1
Cromer Cl PL6 125 A7
Cromer Wlk PL6 125 A7
Cromwell Gate PL6 125 C7
Cromwell Rd
  Plymouth PL4 149 C3
  St Austell PL25 114 F3
Crookeder Cl PL9 136 A5
Crookedor La PL11 65 D5
Crooklets EX23 104 C7
Crooklets Rd EX23 104 D6
Cross PL30 47 F1
Cross Cl TR7 111 C7
Cross Comm TR12 102 F2
CROSSGATE 19 A7
Cross Gn PL15 19 F7
Cross Hill PL2 127 E4
Cross La
  Bodmin PL31 109 E5
  7 St Austell PL25 114 C3
CROSS LANES 99 C4
Cross Lanes
  Chacewater TR4 69 B1
  Cross Lanes TR12 99 C4
  Launceston PL15 106 C8
  Stratton EX23 4 F1
Crossmount TR7 111 D7
Cross Park Ave PL6 124 F1
Cross Park Rd PL6 124 F1
Cross Park Terr PL26 73 C4
Cross Park Way PL6 124 F1
Cross Pk
  Buckland Monachorum PL20 42 A3
  Crafthole PL11 65 B5
Crossroads Cl PL28 31 F8
Cross St
  Camborne TR14 138 D2
  Hayle TR27 142 D6
  Helston TR13 146 B6
  Padstow PL28 107 D5
  13 Penzance TR18 143 E6
  3 Redruth TR15 140 B4
  Wadebridge PL27 108 B5
Cross Terr PL18 40 F5
Cross The
  Camborne TR14 138 D2
Cross The *continued*
  St Dominick PL12 40 D2
  St Newlyn East TR8 56 B7
CROSSTOWN 2 B1
Crosswalla Fields TR13 146 C7
Crosswater EX23 2 C1
Crossway PL7 130 D7
Crossway Ave PL4 129 B3
Crossways TR11 144 F2
CROWAN 79 C1
Crowan Prim Sch TR14 79 C2
CROWLAS 89 C8
Crowlas Ind Est TR20 89 B8
Crown Cl TR7 111 A4
Crown Cres TR8 56 B7
Crowndale Ave PL3 129 A6
Crown Gdns PL6 125 A1
CROWNHILL 124 F2
Crownhill Ct PL6 124 F2
Crownhill Fort★ PL6 124 F3
Crownhill Fort Rd PL6 124 F3
Crownhill Rd PL5 124 C3
Crown Rd PL26 58 D8
Crown Terr PL26 58 D8
CROWNTOWN 91 B5
Crow Pk PL3 128 F5
Crows-an-Eglos 5 TR26 77 A6
CROWS-AN-WRA 96 F8
CROW'S NEST 38 B4
Croydon Gdns PL5 123 E4
Crozier Rd 6 PL4 128 F4
CRUGMEER 107 A7
CRUMPLEHORN 62 D2
Crun-Melyn Parc TR27 142 B4
Crusoe Flats 48 TR26 141 B6
Cryben TR12 92 C1
Cryon View TR1 69 E3
CUBERT 55 D8
Cubert Sch TR8 43 D1
Cuby Cl TR2 72 A3
Cuby Rd TR2 71 F4
Cuckoo La TR20 77 A3
Cuddenbeake Terr PL12 65 B8
Cuffe Rd PL3 128 C4
Culbin Gn PL6 129 D7
Culdrose Airfield TR12 146 E1
Culdrose Cl PL5 123 E4
Cullen View TR2 71 C6
Culme Rd PL3 129 A5
Cul-Rian PL26 58 D7
Culroy Flats 12 TR1 137 C4
Culver Cl PL6 129 A8
Culver Ct PL12 122 F2
Culverland Pk PL14 113 C7
Culverland Rd PL14 113 B8
Culver Rd PL12 122 F2
Culvers Mdw PL15 106 B8
Culver Way PL6 129 A7
Culverwood Cl PL7 131 C6
Culvery The PL27 108 B4
Cumberland Rd PL1 127 F1
Cumberland St PL1 127 E2
Cumble Tor La PL12 53 D2
Cundy Cl PL7 130 A7
Cundy's La PL26 58 D4
Cunliffe Ave PL9 135 A6
Cunnack Cl TR13 146 C7
Cunningham Pk TR10 81 C1
Cunningham Rd PL5 124 C8
Cunningham Way PL12 122 D3
CURGURRELL 83 C4
Curlew Cl TR7 110 B5
Curlew Mews PL3 129 C4
Curlew Pk Ind Est TR4 69 C3
Curlews TR8 43 B1
Curnow Sch TR15 140 B6
Curnows Rd TR27 142 C5
Currian Hill PL26 58 D8
Currian Rd PL26 58 D7
CURRIAN VALE 58 D8
CURRY LANE 12 E4
Curtice Cl PL25 114 E7
Curtis St PL1 127 E1
Curtis VC Cl TR8 56 B7
CURY 99 B4
Cury CE Prim Sch TR12 99 A4
CUSGARNE 81 B7
Cusgarne Hill TR4, TR16 81 B8
Cusgarne Prim Sch TR4 81 C7
Custom House Ct TR18 143 F5
Custom House La
  16 Penzance TR18 143 E5
  Plymouth PL1 148 B1
Customs House Hill PL23 116 D4
CUSVEORTH COOMBES 69 B2
Cutcrew La PL12 52 E3
Cuth Avallon TR1 137 C4
Cutmere Hill PL12 52 D3
Cutmere La PL12 52 D3
CUTTIVETT 53 B5
Cuxhaven Way TR20 88 F6
Cuxton Mdws PL20 41 F3
Cypress Ave PL25 115 F4
Cypress Cl 6 PL7 131 C5
Cyril Rd TR1 137 C5

D

Dabryn Way PL26 58 B4
DADBROOK 132 E4
Daglands Hill PL23 116 C4
Daglands Rd PL23 116 C4
DairyLand Farm World★ TR8 44 F1
Daisymount Dr PL28 31 F7
Dale Ave PL6 129 C7
Dale Cl TR7 111 A4
Dale Gdns PL4 128 D4
Dale Rd
  Newquay TR7 111 A4
  Plymouth PL4 128 D4
Daleswood Rd PL19 147 A4
Dalton Gdns PL5 123 E3
Damerel Cl PL1 127 F2
Dandre Apartments TR7 111 A7
Dane Rd TR7 110 D7
Daniel Cl PL25 115 A4
Daniell Ct TR1 137 C3
Daniell Gdns TR1 137 C3
Daniell Rd TR1 137 B3
Daniell St TR1 137 C3
Daniel Pl TR18 143 E4
Daniels La PL25 115 B4
Daniels Sail Loft TR10 144 D7
Danmore Cl PL34 14 C7
Danum Dr PL7 131 B3
DARITE 38 B4
Darite Prim Sch PL14 38 A4
Darkey La PL16 19 F4
Dark La
  Camelford PL32 105 C4
  Liskeard PL14 113 D6
  Lostwithiel PL22 112 C1
Darklake Cl PL6 125 E5
Darklake La PL6 125 D8
Darklake View PL6 125 E5
Dark Street La PL7 130 E4
Darlington Rd TR20 88 F6
Darloe La PL13 117 C3
DARRACCOTT 2 D4
Darracott Hill EX39 2 E3
Dart Cl
  Plymouth PL3 129 D7
  St Giles on the Heath PL15 13 F1
Dartington Wlk PL6 129 E8
Dartmeet Ave PL3 129 B6
Dartmoor View
  Plymouth PL4 129 C3
  Saltash PL12 122 E4
Dartmouth Wlk PL6 129 E8
Darwin Cres PL3 129 D5
Dashwood Ho TR11 145 A6
Daubuz Cl TR1 137 C6
Daubuz Ct TR1 137 D5
Daucus Cl PL19 147 B4
Davenham Cl PL6 125 B6
Davey's Cl TR11 144 E1
David Cl PL7 130 F6
David Penhaligon Way TR1 137 D3
David Southgate Ct PL1 148 A2
DAVIDSTOW 16 A6
Davidstow Airfield & Cornwall at War Mus★ Pl32 15 F5
Davy Cl
  Torpoint PL11 126 F3
  Tremar PL14 38 A3
Davy Rd PL6 125 C4
Davys Row PL14 37 E4
Dawe Cres PL31 109 C3
Dawes Cl PL14 50 E7
Dawes La
  Looe PL13 117 D5
  Millbrook PL10 132 E5
  Plymouth PL9 136 D7
Dawlish Wlk PL6 129 E8
Dawney Terr PL11 65 B5
Dawn Rd PL13 117 D2
Daws Ct PL12 123 A2
DAW'S HOUSE 18 E1
Daw's Mdw PL32 105 E4
Dawson Cl PL5 123 E1
Daymer La PL27 21 D4
Daymond Rd PL5 123 D2
Dayton Cl PL6 124 E3
Deacon Dr PL12 122 F1
Deacons Gn PL19 147 A3
Dean Cross PL9 135 E7
Dean Cross Rd PL9 135 E7
Dean Hill
  Liskeard PL14 113 B6
  Plymouth PL9 135 E7
Dean La PL14 113 B6
Dean Park Rd PL9 135 D7
Dean Rd PL7 130 D6
Dean St PL14 113 B5
Dean Terr PL14 113 B6
Debden Cl PL5 123 D4
Deeble Cl
  Plymouth PL7 130 E7
  Threemilestone TR3 69 C3
Deeble Dr 20 PL24 60 B4
Deep La PL7 131 C3
Deer Leap PL19 147 D4
Deer Park Cl PL19 147 C5
Deer Park Cres PL19 147 C5
Deer Park Dr PL3 129 D7
Deerpark Forest Trail★ PL14 50 C3
Deer Park La PL19 147 C5
Deer Park Rd PL19 147 C5
Deer Pk
  Newquay TR7 110 D6
  Saltash PL12 122 F3
Defoe Cl PL5 124 C1
Degibna La TR12, TR13 146 C2
DELABOLE 14 D3
Delabole Prim Sch PL33 14 D2
Delacombe Cl PL7 130 F7
De-la-Hay Ave PL3 148 A4
Delamere Rd PL6 129 D7
Delavue Terr PL32 105 C3
Delaware Cotts PL18 40 F6
Delaware Ct PL18 40 F5
Delaware Gdns PL2 127 F7
Delaware Prim Sch PL18 40 F5
Delaware Rd PL18 40 F6
Delgany Dr PL6 125 A5
Dell Cl TR18 143 C3
Dell Mdw PL15 18 B8
Dell The
  Plymouth PL7 130 B6
  Tavistock PL19 147 B6
  Truro TR1 137 C5
DEMELZA 46 E6
Denas Water TR2 71 A5
Dengie Cl PL7 131 B5
Denham Cl PL5 124 C2
Dennis Cl PL5 127 C7
Dennis Gdns PL15 18 C2
Dennis La PL28 107 D4
Dennison Ave PL25 115 A4
Dennison Rd PL31 109 D5
Dennis Rd
  Liskeard PL14 113 D6
  Padstow PL28 107 D5
Dennybowl La PL12 52 E3
Dens Meadow PL12 52 F6
Denyer Ct TR11 145 A6
Denys View TR9 45 F2
De Pass Gdns TR11 145 C3
De Pass Rd TR11 145 C2
Deptford Pl PL4 149 A4
Derby Rd PL5 124 C4
Derby's La PL26 85 C5
Dereham Terr 6 TR1 137 B4
Derowen Dr TR27 142 B3
DERRIFORD 125 B4
Derriford Bsns Pk PL6 125 A4
Derriford Health & L Ctr PL6 125 B3
Derriford Hospl PL6 125 B4
Derriford Pk PL6 125 A3
Derriford Rd PL6 125 B4
DERRIL 8 D6
Derriton Rd EX22 8 F6
Derry Ave PL4 148 C4
Derry's Cross PL1 148 B2
Derwent Ave PL3 129 C5
Desborough La PL4 149 C3
Desborough Rd PL4 149 C3
Deva Ho TR7 111 A6
DEVERAL 78 D2
Deveral Rd TR27 78 D2
Deveron Cl PL7 131 A5
Devington Ct TR11 145 C2
Devington Hall TR1 137 E5
Deviock Hill PL11 64 C5
Devonia Cl PL7 130 E7
DEVONPORT 127 D4
Devonport High Sch for Boys PL1 128 A2
Devonport High Sch for Girls PL2 128 C6
Devonport Hill
  Kingsand PL10 133 A2
  Plymouth PL1 127 F1
Devonport Leat PL6 121 B5
Devonport Rd PL3 127 F3
Devonport Sta PL1 127 F3
Devon Progressive Sch PL19 42 A5
Devonshire Ct PL11 127 B3
Devonshire Ho
  Plymouth PL1 148 B2
  2 Tavistock PL19 147 B5
Devonshire St PL4 149 A3
Devon Terr PL3 128 E5
Devon Tors Rd 9 PL20 42 C3
DEVORAN 81 F6
Devoran La TR3 81 F6
Devoran Sch TR3 81 F6
Diamond Ave PL4 149 B4
Diana Cl TR11 144 E2
Dickens Rd PL5 124 B1
Dickiemoor La PL5 124 C2
Dickna St PL15 13 F1
Dicky La TR3 82 D6
Diddies La EX23 4 E1
Diddies Rd EX23 4 E1
Dieppe Cl PL1 127 F2
Digey Gr PL5 123 F5
Digey Flats 49 TR26 141 B6
Digey The 25 TR26 141 B6
Diggory's Field 4 PL14 38 A3
Dinas Ct PL11 64 C5
Dinas Rd 1 TR9 45 D6
Dingle Cl PL17 28 D1
Dingle Rd
  Plymouth, North Prospect PL2 128 A6
  Plymouth, Plympton PL7 130 C6
Dingles Cl TR3 81 B4
Dingle's Folly PL13 117 C3
Dingles Way PL27 21 E3
Dingwall Ave PL5 124 E3
DINWORTHY 3 F2
Dipper Cl EX23 5 A6
Dipper Dr PL19 147 D2
Dipper La EX23 5 A7
Dirty La PL12 122 B5
Discovery Wharf 20 PL4 149 A2
Distine Cl PL3 129 B7
Dithmarschen Way PL25 114 B2
Dittisham Wlk PL6 129 E8
Ditton Ct PL6 129 A8
Dixon Pl PL2 127 F4
DIZZARD 6 B1

Dobbin Cl PL28 . . . . **20** F2
Dobbin La PL28 . . . . **20** F2
Dobbin Rd PL28. . . . . **20** F2
Dobbs La TR1. . . . . **137** A4
Dobell Rd PL25 . . . . **114** E4
DOBWALLS **50** E8
Dobwalls Prim Sch PL14 . **50** E7
Dockacre Rd PL15 . . . . . . **106** C6
Dockey 1 PL15. . . . . **106** C5
Dock La PL18 . . . . **143** F5
Dockray Cl PL6 . . . . **125** D4
Dockyard Sta PL2. . . . . . . **127** E4
DOCTON **2** F8
Doctors Hill
  8 Boscastle PL35. . . . . **9** C1
  5 St Keverne TR12. . . . . . **101** C4
Doctors La PL14. . . . . **113** C6
Doctor's La PL14. . . . . . . **113** C6
Doddridge Cl PL9. . . . . . . **135** F4
Dodson's Gap TR12 . . . . . . **99** B7
Doidges Farm Cl PL6. . . . **129** B8
Dola La TR20 . . . . **89** E5
Dolcoath Ave TR14. . . . . . **138** F3
Dolcoath Cl TR14 . . . . **138** F3
Dolcoath Ind Pk TR14 . . . **139** A4
Dolcoath Rd TR14. . . . . . . **138** F3
Dolgey Post PL27 . . . . **32** A4
Dolphin PL29 . . . . **22** D7
Dolphin Cl PL9. . . . . **135** F6
Dolphin Court Rd PL9 . . . **135** F6
Dolphin Ho 18 PL4 . . . . . **149** A2
Dolphin Sq PL9 . . . . **135** F6
Dolvin Rd PL19 . . . . **147** C5
Domellick Cnr PL26 . . . . . **46** B1
Domellick Hill PL26 . . . . . **46** B1
Doniert's Cl 11 PL14. . . . **113** B5
Donkey La
  Millbrook PL10. . . . . **132** C4
  Portwrinkle PL11. . . . . . . **65** A4
Donkey Pk PL28 . . . . **31** F8
Donnington Dr PL3 . . . . . **129** C7
Donnington Rd TR18 . . . . **143** C3
Donovan Way PL31. . . . . . **109** B4
Dopps Terr TR15. . . . . **140** C5
Dorchester Ave PL5 . . . . . **124** D4
Dorchester Ct TR14 . . . . . **138** E4
Doreena Rd PL9 . . . . **136** C7
Dormy Ave PL3 . . . . **128** F5
Dorset Pk PL15 . . . . **13** A2
Dorsmouth Terr PL7 . . . . **130** E4
DOUBLEBOIS **50** C8
Doublebois Ind Est PL14 . **50** D7
Doubletrees PL24. . . . . **60** B4
Doubletrees Ct 2 PL24. . . **60** B4
Doubletrees Sch 21 PL24. **60** B4
Douglas Cl PL26 . . . . **47** A3
Douglas Dr PL9 . . . . **136** A6
Douglass Rd PL3. . . . . **129** C6
Doulton Rd PL25 . . . . **115** A4
DOUSLAND **42** F3
Dousland Ho PL20. . . . . . . **42** E3
Dousland Rd PL20. . . . . . . **42** D3
Dousland Terr PL20. . . . . . **42** E3
Dovedale Rd PL2. . . . . **128** A4
Dove Gdns PL3 . . . . **129** D7
Dover Rd PL6. . . . . **125** E3
Dove St 16 TR26 . . . . **141** B5
Dower's Terr TR16. . . . . . . **80** B5
Down Cl PL12. . . . . **122** C2
DOWNDERRY **64** C5
Downfield Dr PL7 . . . . . . **130** F5
Downfield Way PL7 . . . . . **130** F5
Downfield Wlk PL7. . . . . . **130** F5
DOWNGATE
  Kelly Bray **40** A7
  Pensilva. **38** D5
Downgate Gdns PL2. . . . . **128** D8
Downham Gdns PL5. . . . . **124** C7
Downhorne Pk PL9 . . . . . **135** F6
DOWNINNEY **11** B1
Downlea PL19 . . . . **147** D4
Down Park Dr PL19 . . . . . **147** D4
Down Parks EX23 . . . .**5** B7
Down Rd
  Plymouth PL7. . . . . **131** C5
  Tavistock PL19. . . . . **147** D4
Downs Cl PL26. . . . . **58** C8
Downs Hill PL23. . . . . **61** B5
Downside Ave PL6 . . . . . . **129** C7
Downside Cl TR7. . . . . **111** A4
Downs La PL13 . . . . **117** B3
Downs Lane Pk PL13 . . . . **117** B3
Downs Rd PL13 . . . . **117** C4
Downs The PL13 . . . . **117** C3
Downstream Cl PL28. . . . **107** C5
Downs View
  Bude EX23 . . . . **104** D7
  Looe PL13 . . . . **117** C3
Down The PL20 . . . . **41** C1
DOWN THOMAS **135** C1
Downton Cl PL1 . . . . **148** A4
Dowren Ho TR27. . . . . **142** B5
Dozmere TR3. . . . . **82** C5
Dozmere St TR3. . . . . **82** C5
Dracaena Ave
  Falmouth TR11. . . . . **144** F5
  Hayle TR27. . . . . **142** E6
Dracaena Cres TR27 . . . . **142** E6
Dracaena Pl TR11. . . . . . . **144** F4
Dracaena View TR11. . . . . **144** F5
Dragon L Ctr The PL31. . . **109** C7
Drake Cir PL1, PL4. . . . . . **149** A3
Drakecircus Sh Ctr PL1 . **149** A3

Drake Ct
  Plymouth, Ernesettle
    PL5 . . . . **123** E4
  Plymouth, St Jude's PL4 . **149** B3
Drakefield Dr PL12. . . . . . **123** A3
Drake Gdns PL19. . . . . . . **147** C4
Drake Prim Sch PL2. . . . . **127** E6
Drake Rd
  Padstow PL28 . . . . **107** C5
  Tavistock PL19. . . . . **147** C6
Drakes Cl PL6 . . . . **124** F4
Drake's Pk 3 PL20. . . . . . **41** B1
Drake Villas PL19 . . . . . . **147** A4
Drakewalls Gdns PL18. . . **40** F5
Drakewalls Pl PL18. . . . . . **40** F5
Drake Way PL9 . . . . **135** E7
Drang The TR9 . . . . **45** E1
Drannack La TR27. . . . . . . **78** D4
Drannack Mill Lane TR27. **78** C3
Draper Terr 3 PL19. . . . . **147** B5
DRAWBRIDGE **49** F8
Drax Gdns PL6. . . . . **128** E8
Draycott Terr TR26. . . . . . **141** C4
Drayton Rd PL5 . . . . **124** C1
Dreysen Ct TR15 . . . . **139** C8
DRIFT. **87** F3
Drift Cl TR20. . . . . **87** F3
Drift La PL14 . . . . **49** C7
Drillfield La 9 TR26. . . . . **141** B5
Drinnick Terr PL26. . . . . . **58** D6
Drive The
  Helston TR13 . . . . **146** D7
  Plymouth PL3. . . . . **128** E7
Driving La PL24. . . . . **60** C6
Drogeada Cl PL15. . . . . . . **27** D3
Droskyn Castle 19 TR6 . . **55** A5
Droskyn Cl 22 TR6. . . . . . **55** A5
Droskyn House Villas TR6 **55** A5
Droskyn Way TR6. . . . . **55** A5
Druckham Pl PL15 . . . . . **106** D5
Druckham Terr PL15. . . . **106** C5
Druid's Lodge TR15 . . . . **139** D5
Druid's Rd
  Camborne TR15 . . . . . . **139** D5
  Redruth TR15. . . . . **139** D6
Drummer's Hill PL26 . . . **114** C8
Drummond Cl PL2 . . . . . . **127** F2
Drummond Pl PL1 . . . . . . **127** F3
Drummond Way PL20 . . . **119** E4
Drump Rd TR15 . . . . **140** C5
Drunken Bridge Hill PL7 **130** D4
Dryburgh Cres PL2. . . . . **128** A8
Dryden Ave PL5 . . . . **124** C1
DRYM. **91** A8
Drym La
  Leedstown TR14 . . . . **78** F1
  Nancegollan TR14 . . . . . . **91** A8
Drym Rd TR13 . . . . **91** B7
Dualstone Cross EX22. . . . **8** D3
Ducane Wlk PL6 . . . . **125** B1
Duchy Ave TR7 . . . . **111** C7
Duchy Cl
  Launceston PL15 . . . . . . **106** C7
  St Austell PL25 . . . . **114** F3
Duchy Coll
  St Breock PL27 . . . . **33** C7
  Stoke Climsland PL17 . . . **28** D1
Duchy Coll Rosewarne
  TR14. . . . . **138** D5
Duchy Cotts PL17 . . . . **28** D1
Duchy Hospl TR1. . . . . **69** E4
Duchy Terr
  Minions TR12. . . . . **38** B6
  Upton Cross PL14 . . . . . . **38** D7
Duck La PL12 . . . . **53** E2
Duck St
  9 Mousehole TR19. . . . . **88** C1
  St Austell PL25 . . . . **115** B2
Duckworth St 3 PL2. . . . **128** A4
Ducky La PL12 . . . . **53** C3
Ducky Row PL17 . . . . **40** D4
Dudley Gdns PL6. . . . . . . **129** B8
Dudley Rd PL7 . . . . **130** B5
Dudman Rd TR1 . . . . **69** F3
Dudnance La TR15 . . . . . **139** B4
Duke's Ct PL26 . . . . **46** F3
Dukes Dr PL19 . . . . **41** B4
Dukes Ryde The 1 PL9. . **135** F7
Duke St
  Launceston PL15 . . . . . . **106** A8
  Lostwithiel PL22 . . . . . . **112** C2
  Padstow PL28 . . . . **107** D5
  St Austell PL25 . . . . **114** C3
  Tavistock PL19. . . . . **147** C6
  11 Truro TR1. . . . . **137** D4
Duke's Way TR7 . . . . **111** A5
DULOE **51** A4
Duloe CE VA Jun & Inf Sch
  PL14 . . . . **51** A1
Duloe Gdns PL2. . . . . **128** C8
Dumbarton Terr 7 TR19. **88** C3
Dumfries Ave PL5. . . . . . . **124** D3
Duncannon Dr TR11. . . . **144** F4
Duncan St PL1 . . . . **127** E1
Dunclair Pk PL3 . . . . **129** D5
Duncombe Ave PL5 . . . . . **124** A2
Dundas St 4 PL2 . . . . . . **128** A4
Dundonald St PL2. . . . . . **127** F4
Dungarth Gn PL14. . . . . . **113** D6
Dungarth Rd PL14. . . . . . **113** D6
Dunhead View PL15. . . . . **28** B6
Dunheved Fields PL15. . . **106** C4
Dunheved Rd
  Launceston PL15 . . . . . . **106** C5
  Saltash PL12 . . . . **122** F2
Dunkeswell Cl PL2. . . . . . **127** F8

Dunley Wlk PL6. . . . . **125** C1
DUNMERE **34** D2
Dunmere Cl 1 PL24. . . . . **60** C4
Dunmere Rd PL31. . . . . . **109** B5
Dunnet Rd PL6. . . . . **124** D7
Dunn St 10 PL35. . . . . **9** C1
Dunraven Dr PL6. . . . . . . **125** A6
Dunsdon Cross EX22 . . . . . **5** F3
DUNSLEY. **38** C6
Dunstable Rd PL26 . . . . . **58** D6
Dunstan Cl TR10. . . . . . . **144** C8
Dunstan La PL12 . . . . **40** A1
Dunstanville Terr 12
  TR11. . . . . **145** A5
Dunster Cl PL7. . . . . **131** C4
Dunston Cl PL26 . . . . **58** C8
Dunstone Ave PL9 . . . . . . **136** A7
Dunstone Cl PL9 . . . . **135** F7
Dunstone Dr PL9. . . . . . . **135** F7
Dunstone La PL9. . . . . . . **136** B7
Dunstone Prim Sch PL9 **136** A8
Dunstone Rd
  Plymouth, Plymstock PL9 . **135** F7
  Plymouth, St Budeaux PL5. **123** F3
Dunstone View PL9 . . . . . **136** A7
DUNTERTON **28** F6
Duntz Hill PL16 . . . . **19** F4
Dunvegan Rd TR10. . . . . **144** B8
Dunveth Industrial Estate
  PL27 . . . . **33** C7
Dunveth Rd PL27. . . . . . . **108** A5
Dupath La PL17. . . . . **40** A4
DUPORTH **115** A1
Duporth Bay PL26. . . . . . **115** A1
Duporth Rd PL24, PL26. . **115** A2
Dural Cross EX22 . . . . **3** E3
Durban Rd PL3 . . . . **128** D5
DURGAN **93** D2
Durgan Crossroads TR11. **93** D3
Durgan La TR10. . . . . **144** C8
Durham Ave PL4. . . . . . . **149** C4
Durley Dene TR26. . . . . . . **77** E4
Durnford St PL1 . . . . **128** A1
Durnford Street Ope
  PL1. . . . . **128** A1
Durning Rd TR5. . . . . **54** C1
Durrant Cl PL1. . . . . **127** E3
Durris Cl PL6 . . . . **125** A6
Durris Gdns PL6. . . . . **125** D4
Durston Rd EX23. . . . . . . **104** F7
Durwent Cl PL9 . . . . **135** A6
DUTSON **106** E8
Dutson Rd PL15. . . . . **106** E8
Dutson Terr PL15. . . . . . . **106** C7
Dux Cross EX22. . . . . **8** C4
Duxford Cl PL5 . . . . **123** E5
Dye House Cotts PL14. . . **36** F2
Dymond Cl PL32 . . . . **105** B2
Dymond Ct (Kingdom Pl)
  PL12. . . . . **122** F2
Dynas-la Rd TR26. . . . . . . **141** B4
Dynevor Cl PL3 . . . . **128** F7

E

Eagle Rd PL7 . . . . **131** C4
Earle's Retreat TR11 . . . . **145** B3
Earl's Acre PL3 . . . . **128** C4
Earl's Dr The
  Cawsand PL10. . . . . **133** A1
  Kingsand PL10. . . . . **133** B3
Earls Mill Rd PL7. . . . . . . **130** E6
Earls Rise TR7 . . . . **111** B5
Earls Wood Cl PL6 . . . . . **125** F3
Earls Wood Dr PL6 . . . . . **125** F3
Eastbourne Cl PL25 . . . . **114** E3
Eastbourne Rd PL25. . . . **114** D3
East Bridge 4 TR4. . . . . . **69** A3
Eastbury Ave PL5 . . . . . . **124** A2
East Camps Bay PL11. . . . **64** D4
East Charles St TR14 . . . **138** E2
East Cl TR13 . . . . **146** D7
East Cliff PL13. . . . . **117** D3
Eastcliff Ave TR4. . . . . **68** A7
Eastcliffe Rd PL24. . . . . . . **60** C5
East Cliff La TR17 . . . . **89** C5
Eastcote Cl PL6. . . . . **125** B6
EASTCOTT. **3** A3
Eastcott Cross EX23 . . . . . **3** A2
Eastella Rd PL20 . . . . **42** D2
East End TR15 . . . . **140** C5
Easterdown Cl PL9 . . . . . **135** F7
Eastern Ave PL14 . . . . . . **113** D6
Eastern Gn
  Gulval TR18 . . . . **88** E6
  Penzance TR18. . . . . **143** F7
Eastern Green Pk TR18. . . **88** E6
Eastern La TR14 . . . . **138** D4
Eastern Wood Rd PL7. . . **131** D4
East Fairholme Rd EX23 . **104** F7
Eastfield Ave PL9 . . . . . . **135** C6
Eastfield Cres PL3 . . . . . . **129** A6
Eastfield Way PL25. . . . . **114** F5
East Hill
  Camborne TR14 . . . . . . **139** A5
  St Austell PL25 . . . . **114** D3
Eastlake Ho 5 PL1. . . . . . **149** A2
Eastlake St 4 PL1 . . . . . . **148** C3
Eastland Cl TR1. . . . . **137** F4
EAST LOOE **117** D3
EAST PANSON **13** F3
East Park Ave PL4. . . . . . **148** C4
East Pk
  Pensilva PL14 . . . . **38** D4
  Redruth TR15. . . . . **140** D6

East Pool Pk TR15 . . . . . **139** D6
EAST PORTHOLLAND **84** E5
East Quay TR27 . . . . **142** B6
East Quay Ho PL13 . . . . . **117** D3
East Rd
  Kilkhampton EX23 . . . . . . **5** A6
  Menheniot PL14. . . . . . . **52** A5
  Quintrell Downs TR8 . . . . **44** E3
  Stithians TR3 . . . . **80** F3
East Rise TR11. . . . . **144** F3
East Rosewin Row 10
  TR1 . . . . **137** D5
East St
  Newquay TR7. . . . . **110** E6
  Plymouth PL1. . . . . **148** A2
  Polruan PL23. . . . . **116** D3
  1 St Columb Major TR9 . . **45** E4
EAST TAPHOUSE **50** B6
East Terr TR27 . . . . **142** B6
East View PL14 . . . . **51** F5
East Wharf PL26 . . . . **73** C3
East Wheel Rose Sta★
  TR8. . . . . **56** C6
Eastwood Park Ind Est
  TR10. . . . . **144** D7
Eastwood Rd TR10 . . . . . **144** D7
EAST YOULSTONE **3** C2
East Youlstone Cross EX23 **3** C2
Ebenezer Pl 12 TR18. . . . **143** C1
Ebrington St PL4. . . . . . . **149** A3
Echo Cres PL5 . . . . **124** D2
Eddystone Cl PL3 . . . . . . **129** C6
Eddystone Ct PL13 . . . . . **117** D2
Eddystone Pl 3 PL27 . . . **108** B5
Eddystone Rd
  Down Thomas PL9. . . . . **135** C1
  St Austell PL25 . . . . **114** E5
  Wadebridge PL27 . . . . . **108** B6
Eddystone Rise PL14 . . . **113** D7
Eddystone Road Trad & Ind
  Est PL27. . . . . **108** B6
Eddystone Terr
  Plymouth PL1. . . . . **148** B1
  2 Wadebridge PL27 . . . **108** B5
Eden Cl 11 PL24. . . . . **60** B4
Eden Gdns 14 TR18 . . . . **143** C1
Eden Project★ PL24,
  PL26. . . . . **115** D8
Edenside PL3 . . . . **128** F6
Eden Terr 13 TR18 . . . . . **143** C1
Edgar Rd
  Jacobstow EX23 . . . . **11** A6
  Wainhouse Corner EX23 . . **10** F6
Edgar Terr PL4 . . . . **129** A4
Edgcumbe Ave
  Lostwithiel PL22 . . . . . . **112** B1
  Roche PL26 . . . . **46** F3
  Saltash PL12 . . . . **122** C5
  St Austell PL25 . . . . **114** A3
  St Dominick PL12. . . . . . . **40** D2
Edgcumbe St PL1 . . . . . . **128** A1
Edgcumbe Terr
  Milton Abbot PL19 . . . . . . **29** C6
  1 Par PL24. . . . . **60** D5
Edgecombe Way PL18. . . **40** E5
Edgecumbe Terr 14 PL20. **41** B1
Edgemoor Cl PL14 . . . . . . **38** A3
Edinburgh Cl PL25 . . . . . **115** C3
Edinburgh St PL1 . . . . . . **127** E1
Edith Ave PL4. . . . . **149** C4
Edith St PL5 . . . . **123** D1
EDMONTON **33** B7
Edmund Rd TR15. . . . . . . **140** B6
Edna Terr PL4 . . . . **149** C3
Ednovean La TR20 . . . . . . **89** E4
Edward Hain Com Hospl
  TR26 . . . . **141** B5
Edwards Cl PL7. . . . . **131** B4
Edwards Cres PL12. . . . . **122** C2
Edwards Dr PL7. . . . . **131** B5
Edwards Rd
  Devoran TR3 . . . . **81** F6
  St Giles on the Heath PL15 . **13** F1
Edward St
  Camborne TR14 . . . . . . **138** F4
  Truro TR1. . . . . **137** C4
Edymeade Ct PL15 . . . . . **106** C5
Edymeade Gdn
  9 Launceston PL15 . . . . **106** C5
  11 PL15. . . . . **106** C5
Effingham Cres PL3. . . . . **128** D7
EFFORD **129** C5
Efford Cres PL3. . . . . **129** B6
Efford Down Pk EX23 . . . **104** C5
Efford Farm Bsns Pk
  EX23. . . . . **104** C4
Efford Farm Cotts EX23 . **104** C4
Efford Fort PL3 . . . . **129** C6
Efford La PL3 . . . . **129** B5
Efford Pathway PL3. . . . . **129** C6
Efford Rd PL3. . . . . **129** B6
Efford Wlk PL3 . . . . **129** B6
Egerton Cres PL4 . . . . . . **149** C3
Egerton Pl PL4. . . . . **149** C3
Egerton Rd
  Padstow PL28 . . . . **107** D4

Egerton Rd continued
  Plymouth PL4. . . . . **149** C3
EGGBEARE **19** A7
EGGBUCKLAND **129** C8
Eggbuckland Rd PL3 . . . **129** C7
Eglos Ct PL30. . . . . **23** E7
Egloshayle Rd
  Hayle TR27. . . . . **142** E6
  Wadebridge PL27 . . . . . **108** D5
EGLOSKERRY **18** A5
Egloskerry Prim Sch PL15 **18** A5
Eglos Mdw TR11 . . . . **82** A3
Eglos Parc
  Mullion TR12 . . . . **99** A2
  Wadebridge PL27 . . . . . **108** D5
Eglos Rd
  Ludgvan TR20 . . . . **89** A7
  Shortlanesend TR4. . . . . . **69** F6
  St Erme TR4. . . . . **70** D8
Eglos View 2 PL35. . . . . . . **9** C1
EGOSHAYLE **108** D6
Egret Cl PL10. . . . . **133** A6
Eider Wlk TR27 . . . . **77** E3
Eight Acre Cl 1 PL7. . . . . **131** C5
Elaine Cl PL7 . . . . **130** B5
Elbow La PL19 . . . . **147** C6
ELBURTON **136** B6
Elburton Prim Sch PL9. . **136** C7
Elburton Rd PL9 . . . . **136** B8
Eldad Hill PL1 . . . . **148** A3
Elder Cl 2 PL7 . . . . **131** B5
Elderfield Cl 7 PL24. . . . . **60** D5
Eleanor Ho PL1 . . . . **148** A2
Elerkey Cl TR2. . . . . **83** F6
Elerkey La TR2. . . . . **83** F6
Eleven Doors PL25 . . . . . **115** B2
Elford Cres PL7. . . . . **130** E7
Elford Dr PL9 . . . . **135** C7
Elford Pk PL20 . . . . **42** D2
Elgin Cres PL5 . . . . **124** E3
Elim Cl PL3. . . . . **128** E5
Elim Terr PL3. . . . . **128** E5
Eliot Cl PL15. . . . . **18** C2
Eliot Ct TR7 . . . . **110** F6
Eliot Dr PL12 . . . . **65** B8
Eliot Gdns TR7. . . . . **110** F6
Eliot Rd
  St Austell PL25 . . . . **114** E4
  Truro TR1. . . . . **137** C5
Eliot St PL5. . . . . **127** E8
Elizabeth Cl
  Bodmin PL31. . . . . **109** D4
  Threemilestone TR3. . . . . **69** C3
Elizabeth Ct
  Bugle PL26. . . . . **47** C1
  2 Plymouth PL1. . . . . . . **149** A2
Elizabeth House Mus & Arts
  Gall★ PL4. . . . . **149** A2
Elizabeth Pl PL4 . . . . **149** A4
Elizabeth Rd
  Bude EX23 . . . . **104** F5
  St Austell PL25 . . . . **114** E3
Elizabeth Terr TR17 . . . . . **89** B5
Ellen Cl TR4 . . . . **68** C6
Ellenglaze Ct TR8 . . . . . . **55** D8
Ellenglaze La TR8. . . . . . . **55** D8
Ellenglaze Mdw TR8 . . . . **55** D8
Elliot Sq PL11. . . . . **127** B3
Elliot St PL1 . . . . **148** B1
Elliott Cl PL12 . . . . **122** D2
Elliott Terr PL1 . . . . **148** C1
Elliot Terrace La PL1. . . . **148** C1
Elliot Way PL4. . . . . **129** B1
Ellis Cl TR27 . . . . **142** C5
Ellis Mdw TR27 . . . . **78** D6
Elliston Gdns 3 TR13 . . . **98** C8
Ellis Way TR27 . . . . **142** C5
Elm Cl
  Callington PL17 . . . . **39** F4
  Camborne TR15 . . . . . . **139** D6
  Newquay TR7. . . . . **110** F4
  Tavistock PL19. . . . . **147** C3
Elm Cotts PL12 . . . . **122** C3
Elm Court Gdns TR1. . . . **137** D5
Elm Cres PL3, PL4 . . . . . **129** A4
Elm Croft PL2. . . . . **128** B7
Elm Ct TR1 . . . . **137** D5
Elm Dr
  Bude EX23 . . . . **104** F5
  8 St Columb Major TR9 . . **45** D6
Elmgate Crossways PL12 . **65** E8
Elm Gr
  Feock TR3 . . . . **82** C5
  Plymouth, Eggbuckland
    PL6 . . . . **129** B8
  Plymouth, Plympton PL7 . **130** B5
Elm Grove Cotts TR10 . . . **93** C6
Elmlea EX23 . . . . **104** F5
Elm Mdw TR3. . . . . **82** C5
Elm Meadow Dr PL13 . . **117** D4
Elm Pk PL10 . . . . **133** B6
Elm Rd
  Plymouth, Glenholt PL6. . **125** D6
  Plymouth, Mannamead PL4 . **128** F4
Elms Close Terr 25 TR18. **143** C2
ELMSCOTT **2** E8
Elmsleigh PL25 . . . . **114** B3
Elmsleigh Rd PL27. . . . . **108** B6
Elms The
  Perranuthnoe TR20 . . . . . **89** D4
  Plymouth PL3. . . . . **128** A3
Elm Terr
  8 Mullion TR12. . . . . **99** A2
  1 Plymouth PL3 . . . . **128** F5
  St Austell PL25 . . . . **114** C4
Elm Tree Rd PL13 . . . . . . **117** D4
Elmwood Cl PL6 . . . . **125** D5

Elowen Cl TR11 . . . . 144 E2
Elphinstone Rd PL2 . . . . 128 C7
Elspeth Sitters Ho 11
  PL4 . . . . 149 A2
Elwell Rd PL12 . . . . 123 A2
Elwick Gdns PL3 . . . . 129 B5
Embankment La PL4 . . . 129 B2
Embankment Rd PL4 . . . 129 B2
Embankment Road Lane N
  PL4 . . . . 129 B2
Emily Gdns PL4 . . . . 149 B4
Emlyn Fields PL25 . . . . . 114 F6
Emma Pl PL1 . . . . 128 A1
Emma Place Ope PL1 . . . 128 A1
EMPACOMBE 133 D6
Empire Way TR11 . . . . . . 144 E4
Empress Ave 23 TR18 . . 143 E6
Emslie Rd TR11 . . . . 145 C2
Endeavour Ct PL1 . . . . . 128 A3
Endsleigh Dr PL15, PL19 . . 28 F5
Endsleigh Gdns 2 PL4 . 149 A4
Endsleigh Gdns Nursery★
  PL19 . . . . 29 B5
Endsleigh Park Rd PL3 . 128 D6
Endsleigh Pk EX23 . . . . . . 7 B6
Endsleigh Pl PL4 . . . . . . 149 A4
Endsleigh Rd PL9 . . . . . 135 C7
Endsleigh Terr PL14 . . . 113 C6
Eningdale Rd PL19 . . . . . 147 A4
Ennerdale Gdns PL6 . . . 124 E5
ENNISCAVEN 46 D2
Ennis Cl TR4 . . . . 56 D1
Ennor's Rd TR7 . . . . 110 D6
Epping Cres PL6 . . . . 129 D7
Epworth Cl TR1 . . . . 137 E4
Epworth Terr 4 PL2 . . . 127 F5
Erdiston Ct EX23 . . . . . . 104 D6
Ergue-Gaberic Way
  EX23 . . . . 104 D5
Eric Rd
  Calstock PL18 . . . . 41 B3
  Plymouth PL4 . . . . 149 C3
Erisey Terr TR11 . . . . . . 145 B4
Erith Ave PL2 . . . . 127 C4
Erle Cl PL7 . . . . 130 F3
Erlstoke Cl PL6 . . . . 125 D1
Erme Gdns PL3 . . . . 129 C5
Ermington Terr PL4 . . . . 128 E4
ERNESETTLE 123 E3
Ernesettle Cres PL5 . . . 123 E3
Ernesettle Gn PL5 . . . . . 123 E4
Ernesettle La PL5 . . . . . 123 D4
Ernesettle Prim Sch PL5 123 E4
Ernesettle Rd PL5 . . . . . 123 E3
Erow Glas PL10 . . . . 144 C8
Esmonde Gdns PL5 . . . . 127 B8
Esmonde Rd TR13 . . . . . 146 D4
Esperanza Ct TR11 . . . . 144 F6
Esplanade PL23 . . . . 116 C3
Esplanade Rd TR7 . . . . . 110 A6
Esplanade The PL1 . . . . 148 C1
Essa Rd PL12 . . . . 122 F2
Essex Dr TR15 . . . . 139 B8
Essex St PL1 . . . . 148 B4
Esso Wharf Rd PL4 . . . . 149 C1
Eston Cl TR10 . . . . 93 C8
ESTOVER 125 E4
Estover Cl
  PL6 . . . . 125 F5
  Plymouth PL6 . . . . 125 F5
Estover Ind Est PL6 . . . 125 E4
Estover Rd PL6 . . . . 125 F4
Estuary View
  2 Falmouth TR11 . . . 145 B5
  Lelant TR26 . . . . 77 E3
  Newquay TR7 . . . . 110 D5
Estuary Way PL5 . . . . . . 127 C7
Eton Ave PL1 . . . . 148 C4
Eton Pl PL1 . . . . 148 C4
Eton St PL1 . . . . 148 C4
Eton Terr 3 PL1 . . . . . . 148 B3
Euny Cl TR15 . . . . 140 A4
Eureka Vale 7 TR6 . . . . 55 A5
Europa Ct TR8 . . . . 31 C2
Evans Ct PL1 . . . . 148 A3
Evans Pl PL2 . . . . 128 B5
Evans Way TR20 . . . . 90 C4
Evea Cl TR1 . . . . 69 F3
Evely Cl PL14 . . . . 113 D7
Evelyn Pl PL4 . . . . 149 A4
Evelyn St PL5 . . . . 123 D1
Evenden Ct PL11 . . . . . . 127 A3
Example Cross PL15 . . . . 27 B6
Exchange (Gall) The★ 37
  TR18 . . . . 143 E5
Exchange St PL4 . . . . . . 149 A2
Exe Gdns PL3 . . . . 129 C7
Exeter Cl PL5 . . . . 123 D4
Exeter Ct 6 PL15 . . . . . 106 C6
Exeter St
  Launceston PL15 . . . . 106 C6
  Plymouth, Barbican PL4 . 149 A3
  Plymouth, St Jude's PL4 149 B2
Exmouth Ct PL1 . . . . 127 F3
Exmouth Rd PL1 . . . . . . 127 F4
Explorer Ct PL2 . . . . 128 B5

F

Factory Cotts PL14 . . . . . 51 F5
Fairbourne Rd PL25 . . . . 114 F4
Fair Cross TR2 . . . . 72 C6
Fairfax Rd TR2 . . . . 70 F5
Fairfax Terr 5 PL2 . . . . 127 F4
Fairfield
  Plymouth PL7 . . . . 130 E7
  St Germans PL12 . . . . . 65 A8
Fair Field TR20 . . . . 89 B8
Fairfield Ave PL2 . . . . . . 128 C7
Fairfield Cl
  Lelant TR26 . . . . 77 E4
  St Austell PL25 . . . . . . 115 A4
Fairfield Pk PL15 . . . . . . 26 C7
Fairfield Rd
  Bude EX23 . . . . 104 E5
  Falmouth TR11 . . . . . . 144 F4
Fairfields PL13 . . . . 117 D5
Fairlight PL14 . . . . 113 D5
Fairmantle St TR1 . . . . . 137 D4
Fairmead Cl PL12 . . . . . . 53 E4
Fairmead Mews PL12 . . 122 C3
Fairmeadow TR10 . . . . . 144 B7
Fairmead Rd PL12 . . . . . 122 C2
Fair Park Cl PL15 . . . . . . 106 D5
Fairpark Rd
  Liskeard PL14 . . . . 113 C5
  Wadebridge PL27 . . . . 108 B5
Fair Park View TR8 . . . . . 56 F5
Fair Pk Cl 10 PL15 . . . . 106 C5
Fair St TR9 . . . . 45 E6
Fair View
  Bodmin PL31 . . . . 109 B4
  Lanivet PL26 . . . . 47 E4
Fairview Ave PL3 . . . . . . 129 D5
Fairview Pk 5 TR9 . . . . 45 E2
Fairview Terr TR7 . . . . . . 110 E6
Fair View Terr TR4 . . . . . 55 D8
Fairview Way PL3 . . . . . . 129 E5
Fairway
  Saltash PL12 . . . . 122 C2
  St Austell PL25 . . . . . . 115 D3
Fairways The PL30 . . . . . 48 C7
Fairway The TR11 . . . . . . 93 C2
FAIRY CROSS 49 B5
Falcon Terr EX23 . . . . . . 104 D5
FALMOUTH 145 C4
Falmouth Art Gall★
  TR11 . . . . 145 B4
Falmouth Bsns TR11 . . 144 E3
Falmouth Com Sch
  TR11 . . . . 144 D5
Falmouth Docks Sta
  TR11 . . . . 145 D3
Falmouth Hospl TR11 . . 144 F4
Falmouth Marine Sch 17
  TR11 . . . . 145 A4
Falmouth Pl TR19 . . . . . . 86 F8
Falmouth Prim Academy
  TR11 . . . . 145 A5
Falmouth Rd
  Helston TR13 . . . . 146 D7
  Penryn TR10 . . . . 144 E7
  Redruth TR15 . . . . 140 C4
  Truro TR1 . . . . 137 C3
Falmouth Town Sta
  TR11 . . . . 145 C3
Falmouth University
  (Tremough Campus)
  TR10 . . . . 144 A8
Falmouth University
  (Wellington Annexe)
  TR11 . . . . 145 B4
Falmouth University
  (Woodlane Campus)
  TR11 . . . . 145 B3
Falmouth Watersports Ctr 15
  TR11 . . . . 145 B4
Falmouth Wharves TR11 145 A6
Fanshawe Way PL9 . . . . 135 C6
Faraday Mill Bsns Pk
  PL4 . . . . 129 B1
Farfield Pl TR7 . . . . 110 B5
Faringdon Rd PL4 . . . . . 129 B3
Farley Cl TR1 . . . . 137 C3
Farm Cl PL7 . . . . 130 C7
Farmers Cl PL14 . . . . 50 B6
Farmers Ct TR20 . . . . 89 B8
Farmer's La PL14 . . . . . . 50 B6
Farmers Mdw 8 TR18 . 143 C2
Farm La
  Plymouth PL5 . . . . 124 B2
  Saltash PL12 . . . . 122 D1
FARMS COMMON 79 F1
Farm Town TR15 . . . . . . 140 C3
Farnley Cl PL6 . . . . 125 B6
Farrar Cl TR27 . . . . 142 E8
Farriers Cotts PL7 . . . . . 130 E7
Farriers Gn PL32 . . . . . . 105 B2
Farriers The PL19 . . . . . . 30 A3
Farrow Fordh PL26 . . . . . 46 F3
Faugan La TR18 . . . . 143 B1
Faugan Rd TR18 . . . . 143 B1
Faukener Cl TR11 . . . . . . 144 F4
Fayre View PL12 . . . . 122 B1
Fearnside Way PL12 . . . 122 C3
Federation Rd PL3 . . . . . 129 C4
Fegan Rd PL5 . . . . 123 B1
Feliskirk La TR17 . . . . . . 89 B6
Felixstowe Ave TR7 . . . . 111 E2
Fellowes Pl PL1 . . . . 128 A4
Fenten Cl EX23 . . . . 104 E7
Fenten Pk PL12 . . . . 122 F3

Fenteroon Rd PL32 . . . . 105 C2
FENTONADLE 24 A5
Fentonluna La PL28 . . . 107 D6
Fenwick Rd TR11 . . . . . . 145 B2
FEOCK 82 C5
Fern Cl PL7 . . . . 131 C5
Ferndale Ave PL2 . . . . . . 127 E7
Ferndale Cl PL6 . . . . 125 D8
Ferndale Rd
  Falmouth TR11 . . . . . . 145 A2
  Plymouth PL2 . . . . 127 F7
Ferndale Terr PL14 . . . . 113 B6
Fern Glen 18 TR26 . . . 141 A5
Fernhill Rd TR7 . . . . 110 C6
Fern Lee Terr 19 TR26 . 141 B5
Fernleigh Cres PL27 . . . 108 C4
Fernleigh Gdns PL27 . . . 108 C4
Fernleigh La PL27 . . . . . 108 C4
Fernleigh Rd
  Plymouth PL3 . . . . 128 F5
  Wadebridge PL27 . . . . 108 C4
Fernleigh Terr
  Gunnislake PL18 . . . . . 40 E5
  Nanpean PL26 . . . . 58 C6
Fern Mdw PL19 . . . . 147 D6
Fernside Pk PL14 . . . . . . 38 A3
Fernside Rd TR14 . . . . . . 138 B1
FERNSPLATT 81 C8
Ferrers Rd PL5 . . . . 123 E1
Ferretts Cross EX23 . . . . 11 A6
Ferris Town TR1 . . . . 137 C4
Ferris Way PL23 . . . . 116 E2
Ferry La PL11 . . . . 126 D5
Ferry Rd PL1 . . . . 127 E5
Ferry St PL11 . . . . 127 C3
Festival Villas TR3 . . . . . 69 D3
Fettling Lane 3 PL25 . . 115 A3
Feversham Cl PL7 . . . . . 131 B6
FIDDLERS GREEN 56 B5
Field Cl PL22 . . . . 112 D2
Field Pl TR11 . . . . 93 D3
Field The TR 20 . . . . 76 F2
Fifield Ho PL26 . . . . 58 B4
Fillace La PL20 . . . . 42 C4
Fillace Pk PL20 . . . . 42 C4
Filtrick La TR16 . . . . 139 E1
Finch Cl PL3 . . . . 129 D4
Finches Cl PL9 . . . . 136 C7
Findon Gdns PL6 . . . . . . 125 D4
Finewell St PL1 . . . . 148 C2
Finnigan Rd PL4 . . . . . . 129 B1
Finnygook La PL11 . . . . . 65 A4
Finsbury Rise PL26 . . . . . 46 F3
Fir Cl
  Goonhavern TR4 . . . . . 55 D4
  Helston TR13 . . . . 146 B7
  St Austell PL25 . . . . . . 114 B3
Fir Cres PL26 . . . . 58 D5
Fircroft Rd PL2 . . . . 128 B7
Firebeacon Cross EX39 . . 2 F7
Firestone Cl PL6 . . . . . . 125 E1
Fir Gr 8 TR3 . . . . 81 F7
Firsleigh Pk PL26 . . . . . . 46 F3
First Ave
  Plymouth, Billacombe
    PL9 . . . . 135 F8
  Plymouth, Stoke PL1 . . 128 A2
Firs The PL26 . . . . 58 E8
Fisgard Way PL11 . . . . . . 126 D3
Fisher Cl PL27 . . . . 108 D6
Fisher Rd PL2 . . . . 128 A5
Fish Mkt PL4 . . . . 149 B2
Fish Quay PL4 . . . . 149 A2
Fish St 9 TR26 . . . . 141 B6
Fish Strand Hill TR11 . . 145 B4
Fish Strand Quay TR11 . 145 B4
Fistral Cl PL11 . . . . 126 F4
Fistral Cres TR7 . . . . 110 A5
Fistral Ct TR7 . . . . 110 A5
Fistral Sands Apartments
  TR7 . . . . 110 D7
Fitzroy Rd PL1 . . . . 128 A3
Fitzroy Terr 7 PL1 . . . . 128 A3
Fitzsimmons Cl 7 TR13 146 C5
Five Fields La TR11 . . . . 145 A3
Five Wells La TR13 . . . . . 146 B5
Flamank Pk PL31 . . . . . . 109 C4
Flambards Experience The★
  TR13 . . . . 146 E4
Flamborough Rd PL6 . . . 125 A7
Flamborough Way PL6 . 125 A6
Flamsteed Cres PL5 . . . 123 E1
Fleet St PL2 . . . . 127 E6
Fleetwood Gdns PL6 . . . 125 A7
Fletcher Cres PL9 . . . . . 136 B6
FLETCHERSBRIDGE 48 F8
Fletcher Way PL9 . . . . . . 136 A6
Fletemoor Rd PL5 . . . . . 123 E1
Fletewood Sch PL4 . . . . 148 C4
FLEXBURY 104 E6
Flexbury Ave EX23 . . . . 104 E7
Flexbury Mews EX23 . . . 104 E7
Flexbury Park Cl EX23 . . 104 E6
Flexbury Park Rd EX23 . 104 E6
Flexbury Pk EX23 . . . . . 104 E7
Flora Cotts PL1 . . . . 148 B2
Flora Ct PL1 . . . . 148 B3
Flora St PL1 . . . . 148 B2
Florence Hill PL17 . . . . . 39 F5
Florence Pl
  Falmouth TR11 . . . . . . 145 B3
  Newlyn TR18 . . . . 143 C3
  Plymouth PL4 . . . . 149 C3
Florence Rd PL17 . . . . . . 39 F5
Florence Road Bsns Pk
  PL17 . . . . 39 F6
Florence Road Ind Est
  PL17 . . . . 39 F6

Florence St PL5 . . . . 123 D1
Florence Terr TR11 . . . . 145 B3
Florida Gdns PL3 . . . . . . 129 C6
Floyd Cl PL2 . . . . 127 F7
FLUSHING
  Manaccan 101 B8
  Penryn 145 C6
Flushing Prim Sch TR11 145 B6
Focus Sch - Plymouth
  Campus PL5 . . . . 123 B1
Folders La PL30 . . . . 23 F6
Foliot Ave PL2 . . . . 128 A6
Foliot Rd PL2 . . . . 128 A6
Folkstone Cl PL26 . . . . . 58 E6
FONSTON 11 C2
Forbes Cl TR18 . . . . 143 B1
Forbes Rd TR18 . . . . 143 B1
FORD 128 A5
Ford Cl PL22 . . . . 49 E3
Ford Cl PL14 . . . . 39 A2
FORDER
  Cawsand 132 F1
  Saltash 122 C1
Forder Hill PL10 . . . . 132 F1
Forder Hts PL6 . . . . 125 B1
Forder La PL10 . . . . 132 F1
Forder Valley Rd PL6 . . . 129 D8
Ford Hill PL2 . . . . 128 A5
FORD PARK 128 D4
Ford Park La PL4 . . . . . . 128 E4
Ford Park Rd PL4 . . . . . . 128 E4
Ford Pk PL4 . . . . 128 E4
Ford Prim Sch PL2 . . . . 127 F5
Fords Hill PL12 . . . . 100 D7
Ford's Row PL15 . . . . . . 140 B5
Ford St PL19 . . . . 147 B5
Foredown Pk PL14 . . . . . 38 C3
Fore St
  Ashton TR13 . . . . 90 E3
  Barripper TR14 . . . . . . 79 B5
  Bere Alston PL20 . . . . . 41 B1
  Bere Ferrers PL20 . . . . 119 F3
  Bodmin PL31 . . . . 109 D5
  Boscastle PL35 . . . . . . 9 C1
  Bugle PL26 . . . . 47 C1
  6 Callington PL17 . . . 39 E4
  Calstock PL18 . . . . 41 A3
  Camborne TR15 . . . . . 139 B6
  Camelford PL32 . . . . . 105 D4
  Cargreen PL12 . . . . . . 119 A4
  Carharrack TR16 . . . . . 80 F8
  Chacewater TR4 . . . . . 69 A3
  Constantine TR11 . . . . 92 A3
  Crumplehorn PL13 . . . 62 D1
  Fowey PL23 . . . . 116 D4
  Golant PL23 . . . . 61 B5
  Goldsithney TR20 . . . . 89 E5
  Grampound Road TR2 . 57 E1
  Grampound TR2 . . . . . 72 A7
  Gunnislake PL18 . . . . . 40 F5
  Hayle TR27 . . . . 142 D6
  Herodsfoot PL14 . . . . . 50 E3
  Kingsand PL10 . . . . . . 133 A2
  Lelant TR26 . . . . 77 E4
  Lerryn PL22 . . . . 61 C7
  Lifton PL16 . . . . 19 F4
  Liskeard PL14 . . . . 113 C6
  Looe PL13 . . . . 117 C3
  Lostwithiel PL22 . . . . . 112 C2
  Madron TR20 . . . . 88 B7
  Marazion TR17 . . . . . . 89 C5
  Mevagissey PL26 . . . . . 73 C3
  Millbrook PL10 . . . . . . 132 E5
  Milton Abbot PL19 . . . . 29 C6
  Mount Hawke TR4 . . . . 68 C6
  13 Mousehole TR19 . . 88 C1
  Nanpean PL26 . . . . 58 D7
  Newlyn TR18 . . . . 143 C1
  Newquay TR7 . . . . 110 D6
  Par PL24 . . . . 60 B5
  Penponds TR14 . . . . . . 138 B1
  Pensilva PL14 . . . . 38 E4
  Plymouth, Devonport PL1 127 E4
  Plymouth, Plympton PL7 130 E4
  Plymouth, Tamerton Foliot
    PL5 . . . . 124 B2
  Polgooth PL26 . . . . 59 A1
  Polruan PL23 . . . . 116 D2
  4 Porthleven TR13 . . 98 B8
  Port Isaac PL29 . . . . . . 22 D7
  Praze-an-Beeble TR14 . 79 B2
  Probus TR2 . . . . 71 C6
  Redruth TR15 . . . . 140 B5
  Roche PL26 . . . . 46 F2
  Saltash PL12 . . . . 122 F2
  St Austell PL25 . . . . . . 114 C3
  St Cleer PL14 . . . . 37 F3
  St Columb Major TR9 . 45 E6
  St Day TR16 . . . . 68 D1
  St Dennis PL26 . . . . . . 58 C8
  St Erth TR27 . . . . 142 A1
  St Germans PL12 . . . . . 65 A8
  St Ives TR26 . . . . 141 B6
  St Just TR19 . . . . 86 F6
  7 Stratton EX23 . . . . . 4 E1
  St Stephen PL26 . . . . . 58 B4
  St Teath PL30 . . . . 23 E7
  Tintagel PL34 . . . . 14 C7
  Torpoint PL11 . . . . 127 B3
  Tregony TR2 . . . . 71 F3
  Troon TR14 . . . . 79 E5
  9 Tywardreath PL24 . 60 D5
Forest Ave PL2 . . . . 128 C7
Foresters Rd PL9 . . . . . . 135 D7
Forest Hos TR4 . . . . 70 D8
Forest View PL6 . . . . 125 D7
FORGE 68 A4

Forge Ind Pk TR14 . . . . . 138 E5
Forge La PL12 . . . . 122 C4
Forge The TR3 . . . . 82 A7
Forge Way TR14 . . . . 69 F6
Forlaze Rd PL27 . . . . 21 D2
Formal Ind Pk TR14 . . . 138 B4
FORRABURY 9 C2
Forrabury Hill 5 PL35 . . 9 C1
Forreglos Dr 10 TR17 . . 89 C5
Forresters Dr PL6 . . . . . 125 D7
Forsters Ct TR2 . . . . 72 A7
Forsythia Dr PL12 . . . . . 122 C3
Fort Austin Ave PL6 . . . 125 C1
Fortescue Cl PL26 . . . . . 58 D6
Fortescue Pl
  Lostwithiel PL22 . . . . . 112 D3
  Plymouth PL3 . . . . 129 A6
Fortescue Terr PL19 . . . 147 A6
Forth an Cos TR3 . . . . . . 81 B4
Forth-an-Eglas TR16 . . . 68 D1
Forth-an-Nance TR16 . . . 67 C6
Forth-an-Praze
  Illogan TR15 . . . . 139 D8
  St Day TR16 . . . . 68 D1
Forth-an-Ryn TR15 . . . . 140 D4
Forth an Streth TR27 . . . 142 E7
Forth an Tewennow
  TR27 . . . . 142 D7
Forth-an-Tre TR27 . . . . . 142 E7
Forth an Ula TR27 . . . . . 142 E7
Forth an Venegh PL31 . . 109 E3
Forth an Vre TR14 . . . . . 139 A3
Forth Coth TR3 . . . . 82 A7
Forthcrom TR12 . . . . 92 C1
Forth Dall 21 TR16 . . . . 67 E4
Forth Gdns PL3 . . . . 129 D6
Forth Gwedhen TR13 . . . 146 D8
Forth Kegyn TR15 . . . . . 139 B4
Forthnoweth TR15 . . . . . 140 B5
Forth Noweth 4 TR3 . . 81 F7
Forth Scol
  Camborne TR15 . . . . . 139 D7
  6 Porthleven TR13 . . 98 C8
Forthvean
  Camborne TR14 . . . . . 138 D1
  Portreath TR16 . . . . . . 67 C5
Forthvean Cres TR14 . . . 68 A6
Forthvean Rd TR4, TR16 . 67 F7
Forth Veor TR15 . . . . 140 E7
Forthvras TR15 . . . . 139 B8
Fort Picklecombe PL10 . 133 F4
Fort Terr PL6 . . . . 124 F3
Fort The PL10 . . . . 133 A1
Fosbrooke Ct 10 PL3 . . 128 F6
FOSS 133 A5
Foster Dr PL31 . . . . 109 C3
Fosters La PL34 . . . . 14 C7
Fosters Mdw PL18 . . . . . 40 D6
Fosters Way EX23 . . . . . 104 F6
Foulston Ave PL5 . . . . . . 127 B8
Foulston Way PL31 . . . . 109 B4
FOUNDRY 142 B5
Foundry Dr PL25 . . . . . . 115 B3
Foundry Flats TR27 . . . . 142 B5
Foundry Gdns PL15 . . . . 106 B6
Foundry Hill
  Hayle TR27 . . . . 142 B4
  Stithians TR3 . . . . 80 F3
Foundry Ho 3 TR27 . . . 142 B5
Foundry La
  Hayle TR27 . . . . 142 B5
  Newlyn TR18 . . . . 143 C2
Foundry Mews PL19 . . . 147 D6
Foundry Rd TR14 . . . . . . 138 E3
Foundry Row
  Marhamchurch EX23 . . 7 B6
  5 Redruth TR15 . . . . 140 B5
Foundry Sq TR27 . . . . . . 142 B5
Foundry St 6 PL27 . . . 108 B5
Fountain Ct 28 TR18 . . 143 E6
Fountains Cres PL2 . . . . 128 C8
Four Acres Rd TR2 . . . . . 83 F6
Fourgates Est PL14 . . . . 51 F5
FOUR LANES 80 A5
Four Lanes' End TR19 . . . 97 F6
Fourlanesend Com Prim Sch
  PL10 . . . . 132 F3
Four Turnings PL23 . . . . 60 D7
Fowenn Ct 12 PL14 . . . 113 B6
FOWEY 116 B4
Fowey Com L Ctr PL23 . 116 B4
Fowey Cres 27 PL17 . . . 39 F4
Fowey Gdns PL3 . . . . . . 129 D6
Fowey Hospl PL23 . . . . . 116 C5
Fowey Mus★ PL23 . . . . . 116 B4
Fowey Prim Sch PL23 . . 116 C4
Fowey River Academy
  PL23 . . . . 116 B4
Fowlfield Row PL13 . . . . 90 F3
Foxdown PL27 . . . . 108 D5
Foxes Field PL18 . . . . . . 88 E6
Foxes La 5 TR19 . . . . . . 88 C1
Foxes Row TR18 . . . . 80 E8
Fox Field Cl PL3 . . . . 129 C5
Foxglove Cl
  Launceston PL15 . . . . 106 E4
  PL26 . . . . 46 F3
Foxglove Cres PL28 . . . . 31 F7
Foxglove Way PL12 . . . . 122 B3
FOXHOLE 58 D5
Foxhole La PL26 . . . . 85 D5
Foxhole Prim Sch PL26 . 58 D5
Fox's La TR11 . . . . 145 B3
Foxstanton Dr TR10 . . . 144 D7

Foxs Yd TR10 . . . . 144 D7
Foxtor Cl PL5 . . . . 124 B3
Foxwood Gdns
　Plymouth, Plymstock PL9 . 135 F5
　Plymouth, Southway PL6 . . 124 E5
Foyle Cl PL7 . . . . 131 A5
FRADDAM 78 D1
FRADDON 45 E1
Fradgan Pl TR18 . . . . 143 C2
Fradgan The 12 TR18 . . . . . 143 C2
Frances St TR1 . . . . 137 C4
Francis La PL27 . . . . 21 D5
Francis Rd PL27 . . . . 21 D5
Francis St PL1 . . . . 148 A3
Frankfort Gate 9 PL1 . . . . 148 B3
Frankland Cl TR11 . . . . 144 F3
Franklin Cl PL27 . . . . 108 D6
Franklyn Cl PL25 . . . . 114 F5
Franklyns' PL6 . . . . 125 A4
Franklyns Cl PL6 . . . . 125 A4
Franwill Terr 16 TR18 . . . . 143 C1
Fraser Pl PL5 . . . . 124 C7
Fraser Rd PL5 . . . . 124 C7
Fraser Sq PL5 . . . . 124 C7
FREATHY 65 E3
Frederick Street E PL1 . . . . 148 B3
Frederick Street W 6
　PL1 . . . . 148 B3
Fredington Gr PL2 . . . . 128 B6
Freedom Sq PL4 . . . . 149 B4
Freeman Collins Dr
　TR11 . . . . 144 F4
Freemans Wharf PL1 . . . . 134 A8
Fremantle Gdns 4 PL2 . . . 127 F4
Fremantle Pl PL2 . . . . 127 F4
Frenchman's La PL12 . . . . . 53 C4
Frensham Ave PL6 . . . . 125 C7
Frensham Gdns PL6 . . . . . . 125 C7
Freshbrook Cl TR18 . . . . . . 88 E6
Freshford Cl PL6 . . . . 125 C1
Freshford Wlk PL6 . . . . 125 C1
Freshwater La TR2 . . . . 95 B6
Frewin Gdns PL6 . . . . 125 B6
Friar's La TR12 . . . . 102 F6
Friars' La PL1 . . . . 149 A2
Friar's La TR12 . . . . 103 B5
Friars Wlk PL19 . . . . 147 E2
Friary Pk PL4 . . . . 149 B3
Friary St PL4 . . . . 149 B3
Frith Rd PL12 . . . . 122 D3
Frobisher App PL5 . . . . 124 D2
Frobisher Dr PL12 . . . . 122 E2
Frobisher Terr 9 TR11 . . . 145 A5
Frobisher Way
　Tavistock PL19 . . . . 147 B5
　Torpoint PL11 . . . . 126 D3
Frog La TR2 . . . . 71 F3
Frogmore Ave PL6 . . . . 129 B7
Frogmore Ct PL6 . . . . 129 B7
FROGPOOL 81 C7
FROGWELL 39 D3
Frogwell Rd PL17 . . . . 39 E4
Frome Cl PL7 . . . . 131 A4
Frontfield Cres PL6 . . . . . . 124 E5
Front Rd PL11 . . . . 64 C4
Frost Cl TR11 . . . . 144 E5
Fuggoe Croft TR26 . . . . . . 141 C3
Fuggoe La TR26 . . . . 141 C2
Fullaford Rd PL17 . . . . 40 A4
Fuller Rd TR6 . . . . 55 A5
Fullerton Rd PL2 . . . . 128 A5
Fuller-Tre Cl PL26 . . . . 46 F3
Furland Cl PL9 . . . . 135 C5
Furneaux Ave PL2 . . . . 128 B6
Furneaux Rd PL2 . . . . 128 B6
Furniss Cl 6 TR1 . . . . 137 D4
Furry The TR13 . . . . 146 B5
Furry Way TR13 . . . . 146 B5
Fursdon Cl PL9 . . . . 136 C6
Furse Pk PL5 . . . . 127 C7
Furzeacre Cl PL7 . . . . 131 A7
Furze Cross EX22 . . . . 8 B5
Furzedown Terr PL13 . . . . . 117 C4
Furze Gdns EX23 . . . . 2 D1
Furzehatt Ave PL9 . . . . . . 136 A6
Furzehatt Park Rd PL9 . . . 136 A6
Furzehatt Rd PL9 . . . . 135 F6
Furzehatt Rise PL9 . . . . . . 136 A6
Furzehatt Villas PL9 . . . . . 135 F6
Furzehatt Way PL9 . . . . . . 136 A6
Furzehill Rd PL4 . . . . 128 F4
Furze Pk
　Polruan PL23 . . . . 116 D2
　St Issey PL27 . . . . 32 D5
　Trelights PL29 . . . . 22 D6
FutureWorld@Goonhilly *
　TR12 . . . . 99 F4

G

Gabriel St 5 TR26 . . . . . . 141 B5
Gadiwall Rise TR27 . . . . . . 77 E3
Gainsborough Ct TR7 . . . . 110 D5
Gainsborough Ho PL19 . . . 147 B6
Gains Cross EX22 . . . . 5 F3
Galileo Cl PL7 . . . . 130 E6
Gallacher Way PL12 . . . . . . 122 B3
Galland Rd TR1 . . . . 69 F4
Gallant's Dr PL23 . . . . 116 B3
Galleon Ct TR7 . . . . 110 D4
Galleries The 46 TR26 . . . 141 B6
Gallery La
　Landrake PL12 . . . . 53 A1

Gallery La continued
　St Germans PL12 . . . . 65 A8
Galligan Cl TR19 . . . . 97 A6
Galligan La TR19 . . . . 97 A6
Gallops The PL12 . . . . 122 D4
Galsworthy Cl PL5 . . . . 124 C2
Galva Rd PL7 . . . . 131 C8
GAM 24 A1
Gander La TR13 . . . . 146 B6
Ganges Cl TR11 . . . . 82 C2
Ganges Rd PL2 . . . . 128 A5
Ganna Park Rd PL3 . . . . . . 128 D6
Gannel Rd TR7 . . . . 110 E4
Gannel View Cl TR8 . . . . . . 111 B3
Gannet Dr PL25 . . . . 114 F4
Gara Cl PL9 . . . . 136 B6
Garby La TR15 . . . . 140 C3
Garcia Terr PL15 . . . . 106 A4
Garden Cl PL7 . . . . 131 D5
Garden Cres PL1 . . . . 148 B1
Gardeners Way PL27 . . . . . 32 E6
Garden House The * PL20 . 42 A3
Garden La PL19 . . . . 147 B5
Garden Mdw TR11 . . . . . . 144 E3
Garden Park Cl PL9 . . . . . . 136 C7
Garden St PL4 . . . . 127 E4
Garden Village PL9 . . . . . . 135 F8
Garden Way TR8 . . . . 111 B3
Garden Wk PL26 . . . . 115 A1
Gards La PL5 . . . . 123 E2
Garfield Terr PL1, PL3 . . . . 128 A3
Garland Pl TR14 . . . . 138 D4
Garlidna 24 TR18 . . . . 143 E6
GARRAS 99 D6
Garras Prim Sch TR12 . . . . 99 D7
Garrett St PL10 . . . . 133 A1
Garrick Cl PL5 . . . . 124 C2
Garris Cotts TR20 . . . . 88 E8
Garrison Cl PL1 . . . . 127 E1
Garro La PL9 . . . . 99 A1
Garston Cl PL9 . . . . 136 A8
Garth-an-Creet TR26 . . . . . 77 A7
Garth Marhas TR14 . . . . . . 138 C3
Garth Morcom PL14 . . . . . . 113 B5
Garth Rd TR18 . . . . 143 B3
Gascoyne Ct PL4 . . . . 149 A3
Gascoyne Pl PL4 . . . . 149 A3
Gas Hill TR1 . . . . 137 E2
Gashouse La PL4 . . . . 149 B2
Gasking St PL4 . . . . 149 A3
Gas La 8 TR15 . . . . 140 B4
Gas St TR14 . . . . 138 D3
Gateway St TR27 . . . . 77 E2
GATHERLEY 19 E1
Gavercoombe Pk 2 PL34 . . 14 C7
Gay's Hill TR12, TR13 . . . . 146 E4
Gdynia Way PL4 . . . . 149 C2
GEAR 99 F7
Gear Hill
　Madron TR20 . . . . 88 C8
　Mawgan TR12 . . . . 99 E8
Gear La TR20 . . . . 88 B8
Gears La TR17, TR20 . . . . . 89 D6
Geasons La PL7 . . . . 130 E5
Geevor Cotts TR19 . . . . 86 F8
Geevor Tin Mine Mus *
　TR19 . . . . 74 F1
Geffery Cl PL12 . . . . 53 C3
Gems Bolitho Sch TR18 . . 143 C5
Gendalls Way PL15 . . . . . . 106 B8
Gennys Cl PL18 . . . . 40 E6
George Ave PL7 . . . . 130 F6
George Cross PL7 . . . . 130 F6
George Downing Ho
　PL6 . . . . 125 A1
George Fox Cl PL15 . . . . . . 106 A4
George La PL7 . . . . 130 F5
George Pl PL1 . . . . 148 A2
Georges La PL11 . . . . 65 C6
Georges Paddock PL15 . . . . 27 B3
George Sq PL1 . . . . 127 F1
George St
　Plymouth PL1 . . . . 127 F1
　Truro TR1 . . . . 137 C4
GEORGIA 76 E3
Georgia Cres PL3 . . . . 129 C6
Geraldine Terr PL12 . . . . . 122 C1
GERMOE 90 C4
GERMOE CROSS ROADS . . 90 C3
Germoe Cty Prim Sch
　TR20 . . . . 90 C4
GERRANS 83 B2
Gerrans Cl PL25 . . . . 115 B5
Gerrans Hill TR2 . . . . 83 B2
Gerrans Parish Her Ctr *
　TR2 . . . . 83 B2
Gerrans Prim Sch TR2 . . . . 83 B1
Gerrans Sq TR2 . . . . 83 B2
Gewans Mdw PL25 . . . . . . 114 E2
Ghost Hill TR12 . . . . 99 A1
Gibbon La PL4 . . . . 149 A3
Gibbons Fields 9 TR12 . . . 99 A2
Gibbon St PL4 . . . . 149 A3
Gibbs La PL35 . . . . 9 C1
Gibraltar Terr 6 TR2 . . . . . 95 A6
Gibralter Sq 6 EX23 . . . . . . 4 E1
Gibson Way PL13 . . . . 91 B1
Gifford Pl PL3 . . . . 128 D4
Gifford Terrace Rd PL3 . . . 128 E5
Gig La TR3 . . . . 82 A7
Gilbert Cl PL26 . . . . 58 B4
Gilbert Pl PL7 . . . . 131 B6
Gilbert La PL2 . . . . 128 C5
Gilbert Rd PL31 . . . . 109 F4
Gilbert's Coombe 140 A8
GILLAN 101 C8
Gill-an-Creet TR26 . . . . 77 A7

Gillbard Centenary Flats
　PL15 . . . . 106 B5
Gillbard Centenary Homes
　PL15 . . . . 106 B5
Gilley La PL26 . . . . 73 A4
Gill Pk PL3 . . . . 129 B5
Gills Cl TR10 . . . . 144 B6
Gilly Fields TR15 . . . . 140 B3
Gilly Gabben Ind Est TR12 99 B7
Gilly Hill
　Cury TR12 . . . . 99 B5
　Redruth TR15 . . . . 140 C3
Gilly La TR26 . . . . 77 C1
Gilston Rd PL12 . . . . 122 D4
Gilwell Ave PL9 . . . . 136 B7
Gilwell Pl PL4 . . . . 149 A3
Gilwell St PL4 . . . . 149 A3
Gipsy La
　Liskeard PL14 . . . . 113 A5
　Sithney TR13 . . . . 91 C2
Gitchell La
　Crowlas TR20 . . . . 89 C8
　St Erth TR26 . . . . 77 C1
Glade Cl PL6 . . . . 125 A4
Glade The
　Crapstone PL20 . . . . 42 B2
　St Minver PL27 . . . . 22 A3
Gladstone Rd PL30 . . . . . . 109 C2
Gladstone Terr
　Longrock TR20 . . . . 88 F6
　3 Redruth TR15 . . . . . . 140 C5
Gladwell Gdns 10 EX23 . . . . 4 D1
Glamis Rd TR7 . . . . 111 B6
Glantis Cres TR9 . . . . 45 E2
Glanville Rd PL19 . . . . 147 B6
Glanville St PL1, PL4 . . . . . 148 C3
Glanville Terr PL12 . . . . . . 122 F3
Glasney Pl TR10 . . . . 144 C7
Glasney Rd TR11 . . . . 145 A5
Glasney Terr TR10 . . . . . . 144 D7
Glebe Ave PL12 . . . . 122 F3
Glebe Cl
　Mawgan TR12 . . . . 99 D7
　Pelynt PL13 . . . . 62 D5
　6 St Columb Major TR9 . 45 E6
Glebe Cres PL27 . . . . 32 D6
Glebe Dr PL26 . . . . 46 F3
Glebe Est PL14 . . . . 38 F2
Glebelands
　Callington PL17 . . . . 39 E5
　Looe PL13 . . . . 117 D5
Glebe Mdw PL17 . . . . 39 E5
Glebe Parc PL30 . . . . 23 E3
Glebe Pl TR12 . . . . 103 B5
Glebe Row PL27 . . . . 142 D7
Glebe Terr
　Constantine TR11 . . . . . . 92 F4
　Ruan Minor TR12 . . . . . . 103 B5
Glebe The
　Camborne TR14 . . . . 138 C3
　Cubert TR8 . . . . 55 B8
　St Mellion PL12 . . . . 53 D8
　Tregony TR2 . . . . 71 F4
　Week St Mary EX22 . . . . . 11 E8
Glenavon Rd PL3 . . . . 128 E5
Glenburn Cl PL3 . . . . 128 E7
Glencross Ct 3 PL14 . . . . 113 C6
Glen-Dale Cl 3 PL25 . . . . 115 A5
Glendale Cres TR4 . . . . 68 C6
Glen Dale Cres TR15 . . . . 140 D4
Glen-Dale Cres PL25 . . . . 115 A5
Glendale Terr PL26 . . . . . . 58 E3
Glendower Rd PL3 . . . . . . 128 D5
Glendurgan Gdn * TR11 . . 93 D2
Gleneagle Ave 4 PL3 . . . . 128 F6
Gleneagle Rd PL3 . . . . 128 F6
Gleneagle Villas 3 PL3 . . 128 F6
Glenfeadon Terr TR16 . . . . 67 C6
Glenfield Cl PL6 . . . . 125 D6
Glenfield Rd PL6 . . . . 125 D6
Glenfield Way PL6 . . . . . . 125 D6
GLENHOLT 125 D6
Glenholt Cl PL6 . . . . 125 D6
Glenholt Rd PL6 . . . . 125 D6
Glenhurst Rd 5 PL3 . . . . . 128 E6
Glen Leigh TR15 . . . . 140 A6
Glenleigh Pk PL26 . . . . 58 E1
Glenmoor La TR12 . . . . 99 A1
Glenmore Ave PL2 . . . . . . 127 F5
Glenmore Terr
　7 Liskeard PL14 . . . . . . 113 D6
　Mabe Burnthouse TR10 . . 81 A1
Glennaven Cl PL7 . . . . 131 C6
Glen Park Ave PL4 . . . . . . 148 C4
Glen Park Prim Sch
　Plymouth PL7 . . . . 130 E6
　6 Plymouth PL7 . . . . . . 131 B5
Glen Pk PL14 . . . . 38 D4
Glen Rd
　Plymouth, Mannamead
　PL3 . . . . 128 F5
　Plymouth, Plympton PL7 . 130 F6
　Wadebridge PL27 . . . . . . 108 B5
Glenside Rise PL7 . . . . . . 130 E6
Glenthorne Rd TR3 . . . . . . 69 C3
Glentor Rd PL3 . . . . 128 E7
Glentowan Rd PL26 . . . . . . 73 C6
Glen Vale PL15 . . . . 139 E6
Glenview PL25 . . . . 114 B3
Glen View
　Callington PL17 . . . . 39 E5
　Penryn TR10 . . . . 144 B8
　Tywardreath PL24 . . . . . . 60 D5
　Wadebridge PL27 . . . . . . 108 B4
Glenwood Rd PL3 . . . . 128 E6
Globerdon Rd PL14 . . . . . . 38 E4
Globe Sq PL14 . . . . 139 F2
Gloucester Ave PL25 . . . . 115 C3

Gloucester Cres TR18 . . . . 143 B1
Gloucester Ct PL1 . . . . . . 148 C4
Gloucester Pl
　27 Newlyn TR18 . . . . . . 143 C2
　Plymouth PL1 . . . . 148 C4
Gloucester Rd TR18 . . . . . 143 C2
GLOWETH 69 E3
Gloweth View TR1 . . . . 69 E3
Gloweth Villas TR1 . . . . . . 69 E3
GLUVIAN 45 E7
Gluyas The TR11 . . . . 144 E1
Glynn Ave 8 TR13 . . . . . . 146 C5
Glynn House Short Stay Sch
　TR1 . . . . 137 A4
Glynn Rd
　Liskeard PL14 . . . . 113 A5
　Padstow PL28 . . . . 107 D5
Glyn Way TR3 . . . . 69 D3
Goad Ave
　Plymouth PL4 . . . . 149 C2
　Torpoint PL11 . . . . 126 C3
Goad Cl PL11 . . . . 126 F3
Godding Gdns PL6 . . . . . . 124 E6
Godolphin Ave TR17 . . . . . 89 B5
Godolphin Cl TR17 . . . . 89 B6
Godolphin Cres TR13 . . . . . 90 E6
GODOLPHIN CROSS 90 E6
Godolphin Ct 5 TR14 . . . . 138 D3
Godolphin Dr TR17 . . . . . . 89 B5
Godolphin Ho * TR13 . . . . . 90 E6
Godolphin Ho PL19 . . . . . . 147 C5
Godolphin Pk 11 PL17 . . . . 39 E4
Godolphin Pl TR17 . . . . 89 B5
Godolphin Prim Sch TR13 90 E6
Godolphin Rd
　Falmouth TR11 . . . . 144 F5
　Helston TR13 . . . . 146 C6
　Longrock TR20 . . . . 88 F6
Godolphin Terr TR17 . . . . . 89 B5
Godolphin View TR14 . . . . 138 D1
Godolphin Way TR7 . . . . . 111 B7
Godrevy Ct TR26 . . . . 141 D2
Godrevy Ho TR1 . . . . 69 E4
Godrevy Terr 28 TR26 . . . 141 B6
GODREVY TOWANS 66 B3
GOLANT 61 A5
GOLBERDON 39 C6
Goldbank Bglws PL30 . . . . 34 C2
Golden Bank Pk TR11 . . . . 144 E1
Golden Sands 11 TR6 . . . . 55 A5
Goldfinch Cl PL15 . . . . 106 E4
Goldfinch Gdns PL19 . . . . 147 D2
Goldfinch Gr PL12 . . . . . . 122 D4
Goldmartin Cl TR11 . . . . . . 93 D3
Goldmartin Sq TR11 . . . . . 93 D3
GOLDSITHNEY 89 D5
Goldsmith Gdns PL5 . . . . . 124 D3
Goldsworthy Dr EX23 . . . . 104 F5
Goldsworthy Way PL27 . . . 108 B5
Golf House Rd EX23 . . . . . 104 D6
Golf Terr TR7 . . . . 110 C6
Golf View TR14 . . . . 79 B2
Golitha Falls National Nature
　Reserve * PL14 . . . . 37 D3
Golitha Rise PL14 . . . . 113 E6
GOLLAWATER 55 A1
Golva Cl TR13 . . . . 91 C4
GONAMENA 38 B5
Gonvena Hill PL27 . . . . . . 108 D6
Gonvena Ho PL27 . . . . 108 C6
Goodern Drive TR3 . . . . . . 69 E3
Goodeve Cl 7 PL9 . . . . . . 135 E6
Goodmans La PL14 . . . . . . 38 D4
Goodwin Ave PL6 . . . . 125 A6
Goodwin Cres PL2 . . . . . . 128 A6
Goonabarn Cotts TR26 . . . 58 C5
Goonbarrow Mdw PL26 . . . 47 C1
GOONBELL 68 D8
GOON GUMPAS 68 E1
Goongumpas La TR16 . . . . . 68 E1
GOONHAVERN 55 E4
Goonhavern Ind Est TR4 . . 55 D4
Goonhavern Prim Sch
　TR4 . . . . 55 D4
Goonhilly Cl TR4 . . . . 55 D4
GOONHUSBAND 146 C1
Goonlaze Terr TR3 . . . . 80 D4
GOONOWN 54 D1
Goonown La TR5 . . . . 54 D1
Goonown Rd
　Goonbell TR5 . . . . 68 D8
　St Agnes TR5 . . . . 54 D1
Goonrea PL13 . . . . 117 B4
GOONVREA 68 B8
Goonvrea TR3 . . . . 81 D5
Goonvrea Ct TR7 . . . . 110 F4
Goonvrea Rd TR5 . . . . 54 C1
Goonwartha Cl PL13 . . . . . 117 C4
Goonwartha Rd PL13 . . . . 117 B3
Gooseberry La
　Pensilva PL14 . . . . 38 E4
　Plymouth PL1 . . . . 148 B2
Gooseford La PL11 . . . . . . 132 C8
GOOSEHAM 2 E3
Goosewell Hill PL6 . . . . . . 125 D8
Goosewell Park Rd PL9 . . 135 F6
Goosewell Prim Sch PL9 135 F6
Goosewell Rd PL9 . . . . . . 135 F6
Goosewell Terr PL9 . . . . . 135 F6
Gordon Ct PL12 . . . . 122 D2
Gordon Pl 8 TR9 . . . . 45 E6
Gordons Ct TR3 . . . . 80 F3
Gordon Terr PL4 . . . . 128 E4
GORRAN CHURCHTOWN . . 73 B1
GORRAN HAVEN 85 D5

GORRAN HIGH LANES 72 F2
Gorran Sch PL26 . . . . 85 B5
Gorse Cl TR7 . . . . 111 A4
Gorsey Cl PL5 . . . . 124 E2
Gorvin Cross EX39 . . . . 3 E6
Goss Moor National Nature
　Reserve * PL26 . . . . 46 B2
Goswela Cl PL9 . . . . 135 F5
Goswela Gdns PL9 . . . . . . 135 F5
Gotch Gdns PL14 . . . . 50 B6
GOTHERS 46 D1
Gothers Hill PL26 . . . . 46 D1
Gothers Rd
　St Dennis, Gothers PL26 . . 46 D1
　St Dennis, Hendra PL26 . . 58 C8
Goudges La PL26 . . . . 58 E8
Gounce The 14 TR6 . . . . . . 55 A5
Gover Cl TR3 . . . . 68 C6
Gover La TR7 . . . . 110 D6
Gover Rd PL25 . . . . 114 B4
Goverseth Hill PL26 . . . . . . 58 D6
Goverseth Rd PL26 . . . . . . 58 D6
Goverseth Terr PL26 . . . . . 58 D6
GOVER VALLEY 59 A4
Gower Ridge Rd PL9 . . . . . 135 D6
Goyne's Field TR4 . . . . 68 A7
Gracca Terr PL26 . . . . 47 C1
Grade-Ruan CE Prim Sch
　TR12 . . . . 103 B5
Grafton Rd PL4 . . . . 128 E4
Graham Ave PL25 . . . . 114 E4
Graham Rd TR15 . . . . 140 C5
Grainge Rd PL6 . . . . 125 A1
GRAMPOUND 72 B7
GRAMPOUND ROAD 57 E1
Grampound Road Ind Est
　TR2 . . . . 57 E1
Grampound Road Village CE
　Prim Sch TR2 . . . . 57 E1
Grampound-with-Creed CE
　Sch TR2 . . . . 72 A7
Granby Ct PL1 . . . . 127 E2
Granby Gn PL1 . . . . 127 E2
Granby Pl PL1 . . . . 127 E2
Granby St PL1 . . . . 127 E2
Granby Way PL1 . . . . 127 E2
Grand Hotel Rd PL1 . . . . . 148 B1
Grand Par PL1 . . . . 148 B1
Grange Rd
　Helston TR13 . . . . 146 B5
　Plymouth PL7 . . . . 131 A4
　Yelverton PL20 . . . . 42 C3
Grange The TR14 . . . . 138 C2
Granite Way PL17 . . . . 39 F4
Grannery Ct EX23 . . . . . . 104 D5
Granny's Gn PL31 . . . . . . 109 E3
Granny's La TR6 . . . . 55 A4
Grantham Cl PL7 . . . . 130 B4
Grantley Gdns PL3 . . . . . . 129 A5
Grant's Ct PL25 . . . . 114 C3
Grant's Wlk 4 PL25 . . . . . 114 C3
Granville Terr EX23 . . . . . . 104 D5
Grasmere Cl PL6 . . . . 124 E5
Grasmere La PL14 . . . . 38 B5
Grassendale Ave PL2 . . . . 127 F7
Grass La PL2 . . . . 128 C6
Grassmere Way PL12 . . . . 122 D4
Grass Valley Pk PL31 . . . . 109 F1
Gratton Cross PL20 . . . . . . 42 D2
Gratton La PL20 . . . . 42 D2
Gratton Pl PL6 . . . . 125 A1
Gravesend Gdns PL11 . . . 127 B3
Gravesend Wlk PL5 . . . . . 123 D4
Graybridge Rd PL20 . . . . . . 42 C4
Gray Cres PL5 . . . . 127 C8
Great Berry Rd PL6 . . . . . . 124 F1
GREAT BOSULLOW 87 D8
Great Charles Cl PL26 . . . . 58 B4
Great Churchway PL9 . . . . 136 A7
Greatfield Rd PL3 . . . . 129 B7
Greatlands Cres PL2 . . . . . 128 A6
Greatlands Pl 5 PL2 . . . . . 128 A5
Great Mdw PL14 . . . . 36 F2
Great Mills Ind Parc
　PL25 . . . . 115 D4
Great Mis Tor Cl 5 PL20 . 42 C3
Great Orchard Cl PL9 . . . . 135 E5
Great Park Cl 4 PL7 . . . . . 131 C5
Great Western Commercial
　Village PL22 . . . . 112 D2
Great Western Rd PL1 . . . 148 B2
Great Wheal Seton TR14 . 138 F6
Greatwood TR11 . . . . 82 C3
Great Woodford Dr PL7 . . 130 B6
Grebe Cl PL7 . . . . 130 F5
Greeb Way TR20 . . . . 89 D4
Green Acre PL15 . . . . 28 A5
Greenacres
　Bodmin PL30 . . . . 34 C2
　Plymouth PL9 . . . . 135 F8
Greenbank
　Connor Downs TR27 . . . . 78 D6
　1 Penzance TR18 . . . . . 143 D5
　Plymouth PL4 . . . . 149 B4
　Polruan PL23 . . . . 116 D2
Greenbank Ave PL4 . . . . . 149 B3
Greenbank Cl TR2 . . . . 57 E1
Greenbank Cottages
　PL4 . . . . 149 B4
Greenbank Cres TR2 . . . . 111 C7
Greenbank La PL14 . . . . . . 113 C6
Greenbank Rd
　Devoran TR3 . . . . 81 F6
　Liskeard PL14 . . . . 113 C6
　Plymouth PL4 . . . . 149 B4
Greenbanks Rd PL27 . . . . . 21 E2
Greenbank Terr
　1 Callington PL17 . . . . . 39 F4

Greenbank Terr *continued*
Plymouth PL4 . . . . 149 B4
GREEN BOTTOM 69 B4
Green Cl
Feock TR3 . . . . 82 C5
Truro TR1 . . . . 137 B3
Green Cres TR13 . . . . 146 D7
Greendale Rd PL2 . . . . 128 A7
Green Field Cl TR12 . . . . . . 102 F2
Greenfield Rd PL12 . . . . 122 D2
Greenfields Cl TR11 . . . . 93 D3
Greenfield Terr TR16 . . . . . . 67 D6
Greenfinch Cres PL12 . . . . . 122 E4
Green Hill
Lamerton PL19 . . . . 30 A3
St Martin TR12 . . . . 100 D6
Tavistock PL19 . . . . 147 D5
Wadebridge PL27 . . . . 108 E5
Greenhill Cl PL9 . . . . 135 F5
Greenhill Rd PL9 . . . . 136 A5
Greenhills PL32 . . . . 105 C5
Green Hill Terr TR12 . . . . . 100 D6
Green Hill Villas PL27 . . . . 108 E5
Green La
Bodmin PL31 . . . . 109 F2
Boscastle PL35 . . . . 9 C1
Crantock TR8 . . . . 43 D3
Fowey PL23 . . . . 116 C5
Gwithian TR27 . . . . 66 B2
Kingsand PL10 . . . . 133 A2
Lelant TR26 . . . . 77 E4
Lizard TR12 . . . . 103 A2
Marazion TR17 . . . . 89 B6
Penryn TR10 . . . . 144 B8
Porthleven TR13 . . . . 91 B1
Portreath TR16 . . . . 67 C6
Redruth, Plain-an-Gwarry
TR15 . . . . 140 B5
Redruth, Wheal Rose TR16 . . 68 C4
Rock PL27 . . . . 21 D2
Tavistock PL19 . . . . 147 E5
Truro TR1 . . . . 137 B3
Veryan TR2 . . . . 83 F6
Yelverton PL20 . . . . 42 C1
Greenland PL10 . . . . 132 F5
Greenlands Est PL19 . . . . . . 147 D5
Green Lane Cl TR10 . . . . . . 144 B8
Green Lane Hill TR18 . . . . . 143 F8
Green Lane Vean TR15 . . . . 140 B5
Green Lane W TR17 . . . . 89 B6
Green La The TR27 . . . . 77 F1
Greenlees Dr PL7 . . . . 131 B3
Greenmarket The **26**
TR18 . . . . 143 E5
Green Mdws PL32 . . . . 105 C4
Green Parc Rd TR27 . . . . . . 142 D5
Green Park Ave PL4 . . . . . . 128 D4
Green Park Rd PL9 . . . . 135 E5
Green Pk PL10 . . . . 133 A2
GREENSPLAT 59 A6
Greensplat Rd PL25 . . . . . . 114 A6
Green St
Penzance TR18 . . . . 143 F4
Truro TR1 . . . . 137 B3
Greens The TR19 . . . . 96 C7
Greensway Rd PL19 . . . . . . 147 A4
Green The
Bridgerule EX22 . . . . 8 A5
Carnon Downs TR3 . . . . 82 A5
5 Horrabridge PL20 . . . . . . 42 C5
Kingsand PL10 . . . . 133 A2
Liskeard PL14 . . . . 113 B5
Meavy PL20 . . . . 42 F2
Milton Combe PL20 . . . . . . 120 F8
Nancegollan TR13 . . . . 91 B7
Plymouth, Ernesettle PL5 . . 123 E3
Plymouth, Hooe PL9 . . . . . . 135 B6
Probus TR2 . . . . 71 C6
Saltash PL12 . . . . 122 C3
St Buryan TR19 . . . . 97 A6
St Martin TR12 . . . . 100 D6
6 Trewoon PL25 . . . . 59 A3
Greenway Ave PL7 . . . . 130 B6
Greenway Cl **2** PL20 . . . . . 42 C5
Greenwich Pl PL12 . . . . 122 F3
Greenwith Cl TR1 . . . . 137 B3
Greenwith Cres TR3 . . . . . . 81 D6
Greenwith Hill TR3 . . . . 81 D6
Greenwith Rd TR3 . . . . 81 D6
Greenwix Parc PL30 . . . . . . 34 D8
Greenwood Cres TR10 . . . . 144 A8
Greenwood Park Cl PL7 . . . 131 B6
Greenwood Park Rd PL7 . . . 131 B6
Greenwood Rd TR10 . . . . . 144 A8
Gregor Rd TR1 . . . . 137 B3
Gregory's Ct **10** PL31 . . . . . 109 D5
Gregory's Mdw PL15 . . . . . 106 F3
Grenfell Ave PL12 . . . . 122 D3
Grenfell Gdns PL12 . . . . . . 122 C3
Grenfell St **19** TR19 . . . . . . 88 C1
Grenifer Rd TR15 . . . . 139 D7
Grenna La TR3 . . . . 81 D7
GRENOFEN 42 A6
Grenofen Cl PL19 . . . . 42 A6
Grenville Cl PL17 . . . . 39 F4
Grenville Cres TR11 . . . . . . 144 F5
Grenville Ct
Plymouth PL7 . . . . 131 C6
2 St Austell PL25 . . . . . . 114 C3
Grenville Dr
6 St Agnes TR5 . . . . 54 D1
Tavistock PL19 . . . . 147 B3
Grenville Gdns TR14 . . . . . . 79 C5
Grenville Mdws
Lostwithiel PL22 . . . . 112 E2
St Austell PL26 . . . . 58 D7
Grenville Meadow PL19 . . . 147 B3
Grenville Pk PL20 . . . . 42 D2

Grenville Rd
Falmouth TR11 . . . . 145 A5
Helston TR13 . . . . 146 D5
Lostwithiel PL22 . . . . 112 D2
Padstow PL28 . . . . 107 C4
Plymouth PL4 . . . . 149 D3
Truro TR1 . . . . 137 B5
Grenville Road Lane S
PL4 . . . . 129 B2
Grenville Wlk PL13 . . . . 62 D2
Gresham Cl
Newquay TR7 . . . . 110 F4
Plymouth PL5 . . . . 124 C7
Greyfriars TR11 . . . . 145 C2
Greys Terr **1** TR16 . . . . 140 F1
Greystoke Ave PL6 . . . . 129 D7
Greystone Ave PL26 . . . . . . 58 E5
Greystones TR9 . . . . 57 E8
Gribbas Cl TR3 . . . . 80 F3
Gribbas Cnr TR3 . . . . 80 F3
Gribben Cl PL25 . . . . 114 E6
Gribben Rd PL25 . . . . 114 E6
Gribbon Way PL24 . . . . 60 C4
Griffins The PL14 . . . . 113 D6
Griffin Way PL9 . . . . 136 C6
Griggs Cl PL7 . . . . 131 B4
Griggs Hill PL27 . . . . 77 E3
GRIMSCOTT 5 A2
Grimscott Est EX23 . . . . 5 B2
Grimspound Cl PL6 . . . . 129 E8
Grimstone Terr PL20 . . . . . . 42 B2
Grist La PL27 . . . . 78 C5
Grizedale Rd PL6 . . . . 129 D7
Grose Hill Cres **11** PL26 . . . 59 D7
Grose Mdws PL26 . . . . 58 B8
Grosvenor Ave TR7 . . . . 110 E6
Grosvenor Cotts **1** PL4 . . . 128 F4
Grosvenor Pl PL25 . . . . 114 B4
Grosvenor Rd PL6 . . . . 124 C7
Grove Cotts TR7 . . . . 57 C1
Grove Dr **4** PL14 . . . . 51 A7
Grove Hill
Mawnan Smith TR11 . . . . . . 93 D3
St Mawes TR2 . . . . 95 A6
Grovehill Cres TR11 . . . . . . 145 C3
Grovehill Dr TR11 . . . . 145 C3
Grovehill Ho TR11 . . . . 145 B3
Grove La TR20 . . . . 89 F5
Grove Park Ct PL14 . . . . . . 113 B4
Grove Pk
Par PL24 . . . . 60 C6
Tavistock PL19 . . . . 147 D5
Torpoint PL11 . . . . 126 E3
Grove Pl **3** TR11 . . . . 145 C3
Grove Rd
Par PL24 . . . . 115 F6
St Austell PL25 . . . . 114 C4
Grove The
Plymouth, Plymstock
PL9 . . . . 135 D8
Plymouth, Stoke PL3 . . . . . 128 A4
Grovewood Ct TR9 . . . . 45 E1
GRUMBLA 87 C4
Grylls Parc TR13 . . . . 146 B6
Grylls Pk PL13 . . . . 62 A7
Guardian Ct **6** PL31 . . . . . 109 E5
Gue The **2** TR13 . . . . 98 C8
GUILDFORD 142 E6
Guildford Cl
Foxhole PL26 . . . . 58 D6
Plymouth PL5 . . . . 124 D7
Guildford Rd TR27 . . . . 142 E6
Guildford Road Ind Est
TR27 . . . . 142 E6
Guildford St PL4 . . . . 149 A3
Guildhall La PL22 . . . . 112 C2
Guildhall Sq PL1 . . . . 148 C2
Guineaport Parc PL27 . . . . . 108 C5
Guineaport Rd PL27 . . . . . . 108 C5
Guipavas Rd PL17 . . . . 39 F4
Guisseny Pl TR13 . . . . 91 B1
Gulland Rd PL27 . . . . 21 D6
Gull Rock
Newquay TR7 . . . . 110 A5
Wadebridge PL27 . . . . 21 D2
GULVAL 88 E6
Gulval Almshouses TR18 . . 143 F8
Gulval Cross TR18 . . . . 143 F8
Gulval Prim Sch TR18 . . . . . 88 E6
Gulworthy Cotts PL19 . . . . . 41 B7
Gulworthy Cross PL19 . . . . . 41 B7
Gulworthy Prim Sch PL19 . . 41 B7
Gun Hill Rd TR8 . . . . 43 B1
GUNNISLAKE 40 F5
Gunnislake Prim Sch
PL18 . . . . 40 F6
Gunnislake Rural Workshops
PL18 . . . . 40 F5
Gunnislake Sta PL18 . . . . . . 40 F5
Gunpool La **9** PL35 . . . . 9 C1
Gunver PL28 . . . . 31 F7
GUNWALLOE 98 E5
Gunwennap PL32 . . . . 10 B2
Gunwin Ct PL26 . . . . 58 D8
Gurly Hill TR20 . . . . 90 A7
Gurnard Wlk PL3 . . . . 129 C6
Gurney Cl
Bude EX23 . . . . 104 E7
Torpoint PL11 . . . . 126 F3
Gurney's La **2** TR14 . . . . . 138 D3
Gurneys Mews **6** TR14 . . . 138 D3
Gurnick Est TR18 . . . . 143 B2
Gurnick Rd TR18 . . . . 143 B1
Gurnick St **24** TR19 . . . . . . 88 C1
Gustavus Rd TR14 . . . . 138 D3
Gustory Rd TR8 . . . . 43 D3
Guy Miles Way PL5 . . . . . . 124 B3

GWALLON 89 C6
Gwallon La TR17 . . . . 89 C6
Gwallon Rd PL25 . . . . 114 C5
Gwarnick Rd TR1 . . . . 137 B4
Gwarth an Drae TR13 . . . . . 146 C8
Gwarth an Dre TR27 . . . . . 142 E8
GWAVAS 91 D4
Gwavas Bglws **4** TR18 . . . 143 C1
Gwavas La TR18 . . . . 88 C2
Gwavas Quay **7** TR18 . . . . 143 C2
Gwavas Rd TR18 . . . . 143 C1
Gwavas St **9** TR18 . . . . . . 143 C2
Gwavas St **9** TR18 . . . . . . 143 E6
Gweal Darras TR10 . . . . 81 C1
Gwealdues TR13 . . . . 146 D7
Gwealfolds Rd TR13 . . . . . . 146 C7
Gweal Gollas TR27 . . . . 142 E8
Gwealhellis Warren
TR13 . . . . 146 B7
Gwealmayowe Pk TR13 . . . 146 D8
Gweal Pawl TR15 . . . . 140 A4
Gweal Wartha TR13 . . . . . . 146 B8
Gwedhennek TR18 . . . . . . 143 F7
GWEEK 92 C1
Gweek Dr
Gweek TR13 . . . . 92 C1
Mawgan TR12 . . . . 99 D8
Gweek La TR13 . . . . 92 A3
Gwel an Garrek **2** TR12 . . 99 A1
Gwel-an-mor
1 Marazion TR17 . . . . . . 89 C5
St Austell PL25 . . . . 115 A5
Trenance TR8 . . . . 31 C2
Gwel-an-mor Apartments
TR26 . . . . 141 C4
Gwelanmor Cl TR26 . . . . . . 141 D2
Gwelanmor Rd TR26 . . . . . 141 D2
Gwel-an-Nans Cl **2**
PL14 . . . . 113 B5
Gwel-an-Scol TR3 . . . . 82 C5
Gwel-an-Skol TR14 . . . . . . 138 E5
Gwel an Wheal TR26 . . . . . 141 A4
Gwel an Wheal Cres
TR26 . . . . 141 A4
Gwel Avon Bsns Pk PL12 . . 122 D4
Gwelavon Cl PL25 . . . . 108 D5
Gwelenys Rd **3** TR19 . . . . . 88 C1
Gwel Eryon **3** TR14 . . . . . 138 F2
Gwel Gwarthe TR16 . . . . . . 68 C3
Gwell-an-Nans TR2 . . . . 71 C6
Gwel Lewern TR18 . . . . 88 E6
Gwel Marten Flats TR26 . . 141 E2
Gwelmenhir Pk **8** PL14 . . . 38 A3
Gwel Mengleth PL27 . . . . . 108 D5
Gwelmor TR14 . . . . 138 E2
Gwel-Mor **9** TR19 . . . . 75 A1
Gwel-Tek TR27 . . . . 142 D8
Gwel Trencrom TR27 . . . . . 142 B3
Gwendra La PL26 . . . . 58 E8
Gwendroc Cl TR1 . . . . 137 D3
Gwendroc Ho TR1 . . . . 137 D3
Gwendroc House Mews
TR1 . . . . 137 D3
Gwendrock Villas PL27 . . . 108 C5
Gwendrona Cl TR13 . . . . . 146 D8
Gwendrona Way TR13 . . . . 146 D8
GWENNAP 80 F7
Gwindra Ind Est PL26 . . . . . 58 C3
Gwindra Rd PL26 . . . . 58 B4
GWINEAR 78 C4
Gwinear La TR27 . . . . 78 E4
Gwinear Prim Sch TR27 . . . 78 E4
Gwinear Rd TR27 . . . . 78 C5
GWITHIAN 66 B2
Gwithian Cl
St Austell PL25 . . . . 114 E7
Torpoint PL11 . . . . 126 F4
Gwithian Green Nature
Reserve ★ TR27 . . . . 78 C8
Gwithian Rd
Connor Downs TR27 . . . . . 78 D6
St Austell PL25 . . . . 114 E7
Gwithian Sands Chalet Pk
TR27 . . . . 66 B1
GWITHIAN TOWANS 66 A2
Gwithian Towers Nature
Reserve ★ TR27 . . . . 78 B8
Gwyn Rd PL4 . . . . 149 C4
Gwythian Way TR16 . . . . . . 55 A4
Gyllng Hall TR11 . . . . 145 B3
Gyllng St TR11 . . . . 145 B4
Gyllyng Street Hill TR11 . . 145 B2
Gyllyngvase Rd TR11 . . . . . 145 C2
Gyllyngvase Terr TR11 . . . . 145 C2
Gypsy La PL33 . . . . 14 C1

H

Haddington Rd PL2 . . . . . 127 F4
Haddon Way PL25 . . . . 115 D3
Haddy's Row PL14 . . . . 39 A2
Haig Pl **8** PL18 . . . . 143 C7
Hain Wlk TR26 . . . . 141 D4
HALAMANNING 90 A6
Halbullock View TR1 . . . . . 69 E3
Halcyon Ct PL2 . . . . 128 A6
Halcyon Rd PL2 . . . . 128 A6
Haldon Pl PL5 . . . . 124 A3
HALE MILLS 69 A1
Haley Barton **4** PL2 . . . . . 128 A5
HALGABRON 14 E7
Halgavor La PL31 . . . . 109 E2
Halgavor Pk PL31 . . . . 109 F1
Halgavor Rd PL30, PL31 . . 109 D2
Halgavor View PL31 . . . . . 109 F2

Halifax Rd PL27 . . . . 31 F3
Halimote Rd PL26 . . . . 58 C8
Hallane Rd PL25 . . . . 115 A6
Hallaze Rd PL26 . . . . 59 D7
Hallan Vean TR19 . . . . 96 A6
Hallaze Rd PL26 . . . . 59 D7
Hallerton Cl PL6 . . . . 125 E2
Hallett Cl PL12 . . . . 122 B3
Hallett Way EX23 . . . . 104 F7
HALLEW 47 C2
Hallew Rd PL26 . . . . 58 C7
Halley Gdns PL5 . . . . 123 E1
Hall for Cornwall (Theatre)
The ★ **21** TR1 . . . . 137 D4
HALLIVICK 58 A4
Halloon Ave **9** TR9 . . . . . . 45 E2
Hall Rd PL26 . . . . 58 C8
Hall Terr PL23 . . . . 116 E5
HALLWORTHY 16 D6
HALSETOWN 77 A5
Halt Rd
Goonhavern TR4 . . . . 55 D4
St Newlyn East TR8 . . . . . . 56 B7
Halvana TR15 . . . . 140 D3
Halvarras Pk TR3 . . . . 82 B8
Halvarras Rd TR3 . . . . 82 B8
Halveor Cl **5** TR9 . . . . 45 E6
Halveor Ct TR6 . . . . 55 B5
Halveor La TR9 . . . . 45 D6
HALVOSSO 93 A8
HALWIN 92 B8
Halwin La TR13 . . . . 92 B8
Halwin Prim Sch TR13 . . . . 92 C8
Halwyn Cl **12** TR3 . . . . . . 81 F7
Halwyn Hill TR8 . . . . 110 A3
Halwyn Pl TR1 . . . . 137 B4
Halwyn Rd TR8 . . . . 110 A3
Halwyn Terr TR1 . . . . 137 B3
Halye Vw TR27 . . . . 108 A6
HAM 128 A8
Hamble Cl PL3 . . . . 129 D7
Ham Cl PL2 . . . . 128 B8
Ham Dr PL2 . . . . 128 B8
Ham Field PL27 . . . . 21 D5
Ham Gn PL2 . . . . 128 A7
Ham Green La PL2 . . . . . . 128 A8
Ham Ho PL2 . . . . 128 A8
Ham Green PL2 . . . . 128 A7
Hamilton Cl TR27 . . . . 142 B4
Hamilton Gdns PL4 . . . . . . 128 D4
Hamilton Pl TR11 . . . . 145 D3
Ham La PL2 . . . . 128 A8
Hammer Dr PL25 . . . . 114 E7
Hammill's Cl **13** TR13 . . . . 98 C8
Hammills Dr **12** TR13 . . . . 98 C8
Hamoaze Ave PL5 . . . . 127 D8
Hamoaze Pl PL1 . . . . 127 D2
Hamoaze Rd PL11 . . . . 127 B2
Hampton Cl TR7 . . . . 110 D6
Hampton St PL4 . . . . 149 A3
Hancock Cl PL6 . . . . 124 D6
Hancock La PL12 . . . . 95 A6
Hangmans La PL17 . . . . 39 F4
Hangmans Wlk **32** PL17 . . 39 F4
Hannaford Rd PL16 . . . . 19 F3
HANNAFORE 117 C2
Hannafore La PL13 . . . . . . 117 C3
Hannafore Rd PL13 . . . . . . 117 D2
Hanover Cl
17 Perranporth TR6 . . . . . 55 A5
Plymouth PL3 . . . . 129 B5
Hanover Ct
Camborne TR14 . . . . 138 E4
10 Penzance TR18 . . . . . . 143 E5
16 Plymouth PL1 . . . . 149 A2
Hanover Ho EX23 . . . . 4 D4
Hanover Pk TR9 . . . . 45 F2
Hanover Rd PL3 . . . . 129 C4
Hanson Dr PL23 . . . . 116 C3
Hanson Rd PL14 . . . . 113 D6
Harbour Ave
Plymouth, Camels Head
PL5 . . . . 127 E8
Plymouth PL4 . . . . 149 A2
Harbour Ct
Falmouth TR11 . . . . 145 B4
15 Penzance TR18 . . . . . . 143 E5
Portreath TR16 . . . . 67 C6
Harbour Lights **11** TR18 . . 143 C1
Harbour Mews TR19 . . . . . . 96 B7
Harbour Rd
Par PL24 . . . . 60 C4
Porthleven TR13 . . . . 98 B8
Wadebridge PL27 . . . . 108 C5
Harbourside **12** TR13 . . . . . 98 B8
Harbour Side PL13 . . . . . . 117 C3
Harbour St PL11 . . . . 127 B3
Harbour Terr
Falmouth TR11 . . . . 145 B5
Portreath TR16 . . . . 67 C6
Harbour View
Fowey PL23 . . . . 116 C4
Hayle TR27 . . . . 142 B5
Marazion TR17 . . . . 89 B5
Penryn TR10 . . . . 144 B8
Plymouth PL9 . . . . 135 A7
5 Porthleven PL13 . . . . . . 98 B8
Saltash PL12 . . . . 122 E2
Truro TR1 . . . . 137 E3
Harbour View Cres TR18 143 E6
HARCOURT 82 B4
Harcourt Cl TR1 . . . . 69 F3
Harding Mdw PL13 . . . . . . 63 F8
Hardings Cl PL12 . . . . 122 E3
HARDISWORTHY 2 D7
Hardisworthy Cross EX39 . . . 2 E7
Hardwick Farm PL7 . . . . . 130 C3
Hardy Cres PL25 . . . . 124 E1

Gre–Haw **161**

Hardy Ho TR3 . . . . 80 F3
Harebell Cl PL12 . . . . 122 D4
Harefield Cres TR14 . . . . . 138 D4
Hareston Cl PL7 . . . . 131 B3
Harewood Cl PL7 . . . . 130 E5
Harewood Cres PL5 . . . . . 124 B2
Harewood Rd PL18 . . . . . . 41 A3
Hargood Terr **6** PL2 . . . . . 127 F4
Hargreaves Cl PL5 . . . . . . 123 F2
Harlech Cl PL3 . . . . 129 A7
Harleigh Rd PL31 . . . . 109 E3
Harleigh Terr PL31 . . . . . . 109 E3
Harlequins **27** TR26 . . . . . 141 B5
HARLYN 20 D2
Harlyn Barton PL28 . . . . . . 20 D2
Harlyn Cotts PL28 . . . . 20 D2
Harlyn Drive PL2 . . . . 128 D8
Harlyn Rd PL28 . . . . 20 D1
Harmer PL31 . . . . 109 D6
Harmony Cl
Redruth TR15 . . . . 140 B6
Roche PL26 . . . . 46 F3
Harmony Mdw PL26 . . . . . . 46 F3
Harmony Rd PL26 . . . . 46 F3
Harmony Terr
4 Illogan TR16 . . . . 67 E4
Truro TR1 . . . . 137 E2
Harnorlen Rd PL2 . . . . 128 D7
Haroldsleigh Ave PL5 . . . . 124 E2
Harpers Mdw PL15 . . . . . . 27 B7
Harriet Gdns PL7 . . . . 130 B6
Harriet Pl TR11 . . . . 145 A5
Harris Cl TR17 . . . . 39 F6
Harris Ct
1 Penryn TR10 . . . . 144 C7
Plymouth PL9 . . . . 135 B6
Harrison Gdns TR15 . . . . . 139 D7
Harrison St **7** PL2 . . . . . . 127 F4
Harrison Terr TR1 . . . . 137 B4
Harriss Hill TR3 . . . . 82 A7
HARROWBARROW 40 D5
Harrowbarrow Prim Sch
PL17 . . . . 40 D4
Harrowbeer La PL20 . . . . . 42 C3
Hartland Forest Golf &
Leisure Parc EX39 . . . . 3 E6
Hartland Rd PL29 . . . . 22 E7
Hartland Terr EX23 . . . . . 104 D6
HARTLEY 128 E7
Hartley Ave PL3 . . . . 129 A6
Hartley Ct PL3 . . . . 129 A6
Hartley Park Gdns PL3 . . . 128 F6
Hartley Rd PL3 . . . . 128 E6
HARTLEY VALE 129 A8
Hartmeade PL14 . . . . 52 A5
Hartwell Ave PL9 . . . . 136 D7
Harvenna Cl TR9 . . . . 45 E1
Harvenna Hts TR9 . . . . 45 E1
Harvest Moon TR7 . . . . . . 110 D7
Harvey Ave PL4 . . . . 129 B1
Harvey Rd TR1 . . . . 137 D2
Harvey St PL11 . . . . 127 B3
Harvey's Towans TR27 . . . 142 A7
Harvey's Way TR27 . . . . . . 142 C5
Harwell Ct **8** PL1 . . . . 148 B3
Harwell St PL1 . . . . 148 B3
Harwood Ave PL5 . . . . 124 C7
Hastings St PL1 . . . . 148 B3
Hastings Terr PL1 . . . . 148 B3
Haswell Cl PL6 . . . . 129 A8
Hatch's Hill TR27 . . . . 78 C5
Hatfield Cres TR7 . . . . 110 B5
Hat La PL10 . . . . 132 F2
Havelock Terr PL2 . . . . . . 127 F3
Haven Ct TR27 . . . . 142 C5
Haven Pk PL14 . . . . 39 A2
Haven Rd EX23 . . . . 10 C6
Havett Cl PL14 . . . . 50 E8
Havett Rd PL14 . . . . 50 E8
Haviland Rd PL14 . . . . . . 113 E4
Hawarden Cotts PL4 . . . . . 129 B1
Haweswater Cl PL6 . . . . . . 124 E4
Hawke Cl TR7 . . . . 110 D6
Hawkens Way **9** TR9 . . . . . 45 D6
Hawke Rd TR13 . . . . 146 D4
Hawkers Ave PL4 . . . . 149 A2
Hawkers Ct EX23 . . . . 104 D7
Hawkers La PL3 . . . . 128 E5
Hawkeys Mews TR15 . . . . 140 D2
Hawkinge Gdns PL5 . . . . . 123 E4
Hawkins Cl PL6 . . . . 125 A5
Hawkins Ct **2** TR18 . . . . . 143 D5
Hawkins Rd
Newquay TR7 . . . . 110 E5
Padstow PL28 . . . . 107 C5
Penzance TR18 . . . . 143 D5
Hawkins Way **12** TR11 . . . 145 A4
Hawks Pk PL12 . . . . 122 C2
Hawk's Tor Dr PL15 . . . . . . 27 B7
Hawthorn Ave
Bude EX23 . . . . 104 E4
Torpoint PL11 . . . . 126 F3
Hawthorn Cl
Bude EX23 . . . . 104 E4
Camelford PL32 . . . . 105 D4
Plymouth, Hooe PL9 . . . . . 135 C5
Plymouth, Woolwell PL6 . . 125 D7
Redruth TR15 . . . . 140 B6
St Austell PL25 . . . . 114 F6
7 St Columb Major TR9 . . 45 D6
Hawthorn Gr PL2 . . . . 128 C7
Hawthorn Rd PL19 . . . . . . 147 C2
Hawthorns PL12 . . . . 122 D2

Hawthorn Way
Plymouth PL3 . . . . **129** B7
Threemilestone TR3 . . . . **69** C3
Haxter Cl PL6 . . . . **121** B1
Haydon Gr PL5 . . . . **123** C1
Haydown Cl PL30 . . . . **24** B4
HAYE **39** D4
Haye Common Dr PL15 . **106** D3
Haye La PL17 . . . . **39** E5
Haye Rd
Callington PL17 . . . . **39** D4
Plymouth PL7, PL9 . . . . . **130** C4
Haye Rd S PL9 . . . . **136** C7
Hayes Pl PL9 . . . . **129** B8
Hayes Rd PL9 . . . . **135** C7
Hay La
Looe PL13 . . . . **117** E4
Sheviock PL11 . . . . **65** B6
HAYLE **142** C6
Hayle Community School
TR27 . . . . **142** D5
Hayle Ind Pk TR27 . . . . . . **142** F7
Hayle Rd TR27 . . . . **78** C1
Hayle Sta TR27 . . . . **142** B5
Hayle Terr TR27 . . . . **142** C6
Hayman Way TR11 . . . . . **144** E5
Hayne Corfe Cres TR1 . . **137** A4
Hayne Corfe Gdns TR1 . **137** A4
Haystone Pl PL1 . . . . **148** B4
Haytor Cl PL5 . . . . **124** B3
Hazel Cl
Plymouth PL6 . . . . **125** B6
St Austell PL25 . . . . **115** A6
Hazel Dr PL9 . . . . **136** C7
Hazel Gr
Plymouth PL9 . . . . **136** C7
Yelverton PL20 . . . . **42** D3
Hazelmead PL14 . . . . **113** B5
Hazelmere Dr PL25 . . . . . **115** B4
Hazel Rd PL19 . . . . **147** C2
Hazelwood Cres PL9 . . . . **136** D7
Hazelwood Dr PL6 . . . . . **125** D8
Hazelwood Rd PL17 . . . . . **39** F4
Heabrook Parc [2] PL18 . **143** C7
Hea Cl TR18 . . . . **143** C7
Hea Cotts [5] TR18 . . . . . . **143** C7
Head La TR5 . . . . **68** D8
Headland Cl TR26 . . . . . . **141** E2
Headland Cotts
Coverack TR12 . . . . **103** H7
Newquay TR7 . . . . **110** C8
Headland Ct TR26 . . . . . . **141** E2
Headland Pk PL4 . . . . **149** A4
Headland Point PL7 . . . . **110** C7
Headland Rd
Carbis Bay TR26 . . . . **141** E2
Newquay TR7 . . . . **110** C7
Headlands The TR6 . . . . . **55** A5
Headleigh Rd TR4 . . . . . . **110** F5
Headon Cross EX23 . . . . . **11** A5
Healy Ct [9] PL2 . . . . **127** F4
Healy Pl PL2 . . . . **127** F4
HEAMOOR **143** B7
Heamoor Prim Sch TR18 **143** B6
Heanton Terr
Millbrook PL10 . . . . **132** E6
Redruth TR15 . . . . **140** C4
Heanton Villas TR15 . . . . **140** C4
Hea Rd TR18 . . . . **143** C7
Hearl Rd PL12 . . . . **122** B3
Heatherbell Gdns TR26 . . **141** E1
Heather Cl
Heamoor TR18 . . . . **143** B7
Tavistock PL19 . . . . **147** D4
Heather La TR27 . . . . **77** D2
Heather Mdw TR9 . . . . **45** E1
Heather Way TR20 . . . . . . **89** F4
Heathers The
Foxhole PL26 . . . . **58** E5
Plymouth PL6 . . . . **125** D7
Heather Vean TR3 . . . . **69** D4
Heathfield Gdns TR15 . . . **140** E7
Heathfield Pk PL26 . . . . . . **42** D3
Heathfield Rd PL4 . . . . . . **129** B3
Heathlands Bsns Pk
PL14 . . . . **113** C5
Heathlands Ind Est [9]
PL14 . . . . **113** C5
Heathlands Rd PL14 . . . . . **113** C5
Heath Terr PL18 . . . . **40** F5
Heavitree Rd PL10 . . . . . . **133** A2
Hedgerow Cl PL6 . . . . **125** E8
Hedgerow La PL26 . . . . . . **58** B4
Hedgerows The PL12 . . . . **122** B3
Hedingham Cl PL7 . . . . . . **131** C4
Hedingham Gdns PL6 . . . **125** B7
Helca Dr TR26 . . . . **141** C3
HELE **13** C2
HELEBRIDGE **7** A6
Helebridge Rd EX23 . . . . . . **7** B6
Hele Cross PL15 . . . . **13** E3
Hele Gdns PL7 . . . . **131** A4
Hele La PL6 . . . . **121** F2
Helena Ct [7] PL26 . . . . **59** D7
Hele Rd
Bude EX23 . . . . **104** F1
Marhamchurch EX23 . . . . . **7** A6
Hele's Sch PL7 . . . . **130** C6
Hele's Terr PL4 . . . . **129** B2
HELFORD **93** B1
HELFORD PASSAGE **93** C2
Heligan Ho PL26 . . . . **73** A5
HELLAND **35** A5
HELLANDBRIDGE **34** F6
Helland Rd PL31 . . . . **109** E6

Hellescoth Way TR13 . . . . **146** D8
Hellescott Rd PL15 . . . . . . **18** B7
Hellesvean [2] TR26 . . . . . **77** A6
Hellesvean Cl [3] TR26 . . . **77** A6
HELLESVEOR **77** A7
Helleur Cl [4] PL24 . . . . **60** B4
Hellis Wartha TR13 . . . . . **146** D5
Helman Tor View PL31 . . **109** E2
Helnoweth Cotts TR18 . . . **143** F8
Helnoweth Gdns TR18 . . . **143** F8
Helnoweth Hill TR18 . . . . **143** F8
Helscott Rd EX23 . . . . **7** A6
HELSTON **146** D6
Helston Com Coll TR13 . . **146** C7
Helston Com Hospl
TR13 . . . . **146** D3
HELSTONE **24** B8
Helston Folk Mus★
TR13 . . . . **146** B5
Helston Rd TR10 . . . . **144** C8
Helston Sp Ctr TR13 . . . . **146** C7
Hembal [5] PL25 . . . . **59** A3
Hembal La PL25 . . . . **59** A3
Hembal Rd [4] PL25 . . . . . . **59** A3
HEMERDON **131** D7
Hemerdon House★ PL7 **131** E7
Hemerdon Hts PL7 . . . . . . **131** A6
Hemerdon La PL7 . . . . **131** C8
Hemerdon Way PL7 . . . . . **130** D6
HENAFORD **2** F5
Hendergulling PL13 . . . . . . **62** F4
Henders Cnr [6] PL3 . . . . . **128** F6
Henderson Pl PL2 . . . . **127** F6
HENDRA
Bodmin **46** F7
Camelford **105** A4
Mullion **102** F7
St Dennis **58** C8
Hendra Barton TR1 . . . . . **137** B5
Hendra Cl
Ashton TR13 . . . . **90** E3
Liskeard PL14 . . . . **38** A4
Stithians TR3 . . . . **80** E4
[5] Truro TR1 . . . . **137** C5
Hendra Garth PL15 . . . . . . **17** C6
Hendra Gdns PL15 . . . . . **106** B5
Hendra Hts PL26 . . . . **58** C8
Hendra La
Ashton TR13 . . . . **90** D2
Truro TR1 . . . . **137** C5
Hendra Parc PL14 . . . . . . **113** E7
Hendra Pk PL15 . . . . **106** B5
Hendra Prazey PL26 . . . . . **58** B8
Hendra Rd
St Dennis PL26 . . . . **58** C8
Stithians TR3 . . . . **80** E4
Truro TR1 . . . . **137** C5
Hendras Ct TR26 . . . . **141** E2
Hendras Parc TR26 . . . . . **141** D2
Hendra Terr TR3 . . . . **80** E4
Hendra Tor View PL15 . . . . **26** C7
Hendra Vale PL15 . . . . . . **106** B4
Hendra Vean
Carbis Bay TR26 . . . . **141** E1
Truro TR1 . . . . **137** B5
Hendrawna La TR6 . . . . . . **55** B4
Hendwell Cl PL6 . . . . **124** E6
Henfor Cl [12] TR17 . . . . . . **89** C5
HENFORD **13** F5
Henfordh Grange PL14 . . **113** A6
Henfor Mews [6] TR17 . . . **89** C5
Henfor Terr [13] TR17 . . . . **89** C5
Hengar PL30 . . . . **23** F3
Henley Cl TR4 . . . . **68** C6
Henley Cres TR4 . . . . **68** C6
Henley Dr
Mount Hawke TR4 . . . . . . **68** C6
Plymouth PL5 . . . . **124** C7
Henliston Dr TR13 . . . . . . **146** C4
Henry Scott Tuke Ho [5]
TR11 . . . . **145** A4
Hensbarrow Mdws PL26 . . **58** D5
Hensbury La PL20 . . . . . . **119** F4
Henscol TR16 . . . . **80** D6
Henscol Praze TR16 . . . . . **80** D6
Henscol Vale PL14 . . . . . . **113** A6
Henshorn Ct TR13 . . . . . . **146** C7
Hental [3] TR6 . . . . **55** A4
Henver Cl TR27 . . . . **78** E3
Henver Ct TR7 . . . . **111** C7
Henver Gdns TR27 . . . . . . **78** E3
Henver La TR4 . . . . **56** A3
Henver Rd TR7 . . . . **111** B7
Henvor Cl TR15 . . . . **140** D6
Henvor Terr TR15 . . . . **140** E7
HENWOOD **38** B8
Henwood Cres TR7 . . . . . **111** D7
Hen Wythva TR14 . . . . . . **138** E2
Herbert Pl PL2 . . . . **127** E4
Herbert St PL2 . . . . **127** E4
Hereford Rd PL5 . . . . **124** B5
Heritage Cl PL12 . . . . **122** C3
Heritage Pk PL19 . . . . **147** D6
Herland Hill TR27 . . . . **78** D4
Herland Rd TR13 . . . . **90** E6
Hermes Cl TR13 . . . . **146** D5
Hermes Rd TR13 . . . . **146** C4
Hermitage Ct [1] PL4 . . . . **128** E4
Hermitage Rd
Plymouth PL3 . . . . **128** E5
Roche PL26 . . . . **46** F3
HERNISS **80** F1
HERODSFOOT **50** E3
Heron Cl
Millbrook PL10 . . . . **132** F6
Tresillian TR2 . . . . **70** F5
Herons Ct [13] TR6 . . . . . . **55** A5
Heron Way TR1 . . . . **137** E1

Herring Cl PL14 . . . . **113** D7
Herring Rd PL14 . . . . **113** D7
Herschel Gdns PL5 . . . . . **123** E1
Hersham Cross EX23 . . . . . **5** B2
Hertland Wlk PL2 . . . . **128** A7
Hessary Dr PL6 . . . . **121** C1
Hessary Ho [1] PL14 . . . . **113** D6
Hessary View
Saltash PL12 . . . . **122** E4
Tavistock PL19 . . . . **147** B6
HESSENFORD **64** C8
Hessenford Rd PL13, PL11 . **64** B6
Hetling Cl PL1 . . . . **148** B3
HEWAS WATER **72** D8
Hewer's Row PL4 . . . . **149** A3
Hewitt Cl PL12 . . . . **122** C1
Hexham Pl PL2 . . . . **128** A8
Hexton Hill Rd PL9 . . . . . **135** B6
Hexton Quay PL9 . . . . **135** C6
Heybrook Ave PL5 . . . . . . **123** D1
Heybrook Mews TR7 . . . . **110** D6
Hibernia Rd TR13 . . . . **146** D4
Hibernia Terr PL5 . . . . **127** E8
Hichens La TR11 . . . . **145** A5
Hichens Rd TR13 . . . . **146** D4
Hickory Dr PL7 . . . . **131** B5
Hicks Cl TR2 . . . . **71** C6
Hick's La PL4 . . . . **149** A3
Hidden Valley Discovery Pk★
PL15 . . . . **18** A3
High Atlantic TR8 . . . . **44** C6
Highbank Cl PL19 . . . . . . **147** A4
Highbridge Ct PL7 . . . . . . **130** E5
Highburrow [24] TR13 . . . . **98** C8
Highburrow Ct TR15 . . . . **139** C5
Highburrow La TR15 . . . . **139** C5
Highbury PL17 . . . . **38** E8
Highbury Cres PL7 . . . . . **130** D7
Highclere Gdns PL6 . . . . **125** B8
Highcliffe PL27 . . . . **21** D5
High Cross
Lanivet PL30 . . . . **47** F5
Porth Navas TR11 . . . . **93** A4
[12] St Columb Major TR9 . . **45** D6
Truro TR1 . . . . **137** D4
High Cross St PL25 . . . . . **114** D4
Higher Albion Row PL16 . **80** E8
Higher Anderton Rd
PL10 . . . . **132** F5
HIGHER BAL **54** B2
Higher Beech Terr PL13 . **117** C4
Higher Besore Rd TR3 . . . . **69** D4
Higher Bodiniel Rd PL31 **109** C7
Higher Bojewyan TR19 . . . **75** B1
Higher Bolenna [14] TR6 . . **55** A4
Higher Bore St PL31 . . . . **109** C5
Higher Boscaswell **75** A1
Higher Boskerris TR26 . . **141** D1
HIGHER BREA **139** B3
Higher Bridge Pk PL27 . . **108** D5
Higher Broad La TR15 . . . **139** D7
Higher Bugle
Bugle PL26 . . . . **47** C1
Stenalees PL26 . . . . **59** C8
Higher Burrow Cl TR26 . . **141** A4
HIGHER CARNKIE **139** F2
Higher Chapel St PL13 . . **117** D3
Higher Church St PL14 . . **38** B3
Higher Churchtown TR16 **142** D6
Higher Churchway PL9 . . **136** A7
Higher Cl PL27 . . . . **108** E4
Higher Cleaverfield
PL15 . . . . **106** C7
HIGHERCLIFF **63** B8
HIGHER COMPTON **129** A6
Higher Compton Rd PL3 . **128** F6
HIGHER CONDURROW . . . **139** A1
Higher Cotts TR2 . . . . **57** C1
HIGHER CRACKINGTON . . **10** C6
Higher Cross La PL32 . . . . **105** E4
Higher Daws La PL15 . . . . . **18** E2
HIGHER DOWNS **89** F5
Higher East St [9] TR9 . . . . **45** E6
Higher Efford Rd PL3 . . . . **129** B5
Higher Elms PL27 . . . . **21** F3
Higher Fernleigh Rd
PL27 . . . . **108** C4
Higher Fore St
Marazion TR17 . . . . **89** C5
Redruth TR15 . . . . **140** C5
Higher Glen Pk PL14 . . . . . **38** D4
Higher Goongumpas La
TR16 . . . . **68** F1
Higher Green St TR18 . . . **143** D1
Higher Grumbla TR20 . . . . **87** C4
Higher Gwavas Rd [3]
TR18 . . . . **143** C1
Higher Kelly PL18 . . . . **41** A3
Higher La
Ashton TR13 . . . . **90** E3
Mawgan TR12 . . . . **99** D7
Plymouth PL1 . . . . **148** C2
Wadebridge PL27 . . . . . . **108** E4
Higher Lariggan TR18 . . . **143** D4
HIGHER LARRICK **27** E5
Higher Lavorrick PL26 . . . **73** C4
Higher Lidden Rd TR18 . . **143** C3
Higher Lux St PL14 . . . . . **113** C6
Higher Market St
Looe PL13 . . . . **117** D3
Penryn TR10 . . . . **144** C7
Higher Mdw PL14 . . . . **50** E7
Higher Medrose PL33 . . . . **14** E3
Higher Middle Hill PL14 . . **38** D4
Higher Moor TR12 . . . . . . **103** A5
Higher Mount Ambrose La
TR15 . . . . **140** D6
Higher Mowles PL3 . . . . . **129** B6

Higher Newham La TR1 . **137** D2
Higher Park Cl PL7 . . . . . **131** B3
Higher Park Stenak TR16 . **80** F8
Higher Pengegon TR14 . . **138** F2
Higher Penponds Rd
TR14 . . . . **79** B5
Higher Peverell Rd TR18 **143** E7
Higher Polsue Way TR2 . . **70** F5
Higher Port View PL12 . . **122** F2
Higher Pumpfield Row
TR15 . . . . **139** B6
Higher Railway Terr TR16 **80** F8
Higher Rd
Breage TR13 . . . . **90** F3
Pensilva PL14 . . . . **38** D4
Higher Redannick TR1 . . **137** B3
HIGHER ROSEWARNE . . . **138** D5
Higher Row
Ashton TR13 . . . . **90** E3
Kingsand PL10 . . . . **133** A2
Higher Silver Hill TR13 . . **146** C6
Higher Stennack TR26 . . . **141** A5
Higher Stert Terr PL4 . . . **149** C3
Higher Tamar Terr PL18 . . **41** A7
Higher Terr TR3 . . . . **81** B4
HIGHER TOLCARNE **45** B8
Higher Tower Rd TR7 . . . **110** C6
HIGHERTOWN
Camelford **24** E8
Truro **69** F3
Highertown
Portscatho TR2 . . . . **83** B2
Truro TR1 . . . . **69** F3
Highertown Pk PL12 . . . . . **53** C3
Higher Tregenna Rd
TR26 . . . . **141** B3
Higher Treglyn PL27 . . . . . **22** B3
Higher Trehaverne TR1 . **137** C6
Higher Tremena TR15 . . . **114** C4
Higher Tresavean Terr
TR16 . . . . **139** C4
Higher Trevithick TR27 . . **142** D5
Higher Trevorian Barns
TR19 . . . . **97** B7
Higher Trewidden Rd
TR26 . . . . **141** B4
HIGHER TREWINCE **44** E6
Higher Trezaise PL26 . . . . **47** A1
Higher Tristram PL27 . . . . **21** D5
Higher Vicarage La [7]
TR12 . . . . **99** A1
Higher Well La TR13 . . . . **146** C6
Higher Well Pk PL26 . . . . . **73** C3
Higher West End PL26 . . . . **73** C4
Higher Whiterock PL27 . . **108** B5
Higher Woodford La
PL7 . . . . **130** C7
Higher Woodside PL25 . . **114** A4
Highfield Ave
St Austell PL25 . . . . **114** D3
[13] St Columb Major TR9 . . **45** D6
Highfield Cl
Plymouth PL3 . . . . **129** C5
St Austell PL25 . . . . **114** D3
Highfield Ct [9] TR5 . . . . . **54** D1
Highfield Park Rd PL15 . . **106** A5
Highfield Pk PL12 . . . . **122** B3
Highfield Rd
Camelford PL32 . . . . **105** C3
Falmouth TR11 . . . . **144** F4
Mount Hawke TR4 . . . . . . **68** C6
Highfield Rd Ind Est
PL32 . . . . **105** C3
Highfields [19] TR18 . . . . . **143** C2
Highgate Hill [1] TR9 . . . . **45** E1
Highglen Dr PL7 . . . . **131** B7
Highgrove PL15 . . . . **27** A6
Highland Pk
Penryn TR10 . . . . **144** B8
Redruth TR15 . . . . **140** C5
Highlands PL9 . . . . **136** B3
HIGHLANES **32** B7
HIGH LANES **142** D5
High Lanes
Cubert TR8 . . . . **55** E8
Hayle TR27 . . . . **142** D5
High Pk PL12 . . . . **52** F6
High St
Boscastle PL35 . . . . **9** D1
Camelford PL32 . . . . **105** C3
Chacewater TR4 . . . . **68** F3
Delabole PL33 . . . . **14** D3
Falmouth TR11 . . . . **145** B5
Launceston PL15 . . . . **106** C6
Padstow PL28 . . . . **107** D5
Penzance TR18 . . . . **143** E5
[14] PL15 . . . . **106** C6
[3] Plymouth PL1 . . . . . . **149** A2
Plymouth, Stonehouse PL1 **128** A2
Probus TR2 . . . . **71** C6
St Ives TR26 . . . . **141** B6
St Keverne TR12 . . . . **101** C4
HIGH STREET **58** D3
High Street Ind Est PL26 . **58** D3
High Street Prim Sch
PL1 . . . . **128** A2
High Street & Waterloo
Street Flats PL1 . . . . . . **128** A1
Hightrip La PL17 . . . . **39** F7
High Trip La PL17 . . . . **40** A8
Highview TR4 . . . . **68** E5
Highview Cl TR14 . . . . **38** A2
Highview Cres TR4 . . . . . . **68** E5
High View Prim Sch PL3 **129** D6
Highway PL14 . . . . **50** B6
Highway La PL15 . . . . **140** D7

Highwood Pk PL14 . . . . . . **50** E7
Higman Cl PL14 . . . . **50** E7
Hilda Rd PL25 . . . . **114** E7
Hilgrove Rd TR7 . . . . **111** A6
HILL **10** B5
Hill Church TR4 . . . . **68** F2
Hill Cl
Heamoor TR18 . . . . **143** B7
Plymouth PL7 . . . . **130** D4
St Breward PL30 . . . . **24** B3
Hillcrest
Helston TR13 . . . . **146** C7
Shortlanesend TR4 . . . . . . **69** F6
Hill Crest PL3 . . . . **128** E5
Hillcrest Ave TR1 . . . . **137** A5
Hillcrest Cl
Plymouth PL7 . . . . **131** A5
[14] St Columb Major TR9 . . **45** E6
Hillcrest Dr PL7 . . . . **131** A4
Hillcrest Rd TR27 . . . . **142** D6
Hilldale Rd PL9 . . . . **135** E6
Hilldean Cl PL5 . . . . **124** C7
Hill Gdns PL12 . . . . **119** A2
Hill Hay Cl PL23 . . . . **116** A4
Hillhead TR2 . . . . **95** A6
Hill Head TR10 . . . . **144** D6
Hillhead Gdns PL32 . . . . . **105** D4
Hillhead Rd TR11 . . . . **144** C5
Hill La PL3 . . . . **128** F7
Hillocks The PL13 . . . . . . **117** D4
Hillpark Cotts PL15 . . . . . **106** D6
Hill Park Cres
Plymouth PL4 . . . . **149** A4
St Austell PL25 . . . . **114** A2
Hill Park Mews PL4 . . . . . **149** B4
Hill Path PL5 . . . . **123** F5
Hill Pk PL27 . . . . **108** D6
Hill Rd PL27 . . . . **108** C5
Hillsborough [2] PL4 . . . . **128** F4
Hillsborough Cross EX22 . . **8** D7
Hillsdale Bglws TR13 . . . . **90** F5
Hillsdunne Rd PL3 . . . . . . **128** E6
Hillside
Grampound Road TR2 . . . . **57** E1
Lanivet PL30 . . . . **47** E7
Portreath TR16 . . . . **67** C6
St Austell PL25 . . . . **115** B3
Trewellard TR19 . . . . **86** F8
Hillside Ave
Par PL24 . . . . **60** B4
Plymouth PL4 . . . . **128** D4
Saltash PL12 . . . . **122** F3
Hillside Cl PL20 . . . . **41** F3
Hillside Cres PL9 . . . . **135** F8
Hillside Ct
Angarrack TR27 . . . . **78** C5
[21] Yelverton PL20 . . . . . **41** B1
Hillside Gdns PL22 . . . . . . **112** C2
Hillside Ind Est TR16 . . . . **140** E8
Hillside Mdw TR10 . . . . . **144** D7
Hillside Mdws PL26 . . . . . **58** D5
Hillside Parc TR20 . . . . . . **88** B7
Hillside Pk PL31 . . . . **109** D6
Hillside Rd
Falmouth TR11 . . . . **144** F2
Saltash PL12 . . . . **122** E3
St Austell PL25 . . . . **114** D5
Hillside Terr
Carharrack TR16 . . . . **80** E8
Downderry PL11 . . . . **64** C5
Looe PL13 . . . . **117** D4
[22] Newlyn TR18 . . . . . . **143** C2
[2] Redruth TR15 . . . . . . **140** C5
Hillside Villas PL13 . . . . . **117** F5
Hillson Cl PL29 . . . . **22** E7
Hill St
Padstow PL28 . . . . **107** D5
Plymouth PL4 . . . . **149** A3
Hillsview PL13 . . . . **62** D2
Hill Top Crest PL5 . . . . . . **123** E2
Hill View PL20 . . . . **41** F3
Hilton Ave PL5 . . . . **124** D1
Hilton Rd EX23 . . . . **7** B6
Hingston Ct PL6 . . . . **129** A8
HINGSTON DOWN **40** B6
Hinton Ct PL6 . . . . **125** C1
Hirmandale Rd PL5 . . . . . **123** F3
Hirst Ho TR14 . . . . **139** A4
Hobart St PL1 . . . . **148** A2
Hobbacott La EX23 . . . . **7** B6
Hobbs Cres PL12 . . . . **122** C3
Hockens La PL23 . . . . **116** C2
Hockin Cl PL17 . . . . **39** E6
Hockings Ho PL14 . . . . **37** F3
Hodders Way PL12 . . . . . . **119** A2
Hodge Cl PL12 . . . . **122** C2
Hoe App PL1 . . . . **148** C2
Hoe Ct PL1 . . . . **148** C2
Hoegate Ct PL1 . . . . **148** C2
Hoegate Pl PL1 . . . . **148** C2
Hoegate St PL1 . . . . **149** A2
Hoe Gdns PL1 . . . . **148** C2
Hoe Rd PL1 . . . . **148** C1
Hoe St PL1 . . . . **148** C2
Hoe The PL1 . . . . **148** C1
Hogarth Cl PL9 . . . . **136** B6
Hogarth Ho [2] PL19 . . . . **147** B6
Hogarth Wlk PL9 . . . . **136** B6
Holborn Pl PL7 . . . . **130** E6
Holborn St PL4 . . . . **149** B2
Holcombe Dr PL9 . . . . **135** F5
Holcroft Cl PL12 . . . . **122** D2
Holdsworth St PL4 . . . . . . **148** B4
Holebay Cl PL9 . . . . **136** A5
Hole Cross PL20 . . . . **119** E7
HOLESTROW **102** E2
Hollabury Rd EX23 . . . . . . **104** F7
Hollacombe Brake PL9 . . **136** C1

HOLLACOMBE HILL 136 A2
Holland Rd
 Plymouth, Chaddlewood
 PL7 . . . . 131 D5
 Plymouth, Peverell PL3 . . 128 E6
 Plymouth, Plymstock PL9 . 135 F6
 Widegates PL13 . . . . 63 E7
Hollies Cl PL15 . . . . . . 106 B7
Hollies Rd PL15 . . . . . . 106 A7
Hollies The TR27 . . . . . 142 B4
Hollong Pk PL11 . . . . . . 65 E5
Holloway Gdns PL9 . . . . 136 A5
Hollowell Ho **1** PL35 . . . . 9 C2
Hollow Hayes PL6 . . . . . 129 B8
Hollow's Terr TR27 . . . . 142 E7
Hollows The PL9 . . . . . . 136 B8
Holly Cl TR3 . . . . 69 C3
Hollycroft Rd PL3 . . . . . 129 C4
Holly Ct PL6 . . . . 129 E7
Holly Park Cl PL5 . . . . . 124 A5
Holly Park Dr PL5 . . . . . 124 A5
Holly Terr **9** PL18 . . . . . 143 C7
Hollywood Terr PL1 . . . . 148 A3
Holman Ave TR14 . . . . . 138 C4
Holman Cl PL2 . . . . 128 C8
Holman Rd PL14 . . . . . . 113 E6
Holmans Bldgs PL1 . . . . 127 D2
Holmans Mdw PL15 . . . . 19 C1
Holman's Pl **1** TR13 . . . . 98 C8
Holman's Terr TR16 . . . . 80 B5
HOLMBUSH 115 B4
Holmbush Arch Rd PL25 . 115 B3
Holmbush Hill PL17 . . . . . 39 F7
Holmbush Rd PL25 . . . . 115 C4
Holmbush Ind Est PL25 . . 115 B4
Holmer Down PL6 . . . . . 125 D7
Holmes Ave PL3 . . . . . . 129 B5
Holmwood Ave PL9 . . . . 135 E5
Holne Chase PL6 . . . . . . 125 B7
Holnicote Rd EX23 . . . . 104 E5
Holt Cres TR7 . . . . 110 D5
Holtwood Rd PL6 . . . . . 125 D6
Holwell Cl PL9 . . . . 136 A5
Holy Cross RC Prim Sch
 PL4 . . . . 149 A3
Holyrood Pl PL1 . . . . . . 148 C2
Holyway Cross PL15 . . . . 18 A1
HOLYWELL 43 B2
Holywell Bay Fun Pk★
 TR8 . . . . 43 C1
Holywell Ct TR3 . . . . . . 82 B8
Holywell Rd
 Cubert TR8 . . . . 55 D8
 Holywell TR8 . . . . 43 C1
 Liskeard PL14 . . . . 113 E6
 Newquay TR7 . . . . 110 F6
 Playing Place TR3 . . . . . 82 B8
Home Farm Rd PL9 . . . . 135 E8
Homefield Pk PL31 . . . . 109 F3
Home Park Ave PL3 . . . . 128 E6
Home Park (Plymouth Argyle
 FC) PL2 . . . . 128 C5
Home Park Rd PL12 . . . . 123 A3
Home Pk
 Landrake PL12 . . . . 53 C3
 Plymouth PL2 . . . . 127 F4
Homer Park Lane S PL9 . 135 C5
Homer Park Rd PL28 . . . 20 F2
Homer Pk
 Plymouth PL9 . . . . 135 C5
 Saltash PL12 . . . . 122 D3
Homer Rise PL9 . . . . . . 136 B7
Homer Water Pk PL26 . . 58 B4
Homestead Ct TR11 . . . . 144 F6
Home Sweet Home Terr
 PL4 . . . . 149 C2
Homeyard Homes The
 TR2 . . . . 83 F6
Honcray PL9 . . . . 135 D8
Honey St PL31 . . . . 109 E4
Honeysuckle Cl
 Plymouth PL6 . . . . 125 E7
 Saltash PL12 . . . . 122 D3
Honeysuckle Gdns PL15 . 106 E4
HONICKNOWLE 124 B2
Honicknowle Gn PL5 . . . 124 B2
Honicknowle La PL5 . . . . 124 B1
Honicombe Cnr PL17 . . . 40 E5
Honicombe Pk PL17 . . . . 40 E5
Honiton Cl PL5 . . . . 124 B3
Honiton Wlk PL5 . . . . . . 124 B4
Hood Hill TR14 . . . . 79 A6
HOOE 135 C5
Hooe Hill PL9 . . . . 135 C5
Hooe La PL9 . . . . 135 D3
Hooe Manor PL9 . . . . . . 135 C5
Hooe Prim Academy
 PL9 . . . . 135 B5
Hooe Rd PL9 . . . . 135 C5
Hooksbury Ave PL7 . . . . 131 B3
Hooper Ct PL14 . . . . . . 113 C8
Hooper La TR14 . . . . . . 138 D2
Hoopers Cl PL12 . . . . . . 53 C3
Hoopers La PL18 . . . . . . 40 F6
Hooper St PL11 . . . . . . 127 C3
Hope Terr TR7 . . . . 110 D6
Hopton Cl
 Bude EX23 . . . . 104 F5
 Plymouth PL6 . . . . 128 F8
Hornapark Cl PL16 . . . . 19 F3
Hornbrook Gdns PL6 . . . 124 D6
Hornby Cl PL1 . . . . 148 A3
Hornby St **2** PL2 . . . . . . 127 F4
Hornchurch La PL5 . . . . 123 E4
Hornchurch Rd PL5 . . . . 123 E5
Horn Cross PL9 . . . . . . 135 E7
Horn Cross Rd PL9 . . . . 135 F7

Hornick Hill PL26 . . . . . . 58 E4
HORNINGTOPS 51 E3
Horn La
 Liskeard PL14 . . . . 113 B6
 Plymouth PL30 . . . . 135 F7
Horn Lane Flats **4** PL9 . . 135 F7
HORRABRIDGE 42 C5
Horrabridge Com Prim Sch
 PL20 . . . . 42 C4
HORSEBRIDGE 29 C1
HORSEDOWNS 78 F1
Horse & Jockey La **2**
 TR13 . . . . 146 C5
Horsepool La PL11 . . . . . 65 B6
Horsepool Rd
 Connor Downs TR27 . . . . 78 E6
 Sheviock PL11 . . . . 65 B6
Horseshoe Cl PL26 . . . . . 47 A3
Horsewhim Dr PL17 . . . . 39 E6
Horse Whim Dr PL25 . . . 115 B5
Horsham La
 Plymouth, Honicknowle
 PL5 . . . . 124 C2
 Plymouth, Tamerton Foliot
 PL5 . . . . 124 C7
Horsley Rise PL25 . . . . . 114 D3
Horswell Cl PL7 . . . . . . 131 B5
Horton Cross EX22 . . . . . . 3 F3
Hosford Cl PL9 . . . . 136 A4
Hosken's Mdw TR19 . . . . 97 A6
Hospital Rd
 Plymouth PL4 . . . . 149 B4
 Stratton EX23 . . . . 4 D1
Hotham Pl PL1 . . . . 148 A4
Houldsworth Rd PL9 . . . 135 C7
Hounster Dr PL10 . . . . . 132 D4
Hounster Hill PL10 . . . . 132 D4
Housel Bay Rd TR12 . . . 102 F2
Housman Cl PL5 . . . . . . 124 D3
Howard Cl
 Plymouth PL5 . . . . 123 F2
 Saltash PL12 . . . . 122 D3
 Tavistock PL19 . . . . . . 147 A5
Howard La EX23 . . . . 7 C8
Howard Rd PL9 . . . . 135 E8
Howards Way EX23 . . . . 104 D5
Howe Downs TR14 . . . . . 79 A2
Howell's Rd **10** EX23 . . . . . 4 E1
Howeson La PL6 . . . . . . 125 A4
HTP Apartments TR1 . . . 137 E4
Hts The PL19 . . . . 147 A6
HUDDISFORD 3 F6
Hudson Cross EX22 . . . . . 5 E4
Hudson Rd PL27 . . . . 31 F3
Hughville St TR14 . . . . . 138 D4
Hugus Rd TR3 . . . . 69 D3
Hull's La TR11 . . . . 145 C3
Humber Cl PL3 . . . . 129 D6
Humphrey's Cl PL14. . . . . 37 F3
Humphry Davy La PL12 . . 142 D5
Humphry Davy Sch TR18 143 E6
Hungerford Rd PL2 . . . . 128 B5
Hunkin Cl TR1 . . . . 137 C5
Hunter Cl PL6 . . . . 124 F2
Huntersfield TR14 . . . . . 138 F7
Hunter's Oak PL20 . . . . . 41 D2
Huntfield Gdns **15** EX23 . . 4 E1
Huntingdon Gdns PL5 . . 124 D4
Huntley Pl PL3 . . . . 129 C4
Hurdon Rd PL15 . . . . . . 106 D2
Hurdon Way PL15 . . . . . 106 C3
Hurdwick Rd PL19 . . . . . 147 A5
Hurland Rd TR1 . . . . . . 137 D3
Hurlers Cl **11** PL14 . . . . 113 C5
Hurlers The★ PL14 . . . . . 38 A6
Hurlings The TR9 . . . . . . 45 E5
Hurrabrook Cl PL6 . . . . 125 E2
Hurrabrook Gdns PL6 . . 125 E2
Hurrell Cl PL6 . . . . 124 D6
Hurrell Ct PL5 . . . . 129 C5
Hursley Bsns Pk PL6 . . . 121 D1
Hurst Cl PL9 . . . . 135 F5
Hustyns PL27 . . . . 33 D3
Hutchings Cl PL6 . . . . . 124 D6
Huthnance Cl TR1 . . . . . 137 F5
Hutton Hts TR1 . . . . 69 F3
Huxham Cl PL6 . . . . 129 A8
Huxley Cl PL7 . . . . 130 F7
Hyde Park Inf School **1**
 PL3 . . . . 128 E5
Hyde Park Junior School **2**
 PL33 . . . . 128 E5
Hyde Park Rd PL3 . . . . . 128 E5

I

IDLESS 70 B6
Idless La TR4 . . . . 69 F6
Idless Wood Forest Walk★
 TR4 . . . . 69 F6
Ilbert Cotts PL7 . . . . . . 130 E4
Ilbert St PL1 . . . . 148 B4
ILLOGAN 67 E4
Illogan Downs TR15 . . . . 139 B8
ILLOGAN HIGHWAY 139 C5
Illogan Pk **8** TR16 . . . . . 67 E4
Illogan Prim Sch TR16 . . 67 D5
Imperial Ct TR11 . . . . . . 145 D3
Ince Cl PL11 . . . . 126 F4
Inchkeith Rd PL6 . . . . . 124 F7
INDIAN QUEENS 45 E1

Indian Queens Ind Est
 TR9 . . . . 45 F2
Indian Queens Prim Sch
 TR9 . . . . 45 E1
Industrial Est The TR6 . . 55 B4
Infirmary Hill TR1 . . . . . 137 C4
Ingra Rd PL3 . . . . 129 A6
Ingra Tor Cl **2** PL20 . . . . 42 C3
Ingra Wlk PL6 . . . . 125 B8
Innes Ho PL1 . . . . 148 B3
Inney Cl PL17 . . . . 39 F4
Inow Terr TR1 . . . . 93 A2
Institute Hill TR13 . . . . . 98 B8
Instow Wlk PL5 . . . . . . 124 A3
Inswell Ct PL19 . . . . . . 147 A6
INSWORKE 132 F6
Insworke Cl PL10 . . . . . 133 A6
Insworke Cres PL10 . . . . 132 F6
Insworke Pl PL10 . . . . . 133 A6
Inverdene PL3 . . . . 128 D5
Ipswich Cl PL5 . . . . 124 C4
Iron Mine La PL20 . . . . . 42 E3
Isacombe Oaks PL17 . . . . 39 F6
Island Cres TR7 . . . . . . 110 E6
Island Lanes PL31 . . . . . 109 F1
Island Point TR8 . . . . . . 44 C6
Island Rd **4** TR26 . . . . . 141 B6
Island Sq **8** TR26 . . . . . 141 B6
Islington Wharf TR10 . . . 144 D8
Ivanhoe **6** TR7 . . . . 110 F6
Ivanhoe Rd PL5 . . . . . . 123 D2
Ivey Terr PL14 . . . . 113 D7
Ivy Cotts PL18 . . . . 40 F6
Ivydale PL6 . . . . 106 B6
Ivydale Rd PL4 . . . . 128 F4
Ivydene Flats TR7 . . . . . 111 D7
Ivy La TR18 . . . . 143 C5
Ivyleaf Holiday Pk EX23 . . 4 F3

J

Jack Bice Cl PL14 . . . . . 113 E5
Jackett's Steps **6** TR11 . 145 B5
Jack La TR18 . . . . 143 C2
Jackman's Mdw PL10 . . . 133 A3
Jacks Cl TR10 . . . . 144 D7
Jack's La PL11 . . . . 132 B8
Jackson Cl PL5 . . . . 127 F8
Jackson Pl PL2 . . . . 127 F4
Jackson Way PL2 . . . . . 122 E3
Jack Stephens Est TR18 . 143 D6
Jacob's Ladder TR11 . . . 145 B4
JACOBSTOW 11 B6
Jacobstow Prim Sch
 EX23 . . . . 11 A6
Jago Ave PL11 . . . . 127 B3
Jago Cl PL31 . . . . 109 B3
Jago's Slip TR11 . . . . . . 145 B5
Jake's La **1** TR4 . . . . 69 A3
Jamaica Inn Mus★ PL15 . 25 E3
Jamaica Pl **14** TR18 . . . . 143 C7
Jamaica Terr **13** TR18 . . . 143 C7
James Cl PL9 . . . . 136 B6
James Pl TR1 . . . . 137 D4
James Rd PL19 . . . . 147 E2
James's Cross EX23 . . . . . 2 C2
James St
 Plymouth, Mount Wise
 PL1 . . . . 127 E1
 Plymouth PL4 . . . . 148 C4
Jane's Ct **9** TR11 . . . . . 145 B5
Jan Luke Way TR14 . . . . 138 F3
Jasmine Gdns
 Plymouth, Chaddlewood
 PL7 . . . . 131 B5
 Plymouth, Glenholt PL6 . . 125 E6
Jasmine Way PL28 . . . . . 31 F7
Jasper Parc PL14 . . . . . . 37 F3
Jays Cross PL15 . . . . . . 19 C6
Jean Cres PL3 . . . . 129 B6
Jeanne Rees Ct **9** PL14 . 113 B5
Jedburgh Cres PL2 . . . . 128 A8
Jeffery Cl PL6 . . . . 124 D6
Jelbert Way TR18 . . . . . . 88 E6
Jellicoe Rd PL5 . . . . . . 124 E1
Jenkins Cl PL9 . . . . 136 A5
Jenkins Terr **5** TR15 . . . 140 C5
Jenner Gdns TR9 . . . . . . 45 D6
Jenner Parc TR9 . . . . . . 45 D6
Jennings Rd TR10 . . . . . 144 A6
Jennings St TR18 . . . . . 143 E5
Jenns Cross EX22 . . . . . . 5 F7
Jennycliff La PL9 . . . . . 135 A6
Jennys Combe Cl PL9 . . 135 F4
Jephson Rd PL4 . . . . . . 129 B3
Jericho La TR27 . . . . . . 142 D1
Jeryon Cl PL25 . . . . 114 E4
Jessops PL7 . . . . 130 D7
Jethan Dr TR14 . . . . . . 138 B4
Jetty St PL26 . . . . 73 C3
Jewell's Terr TR16 . . . . . 80 B5
JEWEL'S CROSS 7 F6
Jinkin Ave PL4 . . . . 149 B4
John Ellis Ct TR27 . . . . . 142 C5
John La PL4 . . . . 148 C4
John's Cnr TR20 . . . . . . 89 F5
Johnson Cl **2** PL20 . . . . . 41 B1
Johnson Pk PL18 . . . . . . 40 F6
John Sparke Ho **17** PL1 . 149 A2
Johns Pk PL15 . . . . 140 B6
John St
 Plymouth PL1 . . . . 127 E3
 Truro TR1 . . . . 137 C4
JOLLY'S BOTTOM 69 A4
Jon Davey Dr TR16 . . . . 140 C7
Jopes Cl **2** PL14 . . . . . . 38 A3

JOPPA
 Hayle 142 E4
 St Just 87 A4
Jordan La PL20 . . . . 42 C5
Jorys Mdw PL30 . . . . 23 E3
Joseph's Ct **27** TR6 . . . . . 55 A5
Joseph's La TR18 . . . . . 143 C8
Jubilee Bglws **20** TR18 . . 143 C1
Jubilee Cl
 Cubert TR4 . . . . 55 D8
 Duloe PL14 . . . . 51 A1
 8 Kilkhampton EX23 . . . . 5 A6
 Saltash PL12 . . . . 122 D2
Jubilee Cotts
 Landrake PL12 . . . . 53 C3
 Saltash PL12 . . . . 122 C1
Jubilee Ct **15** TR26 . . . . . 77 A6
Jubilee Hill PL13 . . . . . . 62 D5
Jubilee Mdw PL25 . . . . . 115 C5
Jubilee Pl
 Camborne TR14 . . . . . . 138 E3
 Plymouth PL3 . . . . 129 C4
Jubilee Poll TR18 . . . . . 143 F4
Jubilee Rd
 Falmouth TR11 . . . . . . 145 A5
 Pensilva PL14 . . . . 38 C4
 Plymouth PL5 . . . . 123 F3
 Threemilestone TR3 . . . . 69 C3
 Wadebridge PL27 . . . . . 108 C5
Jubilee St TR7 . . . . 110 D6
Jubilee Terr
 Bodmin PL31 . . . . 109 B5
 3 Camborne TR14 . . . . 138 E2
 Goonhavern TR4 . . . . . . 55 D5
 Helston TR13 . . . . 146 C4
 Plymouth PL4 . . . . 129 B2
Julian St PL4 . . . . 149 C2
Julian Wlk PL6 . . . . 125 E6
Jump Cl PL6 . . . . 121 C1
Junction Gdns PL4 . . . . 149 C3
Juniper Way PL7 . . . . . . 131 B5

K

Kailem Cl TR9 . . . . 45 D5
Karenza Ct TR14 . . . . . . 141 E2
Kathleaven St PL5 . . . . . 123 D1
Kay Cl PL7 . . . . 130 F7
Kay Cres PL31 . . . . 109 B3
Kay Gdns PL27 . . . . 108 E5
Kays Mews **7** PL34 . . . . . 14 C7
Kea Com Prim Sch TR3 . . 70 A1
Keason Est PL14 . . . . 39 A2
Keason Hill PL12 . . . . . . 53 C8
Keast Cl **2** TR9 . . . . 45 E1
Keat St PL2 . . . . 127 E4
Keay Heights PL25 . . . . 114 E6
Kedlestone Ave PL5 . . . . 124 A3
Keeble Pk TR3 . . . . 81 E6
Keep The PL12 . . . . 122 C2
KEHELLAND 66 F2
Kehelland Village Prim Sch
 TR14 . . . . 66 F2
Keigwen Pl TR19 . . . . . . 88 C3
Kel Avon Cl TR1 . . . . . . 137 F5
Kellaway Pk TR13 . . . . . 146 D6
Kelley Rd TR11 . . . . 144 E5
Kelliwith TR3 . . . . 82 B6
Kellow Hill PL13 . . . . . . 62 D2
Kellow Pk PL11 . . . . 65 A7
Kellow Rd PL26 . . . . 58 C8
KELLY 29 B8
KELLY BRAY 39 F6
Kelly Cl PL5 . . . . 127 C7
Kelly Coll PL19 . . . . 147 D7
Kelly Coll Prep Sch
 PL19 . . . . 147 D7
Kelly Pk PL30 . . . . 34 C8
Kelvin Ave PL4 . . . . 149 C4
Kelwyn Ct TR26 . . . . . . 141 C2
KELYNACK 86 F4
Kemp Cl TR1 . . . . 137 D4
Kempe Cl PL2 . . . . 127 F6
Kemp's Cl **7** TR5 . . . . . . 54 C1
Kempton Pk PL11 . . . . . 127 B2
Kemyell Pl PL2 . . . . 127 E4
Kendal Gn TR2 . . . . 57 C1
Kendall Park PL23 . . . . . 61 B3
Kendall Pk PL23 . . . . . . 116 D2
Kendal Pl PL5 . . . . 124 E4
Kenidjack Cl TR26 . . . . . 141 E1
Kenilworth Rd PL2 . . . . 128 B7
Kenilworth Way PL26 . . . 58 E5
Kenley Gdns PL5 . . . . . 123 F4
Kenmare Dr PL7 . . . . . . 131 A5
Kennall Pk TR3 . . . . 81 B4
Kennall Vale TR3 . . . . . . 81 B4
Kennall Vale Prim Sch
 TR3 . . . . 81 B4
Kenna Pk TR1 . . . . 69 F3
KENNARDS HOUSE 18 B2
Kenn Cl PL5 . . . . 124 B3
Kennedy Cl TR15 . . . . . 139 B8
KENNEGGY 90 A3
KENNEGGY DOWNS 90 B4
Kennel Hill PL7 . . . . 130 D4
Kennel Hill Cl PL7 . . . . . 130 C4
Kennerley Terr **16** TR2 . . 95 A6
Kennet Cl PL3 . . . . 129 B6
Kenneth Launder Ct **10**
 PL14 . . . . 113 B5
Kensa Way PL27 . . . . . . 78 E6
Kensey Cl PL15 . . . . . . 106 D6
Kensey Pl **3** PL15 . . . . . 106 C6
Kensey Valley Mdw
 PL15 . . . . 106 D6
Kensey View PL15 . . . . . 106 D5

Kensington Pl **8** PL4. . . . 128 F4
Kensington Rd PL4 . . . . 149 B4
Kenstella Rd TR18 . . . . . 143 C2
Kent Ave PL25 . . . . 115 D3
Kent Cl PL26 . . . . 58 C8
Kent Rd PL2 . . . . 127 F5
KENTS 10 F6
KENWYN 137 C6
Kenwyn Church Rd TR1 . 137 B6
Kenwyn Cl
 Bude EX23 . . . . 104 D7
 Truro TR1 . . . . 137 B6
Kenwyn Hill TR1 . . . . . . 137 B6
Kenwyn Mews TR1 . . . . 137 C4
Kenwyn Pk
 St Kew Highway PL30 . . . 23 B2
 Truro TR1 . . . . 137 B6
Kenwyn Rd TR1 . . . . . . 137 C5
Kenwyn St TR1 . . . . 137 C4
Kenython La TR19 . . . . . 86 F7
Keppel Pl PL2 . . . . 127 F4
Keppel St PL2 . . . . 127 F4
Keppel Terr **8** PL2 . . . . . 127 F4
Kerensa Gdns
 St Agnes TR5 . . . . 68 D8
 13 TR5 . . . . 54 D1
Kerensa Gn TR11 . . . . . 144 E5
Kergilliack Rd TR18 . . . . 144 D5
Kerhuon Ct PL31 . . . . . 109 D5
Kerley Gr TR1 . . . . 69 F3
Kerley Hill TR4 . . . . 69 A3
Kerley Vale TR4 . . . . . . 69 A3
Kernick Bsns Pk TR10 . . 144 A6
Kernick Gdns TR10 . . . . 144 A6
Kernick Ind Est TR10 . . . 144 A7
Kernick Rd TR10 . . . . . . 144 B7
Kernick Way TR27 . . . . . 142 E8
Kernow Cl
 Bodmin PL31 . . . . 109 F5
 Torpoint PL11 . . . . 126 E3
 Wadebridge PL27 . . . . . 108 B5
Kernow Cres EX23 . . . . . 104 E4
Kernow Ct
 Newquay TR7 . . . . 110 E6
 Torpoint PL11 . . . . 126 E3
Kernow Mill★ PL12 . . . . 52 E1
Kernyk Lowen TR14 . . . . 138 F5
Kerrier Way TR14 . . . . . 138 E3
KERRIS 97 E8
Kerris Gr TR1 . . . . 137 B5
KERROW MOOR 59 D8
Ker St Ope PL1 . . . . 127 E2
Kersbrook Cross PL17 . . 27 F2
Kersey Cl TR11 . . . . 145 C7
Kersey Rd TR11 . . . . . . 145 B7
Ker St PL1 . . . . 127 E1
Keryor Cl PL25 . . . . 114 F3
Kestell Pk PL31 . . . . . . 109 E2
Kestenenn **16** PL31 . . . . 109 D5
KESTLE 73 A4
Kestle Cl PL31 . . . . 109 E5
Kestle Dr TR1 . . . . 69 F3
KESTLE MILL 111 F1
Keston Gdns PL27 . . . . . 108 A6
Kestor Cl PL21 . . . . 128 A7
Kestral Units PL5 . . . . . 124 A1
Kestral Way **10** TR16 . . . 67 E4
Kestrel Cl
 Plymouth PL6 . . . . 125 D8
 7 Porthleven TR13 . . . . 98 B8
Kestrel Pk PL19 . . . . . . 147 D2
Keswick Cres PL6 . . . . . 125 D2
Keveral La PL11 . . . . 64 B5
Kew Cl TR7 . . . . 111 A4
Kew Klavji **11** PL31 . . . . 109 E5
Kew Lastanen TR1 . . . . . 137 F5
Kew Noweth TR14 . . . . . 138 D2
Kew Pendra TR19 . . . . . 97 A6
Kew Pendra TR19 . . . . . 97 A6
Kew Vean TR26 . . . . . . 141 C3
KEYBRIDGE 35 B8
Keyes Cl PL1 . . . . 127 E2
KEYHAM 127 E5
Keyham Ct PL2 . . . . 127 E6
Keyham Rd PL2 . . . . . . 127 E6
Keyham St PL5 . . . . 127 E8
Keyham Sta PL2 . . . . . . 127 E6
Khyber Cl PL1 . . . . 127 A3
Kibbiscombe Terr PL14. . 63 A8
Kidwelly Cl PL7 . . . . . . 131 C4
Kiel Pl PL3 . . . . 129 D5
Kilhallon PL24 . . . . 60 C5
Kilhallon Woodlands
 PL24. . . . . 60 C5
KILKHAMPTON 5 A6
Kilkhampton Prim Sch
 EX23 . . . . 5 A6
KILLATOWN 37 B1
Killatree Cross EX22 . . . . 8 F7
Killerton Rd EX23 . . . . . 104 E5
Killicourt TR3. . . . . 82 A7
Killiers Ct TR15 . . . . . . 139 C7
Killiersfield TR15 . . . . . 139 C6
Killigrew Ave PL12 . . . . 122 D1
Killigrew Gdns TR4 . . . . 70 D8
Killigrew Pl **9** TR11. . . . 145 A4
Killigrew Rd TR11 . . . . . 113 D6
Killigrew St TR11 . . . . . 145 A4
KILLIVOSE 79 C5
Killivose Gdns TR14 . . . 138 D1
Killivose Rd TR14 . . . . . 138 D1
Killyvarder Way PL25. . . 115 B6
Kilmar Cl PL14 . . . . 37 F3
Kilmar Rd PL14 . . . . . . 113 E6
Kilmar Way PL14 . . . . . . 37 F3

Kilminorth Woods Nature
  Reserve★ PL13 .... 117 A4
Kilna La PL12 .... 53 A2
Kiln Cl
  Cawsand PL10 .... 133 A1
  Mevagissey PL26 .... 73 C4
  Plymouth PL5 .... 127 C8
Kiln Mdws TR12 .... 92 C1
Kilworthy Hill PL19 ..... 147 C6
Kilworthy Rd PL19 ...... 147 C6
Kimber Ct TR11 .... 145 B2
Kimberley Ct TR7 .... 110 D6
Kimberley Foster Cl PL11. 65 B5
Kimberley Park Rd TR11. 145 A4
Kimberley Pl TR1 .... 145 A4
Kimberly Cl TR7 .... 110 D6
Kimberly Dr PL6 .... 125 B1
Kiming EX23 .... 104 E4
Kimlers Way PL13 .... 117 D6
King Arthurs Terr ⑤ PL34 14 C7
KINGBEARE 27 A1
King Charles Prim Sch
  TR11 .... 145 A3
King Edward Cres TR7 .. 110 D7
King Edward Mine Mus★
  TR14 .... 79 E5
King Edward Rd PL12 ... 122 F2
Kingfisher Cl
  Plymouth PL6 .... 125 E6
  Tavistock PL19 .... 147 D2
Kingfisher Dr PL25 ..... 115 A4
Kingfisher Way PL9 .... 135 C7
King George V Memorial Wlk
  TR27 .... 142 C6
KINGSAND 133 A2
King's Ave
  Falmouth TR11 .... 144 F4
  St Austell PL25 .... 114 D3
Kingsbury Ho TR11 ..... 145 A6
Kings Cross EX39 .... 2 E5
Kings Ct PL1 .... 128 A3
King's Hill EX23 .... 104 E3
Kings Hill Cl EX23 ...... 104 E4
King's Hill Ind Est EX23 . 104 E3
Kings Hill Mdw EX23 ... 104 E3
Kingsland Gardens Cl
  PL3 .... 128 E6
Kingsley Ave PL11 ...... 127 B2
Kingsley Cl TR1 .... 69 E3
Kingsley Cove TR4 ...... 68 A7
Kingsley Ct TR9 .... 57 E8
Kingsley Meade TR8 .... 111 B5
Kingsley Rd PL4 .... 128 E4
Kingsley Terr TR1 .... 67 C6
Kingsley Way TR13 ..... 146 C5
Kingsmill Rd PL12 ...... 122 C5
Kings Pippin PL26 .... 58 E5
Kings Rd
  Marazion TR17 .... 89 B5
  Plymouth, Devonport PL1. 127 F2
  Plymouth, West Park PL5 . 123 F3
  ④ St Mawes TR2 ...... 95 A6
King's Rd
  Camborne TR14 .... 138 D4
  Penzance TR18 .... 143 D5
  Plymouth PL1 .... 128 A2
Kings Sch PL3 .... 128 E6
King's St PL22 .... 112 C2
King St
  Bude EX23 .... 104 E5
  Gunnislake PL18 .... 41 A6
  Millbrook PL10 .... 132 E5
  Newquay TR7 .... 110 D6
  Plymouth PL1 .... 148 B3
  Redruth TR15 .... 140 B5
  Tavistock PL19 .... 147 B6
  Torpoint PL11 .... 127 C3
  Truro TR1 .... 137 D4
KING'S TAMERTON 123 F2
King's Tamerton Rd PL5. 123 F2
Kingston Cl PL7 .... 131 A5
Kingston Dr PL7 .... 131 B5
Kingston Rd PL17 .... 28 E1
Kings Tor PL20 .... 42 E4
Kingsway PL16 .... 133 B2
Kingsway Gdns PL6 .... 124 F3
Kingswear Cres PL6 .... 125 B1
Kings Wood★ PL26 ..... 73 B7
Kingswood Est PL14 .... 38 C1
Kingswood Park Ave
  PL3 .... 128 D6
Kingswood Rd PL18 ..... 41 A6
Kinnard Cres PL6 ...... 124 F7
Kinross Ave PL4 .... 129 A4
Kinsale Rd PL5 .... 123 F3
Kinsman Est PL31 ...... 109 C3
Kinterbury Rd PL5 ...... 127 B8
Kinterbury St PL1 ...... 149 A2
Kinterbury Terr PL5 .... 127 B8
Kinver Cl PL6 .... 125 D4
Kipling Gdns PL5 ...... 124 D2
Kirby Rd TR1 .... 137 A4
Kirkby Pl PL4 .... 148 C4
Kirkby Terr PL4 .... 148 C4
Kirkdale Gdns PL2 ..... 128 B7
Kirkella Rd PL20 .... 42 D2
Kirkland Cl PL6 .... 125 C7
Kirkstall Cl PL2 .... 128 A8
Kirkwall Rd PL5 .... 124 E3
Kirland Bower PL30 ..... 48 B7
Kirland Rd PL30 .... 109 B2
Kirton Pl PL3 .... 129 B5
Kit Hill Cres PL17 ...... 27 C8
Kit Hill Ctry Pk★ PL17 .. 40 A6

Kit Hill Vw PL15 .... 106 D4
Kitley Way PL5 .... 123 D1
Kitter Dr PL9 .... 136 A5
Kittiwake Cl TR27 ...... 77 E3
Kitts Ct ⑰ TR18 .... 143 E6
Kleinfontein Terr PL14 .. 38 D4
Knapmedown PL15 ...... 11 B1
Knapps Cl PL9 .... 136 C6
Knave-Go-By TR14 ...... 79 D5
Kneele Gdns PL3 .... 128 E8
Knighton Rd PL4 .... 149 C3
Knighton Terr ⑥ PL20. .. 42 C5
Knightor Cl PL25 .... 59 E6
Knights Cl ① PL34 ...... 14 C7
Knights Ct PL22 .... 112 B3
Knights Hill TR1 .... 137 B6
Knight's Mdws TR3 ...... 81 F7
KNIGHTSMILL 23 F7
Knights Way TR15 ...... 140 D7
Knill Cl TR26 .... 141 C2
Knill Cross PL10 .... 132 E5
Knill Cross Cotts PL10 .. 132 E5
Knoll Pk TR1 .... 137 F4
Knoll The PL7 .... 130 B6
Knowland Cl PL1 ...... 127 F3
Knowle Ave PL2 .... 127 E6
Knowle Terr PL20 .... 42 E4
Koth Karrji PL30 .... 23 E7
KUGGAR 103 B6
Kyl Cober Parc PL17 ..... 28 E1
Kynance Cl PL11 ...... 126 F4
Kynance Ho TR1 .... 69 E4
Kynance Terr TR12 ..... 102 F2

L

Labatt Cl PL6 .... 125 D3
Labernum Terr ① EX23 ... 5 A6
Laburnum Cl TR11 ..... 144 F5
Laburnum Cotts PL19 .. 147 C6
Laburnum Dr TR11 ..... 144 F5
Lacey Cl TR14 .... 79 E5
LADOCK 57 C1
Ladock CE Prim Sch TR2. 57 C2
Ladock Rd
  Ladock TR2 .... 57 C1
  Probus TR2 .... 71 C7
Lady Beam Ct PL17 ..... 39 F6
Ladycross PL15 .... 18 F7
Ladyfern Rd PL6 .... 121 C1
Lady Modiford's CE Prim Sch
  PL20 .... 42 E4
LADY NANCE 44 F3
Ladysmith Ct PL4 ...... 149 C4
Ladysmith Rd PL4 ...... 129 B3
Lady St TR13 .... 146 B5
Ladywell PL28 .... 107 D5
Ladywell Pl PL4 .... 149 B3
Laflouder Fields TR12 ... 99 A2
Laflouder La TR12 ...... 99 A2
Lafrowda Cl TR19 .... 86 E6
Lafrowda Terr TR19 ..... 86 F6
Laguna Ct TR15 .... 140 B5
LAIRA 129 C4
Laira Ave PL3 .... 129 C4
Laira Bridge Rd PL4 .... 129 B1
Laira Gdns PL3 .... 129 C4
Laira Green Prim Sch
  PL3 .... 129 C4
Laira Park Cres PL4 .... 129 B4
Laira Park Pl PL4 ...... 129 B4
Laira Park Rd PL4 ...... 129 B4
Laira Pl PL4 .... 149 C2
Laira St PL4 .... 149 C3
Laity Dr TR14 .... 138 F3
Laity Fields TR14 ...... 138 F3
Laity Rd TR14 .... 79 E4
Laity La TR26 .... 77 C4
Laity Wlk PL6 .... 124 D6
LAKE 42 E3
Lake La
  Dousland PL20 .... 42 E4
  Liskeard PL14 .... 113 D5
Lake Mews PL10 ...... 132 E5
Lake Rd PL9 .... 135 B6
Lakeside PL19 .... 147 B6
Lakeside Dr PL5 ...... 123 E5
Lake View PL12 .... 53 C8
Lake View Cl PL5 ...... 124 B6
Lakeview Dr PL5 ...... 124 B5
Lalebrick Rd PL9 ...... 135 B5
LAMANVA 93 C6
Lamanva Cl ⑯ TR16. ... 67 E4
Lamanva Rd ⑰ TR16. ... 67 E4
Lambert Rd PL5 .... 124 B6
Lambert Terr ④ TR11. .. 145 A5
Lambhay Hill PL1 ...... 149 A1
Lambhay St PL1 .... 149 A1
LAMBOURNE 55 B2
Lambourne Ave ⑦ TR5 .. 54 D1
Lamb Pk ⑤ PL24 .... 60 C4
Lambs La TR11 .... 144 E5
LAMELLION 113 A4
Lamellyn Dr TR1 .... 69 F3
Lamellyn Rd PL24 ...... 60 B4
Lamerhooe Cross PL19 .. 29 C1
Lamerhooe Dr
  Horsebridge PL19 ..... 29 C1
  Luckett PL19 .... 40 C8
LAMERTON 30 B3
Lamerton CE Prim Sch
  PL19 .... 30 B3
Lamerton Cl PL5 .... 124 B3
Lametton Gn PL14 ...... 51 B4
Lamledra Hill PL26 ..... 85 D5
Lamorak Cl PL26 .... 73 B3
LAMORICK 47 E7

LAMORNA 97 E5
Lamorna Cl TR27 .... 78 D6
Lamorna Ct TR16 .... 67 D6
Lamorna Dr ⑪ PL17. .... 39 F4
Lamorna Parc ⑫ PL17. .. 39 F4
Lamorna Pk
  St Austell PL25 ...... 114 E7
  Torpoint PL11 .... 126 E4
Lamorne Cl ④ TR6 ...... 55 A4
LAMORRAN 83 C8
Lampen Rd PL14 .... 36 F2
Lampen Terr PL14 ...... 36 F2
LANA 13 D7
Lana Cotts EX22 .... 13 C7
Lanadwell St PL28 ..... 107 D5
Lanaton Rd TR10 ...... 144 A8
Lancamshire La TR20 ... 89 F5
Lancaster Cres PL27 .... 31 F3
Lancaster Gdns PL5 .... 124 D4
Lanchard La PL14 ...... 113 B5
Lanchard Rd PL14 ..... 113 B5
Lanchard Rise PL14 .... 113 B5
Landaviddy La PL13 ..... 62 D2
Lander Ct TR1 .... 137 D3
Lander Rd PL12 .... 122 F3
Landeryon Gdns TR18 .. 143 D5
Landewednack Prim Sch
  TR12 .... 102 F2
Landithy TR20 .... 143 A8
Landlake Cross PL15 .... 28 A8
Landlake Rd PL15 ..... 106 B2
LANDRAKE 53 B3
Landrake Cl PL5 .... 127 C8
Landreath Pl PL24 ...... 60 B5
Landrew Rd PL25 ...... 114 F6
LANDREYNE 27 C2
Land's End Airport TR19. 86 F3
Lands End Rd TR19 ..... 97 A6
Lands Pk PL9 .... 135 F7
LANDULPH 123 A7
Landulph Cross PL12 ... 118 F1
Landulph Gdns PL5 .... 127 C8
Landulph Sch PL12 .... 118 F1
LANE 111 B3
LANEAST 17 B2
Lane End Cross PL19 .... 29 D2
Lanepark La TR3 .... 2 D5
Lane Reddin Terr ㉑
  TR18 .... 143 C2
LANESCOT 60 D6
Lane The PL7 .... 130 D6
Langage Cross PL7 ..... 131 F6
Langage Ind Est PL7 .. 131 C4
Langage Pk PL7 .... 131 C4
Langage Science Pk
  PL7 .... 131 D5
Langarth Cl TR3 .... 69 D4
Langdale Cl PL6 .... 125 D1
Langdale Gdns PL6 .... 125 D1
LANGDON 11 C3
Langdon Cross PL15 .... 18 D8
Langdon Ct PL9 .... 136 B6
Langdon Down Way
  PL11 .... 126 E3
Langerwell Cl PL12 .... 122 C3
Langerwell La PL12 .... 122 C3
Langfords Mdw ④ PL35 .. 9 C1
Lang Gdns PL18 .... 41 A3
Lang Gr
  Plymouth PL7 .... 136 C7
  Tavistock PL19 ...... 147 D5
Langham Pl PL4 ...... 149 C3
Langhill Rd PL3 .... 128 D5
Langley Cl PL6 .... 125 A7
Langley Cres PL6 ..... 124 F7
Langman Ct ⑬ PL20. ... 41 B1
Langmead Cl PL6 ..... 129 C8
Langmead Rd PL6 .... 129 C8
Langmore Cl PL6 ..... 129 A7
LANGORE 18 D5
Langorran Rd TR14 .... 138 B3
Lang Rd PL14 .... 113 B4
Langreek Bglws PL13 ... 62 C2
Langreek Rd PL13 ..... 62 C2
Langstone Rd PL2 ..... 128 C7
Langstone Terr PL2 .... 128 C7
Langton Rd
  Falmouth TR11 ...... 145 A6
  ⑧ Yelverton PL20. .... 42 C3
Langton Terr ⑧ TR11 .. 145 A5
Languroc Rd TR8 ...... 110 A3
Langurtho Rd PL23 .... 116 B4
Langweath Est TR12 .... 99 D7
Langweath Gdns TR27 .. 77 E3
Langweath La TR12 ..... 99 D7
Langwedh TR16 .... 67 D4
Lanhenvor Ave TR7 .... 110 E5
Lanherne Ave TR8 ...... 45 A8
Lanheverne Parc ④
  TR12 .... 101 C4
Lanhydrock Rd PL4 .... 129 B2
Lanhydrock View PL31 . 109 D3
LANIVET 47 F6
Lanivet Prim Sch PL30 .. 47 E7
LANJETH 58 E3
LANJEW 46 F7
Lanjowan TR13 .... 146 B6
LANK 24 B2
Lankelly Cl PL23 ...... 116 B4
Lankelly La PL23 ...... 116 A4
LANLIVERY 48 C1
Lanlivery Prim Sch PL30. 48 D2
Lanivoie Mdw TR8 ...... 55 D8
Lanmoor Est TR16 ...... 80 D6
Lannarth Glas TR16 .... 140 E1
LANNER 80 D6

Lanner Gn TR16 .... 140 E1
Lanner Hill
  Redruth, Pennance TR16 . 140 E1
  Redruth TR15 .... 140 D1
Lanner Moor Terr TR16.. 80 E6
Lanner Prim Sch TR16. .. 80 D6
Lanner Sq TR16 .... 80 D6
Lannoweth Rd TR18 ... 143 F6
Lanoweth TR10 .... 81 D2
LANREATH 62 B7
Lansallos St PL13 ...... 62 D1
Lansdown Cl EX23 ..... 104 D5
Lansdowne TR26 ...... 141 B4
Lansdowne Cl TR18 .... 143 C5
Lansdowne Ct TR18 ... 143 B5
Lansdowne Pl TR18 ... 143 C4
Lansdowne Rd
  Callington PL17 .... 39 E4
  Falmouth TR11 ...... 145 C3
  Penzance TR18 ...... 143 C5
  Plymouth PL6 .... 124 F2
Lansdown Rd
  Bude EX23 .... 104 D5
  Wadebridge PL27 .... 108 B5
LANSTEPHAN 106 C8
Lantallack Cross PL12 ... 53 A3
LANTEGLOS 14 F1
LANTEGLOS HIGHWAY . 61 E4
Lanteglos Est TR27 ..... 77 F1
Lanuthnoe Est TR27 .... 77 F1
Lanvean Bglws TR8 ...... 45 B8
Lanwithan Ct PL22 .... 112 D2
Lanwithan Rd PL22 .... 112 E1
Lanxon Cres PL30 ...... 48 C2
Lanyon Ct PL14 .... 37 F3
Lanyon Rd TR3 .... 82 B8
Lapthorn Cl PL9 ...... 135 C7
Larch Cl PL12 .... 122 C3
Larch Dr PL6 .... 125 E7
Larcombe Rd PL25 .... 115 A6
Laregan Hill TR18 ..... 143 C3
Lariggan Cres TR18 .... 143 D4
Lariggan Rd TR18 ..... 143 D4
Larkfield Cl PL26 .... 58 E5
Larkfield Rise ⑬ TR2. ... 95 A6
Larkhall Rise PL3 ..... 129 B5
Larkham Cl PL7 .... 130 C6
Larkham La PL7 ...... 130 C6
Lark Hill PL2 .... 128 A6
LATCHLEY 40 D8
Latham Cl PL6 .... 129 A7
Latimer Cl PL7 .... 131 B5
Latimer Wlk PL6 ...... 124 E7
Launcells Cross EX23 .... 5 B1
LAUNCESTON 106 D5
Launceston Castle★
  PL15 .... 106 C6
Launceston Cl
  Bodmin PL31 .... 109 F4
  Plymouth PL6 .... 125 B7
Launceston Coll PL15 .. 106 C4
Launceston Hospl PL15. 106 C4
Launceston Prim Sch
  PL15 .... 106 C5
Launceston Rd
  Bodmin PL31 .... 35 B1
  Kelly Bray PL17 .... 39 E6
Launceston Ret Pk PL15 106 C4
Launceston Sta★ PL15 . 106 B6
Launceston Steam Rly★
  PL15 .... 18 E3
Laura Cl PL34 .... 14 D7
Laura Dr PL25 .... 115 A5
Laurel Cl PL2 .... 128 A7
Laurel Dene PL2 ...... 128 A7
Laurel Dr PL6 .... 125 E5
Laurel La PL17 .... 39 E6
Laurel Rd PL2 .... 128 A7
Laurels The PL18 .... 40 E6
La Vague TR3 .... 82 C5
Lavington Cl PL7 ..... 131 B5
Lavinia Dr PL7 .... 130 C5
Lavorrick Orchs PL26 ... 73 C4
LAWHITTON 19 C1
Lawn Cl ② PL7 .... 131 B5
Lawn Steps TR11 ..... 145 B4
Lawns The
  Plymouth PL5 ...... 124 E1
  Torpoint PL11 ...... 127 A4
Lawn The
  Par PL24 .... 60 B5
  Tavistock PL19 ..... 147 D6
Lawrence House Mus★
  PL15 .... 106 C6
Lawrence Rd
  Plymouth PL9 ...... 135 A6
  St Agnes TR5 .... 54 C1
Lawry Cl ⑥ PL14 ..... 113 B5
Lawton Cl TR7 .... 110 B5
Law Wlk PL6 .... 124 D6
Leader Rd TR7 .... 111 E7
Leafield PL31 .... 35 B2
Leander Way PL5 .... 124 D2
Leanway PL12 .... 122 E2
Leap Pk TR3 .... 69 C3
Leas The TR1 .... 137 E5
Leat Cl PL20 .... 42 E5
Leatfield PL26 .... 73 C3
Leatfield Dr PL6 ..... 124 F4
Leatherby Cl PL6 ..... 124 E7
Leather Tor Cl ④ PL20. .. 42 C3
Leat Rd
  Lifton PL16 .... 19 F3
  Pendeen TR19 .... 75 A1
Leatside PL6 .... 121 C1
Leats The TR1 .... 137 C4

Leat The ⑨ EX23 .... 4 E1
Leat View PL12 .... 122 B3
Leat Wlk
  Plymouth PL3 .... 128 E6
  Roborough PL6 ...... 121 D1
  Saltash PL12 .... 122 D4
Leaves Yd PL3 .... 129 B7
Lea Way EX23 .... 104 F6
LEBURNICK 28 D8
Leburnick Cross PL15 ... 28 D8
Ledgate La PL7 ...... 131 F8
Ledra Cl TR12 .... 103 A4
Ledrah Gdns PL25 .... 114 B3
Ledrah Rd PL25 ...... 114 B3
LEEDSTOWN 78 E1
Leedstown Prim Sch
  TR27 .... 78 E1
Leeside Ct ⑦ PL2 .... 128 A4
Lefra Orch TR19 .... 97 B6
Legendry Land's End★
  TR19 .... 96 A5
Leggos Ct ⑩ TR15 .... 140 B5
Legion La ③ PL24 ..... 60 D5
Legis Wlk PL6 .... 125 B8
LEIGHAM 129 E8
Leigham Ct PL1 ...... 148 B2
Leigham Manor Dr PL6. 129 F8
Leigham Prim Sch PL6. 125 E1
Leigham St PL1 ...... 148 B1
Leigham Terrace La PL1. 148 B2
Leigh Ct PL6 .... 129 A8
Leigh La
  Hatt PL12 .... 53 D6
  Roborough PL6 ...... 121 D6
Leighton Rd PL3 ..... 128 F8
LELANT 77 E4
LELANT DOWNS 77 D2
Lelant Mdws TR26 .... 77 E3
Lelant Saltings Sta TR26. 77 E3
Lelant Sta TR26 ...... 77 E4
Lemellen Gdns PL30 ... 23 B2
Lemin Parc TR27 ...... 78 E3
Lemin's Ct TR15 ..... 140 B5
Lemon Hill TR11 ...... 82 A3
Lemon Hill Gdns TR11.. 82 A3
Lemon Mews Rd TR1. .. 137 D4
Lemon Quay TR1 ..... 137 D4
Lemon Row TR1 ...... 137 D3
Lemon St
  St Keverne TR12 ..... 101 D4
  ⑲ Truro TR1 .... 137 D4
Lemon Terr TR4 .... 81 D8
Lender La ⑤ TR12 ..... 99 A2
Lendra La PL17 .... 39 D4
Lenton Rd PL3 .... 128 F8
Leonards La PL20 ...... 88 A3
Lerrin CE Prim Sch PL22. 61 D8
Lerryn View PL22 ...... 61 C8
Lerwick Rd PL27 ...... 31 F3
LESCROW 116 B6
Lescudjack Cres TR18 .. 143 F6
Lescudjack Rd TR18 ... 143 E6
Lescudjack Terr TR18 .. 143 F6
Lesingey La TR20 ...... 88 A3
Leskinnick Pl ⑭ TR18 .. 143 E6
Leskinnick Terr TR18 .. 143 E6
Leslie Ct TR13 .... 146 B6
LESNEWTH 10 A1
Lesnewth ⑱ PL24 ...... 60 B4
Lester Cl PL3 .... 129 B6
Lestraynes La TR10 .... 92 E8
Lethlean Cl TR27 ..... 142 D7
Lethlean La TR27 .... 142 D7
Lethlean Towans TR27 . 142 D8
LEVALSA MEOR 73 B8
Levant Cl TR19 .... 86 F8
Levant Mine & Beam
  Engine★ TR19 .... 74 E1
Levant Rd TR19 .... 86 F8
Leven Cotts EX23 ..... 104 D5
Leverlake Rd EX23 ...... 6 F4
Levine View TR11 .... 144 E1
LEWANNICK 27 B7
Lewannick Cl PL15 ..... 27 B7
Lewannick Com Prim Sch
  PL15 .... 27 B7
Lewarne Cres TR7 .... 111 C7
Lewarne Rd TR7 ...... 111 C8
Lewes Gdns PL5 ...... 124 C4
Lewis Way PL25 ...... 114 E6
Lewman Cl TR2 .... 71 C6
Lewman Rd TR2 .... 71 C6
Leworthy Cross EX22 .... 8 E4
LEY 36 E1
Ley La PL20 .... 119 D6
Leypark Ct PL6 ...... 125 E2
Leypark Dr PL6 ...... 125 E2
Leypark Wlk PL6 ..... 125 E2
Leys La TR17 .... 89 B5
LEZANT 28 B6
Libby Ct PL12 .... 122 C5
Liberator Row ④ PL27 .. 31 F3
Lidden Cl TR18 ...... 143 C3
Lidden Cres TR18 .... 143 C3
Lidden Rd TR18 ...... 143 C3
Liddicoat Rd PL22 .... 112 D3
Liddle Way PL7 ...... 131 B6
Lifeboat Hill ㉜ TR26 .. 141 B6
LIFTON 19 F3
Lifton Pk PL20 .... 119 D6
Liftondown Cross PL16.. 19 D4
LIFTONDOWN 19 D4
Lifton Prim Sch PL16... 19 F4
Liggars Farm Est PL14 .. 50 F5
Lighterage Hill TR1 ... 137 E2
Lighthouse Hill TR16 ... 67 C6
Lighthouse La PL26 ..... 85 C5
Lighthouse Rd TR12. .. 102 F2
Lilac Cl PL9 .... 135 C5
Lily Way PL28 .... 31 F1

Limerick Pl PL4 149 C3
Limes La
Liskeard PL14 113 B5
Tavistock PL19 147 A6
Limes The PL6 124 F2
Limetree Rd PL3 128 D7
Lime Tree Way PL15 27 D4
Limmicks Rd PL13 117 D6
Lincoln Ave PL4 149 C4
Lincoln Row 6 PL27 31 F3
Linden Ave TR7 110 E5
Linden Cres TR7 110 E5
Linden Terr PL4 149 C3
Lindsay Fields TR9 45 E1
Lingard Cl PL14 113 A6
Lingfield Ave PL26 58 E1
Linhay Cl PL25 115 D6
Linkadells PL7 130 D6
Link Cl TR11 144 F4
Linketty La PL7 130 C5
Linketty Lane E PL6 125 A1
Linketty Lane W PL6 128 F8
LINKINHORNE 39 B8
Link Rd PL15 106 B3
Links The
Falmouth TR11 144 F1
Praa Sands TR20 90 C4
Links View EX23 104 F6
Linley Cl TR3 69 D3
Linnet Ct PL12 122 C2
Linton Cl PL5 124 C8
Linton La EX39 2 E5
Linton Rd PL5 124 C7
Linton Sq PL5 124 C8
Lippell Dr PL9 135 E6
Lipsom Co-operative Academy PL4 129 A4
LIPSON 149 C4
Lipson Ave PL4 149 C4
Lipson Com Coll PL4 129 C4
Lipson Ct PL4 149 B3
Lipson Rd PL4 149 B4
Lipson Sp Ctr PL4 129 B4
Lipson Terr PL4 149 C4
LIPSON VALE 129 A4
Lipson Vale PL4 129 A4
Lipstone Cres PL4 149 C4
Lisbon Terr TR19 97 A6
Liscawn Terr PL11 127 B3
Liscombe Cl PL18 41 A7
Lishaperhill Cross EX22 5 E2
LISKEARD 113 E6
Liskeard Bsns Pk PL14 113 E6
Liskeard Com Hospl PL14 113 E7
Liskeard & District Mus★ PL14 113 C6
Liskeard Hill PL14 36 F2
Liskeard Hillfort Prim Sch PL14 113 A6
Liskeard Rd
Callington PL17 39 E4
Saltash PL12 122 B3
Trematon PL12 53 E3
Liskeard Sch & Com Coll PL14 113 C7
Liskeard Sta PL14 113 B4
Liskerrett Rd PL14 113 D5
Liskey TR6 55 A4
Liskey Hill TR6 55 A4
Liskey Hill Cres 1 TR6 55 A4
Liskey Tourist Pk TR3 69 C4
Lisson Gr PL4 128 F4
Lister Cl PL7 130 F6
Lister Hill 10 TR11 145 A4
Lister St TR11 145 A3
Listowel Dr PL13 117 D4
Listry Rd TR7 110 E5
Litchaton Cres PL7 130 B7
Litchaton Way PL7 130 B7
Litchfield Cl PL7 131 B6
Little Ash Gdns PL5 123 B1
Little Ash Rd PL5 123 B1
LITTLE BOSULLOW 75 D1
Little Bridge Cross EX22 8 A5
Littlebridge Mdw EX22 8 A5
Little Bridge Pk PL27 108 D6
LITTLE BRYNN 46 E5
Little Butts PL9 135 E6
Little Castle St 7 TR1 137 C4
LITTLE COMFORT 28 C7
Little Dean PL14 113 A5
Little Dinas PL28 107 E4
Little Dock La PL5 124 B2
Little Down La PL6 121 E3
Little Down Pk TR7 111 A4
LITTLE FALMOUTH 145 B7
Little Fancy Cl PL6 125 C7
Little Gilly Hill 3 TR15 140 C4
Little Gn PL13 62 D1
Little Gregwartha TR16 80 A5
Little-in-sight 19 TR26 141 A5
LITTLE KIRLAND 109 C1
Little La
Hayle TR27 142 E7
Kingsand PL10 133 A2
Staddiscombe PL9 135 D3
Little Laney PL13 62 D1
Little Mdw
Bodmin PL31 109 D5
Pyworthy EX22 8 E5
Little Mill La TR27 77 E2
Little Oaks TR10 144 B6
Little Orch PL12 53 C3
LITTLE PETHERICK 32 C6
Little Point Cres PL10 132 F5
LITTLE PRIDEAUX 60 B7
Little Stark Cl PL26 58 B4
Littleton Pl PL2 127 F4
Little Treloweer Pk PL26 58 F1
Little Treloweth TR15 139 B6
Little Trelyn PL27 21 E2
Little Trethewey Est TR19 96 E4
Little Trethiggey TR8 111 F2
Little Treverrow PL27 21 E2
Little Western Rly★ TR7 110 F5
Little Woburn Cl PL15 106 C4
Littlewood Cl PL7 131 A4
LIZARD 102 F2
Lizard Cl PL6 124 F7
Lizard Lighthouse Her Ctr★ TR12 102 F1
Lizard Nature Reserve The★ TR12 100 F2
Lizard Wlk PL6 125 A7
Llantillio Dr PL2 128 B8
Llawnroc Cl TR14 138 E2
Llewellyn Cl PL32 105 C3
Lloyds Rd TR12 103 A2
Loatmead Cross EX22 3 E3
LOCKENGATE 47 E4
Lockeridge Rd PL20 41 B1
Lockington Ave PL3 128 F7
Locks Wlk PL1 127 E1
Lockyer Ct PL1 148 C2
Lockyer Mews PL19 147 C6
Lockyer Rd PL3 128 E5
Lockyers Quay PL4 149 B2
Lockyer St PL1 148 C2
Lockyer Terr PL12 123 A3
Lodenek Ave PL28 107 D4
Lodge Dr TR1 137 F6
Lodge Gdns PL6 124 E3
Lodge Hill PL14 113 A3
Lodge La PL8 136 F5
Lodge Way TR9 45 F2
Loe Bar Rd TR13 98 C8
Loe Valley Rd TR13 146 B7
Lofoten Cl PL1 127 E2
Loftus Gdns PL5 123 C2
Logans Ct TR26 141 D2
Loggans Cl TR27 142 E8
Loggans Rd TR27 142 E8
Loggans Way TR27 142 E8
Loggans Wlk TR27 142 E8
Lollabury Rd PL12 122 E3
Lomond Hall TR26 141 D1
LONDON APPRENTICE 59 B1
Longacre
Harrowbarrow PL17 40 C4
Plymouth PL7 130 B7
Long Acre PL12 122 B4
Long-A-Row Cl EX23 10 C6
Long Barn The TR20 89 D8
LONGBRIDGE 129 F7
Longbridge Cl PL6 129 F6
Longbridge Rd
Plymouth, Laira PL3 129 C4
Plymouth, Longbridge PL6 129 E7
Longbrook Barton PL7 130 D5
Longbrook St PL7 130 F4
Longcause PL7 130 F4
Longcause Specl Sch PL7 130 F4
Longcoombe La PL13 62 D3
LONGCROSS 29 F6
Long Cross PL29 22 C6
Longcross Victorian Gdns★ PL29 22 C6
Long Down Gdns PL6 125 E3
LONGDOWNS 81 A1
Longdowns Trad Est TR10 81 A1
Longfield TR11 144 E4
Longfield Cl 25 PL17 39 F4
Longfield Dr PL32 105 C3
Longfield Pl PL4 149 B4
Longfield Rd PL32 105 C3
Longfield Villas PL9 135 D8
Longhouse La PL27 21 E3
Long La
High Street PL26 58 C4
Ludgvan TR20 89 A7
St Erth TR20, TR27 89 E8
LONGLANDS 122 A1
Longlands PL9 135 D8
Longlands La PL12 122 B1
Long Lanes TR20 89 F7
Long Ley PL3 129 B6
Longman's La 3 PL17 39 E4
Long Mdw PL7 130 D7
Long Mdw View PL23 116 B5
Longmeadow Cl PL7 130 E7
Longmeadow Rd PL12 122 E3
Long Moor TR12 103 A5
Long Orch PL20 41 B1
Long Park Cl PL9 135 F5
Longpark Dr EX23 6 F5
Long Park Dr PL6 125 D7
Long Park Rd PL12 122 D2
Longpark Way PL25 114 F5
Long Pk PL15 18 D2
Long Rd PL12 122 B4
LONGROCK 88 F6
Long Rock Business Park TR20 88 F6
Long Rock Industrial Estate TR20 88 F6
Long Row TR19 97 F7
Long Rowden PL3 128 E6
Long Steps PL23 116 C4
LONGSTONE
Carbis Bay 141 E1
St Mabyn 34 F8
Longstone Ave PL6 125 A6
Longstone Cl TR26 141 E1
Longstone Hill TR26 141 E1
Long Terrace Cl 5 PL7 131 C5
Longview Rd PL12 122 D3
Longview Terr PL3 129 B7
Longwood Cl PL7 131 A4
Longwool Mdw EX23 7 B6
LOOE 117 D3
Looe Com Academy PL13 117 D6
Looe Hill
Looe PL13 63 F5
Seaton PL13, PL11 64 A5
Looe Prim Sch PL13 117 D4
Looe St PL4 149 A2
Looe Sta PL13 117 C4
Lookout The 7 TR11 145 B5
Looseleigh Cl PL6 125 A4
Looseleigh La PL6 124 F5
Looseleigh Pk PL6 124 E5
Lopes Dr PL6 121 C1
Lopes Rd
Dousland PL20 42 E3
Plymouth PL2 128 B6
Lopwell Cl PL6 124 F5
Lord Louis Cres PL9 134 F6
Lords Mdw TR2 71 F3
Lorrimore Ave PL2 127 F5
Loscombe Ct TR16 80 A5
Loscombe La TR16 80 A5
Loscombe Rd TR16 139 E1
Lost Gdns of Heligan The★ PL26 73 B5
LOSTWITHIEL 112 E1
Lostwithiel Mus★ PL22 112 C2
Lostwithiel Prim Sch PL22 112 C2
Lostwithiel Rd PL30, PL31 48 C7
Lostwithiel St PL23 116 C4
Lostwithiel Sta PL22 112 D2
Lostwood Rd PL25 114 E4
Lotherton Cl PL7 131 B3
Loughboro Rd PL5 123 C1
LOVATON 42 F1
Love La
Bodmin PL31 109 F5
Hayle TR27 142 E7
Mousehole TR19 88 C1
Penryn TR10 144 D8
Penzance TR18 143 C4
Saltash PL12 122 E2
24 St Ives TR26 141 B6
Lovell Rd PL3 128 F6
Lovely La PL12 65 A8
Loveny Cl PL14 36 F2
Loveny Rd PL14 36 F2
Lovering Rd PL25 114 E6
Lovibond Wlk PL27 108 C5
Lowarth Cl TR13 146 B6
Lowarth Elms 13 TR15 140 B5
Lowarthow Marghas TR15 140 D5
Lowenac Cres TR27 78 E6
Lowenac Gdns TR14 138 C2
Lowen Bre TR1 69 E3
Lowen Ct 7 TR1 137 D4
Lowenek Cl TR11 144 E5
Lowenna Gdns PL13 117 C4
Lowenna Manor PL27 21 E3
Lowen Way TR3 69 C3
Lower Anderton Rd PL10 132 F5
Lower Barncoose TR15 139 F6
Lower Biteford Cross EX39 3 E6
LOWER BODINNAR 87 E7
Lower Bore St PL31 109 D5
LOWER BOSCASWELL 74 F2
Lower Boscaswell Parc TR19 74 F1
LOWER BREA 139 A3
Lower Broad La TR15, TR16 139 C8
Lower Cardrew La TR15 140 B6
Lower Castle Rd TR2 95 A5
Lower Chapel St PL13 117 D3
Lower Church St TR27 142 D6
Lower Cleavefield PL15 106 C7
LOWER CLICKER 51 F4
Lower Clicker Rd PL14 51 F4
LOWER COMPTON 129 A5
Lower Compton Rd PL3 128 F5
Lower Coronation Terr 9 PL17 39 F4
Lower Eastcliff TR4 68 A7
Lower Elms PL27 21 F3
Lower Fairfield PL12 65 A8
Lower Farm Rd PL7 131 A4
Lower Fore St PL12 123 A2
Lower Glen Pk PL14 38 D4
Lower Goongumpas La TR16 68 F1
Lower Goonrea PL13 117 B4
LOWER GREEN 146 A5
Lower Greenbanks PL27 21 E2
Lower Green St TR18 143 D1
Lower Gurnick Rd TR18 143 B3
Lower Hill TR13 146 C6
Lower Hillcrest
Helston TR13 146 C6
9 Perranporth TR6 55 A4
Lower Hillside PL14 50 B6
Lower Hugus Rd TR3 69 C3
Lower Kelly PL18 41 A3
Lower La
Mawgan TR12 99 D7
6 Plymouth PL1 149 A2
Lower Lux St 5 PL14 113 C6
Lower Market St
Looe PL13 117 D3
Penryn TR10 144 C7
Lower Mdw 5 TR4 69 A3
Lower Merritts Hill 22 TR16 67 E4
Lower Middle Hill PL14 38 E4
Lower Molinnis PL26 47 D2
LOWER NINNES 76 B1
Lower Parc TR12 92 C2
Lower Park Dr PL9 135 F4
Lower Pengegon TR14 138 F3
Lower Peverell Rd TR18 143 E7
Lower Pk TR2 70 F5
Lower Polstain Rd TR3 69 D3
LOWER PORTHPEAN 59 E1
Lower Port View PL12 122 F2
LOWER PROSPIDNICK 91 C6
Lower Pumpfield Row TR15 139 B6
Lower Rd PL11 64 C4
Lower Redannick TR1 137 C4
Lower Ridings PL7 131 B7
LOWER ROSE 55 D5
LOWER ROSEWARNE 138 C4
Lower Rosewin Row 9 TR1 137 D5
Lower Row PL10 133 A2
Lower Rowes Terr PL26 58 D5
Lower Saltram PL9 135 C7
Lower Sheffield TR19 97 F7
Lowerside PL2 128 A8
Lower Sq EX22 11 E8
Lower St
Looe PL13 117 D3
Plymouth PL4 149 A3
Lower Tamar Terr PL18 41 A7
Lower Terr TR3 81 B4
LOWERTOWN
Helston 91 E4
Lostwithiel 48 A4
Lower Town PL17 28 E1
Lowertown Cl PL12 53 C3
Lowertown La TR13 146 C7
LOWER TREBULLETT 28 A4
Lower Tregongeeves PL26 59 A1
Lower Tywarnhayle 18 TR6 55 A5
Lower Well La TR13 146 C6
Lower Well Pk PL26 73 C3
Lower Wesley Terr PL14 38 D4
Lower Woodside PL25 114 A4
Lowery Cross PL20 42 F4
Low Lee Rd TR19 88 D1
Lowley Rd PL15 18 E2
Lucas Cl PL31 109 E3
Lucas La PL7 130 D6
Lucas Terr PL4 129 B2
LUCKETT 40 B8
Lucknow Rd PL31 48 D8
Lucknow Road S 2 PL31 48 D8
LUDGVAN 89 A7
Ludgvan Prim Sch TR20 89 B8
Ludlow Rd 2 PL3 128 E6
LUFFINCOTT 13 C5
Luffman Cl PL13 62 D6
Lugger The TR2 83 B2
Lukes Cl TR1 137 F5
Luke's La TR20 89 F6
Lulworth Dr PL6 125 B7
Lundy Cl PL6 124 F7
Lundy Dr EX23 10 C6
Lundy Rd PL29 22 E7
Lusart Dr TR12 102 F2
Lusty Glaze Adventure Ctr TR7 111 A8
Lusty Glaze Rd TR7 111 A7
LUTSFORD 3 A6
Lutsford Cross EX39 3 A6
Lutyens Fold PL19 29 C6
Luxmore Cl PL6 125 E1
Luxon Dr TR7 110 F4
Lux Park L Ctr Pl14 113 C7
Luxstowe Dr 1 PL14 113 C6
Luxstowe Gdns PL14 113 C6
LUXULYAN 48 A1
Luxulyan Rd PL24 115 F7
Luxulyan Sch PL30 48 A1
Luxulyan Sta PL30 47 F1
Lych Cl PL9 135 A6
Lychgate Dr TR1 137 C6
Lydcott Cl PL13 63 F8
Lydcott Cres PL13 63 F8
Lydcot Wlk PL6 125 A1
Lydford Park Rd PL3 128 D5
Lyd Gdns PL19 147 D5
Lydia Way PL4 149 B4
Lympne Ave PL5 123 F5
Lynbridge Ct 5 PL19 147 B5
Lyndhurst Ave PL25 115 A4
Lyndhurst Cl PL2 128 C6
Lyndhurst Rd PL2 128 C6
Lyndon Ct PL12 122 D4
Lyndrick Rd PL3 128 E7
Lynes Cotts 2 PL14 51 A7
Lynher Cl PL15 27 B3
Lynher Ct PL12 122 F1
Lynher Dr PL12 122 F1
Lynher St PL5 123 D2
Lynher View PL17 38 E8
Lynher Way
28 Callington PL17 39 F4
North Hill PL15 27 A4
Lyn-Meynek TR15 140 D4
Lynmouth Cl PL7 130 C7
LYNSTONE 104 D3
Lynstone Cotts EX23 104 D3
Lynstone Rd EX23 104 D4
Lyn Terr 7 TR18 143 C1
Lynwood Ave PL7 130 B6
Lynwood Cl PL31 109 E4
Lynwood Cotts 1 TR19 88 C1
Lynwood Flats TR13 91 A1
Lyons Rd PL25 115 B4
Lytton Pl PL25 114 F4

M

MABE BURNTHOUSE 93 C8
Mabena Cl PL30 34 C8
Mabe Prim Sch TR10 81 C1
Macadam Rd PL4 149 C1
Macaulay Cres PL5 124 C1
McCarthy Dr PL26 58 B4
Macey St PL11 127 C3
Mackenzie Pl PL5 123 C2
Mackerel Cl PL25 114 E7
Mclean Dr PL26 58 D5
Madden Rd PL1 127 F2
Maddever Cres PL14 113 C5
Maddock Cl PL7 131 A4
Maddock Dr PL7 131 B4
Maddocks Cross EX22 3 F2
Madeira Dr EX23 6 F5
Madeira Rd
Falmouth TR11 145 A1
Plymouth PL1 149 A1
Madeira Villas 1 PL20 42 C5
Madeira Wlk TR11 145 A2
MADERS 39 D6
Madford La PL15 106 C5
Madge Ct 3 PL19 147 B6
Madge La PL19 147 B6
Madison Terr TR27 142 E7
Madison Vean TR27 142 E7
MADRON 143 B8
Madron Rd TR18 143 C7
MAENPORTH 93 F4
Maenporth Est TR11 93 E4
Maenporth Rd TR11 93 E4
Maen Valley Pk TR11 93 E5
MAER 104 D8
Maer Down Rd EX23 104 C7
Maer La EX23 104 D8
Magdalen Gdns PL7 130 F3
Magnificent Music Machines Mus★ PL14 51 C3
Magnolia Cl 3 PL7 131 B5
Magnolia Ct 3 PL9 135 F7
Magor Ave TR14 79 E5
Maida Vale Terr PL4 128 F4
Maiden St 1 EX23 4 E1
Maidenwell Rd PL7 130 C5
Maidstone Pl PL5 123 E4
Maine Gdns PL2 127 F7
Main Rd
Crumplehorn PL13 62 D2
Downderry PL11 64 C5
Main St TR18 143 C7
MAINSTONE 125 F2
Mainstone Ave PL4 149 C2
Maitland Dr PL3 128 F8
Maker La PL10 133 B4
Maker Rd PL11 127 A2
Maker View PL3 128 B4
Maker View Rd PL10 133 A6
Malabar Ho TR1 69 F3
Malabar Rd TR1 69 F3
Mallard Cl PL7 130 F5
Mallets Ct PL27 108 C6
Mallory Dr TR7 111 B5
Malmesbury Cl PL2 128 B8
Malory Cl PL5 124 D2
MALPAS 70 D2
Malpas Ho TR1 137 E4
Malpas Rd TR1 137 E2
Malt House Ct TR27 142 D6
Malt House Gdns 2 TR18 143 C2
Malthouse La TR17 89 C5
Malt House The 3 TR18 143 C2
MANACCAN 101 A8
Manaccan Prim Sch TR12 101 A8
MANADON 124 D1
Manadon Cl PL5 124 E1
Manadon Dr PL5 124 E1
Manadon Football Ctr PL2 124 D2
Manadon Hill PL5, PL6 124 E1
Manadon Vale Prim Sch 1 PL5 128 E8
Manaton Cl TR13 146 D8
Manaton Dr PL15 106 C5
Manby Gdns PL5 123 F5
Mandalay Villas 8 TR9 45 E1
Mandeley Cl PL33 14 D2
Manely Way PL17 40 C4
Manewas Way TR7 111 B7
Manfield Way PL25 115 C4
Manifold Gdns PL3 129 D5
Manley Cl PL14 113 B5
Manley Rd PL14 113 B5
Manley Terr 5 PL14 113 B5
MANNAMEAD 128 F5
Mannamead Ave PL3 128 F5
Mannamead Ct 9 PL3 128 F6
Mannamead Rd PL3 128 F6
Man of War View TR12 102 F2
Manor Bourne Rd PL9 135 C1
Manor Cl
Blisland PL30 35 D8
Crackington Haven EX23 10 C6
Falmouth TR11 144 E5
Heamoor TR18 143 D7

Manor Cl *continued*
Helston TR13 146 D8
St Austell PL25 114 F5
Tavistock PL19 147 A6
Manor Cotts TR11 145 D3
Manor Cres TR11 144 E5
Manor Ct [1] TR2 95 A6
Manor Dr TR26 141 C3
Manor Farm PL20 42 E3
Manor Farm Cl [7] TR20 89 E5
Manor Farm Rd PL26 115 A1
Manor Gdns
Camelford PL32 105 D4
Horrabridge PL20 42 B4
Millbrook PL10 132 F6
Plymouth PL1 148 B2
Redruth TR15 140 B6
St Erth TR27 142 A1
Truro TR1 137 E5
Manor La PL3 129 D5
Manor Park Cl PL7 130 F5
Manor Park Dr PL7 131 A4
MANOR PARSLEY 68 B5
Manor Pk
Dousland PL20 42 E3
Duloe PL14 51 A1
Saltash PL12 122 D2
Manor Pl TR18 143 D7
Manor Rd
Bude EX23 104 E4
Camborne TR14 138 C2
Carharrack TR16 80 E8
Falmouth TR11 144 E5
Newquay TR7 110 D6
Plymouth PL9 135 E8
Tavistock PL19 147 B6
Manor St PL1 148 A3
Manor View PL24 60 B4
Manor Way
Heamoor TR18 143 D7
Helston TR13 146 D8
Tavistock PL19 147 B6
Manse Rd [6] TR3 81 F7
Mansion Ho The PL1 134 A8
Manson Pl PL26 58 C8
Manston Cl PL5 123 E5
Mantle Gdns PL5 127 D8
Maple Ave
Camelford PL32 105 E5
Torpoint PL11 127 A3
Maple Cl
Bodmin PL31 109 B4
[23] Callington PL17 39 F4
Plymouth PL6 125 E6
[5] St Columb Major TR9 45 D6
St Dennis PL26 58 B8
Tavistock PL19 147 C3
Maple Ct [2] PL9 135 F7
Maple Gr
Plymouth, Mutley PL4 128 D4
Plymouth, Plympton PL7 130 B5
Maple Way PL6 125 E7
MARAZION 89 B6
Marazion Mus* TR17 89 B5
Marazion Sch TR17 89 C5
Marazion Way PL2 128 D8
Marchant's Cross PL20 42 F1
Marchant's Way PL20 42 F2
Marconi Centre (Mus)* TR13 98 F2
Marconi Cl TR13 146 B6
Marcus Hill TR7 110 E6
Marcwheal [6] TR19 88 C1
Mardon Cl PL6 125 D4
Marett Rd PL5 123 F3
Margaret Ave PL25 114 E3
Margaret Cnr PL31 109 C4
Margaret Cres PL31 109 C4
Margaret Gdns PL27 108 D5
Margaret Pk PL3 128 E8
Margaret Pl TR11 144 F3
Margate La PL30 35 C1
MARHAMCHURCH 7 B6
Marhamchurch CE Prim Sch EX23 7 B6
Maria's La TR19 96 B7
Maribou Ct PL28 31 F7
Marina Ct TR16 67 C5
Marina Rd PL5 123 F3
Marina Terr [7] PL4 128 F4
Marine Academy PL5 123 E1
Marine Cres [5] TR11 145 C3
Marine Ct
Falmouth TR11 145 D3
[26] Perranporth TR6 55 A5
Torpoint PL11 127 B2
Marine Dr
Looe PL13 117 D1
Torpoint PL11 127 B2
Widemouth Bay EX23 6 E5
Marine Par TR2 95 A5
Marine Rd PL9 135 B7
Marine Terr
Boscastle PL35 9 C2
[7] Penzance TR18 143 E4
Maristow Ave PL2 127 F5
Maristow Cl PL6 124 F5
Maristow La PL12 122 F3
Maritime House Discovery Quay [16] TR11 145 C3
Marjorie Ct PL12 122 C4
Market Ave PL1 148 B3
Market Cl PL1 128 A1
Market Ct
Hayle TR27 142 D6
Market Ct *continued*
[9] Launceston PL15 106 C6
Market Hill PL25 114 C4
Market House Arc
[3] Bodmin PL31 109 E5
[10] Launceston PL15 106 C6
Market Inn PL24 60 B5
Market Jew St TR18 143 E5
Market Pl
Camelford PL32 105 D4
Helston TR13 146 B5
Marazion TR17 89 B5
Padstow PL28 107 D5
[25] Penzance TR18 143 E5
St Columb Major TR9 45 E6
[33] St Ives TR26 141 B6
Week St Mary EX22 11 E8
Market Rd
Plymouth PL7 130 D5
Tavistock PL19 147 C5
Market Sq
[18] Callington PL17 39 E4
Hayle TR27 142 D6
Plymouth PL1 148 C3
St Day TR16 68 D1
St Just TR19 86 F6
Market St
Bodmin PL31 109 E5
Devoran TR3 81 F6
Falmouth TR11 145 B4
Fowey PL23 116 D4
Hayle TR27 142 D6
Kingsand PL10 133 A1
[11] Launceston PL15 106 C6
Liskeard PL14 113 C6
Plymouth PL1 128 A1
[6] St Austell PL25 114 C3
St Just TR19 86 F6
[3] Stratton EX23 4 E1
Tavistock PL19 147 C5
Market Strand
Falmouth TR11 145 B4
Padstow PL28 107 D5
[7] Redruth TR15 140 B5
[31] St Ives TR26 141 B6
Market Way
Plymouth PL1 148 C3
[5] Redruth TR15 140 B4
Marks Dr PL31 109 E3
Mark's Way TR7 110 D4
Markwell La PL12 53 C1
Marlborough Ave TR11 145 A3
Marlborough Cl
[1] Falmouth TR11 145 A3
Saltash PL12 122 F1
Marlborough Cres TR11 145 A3
Marlborough Ct [5] TR11 145 A3
Marlborough Gr [2] TR11 145 A3
Marlborough Prim Sch PL1 127 E2
Marlborough Rd
Falmouth TR11 145 B3
Plymouth PL4 149 A4
Marlborough Row PL1 127 E2
Marlborough Sch TR11 145 A3
Marlborough St PL1 127 E2
Marlborough Way PL26 58 E1
Marldon Cl PL5 124 B3
Marlow Cres PL16 29 F8
Marlow Gdns PL9 135 F5
Marriotts Ave TR14 138 B4
Marrowbone Slip PL4 149 B2
Marryat Gdns PL5 124 E1
Marshall Ave PL27 108 D5
Marshall Cl
Roche PL26 46 F3
Tavistock PL19 147 D2
Marshallen Rd TR4 68 C6
Marshall Rd
Bodmin, Nanstallon PL30 34 C2
Bodmin PL31 109 D3
Plymouth PL7 130 A5
Tavistock PL19 147 D2
Marshalls Way PL29 22 D6
Marsh Cl PL6 129 F6
Marshfield View PL11 64 B5
MARSHGATE 10 C2
Marsh La
Angarrack TR27 142 F7
Calstock PL18 41 A3
Hayle TR27 142 E7
Marshlands PL27 34 A6
MARSH MILLS 130 A6
Marsh Mills PL6 129 F7
Marsh Mills Pk PL6 129 F6
Marsh Mills Ret Pk PL6 129 E7
Marsh Mills Sta* PL7 130 A7
Marthas Mdw TR9 45 E1
Marthus Ct [10] PL14 113 C5
Martin Cl TR15 140 D5
Martin Ho [11] TR15 140 B4
Martin La PL4 149 A2
Martins Cl PL14 113 E7
Martin's Ct [2] PL31 109 D5
Martin's La TR15 139 C8
Martin Sq [6] PL17 39 F4
Martin St PL1 148 B2
Martinvale Ave TR15 140 E7
Martinvale Parc TR15 140 E7
Martlesham Pl PL5 123 F4
Martyn's Cl TR4 55 D4
Mary Dean Ave PL5 124 C7
Mary Dean Cl PL5 124 C7
Mary Dean's CE Prim Sch PL5 124 C7
Maryland Gdns PL2 127 F7
Mary Moon Cl PL12 53 B7
Mary Newman's Cottage* PL12 123 A2
Mary Seacole Rd PL1 148 A3
Marythorne Rd [15] PL20 41 B1
Masefield Gdns PL5 124 B1
Masons Row PL18 40 F6
Masterman Rd PL2 127 F4
Matela Cl [10] TR13 98 C8
Matthews Way PL14 51 F6
Maudlin Cl PL14 113 D5
Maudlins La PL19 147 A5
Maunsell Cl PL2 127 F7
Mavisdale PL2 127 F6
Mawes Ct PL18 40 D5
MAWGAN 99 D7
Mawgan TR12 99 D6
Mawgan Cross TR12 99 D7
Mawgan-in-Pydar Com Prim Sch TR8 45 A8
MAWGAN PORTH 31 B2
Mawgan Vu TR9 57 E8
MAWLA 68 B4
MAWNAN 93 E2
MAWNAN SMITH 93 E3
Mawnan Village CE Prim Sch TR11 93 D3
Maxwell Rd PL4 135 B8
MAXWORTHY 12 A3
Maxworthy Cross PL15 12 B4
Maybank Rd PL4 149 C3
Maybrook Dr PL12 122 D2
Mayers Way PL9 135 D6
Mayfair Cres PL6 125 B1
Mayfair Ho PL4 149 A3
Mayfield Cl
Bodmin PL31 35 B2
Port Isaac PL29 22 D7
St Austell PL25 115 A4
Mayfield Cres TR7 110 E5
Mayfield Dr
Port Isaac PL29 22 E7
Roche PL26 47 A3
Mayfield Rd
Falmouth TR11 144 F4
Newquay TR7 110 E5
Port Isaac PL29 22 D7
Mayflower Academy PL2 128 A7
Mayflower Cl
[19] Bere Alston PL20 41 B1
Plymouth PL9 135 F7
Mayflower Dr PL2 128 B5
Mayflower L Ctr PL2 128 C5
Mayflower St PL1 148 C3
May Gdns TR16 80 D6
May La PL13 117 F5
Maymear Terr PL30 23 E3
Mayna Parc PL15 18 B8
Maynarde Cl PL7 131 B5
Maynard Pk PL20 41 B1
Mayne Cl PL15 106 B7
Maynes Row TR14 139 A5
MAYON 96 B6
Mayon Farm TR19 96 B6
Mayon Green Cres TR19 96 B7
May Terr PL4 149 B3
MEAD 2 D4
Mead Cnr EX39 2 D4
Meadfoot Terr [2] PL4 128 F5
Mead Hos The TR18 143 F8
Meadowbank TR11 82 A3
Meadowbank Rd TR11 145 A6
Meadow Brook PL19 147 A4
Meadow Cl
Gloweth TR1 69 E3
Newquay TR7 111 A4
Plymouth PL7 131 D4
Polruan PL23 116 D2
Saltash PL12 122 F3
St Austell PL25 114 F6
St Stephen PL26 58 B4
Meadow Ct
Mevagissey PL26 73 C3
Padstow PL28 107 B4
Stithians TR3 80 E4
St Mabyn PL30 34 C8
Meadow Dr
Bude EX23 104 F6
Camborne TR14 138 C4
Looe PL13 117 D5
Par PL24 115 F5
Saltash PL12 122 D4
Meadowfield Pl PL7 131 B3
Meadow Flats [27] TR26 141 B6
Meadowhead PL27 108 C4
Meadow La TR1 137 D3
Meadowlands PL6 125 D7
Meadowlands Leisure Pool PL19 147 B5
Meadow Pk
[7] Liskeard PL14 113 B5
Plymouth PL9 135 C5
Trewoon PL25 59 A3
Meadow Pl PL31 109 D4
Meadow Plash PL30 35 C8
Meadow Rd PL13 62 A7
Meadow Rise
Foxhole PL26 58 D6
[1] Penwithick PL26 59 D7
Plymouth PL7 131 A4
[12] St Columb Major TR9 45 E6
Meadowside
Launceston PL15 106 A4
Lewannick PL15 27 A6
Newquay TR7 111 A4
Plymouth PL9 135 F7
St Austell PL25 115 C6
Whitstone EX22 12 B8
Meadowside Cl
Hayle TR27 142 A3
St Kew Highway PL30 23 B2
Meadowside Rd TR11 144 F2
Meadow St PL26 73 C3
Meadows The
St Dennis PL26 58 C8
St Dominick PL12 40 D2
St Teath PL30 23 E7
Torpoint PL11 126 E4
Meadowsweet Pk PL12 122 C2
Meadow Terr PL14 37 F3
Meadow The
Illogan TR16 67 D4
Polgooth PL26 59 A1
[47] St Ives TR26 141 B6
Truro TR1 137 B5
Meadow View
Camborne TR14 138 E1
[8] Goldsithney TR20 89 E5
St Minver PL27 21 F3
Meadow View Rd PL7 130 D5
Meadow Villas [8] TR18 143 C1
Meadow Way
Plymouth PL7 130 D7
St Issey PL27 32 E6
Meadow Wlk PL23 116 D2
Mead The PL7 130 D7
Meadway
Looe PL13 117 E4
Saltash PL12 122 E1
St Austell PL25 114 F5
MEADWELL 29 C8
Mearwood La TR11 144 F4
Meaver Rd TR12 99 B1
MEAVY 42 F2
Meavy Ave PL5 124 E2
Meavy Bourne PL20 42 D2
Meavy CE Prim Sch PL20 42 F2
Meavy La PL20 42 D2
Meavy Villas PL20 42 D2
Meavy Way
Plymouth PL5 124 E2
Tavistock PL19 147 D5
MEDDON 3 C4
Meddon Cross
Edistone EX39 3 C5
Welcombe EX39 3 C4
Medland Cres PL6 124 D6
Medland Gdns PL25 114 C4
Medlyn Ct TR13 146 B5
Medrose PL27 21 D2
Medrose St PL33 14 E3
Medrose Terr [21] TR18 143 E6
Medrow PL15 27 A8
Medway Pl PL3 129 D6
Melbourne Cotts PL1 148 B3
Melbourne Gn [2] PL1 148 B3
Melbourne Pl PL1 148 B4
Melbourne Rd PL14 113 B5
Melbourne St PL1 148 B3
Melbourne Terr [17] TR18 143 C7
MELBUR 57 F5
Mellanear Cl TR27 142 B4
Mellanear Ct TR27 142 B4
Mellanear Rd TR27 142 B3
Mellanvrane La TR7 110 F4
Melliars Way EX23 104 F6
MELLINGEY 32 D6
Melrose Ave PL2 128 C8
Melrose Terr [6] TR9 45 E1
Melvill Cres TR11 145 B3
Melvill Ct TR11 145 B2
Melville Pl [1] PL2 128 A5
Melville Rd
Plymouth PL2 128 A5
Threemilestone TR3 69 D3
Melville Terr PL22 112 C2
Melville Terrace La PL2 128 A5
Melvill La TR11 145 B2
Melvill Rd TR11 145 C2
Melyn Cl TR27 142 E8
Memory La PL9 135 E7
Menabilly Cl PL17 39 E3
Menabilly Rd PL25 114 E6
Menacuddle Hill PL25 114 C4
Menacuddle La PL25 114 C4
MENADARVA 66 E2
Menadue Ct TR27 78 E3
Menage St TR13 146 C5
MENAGISSEY 68 C5
Menague PL27 21 E3
Menakarne TR16 80 F8
Menallack Cheese Farm* TR10 93 A6
Mena Park Cl PL9 136 B7
Mena Park Rd PL9 136 B7
MENDENNICK 132 C7
Meneage Cotts [3] TR13 146 C5
Meneage Ho [4] TR13 146 C5
Meneage Parc TR13 146 C5
Meneage Rd TR13 146 C4
Meneage St TR13 146 C5
Meneage Villas PL25 114 B3
Menear Rd PL25 115 A6
Menefreda Way PL27 22 A4
Meneth TR12 92 C1
Meneth Rd TR14 138 F2
Menhaye Gdns TR15 139 D7
Menhay View TR11 144 C3
MENHENIOT 52 A5
Menheniot Cres PL15 18 D5
Menheniot Prim Sch PL14 52 A5
Menheniot Sta PL14 51 F4
Menhinick Cl PL12 53 C3
Menhyr Dr TR26 141 C2
Menna La TR2 57 E5
Mennaye Ct TR18 143 D4
Mennaye Rd TR18 143 D4
Merafield Cl PL7 130 B5
Merafield Dr PL7 130 C4
Merafield Farm Cotts PL7 130 B4
Merafield Rd PL7 130 B4
Merafield Rise PL7 130 C4
Merbein Cotts TR8 44 E8
Merchant's House (Mus)* PL1 148 C2
Merchants Quay PL15 18 E2
Meredith Rd PL2 128 C6
Meres Valley TR12 99 A2
Meridian Ho PL4 149 A3
Merlin Cl PL6 125 E8
Merlins Way PL34 14 D7
Mermaid Ct TR7 111 C8
Merrick Ave TR1 137 E6
MERRIFIELD 7 F4
Merrifield Cl TR1 137 B5
Merrifield Cross EX22 7 F4
Merrill Pl TR11 145 A3
Merritts Hill TR16 67 E4
Merritts Way TR15 139 C7
Merrivale Rd
Plymouth, Ham PL2 128 B7
Plymouth, Honicknowle PL5 124 B3
Merrivale View Rd PL20 42 E3
MERRYMEET 38 C1
Merry Mit Mdw TR11 144 C3
Mersey Cl PL3 129 D6
MERTHER 70 F3
Merther Cl TR13 91 B3
MERTHER LANE 70 F1
Messack Cl TR11 144 E2
Metha Pk TR8 56 C7
Metha Rd TR8 56 C7
METHERELL 40 D4
Methleigh Bottoms TR13 91 A1
Methleigh Parc TR13 91 A1
MEVAGISSEY 73 D3
Mevagissey Aquarium* PL26 73 C3
Mevagissey Ho TR1 69 E4
Mevagissey Mus* PL26 73 C3
Mevagissey Prim Sch PL26 73 C4
Mews Ct PL14 51 F6
Mews The
Launceston PL15 106 A8
Par PL24 60 B5
[3] Penzance TR18 143 E6
Plymouth, Devonport PL1 128 A3
Plymouth, Stonehouse PL1 148 A3
Mexico La TR27 142 C7
Mexico Terr TR27 142 C8
Michael Rd PL3 129 A5
MICHAELSTOW 24 A5
Michell Ave TR7 110 E6
Michell Ct TR7 110 D6
Michigan Way PL3 129 C6
Mid Churchway PL9 136 A7
Mid Cornwall Bsns Ctr PL25 115 E4
MIDDLE CRACKINGTON 10 B6
Middle Down Cl PL9 136 A5
Middlefield Rd PL6 124 D6
Middlefield Cl PL12 122 B2
Middlegates [5] TR5 54 D1
MIDDLE GREADOW 48 B1
MIDDLEHILL 38 D3
Middle Market St PL13 117 D3
MIDDLEMOOR 147 F2
Middle Rd TR15 140 E7
Middle Rosewin Row [8] TR1 137 D5
Middle Row TR13 90 E3
Middle St
Padstow PL28 107 D5
Port Isaac PL29 22 D7
Middle Stennack Cotts [13] TR26 141 A5
Middleton Cres TR7 110 F4
Middletons Row [6] TR15 140 C5
Middleton Wlk PL5 123 D4
Middleway PL24 60 B5
Middlewell Parc PL27 108 B4
Middle Wharf PL26 73 C3
Middle Wlk [1] PL26 115 A1
MIDDLEWOOD 27 B2
Midella Rd PL20 42 D2
Mid Moor PL14 38 B6
Midway Dr TR1 137 E5
Midway Rd PL31 109 A5
Miers Cl PL5 127 C8
Miers Ct PL5 127 C8
Milch Pk PL12 122 C2
MILCOMBE 62 F6
Mildmay St PL4 149 A4
Mile End TR12 102 F4
Milehouse Rd PL2 128 A5
Miles Mitchell Ave PL6 125 A1
Milestone Ct TR3 69 D4
Milford La PL5 124 B5
Military Rd
Millbrook PL10 132 C3
Plymouth PL3 129 C6
Rame PL10 64 C2
St Mawes TR2 95 B4
Milladon La PL12 64 D8
Mill Ball Hill EX23 10 B7
Millbank Mdw TR27 78 E1
MILLBAY 148 B2
Millbay Rd PL1 148 A2
Mill Bridge PL1 148 A3
MILLBROOK 132 E5

Millbrook Bsns Ctr PL11 **132** C6
Millbrook CE Prim Sch
 PL10 . . . . **132** E5
Mill Cl
 Porthleven TR13 . . . . . . **91** A1
 Wadebridge PL27 . . . . . **108** E5
Mill Cotts TR13 . . . . . **146** A6
MILLENDREATH **117** F5
Millennium Apartments
 TR10 . . . . **81** D1
Millennium Way TR13 . **146** D8
Miller Bsns Pk PL14 . . **113** B4
Miller Ct
 Liskeard PL14 . . . . **113** B4
 Plymouth PL1 . . . . **148** A2
Miller Way PL6 . . . . . . **125** E3
Millet Cl TR17 . . . . **89** D5
Millfield TR18 . . . . **88** E6
Mill Flats TR13 . . . . . . **146** B6
Mill Ford Specl Sch PL5 . **123** F4
Mill Gdns PL22 . . . . . . **112** C2
Millham La PL22 . . . . . **112** E3
MILLHILL **30** B1
Mill Hill
 Crumplehorn PL13 . . . . . **62** D1
 Lelant TR27 . . . . **77** E3
 Lostwithiel PL22 . . . . . **112** D2
 St just in Roseland TR2. . **82** F3
Mill Hill Cotts PL11 . . . **30** B1
Millhouse Pk PL11 . . . **127** A2
Mill La
 Camelford PL32 . . . . . . **105** D5
 Coad's Green PL15 . . . . **27** C1
 Grampound TR2 . . . . . . **72** A7
 Helston TR13 . . . . **146** B6
 20 Mousehole TR19 . . . **88** C1
 Porthleven TR13 . . . . . . **91** A1
 St Breward PL30 . . . . . . **24** B3
 St Germans PL12 . . . . . **65** A8
 Torpoint PL11 . . . . **127** A2
 Tregony TR2 . . . . **71** F3
 Truro TR3 . . . . **137** C1
MILLOOK **6** D2
Millpond Ave TR27 . . . **142** B4
MILLPOOL
 Cardinham **35** F5
 Praa Sands **90** B5
Millpool
 Lostwithiel PL22 . . . . . **112** F3
 Rilla Mill PL14 . . . . **38** E8
Millpool Head PL10 . . . **132** E4
Millpool Rd PL10. . . . . **133** A6
Mill Rd
 Millbrook PL10. . . . . . . **133** A5
 Padstow PL28 . . . . **107** D5
 Penponds TR14 . . . . . . **79** B5
 Perranporth TR6 . . . . . **55** B4
 Tideford PL12 . . . . **52** F2
Mill Rd Est PL12 . . . . . **52** F2
Mills Gdns TR16 . . . . . **68** E1
Mill Sq PL28 . . . . **107** D5
Mills Rd PL1. . . . . **127** F2
Mills' St TR16. . . . . . . **68** E1
Mill St PL31 . . . . **109** E5
MILLTOWN
 Cardinham **35** E3
 Lostwithiel **60** F8
Milltown Gdns PL15. . . **18** E6
Mill View Gdns PL10 . . **132** F5
Mill View Rd PL10. . . . **132** F5
Millway Pl PL9 . . . . . . **135** D8
Millwood Dr PL6 . . . . . **125** E1
Milne Pl PL1. . . . . **127** F3
MILTON ABBOT **29** D6
Milton Abbot Sch PL19. . **29** D5
Milton Cl PL5 . . . . **124** D2
MILTON COMBE **120** F8
Milton Cres PL19. . . . . **147** D5
Milton Ct
 Plymouth, Cattedown
  PL4 . . . . **149** C2
 Plymouth, Prince Rock PL4 **129** B1
MILTON GREEN **29** D5
Minack Open Air Theatre★
 TR19 . . . . **96** E2
Mine Hill PL14 . . . . **51** F6
Mine La PL30 . . . . **47** E7
Miners Ct
 Perranporth TR6 . . . . . **55** A4
 Redruth TR15. . . . . . . **140** C5
Miners Row TR15 . . . . **140** C5
Miners Way
 Liskeard PL14 . . . . **113** D7
 12 TR5. . . . . **54** C1
Minerva Cl PL7 . . . . . . **131** A6
MINGOOSE **68** C7
Miniatura Park★ TR4. . **55** E4
MINIONS **38** B6
Minions Heritage Ctr★
 PL14 . . . . **38** B6
Minions Row PL14. . . . **38** B6
Minnie Pl TR11 . . . . . . **145** B3
Minorca La PL26 . . . . . **47** D2
Minses Cl PL9 . . . . **136** C7
Minster Ave EX23 . . . . **104** F4
Minster Mdw TR12. . . . **101** A8
Minster Terr TR12 . . . . **101** A8
Minton Cl PL25 . . . . . . **115** A4
Mirador Pl PL4 . . . . . . **129** C3
Mission The TR18 . . . . **143** F4
Misterton Cl PL9. . . . . **136** B8
MITCHELL **56** F5
Mitchell Cl
 Lizard TR12 . . . . **102** F2
 Plymouth PL9. . . . . **135** D5
Mitchell Ct **11** TR1 . . . . **137** D5
Mitchell Hill TR1. . . . . **137** D5

Mitchell Hill Terr 4
 TR1 . . . . **137** D5
Mitchell La
 Camborne TR14 . . . . . . **138** E3
 Mitchell TR8. . . . . **56** E5
Mitchell Mews **17** TR1. . **137** D4
Mitchell Rd
 Camborne TR14 . . . . . . **138** C3
 St Austell PL25 . . . . . . **114** F4
Mitchell's Boatyard PL26 . **73** C2
Mitchells Cnr **24** TR6. . . **55** A5
MITHIAN **54** F1
MITHIAN DOWNS **68** F8
Mithian Prim Sch TR5. . **54** E1
Mitre Cl PL19 . . . . **147** A3
Mitre Cl **15** PL1 . . . . . . **149** A2
MIXTOW **116** D7
Moat Pk PL6. . . . . **125** C1
Modbury Cl PL5. . . . . . **124** B3
Modus La PL26 . . . . . . **58** E1
Modyford Wlk PL20 . . . **41** F3
Mohun's Cl PL19 . . . . . **147** C4
Mohun's Pk PL19 . . . . **147** C3
Molenick La PL12 . . . . **52** E3
Molesworth Ct **4** PL27. . **108** B5
Molesworth Rd
 Plymouth, Plympton PL7. . **130** C6
 Plymouth, Stoke PL1, PL3 . **128** A3
Molesworth St
 Tintagel PL34. . . . . **14** C7
 Wadebridge PL27 . . . . . **108** B5
Molesworth Terr PL10. . **132** F5
MOLINNIS **47** C2
Molinnis La PL26 . . . . . **47** C2
Molinnis Rd PL26 . . . . **47** C2
Mollison Rd PL5 . . . . . **123** E2
Molyneaux Pl **10** PL1. . . **127** F3
Monastery Cl TR12 . . . **101** D4
MONGLEATH **144** E4
Mongleath Ave TR11 . . **144** E3
Mongleath Cl TR11. . . . **144** E3
Mongleath Rd TR11 . . . **144** E4
Monica Wlk PL4 . . . . . **149** B4
Monkey Sanctuary The★
 PL13. . . . . **63** F5
Monks Hill PL15 . . . . . **28** C4
Monksmead PL15 . . . . **106** D6
Monks Park Cotts PL15. . **106** D6
Monmouth Gdns PL5. . . **124** C4
Monmouth La PL22 . . . **112** D2
Monroe Gdns PL4. . . . **148** B4
Montacute Ave PL5 . . . **124** B2
Montague Ave TR15. . . **140** A6
Monterey Cl EX23 . . . . **104** E4
Monterey Gdns TR1 . . . **137** E5
Montgomery Cl PL12. . . **122** D3
Montgomery Dr PL19. . . **147** A6
Montgomery Rd **2** PL26. . **59** D7
Montpelier Prim Sch
 PL2. . . . . **128** B6
Montpelier Rd PL2. . . . **128** C7
Monument Rd TR13 . . . **146** B5
Monument St PL1. . . . . **127** E1
Monument Way PL31. . . **109** C4
Moonrakers TR26 . . . . **141** D2
Moonsfield **5** PL17 . . . . **39** F4
Moon St PL4. . . . . **149** A3
Moorcroft Cl PL19 . . . . **136** A7
Moor Cross EX22. . . . . **8** D3
Moor Cross Cotts EX23. . **4** C5
Moorfield PL16 . . . . . . **19** C4
Moorfield Ave **4** PL6 . . . **129** C7
Moorfield Rd
 Camborne TR15 . . . . . . **139** C6
 St Giles on the Heath PL15. . **13** F1
Moor La PL5. . . . . **123** E1
Moorland Ave PL7 . . . . **130** F6
Moorland Cl
 Liskeard PL14 . . . . **113** D7
 Pendeen TR19 . . . . **74** F1
 Yelverton PL20. . . . . . . **121** D8
Moorland Ct
 1 St Austell PL25. . . . . . **114** C3
 Yelverton PL20. . . . . . . **42** C2
Moorland Dr PL7 . . . . . **130** E6
Moorland Gdns PL7. . . . **130** F6
Moorland Rd
 Indian Queens TR9 . . . . . **45** F2
 Launceston PL15 . . . . . . **106** A4
 Plymouth PL7. . . . . **130** E5
 St Austell PL25 . . . . . . **114** C3
 Tywardreath PL24 . . . . . **60** C4
Moorland Road Ind Est
 TR9 . . . . **45** F2
Moorlands La PL12. . . . **122** C4
Moorlands Trad Est
 PL12 . . . . **122** C4
Moorland View
 Golberdon PL17 . . . . . . **39** B6
 Liskeard PL14 . . . . **113** D7
 Plymouth, Derriford PL6. . **125** A5
 Plymouth, Plymstock PL9. . **136** B7
 Saltash PL12 . . . . **122** F4
Moorland Way PL18. . . . **40** F5
Moorlan Mdws PL26 . . . **47** A3
Moor Parc TR12 . . . . . . **100** D6
Moor St TR14 . . . . **138** D3
Moors The PL22 . . . . . **112** C1
Moorswater Ind Est PL14. . **51** A7
Moor The TR11 . . . . . . **145** B4
MOORTOWN
 Tavistock **42** D8
 Tetcott **13** C7
Moor View
 Bodmin PL31 . . . . **109** F2
 Plymouth, Keyham PL2. . **127** F5
 Plymouth, Laira PL3. . . . **129** C4
 Plymouth PL9. . . . . **135** D7

Moor View *continued*
 Torpoint PL11. . . . . **127** B3
Moorview Ct PL6. . . . . **125** F5
Moorview Terr PL14. . . . **38** D7
Moor View Terr
 Plymouth PL4. . . . . **128** E4
 Yelverton PL20. . . . . . . **42** D2
Morcom Cl PL25 . . . . . **115** A5
Moresk Cl TR1 . . . . **137** D5
Moresk Gdns TR1. . . . . **137** D5
Moresk Rd TR1. . . . . . . **137** D5
Moreton Ave PL6 . . . . . **124** F1
Morice Sq PL1. . . . . . . **127** E2
Morice St PL1. . . . . **127** E2
MORICE TOWN **127** D3
Morice Town Prim Sch
 PL2 . . . . **127** E4
Morlaix Ave TR1 . . . . . **137** D3
Morlaix Dr PL6 . . . . . . **125** B4
Morla La TR15 . . . . **140** A6
Morleigh Cl PL25 . . . . . **114** F3
Morley Cl PL7 . . . . **130** A5
Morley Ct PL1 . . . . **148** B3
Morley Dr PL20 . . . . . . **42** A2
Morley View Rd PL7 . . . **130** C6
MORNICK **39** B7
Morrab Ct **8** TR7 . . . . . **110** F6
Morrab Pl **34** TR18 . . . . **143** E5
Morrab Rd
 Camborne TR14 . . . . . . **138** C3
 Penzance TR18. . . . . . . **143** E5
Morrab Terr **35** TR18 . . . **143** E5
Morris Gdns TR7. . . . . **110** D4
Morrish Pk PL9 . . . . . . **135** F6
Morshead Rd PL6. . . . . **124** F2
Mortain Rd PL12 . . . . . **122** D4
Mortimore Cl PL12 . . . . **122** D2
MORVAH **75** C2
MORVAL **63** D7
Morvan Trad Est PL25 . . **114** F3
Morven Rd PL25 . . . . . **114** F3
Morview Rd PL13 . . . . . **63** F8
Morwell Gdns PL2. . . . . **128** A6
MORWELLHAM **41** B4
Morwellham Cl PL5. . . . **127** C8
Morwellham Quay★ PL19. **41** B4
Morwenna Gdns TR6. . . **55** B5
Morwenna Rd EX23. . . . **2** D1
Morwenna Terr EX23. . . **104** D6
MORWENSTOW **2** B2
Morweth Cotts PL11 . . . **64** C5
Morweth Ct PL11 . . . . . **64** C5
Moses Cl PL6 . . . . **124** E7
Moses Ct PL6 . . . . **124** E7
Mosquito Cres **3** PL27. . **31** F3
Moss Side Ind Est **30** PL17 . **39** F4
Moss Terr PL23 . . . . . . **116** D3
Mostyn Ave PL4. . . . . . **129** A4
Mote Pk PL12 . . . . **122** C4
Mothecombe Wlk PL6. . **125** E1
Moulton Cl PL7. . . . . . . **131** B5
Moulton Wlk PL7. . . . . **131** B4
MOUNT
 Cardinham **36** B2
 Cubert **55** C7
Mount Agar Rd TR3. . . . **81** F7
MOUNT AMBROSE **140** E7
Mount Ambrose TR15. . . **140** E7
Mountbatten Cl
 Plymouth PL9. . . . . **135** D6
 St Columb Minor TR7. . . **111** E7
Mount Batten Ctr★ PL9. . **134** F7
Mountbatten Rd **5** PL26. . **59** D7
Mountbatten Way PL9. . **135** E6
Mount Bennett Rd 5
 PL24. . . . . **60** D5
Mount Bennett Terr 4
 PL24. . . . . **60** D5
Mount Camel PL32. . . . . **105** C4
Mount Carbis Gdns
 TR15 . . . . **140** C3
Mount Carbis Rd TR15. . **140** D3
MOUNT CHARLES **114** E4
Mount Charles Rd PL25. **114** E4
Mount Charles Sch PL25 **114** F3
Mount Cres PL24. . . . . **60** C6
Mount Edgcumbe House &
 Country Pk★ PL10 . . . . **133** E6
Mount Edgcumbe Terr
 TR11 . . . . **145** B4
Mountfield Terr **6** PL24. . **60** C4
Mount Folly TR27 . . . . . **142** C6
Mount Folly Sq PL31 . . . **109** E4
Mount Ford PL19 . . . . . **147** A5
Mount George Rd TR3. . **82** B7
MOUNT GOULD **129** B2
Mount Gould Ave PL4. . **129** B2
Mount Gould Cres PL4. . **129** B3
Mount Gould Hospl PL4. **129** B3
Mount Gould Rd PL4. . . **129** B3
Mount Gould Way PL4. . **129** B3
MOUNT HAWKE **68** C6
Mount Hawke Academy
 TR4 . . . . **68** C6
Mount Ho PL11 . . . . . . **64** C5
Mount House Sch PL19. . **147** E7
MOUNTJOY **45** A3
MOUNT LANE **13** E6
Mountlea Dr **9** PL24 . . . **60** C4
Mount Lidden TR18 . . . . **143** C4
Mount Pleasant
 Bodmin PL31 . . . . **109** E5
 Boscastle PL35 . . . . **9** D1
 Falmouth TR11. . . . . . . **144** E1
 Hayle TR27 . . . . **142** C6
 Lelant TR26 . . . . **77** E3
 Millbrook PL10. . . . . . . **132** E5
 Newlyn TR18 . . . . **143** C4

Mount Pleasant *continued*
 Par PL24 . . . . **60** B6
 Plymouth PL5. . . . . **124** B2
 39 St Ives TR26 . . . . **141** B6
Mount Pleasant Cl TR18. . **138** E1
Mount Pleasant Gdns
 TR27 . . . . **142** C6
Mount Pleasant Pl PL22 **112** C2
Mount Pleasant Rd
 Camborne TR14 . . . . . . **138** D1
 11 Porthleven TR13 . . . . **98** B8
 Threemilestone TR3. . . . **69** D3
Mount Pleasant Terr
 Mousehole TR19 . . . . . . **88** C1
 PL2. . . . . **128** A4
 Redruth TR15 . . . . **140** E7
Mount Pleasure TR14 . . **138** C1
Mount Prospect Terr
 TR18 . . . . **143** C3
Mount Rd PL24 . . . . . . **60** C4
Mount Royal TR18 . . . . . **143** F6
Mount's Bay Academy
 TR18 . . . . **143** B7
Mounts Bay Rd TR18 . . . **143** C4
Mount's Bay Terr **21** TR13 **98** C8
Mount's Rd **20** TR13 . . . **98** C8
Mount St
 Mevagissey PL26 . . . . . . **73** C3
 Penzance TR18. . . . . . . **143** E6
 Plymouth, Mount Wise PL1 **127** E1
 Plymouth, Mutley PL4 . . **149** A4
Mount Stamper Rd PL25 **114** D7
Mountstephen Cl PL25. . **114** B3
Mount Stephens La
 TR11 . . . . **144** F4
Mount Stone Rd PL1. . . **134** A8
Mount Street Prim Sch
 PL4 . . . . **149** A4
Mount Tamar Cl PL5 . . . **123** E2
Mount Tamar Specl Sch
 PL5 . . . . **123** E2
Mount Tavy Rd PL19 . . . **147** E6
Mount Terr **9** PL4 . . . . . **60** B4
Mount View
 Lane TR11 . . . . **111** B3
 Madron TR20 . . . . **88** A7
Mount View Cotts TR20. **89** A7
Mount View Terr
 5 Marazion TR17 . . . . . . **89** C5
 24 Newlyn TR18. . . . . . . **143** C2
Mount Whistle Rd TR14. **138** C7
MOUNT WISE **127** F1
Mount Wise
 Launceston PL15 . . . . . . **106** C5
 Newquay TR7 . . . . **110** D5
Mount Wise Cotts TR7. . **110** E5
Mount Wise Ct PL1. . . . **127** F1
Mount Wise Prim Sch
 PL1 . . . . **127** E1
Mount Zion **52** TR26 . . . **141** B6
Mourne Villas PL9. . . . . **135** F8
MOUSEHOLE **88** D1
Mousehole La TR11 . . . . **88** C1
Mousehole Prim Sch
 TR19 . . . . **88** C1
Mowbray Mews PL32. . . **10** B1
Mowhay Cl PL7 . . . . **111** A4
Mowhay Cotts PL26 . . . **85** C5
Mowhay La **1** PL17 . . . . **39** E4
Mowhay Mdw
 St John PL11 . . . . **132** B8
 TR9 . . . . **45** E1
 Wadebridge PL27 . . . . . **108** B4
Mowhay Rd PL5. . . . . . **124** A2
Mowie The **13** TR9 . . . . **45** E2
Moyle Rd PL28. . . . . . . **107** E4
MUCHLARNICK **62** E7
Mudges Terr PL18 . . . . . **41** A6
Mudge Way PL7 . . . . . . **130** E5
Mulberry Cl PL6 . . . . . . **125** E7
Mulberry Ct **12** TR11 . . **145** B5
Mulberry Dr PL19 . . . . . **147** C2
Mulberry Quay **11** TR11. **145** B5
Mulberry Rd PL12 . . . . . **122** E1
MULFRA **76** B1
Mulgrave St PL1. . . . . . . **148** C2
Mullet Ave PL3 . . . . **129** C4
Mullet Cl PL3 . . . . **129** C4
Mullet Rd PL3 . . . . **129** C4
MULLION **99** A1
Mullion Cl
 PL25. . . . . **114** C4
 Torpoint PL11 . . . . **126** F4
Mullion Cove TR12 . . . . **102** B7
Mullion Cove Bglws TR12. **98** F1
Mullion Prim Sch TR12. . **99** A1
Mullion Rural Workshops
 TR12 . . . . **99** A1
Mullion Sch TR12 . . . . . **99** B1
Mundys Field TR12. . . . . **103** A5
Muralto Ho PL19 . . . . . . **147** A4
Murdoch Cl
 Redruth TR15. . . . . **140** B6
 Truro TR1. . . . . **137** E6
Murdoch Flyer The★ **12**
 TR15 . . . . **140** B4
Murdoch House & St
 Rumon's Gdn★ **13**
 TR15 . . . . **140** B4
Murdock Rd PL11 . . . . . **126** F3
Murray Villas TR19. . . . . **86** E6
Murtons Terr TR16 . . . . **68** E1
Mus of Witchcraft★ PL35. **9** C2
MUTLEY **128** F4
Mutley Ct PL4 . . . . **149** A4
Mutley Plain PL4. . . . . . **128** E4
Mutley Plain La PL4. . . . **128** E4
Mutley Rd PL3 . . . . **128** E3

Mutton Hill TR27. . . . . . **78** D6
Mutton Row TR10 . . . . . **144** C8
MYLER CHURCHTOWN . . **82** C2
MYLOR BRIDGE **82** A3
Mylor Bridge Prim Sch
 TR11 . . . . **82** A3
Mylor Cl PL2. . . . . **128** D8
My Lords Rd TR9. . . . . . **57** E8
Myrtle Cl PL20 . . . . **42** E3
Myrtle Ct PL26 . . . . **73** C3
Myrtles Ct PL12 . . . . **122** D4
Myrtleville PL2 . . . . **128** A6
Mythyon Ct **4** TR18 . . . **143** C7

N

Nailzee Ho PL13 . . . . . . **117** D2
Nailzee Point PL13. . . . . **117** D2
Nalder's Ct **10** TR1 . . . . **137** C4
Nampara Cl TR26 . . . . . **141** E2
Nampara Ct **7** TR6. . . . . **55** A4
Nampara Row TR6 . . . . **55** A4
Nampara Way TR1 . . . . **137** F4
Nancarrows PL12 . . . . . **122** C2
Nancealverne TR18 . . . . **143** D6
Nancealverne Specl Sch
 TR20. . . . . **143** C6
Nancedden Farm TR20. . **89** A8
NANCEGOLLAN. **91** C7
Nancegollan Ind Est TR13 **91** B7
NANCEMELLIN **66** D1
Nancemere Rd TR1 . . . . **137** D6
Nancevallon TR14. . . . . . **139** B3
Nancherrow Hill TR19. . . **86** F6
Nancherrow Row TR19. . **86** F6
NANCLEDRA **76** F2
Nancledra Prim Sch TR
 26 . . . . **76** F3
Nangitha Cl TR11 . . . . . **144** C3
Nangitha Terr TR11 . . . . **144** C3
Nanhayes Row TR8 . . . . **56** B7
Nanjivey Pl **8** TR26 . . . . **141** A5
Nanjivey Terr **9** TR26 . . . **141** A5
NANPEAN **58** D7
Nanpean Prim Sch PL26. . **58** D6
Nanpusker Cl TR27 . . . . **142** E6
Nanpusker Rd TR27 . . . . **78** C4
Nansalsa Ct TR7 . . . . . . **111** A6
Nansavallon Rd TR1. . . . **69** F3
Nanscober Pl TR13. . . . . **146** B8
Nanscothan **10** TR15 . . . **140** B4
Nans Kestenen TR13 . . . **146** B5
NANSLADRON **73** B7
Nansloe Academy TR13. . **146** C4
Nansloe Ct TR13 . . . . . . **146** D4
Nansmellyon Rd TR12. . **99** A1
NANSTALLON **34** C1
Nanstallon Prim Sch
 PL30 . . . . **34** C1
Nanterrow La TR27. . . . . **66** D1
NANTITHET **99** B5
Nanturras Parc TR20. . . . **89** F5
Nanturras Row TR20 . . . **89** E5
Nanturras Way TR20 . . . **89** E5
Napier St PL1. . . . . **127** F3
Napier Terr PL4. . . . . **128** E4
NARKURS **64** D6
Narkurs Cross PL11 . . . **64** D7
Narrowcliff TR7. . . . . . . **111** A7
Narrow La
 Botusfleming PL12. . . . . **122** C7
 Summercourt TR8 . . . . . **57** C8
Nash Cl PL7 . . . . **131** A5
Nathan Cl TR7 . . . . **111** B5
National Lobster Hatchery★
 PL28 . . . . **107** E5
National Marine Aquarium★
 PL4 . . . . **149** A2
National Maritime Mus
 Cornwall★ TR11 . . . . . . **145** C3
National Seal Sanctuary
 The★ TR12 . . . . **92** C1
NAVARINO **18** B8
Navy Inn Ct **10** TR18 . . . **143** C1
Neal Cl PL7 . . . . **131** B4
Neath Rd PL4. . . . . **149** C4
Neeham Rd TR8 . . . . **56** B7
Nelson Ave PL1. . . . . . . **127** F3
Nelson Gdns **5** PL1. . . . **127** F3
Nelson St PL4 . . . . **149** A4
Nelson Terr PL6 . . . . **125** C4
Nepean St **1** PL2 . . . . . . **127** F3
Neptune Ave PL27 . . . . . **31** F3
Neptune Pk PL9 . . . . . . **135** B8
Neswick St PL1. . . . . **148** B3
Neswick Street Ope PL1. **148** A3
NETHERCOTT **13** E7
Nethercott Cross EX21. . **13** F7
NETHERTON **38** D7
Netherton Est PL20 . . . . **42** A3
Netherton Rd PL28. . . . . **107** D4
Netley Mdw PL26 . . . . . **47** C1
Nettell's Hill TR15 . . . . . **140** B5
Nettlehayes PL9 . . . . . . **136** D7
Netton Cl PL9. . . . . **136** B6
Nevada Cl PL3 . . . . **129** D6
Nevada Pl **16** TR18 . . . . **143** C7
Nevada St TR18 . . . . **143** C7
Nevada Villas **8** PL24 . . **60** C4
Newacott Cross EX22. . . **7** D5
New Barn Hill PL7 . . . . . **130** C4
New Bglws PL30 . . . . . . **36** B3
NEWBRIDGE
 Callington **39** D2

NEWBRIDGE *continued*
Penzance 87 E6
Truro 69 F3
Newbridge Hill PL18 41 A6
Newbridge La TR1, TR3 69 F3
New Bridge St 9 TR1 137 D4
Newbridge Vw TR1 69 E3
Newbridge Way TR1 69 F3
Newbury Cl PL5 124 B4
Newcastle Gdns PL5 124 B5
New Connection St 4 TR14 138 D3
New Cotts
Gunnislake PL18 41 A6
2 Kilkhampton EX23 5 A6
New Ct TR11 145 B4
New Cut TR15 140 B5
New Dairy La TR17 89 B6
NEW DOWNS
St Agnes 54 B2
St Just 86 E6
New George St PL1 148 C3
Newham Est TR1 137 D3
Newham Ind Est TR1 137 D2
Newham La
Helston TR13 146 A7
Lostwithiel PL22 49 A1
Newham Rd TR1 137 E2
New Hill Est TR2 72 A7
New Hos TR14 139 B3
Newhouses PL17 38 E8
New La TR15 140 E7
New Launceston Rd PL19 147 A5
NEWLYN 143 D2
Newlyn Art Gall* TR18 143 C3
Newlyn Halt Sta* TR8 56 C6
Newlyn Prim Sch TR18 143 C3
Newlyn Rd TR19 97 B6
Newman Rd
Plymouth PL5 123 E2
Saltash PL12 122 F3
NEWMILL
Penzance 76 B1
Poundstock 7 A1
Newmills Cl TR1 137 B6
New Mills Farm Pk* PL15 18 D4
New Mills La TR1, TR4 137 A6
Newmills Sta* PL15 18 D4
New Molinnis PL26 47 C2
Newnham Ind Est PL7 130 F6
Newnham Rd PL7 130 F7
Newnham Way PL7 130 F6
New Northernmaye 2 PL15 106 C6
New Park Rd
Plymouth PL7 131 A4
Wadebridge PL27 108 C5
New Passage Hill PL1 127 E3
New Pk
Horrabridge PL20 42 C4
Wadebridge PL27 108 C4
NEW POLZEATH 21 E6
NEWPORT 106 B7
Newport
Callington PL17 39 E4
St Germans PL12 65 A8
Newport Cl 8 PL17 39 F4
Newport Ind Est PL15 106 C6
New Portreath Rd
Illogan TR16 67 F5
Redruth TR16 140 A7
Newport Sq PL15 106 B7
Newport St
Millbrook PL10 132 E5
Plymouth PL1 128 A1
Newport Terr 8 PL17 39 F4
NEWQUAY 110 E7
Newquay Adult Ed Ctr TR7 110 F6
Newquay Airport TR8 44 F8
Newquay Hospl TR7 110 F5
Newquay Junior Academy TR7 110 F6
Newquay Rd
Goonhavern TR4 55 D4
St Columb Major TR9 45 D6
Truro TR1 137 F7
Newquay Sports & Com Ctr TR7 111 B6
Newquay Sta TR7 110 F6
Newquay Tretherras Sch TR7 111 B6
Newquay Zoo TR7 111 A5
New Rd
Barripper TR14 79 B5
Bere Alston PL20 41 B2
Boscastle PL35 9 C2
Cadgwith TR12 103 A4
Callington PL17 39 E4
Camborne TR14 139 B3
Cawsand PL10 133 A1
Kingsand PL10 133 B2
Lifton PL16 19 F4
Liskeard PL14 113 B5
Newlyn TR18 143 C3
Perranporth TR6 55 B4
Port Isaac PL29 22 D7
Roborough PL6 121 D2
Saltash PL12 122 E3
St Columb Major TR9 45 E6
St Hilary TR20 89 F6
Stithians TR3 80 F3
St Just TR19 86 F6
New Rd *continued*
Stratton EX23 4 D1
Summercourt TR8 57 D7
Tregony TR2 71 F3
Troon TR14 79 E4
New Road Cl PL10 133 A2
New Road Hill PL23 116 C4
New Road Terr PL12 53 C3
New Row
Gweek TR12 92 C1
Mylor Bridge TR11 82 A3
Nancledra TR 20 76 F2
Redruth TR16 139 D1
Summercourt TR8 57 B6
New St
Bugle PL26 47 C1
Falmouth TR11 145 B4
Millbrook PL10 132 E5
Padstow PL28 107 D5
Penryn TR10 144 D7
Penzance TR18 143 E5
Plymouth PL1 149 A2
Troon TR14 79 E4
Newtake Rd PL19 147 E2
Newton Ave PL5 123 E2
Newton Ct
Dobwalls PL14 50 E8
Redruth TR15 140 B6
Newton Farm Cotts PL13 62 E3
Newton Gdns PL5 123 F2
Newton Pk 12 TR2 95 A6
Newton Rd
St Mawes TR2 95 A6
Troon TR14 79 E5
Newton's Margate Ind Est PL31 35 B1
NEWTOWN
Coad's Green 27 D5
Praa Sands 90 B4
Newtown PL23 60 F3
NEWTOWN-IN-ST MARTIN 100 E6
Newtown La TR17, TR20 89 A7
New Town La TR18 143 E5
New Windsor Terr 11 TR11 145 A4
New Wood Cl PL6 125 E8
New Zealand Ho PL3 128 B4
Nicholas Ave TR16 80 A5
Nicholas Holman Rd TR14 138 E3
Nicholas Mdw PL17 40 E4
Nicholas Parc 3 TR18 143 C7
Nicholson Rd PL5 124 E2
Nicolls Flats PL15 106 B5
Nightingale Cl PL9 136 C8
Nine Maidens Short Stay Sch TR16 80 A4
Nine Oaks PL20 42 F3
NINNIS BRIDGE 77 B2
No Go By Hill TR19 86 F7
NO MAN'S LAND 63 E7
No Mans' Land Rd TR11 93 D5
Nook The PL19 147 D6
NOONVARES 90 E7
Norfolk Cl PL3 129 C5
Norfolk Rd
Falmouth TR11 145 B4
Plymouth PL3 129 C4
Norman Cotts PL15 106 C7
Normandy Hill PL5 123 B2
Normandy Way
Bodmin PL31 109 F2
Camborne TR14 138 F3
Plymouth PL5 123 C2
Norman's Way PL30 23 E3
NORRIS GREEN 40 E4
Northampton Cl PL5 124 B5
NORTH BEER 12 F3
NORTH BRENTOR 30 E8
North Cl EX23 5 A6
North Cliff 12 TR19 88 C1
North Cnr 1 TR18 143 C2
NORTH CORNER 101 C2
North Cornwall Mus & Gall* PL32 105 C4
North Cornwall Short Stay School PL33 14 F4
NORTHCOTT
Bude 4 C3
St Giles on the Heath 13 D3
Northcott Mouth Rd EX23 104 F8
NORTH COUNTRY 140 B8
NORTH DARLEY 38 D8
North Dimson PL18 40 F6
North Down Cres PL2 127 F6
North Down Gdns PL2 127 F6
North Down Rd PL2 128 B6
Northesk St PL2 128 A4
Northey Cl TR4 69 F6
Northey Rd PL31 109 D4
Northfield Cl TR16 68 E1
Northfield Dr TR1 137 D3
Northgate Pl 1 PL15 106 C6
North Grange Ind Est TR3 81 F6
NORTH HILL 27 B3
North Hill
Blackwater TR4 68 E5
Carharrack TR16 80 F8
Chacewater TR4 68 F3
6 Plymouth PL4 149 A4
North Hill Pk PL25 114 D4
NORTHMOOR 3 F3
North Moor Cross EX22 3 F3
Northolt Ave PL5 123 D4
North Orchard Ct 1 TR20 89 E5
North Par
Camborne TR14 138 E3
Falmouth TR11 145 A6
Penzance TR18 143 E5
Portscatho TR2 83 B2
North Parade Rear TR14 138 D3
North Park Villas PL12 122 C4
NORTH PETHERWIN 18 A8
North Petherwin Ind Est PL15 18 A8
North Petherwin Prim Sch PL15 12 B1
North Pl 15 TR26 141 B6
North Pool Cl TR15 139 C7
North Pool Rd TR15 139 C7
NORTH PROSPECT 128 A6
North Prospect Rd PL2 128 A6
North Quay
Hayle TR27 142 B6
Plymouth PL4 149 A2
North Quay Hill TR7 110 D7
North Quay Par PL28 107 E6
North Rd
Camborne TR14 138 D3
Goldsithney TR20 89 E5
Landrake PL12 53 C3
Lifton PL16 19 F4
Looe PL13 117 C3
Pentewan PL26 73 C6
Redruth TR16 140 E1
Saltash PL12 122 F3
St Teath PL30 23 E7
Torpoint PL11 127 B3
Whitemoor PL26 58 E8
Yelverton PL20 42 C3
North Road E PL4 148 C4
North Road W PL1 148 B4
North Roskear Mdw TR14 138 E5
North Roskear Rd TR14 138 F5
North Row TR19 86 F6
North St
Fowey PL23 116 D4
Launceston PL15 106 A8
Lostwithiel PL22 112 C2
Marazion TR17 89 B5
14 Mousehole TR19 88 C1
Plymouth PL4 149 A3
Redruth TR15 140 B6
St Austell PL25 114 C4
Tavistock PL19 147 C5
Tywardreath PL24 60 D5
NORTH TAMERTON 12 F8
North Terr
2 Penzance TR18 143 E4
12 St Ives TR26 141 B5
Whitemoor PL26 58 E8
Northumberland St PL5 127 E8
Northumberland Terr PL1 148 B1
North View PL13 117 D4
North Way TR8 111 F4
North Weald Gdns PL5 123 E5
Norton Ave PL4 149 C4
Norton Ct 2 PL31 109 E5
Norwich Ave PL5 124 B5
Notre Dame Cl PL6 124 F5
Notre Dame Ho PL1 148 B3
Notre Dame RC Sch PL6 124 F5
Notte St PL1 148 C2
Novorossisk Rd PL6 125 E2
Noweth Pl TR11 144 E5
Nuffield Health Plymouth Hospl PL6 125 B4
NUMPHRA 87 A4
Nunnery Hill PL26 72 F7
Nurseries The TR11 144 D5
Nursery Cl
Plymouth PL5 124 B7
Truro TR1 137 D5
11 Tywardreath PL24 60 D5
Nut La TR27 77 E3
Nut Tree Hill PL12 65 B8

O

Oakapple Cl PL7 130 B7
Oak Apple Cl PL12 122 D4
Oak Ave PL12 40 A1
Oakcroft Rd PL2 128 B6
Oakdene Rise PL9 135 F6
Oakdene Villas 7 TR9 45 E1
Oak Dr
8 Liskeard PL14 113 B5
Plymouth PL6 124 F3
Oakey Orch PL17 40 D4
Oakfield PL15 27 D3
Oakfield Cl PL7 131 C6
Oakfield Pl PL4 129 B1
Oakfield Rd
Falmouth TR11 144 F5
Plymouth PL7 130 C6
Oakfield Terrace Rd PL4 129 B1
Oak Ford PL30 48 C7
Oakham Rd PL5 124 B5
Oakhill PL30 47 C6
Oak La
Truro TR1 69 E4
Whitstone EX22 7 F1
Oakland Pk TR11 144 D5
Oaklands PL19 147 D2
Oaklands Bsns Pk PL13 63 D8
Oaklands Cl PL6 125 C7
Oaklands Ct TR9 45 E6
Oaklands Dr PL12 122 C3
Oaklands Gn PL12 122 D3
Oaklands Ind Est PL14 113 E6
Oaklands Rd PL14 113 E6
Oakleigh Terr TR7 110 F6
Oak Moor Dr PL15 106 D3
Oak Park Terr PL14 113 A6
Oak Pk PL30 23 E3
Oak Rd PL19 147 C2
Oakridge PL12 53 C7
Oak Ridge PL16 19 F4
Oaks The
12 Par PL24 60 C4
Quintrell Downs TR8 111 F3
St Austell PL25 114 B3
Oak Tree Cl PL25 115 B3
Oaktree Ct PL6 124 F1
Oak Tree La PL19 147 C3
Oak Tree Pk PL6 125 D6
Oak Tree School 9 TR4 69 C3
Oak Vale TR2 72 A7
Oak Way TR1 137 D5
Oakwood Cl PL6 125 D7
Oakwood Pk PL31 109 F4
Oakwood Prim Sch PL6 125 A6
Oakwood Rise
Camelford PL32 105 E5
PL32 105 E5
Oates Rd
Helston TR13 146 C6
Marazion TR17 89 C5
Plymouth PL2 128 B5
Observer Cl TR1 137 C3
Ocean Cres 22 TR13 98 C8
Ocean Ct
Plymouth PL1 133 F8
Porthtowan TR4 68 A7
Ocean St PL2 127 E6
Ocean View
Indian Queens TR9 45 E1
Newquay TR7 110 B5
Polruan PL23 116 D2
Porthleven TR13 98 B8
St Austell PL25 114 E7
Ocean View Rd EX23 104 D7
Ocean View Terr TR26 141 A6
Octagon St PL1 148 B3
Octagon The PL1 148 B2
Okehampton Cl PL7 131 B4
Old Bakehouse Flats The TR18 143 F6
Old Barn Ct TR7 110 D4
Old Barns The TR14 66 F2
Old Boat Yard The PL28 107 E6
Old Boys School TR16 67 E5
Old Brewery Yd 4 TR18 143 E5
Old Bridge St TR1 137 D4
Old Butchers Shop The TR20 89 B8
Old Cable La TR19 96 E3
Old Callywith Rd PL31 35 B2
Old Canal Cl EX23 7 B6
Old Carnon Hill TR3 81 F6
Old Chapel The TR4 68 F5
Old Chapel Way PL10 132 F6
Old Chough Flats TR7 111 B7
Old Church Rd TR11 93 E2
Old Church The TR18 143 D4
Old Coach Rd
Lanivet PL26, PL30 47 D6
Playing Place TR3 82 B8
Truro TR3 70 A1
Old Coastguard Cotts PL11 65 A4
Old Coastguard Row TR19 96 B7
Old Corn Mill The TR12 92 C1
Old Dairy The
Plymouth PL3 129 B6
Sancreed TR20 87 E4
Old Drovers Way EX23 4 E1
Old English Ind Est PL20 42 E3
Old Exeter Rd PL19 147 D7
Old Falmouth Rd TR1 137 C1
Old Farm Rd PL5 127 C8
Old Ferry Rd PL12 123 A3
Old Foundry Cl TR19 86 F6
Old Foundry The
Menheniot PL14 51 E6
Tavistock PL19 147 D6
Old George St PL1 148 C2
Old Grammar School Ct PL22 112 C2
Old Greystone Hill PL15, PL19 28 F6
Old Guildhall Mus* PL13 117 D3
Old Hill
Falmouth TR11 144 F6
Grampound TR2 72 A7
Helston TR13 146 A6
Old Hill Cres TR11 144 F5
OLD KEA 82 E8
Old La PL26 46 F3
Old Laira Rd PL3 129 C4
Oldlands Cl PL6 125 B6
Old Launceston Rd PL19 147 B6
Old Laundry The PL1 148 A3
Old Lawn School La PL25 114 B3
Old Market Pl PL31 109 C4
Old Mill Cl PL15 27 B3
Old Mill Ct PL7 130 E5
Old Mill Herbary The* PL30 34 F6
Old Mill La
Camborne TR14 78 F6
Penponds TR14 79 A6
Old Mill The
3 Boscastle PL35 9 C2
Lerryn PL22 61 D8
Old Mine La PL18 40 E6
Old Nursery Cl TR13 91 A1
Old Orchard Cl EX23 7 B6
Old Park Rd PL3 128 D6
Old Paul Hill TR18 143 C2
Old Plymouth Rd PL3 129 E5
Old Portreath Rd
Illogan TR16 67 F5
Redruth TR15 67 F4
Old Post Office Hill 8 EX23 4 E1
Old Pound PL26 58 E6
Old Priory PL7 130 D5
Old Priory Jun Sch PL7 130 D5
Old Quarry Rd PL20 42 A3
Old Quay La PL12 65 B8
Old Rd
Boscastle PL35 9 C2
Liskeard PL14 113 A6
Old Rectory Dr TR9 45 E6
Old Roselyon Cres PL24 60 B5
Old Roselyon Rd PL24 60 C4
Old Sandy La TR16 140 D3
Old School Cl PL27 21 F3
Old School Ct
Padstow PL28 107 D5
Wadebridge PL27 108 B5
Old School Ho The PL10 133 A1
Old Schoolhouse The TR11 145 B4
Old School La PL30 34 D4
Old School Rd PL5 127 C8
Old School The 10 TR5 54 D1
Old Smithy Cl 4 TR17 89 C5
Old Smithy Cotts EX39 2 E4
Old Sta La TR17 89 A6
Old Station Rd
Horrabridge PL20 42 C4
1 Liskeard PL14 51 A7
Old Station The PL20 42 B4
Old Tannery Bsns Pk The 4 PL4 149 A4
Old Tannery La TR2 72 A7
Old Town Hall The PL24 60 B5
Old Town St PL1 148 C3
Old Tram Rd TR3 82 A5
Old Vicarage Cl TR3 80 F4
Old Vicarage Gate TR27 142 A1
Old Vicarage Pl 11 PL25 114 C3
Old Vicarage The TR 26 76 E5
Old Warleigh La PL5 124 B7
Old Well Gdns TR10 144 C8
Old Wharf The PL9 135 C7
Old Woodlands Rd PL5 124 D3
Old Workhouses The TR15 140 B8
Oliver Ct
Liskeard PL14 50 E8
St Mellion PL12 40 A1
Oliver's Terr TR13 146 C5
Olive Villas TR3 81 F6
Olivey Pl TR11 82 A3
Olivia Ct PL4 149 B4
Olympic Way PL6 125 C6
Omaha Rd PL31 109 F3
Onslow Rd PL2 128 C7
Ope's Ct 13 TR11 145 B5
Opies La PL31 109 C5
Opie's Row TR16 80 B5
Opie's Terr TR16 80 A5
Orange La TR26 141 A6
Orchard Ave PL6 129 B7
Orchard Cl
Helston TR13 146 B7
PL15 106 B7
3 Plymouth PL7 131 C5
Poughill EX23 4 D2
St Austell PL25 114 E4
St Giles on the Heath PL15 13 F1
St Mellion PL12 53 C8
Tavistock PL19 41 D8
Tideford PL12 52 F2
Truro TR1 69 F3
Orchard Cotts
Lamerton PL19 30 B3
St Austell PL25 114 F5
Orchard Cres PL9 135 C7
Orchard Ct
Lamerton PL19 30 A3
Penzance TR18 143 C5
Orchard Gr PL25 114 B4
Orchard Ho 11 TR18 143 C2
Orchard La
Helford TR12 93 B1
Plymouth PL7 130 E6
Orchard Pk PL26 47 C2
Orchard Pl 10 TR18 143 C2
Orchard Rd PL2 128 B7
Orchard Terr 20 TR18 143 C2
Orchard The
Gunnislake PL18 41 A6
Lerryn PL22 61 D8
Newquay TR7 111 B7
North Petherwin PL15 18 B8
St Erth TR27 77 E2
Orchardton Terr 2 PL9 135 F5
Orchard Vale TR11 145 C7
Orchard Way
6 Goldsithney TR20 89 E5
2 St Austell PL26 115 A1
Orchard Wlk 13 PL27 108 B5
Orch The PL13 117 D4
Ordnance St PL1 127 E2
Ordulf Rd PL19 147 A5
Oregon Way PL3 129 D6
ORESTON 135 C7
Oreston Com Academy PL9 135 C7

Oreston Rd PL9 135 C8
Orion Dr PL27 31 F3
Osborne Ct PL1 148 C2
Osborne Parc TR13 146 B7
Osborne Pl PL1 148 C2
Osborne Rd PL3 128 A3
Osborne Villas
10 Falmouth TR11 145 C3
2 Plymouth PL3 128 A3
Osprey Gdns PL9 136 C7
OTTERHAM 10 D1
Otterham Com Prim Sch PL32 10 C2
Otterham Pk PL32 16 A8
OTTERHAM STATION 16 A8
OTTERY 30 A2
Ottery Cotts PL19 30 A2
Ottery Park Ind Est PL19 30 A2
Outer Down PL19 30 A3
Outland Rd PL2 128 C7
Overcliff PL29 22 D8
Overton Gdns 3 PL3 128 F5
Overtonn Villas 6 PL15 106 C5
Owen Dr PL7 130 C7
Owen Sivell Cl PL14 113 E6
Oxford Ave PL3 128 E5
Oxford Gdns PL3 128 E5
Oxford Pl PL1 148 C3
Oxford St PL1 148 B3
Oxford Terr 4 PL1 148 B3
Oxland Rd TR16 67 E5
Oxley Vale TR7 111 B5

P

Paardeburg Rd 1 PL31 48 D8
Packet La TR20 89 F5
Packington St PL2 128 A4
Packsaddle TR10 81 D2
Packsaddle Cl TR10 81 D2
Paddock Cl
Plymouth PL9 135 E5
Saltash PL12 122 D4
Paddock The
Helston TR13 146 C7
Redruth TR15 140 D2
Sticker PL26 58 E1
Paddons Row PL19 147 C6
Padnover Terr 22 TR26 141 B5
PADSTOW 107 C4
Padstow Harbour Ind Est PL28 107 E4
Padstow Mus* PL28 107 D5
Padstow Sch PL28 107 C4
Padstow Workshop Units PL28 107 B4
Page's Cross PL15 106 D4
Pagoda Dr PL26 115 A1
Paiges Farm PL9 135 C1
Painton Water EX39 3 A8
Palace Rd PL25 114 D4
Palace St PL1 149 A2
Palm Ct TR1 137 D3
PALMERSBRIDGE 25 F4
Palmers Terr PL34 14 C6
Palmerston St PL1 148 A4
Palmers Way PL27 108 D6
PANCRASWEEK 8 C8
Pannier La TR26 141 C2
Pannier Mkt PL19 147 C5
Panson Cross PL15 13 E3
PANTERSBRIDGE 36 D3
PAR 60 C4
Parade PL1 149 A2
Parade Bsns Pk 4 PL19 147 B4
Parade Hill TR19 88 D1
Parade Ope PL1 149 A2
Parade Pass 29 TR18 143 E5
Parade Rd PL5 124 A3
Parade Sq PL22 112 D2
Parade St TR18 143 E5
Parade The
Helston TR13 146 C5
Liskeard PL14 113 C6
Lostwithiel PL22 112 D2
Millbrook PL10 132 E5
Milton Abbot PL19 29 C6
Mousehole TR19 88 D1
Truro TR1 137 E4
Paradise Park & The World Parrot Trust* TR27 142 A4
Paradise Pk EX22 7 F1
Paradise Pl PL1 128 A2
Paradise Rd
Boscastle PL35 9 C1
Plymouth PL1 128 A2
PARAMOOR 72 E8
Par Beach & St Andrews Rd Nature Reserve* PL24 60 D4
Parc-Abnac TR20 88 B7
Parc-an-Bal Ct TR14 138 E4
Parc-an-Bre Dr PL26 58 C8
Parc-an-Cady Est TR19 97 A6
Parc-an-Challow TR10 144 B8
Parc-an-Creet TR26 77 A7
Parc-an-Dillon Rd TR2 83 B2
Parc-an-Dix La TR27 142 C7
Parc-an-Dower TR13 146 C6
Parcandowr TR2 57 E1
Parc-an-Forth 6 TR26 77 A6
Parc an Gate TR19 88 C1
Parc-an-Gwarry 7 TR3 81 F7
Parc-an-Ithan TR12 102 F2
Parc-an-Maen 11 TR13 98 C8
Parc an Manns TR11 93 D3
Parc-an-Peath TR19 97 A6
Parc-an-Stamps 4 TR26 77 A6
Parc an Yorth TR19 86 F8
Parc-Askell Cl TR12 98 E5
Parc Bean Terr TR26 141 A6
Parc Behan Ct TR2 83 F6
Parc Bowen TR13 92 A3
Parc-Bracket St TR14 138 D3
Parc Brawse TR12 102 F2
Parc Briwer TR10 144 D7
Parc Eglos
Helston TR13 146 B6
St Merryn PL28 31 F8
Parc Eglos Sch TR13 146 C6
Parc Enys TR12 99 B4
PARC ERISSEY 68 A3
Parc Erissey Ind Est TR16 68 A3
Parc Fer Cl EX23 4 E1
Parc Godrevy TR7 110 C5
Parc Holland TR13 146 D8
Parc Ledden TR13 146 C6
Parc Ledrak TR13 146 B8
Parc Letta TR18 143 C7
Parc Mellan TR18 143 D7
Parc Merys TR2 83 B2
Parc Monga Dr TR11 92 F3
Parc Monga Rd TR11 92 F3
Parc Morrep TR20 90 B3
Parc Owles TR26 141 D2
Parc Peneglos TR11 82 A3
Parc Pennkarn PL33 14 E3
Parc Pordic TR27 142 D5
Parc Rowan TR9 57 E8
Parc Shady TR26 77 C1
Parc Stephney TR11 144 C2
Parc Terr 19 TR18 143 C1
Parc Trenance PL28 31 F7
Parc Trethias PL28 31 F7
Parc Vean PL30 34 C1
Parc Venton Cl 2 TR14 138 F2
Parc Villas 17 TR18 143 C1
Parc Wartha Ave TR18 143 D6
Parc Wartha Cres TR18 143 D6
Par Gn PL24 60 C4
Pargolla Rd TR7 110 F6
Park 30 PL15 106 A3
Parka Cl 12 TR9 45 E2
Park-an-Bans TR14 138 E1
Parkancreeg 9 TR3 81 F7
Park an Gonwyn TR26 141 E2
Park an Gorsaf TR14 138 D2
Park an Harvey TR13 146 C6
Park-an-Mengleth TR15 140 D4
Park-an-Pyth 2 TR19 75 A1
Park-an-Tansys TR14 138 F2
Parka Rd
Indian Queens TR9 45 E1
8 St Columb Road TR9 45 E2
Park Ave
Plymouth, Devonport PL1 127 E3
Plymouth, Plymstock PL9 135 D7
St Ives TR26 141 B5
PARK BOTTOM 139 B8
Park Cl
Illogan TR15 139 B8
Nancegollan TR13 91 B7
Plymouth PL7 130 B7
Park Cnr TR18 143 E5
Park Cres
Falmouth TR11 145 A4
Helston TR13 146 B5
Plymouth PL9 135 C7
Ponsanooth TR3 81 B4
Park Ct
Chillaton PL16 29 F8
28 Penzance TR18 143 E5
Park Dr PL31 109 B4
Parkenbutts TR7 111 D7
Parkengear Vean TR2 71 D6
Parkengue TR10 144 A7
Parkenhead La PL28 20 F2
Park Enskellaw 6 TR12 99 A2
Park en Venton TR12 99 A2
Park-en-Vine PL27 32 D6
Parker Cl PL7 130 B5
Parker Rd PL2 128 B6
Parker's Gn PL18 40 F6
Parkesway PL12 122 D2
Park Fenton PL14 113 D5
PARKFIELD 39 A2
Parkfield Dr PL6 125 F1
Park Gwyn PL26 58 B4
Park Hill TR11 145 A4
Park Ho PL25 114 B3
Park Holly TR14 138 B3
Parkins Terr 7 TR1 137 D5
Park La
8 Bere Alston PL20 41 B1
Bugle PL26 47 C1
Camborne TR14 138 E2
Plymouth PL9 135 C7
Parklands
Nanpean PL26 58 C7
14 TR5 54 D1
Parklands Cl TR7 111 D6
Park Leder TR16 68 C3
Park Leven TR16 139 C8
Park Lowen TR26 141 C2
Parknoweth TR12 99 A4
Parknoweth Cl TR8 56 B6
Park Pl
Grampound Road TR2 57 E1
Wadebridge PL27 108 B5
Park Place La 12 PL3 128 A4
Park Rd
Camborne TR14 138 E4
Fowey PL23 116 C4
Illogan TR15 139 B7
Lifton PL16 19 F3
Park Rd *continued*
Liskeard PL14 113 C6
18 Newlyn TR18 143 C1
Plymouth PL3 129 A6
Ponsanooth TR3 81 B4
Redruth TR15 140 C4
St Austell PL25 114 C3
St Dominick PL12 40 D2
Torpoint PL11 127 B3
Wadebridge PL27 108 B5
Whitemoor PL26 58 E8
Park Rd Hos PL22 112 C2
Park Rise TR11 145 A4
Parkryn Rd 4 TR19 88 C1
Parkside PL2 127 F5
Park St PL3 128 A4
Park Stenak TR16 80 F8
Parkstone La PL7 130 F6
Park Street Ope PL3 128 A4
Park Terr
Falmouth TR11 145 A4
Truro TR1 70 D1
Park The
Penryn TR10 144 B7
Tregony TR2 71 F4
Parkvedras Ho 5 TR1 137 B4
Parkvedras Terr 4 TR1 137 B4
Parkventon PL26 47 C2
Park View
Lifton PL16 19 F4
Liskeard PL14 113 C6
Perranarworthal TR3 81 E6
Plymouth PL4 149 C3
Summercourt TR8 57 B7
Truro TR1 137 C3
Parkview Apartments TR7 110 F5
Park View Cl TR3 82 A7
Park View Rd TR13 146 B5
Park View Terr PL27 108 B5
Park Villas TR3 81 B4
Park Way PL25 114 F5
Parkway Ct PL6 129 E7
Parkway Ind Est The PL6 129 E7
Parkway The PL3, PL5, PL6 124 B1
Park Wise TR10 144 C8
Parkwood Cl PL6 121 B2
Parkwood Ct PL19 147 D6
Parkwood Rd PL19 147 D6
Park Wood Rise PL16 19 F4
Parkwoon Cl PL26 46 F3
Par La PL24 60 B4
Par Moor Rd
Par PL24, PL25 60 B3
St Austell PL24, PL25 115 F4
PARNACOTT 8 E8
Parnell Cl PL6 129 A8
Parr La PL4 149 B2
Parr St PL4 149 B2
Parsonage Ct PL16 19 F4
Parsonage Way PL4 149 B2
Parsons Cl PL9 136 A4
Parsons Ct PL10 132 F6
Parsons Gn PL17 39 E6
Par Sta PL24 60 C5
Partwayes PL19 30 A3
Pascoe Cl TR3 69 D4
Pasley St E PL2 127 F4
Pasley St PL2 127 E4
Passage Hill TR11 82 A3
Passage La PL23 116 B5
Passage St PL23 116 D5
Passmore Cl
Blackwater TR4 68 E5
Liskeard PL14 113 D6
Pathfields EX23 104 E5
Pathway Fields The TR27 142 C5
Patna Pl PL1 148 B4
Pato Point PL11 127 A5
Patterdale Cl PL6 125 D3
Patterdale Wlk PL6 125 D3
Pattern Cl 1 PL25 115 A3
Pattinson Cl PL6 125 E2
Pattinson Ct PL6 125 E2
Pattinson Dr PL6 125 F2
PAUL 88 C2
Paull Rd PL31 109 B4
Paulls Row 4 TR15 140 C5
PAUL'S GREEN 90 E8
Paul's Row TR1 137 D5
Paul's Terr TR1 137 D5
Paviland Grange 6 PL1 128 A3
Pavilion Pk TR14 138 F4
Pavilion Rise 5 PL26 115 A1
Pavlova Cl PL14 113 C5
Pavlova Ct 6 PL14 113 C5
Paynter's Cross PL12 53 E7
Paynter's Cross Cotts PL12 53 E7
Paynters La TR16 67 E4
PAYNTER'S LANE END 67 E4
Paynter's Lane End Est TR16 67 D4
Paynter Wlk 5 PL7 131 B5
Peacock Ave PL11 127 A3
Peacock Cl PL7 130 F7
Peacock La PL4 149 A2
Pearce's La 12 TR26 141 A5
Pearce's Row 3 PL24 60 C4
Pearn Cotts 2 PL3 128 F6
Pearn Gdns PL3 129 A7
Pearn Rd PL3 129 A7
Pearn Ridge PL3 129 A7
Pearson Ave 3 PL4 128 F4
Pearson Rd PL4 128 F4
Pebble Ct TR7 111 C7
Pedlars Cl PL15 18 B8
Pedna Carne Mobile Home Pk TR9 57 E8
Pednandrea TR19 86 E6
Pedn-m'n-du TR19 96 A7
Pedn-Moran TR2 95 B6
Pedn-y-ke 1 TR12 99 A1
Peek Moor Cross EX22 13 E4
Peeks Ave PL9 135 F7
Peel St PL1 128 A1
Peguarra Cl PL28 20 E1
Peguarra Ct PL28 20 E1
Pelean Cross TR3 81 B5
Pelham Ct 11 TR11 145 C3
Pellew Cl
7 Falmouth TR11 145 A5
Padstow PL28 107 C5
Pellew Cres TR13 146 C4
Pellew Pl PL2 127 F4
Pellew Rd TR11 145 A5
Pellor Fields TR13 90 F3
PELYNT 62 D5
Pelynt Prim Sch PL13 62 D6
Pembrey Wlk PL5 123 E4
Pembroke Cl 7 PL24 60 C4
Pembroke La PL1 127 E1
Pembroke Rd TR7 111 E7
Pembroke St PL1 127 E1
Pemros Rd PL5 123 C1
Penair Cres TR1 137 F6
Penair Sch TR1 70 D4
Penair View TR1 137 F4
Penally Ct PL35 9 D2
Penally Hill PL35 9 D2
Penally Terr PL35 9 C2
Penalverne Ave TR18 143 D5
Penalverne Cres TR18 143 D5
Penalverne Dr TR18 143 D5
Penalverne Pl TR18 143 D5
Penameyne Ct 5 TR26 141 B6
Pen-an-Gwel TR26 141 A4
Penare Gdns 2 TR18 143 E6
Penare Rd TR18 143 E6
Penare Terr TR18 143 E6
Penarrow Cl TR11 144 E2
Penarrow Rd TR11 145 C8
Penarth PL13 117 B3
Penarth Rd TR11 145 A5
Penarwyn Cres TR18 143 B7
Penarwyn Rd PL24 60 B4
Penarwyn Woods 6 PL24 60 B4
PENBEAGLE 141 A4
Penbeagle Cl 17 TR26 77 A6
Penbeagle Cres 8 TR26 77 A6
Penbeagle Ind Est TR26 77 A6
Penbeagle La TR26 77 A6
Penbeagle Terr 7 TR26 77 A6
Penbeagle Way TR26 141 A4
PENBERTH 97 A3
Penberthy Cross TR27 89 F7
Penberthy Rd
Helston TR13 146 C5
Portreath TR16 67 D6
Penbothidno TR11 92 F3
Pen Brea Cl TR2 95 B6
Penbrea Rd TR18 143 E7
Penbugle La PL31 109 E7
Pencair Ave PL11 126 E2
Pencalenick Specl Sch TR1 70 E4
Pencantol TR4 81 C7
Pencarn Parc TR16 80 A5
Pencarrick Cl TR1 137 B6
PENCARROW 105 D1
Pencarrow* PL30 34 D6
Pencarrow Cl PL17 39 E3
Pencarrow Rd 13 TR16 67 E4
Pencavo Hill PL12 53 A3
Pencoys Prim Sch TR16 80 A5
Pencreber Rd 3 PL20 42 C4
PENCUKE 10 D5
Pendale Sq TR1 137 B4
Pendarves
St Merryn PL28 31 F7
Tresillian TR2 70 F5
Pendarves Rd
Camborne TR14 138 C1
Falmouth TR11 144 F6
Penzance TR18 143 D6
Truro TR1 137 C6
Pendarves St
Camborne, Beacon TR14 138 F1
Troon TR14 79 E4
Pendarves View TR14 138 C1
Pendean Ave PL14 113 B6
Pendean Cl PL14 113 B6
Pendean Ct PL14 113 B6
Pendean Dr PL14 113 B6
PENDEEN 75 A1
Pendeen Cl
Plymouth PL6 124 F6
Threemilestone TR3 69 D3
Pendeen Cres
Plymouth PL6 125 A6
Threemilestone TR3 69 D3
Pendeen Ho TR1 69 E4
Pendeen Pk TR13 146 C8
Pendeen Pl TR7 110 F6
Pendeen Prim Sch TR19 75 A1
Pendeen Rd
Porthleven TR13 91 B1
Threemilestone TR3 69 D3
Truro TR1 137 E3
Pendennis Castle* TR11 145 E2
Pendennis Cl
Penzance TR18 143 E7
Plymouth PL3 128 F8
Pendennis Cl *continued*
Torpoint PL11 126 F3
Pendennis Ct TR11 145 D3
Pendennis Pl TR18 143 F7
Pendennis Rd
Falmouth TR11 145 D3
Looe PL13 117 D5
Penzance TR18 143 E7
Pendennis Rise TR11 145 D3
Pender's La TR15 140 B5
Pendilly Ave PL11 126 F2
Pendilly Dr PL25 114 E7
Pendinnes Gdns PL15 106 B8
PENDOGGETT 23 A6
Pendola Wlk TR26 141 B5
Pendour Pk PL22 112 E2
Pendower Ct TR2 83 D5
Pendower Rd
Looe PL13 117 E4
Veryan TR2 83 F6
Pendower Terr TR14 138 E1
Pendragon Cres TR7 111 A4
Pendragon Ho TR11 145 D3
Pendragon Rd 3 PL14 113 D6
Pendra Loweth TR11 144 D1
Pendray Gdns PL14 50 E7
Pendrea Cl TR18 143 F7
Pendrea Pk TR14 138 F5
Pendrea Pl TR18 143 F7
Pendrea Rd TR18 143 F7
Pendrea Wood TR1 69 F3
PENDRIFT 24 B1
Pendrim Rd PL13 117 D4
Pendruccombe Ct PL15 106 D5
Pen-Eglos 8 TR2 95 A6
PENELEWEY 82 C7
Penforth TR14 138 E2
Penfound Gdns EX23 104 F5
Pengannel Cl TR7 110 D4
Pengarrock Hill TR12 101 D5
Pengarth 1 TR5 54 D1
Pengarth Cl TR1 137 C2
Pengarth Rd TR11 145 A3
Pengarth Rise TR11 145 A3
PENGEGON 138 F2
Pengegon Moor TR14 138 F2
Pengegon Parc TR14 138 F2
Pengegon Way TR14 138 F2
PENGELLY 14 E2
Pengelly
24 Callington PL17 39 F4
Delabole PL33 14 E2
Pengelly Cl PL11 126 F5
Pengelly Cross
Godolphin Cross TR27 90 F7
Wadebridge PL27 108 C1
Pengelly Hill PL11 127 A5
Pengelly Pk PL11 126 F5
Pengelly Pl TR11 144 E5
Pengellys Row TR14 139 A5
Pengelly Way TR3 69 D3
Pengeron Ave 1 TR14 138 F7
Pengersick Est TR20 90 C3
Pengersick La TR20 90 C3
Pengersick Parc TR20 90 C3
Pengliddon PL27 33 B7
PENGOLD 10 A5
Pengover Cl PL14 113 D6
Pengover Gn PL14 51 E8
Pengover Hts PL14 113 D6
Pengover Parc TR15 140 C6
Pengover Pk PL14 113 D6
Pengover Rd PL14 113 E6
Pengrowyn PL26 59 D6
Pengwarras Rd TR14 138 C3
Pengwel 16 TR18 143 C2
PENHALE
Indian Queens 57 D8
Millbrook 132 D7
Mullion 99 D1
Penhale 1 TR6 55 A5
Penhale Cl PL14 37 F3
Penhale Cotts TR3 82 D6
Penhale Est TR15 140 B6
Penhale Gdns TR9 57 D8
Penhale Mdw PL14 37 F3
Penhale Rd
Barripper TR14 79 A4
Carnhell Green TR14 78 F4
Falmouth TR11 144 F1
Penwithick PL26 59 D7
Penhaligon Cl TR15 140 D4
Penhaligon Ct TR1 137 E5
Penhaligon Way PL25 114 F4
PENHALLICK 139 C4
Penhall La TR4 68 C6
PENHALLOW 55 B2
Penhallow TR15 139 B8
Penhallow Cl
Mount Hawke TR4 68 C6
Veryan TR2 83 C5
Penhallow Ct TR7 111 C7
Penhallow Parc PL33 14 D2
Penhallow Rd TR7 111 C7
Penhalls Way TR3 82 B8
PENHALVEAN 80 C4
Penharget Cl PL14 38 D5
Penhaven Cl TR8 56 B7
Penhaven Ct TR7 110 E6
Penhellaz Hill TR13 146 B6
Penhellaz Rd TR13 146 B6
Penhole Cl PL15 27 D3
Penhole Dr PL15 106 D3
Penina Ave TR7 110 F4
Peninsular Pk PL12 122 C4

Penjerrick Gdns★ TR11... 93 D5
Penjerrick Hill
Budock Water TR11..... 144 C1
Falmouth TR11......... 93 E5
Penkenna Cl EX23........ 10 C6
Penkernick Cl TR18...... 143 B1
Penkernick Way TR9..... 45 E6
Penknight La PL22...... 112 A2
Penlean Cl TR15........ 140 D7
Penlea Rd TR10......... 144 B8
Penlee Apartments PL23 116 C3
Penlee Cl
[13] Callington PL17.... 39 F4
Praa Sands TR20....... 90 C3
Tregony TR2............ 71 F4
Penlee Cotts PL10....... 64 C2
Penlee Gdns PL3....... 128 A4
Penlee Ho TR11......... 69 E4
Penlee House Gall & Mus★
TR18................ 143 E5
Penlee Manor Dr TR18.. 143 E4
Penlee Pk PL11........ 126 E4
Penlee Pl [4] PL4...... 128 F4
Penlee Rd PL3......... 128 A4
Penlee St [10] TR18.... 143 E6
Penlee View Terr [3]
TR18................ 143 E4
Penlee Villas TR3....... 82 B8
Penlee Way PL3........ 128 B4
Penlu TR14............ 138 F5
Penlu Ho TR14......... 138 F5
Penluke Cl TR16........ 80 A5
Penmare Cl TR27....... 142 E7
Penmare Ct TR27....... 142 E7
Penmare Terr TR27..... 142 E7
PENMARTH.............. 80 C2
PENMAYNE.............. 21 E3
Penmayne Parc TR16... 140 F1
Penmayne Villas TR27... 21 E3
Penmead Rd PL33........ 14 E2
Penmelen PL32......... 105 C4
Penmeneth TR13....... 146 F8
Penmenner Est [7] TR12. 101 C4
Penmenner Rd TR12.... 102 F2
Penmere Cl
Helston TR13......... 146 B7
Penzance TR18........ 143 E7
Penmere Cres TR11..... 144 F3
Penmere Ct [4] TR11... 145 A3
Penmere Dr TR7........ 110 C5
Penmere Hill [7] TR11.. 145 A3
Penmere Pl
[3] Falmouth TR11.... 145 A3
Penzance TR18........ 143 E7
Penmere Rd
Penzance TR18........ 143 E7
St Austell PL25....... 115 A4
Penmere Sta TR11..... 144 F3
Penmerrin Ct TR7...... 110 E5
Penmeva View PL26.... 73 C3
Penmorvah TR11....... 82 A2
Penmorvah Pl TR14.... 138 E2
Penmorvah Rd TR1..... 137 F6
PENNANCE............ 140 F1
Pennance Hill TR11.... 93 F5
Pennance Ho TR11..... 145 A2
Pennance La TR16..... 140 F1
Pennance Parc TR16... 140 F1
Pennance Rd
Falmouth TR11........ 145 A2
Lanner TR16.......... 80 E7
Redruth TR15........ 140 F1
Pennance Terr TR16... 140 F1
Penn an Drea TR13.... 146 D8
Pennant Farm PL29..... 22 E6
Pennard Villas TR27.... 33 B5
Penn Kernow PL15..... 106 C4
Pennor Dr PL25....... 114 D3
Pennoweth Prim Sch
TR15................ 140 C5
PENNYCOMEQUICK...... 148 B4
Pennycomequick Hill
PL4................. 148 B4
PENNYCROSS.......... 128 C8
Pennycross Cl PL2..... 128 D8
Pennycross Park Rd PL2 128 C7
Pennycross Prim Sch
PL2................. 128 C8
Pennygillam Ind Est
PL15................ 106 A4
Pennygillam Way PL15.. 18 E2
Pennys La PL24....... 115 F5
Penny's La PL9........ 136 D6
PENNYTINNEY.......... 23 A4
Penoweth TR11....... 82 A2
PENPETHY............. 14 F5
PENPILLICK........... 60 D7
PENPOL............... 82 B6
Penpol Ave TR27...... 142 C5
Penpol Hill
Crantock TR8......... 110 B4
Devoran TR3......... 82 B6
PENPOLL.............. 61 D5
Penpol Prim Sch TR27.. 142 C5
Penpol Rd TR27....... 142 C5
Penpol Terr TR27...... 142 B5
Penpol Vean TR27..... 142 C5
PENPONDS............ 138 B1
Penponds Prim Sch TR14. 79 B5
Penponds Rd TR13..... 91 A1
Penpons Cl TR18....... 143 C4
PENPONT.............. 24 A1
Penpont Rd TR15...... 140 D6
Penpont View PL15.... 26 C7
Pen Porth Ave TR26.... 77 A7

Penquite Dr PL31...... 109 F5
Penrice Academy PL25. 115 A3
Penrice Parc PL25..... 115 A3
Penrith Cl PL6........ 125 D3
Penrith Gdns PL6..... 125 D3
Penrith Wlk PL6...... 125 D3
PENROSE
St Breward............ 24 A3
St Eval............... 31 E5
Penrose Ct
Penzance TR18....... 143 F6
[2] South Tehidy TR14. 138 F7
Penrose Parc TR13..... 91 B1
Penrose Rd
Falmouth TR11....... 145 A4
Helston TR13........ 146 C6
Penrose St PL1........ 148 B3
Penrose Terr TR18..... 143 F6
Penrose Villas [5] PL4. 128 F4
Penrose Walks★ TR12,
TR13................ 98 D8
Penruan La TR2........ 95 B6
PENRYN.............. 144 B7
Penryn Coll TR10..... 144 B7
Penryn Com Inf Sch
TR10................ 144 B7
Penryn Jun Sch TR10.. 144 B8
Penryn Mus★ TR10.... 144 C7
Penryn St TR15....... 140 B4
Penryn Sta TR10...... 144 B8
Pensans Com Prim Sch
TR18................ 143 D6
Penscombe Cross PL15.. 28 C6
Penscott La PL26...... 114 C1
PENSILVA............. 38 E5
Pensilva Ind Est PL14.. 38 E5
Pensilva Prim Sch PL14. 38 E5
Pensilva Rd TR1....... 137 E6
Penstowe Rd [5] EX23... 5 A6
Penstrasse Pl [1] PL24. 60 D5
PENSTRAZE........... 69 A5
Penstraze Bsns Ctr TR4. 69 A5
Penstraze La PL26..... 47 A4
Pensylva PL25......... 114 E3
Pentalek Rd TR14..... 138 D1
Pentamar St PL2...... 127 E4
Pentargon Rd [1] PL35.. 9 C1
PENTEWAN............ 73 C6
Pentewan Hill PL26.... 73 D6
Pentewan Rd PL24, PL26. 59 C1
Pentidna La TR27..... 66 B2
Pentillie PL26......... 73 C4
Pentillie Cl [22] PL20.. 41 B1
Pentillie Cres PL4..... 128 D4
Pentillie Gdns
[14] Callington PL17... 39 E4
St Austell PL25...... 114 F6
Pentillie Rd
Bere Alston PL20..... 41 B1
Plymouth PL4........ 128 E4
Pentillie View [23] PL20. 41 B1
Pentillie Way PL26.... 73 C4
PENTIRE............. 43 D4
Pentire Ave TR7....... 110 A5
Pentire Cres TR7...... 110 B5
Pentire Ct TR7....... 110 B6
Pentire Gn TR8........ 43 D3
Pentire Hts TR7...... 110 A5
Pentire Rd
Newquay TR7......... 110 C5
Penryn TR10......... 144 B8
Torpoint PL11........ 126 F3
Pentland Cl PL6...... 124 F7
Pen Tor PL30......... 35 C8
Pentor Ct PL30....... 35 C8
Pentour [3] PL24...... 60 B4
Pentowan Ct TR26..... 141 E2
Pentowan Gdns TR27... 142 E8
Pentowan Rd TR27.... 142 E8
Pentreath Cl
Fowey PL23.......... 116 B5
Lanner TR16........ 80 E7
Penzance TR18....... 143 D7
Pentreath La
Lizard TR12......... 102 F2
Praa Sands TR20..... 90 B3
Pentreath Terr TR16... 80 E7
Pentre Cl PL26....... 46 F3
Pentre Ct EX23........ 4 D4
Pentrevah Ct TR7..... 110 D6
Pentrevah Rd [8] PL26. 59 D7
Pen-Tye PL24......... 78 E3
Pentyre Ct PL4....... 149 C4
Pentyre Terr PL4..... 149 C4
Penvale [3] PL14...... 38 E4
Penvale Cl TR14....... 79 B5
Penvale Cres TR10.... 144 B8
Penvale Ct [8] TR11... 145 A4
Penvale Dr TR10...... 144 B8
Penvean Cl TR10...... 93 C8
Penvean La TR11..... 144 E5
Penvenen [2] TR6...... 55 A5
Penventinnie La TR1... 69 E4
Penventinnie La PL23.. 116 B7
Penventon Terr
Four Lanes TR16..... 80 B6
Redruth TR15....... 140 A4
Penventon View TR13.. 146 B5
Penview Cres TR13.... 146 B5
Penvorder Cotts PL30.. 24 B2
Penvorder La PL30.... 24 B2
Penware Parc TR14.... 138 C1
Penwarne La TR11..... 138 F7
Penwarne La PL26.... 73 C3
Penwarne Rd TR11.... 93 D5
Penwartha TR12...... 101 B2

Penwartha Cl
Constantine TR11..... 92 F3
St Columb Minor TR7.. 111 D7
PENWARTHA COOMBE.... 55 B3
Penwartha Ct TR11.... 92 F3
Penwartha Rd
[15] Illogan TR16..... 67 C4
Perranporth TR6...... 55 B4
Penwartha Vean [14] TR16. 67 E4
PENWEATHERS........ 69 F2
Penwerris Ct TR11.... 145 A6
Penwerris Farm TR11.. 144 F5
Penwerris La TR11.... 145 A6
Penwerris Rd TR1..... 69 F3
Penwerris Rise TR20... 90 B3
Penwerris Terr [10] TR11. 145 A5
Penwethers La TR1.... 69 F3
Penwinnick Cl [9] TR5. 54 C1
Penwinnick Parc [4] TR5. 54 D1
Penwinnick Rd
St Agnes TR5......... 68 D8
St Austell PL25....... 114 B3
Penwith Bsns Ctr TR20. 88 F6
Penwith Cl TR26...... 141 A4
Penwith Coll TR18.... 143 D7
Penwithick Rd PL26... 59 D7
Penwithian Cl TR27... 142 E6
PENWITHICK.......... 59 E7
Penwithick Pk [6] PL26. 59 D7
Penwith Rd PL26...... 141 A4
Penwith St [11] TR18... 143 E6
Penworth Cl PL15..... 106 C5
Penwyth TR12........ 92 C1
Pen y Bryn PL27...... 108 D6
Pen Y Morfa Cl TR8.... 45 A8
PENZANCE........... 143 F5
Penzance L Ctr TR18... 143 D6
Penzance Rd
Helston TR13........ 146 A6
St Buryan TR19...... 97 C7
Penzance School of Art
TR18................ 143 E5
Penzance Sta TR18.... 143 F6
Pepo La TR2.......... 72 A7
Pepper Cl PL12....... 40 C2
Pepper La PL9........ 136 D7
Peppers Ct PL12...... 40 C2
Peppers Hill Cl PL15... 18 F7
Peppers Park Rd PL14.. 113 E6
Pepper St PL19....... 147 C6
Pepys Pl PL5......... 124 E1
PERCUIL............. 83 A1
Percy Davy Cl PL6.... 55 A5
Percy Mews PL28..... 107 C4
Percy St PL5......... 123 D1
Percy Terr PL4....... 129 A4
Pergola Ct [9] TR7.... 110 F6
Perhaver Pk PL26..... 85 D5
Perhaver Way PL26... 85 D5
Periwinkle Dr PL7.... 131 C5
Per Kithen TR12...... 102 F2
Permarin Rd TR10.... 144 C8
PERRANARWORTHAL.... 81 D6
Perran-ar-worthal Prim Sch
TR3................. 81 D6
Perran Cl TR3........ 81 F6
Perrancombe Garden Ct
TR6................. 55 A4
PERRANCOOMBE....... 55 A3
Perran Crossroads TR20. 89 E5
PERRAN DOWNS....... 89 E5
Perran Downs Lane TR20. 89 E5
PERRANPORTH........ 55 B5
Perranporth Cl PL5.... 123 E4
Perranporth Com Prim Sch
[18] TR6............ 55 A4
PERRANUTHNOE....... 89 D4
PERRANWELL......... 55 B3
Goonhavern.......... 55 C3
Perranarworthal..... 81 C6
Perranwell Rd TR4.... 55 D4
Perranwell Sta TR3.... 81 E6
PERRANZABULOE...... 55 B3
Perranzabuloe Mus★ TR6 55 A5
Perrily Mount PL23.... 104 E4
Perry Cl PL19........ 147 B6
Perryman Cl PL7...... 130 E7
Perseverance Cotts [1]
PL7................ 130 E7
Peryn Rd PL19....... 147 A5
Peter Hopper's Hill PL5. 120 C2
Peter's Cl PL9........ 136 C7
Petersfield Cl PL3.... 129 B6
PETER'S FINGER....... 19 C7
Peters Hill PL26...... 58 E4
Peters Park Cl PL5.... 123 E1
Peter's Park La PL5... 123 E1
PETERVILLE.......... 54 D1
Petes Pl [24] PL26.... 141 B5
Petherick Rd EX23.... 104 E7
PETHERWIN GATE...... 18 B7
Pethick Cl PL6....... 124 D6
Pethill Cl PL6........ 125 F2
Pethybridge Dr PL31.. 109 B3
Petroc Ct PL18....... 40 D6
PEVERELL........... 128 D6
Peverell Park Rd PL3.. 128 D6
Peverell Rd
Penzance TR18....... 143 E7
[7] Porthleven TR13.. 98 C8
Peverell Terr
Plymouth PL3........ 128 D5
Porthleven TR13..... 98 B8
Pew Tor Cl [3] PL20... 42 C3
Phernyssick Rd PL25.. 114 F6
Philgray Cl TR27..... 142 E7
Philip Cl PL9........ 136 A6

Philip Gdns PL9...... 135 F6
PHILLACK........... 142 D7
Phillack Hill TR27.... 142 D7
PHILLEIGH........... 83 B6
Phillimore Ct PL6.... 58 D5
Phillimore St [3] PL2. 127 F4
Philpott La PL19..... 147 B2
Phoenix Bsns Pk PL6.. 125 F4
Phoenix Cl [8] PL20.. 42 C4
Phoenix L Ctr PL15... 106 C4
Phoenix St PL1....... 148 A2
Piala Pl PL27........ 142 E7
Piazza [14] TR26..... 141 B6
Piazza The [5] PL31... 109 E5
Pickard Way EX23.... 104 D7
Pickering Villas TR4.. 69 A3
Picketts Yd PL14..... 144 D7
Pick Pie Dr PL6...... 125 E8
PIECE............... 139 D2
Pier La PL10......... 133 A1
Pier St PL1.......... 148 B1
Pigmeadow La PL14... 113 C6
Pike Rd PL3......... 129 D5
Pikes Hill PL23...... 116 C4
Pike's Hill TR11...... 145 B3
Pike St PL14......... 113 C6
Pilchard Works The★
TR18................ 143 C3
Pilgrim Cl PL2....... 128 B6
Pilgrim Ct [11] PL20.. 41 B1
Pilgrim Dr PL20...... 41 B1
Pilgrim Prim Sch PL1. 148 B3
Pilgrims Way PL27.... 78 C1
Pillars Cl TR8....... 56 F5
Pillars Rd
Flushing TR11....... 145 B8
Mylor Bridge TR11... 82 A2
Pillar Wlk PL6....... 124 E7
PILLATON........... 53 B6
PILLATONMILL....... 53 B6
Pill La PL12......... 122 E4
Pillmere Dr PL12..... 122 D4
Pilot Cotts PL28..... 21 B4
Pinch Hill
Bude EX23.......... 104 F2
Marhamchurch EX23.. 7 B7
Pinder Ct PL19...... 147 B5
Pine Cl TR13........ 146 D5
Pine Ct
Par PL24............ 115 F6
Perranarworthal TR3.. 81 D6
Pinehurst Cl PL31.... 109 E3
Pine Lodge Gdns★ PL25 115 D4
Pine Rd PL18........ 143 B4
Pine Trees on the Lizard★
TR12................ 99 F5
Pine View
Gunnislake PL18..... 41 A6
St Dennis PL26...... 46 D1
Pinewood Cl PL7..... 130 F6
Pinewood Dr PL6..... 125 E7
Pinewood Flats PL27.. 21 D5
Pinkhams Cotts PL12. 122 B6
Pink Moors TR16..... 68 D1
Pin La PL1.......... 149 A2
Pinnacle Quay PL4... 149 B2
Pinsla Garden & Nursery★
PL30................ 35 E1
Pinslow Cross PL15... 19 C8
Pintail Ave PL27..... 77 E3
Pipers Cl PL15...... 18 E2
PIPERS POOL........ 17 F3
Piper St PL6........ 125 B5
Piran Cl PL18....... 40 D6
Piran Hts EX23...... 104 C2
Pitick Terr TR11..... 145 B6
Pitland Cnr PL19.... 30 D4
Pit Mdw TR11....... 144 E3
Pits La PL10........ 64 B2
Pitts Cleave Ind Est PL19. 30 D4
PITYME............. 21 F3
Pityme TR12........ 21 F3
Pityme Bsns Ctr PL27. 21 F3
Pityme Farm Rd PL27. 21 F3
Pityme Ind Est PL27.. 21 F3
Pixie's Hall★ TR11... 92 E4
Pixon La PL19....... 147 B4
Pixon Trad Ctr [2] PL19. 147 B4
Place de Brest PL1... 148 C3
Place Parc TR7...... 111 D7
Place Rd PL23....... 116 C4
Place Stables PL23... 116 C4
Place View PL23..... 116 C4
Place View Rd [15] TR2. 95 A6
PLAIDY............. 117 E5
Plaidy La
Looe PL13.......... 117 E4
PL13............... 117 E4
Plaidy Park Rd PL13.. 117 E4
PLAIN-AN-GWARRY.... 140 B6
Plain-an-Gwarry TR15. 140 B5
Plaistow Cl PL5..... 123 E2
Plaistow Cres PL5... 123 E2
Plaistow Hill Inf Sch PL5 123 E2
Planet Pk PL33...... 14 D2
Plantation La TR27.. 142 B5
Plantings Sch The PL3. 128 E6
Platt The PL27...... 108 C5
PLAYING PLACE...... 82 B8
Pleasant Pl [16] TR13. 143 C7
Pleasure Hill Cl PL9.. 135 D8
Plestin Cl PL15..... 106 C7
Pleyber Christ Way PL22 112 C2
Pleydon Cl PL13..... 62 E2
Plintona View PL7... 130 E7
Plougastel Dr PL12.. 122 E3
Plough Ct TR10..... 81 C2
Plough Gn PL12..... 122 C3

Plumer Rd PL6...... 124 F2
PLUSHABRIDGE....... 38 F7
Plymbridge Gdns PL7. 130 C7
Plymbridge La PL6... 125 B4
Plymbridge Rd
Plymouth, Eggbuckland
PL6................ 125 C1
Plymouth, Estover PL6. 125 C1
Plymouth, Mainstone PL6 125 F2
Plymouth, Plympton PL7. 130 C7
Plym Cres PL19...... 147 D5
PLYMOUTH.......... 148 B2
Plymouth Arts Ctr★ PL4 149 A2
Plymouth Athenaeum &
Theatre★ PL1....... 148 B2
Plymouth Business Sch
PL4................ 149 A3
Plymouth City Mkt PL1. 148 B3
Plymouth City Mus & Art
Gal★ PL4.......... 149 A3
Plymouth Coll PL4... 128 E4
Plymouth Coll Inf Sch [1]
PL3................ 128 F5
Plymouth Coll of Art &
Design PL4......... 149 A3
Plymouth Coll of Art &
Design (Sutton Annexe)
PL4................ 149 A3
Plymouth Coll Prep Sch
PL1................ 148 A3
Plymouth Discovery Ctr★
PL3................ 129 F6
Plymouth Eggbuckland Com
Coll PL6........... 129 A8
Plymouth Eggbuckland Vale
Prim Sch PL6....... 129 A8
Plymouth Girls High Sch
PL4................ 149 A4
Plymouth Keyham Barton RC
Prim Sch PL2....... 127 E6
Plymouth Knowle Prim Sch
PL5................ 123 D1
Plymouth Medical & Tech Pk
PL6................ 125 A3
Plymouth Pavilions PL1. 148 B2
Plymouth Rd
Liskeard PL14....... 113 D5
Plymouth PL7........ 130 B6
Tavistock PL19...... 147 B4
Plymouth Road Ind Est
PL19............... 147 C3
Plymouth St Andrew's CE
Prim Sch PL1....... 148 B2
Plymouth St Joseph's RC
Prim Sch PL1....... 127 E2
Plymouth St Paul's RC Prim
Sch PL5............ 123 D1
Plymouth St Peters CE Prim
Sch PL1............ 148 B3
Plymouth Sch of Creative
Arts PL1........... 148 A2
Plymouth Ski & Snowboard
Ctr★ PL6.......... 129 E7
Plymouth Sta PL4.... 148 C4
Plymouth Thornbury Prim
Sch PL6............ 125 D4
Plymouth Trade Pk PL4. 149 C1
Plymouth Whitleigh Prim
Sch PL5............ 124 D4
PLYMPTON.......... 130 E5
Plympton Hill PL7... 130 F3
Plympton St Mary CE Inf Sch
PL7................ 130 D5
PLYMPTON ST
MAURICE........... 130 E4
Plympton St Maurice Prim
Sch PL7............ 130 F3
Plym St PL4......... 149 A3
PLYMSTOCK......... 135 E6
Plymstock Rd PL9.... 135 F8
Plymstock Sch PL9... 135 F8
Plymstock Sp Ctr PL9. 135 F8
Plymtree Dr PL7..... 130 C7
Plym Valley Rly★ PL7. 130 A7
Poad's Trust PL14... 51 F5
Pochin Ho PL25..... 114 F7
Pocklington Rise PL7. 130 E5
Pocohontas Cres [4] TR9. 45 E1
Pode Dr PL7........ 131 B4
POINT.............. 82 B5
Point Neptune PL23.. 116 B3
Point Rd TR3....... 82 A6
Polapit Tamar PL15.. 19 A8
POLBATHIC......... 64 F8
Polbathic Rd TR15... 140 C6
POLBORDER......... 53 D7
Poldark Gdns [7] PL24. 60 B4
Poldark Mine★ TR13.. 92 A6
Poldark Rd [12] TR16. 67 E4
Poldhu Cl TR26..... 141 D1
Poldhu Rd
Liskeard PL14....... 113 C6
Mullion TR12....... 99 A2
Poldice La TR16..... 68 E1
Poldice Terr TR16... 68 E1
Poldrea PL24....... 60 D5
Poldrissick Hill PL12. 53 C2
Poldrissick La PL12.. 53 C2
Poldue Cl TR15..... 140 D6
Polean La PL13..... 117 B4
Polean Trad Est PL13. 117 B4
Polecoverack La TR12. 101 C1
Polgarth
[1] Camborne TR15... 139 C6
Newlyn TR18....... 143 B3

Polgarth Cl TR26......141 D1
Polgaver Ho PL25......115 E3
POLGIGGA..........96 D4
Polgine Cl TR14......79 E5
Polgine La TR14......79 E5
Polglase Wlk TR4......70 D8
Polglaze Cl TR18......143 D7
Polglist PL26........58 D5
Polgoon Cl TR18......143 C5
POLGOOTH..........59 A1
Polgooth Cl TR15....140 D6
Polgover Way **5** PL24...60 B4
Polgrain Rd TR14....138 F6
Polgrean Pl PL24.....60 B5
Polhigey Terr TR16....80 C2
Polhorman La TR12....99 A2
Police Ho TR11.......145 B4
Polisken Way TR4.....56 D1
POLKERRIS...........60 E3
Polkerris Pk PL24....60 C4
Polkerris Rd TR16....80 F8
Polkirt Hill
  Gorran Haven PL26...73 B1
  Mevagissey PL26.....73 C3
Polkirt Hts PL26.....73 C3
Polkyth L Ctr PL25...114 E4
Polkyth Par PL25.....114 E4
Polkyth Rd PL25......114 F4
POLLADRAS..........90 F5
Pollard Cl
  Plymouth PL9.......135 B5
  Saltash PL12.......122 B2
Pollard Rd **7** PL17....39 F4
Pollards Cl
  Goonhavern TR4.....55 D4
  Pensilva PL14.......38 E4
Pollards Way PL12....122 E3
Polmark Dr PL28......20 D2
Polmarth Cl PL25.....114 F6
POLMASSICK.........72 E4
Polmassick Vineyard★
  PL26..............72 E4
POLMEAR............60 E4
Polmear Ct **9** PL27...108 B5
Polmear Hill PL24....60 E4
Polmear Parc PL24....60 D4
Polmear Rd
  St Austell PL25....114 F3
  Tywardreath PL24....60 D4
Polmeere Ho TR18....143 E7
Polmeere Rd TR18....143 E7
Polmena La PL22......112 E1
Polmennor Dr TR26...141 D1
Polmennor Rd
  Falmouth TR11.......144 F1
  Heamoor TR18.......143 C8
Polmenor Downs N TR14,
  TR27..............78 F5
Polmenor Downs S TR14.78 F4
Polmeor Cl TR26......141 D1
Polmewan Flats PL26...59 A1
POLMORLA...........108 A4
Polmorla Mews **10** PL27.108 B5
Polmorla Rd PL27....108 B5
Polmorla Wlk PL27...108 C5
Polmor Rd TR20......89 B8
Polpennic Dr PL28....107 C4
POLPEOR...........77 B3
Polpeor Row TR27....77 A3
POLPERRO..........62 E1
Polperro Heritage Mus of
  Smuggling & Fishing★
  PL13..............62 E2
Polperro Model Village★
  PL13..............62 D1
Polperro Pl PL2.....128 D8
Polperro Prim Sch PL13.62 E2
Polperro Rd PL13....117 B4
Polpey La PL24......60 D5
POLRUAN...........116 C2
Polruan Cl TR26......77 C4
Polruan Ct TR1.......137 E2
Polruan Prim Sch PL23.116 D2
Polruan Rd
  Redruth TR15.......140 D6
  Truro TR1..........137 E2
Polruan Terr PL1.....148 A3
POLSCOE...........112 E3
Polscoe Rd PL22.....112 F3
Polsethow TR10......144 B7
Polstain Cres TR3....69 D3
Polstain Rd TR3......69 D3
Polstain Villas TR3...69 D3
Polsue Way TR2......70 F5
Poltair Ave PL25....114 E4
Poltair Cl TR3.......143 C7
Poltair Cres PL25....114 D4
Poltair Ct PL25......114 E4
Poltair Dr TR10......144 B7
Poltair Rd
  Penryn TR10........144 B7
  St Austell PL25....114 D4
Poltair School PL25..114 D4
Poltair Terr **7** TR18..143 C7
Poltamar PL15.......106 D5
POLTESCO..........103 B5
Poltesco La TR12.....103 B5
Poltisco Cl TR1......137 E3
Poltisco Wharf TR1...137 E4
Poltisko Rd TR10.....144 B7
Poltisko Terr TR10...144 B7
Poltreen Cl TR26....141 D1
Polurrian Rd TR12....99 A1
Polvarth Est TR2.....95 B6
Polvarth Rd TR2......95 A6
Polvean Cross PL14...51 A1
Polvean Terr PL14....51 A1
Polvella Cl TR7......110 B5

Polvellan Manor PL13..117 C4
Polvellan Terr PL13...117 C4
Polvelyn Parc TR27...142 E7
Polventon Cl
  Falmouth TR11......144 E4
  Heamoor TR18.......143 C7
Polventon Parc **6** TR12.101 C4
Polvillion Rd PL23...116 B4
Polweath Ct TR18.....143 E7
Polweath Rd TR18....143 E7
Polwhaveral Terr **6**
  TR11..............145 A5
Polwheal Rd TR14....138 F6
Polwhele Rd
  Newquay TR7.......111 A3
  Truro TR1..........137 F6
Polwithen Ct TR26....141 C1
Polwithen Dr TR26....141 C1
Polwithen Gdns TR26..141 C1
Polwithen Rd
  Falmouth TR11......145 A4
  Penryn TR10........144 B7
  Penzance TR18......143 D5
Polwrath Terr PL14....38 A4
Polwyn Cl TR18......143 B7
Poly Arts & Science
  TR11..............145 B4
Polyear Ct TR18......59 A1
Polyne Cotts PL13....62 F3
POLYPHANT.........17 F1
Polzeath Ct PL27.....21 D6
Polzeath Gdns PL2...128 D8
POMPHLETT.........135 E8
Pomphlett Cl PL9....135 D8
Pomphlett Farm Ind Est
  PL9...............129 E1
Pomphlett Gdns PL9...135 D8
Pomphlett Prim Sch PL9 135 E8
Pomphlett Rd PL9....135 E8
Ponchin Dr
  St Austell PL25....114 E7
Pondbridge Hill **1** PL14.113 C5
Pondfield Rd PL12....122 B3
Pondhu Cres PL25....114 B3
Pondhu Prim Sch PL25.114 B2
Pondhu Rd PL25......114 C3
Pond La TR15........140 A6
Pond Lanes End PL15.140 B6
Ponds Hill TR19......75 B1
Pond View Terr PL26...58 D5
Pond Wlk TR27.......142 D7
PONIOU............76 A5
Poniou La TR20......88 F6
Poniou Rd TR20......88 F6
Poniou Way TR20.....88 F6
Ponsandane Farm Mews
  TR18..............143 F7
PONSANOOTH........81 B5
Ponsharden TR11.....144 E7
Ponsharden Cotts TR11.144 F6
Ponsharden Ind Est
  TR11..............144 E6
Ponsmere Ct **9** TR6....55 A5
Ponsmere Rd TR6.....55 A5
Ponsonby Rd PL3....128 B4
PONSONGATH........103 C3
Ponstantual Hill TR12.99 D7
Ponsvale TR3........81 B4
PONT.............61 D3
Pontsmill Rd PL24....60 C6
POOL.............139 B4
Pool Bsns & Enterprise Coll
  TR15..............139 B4
Pool Bsns Pk TR15...139 B4
Poole Park Rd PL5...127 C8
Pool Hall PL14.......51 F5
Pool Ind Est TR15...139 C5
Pool's Ct TR27......142 E4
Pool St PL31........109 E5
Poplar Cl PL7.......131 B5
Poplars Ct **16** TR6....55 A5
Poplar Terr TR11.....145 B7
Popplestone Pk PL8..136 F5
Porcupine Rd PL24....60 C6
Pordenack Cl TR26...141 E2
Porfell Wildlife Park &
  Sanctuary★ PL14....50 A2
Porhan Gn TR11......144 E6
PORKELLIS.........92 B8
Pork St TR12........100 D4
Porsham Cl PL6......121 B1
Porsham La PL5......124 B8
Porspoder Pl PL10...133 A2
Portbigham PL13.....117 C3
Portbyhan Rd PL13...117 C3
PORTEATH..........22 A6
Porteath Bee Ctr★ PL27.22 A6
Porteous Cl PL1......127 F3
Porter Way PL12.....122 C3
PORT GAVERNE......22 E7
PORTH............111 C8
PORTHALLOW
  Looe..............62 F2
  St Keverne........101 D6
Porth Bean Ct TR7...111 B8
Porth Bean Rd TR7...111 C7
Porthcollum La TR27...78 A1
PORTHCOTHAN.......31 C6
PORTHCURNO........96 E3
Porthcurno Telegraph Mus★
  TR19..............96 E3
Portheast Cl PL26....85 C5
Portheast Way PL26...85 C5
Portherras Cross TR19.75 A1

Portherras Terr **11** TR19.75 A1
Portherras Villas **10** TR19.75 A1
Porthgwidden TR3.....82 C4
Porthgwidden Studios
  TR26..............141 C6
Porthia Cl TR26.....141 A4
Porthia Cres TR26...141 A4
Porthia Rd **12** TR26...77 A6
PORTHILLY.........21 D2
Porthilly Cvn Site PL27.21 D2
Porthilly La PL27....21 D2
Porthilly View PL28..107 E4
PORTH KEA.........70 B1
Porthkerris Divers★
  TR12..............101 E5
PORTHLEVEN........98 B8
Porthleven Cty Prim Sch
  TR13..............91 B1
Porthleven Rd TR13..146 A5
Porthmellon Gdns PL17.39 F4
PORTHMEOR.........75 F4
Porthmeor Ct **51** TR26.141 B6
Porthmeor Hill TR26.141 A6
Porthmeor Rd
  St Austell PL25....115 B3
  6 St Ives TR26...141 B6
Porthmeor Sq **21** TR26.141 B6
Porthmeor Studios **50**
  TR26..............141 B6
Porthminster Terr **23**
  TR26..............141 B5
PORTH NAVAS.......93 B2
PORTHOUSTOCK......101 E4
Porth Par TR7.......111 C8
Porthpean Beach Rd PL26 59 E1
Porthpean Rd PL24, PL26.114 F2
Porthrepta Rd TR26..141 C1
Porth Sawle Flats TR2..83 B2
PORTHTOWAN.......68 A6
Porth View TR2......95 B6
Porth Way TR7......111 B7
PORTINGTON........29 E3
PORT ISAAC.........21 D2
Port Isaac Prim Sch PL29 22 E7
Port La PL15........27 B2
Portland Cl PL14....113 D7
Portland Ct **9** PL1...127 F3
Portland Gdns TR11..144 F4
Portland Pl **23** TR19..88 C1
Portland Rd PL1......127 F3
Portland Sq PL4.....148 C4
Portland Square Lane N
  PL4...............149 A4
Portland Terr PL14...113 C7
Portland Villas PL4..148 C4
PORTLOE...........84 B3
PORTLOOE..........117 A2
PORTMELLON.......73 C3
Portmellon Pk PL26...73 C3
PORT QUIN.........22 B7
PORTREATH.........67 C6
Portreath Com Prim Sch
  TR16..............67 D6
PORTSCATHO........83 B2
Portuan Rd PL13.....117 D1
Portway PL9.........136 D7
PORTWRINKLE.......65 B4
Posses La TR18......88 E6
Possession La PL12...53 C3
Post Box Row TR14...139 B3
Potters La PL35......9 C1
Potters Mews TR4....55 D4
Potters Way PL7.....130 D5
Pottery Est PL10....132 E6
Pottery Rd PL1......127 D3
POUGHILL..........4 D2
Poughill Rd EX23....104 F7
Poultney Cl PL7.....131 A5
Pounda PL14.........51 B4
Pound Dean PL14.....113 A5
Poundfield Cl **2** EX23..4 D1
Poundfield Hill **1** EX23..4 D1
Poundfield La EX23....4 D1
Pound Hill PL12......53 C3
Pound La
  Bodmin PL31.......109 E5
  Stoke Climsland PL17..28 E1
  Threemilestone TR3...69 E1
Pound Pk PL14.......51 F5
Pound Rd PL20.......42 B3
Pound's Cross PL6...120 E5
Pounds Park Rd
  1 Bere Alston PL20...41 B1
  Plymouth PL3.......128 D7
Pounds Pk PL12......122 F3
Pound St
  Liskeard PL14......113 C6
  Plymouth PL1......134 A8
POUNDSTOCK........6 E2
Poundstock Cl PL30...35 F3
Powderham Rd PL3...128 F7
Powis Gdns PL5......124 B2
Powisland Dr PL6....125 A5
PRAA SANDS........90 C3
Praed Pl TR26.......77 E4
Praed's La TR17......89 C5
Pras Coth TR16......68 C3
PRAZE-AN-BEEBLE....79 C2
Praze-an-Creet TR26...77 A7
Praze-an-Cronor TR9...45 E5
Praze Bsns Pk TR14...79 B2
Prazegooth La TR12..103 A4
Praze Mdw TR10.....144 C8
Praze Rd
  Leedstown TR27.....78 E5
  Newquay TR7.......111 B7
  Porthleven TR13....91 B1
  Praze-an-Beeble TR14.79 A2

Praze The TR10......144 C8
Predannack Airfield★
  TR12..............102 D6
Predannack Rd **4** TR12..99 A1
Preeze Cross PL30....35 E6
Prestonbury Cl PL6...125 B7
Prevenna Rd **2** TR19..88 C1
Prideaux Cl PL12....122 C5
Prideaux Place★ PL28.107 C6
Prideaux Rd PL24.....60 B6
Pridham La PL2......128 C2
Pridmouth Rd PL24...60 B6
Priestacott Pk **5** EX23..5 A6
Priesthood Terr PL10.132 E5
Priestley Ave PL5...123 E2
Primitive Row TR14..139 A5
Primrose Cl
  Camborne TR14.....138 B4
  9 Goldsithney TR20..89 E5
  Roche PL26.........47 A3
  Torpoint PL11......126 E4
Primrose Cotts TR2...71 C6
Primrose Ct TR26....141 B4
Primrose Dr PL28.....31 F7
Primrose Gdns
  Illogan TR16.......67 D4
  Tavistock PL19.....147 E4
Primrose Hill TR20...89 E5
Primrose La **4** TR20...89 E5
Primrose Rd EX23....104 F5
Primrose Terr
  Newlyn TR18.......143 D1
  Portreath TR16.....67 D6
  Tresillian TR2......70 F5
Primrose Valley TR26.141 C4
Primrose Way PL15....27 A6
Primrose Wlk PL12...122 C3
Prince Charles Cl PL15.106 C7
Prince Charles Ho PL25.114 E5
Prince Charles Pk PL25.114 E5
Prince Charles Rd PL25.114 E5
Prince Maurice Ct PL4.149 B3
Prince Maurice Rd PL4.128 F4
Prince of Wales Quarry
  Trail★ PL34.........14 E5
Prince Philip Rd PL15.106 C7
PRINCE ROCK.......129 B3
Prince Rock Prim Sch
  PL4...............129 B2
Princes Rd PL6......125 E6
Princes Row PL14.....38 B6
Princess Ave
  Plymouth, Plymstock PL9.135 E6
  Plymouth, West Park PL5.124 A3
Princess Cres PL9....135 E6
Princess Ct **12** TR18..143 E5
Princess Parc TR9....45 E1
Princess Rd PL14.....38 E4
Princess St PL1......148 C2
Princess Street Ope PL1.148 C2
Princes St
  Bude EX23.........104 D6
  Looe PL13.........117 C3
  Penzance TR18......143 E5
  Plymouth PL1......127 E2
Prince's St TR1......137 D4
Princess Terr **7** TR18..38 E4
Princess Villas PL17...28 B1
Princess Way PL1....148 C2
Prior's Barn PL31...109 F4
Priors Cl **10** TR26....77 A6
Priors Row TR13......90 E3
Priory Cl
  Par PL24...........60 C5
  Tavistock PL19.....147 D3
Priory Cotts PL15...106 B6
Priory Dr PL7.......130 D5
Priory Gdns PL19....147 D3
Priory La PL15......106 B7
Priory Lawn Terr PL3.129 A6
Priory Mews PL15....106 B7
Priory Mill PL7......130 D5
Priory Park Rd PL15.106 B6
Priory Rd
  Bodmin PL31.......109 F4
  Plymouth PL3.......129 A6
  St Austell PL25....114 C4
  St Columb Minor TR7, TR8.111 E7
Priory Ridge PL7....130 D5
Prislow Cl TR11.....144 E2
Prislow Fields TR11..144 E2
Prislow La TR11.....144 E2
PROBUS...........71 C6
Probus Com Prim Sch
  TR2...............71 C6
Prospect Bldgs TR7..110 E6
Prospect Cl TR27....142 D6
Prospect Gdns TR1...137 E6
Prospect La PL12....122 C3
Prospect Pl
  Ashton TR13........90 E3
  3 Falmouth TR11..145 B5
  Hayle TR27.........142 D6
  Helston TR13.......146 C5
  Mevagissey PL26....73 C4
  25 Penzance TR18..143 E6
  Plymouth PL1......148 B2
  8 Porthleven TR13..98 B8
  5 Truro TR1.......137 D5
Prospect Row PL1....127 E1
Prospect St PL4.....149 A3
Prospect Terr
  Bodmin PL31.......109 E4
  Gunnislake PL18....41 A4
  Gunnislake, St Ann's Chapel
  PL18..............40 E5

Prospect Wlk PL12...122 C3
Prosper Cl PL26......47 A2
Prosper Hill TR27....66 B1
Prosper Rd PL26.....47 A2
Prouse Cres PL2.....128 C8
Prouse Rise PL12....122 E2
Prouts Ct **4** PL15...106 C6
Prouts Mews **5** PL15.106 C6
Prouts Way PL12.....18 C2
Providence Pl
  Calstock PL18......41 A3
  Plymouth PL1......128 A3
Providence St PL4...149 A4
Provis Rd PL18......143 C4
Prynne Cl PL1.......148 B3
Puckator La PL14.....38 A2
Puffin Close EX23...104 F5
Puggis Hill TR14....138 A5
Pulla Cross TR4.....81 B6
Putnam Cl PL14......113 D5
Pydar Cl TR7........111 B5
Pydar Mews **8** TR1...137 C4
Pydar St TR1........137 C5
Pym St
  Plymouth PL1......127 F3
  Tavistock PL19.....147 C6
Pyramid Cl PL25......58 F4
PYWORTHY..........8 E5
Pyworthy CE Prim Sch
  EX22..............8 E5
PZ Gall★ TR18......143 F4

Q

Quakers Rd TR4, TR3..81 B6
Quant Pk PL19......147 C6
Quarry Cl EX23.....104 E7
Quarry Cnr PL20.....41 C2
Quarry Cotts
  Plymouth, Honicknowle
  PL5...............124 B2
  Plymouth PL1......148 A3
Quarry Cres PL15...106 A3
Quarry Ct TR11.....145 B4
Quarry Gdns TR18...143 D5
Quarry Hill
  Falmouth TR11.....145 B4
  Gulval TR18........88 E7
Quarry House Flats TR1.137 E3
Quarry La
  Gunnislake PL18....40 F6
  Landrake PL12......53 D3
  Launceston PL15....18 E2
  Sheffield TR19......97 F7
  St Germans PL12....65 A8
Quarrymans Cotts PL7.33 B7
Quarry Park Ave PL9.135 D7
Quarry Park Rd
  Newquay TR7.......110 F5
  Plymouth, Peverell PL3.128 D5
  Plymouth, Plymstock PL9.135 D7
Quarry Park Terr PL31.109 C4
Quarry Rd
  Pensilva PL14......38 E4
  Perranporth TR6....55 B4
Quarry St
  St Germans PL12....65 A8
  Torpoint PL11......127 C3
Quarterdeck The PL1.134 A8
Quay Hill
  Falmouth TR11.....145 C4
  Penryn TR10........144 D7
Quay La PL12........53 D1
Quay Mews **8** TR1...137 D4
Quay Rd
  Crumplehorn PL13...62 D1
  Devoran TR3........81 F6
  Landrake PL12......53 A2
  Looe PL13.........117 C3
  Mylor Bridge TR11...82 B4
  Plymouth PL1......149 A2
  St Agnes TR5.......54 C2
  St Austell PL25....115 B2
  St Germans PL12....65 B8
  Tideford PL12......52 F2
Quayside **6** PL19....147 B5
Quay St
  Falmouth TR11.....145 C4
  Looe PL13.........117 C3
  Lostwithiel PL22...112 C2
  11 Mousehole TR19..88 C1
  Penzance TR18......143 E4
  St Ives TR26.......141 C6
  20 Truro TR1......137 D4
Quay The
  Pentewan PL26......73 C6
  Penzance TR18......143 F5
  Plymouth PL9.......135 C7
  Polruan PL23.......116 D3
  Portscatho TR2.....83 B2
  St Germans PL12....65 B8
  St Mawes TR2.......95 A6
Queen Anne Gdns TR11.144 E3
Queen Anne's Quay PL4.149 B2
Queen Elizabeth Rd
  PL15..............106 C7
Queen Mary Ct TR11..145 B2
Queen Mary Rd TR11.145 B2
Queens Cl
  5 Indian Queens TR9..45 E1
  Plymouth PL6......125 E6
  St Austell PL26.....46 F3
Queen's Cres PL31...109 B3

Queen's Ct 6 TR18 . . . . . 143 E4
Queen's Gate
  Plymouth, Lipson PL4 . . . . 149 B4
  Plymouth, Stoke PL3 . . . . 148 A4
Queen's Gate Mews PL4. 149 B4
Queen's Gate Villas PL4. 149 B4
Queen's Gate Villas Rd
  PL4 . . . . . 149 B4
Queens Pk PL27 . . . . . 108 C4
Queens Rd
  Plymouth PL5 . . . . . 123 F3
  St Austell PL25 . . . . . 114 E3
Queen's Rd PL4 . . . . . 149 B4
Queen's Sq 24 TR18 . . . . 143 E5
Queen St
  Bude EX23 . . . . . 104 D6
  Goldsithney TR20 . . . . . 89 E5
  Lostwithiel PL22 . . . . . 112 C2
  Penzance TR18 . . . . . 143 E5
  Plymouth PL1 . . . . . 127 D2
  St Just TR19 . . . . . 86 E6
Queen's Way
  2 Goldsithney TR20 . . . . . 89 E5
  Hayle TR27 . . . . . 142 C5
Queen Terr PL17 . . . . . 40 C4
Quenchwell Rd TR3 . . . . . 81 F7
QUETHIOCK 52 C7
Quethiock Prim Sch PL14 52 C7
Quillet Rd TR18 . . . . . 143 B3
Quilver Cl PL6 . . . . . 85 D5
Quimperle Way PL14 . . . . 113 E6
Quintrell Cl TR8 . . . . . 44 E3
QUINTRELL DOWNS 44 E3
Quintrell Downs Sta TR8 111 F3
Quintrell Gdns TR8 . . . . . 44 E3
Quintrell Rd TR7, TR8 . . . . 111 E5
QUITHER 30 A8
QUOIT 45 F4

R

Rabys Row TR16 . . . . . 140 F8
Race Hill
  Launceston PL15 . . . . . 106 C5
  Truro TR4 . . . . . 81 C8
Race Hill Terr PL15 . . . . . 106 C5
Rachel's Way 17 TR9 . . . . 45 E6
Radcliffe Cl PL6 . . . . . 124 E6
Radford Ave PL4 . . . . . 129 B1
Radford La PL10 . . . . . 132 D4
Radford Park Dr PL9 . . . . 135 D6
Radford Park Rd PL9 . . . . 135 D6
Radford Rd PL1 . . . . . 148 B1
Radford View PL9 . . . . . 135 D6
Radiant Ho PL1 . . . . . 148 B2
Radland Cross PL12 . . . . . 40 C3
Radnor Cl PL31 . . . . . 109 F4
Radnor Hall PL4 . . . . . 149 A3
Radnor Pl PL4 . . . . . 149 A3
Radnor Rd
  Redruth, North Country
   TR16 . . . . . 140 C8
  Redruth, Scorrier TR16 . . . . 68 D3
Radnor St PL4 . . . . . 149 A3
Raginnis Hill 25 TR19 . . . . 88 C1
Raglan Ct PL1 . . . . . 127 F2
Raglan Gdns PL1 . . . . . 127 F2
Raglan Rd PL1 . . . . . 127 F2
Rail Way PL15 . . . . . 17 F5
Railway Cotts
  Camborne TR14 . . . . . 139 A3
  Falmouth TR11 . . . . . 145 D3
  6 Plymouth, Ford PL2 . . . . 127 F5
  Plymouth, Plymstock PL9 .135 D7
  Tavistock PL19 . . . . . 147 B6
Railway Cres PL14 . . . . . 38 A4
Railway Terr
  Bodmin PL31 . . . . . 109 D5
  Carharrack TR16 . . . . . 80 F8
Railway Villas TR15 . . . . . 139 F6
Rainham Cl TR15 . . . . . 139 C8
Rainyfields PL28 . . . . . 107 D5
Rainy Fields Cl PL28 . . . . . 107 D5
Raleigh Cl PL28 . . . . . 107 C4
Raleigh Ct PL7 . . . . . 131 B6
Raleigh Pl 13 TR11 . . . . . 145 A4
Raleigh Rd PL28 . . . . . 107 C5
Raleigh St PL1 . . . . . 148 B3
Ralph's Ct PL19 . . . . . 147 B5
Ramage Cl PL6 . . . . . 125 F3
RAME
  Cawsand 64 B2
  Stithians 92 E8
Rame Croft TR10 . . . . . 80 E1
Ramehead Cotts PL10 . . . . 64 B1
Ramehead La PL10 . . . . . 64 B1
Rame La
  Cawsand PL10 . . . . . 132 F1
  Rame PL10 . . . . . 64 B2
Rame Terr TR10 . . . . . 80 E1
Rame View PL13 . . . . . 117 E5
Ramillies Ave PL5 . . . . . 124 A4
Ramoth Way TR6 . . . . . 55 B5
Ramsey Gdns PL5 . . . . . 124 D1
Ranch View PL15 . . . . . 106 A5
Randwick Park Rd PL9 .135 D7
Ranelagh Ct TR7 . . . . . 111 C7
Ranelagh Mews PL31 . . . . 109 D5
Ranelagh Rd PL25 . . . . . 114 F4
Ranneys Cl PL13 . . . . . 117 D6
Ransum Way PL4 . . . . . 149 B4
Raphael Cl PL9 . . . . . 136 B5
Raphael Dr PL9 . . . . . 136 A6
Raphael Rd PL13 . . . . . 62 C1

Rapson Rd PL14 . . . . . 113 D6
Rashleigh Ave
  Plymouth PL7 . . . . . 130 F7
  Saltash PL12 . . . . . 122 D1
Rashleigh Ct PL25 . . . . . 115 C3
Rashleigh La PL23 . . . . . 116 A4
Rashleigh Mews PL25 . . . . 115 A3
Rashleigh Pl PL25 . . . . . 114 F4
Rashleigh Road 6 PL26. 115 A1
Rashleigh Vale TR1 . . . . . 137 E4
Ratcliffes PL7 . . . . . 146 A5
Rattle St PL26 . . . . . 85 D5
Rawley Ct PL7 . . . . . 110 E5
Rawley La PL7 . . . . . 110 E5
Rawlin Cl PL6 . . . . . 129 C8
Rawlings La PL23 . . . . . 116 D5
Raymond Rd TR15 . . . . . 140 C4
Raymond Way PL7 . . . . . 130 D6
Raynham Rd PL3 . . . . . 128 B4
Read Cl TR10 . . . . . 144 B7
Reading Wlk PL5 . . . . . 124 C4
READYMONEY 116 B3
Readymoney Rd PL23 . . . . 116 B3
REAWLA 78 E3
Reawla La TR27 . . . . . 78 E3
Rebecca Cl PL24 . . . . . 60 B6
Recreation Rd PL2 . . . . . 128 C7
Recreation Road Ind Est
  PL2 . . . . . 128 C7
Rectory Gdns
  Camborne TR14 . . . . . 138 C2
  Lanreath PL13 . . . . . 62 B8
  St Stephen PL26 . . . . . 58 B4
Rectory La PL30 . . . . . 34 D7
Rectory Rd
  Camborne TR14 . . . . . 138 C2
  Lanivet PL30 . . . . . 47 F6
  Plymouth PL1 . . . . . 128 A2
  St Buryan TR19 . . . . . 97 B6
  St Dennis PL26 . . . . . 46 B1
  St Stephen PL26 . . . . . 58 B4
Rectory The TR1 . . . . . 137 C5
Redannack 2 TR12 . . . . . 99 A2
Redannack N 1 TR12 . . . . 99 A2
Redannack Cres TR1 . . . . . 137 B3
Redannick La TR1 . . . . . 137 B4
Redbrooke Rd TR14 . . . . . 138 E2
Redbrooke Terr TR14 . . . . 138 E2
Reddicliff Cl PL9 . . . . . 135 E5
Reddicliff Rd PL9 . . . . . 135 D5
Reddington Rd PL3 . . . . . 129 B7
Redfern Ct 2 TR26 . . . . . 141 B5
Redhill Cl PL5 . . . . . 123 E4
Redinnick Gdns 4 TR18. 143 E4
Redinnick Pl TR18 . . . . . 143 D4
Redinnick Terr 1 TR18.. 143 E4
Red La
  Bugle PL26 . . . . . 47 C2
  Rosudgeon TR20 . . . . . 89 F5
REDMONSFORD 3 F2
Redmoor Cl TR14 . . . . . 138 C2
Redmoor Rd PL19 . . . . . 147 A7
Redmore Cl PL17 . . . . . 39 E6
RED POST 7 F8
Redruth Cl PL5 . . . . . 124 A5
Redruth Highway TR15.. 140 E7
Redruth Old Cornwall
  Society Mus★ TR16 . . . . . 67 F5
Redruth Rd TR13 . . . . . 146 D7
Redruth Sch TR15 . . . . . 140 A5
Redruth Sta TR15 . . . . . 140 C5
Redvale Rd PL30 . . . . . 23 E3
Redvers Gr PL7 . . . . . 130 E4
Redvers Hts TR15 . . . . . 140 B3
Redwing Dr PL6 . . . . . 125 D8
Redwood Cl EX23 . . . . . 104 E5
Redwood Dr PL7 . . . . . 131 B5
Redwood Gr EX23 . . . . . 104 E5
Reeds Pk PL22 . . . . . 112 D2
Reeds Way TR7 . . . . . 110 D5
Reen Hill TR6 . . . . . 55 B4
Reen La TR6 . . . . . 55 B5
Reens Cres TR18 . . . . . 143 D7
Reens Rd TR18 . . . . . 143 C7
Reeves Cl TR13 . . . . . 91 B1
Regal Ct PL12 . . . . . 122 F2
Regan Ct TR10 . . . . . 144 A7
Regency Ho PL25 . . . . . 115 E3
Regent Bldgs 36 TR18... 143 E5
Regent Ct PL4 . . . . . 149 A3
Regent Sq 21 TR18 . . . . . 143 E5
Regent St PL4 . . . . . 149 A3
Regent Terr
  Penzance TR18 . . . . . 143 E4
  St Just TR19 . . . . . 86 E6
Reigate Rd PL9 . . . . . 135 E8
REJERRAH 55 F7
RELEATH 91 E8
Relistian La TR27 . . . . . 78 E3
Relistian Pk TR27 . . . . . 78 E3
RELUBBUS 90 A7
Relubbus Hill TR20 . . . . . 90 A6
Relubbus La TR20 . . . . . 90 A6
Renaissance Gdns 2 PL2. 128 C2
Rendlesham Gdns PL6 . . 125 E3
Rendle St
  Delabole PL33 . . . . . 14 E3
  Plymouth PL1 . . . . . 148 B3
Renney Rd PL9 . . . . . 135 C1
Rennie Ave PL5 . . . . . 123 C1
Renoir Cl PL9 . . . . . 136 A6
Renown St PL2 . . . . . 127 E6
Reperry Cross PL30 . . . . . 47 F6
Reppersfield Row PL13.. 90 F3

RESCASSA 72 F1
RESCORLA 59 D8
Rescorla Ct TR27 . . . . . 142 C5
Research Way PL6 . . . . . 125 C4
Reservoir Cres PL9 . . . . . 136 B7
Reservoir La 1 PL3 . . . . . 128 F6
Reservoir Rd
  Plymouth, Hartley PL3 . . . . 128 F6
  Plymouth, Plymstock PL9 .136 B7
Reservoir Way PL9 . . . . . 136 B7
RESKADINNICK 138 B5
Reskadinnick Rd TR14... 138 B4
RESKIVERS 71 F3
Resolution Ho PL4 . . . . . 149 B3
Respryn Cl PL14 . . . . . 113 D6
Respryn Rd PL31 . . . . . 48 D8
RESTORMEL 112 C5
Restormel Ind Est PL22.. 112 D2
Restormel Castle★ PL22 112 C5
Restormel Rd
  Looe PL13 . . . . . 117 D4
  Lostwithiel PL22 . . . . . 112 C4
  Newlyn TR18 . . . . . 143 C3
  Plymouth PL4 . . . . . 148 C4
Restormel Terr
  Falmouth TR11 . . . . . 145 B3
  Plymouth PL4 . . . . . 148 C4
Restronguet Hill TR11... 82 B4
RESTRONGUET
  PASSAGE 82 A4
RESUGGA GREEN 59 D7
Resugga Green Residential
  Homes Pk PL26 . . . . . 59 D7
Reswythen Wlk 4 TR14. 138 F7
Retallack Gdns 3 TR20.. 89 E5
Retallick Mdws PL25 . . . . 115 B5
Retanning La PL26 . . . . . 58 E1
Retreat The
  8 Chacewater TR4 . . . . . 69 A3
  Plymouth PL3 . . . . . 129 B7
  St Columb Major TR9 . . . . 45 E6
Revell Park Rd PL7 . . . . . 130 D6
Revel Rd PL3 . . . . . 129 A6
Reynolds Gr PL5 . . . . . 127 C8
Reynolds Rd PL7 . . . . . 130 C6
REZARE 28 C4
Rheola Gdns PL6 . . . . . 125 D3
Rhind St PL31 . . . . . 109 E5
Rhodes Cl PL7 . . . . . 130 E7
Rhubarb Hill TR8 . . . . . 43 B1
Rialton Hts TR7 . . . . . 111 E7
Rialton Rd TR7, TR8 . . . . 111 E6
Ribble Gdns PL3 . . . . . 129 D7
Rice La PL26 . . . . . 85 C5
Richard Lander Sch TR3.. 69 D3
Richards Cres TR1 . . . . . 69 F3
Richards La TR16 . . . . . 67 E4
Richards Row PL3 . . . . . 128 F7
Richards Terr PL10 . . . . . 132 E5
Richmond Hill TR1 . . . . . 137 B4
Richmond Pl
  40 St Ives TR26 . . . . . 141 B6
  3 Truro TR1 . . . . . 137 B4
Richmond Rd
  Pelynt PL13 . . . . . 62 D6
  Plymouth PL6 . . . . . 125 A2
Richmond St
  Heamoor TR18 . . . . . 143 C7
  Penzance TR18 . . . . . 143 E6
Richmond Terr
  Buckland Monachorum
   PL20 . . . . . 41 F3
  Truro TR1 . . . . . 137 B4
Richmond Way TR26 . . . . 141 D1
Richmond Wlk PL1 . . . . . 127 F1
Ricketts Rd PL26 . . . . . 59 A1
Rick Mdw PL15 . . . . . 18 E6
Ride The PL7, PL9 . . . . . 129 D2
Ridge Cross PL9 . . . . . 136 A3
Ridgegrove Hill PL15 . . . . 106 D6
Ridgegrove La PL15 . . . . . 106 C7
Ridge Ho PL4 . . . . . 129 A4
Ridge Park Ave PL4 . . . . . 128 D4
Ridge Park Rd PL7 . . . . . 130 E5
Ridge Pk PL7 . . . . . 130 E5
Ridge Rd PL7 . . . . . 130 E3
Ridgevale Cl TR18 . . . . . 143 F8
Ridgevale La TR18 . . . . . 143 F8
Ridgeway
  28 Perranporth TR6 . . . . . 55 A5
  Plymouth, Plympton PL7 . 130 D5
  Plymouth, Plympton St Maurice
   PL7 . . . . . 130 F5
  Probus TR2 . . . . . 71 C6
  Saltash PL12 . . . . . 122 D1
Ridgeway Sch PL7 . . . . . 130 E5
Ridgeway Sp Ctr PL7 . . . . 130 E5
Ridgewell Terr TR9 . . . . . 57 E8
Ridgewood Cl PL26 . . . . . 114 F1
Riflemans Walk PL6 . . . . . 125 B7
Riga Terr PL3 . . . . . 129 C4
Rigdale Cl PL6 . . . . . 129 A7
RILLA MILL 38 E8
Ringmore Way PL5 . . . . . 124 B3
Ringway Flats 9 PL31... 109 D5
RINSEY 90 D2
Rinsey La TR13 . . . . . 90 D2
Risdon Ave PL4 . . . . . 129 B1
Rivendell PL27 . . . . . 108 C4
River Ct
  Saltash PL12 . . . . . 122 D5
  Tavistock PL19 . . . . . 147 D6
Riverford PL6 . . . . . 125 F5
Riverford Cl PL6 . . . . . 125 D7
River Pk 11 PL20 . . . . . 42 C4
Riversdale Pl 8 PL27 . . . . 108 B5
RIVERSIDE 123 A1

Riverside
  Angarrack TR27 . . . . . 78 C4
  3 Chacewater TR4 . . . . . 69 A3
  Lelant TR26 . . . . . 77 E4
  Padstow PL28 . . . . . 107 E5
Riverside Ave TR7 . . . . . 110 A5
Riverside Bsns Pk PL1 .. 127 E3
Riverside Cl 1 PL20 . . . . . 42 C4
Riverside Com Prim Sch
  PL5 . . . . . 127 C8
Riverside Cott PL12 . . . . . 122 C1
Riverside Cres TR7 . . . . . 110 A5
Riverside Ct PL22 . . . . . 112 C2
Riverside Ho TR1 . . . . . 137 D1
Riverside Mews
  Angarrack TR27 . . . . . 78 C5
  Saltash PL12 . . . . . 123 A3
Riverside Mills PL15 . . . . . 106 B7
Riverside Pl PL1 . . . . . 127 D2
Riverside View TR1 . . . . . 137 E3
Riverside Wlk PL5 . . . . . 124 B6
River St
  Mevagissey PL26 . . . . . 73 C3
  Portscatho TR2 . . . . . 83 B2
  Truro TR1 . . . . . 137 C4
Rivers The PL12 . . . . . 122 E1
Riverview TR11 . . . . . 145 A6
River View
  Flushing TR11 . . . . . 145 B7
  Gunnislake PL18 . . . . . 40 E5
  Lerryn PL22 . . . . . 61 C7
  Plymouth PL4 . . . . . 129 B1
  Saltash PL12 . . . . . 122 F3
  Tresillian TR2 . . . . . 70 E4
River View La PL4 . . . . . 129 B1
River Wlk PL25 . . . . . 114 B3
Riviera Apartments
  TR26 . . . . . 141 D2
Riviera Cl 8 TR12 . . . . . 99 A1
Riviera Est TR1 . . . . . 70 D1
Riviera La TR2 . . . . . 95 A6
RIVIERE TOWANS 142 B7
Riviere Towans TR27 . . . . 142 B7
Roach's Ct TR26 . . . . . 141 E1
Roach's Row TR15 . . . . . 140 B5
Robartes Ct 13 TR1 . . . . . 137 C4
Robartes Gardens Flats
  PL25 . . . . . 114 E4
Robartes Gdns PL25 . . . . 114 E4
Robartes Jun Sch PL31.. 109 D4
Robartes Pl PL25 . . . . . 114 E5
Robartes Rd
  Bodmin PL31 . . . . . 109 D4
  Newquay TR7 . . . . . 110 F5
  St Dennis PL26 . . . . . 58 C8
Robartes Terr
  3 Illogan TR16 . . . . . 67 E4
  Lostwithiel PL22 . . . . . 112 C3
Robert Adams Cl PL7.... 130 B5
Robert Eliot Ct PL25 . . . . 114 B3
Robert Hichens Rd TR11. 145 A5
Roberts Ave PL11 . . . . . 127 B3
Roberts Rd PL5 . . . . . 127 D8
Robin Dr PL15 . . . . . 106 E4
Robins Cl 13 PL24 . . . . . 60 B4
Robinsons Av TR15 . . . . . 139 B5
Robins Way PL9 . . . . . 135 E8
ROBOROUGH 121 D1
Roborough Ave PL6 . . . . . 125 B5
Roborough Cl PL6 . . . . . 125 B5
Roborough Down La PL6 121 F5
Roborough La PL5 . . . . . 124 D8
Robyns Cl PL7 . . . . . 131 B5
ROCHE 46 F3
Roche Com Prim Sch
  PL26 . . . . . 46 F2
Roche Rd
  Bugle PL26 . . . . . 47 C2
  Stenalees PL26 . . . . . 59 C7
Roche Rural Workshops
  PL26 . . . . . 47 A4
Roche Sta PL26 . . . . . 47 A4
Rochester Rd
  3 Plymouth PL4 . . . . . 128 E4
  7 Plymouth PL4 . . . . . 149 A4
Rochford Cres PL5 . . . . . 123 F5
ROCK 21 D2
Rock Cl 1 TR14 . . . . . 138 F2
Rock Close Ho TR27 . . . . 142 A1
Rockfield Ave PL6 . . . . . 124 F6
Rock Gdns PL9 . . . . . 129 D1
Rockhaven Gdns PL27... 21 F5
ROCKHEAD 14 E3
Rockhead St PL33 . . . . . 14 E3
Rock Hill PL5 . . . . . 124 C7
Rockingham Rd PL3 . . . . 129 A5
Rock La PL31 . . . . . 109 C4
Rock Rd
  Newlyn TR18 . . . . . 143 C3
  St Minver PL27 . . . . . 21 E2
Rock Terr
  Heamoor TR18 . . . . . 143 C7
  Plymouth PL7 . . . . . 130 D4
Rock Twrs PL13 . . . . . 117 D2
Rock View Parc PL26 . . . . 47 A3
Rock Villas PL27 . . . . . 21 D2
Rockville Pk PL9 . . . . . 135 E8
Rockwood Rd PL6 . . . . . 125 E7
Rocky Hill PL19 . . . . . 147 B5
Rocky La
  Praa Sands TR20 . . . . . 90 C6
  St Agnes TR5 . . . . . 54 C2
  Veryan TR2 . . . . . 83 D7
Rocky Park Ave PL9 . . . . . 135 E8
Rocky Park Rd PL9 . . . . . 135 E8
Rodda Cl PL18 . . . . . 41 A7
Rodda's Rd TR4 . . . . . 68 C6
Roddick Way 8 PL7 . . . . . 131 C5

Rodings The PL14 . . . . . 51 F5
Rodney St PL5 . . . . . 127 D8
Rodwell Cl TR15 . . . . . 140 D5
Rodwill Cl TR27 . . . . . 78 E1
Roebuck Villas TR11 . . . . 145 D3
Roekindale Cl TR15 . . . . . 139 D6
Roeselare Ave PL11 . . . . . 127 A3
Roeselare Cl PL11 . . . . . 127 A3
Rogate Dr PL6 . . . . . 125 D4
Rogate Wlk PL6 . . . . . 125 D4
Rogers Dr PL12 . . . . . 122 D4
Roland Bailey Gdns
  PL19 . . . . . 147 A6
Rollis Park Cl PL9 . . . . . 135 C8
Rollis Park Rd PL9 . . . . . 135 C8
Rolston Cl PL6 . . . . . 124 D6
Roma Cl TR7 . . . . . 111 C7
Roma Ct TR27 . . . . . 142 B5
Roman Bridge PL13 . . . . . 62 D1
Roman Dr PL31 . . . . . 109 F2
Roman Rd PL5 . . . . . 123 E2
Roman Way PL5 . . . . . 123 E2
Romilly Gdns PL7 . . . . . 130 B5
Romney Cl PL5 . . . . . 124 B1
Ronald Terr PL2 . . . . . 127 F5
Ronsdale Cl PL9 . . . . . 135 D8
Roope Cl PL5 . . . . . 127 C7
Ropehaven Cl PL25 . . . . . 114 E6
Ropehaven Rd PL25 . . . . 114 E6
Roper Ave PL9 . . . . . 135 D8
Ropewalk Ct 2 TR11.... 145 C3
Ropewalk Rd TR3 . . . . . 137 C1
Ropewalk The TR18 . . . . . 143 C4
Rope Wlk
  Mount Hawke TR4 . . . . . 68 C3
  Padstow PL28 . . . . . 107 D5
  3 St Austell PL26 . . . . . 115 A1
Rope Wlk The
  3 St Ives TR26 . . . . . 141 B6
  9 St Mawes TR2 . . . . . 95 A6
Rorkes Cl PL5 . . . . . 123 E2
Roscadghill Parc 1
  TR18 . . . . . 143 C7
Roscadghill Rd TR18.... 143 C6
Roscarrack Cl TR11 . . . . . 144 E2
Roscarrack Rd TR11 . . . . 144 E3
Roscarrick Villas TR11... 93 D3
Roscarrock Hill PL29 . . . . 22 D7
ROSCROGGAN 138 D7
ROSE 55 C5
Rose Acre Dr 8 TR15 ...140 C5
ROSE-AN-GROUSE 77 D2
Roseannon TR11 . . . . . 93 D3
Rosebery Ave PL4 . . . . . 149 C4
Rosebery La PL4 . . . . . 149 C4
Rosebery Rd PL4 . . . . . 149 C4
ROSECARE 10 D6
Roseclave Cl PL7 . . . . . 131 C6
Rosecott Pk 4 EX23 . . . . . 5 A6
Rose Cotts
  Camborne TR14 . . . . . 138 C3
  Plymouth PL6 . . . . . 129 B8
  Stithians TR3 . . . . . 80 F3
Rosecraddon View PL14.. 38 A2
Rose Ct PL25 . . . . . 115 A5
Rosedale Ave PL2 . . . . . 128 D7
Rosedale Gdns PL31 . . . . 35 B2
Rosedale Rd TR1 . . . . . 137 C5
Rosedene Farm TR3 . . . . 69 C4
ROSEDINNICK 45 E8
Rosedown Ave PL2 . . . . . 128 A7
Rose Eglos TR11 . . . . . 144 C2
Rose Eglos Cl TR11 . . . . . 144 C2
Rose Gdns PL6 . . . . . 125 E6
ROSEHILL
  Goonhavern 55 D5
  Lostwithiel 112 C1
Rosehill
  Ladock TR2 . . . . . 57 C1
  Lanivet PL30 . . . . . 47 C6
  Marazion TR17 . . . . . 89 B5
  Mylor Bridge TR11 . . . . . 82 A2
Rose Hill
  Altarnun PL15 . . . . . 26 C8
  Fowey PL23 . . . . . 116 C4
  Par PL24 . . . . . 60 B5
  Porthtowan TR4 . . . . . 68 A6
  Port Isaac PL29 . . . . . 22 D7
  Redruth TR15 . . . . . 140 B5
  Sticker PL26 . . . . . 58 F1
Rose Hill Cl PL22 . . . . . 112 C2
Rosehill Gdns TR18 . . . . . 143 B6
Rosehill Mdw TR18 . . . . . 143 B6
Rose Hill Terr PL17 . . . . . 41 A3
Rosehip Cl PL6 . . . . . 125 E7
Rose In The Bush Pk
  TR12 . . . . . 99 B8
Rose La 23 TR26 . . . . . 141 B6
ROSELAND 51 E6
Roseland Cres
  6 Chacewater TR4 . . . . . 69 A3
  Tregony TR2 . . . . . 71 F3
Roseland Flats TR2 . . . . . 82 E1
Roseland Gdns
  Bodmin PL31 . . . . . 109 E6
  Redruth TR15 . . . . . 140 D6
  Veryan TR2 . . . . . 83 F6
Roseland Pk TR14 . . . . . 138 D4
Roselands Rd PL31 . . . . . 109 F6
Roseland Terr TR4 . . . . . 55 F2
Roselare Cl 5 PL25 . . . . . 114 E7
Roselidden Parc TR13... 146 B7
Roseline Est TR13 . . . . . 80 D1
Roselyon Pl PL24 . . . . . 60 C5
Roselyon Sch PL24 . . . . . 60 C4
Rose Mdw TR3 . . . . . 80 F3

Rose Mdws TR4. . . . . 55 D4
Rosemellen Terr PL14. . . 113 B4
Rosemellin TR14. . . . . . . 138 E4
ROSEMELLING. 59 F8
Rosemellin Prim Sch
TR14. . . . . 138 E4
ROSEMERGY. 75 D3
Rosemorran 28 TR26 . . . 141 B5
Rosemullion 4 TR6. . . . 55 A5
Rosemullion Gdns 3
TR14. . . . . 138 F7
Rose Mullion Gdns PL17. . 39 F5
Rosemullion Ho TR1 . . . . 69 E4
Rosemundy TR5 . . . . 54 D1
ROSENANNON. 33 A1
Rosenannon La TR15. . . 139 B8
Rosenannon Rd TR15. . . 139 B8
Rose Row TR15 . . . . 140 B5
ROSERROW. 21 E5
Rose Terr
Gunnislake PL18 . . . . 40 E5
Mitchell TR8. . . . . 56 F5
22 Penzance TR18. . . . . 143 E6
Rosevale TR18. . . . . 143 D4
Rosevale Cres TR14. . . . 138 C4
Rosevale Gdns PL30. . . . 59 C8
Rosevalley TR3 . . . . 69 D3
Rose Valley TR19 . . . . 75 B2
Rosevallon La PL31 . . . . 109 C5
ROSEVEAN. 47 D1
Rosevean Ave TR14 . . . . 138 E3
Rosevean Cl TR14. . . . . . 138 E3
Rosevean Ct 8 PL3 . . . . 128 F6
Rosevean Gdns PL3 . . . . 128 F6
Rosevean Ho 7 PL3. . . . 128 F6
Rosevean Rd TR18 . . . . . 143 E6
Rosevean Terr TR18. . . . 143 E6
ROSEVEAR. 99 C7
Roseveare Cl PL9 . . . . . . 136 A8
Roseveare Dr PL26 . . . . . 46 D1
Roseveare Mobile Home Pk
PL26. . . . . 46 D1
Rosevear Rd PL26. . . . . . 47 C1
ROSEVINE. 83 B3
Rosewall Cotts 16 TR26. 141 A5
Rosewall Terr 17 TR26 . . 141 A5
ROSEWARNE. 78 F3
Rosewarne TR13. . . . . 91 A1
Rosewarne Cl TR14. . . . . 138 D4
Rosewarne Gdns TR14 . . 138 D3
Rosewarne Mews TR14. . 138 D4
Rosewarne Pk TR14. . . . 138 E4
Rosewarne Rd
1 Camborne TR14 . . . . . 138 D3
Carnhell Green TR27. . . . 78 F4
Rosewarne Terr TR14 . . . 138 D5
Rosewarne (Trng Ctr)
TR14. . . . . 138 D5
Rosewin Mews 3 TR9. . . 45 E6
Rosewin Row
2 St Columb Major TR9 . 45 E6
Truro TR1. . . . . 137 D5
Rosewithian Cl TR27. . . . 78 E6
Rosewood Cl PL9 . . . . . . 135 F5
ROSEWORTHY
Camborne 78 F6
Shortlanesend. 69 E6
ROSEWORTHY BARTON . . 78 F6
Roseworthy Hill TR14 . . . 78 F6
Rosina Way PL26. . . . . . . 59 D7
Roskear TR14. . . . . 138 E4
ROSKEAR CROFT 138 E6
Roskear Croft TR14 . . . . 138 E6
Roskear Fields TR14 . . . . 138 E4
Roskear Parc TR14. . . . . 138 F5
Roskear Rd TR14. . . . . . . 138 E3
Roskear Sch TR14. . . . . . 138 F3
Roskilling TR13. . . . . 146 D7
Roskilling Wartha TR13 . 146 D7
Roskilly Cotts TR14 . . . . 88 C2
Roskilly's Ice Cream &
Organic Farm★ TR12. . 101 D3
Roskrow TR16. . . . . 80 A5
Roskruge Cl TR13. . . . . . 146 D8
Ros Lyn TR26 . . . . 141 C1
Roslyn Cl
St Austell PL25 . . . . 114 F5
2 St Austell PL25. . . . . 115 A5
Rosparc TR2. . . . . 71 D6
Rosparvah Gdns TR18 . . 143 C7
Rospeath Cres PL2. . . . . 128 D8
Rospeath La TR20. . . . . . 89 C7
Rossett Gdns PL31 . . . . . 35 B1
Rossiter Ho TR19 . . . . . . 96 B6
Rosslyn Park Rd PL3 . . . 128 C5
Ross St PL2. . . . . 127 E4
Rossventon TR4 . . . . 69 A1
Rostalek PL30 . . . . 24 B2
ROSUDGEON. 89 F4
Rotair Rd TR14. . . . . 138 E3
Rothbury Cl PL6 . . . . 125 E4
Rothbury Gdns PL6 . . . . 125 D4
Rothesay Gdns PL5 . . . . 124 D3
Rougemont Cl PL3. . . . . . 129 B7
Rough La TR3. . . . . 81 B4
Rough St TR16. . . . . 80 D6
Roughtor Dr PL32. . . . . . 105 C3
Roughtor Rd PL32. . . . . . 15 D1
Roughtor View PL33 . . . . 14 D2
Roundhayes Farm Cotts
EX23. . . . . 10 C5
Round Ring TR10 . . . . . . 144 D8
Round's La PL34 . . . . 14 D7
Rous Rd PL12. . . . . 40 C2
ROW. 24 B3
Rowan Cl
Bodmin PL31. . . . . 109 B4
Plymouth PL7. . . . . 131 B5

Rowan Cl continued
Tavistock PL19. . . . . . . 147 C3
Rowan Ct PL12. . . . . 122 C2
Rowans The
Bude EX23. . . . . 104 E4
Lifton PL16. . . . . 19 F4
St Mellion PL12. . . . . . . 53 C8
Rowan Way PL6. . . . . . . 125 E7
Rowan Wood Rd PL19. . . 30 F3
Rowden Cl PL7. . . . . 131 D4
Rowe Ct PL14. . . . . 50 E8
Rowe's La TR13. . . . . 146 E8
Rowe St PL11. . . . . 127 B3
Rowes Terr PL26. . . . . . . 58 D5
Row La PL5. . . . . 123 E2
Rowland Cl PL9. . . . . 135 E5
Rowse Gdns PL18. . . . . . 41 A3
Row The
Launceston PL15. . . . . . 17 F1
Pillaton PL12. . . . . 53 B7
Portloe TR2. . . . . 84 A4
Royal Cornwall Hospl TR1 69 E4
Royal Cornwall Mus★
TR1. . . . . 137 C4
Royal Cornwall
Showground★ Pl27 . . . 33 C6
Royalist Ct 14 TR11. . . . 145 C3
Royal Navy Ave PL2 . . . . 127 F6
Royal Par PL1. . . . . 148 C2
Royal Talbot PL22. . . . . . 112 C2
Royal William Rd PL1 . . 134 A8
Roydon Cl PL15. . . . . 106 B8
Roydon La PL15. . . . . 106 B8
Roydon Rd PL15. . . . . . . 106 B8
Royffe Way PL31. . . . . . . 109 F3
Ruan High Lanes. 83 E6
RUAN LANIHORNE 83 E8
RUAN MAJOR. 102 F6
RUAN MINOR 103 B5
Ruby Terr TR13 . . . . 92 B8
RUDDLEMOOR. 59 B6
Rudyerd Wlk PL3 . . . . . . 129 D6
Rufford Cl PL21. . . . . 128 A7
Rule Cross EX23 . . . . 2 E2
RUMFORD. 32 A5
Ruminella View TR12. . . 103 A4
Rumours Apartments
TR7. . . . . 111 B7
Rundle Ct PL14 . . . . 113 B4
Rundles Ct TR1 . . . . 137 E3
Runnymede Ct PL6. . . . . 125 E2
RUSHFORD. 30 A3
Rush Park Terr PL18 . . . . 40 F7
Ruskin Cres PL5 . . . . 124 D2
Ruskin Ct TR9 . . . . 45 D5
Russell Ave PL3. . . . . 128 F7
Russell Cl
Gunnislake PL18 . . . . . . 41 A7
Plymouth PL9. . . . . 136 B3
Saltash PL12. . . . . 122 C3
Russell Court Gdns PL19 147 B6
Russell Ct
Plymouth PL1. . . . . 148 C2
Saltash PL12. . . . . 122 C3
Tavistock PL19. . . . . . . 147 B6
Russell Mews PL31. . . . . 109 C5
Russell Pl PL1 . . . . 148 B4
Russell St
7 Liskeard PL14. . . . . . 113 C5
Tavistock PL19. . . . . . . 147 C5
Russell Way 4 TR10 . . . 144 C7
Russet Wood PL5 . . . . . . 123 F4
Rutger Pl PL1. . . . . 148 A4
RUTHERNBRIDGE. 34 A1
Ruthern Valley PL30. . . . 34 A1
Ruthven Cl PL6 . . . . 128 F8
RUTHVOES. 45 F3
Ruthy's La PL28. . . . . 107 D5
Rutland Rd PL4 . . . . 128 F4
Rydal Cl PL6. . . . . 125 D2
Ryder Rd PL2 . . . . 127 F4
Rydon La EX22. . . . . 8 F7
Rye Hill
Ponsanooth TR3. . . . . . 81 B4
Saltash PL12. . . . . 122 C2
Rylands Terr PL30. . . . . . 24 B3

S

Saffron Cl PL23. . . . . 116 C4
Sail Loft Flats 2 TR26. . 141 B6
ST AGNES 54 D1
ST AGNES BEACON 54 B1
St Agnes Mus★ TR5. . . . 54 C1
St Agnes Prim Sch TR5. . 54 C1
St Albans Pk PL20. . . . . . 42 D2
ST ALLEN. 56 B1
St Ambrusca Rd TR8 . . . 110 A3
St Andrew's CE Prim Sch
PL20 . . . . 41 F3
St Andrews Cl
12 Bere Alston PL20. . . 41 B1
Ponsanooth TR3. . . . . . 81 B4
Saltash PL12. . . . . 122 C2
St Andrew's Cl PL18. . . . 41 A3
St Andrew's Cross 1
PL1. . . . . 149 A2
St Andrew's Pl PL10. . . . 133 A1
St Andrews Rd PL19. . . . 147 D2
St Andrew's Rd
Par PL24 . . . . 60 C5
12 Stratton EX23. . . . . 4 D1
St Andrew's St
Cawsand PL10 . . . . 133 A1
1 St Ives TR26. . . . . . . 141 B5

St Andrew St
Millbrook PL10. . . . . . . 132 E5
Plymouth PL1. . . . . 148 C2
St Andrews Terr TR3 . . . 81 B4
St Andrew's Terr PL24 . . 60 C5
St Annes TR11 . . . . 93 D3
St Annes Cl
Lelant TR26 . . . . 77 E4
Whitstone EX22. . . . . . . 7 F1
St Annes Rd 17 PL24 . . . 60 B4
St Anne's Rd
Newquay TR7. . . . . 111 A7
Plymouth PL3. . . . . 125 D6
Saltash PL12. . . . . 122 E3
3 Trewoon PL25. . . . . . 59 A3
ST ANN'S CHAPEL. 40 E6
St Ann's Rd EX23. . . . . . . 104 F3
St Anta Rd TR26 . . . . 141 E1
ST ANTHONY. 95 B5
ST ANTHONY-IN-
MENEAGE. 101 C8
St Anthony Way TR11 . . . 145 A2
St Aubyn Ave PL2 . . . . . . 127 F5
St Aubyn Cres TR7 . . . . . 111 A6
St Aubyn Est TR14 . . . . . 79 E5
St Aubyn Rd PL1. . . . . . . 127 E3
St Aubyns TR20 . . . . 89 E5
St Aubyn's Rd TR1 . . . . . 137 D3
St Aubyn St 4 PL1. . . . . 127 E2
St Aubyn's Vean TR1 . . . 137 D3
ST AUSTELL. 114 B5
St Austell Bay Bsns Pk
PL25. . . . . 115 E4
St Austell Brewery Visitor
Ctr★ PL25. . . . . 114 B4
St Austell Com Hospl
PL26 . . . . 114 F1
St Austell Rd PL26 . . . . . 115 C5
St Austell Row 2 TR2. . . 95 A6
St Austell St
Summercourt TR8 . . . . . 57 C6
Truro TR1. . . . . 137 D4
St Austell Sta PL25. . . . . 114 D4
St Barnabas Ct PL1 . . . . 148 A4
St Barnabas Hospl PL12. 122 F2
St Barnabas Terr PL1 . . . 148 A4
St Benedicts Cl 13 PL24 . 60 D5
St Benets Cl PL30 . . . . . . 47 E6
St Blazey. 60 B5
ST BLAZEY GATE 115 F6
St Blazey Rd PL24. . . . . . 60 C4
St Boniface Cl PL2. . . . . . 128 C7
St Boniface Dr PL2 . . . . . 128 C7
St Boniface RC Coll PL5. 124 E1
St Breaca Cl TR13. . . . . . 91 A3
ST BREOCK. 33 C6
St Breock CP Sch PL27. . 108 B5
ST BREWARD 24 B3
St Breward Prim Sch
PL30. . . . . 24 B3
St Bridget Ave PL6 . . . . . 124 F1
ST BUDEAUX. 123 D2
St Budeaux Ferry Rd Sta
PL5 . . . . 127 D8
St Budeaux Foundation Jun
Sch PL5 . . . . 123 F2
St Budeaux Victoria Rd Sta
PL5 . . . . 123 D1
ST BURYAN. 97 B6
St Buryan Hill TR19 . . . . 96 F4
St Buryan Prim Sch TR19. 97 B6
St Cadocs PL28 . . . . 31 F7
St Carantoc Way TR8. . . 43 D3
St Catherine's Castle★
PL23 . . . . 116 B2
St Catherine's CE Prim Sch
PL15 . . . . 106 A4
St Catherines Ct PL23 . . 116 C3
St Clare Flats TR18. . . . . 143 D6
St Clare St TR18 . . . . 143 D6
ST CLEER. 37 F2
St Cleer Dr PL27. . . . . . . 108 D6
St Cleer Prim Sch PL14 . 38 A3
St Cleer Rd PL14. . . . . . . 113 C7
ST CLEMENT. 70 D2
St Clement's Cl TR1. . . . 137 E4
St Clement's Hill TR1 . . . 137 E4
St Clements Parc TR1 . . . 137 E4
St Clement St TR1 . . . . . . 137 E4
St Clements Terr 26 TR19. 88 C1
St Clement's Terr 3
TR1 . . . . 137 D5
St Clement Vean TR1. . . 137 F6
ST CLETHER. 17 A3
St Columb Bsns Ctr TR9 . 45 E6
ST COLUMB MAJOR 45 E6
St Columb Major Academy
TR9. . . . . 45 D6
St Columb Major Bsns Pk
TR9. . . . . 45 E5
St Columb Major Ind Est
TR9. . . . . 45 D5
ST COLUMB MINOR 111 E7
St Columb Minor Academy
TR7. . . . . 111 D7
ST COLUMB ROAD. 45 D2
St Columb Road Ind
Workshops TR9. . . . . . . 45 D2
St Columb Road Sta TR9. 45 D2
St Crewenna Terr TR27. . 78 E1
St Cuthbert Cl PL15 . . . . 106 B7
St Cuthbert's Rd TR7. . . 110 D6
St Cyriac PL30. . . . . 47 F1
St Davids Cl EX23. . . . . . 4 C8
St David's Rd PL19. . . . . 147 E5
ST DAY. 68 E1
St Day & Carharrack Com
Sch TR16. . . . . 68 E1

St Day Rd TR15 . . . . 140 C5
ST DENNIS. 58 C8
St Dennis Ind Est PL26 . . 58 B8
St Dennis Prim Academy
PL26. . . . . 58 C8
St Dominic Cl PL31. . . . . 109 C5
ST DOMINICK 40 D3
St Dominick CE Prim Sch
PL12. . . . . 40 D2
St Dominic Pk PL17. . . . . 40 C4
St Dominic Sq 4 TR1 . . . 137 C4
St Dominic St
8 Penzance TR18. . . . . 143 E6
5 Truro TR1. . . . . 137 C4
St Dunstan's Terr PL4 . . 149 C3
St Edmunds La PL28 . . . . 107 D5
St Edward Gdns PL6. . . . 125 B1
St Edward's CE Prim Sch
PL6. . . . . 125 C1
St Eia St TR26 . . . . 141 C6
St Elizabeth Cl PL7. . . . . 130 F3
St Elvan Cres TR13 . . . . . 91 A1
St Elwyns Rise TR27. . . . 142 B6
ST ENDELLION 22 D5
ST ENODER 57 B7
St Enodoc Cl PL27 . . . . . 108 D6
St ERME 70 E8
St Erme Prim Sch TR4. . . 70 D8
ST ERNEY. 53 B2
ST ERTH. 142 A1
St Erth Com Prim Sch
TR27. . . . . 142 A1
St Erth Hill TR27 . . . . 77 F1
St Erth Ind Est TR27. . . . 77 E2
ST ERTH PRAZE. 142 F1
St Erth Rd PL2 . . . . 128 D7
St Erth Sta TR27 . . . . 77 E2
ST EVAL. 31 F3
St Eval Pl PL5. . . . . 123 E4
ST EWE 72 E5
St Fimbarrus Rd PL23 . . 116 C3
St Francis CE Sch TR11. . 144 E3
St Francis Ct PL3. . . . . . . 124 B3
St Francis Mdw TR8. . . . 56 F5
St Francis Rd TR9 . . . . . . 45 E2
St Francis Rd 5 TR18. . . 143 E6
St Gabriel's Ave PL3 . . . 128 D5
ST GENNYS 10 C8
St George's Arc TR11 . . . 145 B4
St George's Ave PL2 . . . 128 C7
St George's CE Prim Acad
PL1 . . . . 148 A1
St George's Cres PL31. . 109 C4
St Georges Ct
Looe PL13 . . . . 117 D2
1 Plymouth PL2. . . . . . 127 F4
St George's Hill TR6 . . . . 55 A4
St Georges Hill Cl 13 TR6. 55 A4
St George's Pk PL22 . . . 112 C3
St Georges Rd
Nanpean PL26. . . . . 58 D6
Saltash PL12 . . . . 122 D3
St George's Rd
Hayle TR27 . . . . 142 C5
Looe PL13 . . . . 117 D4
Newquay TR7. . . . . 110 D5
Saltash PL12. . . . . 122 E3
Truro TR1. . . . . 137 B5
St George's Terr
Perranporth TR6 . . . . . . 54 F4
Plymouth PL2. . . . . 127 F4
ST GERMANS 65 A8
St Germans Prim Sch
PL12. . . . . 65 A8
St Germans Rd PL17 . . . 39 F3
St Germans Sta PL12. . . 65 B8
St Giles Dr PL27. . . . . . . 108 C6
St Giles Mews PL27. . . . 108 C6
ST GILES ON THE HEATH . 13 E1
St Giles-on-the-Heath Com
Sch PL15 . . . . 13 D1
ST GLUVIAS. 144 D8
St Gluvias Parc TR10 . . . 144 D8
St Gluvias St TR10 . . . . . 144 D7
St Golder Rd TR18 . . . . . 143 B3
St Gothian Sands Nature
Reserve★ TR27 . . . . . . 66 B2
St Grace's Ct TR2 . . . . . . 71 C6
St Helens Wlk PL5 . . . . . 124 C5
St Henry St 4 TR18 . . . . 143 E6
ST HILARY. 89 E6
St Hilary Prim Sch TR20. 89 F6
St Hilary Terr PL4 . . . . . . 149 C3
St Ia St TR26 . . . . 141 D1
St Issen CE Prim Sch
PL27. . . . . 32 D6
ST ISSEY. 32 E6
ST IVE. 38 F2
ST IVE CROSS. 39 A1
St Ive Rd PL14 . . . . 38 E4
ST IVES. 141 C6
St Ives Jun & Inf Schs
TR26. . . . . 141 A5
St Ives La TR27 . . . . 66 B1
St Ives L Ctr TR26. . . . . 141 A5
St Ives Mus★ TR26 . . . . 141 C6
St Ives Mushroom Farm
TR26 . . . . 77 A5
St Ives Rd
Carbis Bay TR26 . . . . . 141 D1
Pendeen TR19 . . . . 75 A1
St Ives Sch TR26 . . . . . . 141 B3
St Ives Sta TR26. . . . . . . 141 B5
St James Ct
Delabole PL33 . . . . 14 E2
Plymouth PL1. . . . . 148 B2
Torpoint PL11. . . . . 127 B3
St James Mews PL1. . . . 148 B2

St James' Place E PL1. . . 148 B2
St James' Place W PL1. . 148 B2
St James Rd PL11. . . . . . 127 B2
St James' St TR18. . . . . . 143 E5
St James's Terr TR10. . . 144 B7
St James View TR9. . . . . 57 D8
ST JIDGEY. 32 F4
ST JOHN. 132 C8
ST JOHNS. 146 A6
St Johns PL19 . . . . 147 C5
St Johns Ave PL19 . . . . . 147 C5
St John's Bridge Rd PL4. 149 B2
St Johns Bsns Pk TR13. . 146 B6
St John's Catholic Prim Sch
4 TR14. . . . . 138 E2
St Johns Cl PL6. . . . . 125 D4
St John's Cl
Helston TR13 . . . . 146 A6
Millbrook PL10. . . . . . . 132 E5
St Johns Ct 7 TR18. . . . 143 E5
St John's Ct
7 Falmouth TR11. . . . . 145 A4
Hayle TR27. . . . . 142 D6
St John's Dr PL9. . . . . . . 135 B6
St Johns Gdns TR11. . . . 145 B6
St Johns La PL11. . . . . . . 132 B8
St Johns Rd PL15 . . . . . . 106 B4
St John's Rd
Helston TR13 . . . . 146 B6
Horrabridge PL20. . . . . 42 C4
Millbrook PL10. . . . . . . 132 F5
Newquay TR7. . . . . 110 D5
Plymouth PL4. . . . . 149 B2
Plymouth, Turnchapel PL9. 135 A6
St John's St
Hayle TR27. . . . . 142 D6
Plymouth PL4. . . . . 149 B2
St John's Terr
Devoran TR3 . . . . 81 F6
8 Pendeen TR19 . . . . . 75 A1
St Johns Wlk TR26 . . . . . 77 A7
St Joseph's Cl PL6 . . . . . 124 F1
St Joseph's Rd PL15. . . . 106 B8
St Joseph's Sch PL15 . . . 106 B7
ST JUDE'S. 149 B3
St Jude's Rd PL4. . . . . . . 149 B2
St Julians Cres PL10 . . . 133 E7
St Julitta PL30 . . . . 48 A1
ST JUST. 86 E6
ST JUST IN ROSELAND . . . 82 F2
St Just Prim Sch TR19. . . 86 E6
St Keri Ct PL15. . . . . 18 A5
ST KEVERNE. 101 C4
St Keverne Cty Prim Sch
TR12. . . . . 101 D4
St Keverne Pl PL2. . . . . . 128 D8
St Keverne Rural Workshops
TR12. . . . . 101 C3
ST KEW. 23 A4
ST KEW HIGHWAY 23 A2
St Kew Prim Sch PL30. . . 22 F3
ST KEYNE. 51 A3
St Keyne Ct PL14 . . . . . . 137 C6
St Keyne Wishing Well Halt
PL14 . . . . 51 C3
ST LAWRENCE. 34 D1
St Lawrence Mews PL4. . 149 A4
St Lawrence Rd
Bodmin PL30, PL31. . . . 109 A4
Plymouth PL4. . . . . 149 A4
St Leonards PL31 . . . . . . 109 C5
St Leonard's Rd
Launceston PL15 . . . . . 106 B8
Plymouth PL4. . . . . 149 C2
St Leonards Terr PL31. . . 109 C5
St Leo Pl PL2. . . . . 127 E4
ST LEVAN. 96 D3
St Levan Cl 8 TR17. . . . . 89 C5
St Levan Prim Sch TR19. 96 E5
St Levan Rd
7 Marazion TR17. . . . . 89 C5
Plymouth PL2. . . . . 127 F5
ST MABYN. 34 C8
St Mabyn CE Prim Sch
PL30. . . . . 34 D8
St Madderns CE Sch
TR20. . . . . 143 A8
St Margarets La PL26. . . 59 A1
St Margarets Rd PL7 . . . 130 B7
St Mark's CE Prim Sch
EX23. . . . . 2 E2
St Marks Rd PL6 . . . . 125 D5
St Marnarch's Cl PL13 . . 62 B8
St Marnarch's Rd PL13. . 62 B8
ST MARTIN
Looe. 117 D7
Mawgan. 100 D6
St Martin-in-Meneage Prim
Sch TR12. . . . . 100 D6
St Martin's Ave PL13 . . . 128 D7
St Martin's CE Prim Sch
PL14 . . . . 113 D5
St Martins Cl
Lewannick PL15. . . . . . . 27 B7
Looe PL13 . . . . 117 D5
St Martin's Cl 2 TR14. . . 138 C2
St Martin's Cres TR14 . . 138 C3
St Martins La PL14 . . . . . 113 E5
St Martins Rd EX23. . . . . 7 B8
St Martin's Rd PL13 . . . . 117 D6
St Martin's Terr TR14 . . . 138 C4
St Marwenne Cl EX23. . . 104 F5
St Maryhaye PL19. . . . . . 147 A5
St Mary's PL13. . . . . 117 D3

St Mary's CE Prim Sch
 Penzance TR18. . . . . **143** E4
 Truro TR1. . . . . **137** C6
St Marys Cl PL7. . . . . **130** D5
St Mary's Cl PL31. . . . . . **109** C4
St Marys Cres PL31. . . . . . **109** C4
St Marys Ct PL7. . . . . **130** D5
St Mary's Ct **2** TR7. . . . . **110** D5
St Mary's Gdns PL31. . . . . **109** C4
St Mary's RC Prim Sch
 Bodmin PL31. . . . . **109** C4
 Falmouth TR11. . . . . . . **144** E3
St Marys Rd PL24. . . . . . . **60** B4
St Mary's RC Sch TR18. . . **143** E7
St Mary's Rd
 Bodmin PL31. . . . . **109** B3
 Launceston PL15. . . . . . **106** C8
 Newquay TR7. . . . . **110** D5
 Plymouth PL7. . . . . **130** C6
St Mary's St
 Penzance TR18. . . . . **143** E6
 12 Truro TR1. . . . . **137** D4
St Mary's Street Mews **10**
 TR1. . . . . **137** D4
St Mary St PL1. . . . . **148** A2
St Mary's Terr
 Penzance TR18. . . . . **143** E5
 4 Truro TR1. . . . . **137** C5
St Matthews Hill PL27. . . **108** D5
St Maurice Ct PL7. . . . . . . **130** F4
St Maurice Mews PL7. . . . **130** E4
St Maurice Rd PL7. . . . . . **130** F3
St Maurice View PL7. . . . **131** B4
ST MAWES **95** B6
St Mawes Castle★ TR2. . . **95** A5
St Mawes Prim Sch TR2. . **95** A6
St Mawes Terr **8** PL2. . . **127** F5
ST MAWGAN **45** A8
St Mawgan Cl PL31. . . . . . **109** F5
St Mellans Terr **5** TR12. . **99** A1
ST MELLION **53** E8
St Mellion CE School
 PL12. . . . . **53** D8
ST MELLION PK **53** C8
St Meriadoc CE Inf Sch
 TR14. . . . . **138** C2
St Meriadoc CE VA Jun Sch
 TR14. . . . . **138** B2
St Meriadoc Rd TR14. . . . **138** C3
ST MERRYN **31** F8
St Merryn Airfield PL28 . . **31** F6
St Merryn Prim Sch PL28. **31** E8
ST MEWAN **59** A2
St Mewan La PL24, PL26. . **59** A3
St Mewan Prim Sch PL26. **59** A2
St Michael Ave PL2. . . . . **127** F5
ST MICHAEL CAERHAYS . . **72** D1
ST MICHAEL PENKEVIL. . . **70** F1
St Michael's Catholic
 Secondary Sch TR14 . . **138** D1
St Michael's CE Prim Sch
 TR13. . . . . **146** C5
St Michaels Cl PL15. . . . . . **19** C1
St Michael's Cl
 Hayle TR27. . . . . **142** B4
 Plymouth PL1. . . . . **127** E1
St Michael's Cotts **11**
 TR18. . . . . **143** E5
St Michaels Ct
 Mawnan Smith TR11 . . . . **93** D3
 18 Penzance TR18. . . . **143** E5
St Michael's Ct **7** PL1. . **127** F3
St Michael's Hospl TR27. **142** B4
St Michael's Mount★
 TR17. . . . . **89** B4
St Michael's RC Small Sch **17**
 TR1. . . . . **137** C4
St Michael's Rd
 Newquay TR7. . . . . **110** D5
 Perranporth TR6 . . . . **55** A4
 Ponsanooth TR3. . . . . **81** C4
 9 Stratton EX23. . . . . . . **4** D1
St Michael's St TR18 . . . **143** E6
St Michael's Terr
 Penzance TR18. . . . . **143** D6
 8 Plymouth, Devonport
 PL1. . . . . **127** F3
 Plymouth PL4. . . . . **148** C4
St Michaels Way PL26. . . . **47** A2
St Michaels Wy PL26. . . . . **46** F2
ST MINVER **21** F3
St Minver Prim Sch PL27. **21** F3
St Modwen Rd PL6. . . . . . **129** F7
St Moritz Ct PL27. . . . . . . **21** D5
St Moritz Villas PL27. . . . **21** D5
St Nazaire App PL1 . . . . . **127** F2
St Nazaire Cl PL1. . . . . . . **127** E2
ST NEOT **36** F2
St Neot Com Prim Sch
 PL14. . . . . **36** F2
ST NEWLYN EAST **56** C7
St Newlyn East Prim Sch
 TR8. . . . . **56** B7
St Nicholas' CE Prim Sch
 PL11. . . . . **64** C4
St Nicholas Cl TR27. . . . . . **78** C6
St Nicholas Cl **1** TR26 . . **141** B6
St Nicholas Pk PL22. . . . . **112** B3
St Nicholas Sch
 Bodmin PL31. . . . . **109** E4
 14 Truro TR1. . . . . **137** D4
St Nonna's Cl PL15. . . . . . **26** C8
St Olaf's Rd **13** EX23. . . . . **4** D1
St Pancras Ave PL2 . . . . . **128** D8
St Paternus Cl PL15. . . . . **27** E8

St Pauls Cl PL3. . . . . **129** C5
St Paul St PL1. . . . . **134** A8
St Peter Cl PL7. . . . . **130** F4
St Peters Ct PL1. . . . . . . **148** A3
St Peter's Hill TR18 . . . . **143** C1
St Peter's RC Prim Sch
 PL5. . . . . **124** B5
St Peters Rd
 Plymouth PL5. . . . . **124** C2
 11 Stratton EX23. . . . . . **4** D1
St Peter's Rd TR11 . . . . . **145** B7
St Peters St **16** TR26. . . **141** B6
St Peters Way TR13 . . . . . **98** C8
St Petroc's CE Prim Sch
 PL31. . . . . **109** E4
St Petroc's Cl PL31. . . . . **109** E4
St Petrocs Mdw PL28. . . . **107** C5
St Petroc's Sch EX23. . . . **104** D7
St Petry TR20. . . . . **89** C5
St Philip St **1** TR18 . . . **143** E6
St Piran Cl PL31. . . . . . . **109** B4
St Pirans Cl **2** TR1. . . . **137** D4
St Piran's Cl PL25. . . . . . **114** F6
St Pirans Ct
 Camborne TR14. . . . . . . **138** D3
 13 Penzance TR18. . . . **143** E5
 Tintagel TR34. . . . . **14** E8
St Piran's Hill TR3 . . . . . . **81** D6
St Pirans Ho **15** TR6. . . . . **55** A5
St Pirans Par **10** TR6. . . . **55** A5
St Pirans Parc **14** TR13. . . **98** C8
St Pirans Rd TR6. . . . . **55** A5
St Piran's Rd TR7 . . . . . . **110** D6
St Piran's Sch TR27. . . . . **142** B4
St Pirans Way TR20 . . . . . **89** D4
St Pol de Leon View TR19 **88** C2
ST RUAN **103** A4
St Rumon's CE Inf Sch
 PL19. . . . . **147** C6
St Sampsons Cl **6** PL24. **60** D5
St Sampson's Terr PL23. . **61** B5
St Saviour's Hill PL23 . . **116** D2
St Saviour's La PL28. . . . **107** D6
St Simon's La PL4. . . . . . **129** B3
St Smithwick Way TR11 . **145** C3
ST STEPHEN. **58** B4
St Stephen Churchtown Prim
 Sch PL26. . . . . **58** B4
ST STEPHENS
 Launceston **106** A8
 Saltash. **122** D2
St Stephens Ct PL15. . . . **106** B7
St Stephen's Hill
 Launceston PL15. . . . . . **106** B8
 Saltash PL12. . . . . **122** C1
St Stephens Prim Sch
 Launceston PL15. . . . . . **106** B8
 Saltash PL12. . . . . **122** E2
St Stephens Rd PL26. . . . . **58** E1
St Stephen's Rd PL12 . . . **122** E2
St Stephen St PL1. . . . . . **127** F1
St Sulien PL30. . . . . **48** A1
St Teresa Ho PL4. . . . . . . **149** A3
St Therese Cl **20** PL17 . . . **39** F4
St Therese's Ct PL1. . . . . **127** F2
ST THOMAS **106** B6
St Thomas Cl
 Plymouth PL7. . . . . **130** F3
 Truro TR1. . . . . **69** F3
St Thomas Hill PL15. . . . **106** B6
St Thomas Rd PL15. . . . . **106** B6
St Thomas' Rd TR7. . . . . **110** F5
St Thomas St TR10. . . . . **144** D7
St Tinney Farm PL32. . . . . **10** D1
St Treath Prim Sch PL30. . **23** E7
ST TUDY **23** E3
St Tudy CE Prim Sch
 PL30. . . . . **23** E3
St Uny CE Sch TR26 . . . . **141** D1
St Uny Cl TR26. . . . . **77** E3
St Uny Cres TR15 . . . . . . **139** F5
ST VEEP. **61** C6
St Vincent St PL2. . . . . . **127** E4
St Warren St **6** TR18. . . **143** E6
ST WENN. **46** D7
St Wenn Sch PL30 . . . . . . **46** D7
St Winnolls Pk PL13. . . . **117** D4
ST WINNOW **61** A8
St Winnow Barton Farm
 Mus★ PL22. . . . . **61** A8
St Winnow CE Prim Sch
 PL22. . . . . **112** F2
Salamanca St PL11. . . . . **127** B3
Salcombe Rd PL4. . . . . . . **149** C4
SALEM **68** F3
Salisbury Ope PL3 . . . . . **128** B5
Salisbury Rd
 Plymouth PL4. . . . . **149** C4
 Truro TR1. . . . . **137** B4
Salisbury Road Jun Sch
 PL4. . . . . **149** C3
Salmon Row **3** TR1. . . . **137** D4
SALTASH. **122** B3
Saltash Bsns Pk PL12. . . **122** C4
Saltash Com Sch PL12. . . **122** C1
Saltash Her Mus★ PL12. . **123** A4
Saltash Ind Est PL12. . . . **122** D4
Saltash L Ctr PL12. . . . . . **122** C3
Saltash Parkway Ind Est
 PL12. . . . . **122** B4
Saltash Rd
 Callington PL17. . . . . **39** F4
 Plymouth, Keyham PL2. . **127** E6
 Plymouth PL3. . . . . **148** C4
Saltash Sta PL12. . . . . . . **123** A2

Saltbox Cl TR11. . . . . **82** A2
Saltbox Rd TR11. . . . . **82** A2
Saltburn Rd PL5. . . . . . . **123** C1
Salt Cellar Hill **10** TR13. . **98** B8
Saltings Cl TR26 . . . . **77** E3
Saltings Reach TR26 . . . . **77** E3
Saltings The TR26. . . . . . **77** E4
Salt Mill PL12. . . . . **122** F4
Saltmill Cl PL12. . . . . . . **122** F3
Saltponds **27** TR19 . . . . . **88** C1
Salts Mdw PL14. . . . . **50** B6
Sampford Gdns PL20. . . . . **42** D5
SAMPFORD SPINEY. **42** E7
Sampford Terr **6** PL20. . **42** C5
Sampson Cl PL18 . . . . **40** D6
Sampson Gdns TR3 . . . . . **81** B4
Sampson's Ct TR27 . . . . . **78** D6
Sampson Way TR3 . . . . . . **69** D3
Sampys Hill TR11 . . . . **93** D3
Samuel Bassett Ave PL6. **125** B7
Samuel Bone Cl PL14 . . . **113** D6
SANCREED **87** E4
Sanctuary Cl TR14 . . . . . **138** C2
Sanctuary La
 Helston TR13. . . . . **146** C6
 12 Stratton EX23. . . . . . **4** E1
Sanctuary Lane Flats
 TR13. . . . . **146** C6
Sand Bay TR11. . . . . **145** C2
Sandercock Cl PL17. . . . . . **39** F7
Sandfield Cres **3** TR14. . **138** C2
Sandford Rd PL9. . . . . . . **135** F8
Sand Hill PL18 . . . . **41** A6
Sand Hill Pk PL18. . . . . . . **40** F5
Sandhole Cross EX39. . . . . **2** D8
Sandhurst Terr **1** TR1. . **137** C5
Sand La PL18. . . . . **41** A3
Sandon Wlk PL6. . . . . . . **125** A1
Sandows La **15** TR26 . . . . **141** A5
Sandpiper Road EX23. . . **104** F5
SANDPLACE **63** C7
Sandplace Rd
 Looe PL13. . . . . **117** C6
 Looe, Sandplace PL13 . . . . **63** B7
 Sandplace Sta PL13. . . . . . **63** B8
Sandra Way PL31 . . . . . . **109** C5
Sandyacres TR27. . . . . **78** B6
SANDY BOTTOM **114** F4
Sandy Cl PL14. . . . . **51** B3
Sandy Cove TR4 . . . . **68** A7
Sandy Ct TR8 . . . . **31** B2
Sandy Hill PL25. . . . . **114** F4
Sandy Hill Academy
 PL25. . . . . **114** F4
Sandyhills PL27. . . . . **21** E2
Sandy La
 Harlyn PL28. . . . . **20** D2
 Redruth TR15, TR16. . . . . **140** D5
 Trevone PL28. . . . . **20** F2
Sandylake La PL22. . . . . . **112** F3
Sandymoor TR14. . . . . . . **139** B3
Sandy Rd
 Plymouth PL7. . . . . **131** C4
 Porthtowan TR4. . . . . **68** A7
Sango Cl PL10 . . . . **132** F6
Sango Rd PL11. . . . . **127** A2
San Sebastian Sq PL1. . . **148** C2
Saracen Cl TR10 . . . . **144** C7
Saracen Cres TR10. . . . . . **144** C7
Saracen Ho **5** TR10. . . . **144** C7
Saracen Pl TR10 . . . . **144** C7
Saracen Way TR10 . . . . . **144** C7
Sarah Cl PL20. . . . . **41** B1
Sarahs Cl PL28. . . . . **107** D4
Sarah's Ct PL28. . . . . **107** D4
Sarah's Gate PL27 . . . . . . **32** C7
Sarah's La PL28. . . . . **107** D4
Sarah's Mdw PL28 . . . . . **107** D4
Sarah's View PL28 . . . . . **107** D4
Sargents Mdw EX23. . . . . . **2** D1
Sarum Cl PL3. . . . . **128** F7
Saunders La PL11. . . . . . . **65** A5
Saunders Wlk PL6 . . . . . **124** D6
Savage Rd PL5. . . . . **127** D7
SAVEOCK. **69** B3
Savery Terr PL4. . . . . **129** A4
Savoy Bldg **3** PL25. . . . **114** C3
Sawles Rd PL25. . . . . **114** B2
Sawmills La TR16. . . . . . . **68** D3
Sawrey St PL1. . . . . **148** A2
Sawyers Ct TR13. . . . . **92** A6
Saxon Rd PL19. . . . . **147** A6
SCARCEWATER **57** E5
Scarletts Well Pk PL31. . . **109** C6
Scarletts Well Rd PL31. . **109** C5
Scarlett's Well Rd PL31. **109** B5
Scarne Ind Est PL15. . . . **106** C3
Scarne Lake Gdns PL15. **106** D3
Scarne Side Gr PL15 . . . **106** D3
Scholars Cl PL14. . . . . **38** F2
Scholar's La TR13. . . . . . . **91** C3
School Cl
 Par PL24. . . . . **60** B4
 Plymouth PL7. . . . . **130** D7
 St Columb Minor TR7. . . . **111** E6
 Tavistock PL19. . . . . **147** D5
School Dr PL6. . . . . **125** D7
School Hill
 Golant PL23. . . . . **61** B5
 Herodsfoot PL14. . . . . . . **50** E3
 Lanjeth PL26. . . . . **58** E4
 Mevagissey PL26. . . . . . . **73** C4
 Padstow PL28 . . . . **107** D5
 Perranarworthal TR3. . . . . **81** D6
 Shortlanesend TR4. . . . . . **69** F6
 South Petherwin PL15. . . . **27** E8

School Hill continued
 St Buryan TR19 . . . . **96** E5
 St Keverne, Porthallow
 TR12. . . . . **101** D6
 St Keverne TR12. . . . . . **101** D4
 St Neot PL14. . . . . **36** F2
School La
 Budock Water TR11 . . . . **144** C3
 Gulval TR18 . . . . **88** E6
 Jacobstow EX23 . . . . **11** A6
 Marazion TR17. . . . . **89** C5
 Plymouth PL7. . . . . **130** E4
 Polruan PL23. . . . . **116** D2
 Redruth TR15. . . . . **140** D5
 St Austell PL25 . . . . **115** C6
 St Erth TR27. . . . . **142** A1
 St Hilary TR20 . . . . **89** F6
 Troon TR14. . . . . **79** E4
 Truro TR1. . . . . **137** C3
School Rd
 Landrake PL12. . . . . **53** C3
 Pensilva PL14 . . . . **38** E5
 Summercourt TR8 . . . . . . **57** B7
 Tavistock PL19. . . . . **147** D2
School Wlk PL27. . . . . . . **108** D6
Sclerder La PL13. . . . . **62** E4
Scoble's Terr **1** TR1. . . . **70** D1
Sconner Rd PL11. . . . . . . **127** A3
Scoria Cl TR16. . . . . **68** D3
SCORRIER **68** D3
Scorrier House Workshops
 TR16. . . . . **68** D2
Scorrier St TR16. . . . . **68** E1
Scott Ave PL5. . . . . **127** C8
Scott Bsns Pk PL2 . . . . . **128** A6
Scott Cl **2** PL14 . . . . **38** E4
Scott Hospl PL2. . . . . **128** A6
Scott Rd PL2. . . . . **128** A6
Scowbuds TR14. . . . . **138** F5
Scrations La PL22. . . . . . **112** C2
SCREDDA **114** D8
Screech Owl Sanctuary★
 TR9. . . . . **46** A3
Seabank TR11. . . . . **145** B2
Seacroft Rd PL5. . . . . **123** C2
Sea Front Ct PL13. . . . . . **117** D3
Seaholme Ct TR11. . . . . . **145** A5
Sea La TR27 . . . . **142** D6
Seapoint Ho TR7. . . . . . . **110** E6
Sea Rd PL25. . . . . **115** D2
SEATON **64** B5
Seaton Ave PL4. . . . . **128** E4
Seaton Bsns Pk PL6. . . . **125** B3
Seaton La PL4 . . . . **128** E4
Seaton Pk PL11 . . . . **64** B5
Seaton Pl PL2. . . . . **127** F5
Sea Urchin TR26. . . . . . . **141** E2
Sea View
 Crackington Haven EX23 . . . **10** C6
 Gunnislake PL18 . . . . **40** E5
Sea View Ave PL4. . . . . . **149** C4
Sea View Cl EX23 . . . . **5** A6
Seaview Cotts **10** TR11 . **145** B5
Sea View Cotts **73** C3
Sea View Cres **11** TR2. . . **95** A6
Sea View Ct TR11. . . . . . **145** B3
Sea View Rd TR11. . . . . . **145** B2
Sea View Pl TR26 . . . . . . **141** C6
Seaview Terr TR8 . . . . **57** E6
Sea View Terr
 Camborne TR14. . . . . . . **138** E2
 Carn Towan TR19 . . . . **96** C7
 Helston TR13. . . . . **146** B6
 6 Newlyn TR18. . . . . . **143** C1
 Par PL24. . . . . **60** B6
 Penwithick PL26 . . . . **59** D7
 Plymouth PL4. . . . . **149** B4
 Redruth TR15. . . . . **140** C5
 20 St Ives TR26. . . . . . **141** B5
Seawell Rd EX23. . . . . . . **104** F7
Second Ave
 Plymouth, Billacombe
 PL9. . . . . **130** A1
 Plymouth, Devonport PL1 . **128** A2
 Plymouth, Weston Mill PL2 **127** E7
Sedley Way PL5. . . . . **124** D3
Sefton Ave PL4. . . . . **129** B3
Sefton Cl PL4. . . . . **149** C4
Segrave Rd PL2. . . . . **128** B6
Seiners Ct **10** TR6. . . . . . **55** A4
Selkirk Ho **5** PL9 . . . . . **135** F7
Selkirk Pl PL5 . . . . **124** E2
SELLAN **87** E5
Selsden Cl PL9. . . . . **136** C6
Sendall's Way PL6 . . . . . **124** F4
Seneschall Pk TR13 . . . . **146** D8
SENNEN. **96** B6
Sennen Cl PL11. . . . . **126** F4
SENNEN COVE **96** B7
Sennen Hts TR19. . . . . **96** B7
Sennen Pl PL2. . . . . **127** E5
Sennen Sch TR19 . . . . **96** C7
Sentry Cl PL27. . . . . **32** D6
Sergeants Hill TR4 . . . . . . **68** F3
Serpell Cl PL6 . . . . **124** E6
Serpells Mdw PL15. . . . . . **17** F1
Sethnoe Way TR13 . . . . . . **91** A3
Seton Gdns TR14. . . . . . . **138** B4
Setons The **6** TR14. . . . **138** F7
Seven Stars La PL5. . . . . **124** C6
Seven Trees Ct PL4 . . . . **149** B4
Severn Pl PL3. . . . . **129** C5
Sewell Ct PL3. . . . . **128** E5
SEWORGAN. **92** C6

Seymour Ave
 Newquay TR7. . . . . **110** E6
 Plymouth PL4. . . . . **149** B4
Seymour Cl TR3 . . . . **69** C3
Seymour Dr PL3 . . . . **128** F5
Seymour Mews PL4 . . . . **149** C4
Seymour Pk PL3. . . . . . . **129** A5
Seymour Pl PL1. . . . . **148** A4
Seymour Rd
 Plymouth, Mannamead
 PL3. . . . . **128** F5
 Plymouth Plympton PL7. . **130** C6
Seymour St PL4. . . . . **149** A3
Shackleton Cres **9** PL27. **31** F3
Shackleton Ct PL5. . . . . . **124** E1
Shackleton Dr TR7. . . . . **111** B5
Shaft Downs La TR27. . . . **78** F3
Shaftesbury Cotts PL4. . . **149** A4
Shaftesbury Ct **3** PL4. . **149** A4
Shakespeare Prim Sch
 PL5. . . . . **124** B2
Shakespeare Rd PL5 . . . . **124** C2
Shaldon Cres PL5. . . . . . **124** B3
Shallowford Cl PL6. . . . . **129** C8
Shallowford Rd PL6. . . . . **129** C8
Shapleys Gdns PL9. . . . . **136** A5
Shapters Rd PL4 . . . . **149** C2
Shapters Way PL4 . . . . . **135** B8
Sharaman Cl PL25 . . . . . **115** A5
Sharlands Rd EX23. . . . . . . **7** B6
Sharon Way PL6 . . . . **125** A5
Sharpitor Gdns PL2 . . . . **128** A7
Sharpitor Row PL20. . . . . **42** E4
Sharrose Rd PL9. . . . . . . **135** B5
Shaw Way PL9. . . . . **135** A7
Shearwood Cl PL7. . . . . . **131** B5
Sheep Fair Mdw **14** PL17. **39** F4
Sheepstor Rd PL6. . . . . . **125** D1
SHEFFIELD **97** F7
Sheila's Ct TR26. . . . . . . **141** D1
Shelburne Cl PL11. . . . . . **144** F3
Shelburne Rd TR11. . . . . **144** F3
Shell Cl PL6. . . . . **125** E1
Shelley Ave PL19. . . . . . . **147** D5
Shelley Rd PL25. . . . . **115** A4
Shelley Way PL5 . . . . **123** D1
Sherborne Cl PL9 . . . . . . **136** C6
Sherford Cres
 Plymouth, Elburton PL9 . . **136** C7
 Plymouth, West Park PL5 **124** A2
Sherford Rd PL9. . . . . **136** D7
Sherford Wlk PL9 . . . . . . **136** E7
Sheridan Rd PL5 . . . . **124** C1
Sherrell Pk PL20. . . . . **41** B1
Sherril Cl PL9. . . . . **135** F4
Sherwell La PL4. . . . . **149** A4
Sherwood Dr PL31. . . . . . **109** C5
SHEVIOCK. **65** B6
Sheviock La PL11. . . . . . . **65** B5
Shilla Pk PL32. . . . . **24** A8
Shilson Terr **7** PL15. . . **106** C5
Shipbuilder Cl PL26. . . . . **73** C4
Shipley Wlk PL6 . . . . **125** A1
Ships & Castles L Ctr
 TR11. . . . . **145** E3
Shirburn Rd PL6. . . . . . . **129** B8
Shire Horse Farm & Carriage
 Mus The★ TR16. . . . . . . **79** F5
Shires Way PL26. . . . . **46** F3
Shirley Gdns PL5. . . . . . . **124** C1
Shoemaker's La PL12 . . . **122** E2
Shoemakers Row PL13. . . **63** B7
Shoot Row TR15 . . . . **140** C5
SHOP
 Morwenstow **2** D1
 St Merryn. **31** F8
Shop Hill **3** TR17. . . . . . **89** C5
Shop Pk PL14. . . . . **38** A2
Shoreline TR7 . . . . **111** B8
Shores La PL27 . . . . **21** E3
Short Cotts PL11. . . . . . . **127** A3
Short Cross Mews TR4 . . . **68** C6
Short Cross Rd TR4. . . . . . **68** C6
Shortlands EX22 . . . . **8** E5
SHORTLANESEND. **69** F6
Shortlanesend Prim Sch
 TR4. . . . . **69** F6
Short Park Rd PL3. . . . . . **128** D5
Shortwood Cres PL9 . . . . **136** A7
Shrewsbury Rd PL5. . . . . **124** C4
Shrubberies Hill TR13. . . . **98** C8
Shute Hill
 Breage TR13 . . . . **90** F3
 Carharrack TR16 . . . . **80** E8
 Lostwithiel PL22 . . . . **112** C2
 Mawnan Smith TR11. . . . . **93** D3
 Pelynt PL13 . . . . **62** D5
Shute La
 Penryn TR10. . . . . **144** C8
 Pensilva PL14. . . . . **38** E4
 6 Porthleven TR13. . . . . **98** B8
Shute Mdw TR10. . . . . . . **144** C7
Shute Park Rd PL9. . . . . . **135** F6
SHUTTA. **117** D4
Shutta Rd PL13. . . . . **117** C4
Sidings The
 Bugle PL26. . . . . **47** C2
 Delabole PL33 . . . . **14** E2
Sidmouth Cotts **9** PL4. . **128** F4
Sidney Terr **7** TR15. . . . **140** C5
Silvanus Jenkin Ave
 PL14. . . . . **113** D6
Silver Birch Cl PL6. . . . . . **125** C7
Silver Ct **1** TR15. . . . . . **140** B4
Silverdale Ct TR7. . . . . . . **110** E6
Silverdale Rd TR11. . . . . **145** A2
Silver Hill TR3 . . . . **81** D6
Silvershell Rd PL29. . . . . . **22** D7

Silvershell View PL29 . . . . **22** D7
Silver St
　Bere Ferrers PL20. . . . . . . **120** A3
　Saltash PL12. . . . . **123** A4
Silver Terr PL10. . . . . **133** A6
Silverton Cl EX23 . . . . . . **104** E5
Silverton Rd EX23 . . . . . . **104** E5
Silver Way TR3 . . . . **69** C3
SILVERWELL **68** F7
Simms Terr PL18. . . . . **41** A6
Simon Cl PL9 . . . . **135** E6
Simpsons Ct 30 TR18 . . . . **143** E5
Singlerose Rd PL26 . . . . . . **59** C7
PL32 . . . . **105** C4
Sir James Smith's Com Sch
　PL32 . . . . **105** C4
Sir John Hunt Com Sports
　Coll PL5. . . . . **124** D4
Sir Robert Geffery's CE Prim
　Sch PL12 . . . . **53** C3
Sir Williams Morles
　Almshouses PL12. . . . . . . **65** A8
Sisna Park Rd PL6 . . . . . . **125** E5
SITHNEY **91** B3
SITHNEY COMMON **91** C3
Sithney Common Hill
　TR13 . . . . **91** C2
SITHNEY GREEN **91** C4
Sithney Old Hill TR13. . . . **146** A6
Sithney Prim Sch TR13 . . . **91** B3
Sithney St PL5. . . . . **123** C1
Six Turnings TR11. . . . . . . **82** A2
Skardale Gdns PL6. . . . . . **129** D8
Skerries Rd PL6. . . . . **124** F7
Skidden Hill 18 TR26 . . . . **141** B5
Skinnard La PL18. . . . . **40** F5
SKINNERS BOTTOM. **68** D5
Skitches Cnr EX23 . . . . **4** D1
Skyburriowe La TR12. . . . . **99** C6
Skylark Rise
　Plymouth PL6. . . . . **125** E8
　Tavistock PL19. . . . . **147** D1
Slade Cl PL9. . . . . **136** A5
Slade Park Rd PL14 . . . . . . **38** E5
SLADESBRIDGE **34** A6
Slades La 2 TR10. . . . . . **144** C7
Slades Rd PL25 . . . . **114** E5
Slate Cl PL33 . . . . **14** D2
Slate La PL1. . . . . **148** A2
Slatelands Cl PL7 . . . . **131** B3
SLAUGHTERBRIDGE **105** D7
Slipway PL27 . . . . **21** D2
Slipway Quay PL12. . . . . . **119** B2
Smallack Cl PL6 . . . . **124** F2
Smallack Dr PL6. . . . . **124** F2
Smallridge Cl PL9. . . . . . . **135** F5
Smallridge La EX23 . . . . **4** F1
Smeaton Sq PL3 . . . . **129** D6
Smeaton's Twr ★ PL1 . . . . **148** C1
Smithfield Ct TR8 . . . . **111** B3
Smithfield Dr PL12. . . . . . **122** B3
Smithick Hill TR11. . . . . . **145** B4
Smith's Cotts PL14 . . . . . . **113** C6
Smiths Way PL12 . . . . **122** B3
Smithy Cl PL12. . . . . **122** C4
Smithy Ct PL32 . . . . **105** D3
Smithy La TR3 . . . . **81** F7
Smugglers Row 8 TR11. . . **145** B5
Snell Dr PL12. . . . . **122** B3
Snowdrop Cres PL15 . . . . . **106** E4
Snow's Pas TR11. . . . . **145** B4
Socotra Dr 7 PL25. . . . . . . **59** A3
Solar Row 6 TR1 . . . . **137** D5
Somer Ct TR11. . . . . **145** B4
Somerset Cotts 10 PL3 . . . **128** A4
Somerset Pl PL3 . . . . **128** A4
Somerset Place La 11
　PL3. . . . . **128** A4
Somerville Rd TR6 . . . . **55** A4
Sona Merg Cl TR18. . . . . . **143** C7
Soper's Hill PL5 . . . . **120** E1
South Albany Rd TR15. . . . **140** C3
Southbourne Cl PL26. . . . . **58** E6
Southbourne Rd PL25 . . . . **114** E2
Southcliff TR11 . . . . **145** C2
South Cliff 18 TR19. . . . . . **88** C1
South Coombe La PL17. . . . **39** F8
SOUTHCOTT **11** A6
Southcott Mdws EX23. . . . . **11** A6
SOUTHDOWN **133** B6
Southdown Cl PL26 . . . . . . **58** E1
Southdown Cotts PL10 . . . **133** B6
Southdown Rd
　Millbrook PL10. . . . . **133** A6
　Sticker PL26. . . . . **58** E1
South Down Rd PL2. . . . . . **128** B6
South Downs TR15 . . . . . . **140** D2
Southdown Terr PL10 . . . . **133** A6
South Dr
　Redruth TR15. . . . . **140** D2
　South Tehidy TR14 . . . . . **138** E8
Southella Rd PL20. . . . . . . **42** D2
Southern Cl PL2 . . . . **127** F7
Southernhaye 8 PL15. . . . **106** C5
Southern Rd 31 PL17. . . . . **39** F4
Southern Terr PL4 . . . . . . **128** F4
Southernway PL9 . . . . **136** A8
Southern Way PL27 . . . . . . **108** C5
Southfield PL12. . . . . **122** C4
Southfield Rd EX23 . . . . . . **104** E5
Southfields EX22. . . . . **8** A5
Southfields Pl 3 TR26 . . . **141** B5
Southgate Ave PL9. . . . . . **135** E4
Southgate Cl PL9 . . . . **135** E4
Southgate Pl 4 PL15. . . . . **106** C5
Southgate St
　Launceston PL15 . . . . **106** C5
　Redruth TR15. . . . . **140** C3

South Harbour TR10 . . . . **144** D7
SOUTH HILL **39** C7
South Hill
　Plymouth, Hooe PL9 . . . . **135** C5
　Plymouth, Stoke PL1. . . . **128** A3
South Hill Rd PL17. . . . . . . **39** E5
SOUTH HOLE **2** D7
Southlea Terr TR3 . . . . **80** F3
Southleigh Ho 15 TR1 . . . **137** C4
Southleigh Mews 14
　TR1. . . . . **137** C4
South Milton St PL4. . . . . **149** C2
South Par 32 TR18 . . . . . . **143** E5
South Park Cl TR15 . . . . . . **140** A4
Southpark Rd PL24. . . . . . . **60** C5
SOUTH PETHERWIN **27** E8
South Petherwin Prim Sch
　PL15 . . . . **27** E8
South Pill **122** E3
South Pk
　Jacobstow EX23 . . . . **11** A6
　Redruth TR15. . . . . **139** F6
　16 St Columb Major TR9 . . . **45** E6
South Pl TR19 . . . . **86** E6
South Place Folly 5
　TR18 . . . . **143** E4
South Place Gdns TR19. . . . **86** E6
South Quay PL28. . . . . . . **107** D5
South Quay Hill TR7. . . . . **110** D6
South Rd
　Goldsithney TR20. . . . . . . **89** E5
　Stithians TR3 . . . . **80** F3
South Roskear Terr
　TR14 . . . . **138** F4
Southside Ope 14 PL1 . . . **149** A2
Southside St PL1. . . . . . . **149** A2
South St
　Fowey PL23. . . . . **116** D4
　Grampound Road TR2 . . . . **57** E1
　Lostwithiel PL22. . . . . . . **112** C2
　St Austell PL25 . . . . **114** C3
SOUTH TEHIDY. **138** E7
South Terr
　Camborne TR14. . . . . **138** D2
　12 Penzance TR18. . . . . . **143** E4
South Towan TR4 . . . . **68** A6
Southview PL10. . . . . **133** A6
South View
　9 Horrabridge PL20. . . . . **42** C4
　Liskeard PL14 . . . . **113** D7
　Penryn TR10. . . . . **144** C8
　Plymouth, Crownhill PL5 . . **124** F3
　Plymouth, Elburton PL9 . . **136** B6
　Porthleven TR13 . . . . **91** A1
South View Cl PL7 . . . . . . **130** D7
South View Dr PL31. . . . . . **109** E5
South View Pk PL7. . . . . . **130** D7
Southview Rd 15 PL24. . . . **60** B4
Southview Terr 8 TR19 . . . **88** C1
South View Terr
　Nancegollan TR13 . . . . . . **91** B7
　Plymouth PL4. . . . . **149** C3
SOUTHWAY. **124** F6
Southway PL28 . . . . **20** F2
South Way TR8 . . . . **111** F3
Southway Dr PL6 . . . . **124** E6
Southway La
　Plymouth, Southway PL6. . **125** B6
　Plymouth, Tamerton Foliot
　PL6 . . . . **124** C6
Southwell Rd PL6. . . . . . . **124** E1
SOUTH WHEATLEY **11** F3
Sovereign Ct PL7 . . . . **130** C5
Spargo Ct TR10 . . . . **93** C8
Spargo's La TR1 . . . . **137** E5
Sparkatown La PL20 . . . . . **42** E3
Sparke Cl PL7. . . . . **131** B4
SPARKWELL **131** F8
Spar La TR15. . . . . **67** D4
Sparnock Grove TR1 . . . . . **69** E3
SPARNON **96** F5
Sparnon Cl
　Redruth TR15. . . . . **140** C4
　St Austell PL25 . . . . **114** B4
Sparnon Cross TR13 . . . . . **90** F5
Sparnon Ct TR15. . . . . . . **140** C4
SPARNON GATE. **67** F4
Sparnon Hill 1 TR15. . . . **140** C4
Sparnon Terr 2 TR15 . . . . **140** C4
Sparry La TR16. . . . . **80** F8
Spaven Mor TR14 . . . . **138** F5
Speares The PL12. . . . . . . **122** B2
Spear's Terr TR11. . . . . . . **144** F1
Speech La TR3. . . . . **81** C4
Speedwell Cl
　Bude EX23 . . . . **104** F5
　Millbrook PL10. . . . . **132** F5
Speedwell Cres PL6. . . . . **129** B7
Speedwell Wlk PL6 . . . . . **129** B7
Spencer Gdns PL12 . . . . . **122** F1
Spencer Rd PL9. . . . . **135** E8
Spernen Ct TR26 . . . . **141** C2
Spernen Wyn Rd TR11. . . . **145** B2
Spicers La 11 EX23. . . . . . . **4** E1
Spindrift TR8 . . . . **44** C6
Spinnaker Quay PL9 . . . . . **134** F7
Spinney The PL7. . . . . **131** A4
Spire Ct PL3. . . . . **129** B5
Spire Hill Pk PL12. . . . . . . **122** C2
Spires The TR1 . . . . **137** C6
Spitfire Row PL27. . . . . **31** F3
Splash Pool EX23 . . . . **104** F5
SPLATT
　Rock. **21** D4
　Warbstow Cross **17** B7
Sportsmans Cl PL15. . . . . . **28** C4
Sportsmans PL32 . . . . . . **105** C3

Sportsmans Rd PL32 . . . . **105** C3
SPRIDDLESTONE **136** C4
Springfield
　Horrabridge PL20 . . . . . . **42** C4
　Portscatho TR2 . . . . **83** B2
　12 Yelverton PL20. . . . . . **42** C4
Springfield Ave PL9. . . . . **136** B6
Springfield Bsns Pk PL15. . **18** E2
Springfield Cl
　Dobwalls PL14. . . . . **50** E7
　Lostwithiel PL22. . . . . . . **112** D2
　Phillack TR27 . . . . **142** D7
　Plymouth PL9. . . . . **136** B7
　Polgooth PL26. . . . . **59** A1
　St Austell PL25 . . . . **114** F5
Springfield Dr PL3. . . . . . **128** A4
Springfield Gate PL13. . . . **117** D5
Springfield La PL9 . . . . . . **136** B7
Springfield Pk
　Barripper TR14 . . . . **79** B5
　Mylor Bridge TR11. . . . . . **82** A3
　Widegates PL13. . . . . **63** E7
Springfield Pl 15 TR9. . . . . **45** E6
Springfield Rd
　Falmouth TR11 . . . . **144** E5
　Goldsithney TR20. . . . . . . **89** E5
　Liskeard PL14 . . . . **113** C6
　Looe PL13 . . . . **117** D5
　Newquay TR7 . . . . **110** F6
　Plymouth PL9. . . . . **136** B6
Springfield Rise PL9 . . . . . **136** B7
Springfields PL26 . . . . **47** C2
Springfields Fun Pk & Pony
　Ctr ★ TR9. . . . . **45** E4
Springfield Way
　Roche PL26 . . . . **46** F3
　St Day TR16. . . . . **68** D1
　Threemilestone TR3. . . . . **69** C3
Springhill PL2. . . . . **128** C8
Spring Hill PL19 . . . . **147** B5
Springhill Gn PL2. . . . . . . **128** C8
Spring Pk PL6 . . . . **125** E7
Springwell View PL1 . . . . **109** F5
Springwood Cl PL7. . . . . . **131** A3
Spruce Gdns PL7 . . . . **131** B5
Spurway Rd PL14 . . . . **113** D5
Square The
　16 Bere Alston PL20. . . . . **41** B1
　Cawsand PL10. . . . . **133** A1
　2 Chacewater TR4 . . . . . . **69** A3
　Grampound Road TR2 . . . . **57** E1
　Gunnislake, St Ann's Chapel
　PL18 . . . . **40** E5
　3 Kilkhampton EX23 . . . . . **5** A6
　Landrake PL12. . . . . **53** C3
　Lizard TR12 . . . . **102** F2
　Ludgvan TR20 . . . . **89** A8
　Manaccan TR12 . . . . **101** A7
　Marazion TR17. . . . . **89** B5
　7 Pendeen TR19 . . . . **75** A1
　Penryn TR10. . . . . **144** D7
　Pentewan PL26 . . . . **73** C6
　Plymouth, Stonehouse PL1 **128** A2
　Portreath TR16 . . . . **67** C6
　Portscatho TR2 . . . . **83** B2
　Praze-an-Beeble TR14 . . . **79** B2
　Probus TR2 . . . . **71** C6
　Redruth TR16. . . . . **80** B5
　Saltash PL12 . . . . **122** C3
　St Keverne TR12 . . . . **101** D4
　3 St Mawes TR2. . . . . **95** A6
　St Stephen PL26 . . . . **58** B4
　St Teath PL30 . . . . **23** E7
　Tregony TR2. . . . . **71** F3
　Veryan TR2 . . . . **83** F6
　Week St Mary EX22. . . . . . **11** E8
Squire La TR16 . . . . **80** F8
Squires La TR13 . . . . **91** C2
Stable Cotts PL7 . . . . **130** F5
Stable Ct PL27. . . . . **108** C5
Stable Hobba Ind Est
　TR18 . . . . **143** B3
Stables The TR14 . . . . **67** B4
STADDISCOMBE. **135** F3
Staddiscombe Rd PL9 . . . **135** F4
Staddon Cres PL9. . . . . . . **135** E6
Staddon Gn PL9 . . . . **135** D6
Staddon La PL9 . . . . **135** E5
Staddon Park Rd PL9 . . . . **135** E6
Staddon Terrace La PL1. . **148** B4
Stafford Cl TR7 . . . . **111** D6
Staggy La TR3 . . . . **81** F7
Stag La
　Plymouth, Elburton PL9. . . **136** B8
　Plymouth, Plympton PL9 . . **130** B1
Stamford Cl PL9 . . . . **135** A6
Stamford Fort Cotts PL9. . **135** A6
Stamford Hill EX23. . . . . . . **4** D1
Stamford La PL9. . . . . **135** A6
Stamps Hill
　Fraddon PL26 . . . . **57** F8
　Indian Queens TR9 . . . . . . **45** F1
Stamps La TR15. . . . . **139** D6
Stamps The PL17. . . . . **40** D5
Stanborough Cross PL9. . . **136** C7
Stanborough Rd PL9 . . . . . **136** B7
Stanbury Ave PL6. . . . . . . **124** F1
Stanbury Cl PL15. . . . . **23** E1
Stanbury Cross EX23 . . . . . . **2** C1
Standarhay Cl PL9 . . . . . . **136** C7
Standarhay Villas PL9 . . . **136** C7
Stanford Cl 5 TR18 . . . . . **143** D5
Stanford Mews TR9. . . . . . **45** E6
Stanford Terr TR18. . . . . . **143** D5
Stangray Ave PL4 . . . . . . **128** D4
Stanharver Cl TR7 . . . . . . **111** E6
Stanhope Rd PL5 . . . . **123** C1
Stanley Ct 4 PL31 . . . . . . **109** D5

Stanley Pl PL4. . . . . **129** B2
Stanley Terr 1 TR15 . . . . . **140** B5
Stanley Way TR15. . . . . . . **140** C6
Stannary Bridge Rd
　PL19. . . . . **147** D6
Stannary La PL7 . . . . **130** E5
Stannary Rd PL26 . . . . **59** C8
Stantons Row PL14 . . . . . . **38** A3
Stanways Rd TR7 . . . . **111** D7
Staple Cl PL6 . . . . **121** C1
Stapleford Gdns PL5 . . . . **123** F5
Stapleton Rd EX23 . . . . . . **104** F4
Star Pk PL18. . . . . **41** A6
START **77** E3
Statham Rd PL31. . . . . . . **109** D4
Station App
　3 Newquay TR7 . . . . **110** F6
　3 St Columb Road TR9 . . . **45** E2
　St Erth TR27. . . . . **77** E2
Station Hill
　Hayle TR27. . . . . **142** B5
　Lelant TR26 . . . . **77** E4
　Praze-an-Beeble TR14 . . . **79** B2
　Redruth TR15. . . . . **140** B4
Station La PL18. . . . . **41** A3
Station Par TR7. . . . . **110** F6
Station Rd
　20 Bere Alston PL20. . . . . **41** B1
　Bere Ferrers PL20. . . . . . **119** E3
　Bugle PL26. . . . . **47** C2
　Camborne TR15. . . . . . . **139** C5
　Carnhell Green TR14 . . . . **78** F4
　Chacewater TR4. . . . . **68** F4
　Fowey PL23. . . . . **116** D5
　Grampound Road TR2 . . . . **57** E1
　Gunnislake PL18 . . . . **40** F6
　Helston TR13. . . . . **146** C7
　Horrabridge PL20 . . . . . . **42** C4
　Kelly Bray PL17 . . . . **39** F6
　Launceston PL15 . . . . . . **106** C6
　Liskeard PL14 . . . . **113** B4
　Looe PL13 . . . . **117** C4
　Mary Tavy PL19 . . . . **30** F5
　North Brentor PL19 . . . . . **30** E8
　Padstow PL28 . . . . **107** D5
　Par PL24 . . . . **60** C5
　Penryn TR10. . . . . **144** B8
　Penzance TR18. . . . . **143** F6
　Perranarworthal TR3. . . . . **81** E6
　Perranporth TR6 . . . . **55** B5
　Plymouth, Elburton PL9. . . **136** C7
　Plymouth, Keyham PL2 . . . **127** E5
　Plymouth, Plympton PL7 . . **130** C5
　Plymouth, Tamerton Foliot
　PL5 . . . . **124** A6
　Redruth TR15. . . . . **140** C5
　Saltash PL12 . . . . **123** A2
　St Columb Major TR9 . . . . **45** E5
　1 St Columb Road TR9 . . . **45** E2
　St Mabyn PL30. . . . . **34** C8
　St Newlyn East TR8 . . . . . **56** B7
　Truro TR1 . . . . **137** B4
　Yelverton PL20. . . . . **42** D2
Station View PL19. . . . . . . **30** E8
Station Yd 6 PL31 . . . . . . **109** D5
Steamers Hill TR27. . . . . . . **78** C5
Steamers Mdw TR27. . . . . . **78** C5
Steeple Cl
　Plymouth PL9. . . . . **135** F4
　St Ives TR26 . . . . **141** B3
Steeple La TR26 . . . . **141** B3
Steeple View Ct TR26 . . . . **141** C1
Steeple Woodland Nature
　Reserve ★ TR26 . . . . **141** B3
Steer Park Rd PL7 . . . . . . **131** C5
Steer Point Cotts PL8 . . . **136** F2
Stefan Cl PL9 . . . . **135** B5
STENALEES **59** B8
Stenalees Hill PL26 . . . . . . **59** C7
Stenlake Pl PL4. . . . . **129** B2
Stenlake Terr PL4. . . . . . . **129** B2
STENNACK **141** A5
Stennack Gdns 14 TR26 . . **141** A5
Stennack Parc TR19. . . . . . **86** F8
Stennack Rd PL25. . . . . . . **115** B4
Stennack The TR26 . . . . . **141** B5
Stentaway Cl PL9 . . . . **135** F8
Stentaway Dr PL9 . . . . **136** A8
Stentaway Rd PL9. . . . . . . **135** F8
STEPASIDE **58** B5
Stephens Rd PL14. . . . . . . **113** E7
Stephney Cl TR11. . . . . . . **144** C2
Steppy Downs Rd TR27. . . . **78** A1
Sterts Theatre ★ PL14. . . . . **38** D7
Stewarts Rd EX22 . . . . **11** E8
STIBB **4** D5
STICKER **58** F1
Stiles The TR8 . . . . **56** B7
Stillman Ct 7 PL4 . . . . . . **149** A2
Stillman St PL4 . . . . **149** A2
Stippy Stappy 11 TR5. . . . . **54** D1
Stirling Ct PL5 . . . . **123** C1
Stirling Rd PL5 . . . . **123** C1
STITHIANS **80** F3
Stithians Com Prim Sch
　TR3 . . . . **80** F4
Stithians Row TR16. . . . . . **80** B5
Stockadon Farm Barns
　PL12. . . . . **118** B4
Stoggy La PL7 . . . . **131** A6
STOKE **128** A3
STOKE CLIMSLAND **28** E1
Stoke Climsland Sch
　PL17. . . . . **28** D1
Stoke Damerel Bsns Ctr 9
　PL3. . . . . **128** A4
Stoke Damerel Com Coll
　PL3. . . . . **128** B4

Sil-Sum 175

Stoke Damerel Prim Sch
　PL1. . . . . **128** A3
Stoke Hill La PL20. . . . . . . **42** B2
Stoke Rd
　Bray Shop PL17. . . . . **28** A1
　Kelly Bray PL17. . . . . **39** E6
　Linkinhorne PL17. . . . . . . **39** A8
　Plymouth PL1. . . . . **148** A3
Stokesay Ave PL6 . . . . . . **125** A5
Stokes La PL1. . . . . **149** A2
Stokes Rd TR1. . . . . **137** C5
Stoke Terr PL17. . . . . **39** E6
Stokingway Cl PL9 . . . . . . **135** E6
Stonebarton Cl PL7 . . . . . **130** C6
Stonebarton Rd PL7. . . . . **130** C6
Stone Chair La TR19 . . . . . **96** B7
Stone Cross PL16 . . . . **19** F5
Stonehall Flats PL1 . . . . . **128** A1
Stone Hill EX23 . . . . **4** E2
STONEHOUSE **128** A1
Stonehouse Bridge PL1 . . **128** A1
Stonehouse St PL1. . . . . . **148** A2
Stonerock Flats PL13. . . . **117** C1
Stones Ct 30 TR26. . . . . . **141** B5
Stonewood Ct 4 TR9 . . . . . **45** E6
Stoney Hill PL25 . . . . **59** A4
Stoney La
　Polgooth PL26. . . . . **59** A1
　St Austell PL25 . . . . **114** C4
Stoney Lands PL12. . . . . . . **53** C3
Stony La
　Bodmin PL31. . . . . **34** D1
　Gunnislake PL18 . . . . **40** F5
Stopford Pl PL1. . . . . **127** F7
STOPTIDE. **21** E2
Stott Cl PL3 . . . . **129** D5
Stour Cl PL3 . . . . **129** D6
STOURSCOMBE. **106** F4
Stourscombe PL15. . . . . . **106** F3
Stourscombe Wood
　PL15. . . . . **106** F4
Stowe Gdns PL5 . . . . **124** B2
STOWFORD. **5** E8
Stowford Cl PL20 . . . . **42** E3
Stowford Cross EX22. . . . . . **5** F8
Stracey Rd TR11. . . . . **145** B2
Strafford Cl EX23 . . . . **104** C3
Strand TR18 . . . . **143** C2
Strand Sh Ctr The EX23. . . **104** D5
Strand St
　Padstow PL28 . . . . **107** D5
　Plymouth PL1. . . . . **134** A8
Strand The
　Bude EX23 . . . . **104** D5
　Falmouth TR11. . . . . **145** C2
　Padstow PL28 . . . . **107** D5
Strangways Terr TR1. . . . . **137** D3
Strangways Villas TR1. . . . **137** D3
STRATTON **4** E1
Stratton Hospl EX23. . . . . . . **4** D1
Stratton Pl TR11 . . . . **145** A6
Stratton Prim Sch EX23 . . . **4** D1
Stratton Rd
　Bude EX23 . . . . **104** F4
　Stratton EX23 . . . . **4** D1
Stratton Terr
　Falmouth TR11. . . . . **145** A6
　Truro TR1. . . . . **137** B4
Stratton Wlk PL2. . . . . . . **128** D8
Strawberry Cl TR15 . . . . . **140** B6
Strawberry Cres TR15. . . . **140** B6
Strawberry Fields TR16. . . **140** E1
Strawberry Gdns TR16 . . . **140** E1
Strawberry La
　Hayle TR27. . . . . **142** D4
　Lelant TR26 . . . . **77** E4
　Redruth TR15. . . . . **140** B6
Stray Park Ct TR14. . . . . . **138** E2
Stray Park Rd TR14 . . . . . **138** E2
Stray Park Way TR14. . . . . **138** F2
Street-an-Garrow 17
　TR26 . . . . **141** B5
Street-an-Pol 3 TR26 . . . **141** B5
Stret Caradoc TR7 . . . . . . **110** C5
Stret Constantine TR7. . . . **110** C5
Stretyn 5 TR3. . . . . **81** F7
Strickland Cotts 6 TR18 . . **143** C2
Stringers Hill TR20. . . . . . . **88** A5
Strode Rd PL7 . . . . **130** F6
Stroma Cl PL6 . . . . **124** F7
Stroud Park Rd PL2 . . . . . **128** C7
Stuart House Arts & Heritage
　Ctr ★ PL14 . . . . **113** C5
Stuart Rd PL3 . . . . **148** A4
Stuart Road Prim Sch
　PL1. . . . . **148** A4
Stuarts Way PL12 . . . . **53** E5
Stucley Rd EX23 . . . . **4** D1
Sturdee Rd PL2. . . . . **128** A5
Sturadon Cross EX23 . . . . . **5** A8
Sugar Mill Bsns Pk PL9 . . **129** C5
SUMMERCOURT **57** C2
Summercourt TR10 . . . . . **144** D7
Summercourt Prim Sch
　TR8 . . . . **57** C2
Summerfield Cl PL26. . . . . **73** B3
Summerfields PL12 . . . . . **122** D1
Summerheath TR10. . . . . . **81** C1
Summerhill Rd PL15 . . . . . **106** A5
Summer La PL13. . . . . **62** D6
Summerlands Cl PL7. . . . . **131** C5
Summerlands Gdns PL7 . . **131** C5
Summerlane Pk PL13 . . . . . **62** D6
Summerleaze Ave EX23 . . **104** D7
Summerleaze Cres EX23 . . **104** D6

Summers Cl PL6 . . . . **129** B7
Summers St PL22 . . . . . . **112** C2
Summerville Cross EX39 . . 3 C6
Suncrest PL14 . . . . **38** A4
Suncrest Est TR9 . . . . **45** E1
Sunderland Cl PL9 . . . . . **135** A6
Sunderland Rd PL27 . . . . **31** F3
Sun Girt La PL14 . . . . . . **113** C5
Sunningdale TR1 . . . . . . **137** A4
Sunningdale Rd PL12 . . . **122** C2
Sunnybank **23** TR13 . . . . . **98** C8
Sunny Bank
　Bodmin PL30 . . . . **48** E8
　Liskeard PL14 . . . . **113** A4
Sunnybanks PL12 . . . . . . **53** E4
Sunny Cnr
　Goldsithney TR20 . . . . . . **89** F5
　Truro TR4 . . . . **81** B7
Sunny Corner La TR19. . . **96** C7
Sunnycroft PL13 . . . . . . **117** C3
Sunny Dene PL5 . . . . **123** D1
Sunnyside
　Carnkie TR13 . . . . **80** D1
　Crantock TR8 . . . . **110** A3
　Menheniot PL14 . . . . **51** F5
　Menheniot PL14 . . . . **52** B5
　2 Perranporth TR6. . . . . **55** A4
　PL11 . . . . **64** F7
　Portscatho TR2 . . . . **83** B2
　7 Redruth TR15 . . . . . . **140** B4
Sunnyside Mdw PL32 . . . **105** D4
Sunnyside Parc TR15 . . . **139** C8
Sunnyside Rd PL14 . . . . . **129** B2
Sunny Terr PL18 . . . . . . **143** B2
Sunnyvale Cl TR16 . . . . . **67** C6
Sunnyvale Rd TR16. . . . . . **67** D6
Sunrising Est PL13 . . . . . **117** D5
Sunset Dr **8** TR13 . . . . . . **98** C8
Sunset Gdns **9** TR13 . . . . **98** C8
Sun Valley Pk TR9 . . . . . . **45** E6
Sunway Cl PL19 . . . . . . **147** A6
Sunwell La
　Antony PL11. . . . . **65** E4
　St John PL11 . . . . **132** A8
Surf View TR7 . . . . **110** A6
Sussex Pl PL1. . . . . **148** C2
Sussex Rd PL2 . . . . **127** F5
Sussex St PL1. . . . . **148** C2
Sussex Terr **5** PL4. . . . . **127** F5
Sutherland Rd PL4 . . . . . **149** A4
Sutton Cl EX23 . . . . **127** F1
Sutton Mews **22** PL4 . . . . **149** A2
Sutton Pl PL4 . . . . **149** B2
Sutton Rd PL4 . . . . **149** B2
Sutton Wharf PL4 . . . . . **149** A2
Swaindale Rd **3** PL3 . . . **128** E6
Swale Cl PL3 . . . . **129** B6
Swallow Cl EX23 . . . . . . **104** D5
Swallowfield Cl PL4 . . . . **60** D5
Swallow Ho **13** TR11. . . . **145** C3
Swallows End PL9 . . . . . **135** E8
Swan Cl PL10 . . . . **133** A6
Swan Gdns PL7 . . . . **130** F5
Swanpool Ct TR11 . . . . . **145** A1
Swanpool Hill TR11 . . . . **145** A2
Swanpool Nature Reserve★
　TR11 . . . . **145** A2
Swanpool Rd TR11 . . . . . **144** F1
Swanpool St TR11 . . . . . **145** A2
SWANVALE **144** F3
Swanvale Rd TR11 . . . . . **144** F3
Sweet Briar Cres TR7 . . . **111** A4
Swift Gdns PL5 . . . . **124** C2
Swinburne Gdns PL5. . . . **124** C1
Swingate Cross EX22. . . . **13** E8
Sycamore Ave
　Plymouth PL4. . . . . **149** C2
　St Austell PL25 . . . . . . **114** E5
　Tavistock PL19 . . . . . . **147** C2
Sycamore Cl
　Bodmin PL31 . . . . **109** B4
　Polgooth PL26 . . . . **59** A1
　Praze-an-Beeble TR14 . . . . **79** B2
　Rock PL27 . . . . **21** E3
Sycamore Dr
　Illogan TR15. . . . . **139** D7
　Plymouth PL6. . . . . **125** C7
　Redruth TR15. . . . . **140** D5
　Torpoint PL11 . . . . **127** A3
Sycamore Gdns TR8. . . . . **57** B7
Sycamore Rd PL12 . . . . . **122** B3
Sycamores The PL25 . . . . **114** C4
Sycamore Way PL6 . . . . . **125** E6
Sydenham Cross PL19 . . . **29** C2
SYDENHAM DAMEREL **29** D2
Sydney Cl
　Plymouth PL7. . . . . **130** E4
　St Austell PL25 . . . . . . **114** C3
Sydney Rd
　Newquay TR7. . . . . **110** D6
　Torpoint PL11 . . . . **127** B3
Sydney St PL1 . . . . **148** B4
Sylvan Cl PL25 . . . . **114** E6
Sylvan Ct PL1. . . . . **128** A3
Sylverton Pl **12** TR18 . . . **143** C7
Symons Cl
　Blackwater TR4 . . . . **68** E5
　St Austell PL25 . . . . . . **115** A5
Symons Hill TR11 . . . . . . **145** A5
Symons Rd PL12 . . . . . . **122** F2
Symons Row PL14 . . . . . . **37** F3
Symons Terr TR15 . . . . . **140** B5
Syra Cl PL30 . . . . **23** B2

T

Tabernacle St TR1 . . . . . **137** D4
Tackbear Rd EX22, EX23. . . .7 E4
Tailyour Rd PL6. . . . . . . **124** F2
Talbot Gdns PL5 . . . . . . **127** D7
Talexandra Terr PL15 . . . **106** D5
Talgos Cl TR16. . . . . **140** E8
TALLAND **62** F2
Talland Ct **29** TR26 . . . . . **141** B5
Talland Hill PL13. . . . . . . **62** E2
Talland Rd TR26 . . . . . . **141** B5
Talland St PL13 . . . . **62** D1
Talmena Ave PL27 . . . . . **108** A5
TALSKIDDY **45** E8
Talveneth
　Camborne TR14 . . . . . . **138** F3
　Pendeen TR19 . . . . **75** A1
　Redruth TR15. . . . . **140** C6
Talvenydh Ct PL31 . . . . . **109** D5
Tamar Ave
　Plymouth PL2. . . . . **127** E5
　Tavistock PL19 . . . . . . **147** D5
Tamar Bridge PL5. . . . . . **123** A2
Tamar Bsns Pk PL15 . . . . **18** E2
Tamar Cl
　18 Bere Alston PL20 . . . . . **41** B1
　29 Callington PL17 . . . . . **39** F4
Tamar Ho PL1 . . . . **127** E1
Tamarisk Cl PL28 . . . . . . **31** F7
Tamarisk La TR7 . . . . . . **111** A4
Tamar Otter & Wildlife Ctr★
　PL15 . . . . **18** B8
Tamar Science Pk PL6 . . **125** C4
Tamarside Sp Complex
　PL5 . . . . **123** F2
Tamar St
　Plymouth PL1. . . . . **127** E3
　Saltash PL12 . . . . **123** A2
　Torpoint PL11 . . . . **127** C3
Tamar Terr
　Calstock PL17 . . . . **41** A3
　Horsebridge PL19 . . . . . **29** C1
　Launceston PL15 . . . . . **106** D5
　Saltash PL12 . . . . **123** A2
Tamar Valley Ctr★ PL18 . . **40** F5
*Tamar Valley Discovery
　Trail*★ PL20. . . . . **41** C1
Tamar Valley Donkey Pk★
　PL18 . . . . **40** D5
Tamar View
　Launceston PL15 . . . . . **106** D5
　Milton Abbot PL19 . . . . . **29** C6
　St Dominick PL12. . . . . . **40** D2
Tamar View Ind Est
　PL12 . . . . **122** D5
Tamar Villas PL9 . . . . . . **135** D7
Tamar Way PL18 . . . . **41** A6
Tamar Wharf PL1 . . . . . . **127** D3
Tamblin Ave PL14. . . . . . . **50** E7
Tamerton Ave PL5 . . . . . **123** D1
Tamerton Cl PL5. . . . . . . **124** A6
TAMERTON FOLIOT. **124** D7
Tamerton Foliot Rd PL6 . . **124** D5
Tamerton Rd PL6 . . . . . . **121** B2
Tangmere Ave PL5. . . . . **123** E5
Tangye Cl TR16 . . . . **67** E5
Tangye Rd TR15 . . . . . . **139** C6
Tanhouse Rd PL22 . . . . . **112** C2
Tanwood View PL31. . . . **109** C5
Tanyard La **19** PL17 . . . . . **39** E4
Tapson Dr PL9 . . . . **135** A6
Taranto Rd TR13 . . . . . . **146** D4
Taroveor Rd TR18. . . . . . **143** E6
Taroveor Terr **3** TR18 . . **143** E5
Tarr PL22. . . . . **49** E3
Tarrandean La TR3. . . . . . **81** E6
Tarten Cross PL12 . . . . . . **53** B4
Tate St Ives (Gall)★
　TR26 . . . . **141** B6
Taunton Ave PL5 . . . . . . **124** B5
Taunton Pl PL5 . . . . **124** B5
Tavern Barn PL23 . . . . . **116** C5
TAVISTOCK **147** E5
Tavistock Coll PL19 . . . . **147** A3
Tavistock Community
　Hospital PL19. . . . . **147** B5
Tavistock Com Prim Sch
　PL19 . . . . **147** B4
Tavistock Cross PL20. . . . **41** C2
Tavistock Mus★ PL19 . . . **147** C5
Tavistock Pl PL4 . . . . . . **149** A3
Tavistock Rd
　Callington PL17 . . . . **39** F4
　Launceston PL15 . . . . . **106** D5
　Launceston, Stourscombe
　　PL15 . . . . **106** E3
　Plymouth Manadon PL5. . **124** E1
　Plymouth PL6. . . . . **125** B5
　Yelverton PL20. . . . . **42** C3
Tavistock St Peter's CE Jun
　Sch PL19 . . . . **147** D5
Tavy Pl PL4. . . . . **128** F4
Tavy Rd
　Saltash PL12 . . . . **123** A3
　Tavistock PL19 . . . . . . **147** D5
Taw Cl PL3 . . . . **129** D6
Tayberry Dr TR16 . . . . . **140** F1
Tay Gdns PL3 . . . . **129** D7
Taylor Rd PL12 . . . . **122** C4
Taylor's Cross EX23 . . . . . .5 B7
Taylor Sq PL19 . . . . **147** B6
Teats Hill Flats PL4 . . . . **149** B1
Teats Hill Rd PL4 . . . . . . **149** B1
Tedder Rd **4** PL26 . . . . . . **59** D7
Tees Cl PL3. . . . . **129** C7

Teetotal St TR26 . . . . . . **141** C6
Tehidy Cl TR14. . . . . **138** F7
Tehidy Country Park★
　TR14 . . . . **67** B4
Tehidy Gdns TR14 . . . . . **138** F7
Tehidy Rd
　Camborne TR14 . . . . . . **138** D4
　Tywardreath PL24. . . . . . **60** D5
Tehidy Terr TR11 . . . . . . **145** A6
Teign Rd PL3 . . . . **129** B6
Telcarne Ct TR27. . . . . . . **78** D6
Telegraph Hill TR16. . . . . **68** E1
Telegraph St TR16 . . . . . . **68** D1
Telegraph Wharf PL1 . . . **134** A8
Telephone La PL26. . . . . . **59** C8
Telford Cres PL5. . . . . . . **123** F2
Temeraire Rd PL5. . . . . . **124** D2
TEMPLE **36** B8
Tenacres La PL14 . . . . . . **38** E4
Tenby Rd PL5. . . . . **123** C1
TENCREEK. **63** A3
Tencreek Ave TR18 . . . . **143** E5
Tenderah Ct TR13. . . . . . **146** C7
Tenderah Rd TR13 . . . . . **146** C6
Tennyson Gdns PL5 . . . . **124** B1
Tern Gdns PL7. . . . . **130** F5
Terrace The
　Chacewater TR4. . . . . . . **68** F3
　Crafthole PL11 . . . . **65** B5
　Dobwalls PL14. . . . . **50** D7
　Downderry PL11 . . . . **64** C5
　East Portholland PL26 . . . . **84** E5
　Harrowbarrow PL17 . . . . . **40** D5
　Penryn TR10. . . . . **144** C3
　Pentewan PL26 . . . . **73** D6
　Port Isaac PL29 . . . . **22** E7
　Portwrinkle PL11. . . . . . . **65** A4
　Rock PL27 . . . . **21** D2
　St Ives TR26 . . . . **141** B5
　Yeolmbridge PL15 . . . . . . **18** E6
Terra Nova Gn PL2. . . . . **128** B5
TERRAS. **58** A4
Terras Hill PL22. . . . . . . **112** C3
Terras Rd PL26 . . . . **58** A4
TETCOTT **13** C7
Tethadene PL30 . . . . **23** E7
Tewington Pl PL25 . . . . **114** B4
Tewkesbury Cl PL2. . . . . **128** A8
Tewynn Ct TR27 . . . . . . **142** E8
Teyla Tor Rd TR26 . . . . . **141** D1
Thackeray Gdns PL5 . . . . **124** B1
Thames Gdns PL3. . . . . . **129** D5
Thanckes Cl PL11 . . . . . . **127** A3
Thanckes Dr PL11. . . . . . **127** A4
The All Saints CE Academy
　PL5 . . . . **124** B1
Theatre Ope PL1. . . . . . . **127** F1
Theatre Royal Plymouth
　PL1 . . . . **148** C2
THE BEACON **10** F6
The Beeches PL18 . . . . . . **40** D5
The Bishops CE Prim Sch
　TR7 . . . . **110** F4
The Crescent PL25 . . . . . **114** E4
The Glebe **11** PL14 . . . . . . **37** F3
The Hayes TR7 . . . . **137** E6
Therlow Rd PL3. . . . . **129** B6
The Roseland Com Coll
　TR2 . . . . **72** A4
The Sidings PL25 . . . . . . **114** E3
Thetford Gdns PL6 . . . . . **129** D8
Theydon Rd TR11 . . . . . **144** F3
Third Ave
　Plymouth, Billacombe
　　PL9 . . . . **130** A1
　Plymouth, Camels Head
　　PL2 . . . . **127** E7
　Plymouth, Stoke PL11 . . . **128** A2
Thirlmere Gdns PL6. . . . . **124** F4
Thistle Cl PL6. . . . . **125** E7
Thomas Bullock Cl PL30. . . **48** C2
Thomas Johnson Ct **6**
　TR1 . . . . **137** C4
Thomas St **4** TR13. . . . . . **98** C8
Thomas Terr **5** TR13. . . . . **98** C8
Thornberry Terr TR18 . . . **143** F6
Thornbury Park Ave PL3 . **128** D6
Thornbury Rd PL6. . . . . . **125** E4
Thorn Cl PL15 . . . . **26** C7
Thorncross PL23 . . . . .4 F2
Thorndon Cross EX22 . . . . .8 F5
Thorn Moor Cross PL15 . . . **19** F7
Thornpark Rd PL25. . . . . **114** E5
Thorn Pk PL3 . . . . **128** F5
Thorn Terr PL14 . . . . **113** B5
Thornton Ave PL4. . . . . . **149** B4
Thornton Cl PL26 . . . . **46** F3
Thornville Terr PL9 . . . . . **135** C7
Thornwell La PL12. . . . . . **53** E2
Thornyville Cl PL9 . . . . . **135** C8
Thornyville Dr PL9 . . . . . **135** D8
Thornyville Villas PL9 . . . **135** C8
Three Bridges Specl Sch **1**
　TR10. . . . . **144** D3
THREE BURROWS **68** F5
Three Corners Cl PL32 . . **105** B2
Three Cross TR13 . . . . . . **91** F5
THREE HAMMERS **17** C6
Three Holes Cross PL27. . . **34** A8
THREEMILESTONE **69** D4
Threemilestone Ind Est
　TR4 . . . . **69** C3

Threemilestone Prim Sch
　TR3 . . . . **69** D3
Threemilestone Ret Pk
　TR3 . . . . **69** C4
THREEWATERS. **34** C1
THURDON 5 D5
Thurlestone Wlk PL6 . . . **129** D8
Tiddy Brook Rd
　Tavistock PL19 . . . . . . **147** E2
　Whitchurch PL19 . . . . . **147** E2
Tiddy Cl
　St Germans PL12 . . . . . . **65** B8
　Tavistock PL19 . . . . . . **147** B3
TIDEFORD **52** F2
Tideford Cross La PL12. . . **52** F3
Tideford Dr
　Landrake PL12. . . . . **53** A2
　St Germans PL12 . . . . . . **65** B8
Tideford Rd PL12 . . . . . . **53** C3
Tidemill Ho TR11 . . . . . . **145** C3
Tides Reach TR7. . . . . . . **111** B7
Tillard Cl PL7. . . . . **131** C5
Tillie St **5** PL17. . . . . **39** E4
Tilly Cl PL9 . . . . **135** F4
Timber Cl PL25 . . . . **114** B4
Tincombe PL12 . . . . **122** C2
Tincroft Rd TR15. . . . . . . **139** B4
Tin La PL4 . . . . **149** A2
Tinners Dr PL27 . . . . **21** D6
Tinners Way
　Callington PL17 . . . . **39** F5
　New Polzeath PL27 . . . . . **21** D6
　16 St Ives TR26. . . . . . . **77** A6
Tinners Wlk TR11 . . . . . . **145** D3
Tinney Dr TR1 . . . . **137** E5
Tinside Lido PL1. . . . . . . **148** C1
TINTAGEL **14** C7
Tintagel Castle★ PL34. . . **14** B8
Tintagel Cres PL2. . . . . . **128** C8
Tintagel Hts PL34 . . . . . . **14** D6
Tintagel Old Post Office★
　PL34 . . . . **14** C7
Tintagel Prim Sch PL34 . . **14** C6
Tintagel Rd PL35. . . . . 9 C1
Tintagel Terr PL22 . . . . . . **22** D7
Tintagel Toy Mus★ PL34 . . **14** C7
Tintagel Visitor Ctr★
　PL34 . . . . **14** C7
Tintern Ave PL4. . . . . . . **149** C2
Tiny Mdws
　Launceston PL15 . . . . . . **18** E1
　South Petherwin PL15. . . **27** F8
Tipple Cross PL15. . . . . . . **19** C6
Tithe Rd PL7. . . . . **130** B7
TITSON 7 D4
Tiverton Cl PL6 . . . . **125** B8
Tobruk Rd PL12. . . . . . . **122** E3
Toby Way TR7 . . . . **110** D7
Toddington Lea PL26. . . . **58** E5
TODPOOL **68** F2
TOLBOROUGH **25** E4
TOLCARNE
　Camborne **79** D5
　Newlyn. **143** C3
Tolcarne Cl PL25 . . . . . . **114** E3
Tolcarne Mews **7** TR7 . . **110** F6
Tolcarne Rd
　Camborne TR14 . . . . **79** D5
　Newquay TR7. . . . . **110** F6
　St Day TR16. . . . . **68** D1
Tolcarne Terr TR18 . . . . **143** C3
Tolcrows Ct TR7 . . . . . . **111** C7
TOLDISH **45** F2
Tolgarrick Rd TR14 . . . . **138** F5
Tolgus Hill TR15 . . . . . . **140** A5
TOLGUS MOUNT. **139** E8
Tolgus Pl TR15 . . . . **140** A6
Tolgus Tin★ TR16 . . . . . . **67** F5
Tolgus Vean TR15. . . . . . **140** A5
Tolgus Wartha TR15 . . . . **140** A6
Tollgate Cl PL14 . . . . **113** B4
Tollox Pl PL3 . . . . **129** B4
Tollyfrank Hill TR2. . . . . . **83** F6
Tolpedn Flats TR26 . . . . **141** E2
Tolponds Rd TR13. . . . . . **91** A1
Tolroy Rd TR27 . . . . **142** D1
Tolskithy **139** E7
Tolskithy La TR15 . . . . . **139** E6
Tolticken Hill TR16. . . . . . **67** E6
Toltuff Cres TR18 . . . . . . **143** C4
Toltuff Rd TR18 . . . . **143** C4
TOLVADDON **138** F6
TOLVADDON DOWNS . . . **139** A7
Tolvaddon Energy Pk
　TR14 . . . . **138** F7
Tolvaddon Rd TR15 . . . . **139** A5
Tolvan Cross TR12 . . . . . . **92** C2
Tolver Pl TR18 . . . . **143** E6
Tolver Rd TR18 . . . . **143** E6
Tolverth Terr TR20 . . . . . . **88** F6
Tolview Terr TR27 . . . . . **142** B4
Tom Lyon Rd PL14 . . . . . **113** E5
Tom Nicolls Cl **7** PL14 . . . **38** A3
Top Hill TR2 . . . . **57** E1
Top of the Town Ctyd
　PL12. . . . . **122** F2
Top Rd PL11 . . . . **64** C5
Tor Bridge High PL6 . . . . **125** D2
Tor Bridge Prim Sch
　PL6 . . . . **125** D2
Torbridge Rd
　6 Horrabridge PL20. . . . . **42** C4
　Plymouth PL7. . . . . **130** E6
Torbryan Cl PL6 . . . . **129** E8
Tor Cl
　Plymouth, Hartley PL3. . . **128** E7

Tor Cl *continued*
　Porthleven TR13 . . . . **91** B1
Tor Cres PL3 . . . . **128** E7
Tor La PL12. . . . . **122** B1
Torland Rd PL3 . . . . **128** E7
Torleven Rd TR13 . . . . . . **91** B2
TORPOINT. **127** C3
Torpoint Com Coll PL11 . **127** A4
Torpoint Com Sch PL11 . . **127** A4
Torpoint Inf Sch PL11 . . . **127** B3
Tor Rd
　Newquay TR7. . . . . **110** E6
　Plymouth PL3. . . . . **128** E7
Torridge Cl PL7 . . . . **131** A6
Torridge Rd PL7 . . . . **130** F6
Torridge Way PL3. . . . . . **129** C5
Torr La PL3. . . . . **128** E7
Torr Rd PL3 . . . . **128** E7
Torr View Ave PL3 . . . . . **128** D7
Tors View Cl PL17. . . . . . . **39** F4
Torver Cl PL6. . . . . **125** D2
Tor View
　Bugle PL26. . . . . **47** C2
　Camelford PL32. . . . . . . **105** C2
　7 Horrabridge PL20. . . . . **42** C4
　Tregadillett PL15 . . . . . . **18** C2
Torwood Cl PL31. . . . . . . **109** D4
Tory Brook Ave PL7 . . . . **130** E6
Tory Brook Ct PL7 . . . . . **130** E6
Tory Way PL7. . . . . **130** D6
TOSBERRY 3 B8
Tosberry Cross EX39 . . . . . . 3 B8
Tothill Ave PL4 . . . . **149** B3
Tothill Rd PL4 . . . . **149** B3
Totnes Cl PL7 . . . . **131** B4
Tovey Cres PL5 . . . . **124** D2
Towan Blystra Rd TR7. . . **111** A5
TOWAN CROSS. **68** B7
Towan Ct PL28. . . . . **31** E8
Towan Rd
　Pentewan PL26 . . . . **73** D8
　Porthtowan TR4. . . . . . . **68** A7
Towans The PL28 . . . . **20** D1
Towans View TR27. . . . . . **78** D6
TOWEDNACK **76** E5
Towednack Rd TR26 . . . . . **77** A6
Tower Cl
　Pelynt PL13 . . . . **62** D6
　Sennen TR19 . . . . **96** B6
Tower Ct PL12 . . . . **122** C2
Towerfield Dr PL6 . . . . . **125** C8
Tower Hill
　Looe PL13 . . . . **117** D3
　Wadebridge PL27 . . . . . **108** E5
Tower Hill Gdns **12** PL31. **109** E5
Tower Hill Rd PL15. . . . . . **13** F1
Tower Mdws TR19 . . . . . . **97** A6
Tower Park Est PL13 . . . . **62** D6
Tower Park Rd PL13 . . . . . **62** C6
Tower Pk
　Fowey PL23 . . . . **116** B3
　Lanivet PL30 . . . . **47** E7
　Pelynt PL13 . . . . **62** D6
Tower Rd
　Newquay TR7. . . . . **110** D6
　St Erme TR9 . . . . **70** D8
Towers Cl PL6 . . . . **125** F2
Tower St PL15 . . . . **106** C6
Tower View PL12 . . . . . . **122** D1
Town Arms Pas PL31. . . . **109** E5
Town End PL31 . . . . **109** C5
Town Farm TR15. . . . . . . **140** C3
Town Farm Cl **5** PL20. . . . **42** C4
Townfield TR15 . . . . **139** C6
Town Hill TR5 . . . . **54** D1
TOWNLAKE. **29** C1
Town Mill Gdns PL19. . . . **147** C6
Town Mills Flats PL15 . . . **106** B7
Town Quay TR1. . . . . **137** D4
Townsend
　Polruan PL23 . . . . **116** D2
　14 Stratton EX23. . . . . . . 4 E1
TOWNSHEND **90** D7
Townshend Ave PL2. . . . **127** E5
Townswell Cl PL12. . . . . . **53** E2
Townswell La PL12. . . . . . **53** E2
TRABOE **100** E4
Traboe Cross TR12. . . . . **100** D3
Tracey Ct PL1. . . . . **148** B3
Trafalgar Fields TR20. . . . **88** B7
Trafalgar Pl **2** PL5 . . . . **127** D8
Trafalgar Pl **3** PL1. . . . . **127** F3
Trafalgar Place La PL1 . . **127** F3
Trafalgar Sq TR1. . . . . . . **137** D4
Trafalgar St PL4 . . . . **149** A3
Traine Brake PL9 . . . . . . **136** C1
Traine Rd PL9 . . . . **136** B1
Traly Cl EX23 . . . . **104** F4
TRAMAGENNA **105** A1
Tram La TR16. . . . . **140** E1
Tramway Rd PL6. . . . . . . **125** E7
TRANNACK **91** D5
Trannack Mill Ind Est
　TR13 . . . . **91** E5
Trannack Prim Sch TR13 . **91** E5
Trannack Terr TR18 . . . . **143** E7
Tranquil La PL31. . . . . . . **109** C5
Transit Way PL5 . . . . **124** E3
Trasdeves Orch **16** PL17. . . **39** F4
Travers Cl PL14 . . . . **113** A6
Treago Gdns PL6 . . . . . . **125** C8
TREAL **103** A6
Trease **3** TR9 . . . . **75** A1
Treassowe Rd TR18 . . . . **143** E6
Treassowe Riding TR20. . . **88** F1
TREATH **93** C1
TREATOR **107** A5
Treator Cotts PL28 . . . . . **107** A5

Trebah Gdns★ TR11 . . . . . 93 C2
Treban Rd TR18 . . . . 143 C4
TREBARBER 44 F5
TREBARTHA 27 A4
Trebartha Cl PL17 . . . . 39 E3
Trebartha Rd TR1 . . . . 137 F5
Trebarthen Terr TR4 . . . . . 55 D5
Trebarva Cl TR15 . . . . 140 A6
TREBARVAH 89 E4
Trebarvah La
Rosudgeon TR20 . . . . 89 E4
TR11 . . . . 92 E4
Trebarvah Rd TR11 . . . . 92 E4
TREBARWITH 14 C5
Trebarwith Cres TR7 . . . . . 110 E6
Trebarwith Rd PL33 . . . . . . 14 D4
TREBEATH 17 F6
Treberran Gdns TR14 . . . . . 138 F6
TREBETHERICK 21 D4
Treboul Cross PL12 . . . . . . 64 F8
Treboul Way PL12 . . . . 65 B8
TREBUDANNON 45 C4
TREBULLETT 28 A5
Treburdon Dr PL26 . . . . 46 F3
TREBURGETT 23 D6
Treburgie Water PL14 . . . . 50 D7
TREBURLEY 28 C4
Treburley Cl PL15 . . . . 28 C4
Treburley Ind Est PL15 . . . 28 C4
TREBURRICK 31 D5
TREBYAN 48 C6
Trebyan Bsns Pk PL30 . . . . 48 C6
Trebyhan Parc TR3 . . . . 80 F3
Treby Rd PL7 . . . . 130 F4
Trecarn Cl PL15 . . . . 106 B5
Trecarne TR11 . . . . 144 E5
Trecarne Cl
Polgooth PL26 . . . . 59 A1
St Austell PL25 . . . . 115 B5
Truro TR1 . . . . 137 E5
Trecarne Gdns PL33 . . . . . . 14 E3
Trecarne View PL14 . . . . . . 37 F3
Trecarrack Rd TR14 . . . . . . 138 F3
Trecarrell PL15 . . . . 106 C4
Trecarrell Cl PL15 . . . . 106 D4
Trecerus Ind Est PL28 . . . 107 B4
Treclago View PL32 . . . . . . 105 C2
TRECROGO 27 E7
Tredanek Cl PL31 . . . . 109 B5
Tredarrup Cross PL15 . . . . 11 A1
Tredarvah Dr TR18 . . . . 143 C5
Tredarvah Rd TR18 . . . . 143 C5
TREDAVOE 143 A2
Tredavoe La TR18 . . . . 143 B1
Tredenham Cl 4 PL24 . . . . 60 C4
Tredenham Rd TR2 . . . . 95 B6
TREDETHY 34 F6
Tredethy Rd PL30 . . . . 34 F6
TREDINNICK
Looe 63 A8
Penzance 76 A1
St Issey 32 D5
Tredinnick Cotts TR 20 . . . 76 A1
Tredinnick La PL12 . . . . 53 B2
Tredinnick Lane-End
PL13 . . . . 64 A8
Tredinnick Way 12 TR6 . . . 55 A4
Tredinnick Wood Cl
TR13 . . . . 146 D8
Tredis Vw PL11 . . . . 65 B5
Tredour Rd TR7 . . . . 110 E4
Tredova Cres TR11 . . . . 145 B2
TREDOWN 2 E5
Tredragon Cl TR8 . . . . 31 C2
Tredragon Rd TR8 . . . . 31 C2
Tredrea Gdns TR3 . . . . 81 D5
Tredrea La TR27 . . . . 77 E2
Tredrea Manor TR3 . . . . . . 81 D5
TREDRIZZICK 21 F4
Tredrizzick Cl PL27 . . . . . . 21 F3
Tredruston Rd PL27 . . . . . . 33 B6
Tredydan Rd PL15 . . . . 106 B6
Tredynas Rd TR11 . . . . 145 D3
Tredyson Pl TR11 . . . . 145 A3
Tre-el-Verne Cl TR1 . . . . . 137 A4
TREEN
Porthcurno 96 F3
Zennor 75 F4
Treen Cotts TR26 . . . . 75 F4
Treen Flats TR14 . . . . 138 F3
Treen Hill TR19 . . . . 96 F4
TREESMILL 60 D6
Treetop Cl PL12 . . . . 122 D4
Treetops Hill PL13 . . . . . . 117 A3
Treeve La TR27 . . . . 78 C6
Treeve Lane Ind Est TR27 . 78 C6
TREFANNY HILL 62 D8
Treffry Ct TR7 . . . . 110 D6
Treffry La PL30 . . . . 48 C6
Treffry Rd TR1 . . . . 137 E6
Treffry Way 12 PL24 . . . . . 60 B4
Trefinnick Rd PL17 . . . . 39 B8
Trefleur Cl 3 PL35 . . . . 9 C1
Trefloyd Cl PL17 . . . . 39 E6
TREFOFDA 24 A8
Treforda Rd TR7 . . . . 110 F4
Treforest Rd PL27 . . . . 108 A6
Treforthlan 7 TR16 . . . . . . 67 E4
Treforthlan Cl 6 TR16 . . . . 67 E4
TREFREW 105 D6
Trefrew Rd PL32 . . . . 105 D5
TREFRIZE 27 E3
Trefusis Cl TR1 . . . . 137 F5
Trefusis Ct TR11 . . . . 145 A6
Trefusis Gdns PL3 . . . . 129 A4
Trefusis Rd
Falmouth TR11 . . . . 144 E2
Flushing TR11 . . . . 145 C6
Trefusis Rd *continued*
Redruth TR15 . . . . 140 C4
Trefusis Terr
Millbrook PL10 . . . . 132 E6
Redruth TR15 . . . . 140 C5
TREGADILLETT 18 C2
Tregadillett Prim Sch
PL15 . . . . 18 C2
Tregaer TR11 . . . . 145 C3
Tregainlands Pk PL30 . . . . 34 D3
TREGAJORRAN 139 D4
Tregalister Gdns PL12 . . . . 65 B8
Tregaller La PL15 . . . . 18 E1
TREGAMERE 45 F7
Treganoon Rd TR15 . . . . . . 140 D7
Tregargus View PL26 . . . . . 58 B4
TREGARLAND 63 C8
TREGARLANDBRIDGE 63 B8
Tregarland Cl
Camborne TR14 . . . . 138 E2
Coad's Green PL15 . . . . 27 D4
Tregarne Terr PL25 . . . . . 114 C4
Tregarrek Cl PL26 . . . . 46 F3
Tregarrian Rd TR14 . . . . . 138 F7
Tregarrick PL13 . . . . 117 B3
Tregarrick Cl TR13 . . . . . . 146 B7
Tregarrick Ct PL13 . . . . . . 117 B3
Tregarrick La PL13 . . . . 62 D6
TREGARRICK MILL 62 D7
Tregarrick Rd PL26 . . . . 46 F3
Tregarrick Way PL13 . . . . . 62 D6
Tregarth 12 PL26 . . . . 59 D7
Tregartha Way PL14 . . . . . 113 D6
Tregarthen 2 TR26 . . . . . . 141 A5
Tregarth Pl TR18 . . . . 143 C4
Tregaskes Parc EX23 . . . . . 104 F5
Tregassack Rd TR20 . . . . . . 88 F7
Tregassick Rd TR2 . . . . 83 B1
TREGASWITH 45 C5
TREGATTA 14 C6
TREGAVARRAS 85 A5
Tregavarras Row PL26 . . . . 85 A5
Tregavethan View TR3 . . . . 69 C4
Tregay La PL14 . . . . 113 C7
Tregeagle Rd PL26 . . . . 47 A2
Tregea Hill TR16 . . . . 67 C6
Tregear Cl TR12 . . . . 99 D6
TREGEARE 17 D5
Tregear Gdns TR1 . . . . 137 C4
Tregease Rd TR5 . . . . 54 C1
Tregea Terr TR16 . . . . 67 C6
Tregellas Cl 10 TR5 . . . . . . 54 C1
Tregellas Rd TR12 . . . . 99 B1
Tregellas Tapastry The★ 12
TR15 . . . . 140 B4
Tregellast Cl TR12 . . . . . . 101 D4
Tregellast Parc TR12 . . . . 101 D4
TREGELLIST 22 E4
Tregembo Hill TR20 . . . . . . 90 A7
Tregender La TR20 . . . . 89 B8
Tregender Rd TR20 . . . . . . 89 B8
Tregenna Cl
Plymouth PL7 . . . . 131 C4
Wainhouse Corner EX23 . . . 10 F6
Tregenna Ct
Camborne TR14 . . . . 138 C2
Falmouth TR11 . . . . 145 C3
Tregenna Fields TR14 . . . . 138 C2
Tregenna Hill 16 TR26 . . . 141 B5
Tregenna La TR14 . . . . 138 C2
Tregenna Parc TR26 . . . . . 141 C3
Tregenna Pl 4 TR26 . . . . . 141 B5
Tregenna Rd PL30 . . . . 35 C8
Tregenna Terr TR26 . . . . . 141 B5
Tregenver Rd TR11 . . . . . . 144 F4
Tregenver Terr TR11 . . . . 144 F4
Tregenver Villas TR11 . . . . 144 F4
TREGESEAL 86 F7
Tregeseal Hill TR19 . . . . . . 86 F7
Tregeseal Row TR19 . . . . . . 86 F6
Tregeseal Terr TR19 . . . . . . 86 F6
TREGEW 145 B8
Tregew Cl TR11 . . . . 145 B7
Tregew Rd
Flushing TR11 . . . . 145 B8
Penryn TR10, TR11 . . . . 81 F2
Treggodick Cotts TR20 . . . 143 A8
Tregian Cl TR1 . . . . 137 F5
Tregidden Hill TR12 . . . . . 100 F5
Tregie TR18 . . . . 143 B3
TREGISKEY 73 C5
Tregiskey Cotts PL26 . . . . . 73 C5
Tregisky La TR12 . . . . 101 C1
Treglenwith Rd TR14 . . . . 138 C4
Treglisson Rural Workshops
TR27 . . . . 78 C3
Treglyn Cl TR18 . . . . 143 B1
Treglyn Farm Cotts PL27 . . 22 B3
Tregoddick Cl TR20 . . . . . . 88 B7
Tregolds La PL28 . . . . 31 F7
TREGOLE 6 E1
TREGOLLS 80 F3
Tregolls Cl TR1 . . . . 137 E5
Tregolls Rd TR1 . . . . 137 F5
Tregolls Sch TR1 . . . . 137 F5
TREGONCE 107 F2
TREGONETHA 46 C6
Tregoney Hill PL26 . . . . 73 C3
Tregongeeves La PL26 . . . . 59 A2
TREGONHAWKE 132 B4
Tregonhay PL14 . . . . 38 C7
Tregonhayne Ct TR2 . . . . . . 72 A4
Tregoniggie Ind Est
TR11 . . . . 144 D4
Tregoning Rd PL11 . . . . . . 126 F2
Tregonissey Cl PL25 . . . . . 114 D5
Tregonissey Rd PL25 . . . . 114 E5
Tregonissy La End PL25 . 114 E6
TREGONNA 32 C7
Tregonning Cl TR13 . . . . . . 90 E3
Tregonning Ct 8 TR6 . . . . . 55 A5
Tregonning Rd TR3 . . . . . . 80 F3
Tregonning Terr TR13 . . . . 90 F5
Tregonning View 17 TR13 . 98 C8
TREGONY 71 F4
Tregony Com Prim Sch
TR2 . . . . 71 F4
Tregony Hill TR2 . . . . 71 F3
Tregony Ind Est TR2 . . . . . . 71 E3
Tregony Rd TR2 . . . . 71 D6
TREGOODWELL 105 F4
TREGORRICK 114 D1
Tregorrick Pk (St Austell
RFC) PL26 . . . . 114 E1
Tregorrick Rd PL26 . . . . . . 114 E1
Tregos Rd TR26 . . . . 141 C2
TREGOSS 46 D3
Tregoss Rd TR7 . . . . 110 F6
Tregothnan Rd
Falmouth TR11 . . . . 145 A5
Truro TR1 . . . . 137 E3
Tregowris Court Cotts
TR12 . . . . 101 B5
Tregrea TR14 . . . . 138 E1
TREGREENWELL 23 F7
Tregrehan Gdns★ PL24 . . 115 E6
TREGREHAN MILLS 115 D6
Treguddock Dr PL27 . . . . . 108 D5
Tregullan TR15 . . . . 139 C8
Tregullan View PL31 . . . . 109 D3
Tregullow Rd TR11 . . . . . . 144 F5
Tregundy Cl 21 TR6 . . . . . . 55 A5
Tregundy Ct 20 TR6 . . . . . . 55 A5
Tregundy La TR6 . . . . 55 A5
Tregundy Rd TR6 . . . . 55 A5
TREGUNE 10 F4
TREGUNNA 33 B8
Tregunna Cl TR13 . . . . 91 B1
Tregunnel Hill TR7 . . . . . . 110 D4
Tregunnick La PL11 . . . . . . 64 B6
Tregunnus La PL11 . . . . 64 D5
Tregunter Mews TR11 . . . 145 D3
Tregurra La TR1 . . . . 137 E6
TREGURRIAN 44 E8
Tregurrian Hill TR8 . . . . . . 44 D8
Tregurtha Farm Cotts
TR17 . . . . 89 D6
Tregurtha View TR20 . . . . . 89 E5
Tregurthen Cl TR14 . . . . . 138 C2
Tregurthen Rd TR14 . . . . . 138 C2
TREGUSTICK 33 D1
Treguth Cl TR8 . . . . 43 B1
Tregwary Rd TR26 . . . . . . 141 A5
Tregye Rd TR3 . . . . 82 A7
Trehaddle TR4 . . . . 81 B7
TREHAN 122 A1
Trehane Rd TR14 . . . . 138 B3
Trehannick Cl PL30 . . . . 23 E7
Trehaverne Cl TR1 . . . . . . 137 C5
Trehaverne La TR1 . . . . . . 137 C5
Trehaverne Terr 3 TR1 . . 137 C5
Trehaverne Vean TR1 . . . . 137 C5
Trehawke La PL14 . . . . 38 C1
Trehayes Mdw TR27 . . . . . . 77 E2
Trehayes Parc TR27 . . . . . 142 E7
Trehaze-Na Cl PL32 . . . . . . 10 C3
Treheath Rd PL14 . . . . 50 E7
Trehill Cross PL12 . . . . 40 C2
Trehill La PL10 . . . . 64 B2
TREHUNIST 52 C6
Trehunsey Cl TR11 . . . . 93 E2
Trehurst TR18 . . . . 143 D4
Trekeen Rd TR10 . . . . 144 B8
TREKEIVESTEPS 37 E4
TREKENNER 28 B5
Trekenner Prim Sch PL15 . 28 C5
TREKENNING 45 D5
Trekenning Rd TR9 . . . . 45 D5
Trekestle Pk PL15 . . . . 18 C2
TREKNOW 14 C5
Trekye Cl TR16 . . . . 80 B5
Trelake La PL34 . . . . 14 D5
Trelake Rd PL25 . . . . 114 B4
TRELAN 100 E1
Trelan TR14 . . . . 138 F3
Trelander Barton TR1 . . . . 137 E5
Trelander E TR1 . . . . 137 F4
Trelander Highway TR1 . . 137 E4
Trelander N TR1 . . . . 137 F4
Trelander S TR1 . . . . 137 F4
Trelander Vean TR1 . . . . . 137 F4
Trelantis PL28 . . . . 20 E1
Trelantis Est PL28 . . . . 31 F8
TRELASH 10 F1
Trelaske La PL13 . . . . 62 F4
Trelavour Prazey PL26 . . . . 58 B8
Trelavour Rd PL26 . . . . 58 C8
Trelavour Sq PL26 . . . . 58 C8
Trelawne Cl 10 TR3 . . . . . . 81 F7
Trelawne Cottage Gdns
PL13 . . . . 62 E4
Trelawne Gdns PL13 . . . . . 62 E5
Trelawne Rd TR3 . . . . 81 F7
Trelawney Apartments
TR7 . . . . 110 F6
Trelawney Ave
Falmouth TR11 . . . . 145 B3
Plymouth PL5 . . . . 123 D1
Poughill EX23 . . . . 4 C3
Redruth TR15 . . . . 140 E7
St Ives TR26 . . . . 141 A5
Trelawney Cl
Bodmin PL31 . . . . 109 C4
Maenporth TR11 . . . . 93 E3
Torpoint PL11 . . . . 126 E3
Warbstow Cross PL15 . . . . . 11 B1
Trelawney Cotts PL15 . . . 106 D5
Trelawney Ct PL27 . . . . 21 E3
Trelawney Est
Madron TR20 . . . . 143 A8
Ponsanooth TR4 . . . . 81 B7
Trelawney Gdns PL14 . . . . 38 D4
Trelawney Hts 19 PL17 . . . 39 F4
Trelawney Parc
St Columb Major TR9 . . . . . 45 D5
Warbstow Cross PL15 . . . . . 11 B1
Trelawney Pl
Hayle TR27 . . . . 142 C6
Penryn TR10 . . . . 144 C8
Plymouth PL5 . . . . 123 D1
Trelawney Rd
Bodmin PL31 . . . . 109 C3
Callington PL17 . . . . 39 F4
Camborne TR14 . . . . 138 D3
Chacewater TR4 . . . . 69 A3
Helston TR13 . . . . 146 C5
Newquay TR7 . . . . 110 E5
Padstow PL28 . . . . 107 D4
Plymouth PL3 . . . . 128 D5
Ponsanooth TR3 . . . . 81 B4
Saltash PL12 . . . . 122 E2
St Austell PL25 . . . . 114 E5
St Ives TR26 . . . . 141 A5
St Mawes TR2 . . . . 95 A6
Truro TR1 . . . . 137 B5
Trelawney Rise
18 Callington PL17 . . . . 39 F4
Torpoint PL11 . . . . 126 E3
Trelawney Terr
Cury TR12 . . . . 99 B4
Looe PL13 . . . . 117 C4
Trelawney Way
Hayle TR27 . . . . 142 C6
Torpoint PL11 . . . . 126 E3
Trelawny Ct TR14 . . . . 138 C3
Trelawny Rd
Falmouth TR11 . . . . 145 B4
Menheniot PL14 . . . . 52 A6
Plymouth PL7 . . . . 130 C6
St Agnes TR5 . . . . 54 C1
Tavistock PL19 . . . . 147 C6
Treleaver Way TR1 . . . . 69 F3
Trelee Cl TR27 . . . . 142 E7
TRELEIGH 140 D8
Treleigh Ave TR15 . . . . . . 140 B6
Treleigh Ind Est TR16 . . . . 140 C7
Treleigh Prim Sch TR16 . . 140 C8
Treleigh Terr TR15 . . . . . . 140 A5
Trelevan Cl PL25 . . . . 114 C3
Treleven Rd EX23 . . . . 104 F4
TRELEW 82 B2
Treliddon La PL11 . . . . 64 C5
Treliever Cross TR10 . . . . . 81 C1
Treliever Rd
Mabe Burnthouse TR10 . . . . 81 C1
Penryn TR10 . . . . 144 B8
TRELIGGA 14 C3
Treligga Downs Rd PL33 . . 14 D2
TRELIGHTS 22 C6
Trelil Cvn Site TR13 . . . . . 146 E7
TRELILL 23 C5
Trelil La TR11 . . . . 144 C2
Trelindon PL15 . . . . 27 E8
Trelinnoe Cl PL15 . . . . 27 E8
Trelinnoe Gdns PL15 . . . . . 27 E8
Treliske Ind Est TR1 . . . . . . 69 E4
Treliske La TR1, TR4 . . . . . . 69 F4
Treliske Rd TR15 . . . . 140 D6
Trelispen Park Dr PL26 . . . 85 C5
Trelispen Pk PL26 . . . . 85 C5
Trelissick Fields TR27 . . . 142 B3
Trelissick Gdns PL17 . . . . . 39 E3
Trelissick Gdns★ TR3 . . . . 82 D6
Trelissick Rd
Falmouth TR11 . . . . 144 F5
Hayle TR27 . . . . 142 B3
Trelissick Woodland Wlk★
TR3 . . . . 82 D6
TRELIVER 46 E8
Treloan La TR2 . . . . 83 B1
Treloar Terr PL15 . . . . 106 B6
Treloggan Ind Est TR7 . . . 111 B4
Treloggan Rd TR7 . . . . 111 A4
Trelorrin Gdns PL3 . . . . . . 128 E5
Trelowarren★ TR12 . . . . . . 99 F6
Trelowarren Ct 13 PL17 . . 39 E4
Trelowarren St TR14 . . . . 138 D3
Treloweck TR14 . . . . 79 A4
Treloweth Cl
Plymouth PL2 . . . . 128 D8
St Erth TR27 . . . . 77 E2
Treloweth Com Prim Sch
TR15 . . . . 139 D6
Treloweth Gdns TR15 . . . . 139 C6
Treloweth La TR27 . . . . 77 E2
Treloweth Rd TR15 . . . . . . 139 C6
Treloweth Terr TR15 . . . . . 139 B7
Treloweth Way TR15 . . . . 139 C7
Trelowth Rd PL26 . . . . 59 A1
Treloyhan Cl TR26 . . . . . . 141 C3
Treloyhan Park Rd TR26 . 141 C3
Trelyn PL27 . . . . 21 E3
Trelyn Rd TR12 . . . . 101 D4
TRELYON 141 B3
Trelyon Ave TR26 . . . . 141 C4
Trelyon Cl TR19 . . . . 97 B6
Tremabe La PL14 . . . . 50 E7
Tremabe Pk PL14 . . . . 50 E7
Tremadart Cl PL14 . . . . 51 A1
Tremadart Farm Barns
PL14 . . . . 51 A1
Tremaddock Cotts PL14 . . 36 F3
Tremaddock Council Hos
PL14 . . . . 36 F3
TREMAIL 16 B5
Tremaine Cl TR18 . . . . 143 C7
Tremalic PL13 . . . . 117 B3
Tremall Parc TR3 . . . . 80 F3
Tremanor Way TR11 . . . . . 144 D5
TREMAR 38 A2
Tremar Cl PL14 . . . . 38 A2
Tremar La
St Cleer PL14 . . . . 37 F3
Tremar PL14 . . . . 38 A3
Tremarle Home Pk TR14 . 138 F5
Tremarne Cl TR3 . . . . 82 C5
Tremar Rd TR26 . . . . 77 A7
Tremarren Rd PL27 . . . . . 108 B5
TREMATON 53 E2
Trematon Cl PL11 . . . . 126 E4
Trematon Terr PL4 . . . . . . 128 E4
TREMAYNE 79 C2
Tremayne Cl TR3 . . . . 81 F6
Tremayne Ho PL31 . . . . . . 109 B4
Tremayne Pk TR14 . . . . . . 138 F2
Tremayne Rd
Carharrack TR16 . . . . 80 F8
St Austell PL25 . . . . 114 E4
Truro TR1 . . . . 137 C5
Tremayne Rise PL19 . . . . . 147 B5
Tremayne Terr PL13 . . . . . . 63 F8
Trembath Cres TR7 . . . . . . 110 E5
Trembear Rd PL25 . . . . . . 114 A4
Trembel Rd TR12 . . . . 99 B2
Trembrase TR19 . . . . 96 C7
TREMBRAZE 113 D8
Tremeadow Terr
Hayle TR27 . . . . 142 B4
Liskeard PL14 . . . . 113 D7
Tremear Gn 6 TR9 . . . . 45 E2
Tremearne Rd 16 TR13 . . . 98 C8
Tremeddan Ct 2 PL14 . . . 113 C6
Tremeddan La PL14 . . . . . 113 C6
Tremeddan Terr PL14 . . . . 113 B4
Tremeer La PL30 . . . . 23 E3
Tremellin La TR27 . . . . 77 F1
Tremena Gdns PL25 . . . . . 114 C4
Tremena Rd PL25 . . . . 114 C4
Tremenheere Ave TR13 . . 146 D8
Tremenheere Rd TR18 . . . 143 E6
Tremenva Ct 1 TR13 . . . . 146 C5
TREMETHICK CROSS 88 A5
Tremewan 1 PL25 . . . . 59 A3
Tremodrett Rd PL26 . . . . . . 46 F3
Tremoh Ct TR2 . . . . 71 C6
TREMOLLETT 27 D2
Tremollett Cotts PL17 . . . . 28 B1
TREMORE 47 C7
Tremore Rd TR15 . . . . 140 D6
Tremorva TR27 . . . . 142 C6
Tremorvah Barton TR1 . . 137 E5
Tremorvah Cres TR1 . . . . 137 E5
Tremorvah Ct
Falmouth TR11 . . . . 144 F1
Truro TR1 . . . . 137 E5
Tremorvah Pk TR11 . . . . . 144 F1
Tremorvah Wood La
TR1 . . . . 137 E5
Tremough Barton Cotts
TR10 . . . . 81 C1
Tremoughdale TR10 . . . . . 144 B8
Trenale La PL34 . . . . 14 D7
Trenalt Terr TR1 . . . . 137 B5
TRENANCE
Newquay 110 E5
Roche 46 F7
St Issey 32 D5
Tregurrian 31 C2
Trenance Ave TR7 . . . . . . 110 F5
Trenance Cl TR13 . . . . 146 B7
Trenance Ct TR7 . . . . 110 E4
Trenance Dr PL19 . . . . 30 A3
Trenance Hill PL25 . . . . . . 114 A5
Trenance La
3 Mullion TR12 . . . . 99 A1
Newquay TR7 . . . . 110 E4
Trenance Learning Academy
TR7 . . . . 110 E5
Trenance Leisure Park &
Gdns★ TR7 . . . . 111 A5
Trenance Pl PL25 . . . . 114 B4
Trenance Rd
Camborne TR14 . . . . 138 E4
Newquay TR7 . . . . 110 E5
St Austell PL25 . . . . 114 B4
TRENANT 37 C3
Trenant TR16 . . . . 68 D1
Trenant Cl PL27 . . . . 21 E5
Trenant Cross PL14 . . . . . . 63 A6
TRENANT GIRT 108 C5
Trenant Ind Est PL27 . . . . 108 D6
Trenant Rd
Looe PL13 . . . . 117 D5
2 Tywardreath PL24 . . . . . . 60 D5
Trenant Vale PL27 . . . . . . 108 D6
TRENARREN 73 E7
Trenarren View PL25 . . . . 115 A6
Trenarth TR10 . . . . 144 C8
Trenarth Rd TR7 . . . . 110 E5
Trenawin La TR27 . . . . 78 E5
TRENCREEK 111 C4
Trencreek Cl TR4 . . . . 56 D1
Trencreek La TR8 . . . . 111 B4
Trencreek Rd TR7, TR8 . . . 111 B4
TRENCROM 77 B3
Trencrom La TR26 . . . . 141 D1
Trencrom Row TR20 . . . . . . 77 B3
TRENDEAL 57 C3
Trendeal Gdns 1 TR18 . . 143 E5

Trendlewood Rd PL6...... 125 D7
Trendreath Cl TR26 ...... 77 E3
Treneague Pk PL27 ...... 108 B4
TRENEAR............. 92 A6
Trenear Cl TR15 .... 140 D6
TRENEERE............ 143 E7
Treneere La TR18 ...... 143 D7
Treneere Rd TR18...... 143 D6
TRENEGLOS........... 16 F7
Treneglos Terr TR4..... 81 C7
Treneglos Terr
  Gulval TR18 .... 88 E6
  Newlyn TR18 .... 143 C3
Trenerry Cl TR1........ 137 D6
TRENERTH........... 78 D2
Trenerth Rd TR27 ...... 78 E2
Trenethick Ave TR13 .... 146 D8
Trenethick Bsns Pk
  TR13 .... 146 C8
Trenethick Cl TR13...... 146 D7
Trenethick Farm TR13 ... 146 B8
Trenethick Parc TR13 ... 146 D8
TRENEWAN........... 62 A4
TRENGALE............ 37 C2
Trengove PL26......... 47 C1
Trengove Cross TR11.... 92 D5
Trengrouse Ave PL11.... 126 F3
Trengrouse Way TR13 ... 146 C5
TRENGUNE............ 11 A4
Trengwainton Gdns★
  TR20 .... 88 A6
Trenhaile Terr TR1 ..... 70 D1
Trenhayle La TR27 ..... 142 B2
Treningle View TR31 .... 109 C3
TRENINNICK.......... 111 A4
Treninnick Hill TR7 ..... 110 F5
Treninnow & Wiggle Chalets
  PL10 .... 132 C2
Trenithick Mdw TR4 .... 68 C6
Trenithon La TR18 ..... 57 C6
Trennance Ct 6 TR12... 99 A1
Trennick La TR1 .... 137 E3
Trennick Row TR1 ..... 137 E3
Trennick Villas Ct TR1... 137 E3
Trenode CE Prim Sch
  PL13 .... 51 F1
Trenouth Cl 5 PL14.... 38 A3
Trenovissick Rd TR24 ... 60 B4
Trenowah Rd PL25...... 115 C5
TRENOWETH.......... 93 B8
Trenoweth Ave TR14 ... 138 B3
Trenoweth Cres TR18 ... 143 B4
Trenoweth Ct TR12..... 102 F2
Trenoweth La TR10 ..... 93 B8
Trenoweth Mdw TR12 .. 102 F2
Trenoweth Rd
  Falmouth TR11........ 144 F2
  Penzance TR18........ 143 B5
Trenoweth Terr TR10 .. 93 B8
Trenoweth Vean TR10... 81 B1
Trenowth Terr TR2..... 57 E1
Trent Cl PL3.......... 129 B6
Trentham Cl PL6 ...... 125 B6
Trentworthy Cross EX22.. 3 E2
TRENWHEAL........... 90 F7
Trenwith La TR26 ...... 141 A4
Trenwith Pl 14 TR26... 141 B5
Trenwith Rd TR14 ..... 138 B3
Trenwith Sq TR26...... 141 A5
Trenwith Terr 11 TR26.. 141 B5
Trenython Rd 10 PL24... 60 B4
Treore Cl PL30........ 23 A6
Treovis Cross PL14..... 38 C8
Tre-Pol PL26.......... 58 F1
TREQUITE............ 23 B3
Treraven La PL27 ...... 108 C3
Trerew Rd TR18........ 143 C4
Trerice★ TR8 .... 44 D1
Trerice Ct 15 PL17 .... 39 E4
Trerice Dr TR7......... 111 B5
Trerice Fields TR14 .... 79 B2
Trerice Holdings TR8 ... 44 C1
Trerice Pl TR26........ 141 A5
Trerice Rd 6 TR26..... 141 A5
Trerice Terr PL26 ..... 58 A8
Trerieve PL11......... 64 C5
TRERISE............. 103 A7
Trerise Rd TR14....... 138 C3
Treroosel Rd PL30 ..... 23 D8
Trerose Coombe PL11... 64 C5
Treruffe Hill TR15...... 140 B4
Treruffe Terr 9 TR15 .. 140 B4
Treryn Cl PL24........ 60 B5
Tresaderns Rd TR15.... 140 A6
Tresahar Rd TR11 ..... 145 A3
Tresamble Hill TR4, TR3 .. 81 B6
TRESARRETT.......... 35 B8
Tresavean Est TR16 .... 80 E6
Tresavean Hill TR16..... 80 E6
Tresavean Terr TR16 ... 80 E6
Tresawla Ct TR14 ..... 138 F6
TRESAWLE........... 71 C5
Tresawle Rd TR11...... 145 A6
Tresawls Ave TR1...... 69 F3
Tresawls Rd TR1, TR4... 69 E4
Tresawna Terr TR11.... 145 B4
Tresawya Dr TR1....... 137 C4
Trescobeas Rd TR11 ... 144 E5
Trescoe Rd TR20....... 88 F6
Tresco Pl TR11 .... 144 F4
Trescore PL28......... 31 F7
TRESCOWE........... 90 B5
Trescowe Rd TR20..... 89 F5

Tresdale Parc TR27..... 78 D6
Treseder's Gdns TR1.... 137 D5
Tresevern Hill TR3...... 80 D4
Tresidder Cl TR1....... 144 E4
TRESILLIAN........... 70 F5
Tresillian Ho TR1 ...... 69 E4
Tresillian Rd TR11 ..... 144 F6
Tresillian St PL4....... 149 C2
TRESINNEY........... 24 C8
Tresithney Rd TR16 .... 80 F8
Treskerby TR16........ 140 F7
Treskewes Est 1 TR12 . 101 C4
Treskewes Ind Est 1
  TR12 .... 101 C3
TRESKILLARD......... 139 C1
Treskilling PL30 .... 59 F8
TRESKINNICK CROSS 6 F1
TRESLOTHAN.......... 79 D4
Treslothan Rd TR14 .... 79 D4
Tresluggan Rd PL5...... 123 D1
Tresooth Ct TR10 ..... 144 D7
Tresooth La TR10 ..... 144 C8
Tresooth Terr TR10.... 144 D7
TRESOWES GREEN..... 90 D4
TRESOWES HILL....... 90 E4
Tresowgar La TR2 ..... 71 B6
TRESPARRETT......... 10 B2
TRESPARRETT POSTS... 10 C4
Tresprison Ct TR13..... 146 E5
TRESWITHIAN......... 138 A3
Treswithian Barns TR14. 138 A3
Treswithian Park Rd
  TR14 .... 138 B3
Treswithian Rd TR14... 138 B3
Tretawn Cl PL30....... 23 B2
Trethannas Gdns TR14.. 79 B2
TRETHELLAN.......... 110 C6
Trethellan Hill TR7..... 110 C5
Trethern Cl TR14....... 79 E4
Tretherras Cl TR7...... 111 A6
Tretherras Rd TR7 ..... 111 A6
TRETHEVEY.......... 14 F8
Trethevy Cl PL14...... 37 F3
Trethevy Quoit★ PL14.. 38 A3
TRETHEWEY.......... 96 E4
Trethewey Cl 10 TR9 .. 45 E6
Trethewey Way TR7.... 110 D5
Trethew Gdns TR14 ... 138 E4
Trethiggey Cres TR8 ... 111 F3
Trethill La PL11 .... 65 C5
Trethorne Leisure Farm★
  PL15 .... 18 B2
Trethorns Ct TR20 .... 89 A8
TRETHOSA........... 58 A5
Trethosa Rd PL26...... 58 B4
Trethowan Hts TR1 .... 69 F3
TRETHOWEL.......... 114 C6
Trethurffe Terr TR9 .... 45 E5
Trethurffe Villas TR2.... 57 C1
TRETHURGY.......... 59 F6
Trethurgy Gdns 17 PL17. 39 E4
Tretoil View PL31...... 109 E2
Tretorvic TR18........ 143 C8
Tretower Cl PL6....... 124 F5
TREVADLOCK......... 27 A6
Trevadlock Hall Pk PL15. 27 A6
TREVAIL............ 43 D1
Trevail Cotts TR8 ..... 43 D1
Trevail Way PL25 ..... 114 E4
Trevale TR18.......... 143 C5
TREVALGA........... 9 B1
Trevalga Cl 5 TR6..... 55 A4
Trevallack Parc 3 TR12. 101 C4
Trevallack View 2 TR12. 101 C4
Trevallion Pk TR3...... 82 B5
Trevallyn Rd PL15...... 106 B4
TREVANCE............ 32 E6
Trevance TR10........ 144 A8
Trevance Pk PL24...... 60 D5
TREVANGER.......... 21 F4
Trevanion Cl PL27...... 108 B4
Trevanion Ct
  Mawnan Smith TR11 ... 93 D3
  1 Newquay TR7...... 110 F6
  Truro TR1.......... 69 F3
Trevanion La PL25 ..... 59 A3
Trevanion Pk PL27 .... 108 C4
Trevanion Rd
  Liskeard PL14........ 113 D5
  St Austell PL25....... 114 D2
  3 Trewoon PL25..... 59 A3
  Wadebridge PL27 ..... 108 B4
Trevanion Terr PL27 ... 108 C4
TREVANSON........... 33 C7
Trevanson Rd PL27..... 108 A6
Trevanson St PL27 .... 108 B6
Trevanson Street PL27.. 108 B6
Trevarner Way PL27.... 108 D6
Trevarno Cl PL25...... 59 A3
Trevarno Estate & Gdns★
  TR13 .... 91 C5
Trevarren Cl TR27...... 78 C6
Trevarnon Cl TR27 .... 78 D6
Trevarnon La TR27 .... 78 D6
Trevarrack Cl TR18..... 143 F8
Trevarrack La TR18 .... 143 F8
Trevarrack Pl TR18..... 143 F8
Trevarrack Rd TR18 ... 143 F8
Trevarrack Row TR18... 88 B6
TREVARREN.......... 45 E3
Trevarren Ave TR16.... 80 A5
TREVARRIAN.......... 31 C1
Trevarrian Hill TR8..... 44 D8
TREVARRICK.......... 72 F2
Trevarrick Ct TR26..... 141 C1
Trevarrick Dr PL25..... 114 B4

Trevarrick Rd PL25...... 114 B3
TREVARTH........... 80 E7
Trevarthen Cl TR27..... 78 D6
Trevarth Est PL26 ..... 73 C4
Trevarthian Ho TR17 ... 89 B5
Trevarthian Rd PL25.... 114 C4
Trevarth Rd TR11 ..... 144 F5
Trevarth Terr TR16..... 80 E7
Trevarweneth Rd 8 PL24. 60 B4
Trevassack Ct TR27 ... 142 D6
Trevassack Hill TR27... 142 E6
Trevassack Manor Pk
  TR27 .... 142 D6
Trevassack Parc TR27.. 142 E6
Trevaunance Cl TR5.... 54 C2
Trevaunance Cove★ TR5. 54 D2
Trevaunance Rd TR5 ... 54 C2
Trevaylor Cl TR1....... 137 E6
Trevaylor Rd TR11 .... 144 F5
Trevean Cl TR14....... 138 B3
Trevean Gdns 3 TR18.. 143 D5
Trevean La TR20 ...... 89 F4
Trevean Rd
  Penzance TR18........ 143 D5
  Truro TR1.......... 69 F3
Trevean Way
  Newquay TR7........ 110 C5
  Rosudgeon TR20 ..... 89 F4
Trevear Cl PL25....... 114 D3
Trevear Rd PL26 ...... 58 B4
Trevecca Cotts PL14 ... 113 C8
Treveglos TR27........ 142 B6
Treveglos Rd TR11..... 144 E1
TREVEIGHAN.......... 23 F6
Trevelga Cl TR7........ 111 A7
Trevelgue Ct TR8 ..... 44 C6
Trevelgue Rd TR7, TR8... 44 C6
Trevellan Rd TR11 .... 82 A3
Trevella Rd EX23...... 104 C7
TREVELLAS........... 54 F2
Trevella Vean TR4 ..... 70 D8
TREVELMOND......... 50 D6
Trevelthan Rd 18 TR16. 67 E4
Trevelva Rd TR1....... 137 E2
Trevelveth Rd TR8 .... 110 B3
Trevelyan Cl 10 TR20... 89 E5
Trevelyan Rd TR15, TR16. 67 E4
Trevelyan Way 5 TR20.. 89 E5
TREVEMPER.......... 110 E2
Trevemper Rd TR7, TR8.. 110 F3
TREVEN............. 14 C6
Trevena Cl TR1........ 143 C4
Trevena Cross TR13 ... 90 F3
Trevena Dr 8 PL34 .... 14 C7
Trevena Gdns TR11 .... 93 D3
Trevena Lodge 6 PL34.. 14 C7
Trevena Rd TR8........ 143 C4
Trevena Terr TR7...... 110 D6
Trevendon PL17....... 28 D1
Treveneague Gdns PL2.. 128 D8
Trevenen Rd TR13 .... 146 C5
Treveneth Cres TR18... 143 C1
Treveneth Pl 1 TR18... 143 C1
Treven La TR27........ 78 B1
Trevenna Cross TR8.... 45 A8
Trevenner Ho 8 TR15.. 140 B5
Trevenner La TR17..... 89 C5
Trevenner Mews 6
  TR15 .... 140 B5
Trevenner Sq TR17..... 89 C5
TREVENNING......... 23 F5
Treven Noweth TR16 ... 68 C3
Trevenson Ct TR15 .... 139 B6
Trevenson La
  Camborne, Pool TR15... 139 A6
  Camborne TR14....... 138 D2
Trevenson Rd
  Camborne TR15....... 139 B5
  Newquay TR7........ 111 B6
Trevenson St TR14 .... 138 D2
Treventon Cl
  Falmouth TR11........ 144 E4
  Portscatho TR2....... 83 B2
Treventon Rd TR2...... 83 B2
Treventon Rise 11 TR9 .. 45 E6
TREVERBYN
  Penwithick........ 59 C7
  St Cleer.......... 37 B2
Treverbyn Academy PL26. 59 C8
Treverbyn Cl
  Liskeard PL14........ 113 E6
  Plymouth PL7........ 130 D6
Treverbyn Gdns PL25... 114 F4
Treverbyn Rd
  Falmouth TR11........ 144 E1
  Padstow PL28 .... 107 E4
  Plymouth PL7........ 130 D6
  St Austell PL25....... 114 E7
  Stenalees PL26 ...... 59 C8
  St Ives TR26........ 141 A5
  Truro TR1.......... 137 E6
Treverbyn Rise TR10 ... 144 A8
Trevere Cl TR27........ 78 C6
Treverno Rd TR14...... 138 E6
TREVERVA........... 93 B6
Treveryn Parc TR11 ... 144 C2
TREVESCAN.......... 96 B5
Trevessa Cl PL2....... 128 D8
Trevethan Cl
  Falmouth TR11........ 145 A4
  TR6 .... 55 B4
Trevethan Ct 2 TR11... 145 A4
Trevethan Gdns 2 TR11. 145 A4
Trevethan Hill 1 TR11.. 145 B5
Trevethan Pk PL20..... 119 F4
Trevethan Rd TR11..... 145 A4
Trevethan Rise TR11 ... 145 A4
Trevethenick Rd TR1 ... 137 E3

Treveth La TR13 ...... 146 D8
TREVETHOE.......... 77 D3
Treveth Tean TR9...... 57 E8
Treveth Ylyn TR14 .... 138 F5
TREVIA.............. 105 B4
TREVIADES........... 93 A3
Trevia La PL32........ 105 B4
Trevian Cl 7 TR6 ..... 55 A4
Trevia Pk Terr PL32.... 105 C3
Treviglas Cl TR7 ...... 111 D7
Treviglas Com Coll TR7.. 111 D7
Treviglas La TR2....... 71 C6
Treviglas Rise TR2 .... 71 C6
TREVIGRO........... 39 C4
Trevilder TR2......... 82 C6
Trevilley La PL30, PL33 .. 23 E8
Trevillick La PL30 ..... 23 F6
Trevilling Rd PL27 ..... 108 B6
Trevillis Pk PL14....... 113 B4
TREVILSON.......... 56 D6
Trevilson Cl TR8 ...... 56 C7
Trevince Parc TR16 .... 80 F8
Trevingey Cl TR15 .... 140 A4
Trevingey Cres TR15 ... 140 A4
Trevingey Parc TR15 ... 140 A4
Trevingey Rd TR15..... 140 A3
TREVISCOE.......... 58 B7
Trevisker Prim Sch PL27. 31 F3
Treviskey Hill TR2..... 84 B3
Trevissome Ct TR11.... 144 F6
Trevithick PL28........ 31 F8
Trevithick Ave PL11 ... 126 F4
Trevithick Cl
  Newquay TR7........ 110 F4
  St Merryn PL28 ...... 31 F8
  Truro TR1.......... 137 E6
Trevithick Cres TR27... 142 D5
Trevithick Ct
  3 Camborne, Illogan Highway
    TR15 .... 139 C6
  Camborne TR14....... 138 C3
  Truro TR1.......... 137 E6
Trevithick Learning Academy
  TR14 .... 138 D1
Trevithick Rd
  Camborne, Illogan Highway
    TR15 .... 139 C6
  Camborne TR14....... 138 D3
  Chacewater TR4....... 69 A3
  Falmouth TR11........ 144 E5
  Plymouth PL5........ 123 E2
  St Austell PL25....... 114 E3
  Truro TR1.......... 137 E5
Trevoarn TR27........ 142 B6
Trevol Bsns Pk PL11.... 126 D3
TREVOLLARD......... 53 D1
Trevollard PL13....... 61 F7
Trevollard La PL12 .... 53 D1
Trevol Pl PL11 .... 126 E3
Trevol Rd PL11........ 126 E3
TREVONE............ 20 E2
Trevone Cres PL25..... 114 A4
Trevone Gdns PL2 .... 128 D8
Trevone Rd PL28...... 20 F2
Trevoney TR11........ 144 C2
Trevorder Cl PL11..... 126 F2
Trevorder Dr PL25 .... 114 E7
Trevorder Rd PL11 .... 126 F2
Trevorgans Cross TR19.. 96 F8
TREVORRICK......... 107 E1
Trevose Ave TR7...... 110 C6
Trevose Cl
  Constantine Bay PL28... 20 C1
  St Agnes TR5....... 54 C1
Trevose Ho TR1....... 69 E4
Trevose Rd TR1....... 69 F4
Trevose Way PL3 ..... 129 C6
Trevowah Mdws TR8.... 110 A3
Trevowah Rd TR8 ..... 43 D3
TREVOWHAN......... 75 C2
Trevozah Cross PL15.... 28 B8
Trevu Ho TR14........ 138 E1
Trevu Rd TR14........ 138 E2
Trevurvas La TR13 .... 90 C3
TREW............... 90 F4
TREWALDER.......... 14 E1
Trewall Hill PL11....... 64 D5
Trewan Hall TR9....... 45 E7
Trewans Terr TR15..... 140 B4
Trewardreva Cross TR11. 92 E4
Trewarlett Cross PL15... 28 A7
TREWARMETT........ 14 D5
Trewarne La TR8....... 111 F3
Trewartha Cl 4 PL14 .. 113 C6
Trewartha Est TR26.... 141 D1
Trewartha Flats TR26... 141 D1
Trewartha Rd TR20..... 90 C3
Trewartha Terr 12 TR18. 143 B6
Trewarton Rd TR10 ... 81 D2
Trewarveneth Farm Cotts
  TR18 .... 88 C2
Trewarveneth St TR18.. 143 C2
TREWASSA........... 15 F5
Trewassa Flats PL32.... 15 F5
Trewavas Cres TR13.... 146 C5
Trewavas Rd TR18 .... 143 C1
Treweath Rd TR18 .... 143 D7
Treweege Row TR3 .... 80 E4
Treweeks Rd TR19 .... 75 A1
Treweese Cross PL14 ... 52 B7
Treweese Rd
  Menheniot PL14....... 52 B7
  Quethiock PL14....... 52 B8
TREWELLARD......... 86 F8
Trewellard Hill TR19 ... 87 A8
Trewellard Ind Est TR19. 86 F8
Trewellard Rd TR19 ... 86 F8

Trewelloe Rd TR20...... 90 C3
Trewelm La TR16 ..... 68 E1
TREWEN............ 17 E2
TREWENNACK........ 146 F8
TREWENNAN......... 23 E8
Trewen Rd TR11....... 144 C2
Trewen Terr TR11...... 144 C2
Trewen La TR20........ 87 E6
TREWETHA.......... 22 E7
Trewetha Farm Lodges
  PL29 .... 22 E7
Trewetha La PL29...... 22 D7
TREWETHERN........ 22 E3
TREWEY............. 76 B5
Trewey Hill TR 26 ..... 76 B4
Trewhella La TR20 .... 89 F7
Trewhella Terr TR20 ... 90 A6
Trewhiddle Rd PL25.... 114 C3
Trewidden Cl TR1...... 137 E5
Trewidden Ct TR1...... 137 E5
Trewidden Gdn★ TR20... 88 A4
Trewidden Rd TR26 ... 141 B5
TREWIDLAND......... 51 C2
Trewidland Prim Sch
  PL14 .... 51 C3
Trewince La
  Grampound Road TR2... 57 E1
  Lostwithiel PL22...... 112 C3
  Porth Navas TR11 .... 93 B3
Trewince Manor TR2.... 95 C6
Trewince Terr 2 TR2... 143 C1
Trewince Villas PL27 ... 32 E6
Trewinnard Ct TR1..... 137 B6
Trewinnard Gr TR1..... 137 B6
Trewinnard La TR27.... 77 E1
Trewinnard Rd TR3 .... 81 D5
Trewinnick Council Hos
  PL27 .... 32 A5
Trewinnick Rd PL27.... 32 A5
Trewinnow Cross PL15.. 27 D6
TREWINT............ 10 F8
Trewint Cres PL13 .... 117 D4
Trewint Est PL14...... 52 A5
Trewint La
  Landrake PL12....... 53 B2
  Rock PL27.......... 21 D3
Trewint Rd PL14...... 52 A6
Trewirgie Cty Jun Sch
  TR15 .... 140 B4
Trewirgie Gdns TR15... 140 B4
Trewirgie Hill TR15 .... 140 B3
Trewirgie Rd TR15 .... 140 B3
Trewirgie Vean TR15... 140 B4
Trewiston La PL27 .... 21 E3
Trewithan Parc PL22.... 112 D2
Trewithen Gdns★ TR2... 71 E6
Trewithen Rd TR26 .... 58 B7
Trewithen Terr TR13 ... 90 D5
TREWITHIAN.......... 83 B4
Trewithick Rd TR13 ... 90 F2
Trewithy Ct PL6....... 124 F1
Trewithy Dr PL6....... 124 F1
TREWOLD............ 9 E1
Trewollock Cl PL26 .... 85 C5
Trewollock La PL26 ... 85 C5
TREWOODLOE........ 39 B6
Trewoolsta Terr 5 PL14. 38 E4
TREWOON
  Mullion............ 99 B2
  St Austell.......... 59 A3
Trewoon Rd PL25...... 99 B2
Treworder Cl EX23....... 4 C1
Treworder La PL27 .... 108 F5
Treworder Rd TR1 .... 137 B3
TREWORGA........... 83 D7
Treworgan View TR4.... 56 D1
TREWORLAS......... 83 B5
Treworlis Cl TR13...... 146 D8
TREWORNAN......... 22 C1
TREWORRICK......... 37 E3
TREWORTHAL........ 83 C5
Treworthal Rd TR3..... 81 D5
Treworvenneth Dr 9
  TR17 .... 89 C5
Trewrickle La PL11..... 65 A5
Trewyn Flats 41 TR26.. 141 B6
Treyew Pl TR16........ 80 F8
Treyew Rd TR1........ 137 B3
TREZAISE........... 47 A2
Trezaise Ave PL26...... 47 A2
Trezaise Cl PL26 ...... 47 A2
Trezaise Rd PL26 ..... 46 F2
Trezaise Sq PL26...... 47 A2
Treza Rd TR13 .... 91 A1
Trezela Rd TR13...... 143 D6
Trinity Cl
  Bere Alston PL20...... 41 B1
  Carnkie TR16....... 80 C2
Trinity Praze TR16 .... 80 C2
Trinity St PL25........ 114 C3
Trinity Way PL19...... 147 A4
Tripp Hill PL14........ 36 F2
TRISPEN............ 56 D7
Trispen Hill TR4....... 56 D1
Tristan Rd TR1........ 137 F5
Triumphal Cres PL7..... 130 A6
TROAN............. 57 C8
Trolver Hill TR3....... 82 B6
Trolvis Vean TR10 ..... 81 A1
Troods Mill PL15...... 106 B7
TROON.............. 79 E5
Troon Moor TR14...... 79 D4
Troon Prim Sch TR14... 79 E4
Troon Row TR13....... 90 F3
Troubridge Rd TR13.... 146 C4
Trowbridge Cl PL5...... 124 C4

Troy Ct PL23 . . . . 116 C4
Truck Hill TR2 . . . . 71 B6
Trunglemoor Cotts TR19 . 88 C2
Trungle Parc TR19 . . . . 88 C2
Trungle Terr TR19 . . . . 88 C2
TRURO 137 E3
Truro Bsns Pk TR3 . . . . . . 69 C3
Truro Dr PL5 . . . . 124 A5
Truro High Sch for Girls
TR1 . . . . 137 C3
Truro Hill TR10 . . . . 144 C8
Truro La TR10 . . . . 144 C8
Truro L Ctr TR1 . . . . 69 E3
Truro Learning Academy
TR1 . . . . 137 A4
Truro & Penryn Coll
Truro TR1 . . . . 69 E3
🟐 Truro TR1 . . . . 137 D4
Truro Prep Sch TR1 . . . . . . 69 F4
Truro Rd
Lanivet PL30 . . . . 47 F7
St Austell PL25 . . . . 114 A2
Truro Sch TR1 . . . . 137 E3
Truro Sta TR1 . . . . 137 B4
Truro Vean Terr TR1 . . . . 137 D5
TRUSCOTT 18 D4
TRUTHAN 56 C2
TRUTHWALL
Marazion 89 D7
St Just 86 E7
Truthwall La TR19 . . . . 86 F7
Tryelyn PL31 . . . . 109 F2
Tryhornek TR26 . . . . 77 D4
Trythall Prim Sch TR 20 . . . 76 B1
TRYTHOGGA 143 F8
Trythogga Hill TR18 . . . . . 143 F8
Trythogga Rd TR18 . . . . . 143 F8
Tubbon Hill TR3 . . . . 81 A4
TUBBS MILL 72 D2
Tucker Cl PL5 . . . . 127 F8
TUCKERMARSH 41 B2
Tuckers Cl TR8 . . . . 111 B4
TUCKINGMILL
Camborne 139 A4
St Breward 24 B4
Tuckingmill Terr TR13 . . . . 91 E4
Tudor Cl PL9 . . . . 135 E5
Tudor Ct PL12 . . . . 123 A2
Tuke Cl TR11 . . . . 144 E5
Tunnels Through Time★
TR7 . . . . 110 D5
Turbill Gdns 🟐 PL7 . . . . 131 B5
TURFDOWN 48 E8
Turfdown Rd PL30 . . . . 48 E8
Turf St PL31 . . . . 109 E5
Turnavean Rd PL25 . . . . . 114 A5
Turnaware Rd TR11 . . . . . 144 E2
TURNCHAPEL 135 B7
Turnpike
Gunnislake/Calstock PL18 . 40 E5
Helston TR13 . . . . 146 C7
Turnpike Hill 🟐 TR17 . . . . 89 C5
Turnpike Pl PL14 . . . . 113 B4
Turnpike Rd
Connor Downs TR27 . . . . . 78 D6
Marazion TR17 . . . . 89 C5
Turnpike The TR19 . . . . . . 86 F6
Turnquay PL9 . . . . 135 C7
Turnstone Way EX23 . . . . 104 F4
Turret Gr PL4 . . . . 128 F4
TUTWELL 29 A2
Tuxton Cl PL7 . . . . 131 C5
TWELVEHEADS 69 B1
Twelvewoods Cl PL14 . . . . 50 E8
Twelvewoods Pl PL14 . . . . 50 E8
Twinbrook Pk TR11 . . . . . . 93 B3
TWO BURROWS 68 E5
Two Hills Pk PL12 . . . . . . 122 C2
Two Trees PL27 . . . . 108 B4
Two Trees Rd PL22 . . . . . 112 F1
Tyacke Rd TR13 . . . . 146 B5
Tybesta
Grampound TR2 . . . . 72 A7
TR2 . . . . 72 A7
Tye Hill Cl PL35 . . . . 59 A3
Tyland Rd PL32 . . . . 105 F4
Tylney Cl PL6 . . . . 125 B6
Tyndale Cl PL5 . . . . 124 B1
Tyringham Pl TR26 . . . . . . 77 E4
Tyringham Rd TR26 . . . . . . 77 E4
Tyringham Row TR26 . . . . . 77 E4
Tyshute La PL26 . . . . 59 A1
Tything Wlk 🟐 PL3 . . . . 128 E6
TYWARDREATH 60 E5
Tywardreath Highway
PL24 . . . . 60 C6
Tywardreath Hill PL24 . . . . 60 D4
Tywardreath Prim Sch
PL24 . . . . 60 D5
Tywarnhale Way TR4 . . . . . 68 A6
Tywarnhayle Rd TR6 . . . . . 55 A5
Tywarnhayle Sq 🟐 TR6 . . 55 A5

U

Uglow Cl TR14 . . . . 138 C3
Ulalia Rd TR7 . . . . 110 F6
Ullswater Cres PL6 . . . . . 124 E4
Umfulla Pl 🟐 TR26 . . . . . 141 B5
Under Chapel Yd TR18 . . . 143 F4
Undercliff TR27 . . . . 142 D7
Undercliff Rd PL9 . . . . . . 135 B7
Underhayes La PL15 . . . . 106 A4
Underhill Rd PL3 . . . . 128 A4
Underhill Villas 🟐 PL3 . . 128 A3
Under La PL15 . . . . 18 C3

Underlane
Boyton PL15 . . . . 13 A3
Marhamchurch EX23 . . . . . . 7 B6
Plymouth, Plympton PL7 . . 130 C5
Plymouth, Plymstock PL9 . 135 E6
Under Rd
Boscastle PL35 . . . . 9 C1
Bridgerule EX22 . . . . 8 A5
Gunnislake PL18 . . . . 41 A6
Underways PL20 . . . . 41 B1
UNDERWOOD 130 C5
Underwood Rd PL7 . . . . . 130 D4
Unicorn Cl PL7 . . . . 130 B6
Union Cnr TR11 . . . . 144 D5
Union Hill
St Columb Major TR9 . . . . 45 E6
🟐 Stratton EX23 . . . . 4 D1
Truro TR1 . . . . 70 D5
Union Pl
Fowey PL23 . . . . 116 D4
Plymouth PL1 . . . . 148 A2
Truro TR1 . . . . 137 D5
Union Rd TR11 . . . . 144 D6
Union Sq TR9 . . . . 45 E6
Union St
Camborne TR14 . . . . 138 D2
🟐 Penzance TR18 . . . . . . 143 E5
Plymouth PL1 . . . . 148 A2
Truro TR1 . . . . 137 C5
UNITED DOWNS 81 A8
United Downs Ind Pk
TR16 . . . . 81 A8
United Rd TR16 . . . . 80 F8
Unit Hos PL27 . . . . 33 B5
Unity Cl PL6 . . . . 125 D5
Unity Rd TR13 . . . . 98 C8
University of Plymouth Bsns
Sch PL4 . . . . 148 C4
University of Plymouth
(Cookworthy Bldg)
PL4 . . . . 149 A3
UPCOTT 2 F4
Upcott Cross EX39 . . . . 2 F5
Upland Cl TR1 . . . . 137 F6
Upland Cres TR1 . . . . 137 E6
Upland Dr PL6 . . . . 125 A5
Uplands
Lostwithiel PL22 . . . . 112 B2
Saltash PL12 . . . . 122 E1
Tavistock PL19 . . . . 147 A4
Uplands Vean TR1 . . . . . . 137 F5
Upper Castle Rd TR2 . . . . . 95 A6
Upper Chapel PL15 . . . . . 106 A4
Upper Dobbin Cl PL28 . . . . 20 F2
Upper Dobbin La PL28 . . . . 20 F2
Upper Eastcliffe Rd PL24 . 60 D4
Upper Hillcrest 🟐 TR6 . . . 55 A4
Upper Knollys Terrace La
PL3 . . . . 128 C4
Upper Lemon Villas TR1 . 137 C3
Upper Ridings PL7 . . . . . . 131 B7
Upper School La TR1 . . . . 137 C3
Upperton La PL6 . . . . 121 F3
Upper Tredrea PL3 . . . . . . 81 D5
UPTON
Bude 104 C2
Upton Cross 38 C7
Upton Cl PL3 . . . . 129 B7
UPTON CROSS 38 D6
Upton Cross EX23 . . . . . . 104 C2
Upton Cross Prim Sch
PL14 . . . . 38 C7
Upton Mdws EX23 . . . . . . 104 C3
Upton Terr EX23 . . . . 104 C2
UPTON TOWANS 78 B6
Upton Twrs Nature Reserve★
TR27 . . . . 78 B6
Urban Terr PL17 . . . . 39 F5
UTC Plymouth PL19 . . . . . 127 E4
Uxbridge Dr PL5 . . . . 123 E4
Uzella Pk PL22 . . . . 112 C2

V

Vaagso Cl PL1 . . . . 127 E2
Valency Row PL35 . . . . 9 C2
Valentine Row 🟐 PL17 . . . 39 E4
Valiant Ave PL5 . . . . 124 A4
Vallard's La PL12 . . . . 53 E4
Valletort Flats PL1 . . . . . 128 A2
Valletort Ho PL1 . . . . 148 A1
Valletort La PL1 . . . . 128 A3
Valletort Pl PL1 . . . . 128 A3
Valletort PL PL1, PL3 . . . . 128 A3
Valletort Terr PL1 . . . . . . 148 A4
Valley Bglws PL13 . . . . . . 117 F5
Valley Cl
Goonhavern TR4 . . . . 55 C3
Truro TR1 . . . . 69 F3
Valley Gdns 🟐 TR16 . . . . 67 E4
Valley La TR3 . . . . 81 F7
Valley Park La PL26 . . . . . 73 C3
Valley Park
Bude EX23 . . . . 104 E5
Carbis Bay TR26 . . . . 141 C2
Mevagissey PL26 . . . . 73 C4
Plymouth PL7 . . . . 130 B5
Saltash PL12 . . . . 122 E2
Truro The TR19 . . . . 96 E3
VALLEY TRUCKLE 105 C2
Valley View
Bodmin PL31 . . . . 109 E3
🟐 Illogan TR16 . . . . 67 E4
Plymouth PL6 . . . . 125 D7
Redruth TR16 . . . . 140 E1
St Keyne PL14 . . . . 51 A4
St Teath PL30 . . . . 23 E7

Valley View continued
Wadebridge PL27 . . . . . . 108 C4
Valley View Cl PL3 . . . . . . 129 B6
Valley View Dr TR1 . . . . . . 69 F3
Valley View Pk
Bodmin PL31 . . . . 34 D2
St Austell PL26 . . . . 47 C2
Valley View Rd PL3 . . . . . 129 B7
Valley View Terr TR3 . . . . . 81 B5
Valley Wlk PL6 . . . . 125 E6
Vanguard Cl PL5 . . . . 124 D1
Vapron Rd PL3 . . . . 128 F6
Varfell La TR20 . . . . 89 A7
Varley La PL14 . . . . 113 B5
Varley Terr 🟐 PL14 . . . . . 113 B5
Vauban Pl PL2 . . . . 127 F4
Vaughan Cl PL2 . . . . 128 C7
Vauxhall Ct 🟐 PL4 . . . . . 149 A2
Vauxhall Quay PL4 . . . . . 149 A2
Vauxhall St PL4 . . . . 149 A2
Vauxhall Street Flats 🟐
PL4 . . . . 149 A2
Vean Rd TR14 . . . . 138 E2
Vean Terr TR14 . . . . 138 E2
Vear Ho TR14 . . . . 138 D2
Vellan Cl TR14 . . . . 79 B5
Vellandrucia TR3 . . . . 80 F3
Vellanhoggan Mews TR18 88 E6
VELLANOWETH 89 A8
Vellan Parc Ave TR27 . . . . 78 C5
Vellan Vrane TR27 . . . . . . 78 C5
Venetian Views TR9 . . . . . 57 D8
Venland Cl 🟐 PL14 . . . . . . 38 A3
Venn Cl 🟐 PL3 . . . . 128 E6
Venn Cres PL3 . . . . 128 E6
Venn Ct PL3 . . . . 128 E6
Venn Gdns PL3 . . . . 128 E7
Venn Gr PL3 . . . . 128 E6
Venn Hill PL19 . . . . 29 C6
Venn La PL2. PL3 . . . . 128 C6
Venn Way PL3 . . . . 128 E7
Vensloe Hill PL14 . . . . 113 B7
VENTERDON 28 D2
Ventnor Terr TR26 . . . . . . 141 A6
Venton Cl PL15 . . . . 18 B8
Venton East Sq TR19 . . . . 86 F6
VENTONGIMPS 55 C2
Venton Lace Rd TR2 . . . . . 57 E1
VENTONLEAGUE 142 F7
Ventonleague Hill TR27 . 142 E7
Ventonleague Row TR27 142 E7
Ventonraze TR16 . . . . 67 E4
Ventonraze Terr 🟐 TR16 . 67 E4
Venton Rd
Falmouth TR11 . . . . 144 E4
St Ives TR26 . . . . 141 C3
Ventonvision Rise TR26 . 77 A7
Veor Rd TR7 . . . . 111 C7
Verden Cl PL3 . . . . 128 E5
Verdun Terr PL14 . . . . . . 113 B5
Vermont Gdns PL2 . . . . . . 127 F7
Verna Pl PL5 . . . . 123 D2
Verna Rd PL5 . . . . 123 E2
Vernigo Cross PL12 . . . . . 40 B1
Vernon Pl TR11 . . . . 145 B4
Vernon Villas PL24 . . . . . . 60 B4
Vernon Way TR10 . . . . . . 144 B7
VERYAN 83 F6
Veryan CE Prim Sch TR2 . 83 F6
VERYAN GREEN 83 F7
Viaduct Hill TR27 . . . . . . 142 E6
Viaduct La TR14 . . . . 138 A1
Vicarage Cl
Budock Water TR11 . . . . . 144 C3
Menheniot PL14 . . . . 51 F5
Vicarage Gdns
Milton Abbot PL19 . . . . . . 29 C6
Plymouth PL5 . . . . 123 B1
Vicarage Hill
Budock Water TR11 . . . . . 144 C3
Mevagissey PL26 . . . . 73 C4
🟐 St Austell PL25 . . . . . . 114 C3
St Day TR16 . . . . 68 C1
🟐 Tintagel PL34 . . . . 14 C7
Vicarage La
Lelant TR26 . . . . 77 E4
Manaccan TR12 . . . . 101 A8
Poundstock EX23 . . . . 6 F2
Vicarage Mdw PL23 . . . . . 116 C3
Vicarage Rd
Bude EX23 . . . . 104 D5
Plymouth PL7 . . . . 130 C6
Porthleven PL13 . . . . 91 A1
St Agnes TR5 . . . . 54 D1
Torpoint PL11 . . . . 127 B2
Tywardreath PL24 . . . . 60 D5
Vicarage Row PL13 . . . . . 90 F3
Vicarage Terr TR11 . . . . . 92 F4
VICTORIA
Lostwithiel 112 B2
Roche 46 F4
Victoria Ave PL1 . . . . 148 A4
Victoria Bsns Pk PL26 . . . 47 A4
Victoria Cl PL14 . . . . 113 C6
Victoria Cotts
Budock Water TR11 . . . . . 144 C3
Falmouth TR11 . . . . 145 B3
Plymouth PL6 . . . . 129 B8
Victoria Ct 🟐 TR18 . . . . . 143 E6
Victoria Gdns
🟐 St Columb Road TR9 . . 45 D2
Threemilestone TR3 . . . . . 69 D3
Victoria La PL12 . . . . 122 F2
Victoria Mews 🟐 TR18 . . 143 E6
Victoria Pk PL27 . . . . 108 D6
Victoria Pl
🟐 Penzance TR18 . . . . . 143 E5

Victoria Pl continued
Plymouth, Devonport PL2 . 127 F4
Plymouth PL1 . . . . 148 A2
Ponsanooth TR3 . . . . 81 B4
🟐 St Austell PL25 . . . . . . 114 C3
🟐 St Ives TR26 . . . . 141 B6
Victoria Quay
🟐 Falmouth TR11 . . . . . 145 B5
Truro TR1 . . . . 70 D1
Victoria Rd
Bude EX23 . . . . 104 D7
Camelford PL32 . . . . 105 E4
Plymouth PL5 . . . . 123 D2
Roche 46 F3
Saltash PL12 . . . . 122 F2
🟐 St Austell PL25 . . . . . . 114 F3
🟐 St Ives TR26 . . . . 141 B6
Threemilestone TR3 . . . . . 69 D3
Victoria Road Prim Sch 🟐
PL5 . . . . 123 D1
Victoria Row TR19 . . . . . . 86 E6
Victoria Sq
Bodmin PL31 . . . . 109 F3
🟐 Penzance TR18 . . . . . 143 E6
Truro TR1 . . . . 137 C4
Victoria St
Camborne TR14 . . . . 138 D2
St Columb Major TR9 . . . . 45 E6
Torpoint PL11 . . . . 127 B3
Victoria Terr
🟐 Liskeard PL14 . . . . . . 113 B5
Plymouth PL4 . . . . 148 C4
Portscatho TR2 . . . . 83 B2
St Breward PL30 . . . . 24 B3
Victory Rd EX22 . . . . 13 A8
Victory St PL2 . . . . 127 E6
Vigo Bridge Rd PL19 . . . . 147 C6
Vigo Mews PL19 . . . . 147 C6
Village Dr PL6 . . . . 121 C1
Village Farm Cl EX23 . . . . . 7 B6
Village The
Buckland Monachorum
PL20 . . . . 41 F3
Duloe PL14 . . . . 51 A1
Villa Marina TR17 . . . . 89 B5
Villiers Cl PL9 . . . . 135 D7
Vincent Way PL12 . . . . . . 122 F2
Vine Cres PL2 . . . . 128 B6
Vinefield Ct TR11 . . . . 145 B7
Vine Gdns PL2 . . . . 128 B6
Vine Pl 🟐 PL24 . . . . 60 D5
Vinery La PL7, PL9 . . . . . . 130 E1
Vineyard The TR3 . . . . 80 F3
Vingoe's La TR20 . . . . 88 B7
Vinstone Way PL5 . . . . . . 123 D1
Violet Dr PL6 . . . . 125 E8
Violet La PL19 . . . . 147 E6
Virgin Hill TR17 . . . . 89 C6
Virginia Gdns PL2 . . . . . . 127 F7
Virgin Pl 🟐 TR19 . . . . 88 C1
Virgin St 🟐 TR26 . . . . . . 141 B6
Visicks Works TR3 . . . . . . 81 E6
Vivian Cl TR7 . . . . 110 E5
Vivian Ct TR1 . . . . 137 D3
Vivian Pk TR14 . . . . 138 F2
Vivian Rd PL31 . . . . 109 B4
Vixen Tor Cl PL20 . . . . 42 C3
VOGUE 68 D1
Vogue Hill TR16 . . . . 68 D1
Vorfield Cl TR15 . . . . 140 B6
Vosporth Hill TR8 . . . . . . 110 A3
Voss Rd PL12 . . . . 53 E1
Vounder Glaze TR19 . . . . . 86 E6
Voundervour La 🟐 TR18. 143 E5
Vyvyan Dr 🟐 TR8 . . . . . . 44 E3
Vyvyan Pl TR13 . . . . 146 C5
Vyvyan St TR14 . . . . 138 D3
Vyvyan's Terr TR14 . . . . . . 79 B2

W

Waddon Cl PL7 . . . . 130 E7
WADEBRIDGE 108 A6
Wadebridge L Ctr PL27 . . 108 C7
Wadebridge Prim Academy
PL27 . . . . 108 C6
Wadebridge Rd
St Mabyn PL30 . . . . 34 C8
St Tudy PL30 . . . . 23 E3
Wadebridge Sch PL27 . . . 108 D6
Wadeland Terr 🟐 PL14 . . . 51 A7
Wadham Cl 🟐 PL14 . . . . . 113 C5
Wadham Dr PL14 . . . . 113 C5
Wadham Ho 🟐 PL14 . . . . 113 C5
Wadham Rd PL14 . . . . 113 C5
Wadham Terr 🟐 PL2 . . . . 128 A5
Wagg La TR2 . . . . 71 C6
Waggon Hill PL7 . . . . 131 A4
WAINHOUSE CORNER 10 E6
Wain Pk PL7 . . . . 130 F4
Wainsway 🟐 TR6 . . . . 55 A4
Wainways EX23 . . . . 10 F6
Wakefield Ave PL5 . . . . . . 123 E1
Wake St PL4 . . . . 148 B4
Walcot Cl PL6 . . . . 125 C4
Waldon Cl PL7 . . . . 131 B5
Walker Lines Ind Est 🟐
PL31 . . . . 48 D8
Walker Terr PL1 . . . . 148 B1
Walkham Bsns Pk PL5 . . . 124 B1
Walkham Cl PL19 . . . . 147 D5
Walkham Mdws PL20 . . . . 42 C3
WALKHAMPTON 42 D4
Walkhampton Rd PL20 . . . 42 C4
Walkhampton Wlk PL6 . . . 125 E1
Walkham Terr 🟐 PL20 . . . 42 C5
Walk Terr PL23 . . . . 116 C4

Walk The PL15 . . . . 106 C6
WALL 78 E3
Wallace Mews 🟐 PL31 . . 109 D5
Wallace Rd
Bodmin PL31 . . . . 109 D5
Plymouth PL7 . . . . 131 A4
Walled Gdn The TR10 . . . 144 A6
Wall Gdns TR27 . . . . 78 E3
Wallpark Cl PL7 . . . . 130 F7
Wall Rd TR27 . . . . 78 E3
Wallsend Ind Est PL4 . . . 149 C1
Wall Vean TR27 . . . . 78 E3
Walnut Cl PL7 . . . . 131 B5
Walnut Dr PL7 . . . . 131 C5
Walnut Gdns PL7 . . . . . . 131 C5
Walreddon PL19 . . . . 147 B4
Walsingham Ct PL7 . . . . . 131 B6
Walsingham Pl 🟐 TR1 . . 137 D4
Walters La PL15 . . . . 18 D5
Walters Rd PL5 . . . . 123 C2
Waltham Pl PL2 . . . . 128 A8
Walton Cres PL5 . . . . 124 C1
Wandle Pl PL3 . . . . 129 D5
Wansford Mdws PL26 . . . . 85 C5
WANSON 6 F3
Wanstead Gr PL5 . . . . . . 124 A2
Wantage Gdns PL1 . . . . . 148 A3
WARBSTOW 11 B1
Warbstow Com Sch PL15 . 11 B1
WARBSTOW CROSS 11 B2
Warburton Gdns PL5 . . . . 123 C1
Ward Cl 🟐 EX23 . . . . 4 D1
Wardlow Cl PL6 . . . . 128 F8
Wardlow Gdns PL6 . . . . . 128 F8
Wardour Wlk PL6 . . . . . . 125 B7
Ward Pl PL3 . . . . 129 B5
Warfelton Cres PL12 . . . . 122 E2
Warfelton Gdns PL12 . . . 122 E2
Warfelton Terr PL12 . . . . 122 E2
Waring Rd PL6 . . . . 124 D7
WARLEGGAN 36 C4
Warleigh Ave PL2 . . . . . . 127 E5
WARLEIGH BARTON 123 F8
Warleigh Cres PL6 . . . . . 124 F5
Warleigh La TR2 . . . . 127 E5
Warleigh Rd 🟐 PL2 . . . . . 128 E4
Warmwell Rd PL5 . . . . . . 123 E4
Warne Cl TR2 . . . . 71 F3
Warran La PL19 . . . . 147 C3
Warraton Cl PL12 . . . . . . 122 D3
Warraton Gn PL12 . . . . . . 122 D3
Warraton La PL12 . . . . . . 122 D3
Warraton Rd PL12 . . . . . . 122 D3
Warren TR26 . . . . 141 B5
Warren Cl 🟐 TR13 . . . . . . 98 C8
Warren La PL5 . . . . 124 A8
Warren Pk PL6 . . . . 125 D7
Warren Rd TR9 . . . . 45 F2
Warrens Field PL32 . . . . . 105 D5
Warren St PL2 . . . . 127 E4
Warren The PL13 . . . . 62 E1
Warspite Gdns PL5 . . . . . 124 D2
Warton Cl PL5 . . . . 124 D3
Warwick Ave
Illogan TR16 . . . . 67 D4
Plymouth PL5 . . . . 124 D3
Warwick Cl PL28 . . . . 31 F8
Warwick Cres 🟐 PL27 . . . 31 F5
Warwick Dr PL25 . . . . . . 115 B5
Warwick Orchard Cl PL5 124 B3
Warwick Rd EX23 . . . . . . 104 E4
Wasdale Cl PL6 . . . . 125 D2
Wasdale Gdns PL6 . . . . . 125 D2
WASHAWAY 34 C4
Washbourne Cl PL1 . . . . . 127 E3
WATERGATE 24 E8
Watergate La PL30 . . . . . . 34 C8
Watergate Rd TR8 . . . . . . 44 C6
Watering Hill Cl PL25 . . . 114 E3
Waterings Rd TR11 . . . . . 82 A2
Water La
Crantock TR8 . . . . 110 A3
Delabole PL33 . . . . 14 E3
Golant PL23 . . . . 61 B5
Hayle TR27 . . . . 142 B3
St Agnes TR5 . . . . 54 D1
WATERLOO 35 D7
Waterloo Cl
Plymouth PL1 . . . . 128 A2
St Mawes TR2 . . . . 95 A6
Waterloo Ct PL1 . . . . 128 A2
Waterloo Pl TR11 . . . . . . 145 B4
Waterloo Rd TR11 . . . . . . 145 B4
Waterloo St
Plymouth PL4 . . . . 149 A4
Plymouth, Stoke PL1 . . . . 128 A3
Waterloo Yard Flats PL1 . 128 A2
Water-ma-Trout TR13 . . . 146 C8
Water-ma-Trout Ind Est
TR13 . . . . 146 C8
Waters Cl TR15 . . . . 140 E7
Waters Edge
Newquay TR7 . . . . 110 A6
Tavistock PL19 . . . . 147 D6
Water's Edge PL28 . . . . . 107 E6
Watersedge Cl PL25 . . . . 114 B4
Waterside Lane PL30 . . . . 47 E7
Waterside Mews PL1 . . . . 127 D3
Watersmead Parc TR11 . . 144 C3
Waterwheel Cl 🟐 PL25 . . 115 A3
Watery La
Bodmin PL31 . . . . 109 D5
Milton Combe PL6 . . . . . . 120 D6
Watson Gdns PL4 . . . . . . 149 B3

Watson Pl PL4 . . . . 149 B2
Watts Park Rd PL2 . . . 128 C7
Watts Rd PL19 . . . . 147 B5
Watts' Rd PL4 . . . . 149 C3
Waveney Gdns PL5 . . 124 C3
Waverley Ct PL25 . . . 115 A5
Waverley Rd PL5 . . . 123 D2
Wavish Pk PL11 . . . 126 E3
Waycott Wlk PL6 . . . 124 D6
Way Cross PL15 . . . 27 B3
Wayfield Rd TR11 . . . 82 B2
Wayside Ct TR7 . . . 111 A4
Wayside Folk Mus★
TR26 . . . . 76 B5
WEARDE 122 F2
Wearde Rd PL12 . . . 122 E1
Webber Hill TR11 . . . 145 B4
Webber St TR11 . . . 145 B4
Webbs Ct [9] PL14 . . 113 C6
Webb St PL23 . . . 116 D4
Wedgewood Rd PL25 . 115 A4
WEEK GREEN . . . 11 E8
WEEK ST MARY . . . 11 E8
Weeks Rise PL32 . . . 105 B2
Weekstone Cross EX22 . 8 C8
Weeth Cl TR14 . . . 138 C3
Weethes Cotts [6] TR18 143 D5
Weeth La TR14 . . . 138 C3
Weeth Prim Sch TR14 . 138 C4
Weeth Rd TR14 . . . 138 C4
Weir Cl PL6 . . . 125 F2
Weir Gdns PL6 . . . 125 F2
Weir Rd PL6 . . . 125 F2
Welbeck Ave PL4 . . . 148 C4
WELCOMBE . . . 2 D5
Welcombe Cross EX39 . 3 B4
Welcome Cl TR4 . . . 56 D1
Welland Gdns PL3 . . 129 C5
Weller Ct TR11 . . . 145 B3
Wellfield Cl
Coad's Green PL15 . . 27 D3
Plymouth PL7 . . . 131 C5
Well Gdns PL1 . . . 148 B3
Wellhay Cl PL9 . . . 136 C6
Wellhouse The [8] PL14 . 113 C6
Wellington Cl TR14 . . 138 C3
Wellington Ct TR2 . . 72 A7
Wellington Gdns TR11 . 145 B4
Wellington Pl
Falmouth TR11 . . . 145 B4
Penzance TR18 . . . 143 D6
Wadebridge PL27 . . 108 C4
Wellington Plantation
TR3 . . . 82 B7
Wellington Rd
Camborne TR14 . . . 138 D3
Porthleven TR13 . . . 91 B1
St Dennis PL26 . . . 58 C8
[2] St Eval PL27 . . . 31 F3
Wellington St
Plymouth PL4 . . . 149 A4
Plymouth, Stoke PL1 . 128 A3
Torpoint PL11 . . . 127 B3
Wellington Terr
Falmouth TR11 . . . 145 B4
Porthleven TR13 . . . 91 B1
[2] Truro TR1 . . . 137 C4
Well La
Constantine TR11 . . 92 F4
Falmouth TR11 . . . 145 B4
Goldsithney TR20 . . 89 F5
Lamorna TR19 . . . 97 E5
Liskeard PL14 . . . 113 C6
St Cleer PL14 . . . 37 F3
St Keverne TR12 . . . 101 D4
TR11 . . . 92 F3
Tregony TR2 . . . 71 F3
Tremar PL14 . . . 38 A3
Welcombe EX39 . . . 2 E5
Well Mdw PL15 . . . 18 A5
Wellpark Rd PL18 . . . 40 F5
Well Park Rd PL11 . . 127 B3
Wellsbourne Pk PL3 . . 129 A6
Wells Ct PL10 . . . 132 E4
Well St
Callington PL17 . . . 39 E4
Delabole PL33 . . . 14 E3
Tregony TR2 . . . 71 F3
Tywardreath PL24 . . 60 D5
Well Way TR7 . . . 111 C7
Welman Rd PL10 . . . 132 F6
Welsby Terr PL14 . . . 37 F3
WELSFORD . . . 3 C8
Welsford Ave PL2 . . . 127 F5
Welway TR6 . . . 55 A4
WEMBURY . . . 136 B1
Wembury Park Rd PL3 . 128 C8
Wembury Rd PL9 . . . 136 A4
WENDRON . . . 91 F6
Wendron CE Prim Sch
TR13 . . . 91 F5
Wendron St TR13 . . . 146 C6
WENFORDBRIDGE . . 24 A2
Wenlock Gdns PL2 . . 128 B8
WENMOUTH CROSS . . 37 A3
Wensum Cl PL7 . . . 131 A4
Wentwood Gdns PL6 . . 125 E3
Wentwood Rd PL6 . . 125 E3
Wentworth
Lynstone EX23 . . . 104 C3
Polzeath PL27 . . . 21 D5
Redruth TR15 . . . 140 C3
Wentworth Pl PL4 . . . 129 B2
Wentworth Way PL12 . 122 C2
WERRINGTON . . . 18 F6

Werrington Dr PL17 . . 39 E4
Werrington Prim Sch
PL15 . . . 18 F7
Wesley Ave PL3 . . . 128 E5
Wesley Cl
Kelly Bray PL17 . . . 39 F6
Stenalees PL26 . . . 59 C8
Wesley Cottage Mus★
PL15 . . . 26 B7
Wesley Ct
Penryn TR10 . . . 144 C8
Pensilva PL14 . . . 38 D4
[25] Porthleven TR13 . . 98 C4
Torpoint PL11 . . . 127 C3
Wesley La PL12 . . . 122 F2
Wesley Pl
[5] Newlyn TR18 . . . 143 C2
Plymouth, Mutley PL3 . 128 E5
[1] Plymouth, Stoke PL2 . 128 A4
St Austell PL25 . . . 114 F3
[7] St Ives TR26 . . . 141 B5
Wesley Rd
Cubert TR8 . . . 55 D8
Pensilva PL14 . . . 38 D4
Saltash PL12 . . . 122 F2
Wesley St
Camborne TR14 . . . 138 E3
[11] Heamoor TR18 . . . 143 C7
Redruth TR15 . . . 140 C3
Wesley Terr
Bugle PL26 . . . 47 C2
Looe PL13 . . . 117 D4
Wesley Way PL15 . . . 26 B7
Wesley Yd TR7 . . . 110 D6
West Ave [4] PL19 . . . 147 B5
West Beach Rd TR4 . . 68 A6
West Beckon Cl EX23 . . 2 D1
WEST BLACKDOWN . . 30 F8
Westborne Hts TR15 . . 140 B3
Westborne Rd TR14 . . 138 B4
Westbourne Dr PL25 . . 114 B3
Westbourne La PL14 . . 113 B6
Westbourne Rd PL3 . . 128 D5
Westbourne Terr
Fraddon TR9 . . . 57 D8
Saltash PL12 . . . 122 F3
Westbridge Cotts PL19 . 147 B4
Westbridge Ind Est [3]
PL19 . . . 147 B4
Westbridge Rd PL25 . . 59 A3
West Bridge Rd PL15 . 106 B7
Westbury Cl PL5 . . . 124 B4
Westby Rd EX23 . . . 104 E5
West Camps Bay PL11 . 64 C4
West Charles St TR14 . 138 D2
West Cl TR13 . . . 146 D7
West Cliff TR4 . . . 68 A6
West Cnr [1] TR3 . . . 81 F7
Westcombe Cres PL9 . 135 D5
West Cornwall Hospl
TR18 . . . 143 D6
Westcott PL27 . . . 108 A6
Westcott Cl PL6 . . . 129 A8
Westcove Ho [2] TR7 . . 110 F6
Westcroft Rd PL5 . . . 123 D1
West Ct TR7 . . . 110 C6
WEST CURRY . . . 12 D4
West Devon Bsns Pk
PL19 . . . 147 B3
West Down Ct PL13 . . 117 C4
Westdown Rd PL33 . . 14 D2
West Down Rd PL2 . . 128 B6
WESTDOWNS . . . 14 C1
Westella Rd PL20 . . . 42 D2
West End
Goldsithney TR20 . . 89 E5
Marazion TR17 . . . 89 B5
Pentewan PL26 . . . 73 C6
Redruth TR15 . . . 140 B4
St Day TR16 . . . 68 D1
West End Cl TR10 . . . 144 C8
West End Cotts PL11 . 64 B8
West End Ct [2] TR15 . 140 B4
West End Ind Est PL10 . 144 B8
West End Sq [7] PL17 . 39 E4
Westend Terr TR10 . . 144 C8
Westeria Terr PL2 . . 128 C7
Westerlands Rd PL27 . 108 B6
Western App PL1 . . . 148 B2
Western Ave [5] PL14 . 51 A7
Western College Rd PL4 128 F5
Western Dr PL3 . . . 129 B4
Western Pl TR10 . . . 144 B8
Western Promenade Rd
TR18 . . . 143 E4
Western Rd PL15 . . . 106 B5
Western Terr
Bodmin PL31 . . . 109 C4
Falmouth TR11 . . . 145 A3
Launceston PL15 . . 106 B5
Western Wood Way PL7 131 D5
West Fairholme Rd EX23 104 E7
Westfield PL7 . . . 131 A6
Westfield Ave PL9 . . 135 C6
Westgate Mews [2] PL15 106 C5
Westgate St PL15 . . . 106 C5
Westground Way PL34 . 14 D7
Westhampnett Pl PL5 . 123 F4
Westhaul Pk PL25 . . 115 E4
Westhays Cl PL9 . . . 135 F4
Westhead Rd PL10 . . 64 B2
Westheath Ave PL30,
PL31 . . . 109 B3
Westheath Rd PL31 . . 109 B3

West Hill
St Austell PL25 . . . 114 C3
Wadebridge PL27 . . 108 A6
West Hill Ct [16] PL25 . 114 C3
West Hill Rd PL4 . . . 128 F4
WEST HOE . . . 148 B1
West Hoe Rd PL1 . . . 148 B1
West Kitty TR5 . . . 54 C1
West La
Crafthole PL11 . . . 65 B5
Delabole PL33 . . . 14 E2
Landrake PL12 . . . 53 B3
Westlake Cl PL11 . . . 126 F3
WEST LOOE . . . 117 C3
West Looe Hill PL13 . . 117 B3
West Looe Sq PL13 . . 117 C3
West Malling Ave PL5 . 123 E5
Westmoor Cl PL7 . . . 131 C6
Westmoor Cres PL25 . . 81 D6
Westmoor Pk PL19 . . 147 C4
WESTON MILL . . . 127 E8
Weston Mill Dr PL5 . . 127 F8
Weston Mill Hill PL5 . . 123 F1
Weston Mill La PL5 . . 124 A1
Weston Mill Prim Sch
PL2 . . . 127 E7
Weston Mill Rd PL5 . . 123 E1
Weston Park Rd PL3 . . 128 D6
Westover Rd PL17 . . . 39 E4
West Pk
Perranarworthal TR3 . 81 D6
Redruth TR15 . . . 139 F6
[13] St Columb Major TR9 . 45 E6
Tideford PL12 . . . 52 F2
Trewidland PL14 . . . 51 C3
West Pl
Falmouth TR11 . . . 145 A3
[45] St Ives TR26 . . . 141 B6
St Just TR19 . . . 86 E6
West Point TR8 . . . 111 C4
West Porthmear Cotts
PL25 . . . 115 B2
West Porthmear Ct PL25 115 B2
WEST PORTHOLLAND . 84 D5
West Quay PL10 . . . 132 E5
West Rd
Looe PL13 . . . 117 C4
Quintrell Downs TR8 . 111 E3
West Rise TR11 . . . 144 F3
West St
Grimscott EX23 . . . 5 B1
Liskeard PL14 . . . 113 B6
Millbrook PL10 . . . 132 E5
Polruan PL23 . . . 116 C2
St Columb Major TR9 . 45 E6
Tavistock PL19 . . . 147 B5
Torpoint PL10 . . . 132 E4
WEST TAPHOUSE . . . 49 E6
West Tehidy TR14 . . . 138 F7
West Terr
Hayle TR27 . . . 142 B6
Newlyn TR18 . . . 143 C3
WEST TOLGUS . . . 139 D8
West Tolgus TR15 . . . 139 D8
West Trevingey TR15 . 140 A3
West Trewirgie Rd TR15 140 B4
Westview TR6 . . . 55 B5
West View
Porthleven TR13 . . . 91 A1
Tavistock PL19 . . . 147 E2
Trevone PL28 . . . 20 E2
West View Rd [5] PL20 . 41 B1
West Villas TR8 . . . 57 B7
Westward PL27 . . . 21 D5
Westward Rd TR26 . . 141 A6
WEST WATERGATE . . 62 E4
Westway PL9 . . . 135 B5
West Week Cl EX22 . . 11 E8
West Wharf PL26 . . . 73 C3
Westwinds PL32 . . . 105 B4
Westwood PL14 . . . 113 B6
Westwood Ave PL6 . . 125 C6
WEST YOULSTONE . . 3 B2
Wetherham La PL30 . . 23 E3
Whalesborough Parc
EX23 . . . 104 F5
Wharf Rd
Penzance TR18 . . . 143 F5
St Ives TR26 . . . 141 B6
Wharfe Cl [8] TR18 . . 143 E5
Wharfside Sh Ctr TR18 . 143 F5
Wharfside Village [9]
TR18 . . . 143 E5
Wharf The
[22] Mousehole TR19 . . 88 C1
St Ives TR26 . . . 141 B6
Wharf Theatre & Gall The★
PL19 . . . 147 B5
Wheal Agar TR15 . . . 139 C6
Wheal Agar [5] TR14 . 138 F7
WHEAL ALFRED . . . 142 F4
Wheal Alfred Rd TR27 . 142 F5
Wheal-an-Wens TR17 . 89 C5
Whealbrake Lodge PL26 58 E8
Wheal Bull PL26 . . . 58 D5
WHEAL BUSY . . . 68 F3
Wheal Busy La TR4 . . 68 F3
Wheal Catherine Cl TR6 55 B5
Wheal Damsel Rd TR16 . 80 E8

Wheal Dance TR16 . . 140 D3
Wheal Dream TR26 . . 141 C6
Wheal Eliza Cl PL25 . . 115 B5
Wheal Fortune La TR15 139 D6
WHEAL FRANCES . . . 55 D3
Wheal Friendly La TR5 . 54 C2
Wheal Gerry TR14 . . 138 E4
Wheal Golden Dr TR8 . 43 C1
Wheal Gorland Rd TR16 . 68 D1
Wheal Harmony Terr
TR15 . . . 140 D2
Wheal Jane Mdws TR3 . 69 C3
Wheal Jewel (Gipsy Site)
TR16 . . . 68 E1
Wheal Kitty TR5 . . . 54 C1
Wheal Kitty La TR5 . . 54 C2
Wheal Kitty Workshops
TR5 . . . 54 D2
Wheal Leisure TR6 . . 55 A5
Wheal Leisure Cl [25] TR6 . 55 A5
Wheal Margery TR26 . . 141 C3
Wheal Maria Cotts PL19 . 29 D1
Wheal Northey PL25 . . 115 B5
Wheal Oak TR13 . . . 146 D8
Wheal Quoit Ave TR5 . 54 C1
Wheal Ramoth [3] TR6 . 55 A5
Wheal Regent Pk PL25 . 115 D3
WHEAL ROSE . . . 68 C3
Wheal Rose [19] TR13 . . 98 C8
Wheal Silver TR15 . . 140 B5
Wheal Speed Rd TR26 . 141 C2
Wheal Sperries Way TR1 . 69 E3
Wheal Tehidy La TR15 . 139 E6
Wheal Trefusis TR15 . . 140 D2
Wheal Trelawney TR16 . 140 D3
Wheal Venture Rd TR26 141 C3
Wheal View PL26 . . . 58 B4
Wheal Virgin Ho TR26 . 77 A6
WHEAL VOR . . . 91 A5
Wheal Vor TR15 . . . 140 D3
Wheal Vyvyan TR11 . . 92 F4
Wheal Whidden TR26 . 141 C2
Wheatfield Cres TR7 . . 111 A4
Wheatridge PL7 . . . 130 B7
Wheel Ayr Terr TR26 . . 141 A6
Wheeler Higman Cl PL26 . 59 C7
Wheelgate House Sch
TR8 . . . 43 D2
Wheelwright Ct PL20 . . 42 E4
Wherry Pl PL23 . . . 116 D2
WHERRY TOWN . . . 143 D4
Wherry Way PL14 . . . 50 E7
Whieldon Rd PL25 . . 115 A4
Whimple St PL1 . . . 148 C2
Whin Bank Rd PL5 . . 124 E2
WHIPSIDERRY . . . 44 C6
Whistley Down PL20 . . 42 B2
Whitby Cres PL6 . . . 125 A1
Whitby Rd PL6 . . . 125 A1
WHITCHURCH . . . 147 D3
Whitchurch Prim Sch
PL19 . . . 147 D2
Whitchurch Rd
Horrabridge PL20 . . 42 C5
Tavistock PL19 . . . 147 C3
Whitcross Hill TR15 . . 139 C3
Whitebarrow Cotts PL14 . 37 A4
Whitecroft Way EX23 . . 5 A6
WHITECROSS
Crowlas TR20 . . . 77 C1
Wadebridge . . . 33 B7
WHITE CROSS
Mullion . . . 99 B4
St Columb Road . . . 45 C2
Whitecross
Blisland PL30 . . . 35 D7
Bodinnick PL23 . . . 116 F6
White Cross
Cury TR12 . . . 99 B4
Redruth TR15 . . . 68 D3
White Cross Ct PL4 . . 149 A3
Whitecross Ind Est TR8 . 45 B2
Whitefield Terr PL4 . . 149 B4
Whiteford Cl [16] PL17 . 39 E4
Whiteford Rd PL3 . . . 128 E6
White Friars La PL4 . . 149 B3
Whitegate PL26 . . . 58 B8
Whitegate Mdws PL26 . 58 B8
Whitegate Rd TR7 . . . 111 A6
Whitegate Sh Complex
TR7 . . . 111 A7
Whitehall Bglws PL30 . 23 B2
Whitehall Dr
[9] Bere Alston PL20 . 41 B1
Plymouth PL9 . . . 136 B7
Whitehall Est PL30 . . 23 B2
White Hart Arc The [3]
PL15 . . . 106 C5
Whitehaven Way PL6 . 125 A4
WHITEHILL . . . 146 C4
Whitehill Cross PL15 . 19 C6
Whitehill Terr TR13 . . 146 C4
White Horse
Crowntown TR13 . . 91 A6
Nancegollan TR13 . . 91 A6
White House Cl TR26 . 141 C2
White La PL1 . . . 149 A2
White Lady Rd PL9 . . 135 D5
White Lodge EX23 . . 10 C7
WHITEMOOR . . . 58 E8
Whitemoor Academy
PL26 . . . 58 E8
White River PL11 . . . 114 C3
White River Pl Sh Ctr
PL25 . . . 114 C3
WHITEROCK . . . 108 A5

Whiterock Cl PL27 . . 108 A5
Whiterock Rd PL27 . . 108 B5
Whiterocks Pk PL18 . . 40 D6
Whiterock Terr PL27 . . 108 B5
White's Cl [3] TR5 . . 54 C1
White Smock Mdw [7] TR5 54 C1
Whitestone Cres PL31 . 109 C3
Whitestone Rd PL31 . . 109 C3
White Walls Ct [16] TR6 . 55 A4
Whitewater Ct PL7 . . 130 E6
WHITEWELL . . . 23 D7
Whitham Pk PL19 . . . 147 C4
WHITLEIGH . . . 124 C5
Whitleigh Ave PL5 . . 124 E2
Whitleigh Cotts PL5 . . 124 E2
Whitleigh Cl PL5 . . . 124 D4
Whitleigh Gn PL5 . . . 124 D4
Whitleigh Villas PL5 . . 124 E2
Whitleigh Way PL5 . . 124 C4
Whitley Cl TR1 . . . 137 D4
Whitley Grange PL14 . 113 A6
Whitlieburn Terr PL13 . 117 C1
Whitpot Hill PL12 . . . 64 F8
Whitsam Cross PL20 . . 41 A1
Whitsand Bay View PL11 . 65 A4
Whitson Cross PL5 . . 124 C7
Whitsoncross La PL5 . . 124 C7
WHITSTONE . . . 7 F1
Whitstone Cty Prim Sch
EX22 . . . 7 F1
Whitstone Head Sch EX22 . 7 F1
Whittington St PL3 . . 148 B4
Whitworth Cl TR5 . . . 54 C1
Whity Cross PL12 . . . 122 A4
Whym Kibbal Crt TR15 . 140 C5
Widegate Nursery PL9 . 136 B5
WIDEGATES . . . 63 F8
WIDEMOUTH BAY . . 6 F5
WIDEWELL . . . 125 B7
Widewell La PL6 . . . 125 C7
Widewell Prim Sch PL6 . 125 B7
Widewell Rd PL6 . . . 125 B7
Widey Court Prim Sch
PL6 . . . 124 F1
Widey Cross PL6 . . . 124 F1
Widey Ct PL6 . . . 124 F1
Widey La PL6 . . . 124 F1
Widey View PL3 . . . 128 F6
Widgeon Way TR27 . . 77 E3
Wilcove La PL11 . . . 126 D5
Wildebeest Rd [7] PL27 . 31 F3
Wilderness Rd PL3 . . 128 E5
Wilderness Trail★ PL30 . 48 C5
Wildflower La TR7 . . . 111 A6
Wilkes Wlk TR1 . . . 137 D4
Wilkinson Cl PL17 . . 39 E6
Wilkinson Rd PL5 . . . 127 D8
Willapark View PL35 . . 9 C1
William Edwards Cl
EX23 . . . 104 E6
William Evans Cl PL6 . . 124 D5
William Laundry Cl PL14 . 52 A5
William Prance Rd PL6 . 125 A3
Williams Ave PL4 . . . 129 B1
Williams Ho PL31 . . . 109 B4
William St
Camborne TR14 . . . 138 D2
Truro TR1 . . . 137 D4
William Young Mews
PL14 . . . 113 E5
Willis Vean TR12 . . . 99 A1
Willoughby Pl PL17 . . 39 E4
Willoughby Way TR27 . 78 D6
Willowby Pk PL20 . . . 42 D2
Willow Cl
[22] Callington PL17 . 39 F4
Mylor Bridge TR11 . . 82 A3
Plymouth PL3 . . . 129 E5
Quintrell Downs TR8 . 44 E3
Willow Cotts PL7 . . . 130 D4
Willow Ct PL6 . . . 129 E7
Willow Dr TR14 . . . 138 B4
Willowfield TR18 . . . 143 C5
Willow Gn PL12 . . . 122 D2
Willow Rd PL19 . . . 147 C3
Willows The
Bugle PL26 . . . 47 C1
Whipsiderry TR7 . . . 44 C6
Willow Way PL14 . . . 113 B5
Willow Wlk PL6 . . . 125 D5
Wills Cl PL6 . . . 124 E7
Wills La [53] TR26 . . . 141 B6
Wills Moor PL26 . . . 85 C5
Will's Row TR15 . . . 139 C8
WILMINSTONE . . . 30 F7
Wilminstone Ind Est
PL19 . . . 147 E7
Wilmot Gdns PL5 . . . 124 D3
Wilsey View PL15 . . . 17 B7
Wilson Cres PL2 . . . 128 B5
Wilson Way
Camborne TR15 . . . 139 D5
[14] Par PL24 . . . 60 B4
Wilsworthy Cross EX22 . 12 C7
Wilton Rd PL1 . . . 128 A3
Wilton St PL1 . . . 148 A4
Wilton Terr PL13 . . . 62 D6
Wiltshire Cl PL4 . . . 128 F4
Winchester Gdns PL5 . 124 A5
Windermere Cres PL6 . 124 F4
Winding Terr TR10 . . . 81 A1
WINDMILL . . . 20 F1
Windmill PL23 . . . 116 C4
Windmill Hill
Launceston PL15 . . 106 C5
Saltash PL12 . . . 122 F4
St Just in Roseland TR2 . 82 F2

Windmill Hill continued
TR2 .... 57 E1
Windmill Hill Terr PL15 . 106 C5
Windmill Ho PL23 ...... 116 C4
Windmill Ind Est PL23.. 116 C4
Windmill La PL15 ...... 106 C5
Windsor Ct
　Falmouth TR11 ...... 145 B4
　Newquay TR7 .... 110 D5
Windsor Dr PL25 ...... 115 C3
Windsor Gr PL31 ...... 109 F5
Windsor Hill 8 TR26 .. 141 B5
Windsor Ho 9 PL31 .. 109 E5
Windsor La
　Kelly Bray PL17 ...... 39 F6
　Saltash PL12 .... 122 E2
Windsor Mews PL31... 109 E5
Windsor Pl
　Liskeard PL14 .... 113 C5
　28 Penzance TR18 .. 143 E6
　Plymouth PL1 .... 148 C2
Windsor Rd PL3 ...... 129 B7
Windsor Terr
　Falmouth TR11 ...... 145 B4
　Penzance TR18 ...... 143 D6
　4 St Ives TR26 ...... 141 A5
Windsor Villas PL1 .. 148 C2
Windsworth PL24 ...... 115 F7
Windy Ridge PL26 ...... 46 D1
Wingfield PL31 .... 35 B2
Wingfield Mans PL3... 128 A3
Wingfield Rd PL3 ...... 148 A4
Wingfield Way PL3 .. 148 A4
Winifred Baker Ct 5
　PL4 .... 149 A4
Winnard's Perch TR9 ... 32 D1
Winnicott Cl PL6 ...... 124 E7
Winnow Cl PL9 .... 135 F4
Winns Row TR13 ...... 146 C6
Winsbury Ct PL6 ...... 125 A1
Winsor Cotts PL15 .. 106 B7
Winsor Est PL13 ...... 62 D5
Winstanley Wlk PL3.. 129 D6
Winston Ave PL4....... 148 C4
Winstowe Terr TR8 ... 110 A3
Winwell Field PL27... 108 D6
Witham Gdns PL3 .... 129 C5
WITHEVEN 11 D3
WITHIEL 47 A8
WITHIELGOOSE MILLS 47 C8
Withnoe La PL10....... 132 B6
Withnoe Terr PL10 .... 65 E3
Withnoe Way Cl PL15 . 106 D3
Wixenford Ct PL9 ..... 135 F8

Woburn Rd PL15........ 106 B4
Woburn Terr PL9 ..... 135 C7
Wodehouse Terr TR11... 145 B4
Wolcocke Cl TR17..... 89 D5
Wollaton Gr PL5 ...... 123 F3
Wolrige Ave PL7 ...... 131 B5
Wolrige Way PL7 ..... 131 A5
Wolsdon Pl PL1........ 148 A3
Wolsdon St PL1........ 148 B3
Wolseley Bsns Pk 2
　PL2 .... 128 A5
Wolseley Cl PL2 ...... 128 A5
Wolseley Rd
　Plymouth, Camels Head
　　PL5 .... 127 F6
　Plymouth, St Budeaux PL5 123 C1
Wolseley Road Flats PL2 127 F6
Wolverwood Cl PL7.... 131 C3
Wolverwood La PL7.... 131 B3
Wombwell Cres PL2... 127 E7
Wood Acre PL12 ...... 122 B4
Woodacre Ct PL12.... 122 B4
Wooda La PL15 ...... 106 B6
Wooda Rd PL15 ...... 106 C6
Woodbine Cotts PL7 .. 130 E4
Woodbine La TR16 .... 67 D4
Woodbury Gdns PL5 .. 124 A3
Woodchurch PL20 .... 42 B3
Wood Cl PL12........ 122 B3
Woodcock Cl PL10 ... 133 A6
Wood Dr
　Saltash PL12 .... 53 C8
　St Mellion PL12 ...... 53 C8
Woodend Rd PL6 .... 125 D7
Woodfield Rd EX23.... 104 E7
WOODFORD
　Plymouth 130 C7
　Shop 4 D8
Woodford Ave PL7.... 130 A7
Woodford Cl PL7....... 130 A7
Woodford Cres PL7 ... 130 A6
Woodford Cross EX23 .. 2 C1
Woodford Gn PL7 ..... 130 B6
Woodford Prim Sch PL7. 130 B6
Woodford Rd PL6...... 125 D6
Woodgate Rd PL14.... 113 A5
Woodgrove Pk PL26... 59 A1
Wood La
　Landrake PL12......... 53 D2
　Truro TR1.............. 137 D3
　Tywardreath PL24.... 60 D5
Woodland Ave
　Penryn TR10........... 144 B6
　Plymouth PL9.......... 136 A8

Woodland Ave continued
　12 Tywardreath PL24 ..... 60 D5
Woodland Cl
　Gunnislake PL18 .... 40 F6
　Lanivet PL30 .... 47 E7
　St Austell PL25 ...... 114 E3
Woodland Ct TR1 ...... 137 E5
Woodland Dr PL7 ..... 130 B4
Woodland Glade PL30.... 47 F7
Woodland Hts TR1 ..... 137 E5
Woodland Rd
　Plymouth PL7.......... 130 C6
　St Austell PL25 ...... 114 E3
Woodland Rise
　Penryn TR10........... 144 B7
　Rilla Mill PL17 .... 38 E8
Woodlands
　Dousland PL20.......... 42 E3
　4 Mullion TR12........ 99 A2
　10 Par PL24............ 60 C4
　Plymouth PL9.......... 135 F6
Woodlands Ct PL5 .... 124 A3
Woodlands End PL6.... 125 D5
Woodlands La PL6 .... 125 F1
Woodlands Sch PL5.... 124 B4
Woodlands Terr 3 TR16 140 F1
Woodlands The TR14... 67 B4
Woodlands View PL13.. 117 B4
Woodland Terr
　Plymouth PL4.......... 149 B4
　4 St Columb Road TR9.. 45 E2
Woodland Terr La PL4 . 149 B4
Woodland View
　Coombe PL26.......... 58 C2
　Lanivet PL30 .... 47 E6
　7 PL26................ 115 A1
Woodland Way
　Gunnislake PL18 ...... 41 A7
　Torpoint PL11 .... 126 F3
Woodlane TR11......... 145 B3
Woodlane Cl TR11 .... 145 B3
Woodlane Cres TR11... 145 B3
Woodlane Dr TR11 .... 145 B3
Woodley Cl 8 EX23 .... 4 D1
Woodman's Cnr PL20 ... 42 D3
Woodpecker Way PL19..147 D2
Woodridge Cl TR27 .... 78 E1
Woods-Browning Ind Est
　PL31.................. 109 F2
Woodside
　Crapstone PL20........ 42 B2
　Penryn TR10.......... 144 B7
　Plymouth PL4......... 149 B4
Woodside Ave PL9..... 135 C6
Woodside Ct PL7 ..... 130 E4

Woodside La PL4 ...... 149 B4
Woodstock Gdns PL5.. 123 D1
Woodvale Terr PL15... 106 C5
Wood View TR10....... 144 B7
Woodview Pk PL9...... 136 A6
Woodville Cl PL2...... 127 F7
Woodville Rd
　Morwenstow EX23..... 2 C1
　Plymouth PL2.......... 127 F6
　Woodford EX23 .... 4 D8
Woodway
　Penryn TR10.......... 144 B7
　Plymouth PL9.......... 136 A7
Woolacombe Cross PL20 . 41 C1
Woolacombe Rd PL20... 41 C1
Woollcombe Ave PL7 .. 130 F4
WOOLLEY 3 A3
WOOLSTON 38 E3
WOOLWELL............. 125 D7
Woolwell Cres PL6..... 125 C8
Woolwell Dr PL6....... 125 C7
Woolwell Rd PL6....... 125 D7
Woon La 3 TR3 .... 81 F7
Worcester Rd PL25..... 115 A4
Wordsworth Cres PL2.. 127 F7
Wordsworth Rd PL2.... 127 F7
Wotton Cross PL12..... 53 B4
Wreford Cl 11 TR9 .... 45 D6
Wren Gdns PL7 .... 130 C6
Wren Ind Est TR1 ..... 69 E4
Wrens Gate PL9....... 135 E8
Wrey Ave PL14......... 113 C7
Wright Cl PL1.......... 127 E3
WRINGSDOWN 18 E6
Wyatts La PL19 ...... 147 B6
Wych Hazel Way TR7... 110 F4
Wycliffe Rd PL3....... 129 B4
Wye Gdns PL3 .... 129 D7
Wykeham Dr PL2 ..... 128 A7
Wyndham La PL1 ..... 148 A3
Wyndham Mews PL1 .. 148 A3
Wyndham Pl PL1....... 148 A3
Wyndham Sq PL1 .... 148 A3
Wyndham Street E PL1.. 148 B3
Wyndham Street W PL1. 148 B3
Wyndhurst Orch PL27.. 108 B6
Wyoming Cl PL3........ 129 C6
Wythburn Gdns PL6... 125 D3

Y

Yardley Gdns PL6 ...... 125 E3
Yarrow Mead PL9...... 136 D7

Yealmpstone Cl PL7.... 131 B4
Yealmpstone Dr PL7 ... 131 B3
Yealmpstone Farm Prim Sch
　PL7 .... 131 B3
Yeats Cl PL5.......... 124 C2
Yellowmead Rd PL2.... 128 A7
Yellow Tor Ct PL12.... 122 C2
Yellow Tor La PL12..... 122 C2
Yellow Tor Rd PL12.... 122 B2
Yellow-Wort TR16 .... 80 C3
YELVERTON 42 D3
Yelverton Bsns Pk PL20 .. 42 B2
Yelverton Cl PL5...... 123 E4
Yelverton Paperweight
　Mus* PL20............. 42 C2
Yelverton Terr
　Tavistock PL19......... 147 D6
　Yelverton PL20........ 42 D2
Yeo Cl PL3........... 129 B5
Yeoland Down PL20.... 121 E8
Yeoland La PL20....... 42 C1
YEOLMBRIDGE 18 F6
Yeomadon Cross EX22 ....8 E4
Yeomans Cl PL14 .... 113 D5
Yeomans Way PL7 .... 131 A4
Yewdale Gdns PL6 .... 125 D2
Yew Tree Ct TR1....... 137 F6
Yonder St PL9 .... 135 B6
York Pl PL2........... 127 F4
York Rd
　Plymouth PL5......... 127 E8
　Plymouth PL11 .... 127 B3
York St
　Penzance TR18....... 143 D6
　Plymouth PL1......... 127 E2
York Terr 7 PL2....... 127 F5
Youldon Way PL20 .... 42 C4

Z

Zaggy La PL17 .... 39 E4
ZELAH 56 A2
ZENNOR 76 B5
Zion St PL1............ 148 C2
Zodiac Ho TR19........ 96 E3